EXPECTATIONS AND ACTIONS:
Expectancy-Value Models in Psychology

EXPECTATIONS AND ACTIONS:
Expectancy-Value Models in Psychology

Edited by

Norman T. Feather
The Flinders University of South Australia

LEA LAWRENCE ERLBAUM ASSOCIATES, PUBLISHERS
1982 Hillsdale, New Jersey

Lawrence Erlbaum Associates, Inc., Publishers
365 Broadway
Hillsdale, New Jersey 07642

Library of Congress Cataloging in Publicating Data
Main entry under title:

Expectations and actions.

Bibliography: p.
Includes index.
1. Expectation (Psychology) 2. Performance.
I. Feather, Norman T. [DNLM: 1. Achievement.
2. Decision making. 3. Models, Psychological.
4. Motivation. 5. Reward. BF 683 E96]
BF323.E8E95   153.8   80-28791
ISBN 0-89859-080-9

Printed in the United States of America

Contents

Preface   ix

1. **Introduction and Overview**
   Norman T. Feather   **1**
   Overview of Chapters   5

PART I: THE CONTEXT OF ACHIEVEMENT MOTIVATION

2. **Old and New Conceptions of How Expected**
   Consequences Influence Actions
   John W. Atkinson   **17**
   Some Historical Issues   17
   Implication of an Inhibitory Tendency
     When the Value of Expected Consequence is Negative   27
   Reconsideration of "Expectancy × Value"
     Within the Framework of the New Dynamics of Action   33

3. **Actions in Relation to Expected Consequences:**
   An Overview of a Research Program
   Norman T. Feather   **53**
   Object Preference   54
   A Theory of Achievement Motivation   57
   Studies of Persistence   61
   Determinants of Expectations   63
   Studies of Affect   68
   Information-Seeking Behavior   71
   Expectations and Performance   74
   Valence and Perceived Control   78
   Expectations and Causal Attribution   80
   Affect and Consistency of Outcome with Sex Roles   85
   Values and Valence   86
   Conclusion   90

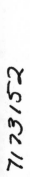

v

4. **Future Orientation, Self-Evaluation, and Achievement Motivation: Use of an Expectancy × Value Theory of Personality Functioning and Change**
    Joel O. Raynor   **97**
    Initial Expectancy × Value Theory
    of Achievement Motivation   97
    A More General Expectancy × Value Theory
    of Achievement Motivation   99
    Empirical Evidence Concerning Contingent
    Future Orientation   101
    Future Orientation and Self-Evaluation   108
    Future-Importance, Self-Importance, and
    Self-Possession of Competence   110
    The Self System and Theory of Achievement Motivation   112
    Sources of Value and Possession of Competence   115
    Time-Linked Sources of Value
    and Expectancy × Value Theory: The Past   116
    Cultural Value and the Theory of Achievement Motivation   119
    Summary   120

5. **The Expectancy-Value Approach within the Theory of Social Motivation: Elaborations, Extensions, Critique**
    Julius Kuhl   **125**
    The Original Theory of Achievement Motivation   126
    Elaborations of the Theory of Achievement Motivation   132
    Critique of Expectancy-Value Theory   149

PART II: THE CONTEXT OF ATTRIBUTION THEORY

6. **An Attributionally Based Theory of Motivation and Emotion: Focus, Range, and Issues**
    Bernard Weiner   **163**
    Abstract   163
    The Search for Causes   164
    Dimensions of Causality   167
    Consequences of Causal Properties   171
    Stability—Expectancy of Success   171
    Locus—Affect   177
    Expectancy and Value as Determinants of Performance   181
    Control—Helping, Evaluation, and Liking   186
    Summary   190
    Theoretical Range   190
    Conclusion   198

PART III: THE CONTEXT OF INFORMATION FEEDBACK

7. **Expectation and What People Learn from Failure**
   Ronnie Janoff-Bulman and Philip Brickman   **207**
   Giving Up and the Pathology of Low Expectations   208
   Persistence and the Pathology of High Expectations   211
   An Experiment in Immunization   216
   Learning When to Continue and When to Quit   218
   A Sequential Model for Testing One's Limits   225
   Conclusions and Directions for Future Research   230

PART IV: THE CONTEXT OF SOCIAL LEARNING THEORY

8. **Social Learning Theory**
   Julian B. Rotter   **241**
   Abstract   241
   Some Basic Principles of Social Learning Theory   242
   Motivation, Incentive, and Emotion   246
   Beliefs, Expressed Social Attitudes, and Social Action   249
   Social Learning Theory and Attribution Theory   254
   The Psychological Situation and Interactionism   255

PART V: THE CONTEXT OF VALUES AND ATTITUDES

9. **Human Values and the Prediction of Action:
   An Expectancy-Valence Analysis**
   Norman T. Feather   **263**
   The Flinders Value Program   265
   Value Systems and Social Interaction   267
   Attitudes, Values, and Behavior   271
   Values and Motives   275
   Values, Valence and Expectancy   277
   Values and Social Movements   280
   Some Issues   284
   Concluding Remarks   286

PART VI: THE CONTEXT OF ORGANIZATIONAL PSYCHOLOGY

10. **Expectancy-Value Models in Organizational Psychology**
    Terence R. Mitchell   **293**
    Theoretical Development   294
    Research Results   298
    Methodological Issues   301
    Empirical Issues   303
    Theoretical Issues   304
    Summary and Conclusions   309

PART VII: THE CONTEXT OF DECISION MAKING

11. **The Experienced Utility of Expected
    Utility Approaches**
    Baruch Fischhoff, Bernard Goitein, and Zur Shapira   **315**
    Formal Models of Decision Making   316
    Prescriptive Validity   322
    Availability of Inputs   325
    Decision Contexts   332
    Conclusion   335

12. **Conflict Theory of Decision Making
    and the Expectancy-Value Approach**
    Leon Mann and Irving Janis   **341**
    Conflict Theory: A Model of Decisional Stress   342
    Conclusion   361

13. **Expectancy-Based Decision Schemes:
    Sidesteps Toward Applications**
    Barbara H. Beach and Lee Roy Beach   **365**
    Probability   367
    Utilities   373
    Subjective Expected Utility   382
    Conclusions   388

14. **Expectancy-Value Approaches:
    Present Status and Future Directions**
    Norman T. Feather   **395**
    New Perspectives on Expectancy-Value Theory   395
    Scope of the Expectancy-Value Approach   397
    The Role of Thought   401
    The Role of Affect   405
    Determinants of Expectations   406
    The Measurement of Expectations   408
    Determinants of Valences   410
    The Measurement of Valences   412
    Interaction of Expectations and Valences   413
    The Combination of Expectations and Valences   414
    The Stream of Behavior   415

    Author Index   421
    Subject Index   431

Preface

This book examines the current status of expectancy-value models in psychology. The focus is upon cognitive models that relate action to the perceived attractiveness or aversiveness of expected consequences. A person's behavior is seen to bear some relation to the expectations the person holds and the subjective value of the consequences that might occur following the action.

The expectancy-value model has a long history in psychology and continues to command attention as an important theoretical approach in the psychology of motivation. Over 20 years ago I reviewed five examples of expectancy-value models in the first such comparison to appear in the literature. Specifically, expectancy-value models developed by Lewin, et al., Tolman, Rotter, Atkinson, and Edwards were compared and discussed along with my own contributions. It was exciting then to realize that similar concepts and models had emerged from quite different areas of psychology—level of aspiration, the rat's performance at a bar-pressing task, social learning and clinical psychology, achievement motivation, SEU decision theory, and the study of object preference. There were some differences to be sure, but the concepts used by each theorist were similar and they have continued to survive right through to the cognitive revolution that marks much of present day psychology.

Despite widespread interest in the expectancy-value (valence) approach, there is no book that looks at its current status and that discusses its strengths and its weaknesses, using contributions from some of the theorists who were involved in its original and subsequent development and from others who have been influenced by it or have had cause to examine the approach closely. This book was planned to meet this need. It contains new discussions by Atkinson, Rotter, and the author that review and update their past contributions. And it includes major new contributions from other authors. The chapters in the book relate to such areas as achievement motivation, attribution theory, information feedback, organizational psychology, the psychology of values and attitudes, and decision theory and in some cases they advance the expectancy-value approach further and, in other cases, point to some of its deficiencies. All of the chapters were especially written for this volume.

In planning this book I have deliberately attempted to include contributions that demonstrate the wide scope of the expectancy-value approach. Thus, the book examines how these models have been applied in a variety of different contexts, as noted previously. There is little question that the analysis of behavior in relation to the perceived attractiveness or aversiveness of expected consequences continues to stimulate ideas and to guide research in diverse areas of psychology. In selecting contributors, however, I have not taken the role of the protective advocate seeking to safeguard a position. There are some strong criticisms of the expectancy-value approach in this volume as well as some friendly discussions of it. My purpose has been to present both positive and negative views, in the belief that progress issues from the consideration of both point and counterpoint, thesis and antithesis.

The book contains an introductory chapter that sets the general scene and signposts the chapters to come. In the final chapter I have attempted to summarize the present status of the expectancy-value approach and to indicate some future directions that might be taken. The book has been planned to sample widely but also to have a basic unity that derives from the focus on the one kind of model. It attempts to evaluate where this model stands in the 1980s. It is primarily addressed to psychologists who are interested in cognitive approaches to motivational theory and in the problem of how actions might relate to intervening cognitive processes that involve as important components, expectations and subjective values (or valences). Given the wide scope of the expectancy-value model, however, the book should be of interest to people working in many different areas, some of which I have already mentioned but will repeat: achievement motivation, attribution theory, social learning theory, coping strategies for dealing with failure, the psychology of attitudes and values, organizational psychology, and decision theory. And, of course, the approach will probably be applied to new areas in the future, given its obvious vitality and its compatability with the current widespread interest among psychologists in cognitive theory.

Whether expectancy-value models are able to handle the problem of how cognition influences action is for the reader to judge. Certainly, however, if cognitive models are to make a contribution to motivational theory they must not leave the person ''buried in thought''. They must provide a convincing analysis of the links between cognition and action. I believe that the expectancy-value approach provides an important lever for dealing with this difficult and complex problem, a problem that many cognitive theorists of the 1970s and 1980s continue to neglect or to gloss over in various ways.

I am sure that all of the contributors to this volume would wish me to thank those who assisted them in bringing their chapters to fruition, including their colleagues and secretarial staff. For my own part, I wish to thank Kay Guest and Carol McNally for their secretarial help, provided under difficult conditions, and Flinders University and the Australian Research Grants Committee for financial support.

To my wife, Daryl, and son, Mark, I owe a special debt of gratitude for their encouragement and understanding during the long period involved in preparing this volume.

NORMAN T. FEATHER

1 Introduction and Overview

Norman T. Feather
The Flinders University of South Australia

This book examines the current status of expectancy-value models in psychology. The distinctive characteristic of this class of models is their attempt to relate action to the perceived attractiveness or aversiveness of expected consequences. What a person does is seen to bear some relation to the expectations that the person holds and the subjective value of the consequences that might occur following the action. We are dealing with a basic question in psychology, the relationship of actions to expectations, where these expectations encompass beliefs about the implications of behavior, and where an important set of these implications consists of consequences that have positive or negative perceived value.

The model that is the center of attention goes by a variety of names. In motivational psychology it is usually referred to as the expectancy-value model, although the alternative and perhaps more accurate term, expectancy-valence model, has also been used. Decision theorists refer to it as the SEU model because the decision rule involves maximizing subjectively expected utilities involved in the choice situation. The terms expectation and expectancy are used interchangeably and they are indexed in terms of the perceived likelihood that an action will be followed by a particular consequence—that is by a subjective probability that the consequence will occur given the response. Similarly, there is a high degree of overlap in the terms used to refer to the subjective value of the expected consequences. Among the concepts that have been employed are incentive values, utilities, valences, and reinforcement values—all of which can be positive or negative.

Some theorists distinguish outcomes from consequences, a given outcome (e.g., success) being associated with a defined set of consequences that may have

1

different levels of perceived likelihood for a person (e.g., more pay, better working conditions). Other theorists distinguish between outcomes at different levels (e.g., level 1 and level 2 outcomes). What is common to all of these analyses is the recognition that actions and their potential consequences are embedded in a complex means-end structure that involves beliefs about the implications of events extending beyond immediate consequences to possible future consequences. People are assumed to possess cognitive structures that concern the implications of their actions, both now and in the future. These implication structures may not always be well-defined, they may be in error, and one would expect them to vary in their details from person to person. But they are assumed to exist and, along with subjective values, valences, or utilities, to be important determinants of goal directed behavior.

In order to provide a concrete image of this cognitive form of analysis I will use a map as an analogy. A map sets out a pattern of interrelationships that schematize the implications of following particular routes. In planning a vacation, passing through some cities and along some roads may be more attractive than other alternatives. Taking some routes may involve additional expense beyond a person's available resources and income. Some roads may be closed or obstructed or they may be difficult to travel given the condition of a person's car. Some locations have to be passed through before others can be reached, given the structure of the geographical environment. All these variables would be expected to influence where one decides to spend the vacation and which route one chooses to take. Theoretical approaches that use the concepts of expectancy and subjective value assume that, just as a geographical map can be inspected for a given purpose, so too can people consult their own conceptual or cognitive maps to examine the likely implications of alternative actions and to evaluate in positive and negative terms their anticipated consequences. The decision taken is then assumed to be some function of the person's expectations and subjective values as they relate to possible courses of action and consequences. The map analogy can be broadened to take account of time perspective because cognitive maps, though available for present use, incorporate the effects of past events and ideas about the future. The cognitive map may also be a distorted impression of reality, affected by one's wishes and fears. And, of course, it could be in error because of insufficient information.

My selection of the map analogy was deliberate and not accidental. Both Tolman and Lewin conceived of the environment as structured and a person's cognitive representation of it as having map-like qualities (Tolman, 1948; Lewin, 1936). Both were concerned with the structured representation of events— Tolman with the concept of expectation and the development of cognitive maps; Lewin with the topological characteristics of both the person and the psychological environment represented in terms of a finite set of interconnected regions. These seminal contributions of both Tolman and Lewin have had a lasting influence on the development of expectancy-value models in psychology. Both theorists emphasize cognitive structures that incorporate a coherent set of events interconnected across space and time.

The concern with cognitive concepts that capture the structured nature of knowledge and experience has a long history in psychology, going back at least to the Gestalt psychologists (Koffka, 1935; Kohler, 1927). In an earlier article I noted some of the concepts that have been used, especially as they relate to the cognitive and behavioral effects of structural discrepancies (Feather, 1971, pp. 14–15). As well as the concept of expectation, other structural concepts that come to mind are hypothesis, schema, prototype, category, belief, naive theory, cell assembly, abstract structure, personal construct, image, plan, script, and balanced structure. All of these concepts depart from a simple stimulus-response associationist analysis of behavior and recognize the individual's capacity to process information so that it becomes organized and set within a context of meaning. These organized residues of experience then become important filters for future information processing, serving as benchmarks, criteria, or reference frames against which new information can be tested. They also guide the form that behavior takes. Such a cognitive analysis moves one far beyond a machine like view of the person reacting on the basis of stimulus-response connections that are either innately programmed or learned. Instead, the model of the person is that of an active processor of information, organizing and constructing experience into meaningful internal representations, and behaving not as an automaton but as a thoughtful, purposeful being.

There is little doubt that, from the present vantage point in history, the old debate in the 1940s and 1950s between the stimulus-response associationists and the cognitive psychologists has ended in a resounding victory for the advocates of cognitive theories. Yet there is a problem that continues to plague some cognitive approaches—an old problem that has drawn comment (e.g., Brunswik, 1943: Guthrie, 1935) and which needs to be raised again. Let us consider an early statement of the problem. In a well known criticism of Tolman's theory, Guthrie (1935) wrote:

> Signs, in Tolman's theory occasion in the rat *realization*, or *cognition*, or *judgment*, or *hypotheses*, or *abstraction*, but *they do not occasion action*. In his concern with what goes on in the rat's mind, Tolman has neglected to predict what the rat will do. So far as the theory is concerned the rat is left buried in thought; if it gets to the food-box at the end that is his concern not the concern of the theory [p. 172].

The point is that some cognitive theories have left a vacuum between cognition and action. Although there are theorists who have tried to fill this vacuum (see Miller, Galanter & Pribram, 1960, for a notable example), others have continued to ignore it, so that the organism still remains buried in thought, trapped within its own knowledge structures.

To be fair to Tolman, he did respond to Guthrie's criticism by developing principles of performance that acknowledged the importance of needs and valences as well as expectations in the prediction of a rat's behavior in a Skinner box (Tolman, 1955). And Lewin (1951) in some of his later work attempted to go beyond the encapsulated life-space to draw links between the "real" world, the cognitive representation of this reality, and behavior in real-life contexts (Cartwright, 1959, 1978).

Tolman's (1955) solution to the problem was in effect to develop an expectancy-value model, incorporating valences or subjective values as well as expectations. Miller, Galanter, and Pribram (1960, Chapter 4) in their seminal work on images, plans, and behavior also pointed to the importance of taking evaluation into account, although their approach was cast in terms of TOTE units (Test-Operate-Test-Exit units) using cybernetic and computer simulation principles in the context of an information-processing analysis. Miller et al. (1960) endorsed the view that "... knowing is for the sake of doing and that doing is rooted in valuing ... [p. 71]" and argued that any psychology that provides less than a recognition of the connection between knowledge, evaluation, and action, that "... allows a reflex being to behave at random, or leaves it lost in thought or overwhelmed by blind passion—can never be completely satisfactory [p. 71]."

Expectancy-value models may be seen as one possible way of filling the theoretical vacuum between knowledge and action by way of bringing in evaluation as an important component. They have in common a reference to higher-order cognitive structures that represent the interconnectedness of events. In expectancy-value models the events concern actions and their expected consequences and these consequences may have different degrees of positive and negative subjective value or valence.

Some 20 years ago I noted that there were a number of expectancy-value models in existence and that they had emerged from diverse areas of psychology (Feather, 1959a)—level of aspiration (Lewin, Dembo, Festinger, & Sears, 1944), the analysis of a rat's bar-pressing performance (Tolman, 1955), the theory of decision making (Edwards, 1954), social learning and clinical psychology (Rotter, 1954), risk-taking behavior and achievement motivation (Atkinson, 1957), and from my own research into committed and wishful choices between alternative goal objects (Feather, 1959b). All of these models used similar concepts and it seemed to me at that time that they presented a major alternative to the drive theories that were then very much in vogue (Hull, 1943; Spence, 1956). They took a different point of view from drive theory. Instead of attempting to explain behavior in terms of stimulus-response connections along with intervening constructs such as drives and incentives, the expectancy-value approaches emphasized the cognitive structuring of reality by an active organism and the purposive quality of its behavior within a means-end framework—a structured set of relationships in which various means or alternative courses of action could be seen as relevant to the attainment of positive goals or the avoidance of negative consequences.

Each of these models assumed that the behavior that occurred in a given situation could be related to a resultant that maximized the combination of expectations and subjective values. The organism was assumed to pursue that course of action associated with a maximum subjectively expected utility, resultant weighted valence, resultant motivation, behavior potential, choice potential, performance vector, or whatever the combination was called. Obviously the general approach assumed that the organism had the capacity to process information so that cognitive expectations about the implications of actions could be formed and be elicited on the basis of past experience and present perception, that it could also assign positive and negative values to the various possible outcomes or consequences of these actions, and that in some sense it could also combine particular expectations and subjective values so as to arrive at some meaningful resultant. In these models, action was therefore assumed to be related to the interplay of knowledge and evaluation within the perceived situation.

In this book we look at expectancy-value models as they have developed in the 20 or so years since my earlier review (Feather, 1959a). How have they weathered these intervening years? In what areas have they been used? What are their strengths and weaknesses? How generally can they be applied to the analysis of action? These are some of the questions that we hope to answer. The chapters in this book cover theoretical and empirical contributions from a number of different areas, and they are international in their character spanning North American, European, and Australian research. In organizing the contents of the book I have not taken the role of the protective advocate. There are positive statements about expectancy-value models, to be sure, but this volume also includes a considerable amount of critical comment and counterpoint—deliberately so, for that is the way we ultimately move forward.

Let us now set the scene by briefly describing the organization of this book and summarizing some of the distinctive contributions of each chapter.

OVERVIEW OF CHAPTERS

The chapters in this book discuss expectancy-value models in relation to seven different contexts: achievement motivation, attribution theory, information feedback, social learning theory, values and attitudes, organizational psychology, and decision making. Psychologists working in each of these contexts have used expectancy-value models to account for important characteristics of motivated behavior such as changes in the direction of behavior following choice or decision, the latency of response and the persistence of behavior in a particular direction, effort expended, and the level or amplitude of performance. Taken together the chapters relating to each of these contexts are intended to provide a wide ranging and scholarly account of the current status of the expectancy-value approach.

The Context of Achievement Motivation

The model of risk-taking behavior proposed by Atkinson (1957) has been an important source of hypotheses about how people with different motives might be expected to behave in achievement situations where both success and failure are possible outcomes. Atkinson's model was an early example of an expectancy-value model and it had considerable influence on subsequent theorizing and research in the achievement motivation area.

The first section of this book contains four chapters that describe developments since the initial statement of the Atkinson model. In Chapter 2, Atkinson discusses the background to the development of his model, bringing to the fore some important historical issues. He outlines his earlier conception of how expected consequences influence actions (the risk-taking model or theory of achievement motivation) and examines in detail how the theoretical statement forced a new and different conception of the motivational significance of an inhibitory tendency—implying that it should be regarded as a tendency *not* to perform an act where the expected consequence is negative. Atkinson then argues that the earlier theory of achievement motivation was limited because it took an episodic view of behavior. He describes new developments that follow from a theory about the dynamics of action that assumes that the person is always engaged in some activity, and that theories of motivation should relate to the ongoing stream of behavior and changes in the stream rather than to situationally bound episodes (Atkinson & Birch, 1970, 1978). He redefines concepts from the early risk-taking model in terms of the new concepts of instigating and inhibitory forces. This redefinition has important implications, one of which is that in accounting for choice or preference, one should look at ratios that involve forces rather than at differences between competing tendencies. It is clear that Atkinson shows great respect for the deductive consequences of a theory.

The next three chapters by Feather (Chapter 3), Raynor (Chapter 4), and Kuhl (Chapter 5) certainly relate to the Atkinson model and to the achievement context but they make many independent contributions in their own right. In Chapter 3, Feather provides a review of his research program that has extended over 20 years. He describes his early investigation of object preference that specified some of the conditions under which valences and subjective probabilities would not be independent (as they are commonly assumed to be by decision theorists), and which studied the effects of differences in the degree of commitment on choice between goal objects. Feather also describes his study of persistence in which persistence in the face of failure was conceptualized in terms of a decision situation involving an initial task and an alternative task, with tendencies to perform the initial task changing on the basis of changes in the subjective probability of success that follow the repeated failure. Studies of the relationship of expectations to motives are also reviewed, as are studies of the effects of motives and expectations on performance. Feather also describes three theoretical approaches to the analysis of affective reactions to success and failure that are suggested by his investigations. He extends the expectancy-value approach to the analysis of information-seeking behavior and shows that this theoretical extension has testable implications. He describes studies that investigate the relationship between valence and perceived control and suggests modifications to the initial Atkinson model that include perceived control as an additional variable. He reviews his series of studies in which causal attributions following success and failure are related to initial expectations of success. He then describes some studies in the sex role and occupational areas that indicate a relationship between affect and consistency and that also have implications for the analysis of the determinants of valence. Finally, Feather discusses the relationship between the general values held by a person and the specific valences assigned to means and to goals within a defined situation. This is a wide-ranging chapter demonstrating a continuing dialogue between theory and research.

Raynor (Chapter 4) describes his extension of the initial Atkinson model to take account of the important distinction between contingent and noncontingent paths and the effects of contingent future orientation on present behavior. He also discusses the role of self evaluation and suggests that the motivation for performing tests of ability usually involves both the goal of doing well and the goal of finding out about one's competence. He distinguishes between arousal in the behavioral system and arousal in the self system, between affective value (''doing well'') and information value (''finding out''), and between five different sources of value that can be linked to the past, the present, or the future. These distinctions enable him to develop a general theory of personality functioning and change that he discusses in relation to a number of specific issues. Raynor's chapter involves a shift from models applied to a particular domain (achievement behavior) to a much more general approach that acknowledges that task situations have significance not only in relation to possible success or failure and their affective consequences but also in relation to self definition and other aspects of personality functioning.

The chapter by Kuhl (Chapter 5) contains a useful review of the main elaborations and extensions of the expectancy-value approach, especially within the achievement context. Kuhl's chapter refers to much of the European work as well as to North American sources. He makes the interesting distinction between action orientation (focusing on action alternatives) and state orientation (focusing on the state itself), and provides some experimental evidence to show that this distinction is a useful one to make in studies concerned with helplessness and the effects of failure and also in relation to the planning of action. Kuhl also describes the method of logical statement analysis that he has used in his recent research and that allows for a more inductive analysis of data. It is clear that he sees advantages in an inductive as opposed to a deductive approach to testing expectancy-value models.

These four chapters together provide an up-to-date statement of developments and new formulations that have special but not exclusive relevance to the expectancy-value analysis of behavior in achievement situations. Their significance extends beyond the achievement context to motivation theory in general. They contribute new ideas and they may also alert researchers to some old ideas that have been lost or neglected.

The Context of Attribution Theory

The second section of this book shows how the expectancy-value approach can be related to one of the dominant interests of social psychologists over the past 10 years—attribution theory. Weiner (Chapter 6) presents a theory of motivation and emotion that is based upon the kind of causal attributions that individuals are assumed to make. He attempts to identify the dimensions of causality and their psychological consequences. In so doing he provides a valuable review of previous theorizing and research into the psychology of causal attribution. He identifies three major causal dimensions: stability, locus, and control, and links these dimensions respectively with expectancy change, esteem-related emotions, and interpersonal judgments—although the determinants of affect are somewhat complex. Weiner shows how his analysis relates to the expectancy-value approach and it is clear that he considers that it has very wide application, encompassing not only achievement-related behavior but also interpersonal behavior, sources of emotion, self-esteem, helplessness, mastery, reinforcement schedules, expectancy changes, hyperactivity, risk preference, and many other topics.

Weiner's interest in affect and control and in classification of causal attributions within a framework of dimensions is coordinate with a similar emphasis by Feather (Chapter 3), though there are differences in approach.

The Context of Information Feedback

One of the important functions of success and failure is to provide information that may be relevant when a person is confronted by the same task or similar tasks in the future. Raynor in Chapter 4 noted that performance at tasks has information value as well as affective value. The third section of this book concerns this question of the information value of outcomes—What people can learn from their experience with tasks.

The focus of the chapter by Janoff-Bulman and Brickman (Chapter 7) is on what people learn from failure. They review research that concerns reactions to failure under conditions where expectations are low and also where these expectations are high, and they indicate that in both cases reactions may be maladaptive or pathological. The authors argue that attempting tasks that might be impossible is an important way of testing one's limits and that achieving and coping in real life requires some knowledge of what is possible and what is impossible. Janoff-Bulman and Brickman describe a wide range of research evidence that is relevant to the major themes of their discussion.

Their chapter contributes an alternative to motivational interpretations of the effects of task performance. Performance provides information, the implications of which depend upon the circumstances. Success can be a relatively unambiguous source of information with fairly clear implications about what a person should do in the future, but failure is more ambiguous in its implications for future action, though it is a necessary part of learning to test one's limits.

The Context of Social Learning

The fourth section of this book is concerned with the social learning theory of personality developed by Rotter (1954)—one of the early examples of the expectancy-value approach noted by Feather (1959a) in his review of the various models. Some of the concepts developed by Rotter have subsequently had wide impact—especially the concept of a generalized expectancy concerning internal or external locus of control.

In Chapter 8 Rotter discusses his theory again, with reference to its present status. He reviews the theory with its basic concepts of behavior potential, expectancy, reinforcement value, and the psychological situation and he also describes the broader concepts of need potential, freedom of movement, need value, and generalized expectancy. Rotter also discusses conceptual relationships between motivation, incentive, and emotion and individual difference variables involved in predicting some kinds of social action. He comments on attribution theory from a social learning perspective and finally discusses the role of the psychological situation and the need to take an interactionist view of behavior in which actions are related to characteristics of the person interacting with his or her meaningful environment. Rotter contributes a useful analysis of some of the problems involved in treating the psychological situation as a systematic variable together with a discussion of experimental considerations that affect the relative importance of situational and individual differences when apportioning variance within a person-situation interaction.

Rotter's chapter draws our attention to the importance of social learning as a basic variable that influences the nature of the person and the individual's definition of the psychological situation at any given time (see also Bandura, 1977; Mischel, 1973).

The Context of Values and Attitudes

The concept of attitude has been an important concern of social psychologists from the very inception of social psychology as a distinctive area of study. In recent years there has been considerable debate about such issues as how behavior relates to a person's attitudes and whether attitude change is followed by behavior change. Some influential models concerning the attitude/behavior relationship have been provided, and at least one of these (Fishbein & Ajzen, 1975) has clear affinities with the expectancy-value approach. Along with this debate there has been a growing awareness of the need to come to grips with the nature of human values, with the conceptual status of values conceived as properties of persons, and with the relationships between values, attitudes, and behavior (Feather, 1975; Rokeach, 1973).

The fifth section of this book contains a chapter by Feather (Chapter 9) that is relevant to these issues. Feather discusses the relationship of behavior to human values in terms of two models, one that employs the concept of person-environment fit, the other involving the use of an expectancy-value (or valence) approach. In the course of his chapter he comments upon the cognitive revolution in psychology, describes in general terms the program of research into human values emanating from Flinders University, and refers to the current status of theory and research into the relationship between values, attitudes, and behavior. It is clear that he favors an expectancy-valence model for guiding research on the values/action relationship. Feather assumes that basic values can induce valences on means and ends within a perceived situation and that an integrated form of these valences (operationalized by using an attitude measure), together with information about a person's expectations about the consequences of the action in question, will predict behavior better than either attitude or expectation alone. He describes continuing research in which this model has been tested in the context of predicting a person's willingness to assist social movement organizations. Feather also discusses two basic issues: whether the model is overly rational, ignoring both the defects that occur in information-processing and the effects of motivational and emotional states under conditions of stress and excitement, and whether the model necessarily assumes that thought precedes action.

This chapter therefore opens up the basic question of the relationship of action to attitudes and values—a question that has been of considerable interest to social psychologists—and provides a new solution to the question in terms of the expectancy-value (valence) approach.

The Context of Organizational Psychology

The sixth section of this book examines the application of expectancy-value models in organizational psychology, following Vroom's (1964) initial development of the instrumentality or expectancy approach for the prediction of occupational choice, effort on the job, and job satisfaction.

In Chapter 10 Mitchell provides a summary of theoretical developments in this area, starting with Vroom's valence and force models and then describing related formulations. He reviews the research results that relate to both the valence and force models, in particular some of the more recent investigations that use these models to predict occupational preference, job satisfaction, job effort, and specific behaviors. Mitchell also raises several important methodological issues that concern the specification of the number and the content of outcomes and the measurement of expectancies, instrumentalities, and valences. He also reviews some issues that concern the empirical and mathematical characteristics of the expectancy models. Finally he raises some theoretical points that relate to the need to test the models "within subjects," to the importance of comparing the predictive power of the models with competing theoretical viewpoints, and to the possibility that the models may be valid only within certain boundary conditions. Mitchell suggests that expectancy-value models might work best in organizational contexts where the behavior is in the repertoire of the subject, where the behavior is under the control of the subject, where rewards are in fact contingent on specific behaviors, and where the time lags between behaviors and outcomes, and between the assessment of predictors and the criterion, are both short.

In addition to providing a summary of the application of expectancy-value models to the analysis of behavior within organizations, Mitchell's chapter raises the important question of how generally these models can be applied and what are the limiting conditions. As he puts it, the question should not be *"Is* expectancy theory right or wrong?" but *"When* is expectancy theory right or wrong?"

The Context of Decision Making

The prime example of the expectancy-value approach in the theory of decision making is the SEU or subjectively expected utility model. In essence, this model proposes that, in making decisions, people weigh the subjective probabilities and the subjective values (or utilities) associated with the various alternative courses of action that are available and that they choose the alternative associated with the maximum SEU; i.e., the option for which the multiplicative combination of subjective probabilities and utilities is a maximum. The model assumes that the subjective probabilities and the utilities (positive and negative) involved in the decision are independent. Edwards (1954, 1961) has described the model in influential reviews, and there is an extensive literature that deals with the model, issuing not only from psychology but also from economics, mathematics, and philosophy. The general model has clearly been an important though controversial contribution to the analysis of decision among alternatives. Sometimes it has been employed normatively to provide prescriptive rules about how people *should* decide. In other cases it has been treated as a valid descriptive model of how people *do* in fact decide.

The seventh and final section of this book makes no attempt to review the extensive literature on the SEU model, but it does contain three chapters that reflect on the current status of this approach and that probe its advantages and limitations.

In Chapter 11, Fischoff, Goitein, and Shapira take a critical look at the SEU approach and its validity as a model. Their general theme is that the model often does not describe the decision making process either as it is designed or executed. They describe research into model fitting and indicate that simple linear models usually do an excellent job of postdicting judges' decisions despite the fact that the judges claim that they are using more complicated strategies. They examine the prescriptive validity of the SEU model by noting a number of cases when people might reject the rules that it implies (when more of a good thing is not better, when utilities and subjective probabilities are not independent, when options are evaluated by noncompensatory criteria, when consequences are not evaluated independently, and when options are not evaluated simultaneously). Fischoff, Goitein, and Shapira also review evidence that people have difficulty both in structuring the relevant options and consequences within a situation and in assessing probabilities—often relying upon relatively simple heuristics whose internal logic bears little relationship to the laws of probability. They also indicate that the assessment of utilities is a difficult matter because people's preferences are not always well defined, and attempts to elicit them may lead to artifactual results. They review some attempts to apply the SEU approach to realistic decision contexts and conclude that the results are by no means impressive. They conclude that one needs to search for alternatives to SEU theory that build upon the insights gained from this approach and that take account of human error.

Mann and Janis (Chapter 12) describe their conflict model of decision making under stress and its relationship to the expectancy-value approach. They argue that their conflict model offers a general theory of decision making and not a theory of choice behavior. Their model is concerned with how people go about making key consequential choices that affect their lives rather than with the actual choices that people make. They note that while the concept of expectancy has no central role in conflict theory it does enter into the analysis in various places: as a source of decisional conflict/stress, as a determinant of decisional coping patterns, as a component of the decisional balance sheet, in relation to the loss of choice alternatives, and in relation to the unexpected consequences of decisional choice. They argue that laboratory studies of the expectancy-value model presuppose a cool, vigilant decision-maker usually involved in hypothetical, inconsequential decisions, but that the principles governing consequential decision making under conflict or stress may be quite different. They suggest some future possibilities for collaboration between the two approaches that may be facilitated by the liberalization of the traditional expectancy-value formulation beyond the rational SEU model from behavioral decision theory—a liberalization that is very apparent in various chapters in this volume. And they argue that a close examination of the stress-inducing conditions that produce departures from the SEU model may provide a better understanding of when the model is valid.

Beach and Beach (Chapter 13) are not so much concerned with the descriptive or predictive adequacy of the expectancy-value approach. Their interest is in the use of the SEU model as a means to other ends—to aid personal or public decision-making, to discover how people think and feel about the components involved in the decisions they are confronted with, or to assist people in evaluating these components more carefully and systematically. They review the research on the components of the model (subjective probability, utility) and on the use of the model itself—referring in the process to some interesting applications to significant questions that have important consequences for people (meteorology, prediction of suicide, medical diagnosis and treatment, evaluating the quality of water supplies, use of public transit systems, occupational choice, family planning). They comment on the fact that few of the decision analytic schemes devised by researchers seem to venture or survive outside the laboratory though they could be of assistance to decision-makers. Like Mann and Janis, they note that the exercise of simply working through some sort of decision scheme may be of benefit in its own right, irrespective of whether or not it is used to arrive at a final decision.

The three chapters by Fischoff, Goitein, and Shapira, by Mann and Janis, and by Beach and Beach are critical toward the SEU model but they are also constructive. They bring out the subtleties and complexities of the decision process and the effects of human frailty and error as reflected in defective information processing and reactions to stress and conflict. They suggest that the rational, considered kind of decision making implied by the SEU model does not adequately reflect a lot of consequential decision-making that goes on in real life under difficult circumstances. The implication is that the SEU model from behavioral decision theory overemphasizes rational, intelligent behavior and, in so doing, provides a limited perspective on human decision-making as it occurs in real-life situations.

The overview of the different sections in this book that I have provided is necessarily one person's summary. It does attempt to capture some of the main ideas presented by the various contributors but there are many points of interest that could not be highlighted and that are left to the reader to discover. It should be clear that the expectancy-value approach has been a vigorous and productive form of analysis in many areas of psychology and that it varies across areas in the degree to which it has been liberalized and extended to meet deficiencies in the theoretical analysis.

In the final chapter of the book (Chapter 14) I discuss some general issues that emerge from the various contributions and that seem to me to be important for the future development of expectancy-value models. This final chapter does not attempt to achieve firm closure. At the present stage of development that goal is unrealistic, given the sometimes overlapping and sometimes competing points of view that exist, and given the continuing evolution of more sophisticated theoretical analyses that examine the relationship of actions to their expected consequences.

REFERENCES

Atkinson, J. W. Motivational determinants of risk-taking behavior. *Psychological Review*, 1957, *64*, 359-372.

Atkinson, J. W., & Birch, D. *The dynamics of action*. New York: Wiley, 1970.

Atkinson, J. W., & Birch, D. *An introduction to motivation*. Princeton, N.J.: D. Van Nostrand, 1978.

Bandura, A. *Social learning theory*. Englewood Cliffs, N.J.: Prentice-Hall, 1977.

Brunswik, E. Organismic achievement and environmental probability. *Psychological Review*. 1943, *50*, 255-272.

Cartwright, D. Lewinian theory as a contemporary systematic framework. In S. Koch (Ed.), *Psychology a study of a science* (Vol. 2), New York: McGraw-Hill, 1959.

Cartwright, D. Theory and practice. *Journal of Social Issues*, 1978, *34*, 168-180.

Edwards, W. The theory of decision making. *Psychological Bulletin*, 1954, *51*, 380-417.

Edwards, W. Behavioral decision theory. *Annual Review of Psychology*, 1961, *12*, 380-417.

Feather, N. T. Subjective probability and decision under uncertainty. *Psychological Review*, 1959, *66*, 150-164. (a)

Feather, N. T. Success probability and choice behavior. *Journal of Experimental Psychology*, 1959, *58*, 257-266. (b)

Feather, N. T. Organization and discrepancy in cognitive structures. *Psychological Review*, 1971, *78*, 355-379.

Feather, N. T. *Values in education and society*. New York: Free Press, 1975.

Fishbein, M., & Ajzen, I. *Belief, attitude, intention, and behavior: An introduction to theory and research*. Reading, Mass.: Addison-Wesley, 1975.

Guthrie, E. R. *The psychology of learning*. New York: Harper, 1935.

Hull, C. L. *Principles of behavior*. New York: Appleton-Century-Crofts, 1943.

Koffka, K. *Principles of gestalt psychology*. New York: Harcourt Brace, 1935.

Kohler, W. *The mentality of apes*. London: Routledge & Kegan Paul, 1927.

Lewin, K. *Principles of topological psychology*. New York: McGraw-Hill, 1936.

Lewin, K. *Field theory in social science*. New York: Harper, 1951.

Lewin, K., Dembo, T., Festinger, L., & Sears, P. S. Level of aspiration. In J. McV. Hunt (Ed.), *Personality and the behavior disorders* (Vol. 1). New York: Ronald, 1944.

Miller, G. A., Galanter, E., & Pribram, K. H. *Plans and the structure of behavior*. New York: Holt, Rinehart & Winston, 1960.

Mischel, W. Toward a cognitive social reconceptualization of personality. *Psychological Review*, 1973, *80*, 252-283.

Rokeach, M. *The nature of human values*. New York: Free Press, 1973.

Rotter, J. B. *Social learning and clinical psychology*. New York: Prentice-Hall, 1954.

Spence, K. W. *Behavior theory and conditioning*. New Haven: Yale University Press, 1956.

Tolman, E. C. Cognitive maps in rats and men. *Psychological Review*, 1948, *55*, 189-208.

Tolman, E. C. Principles of performance. *Psychological Review*, 1955, *62*, 315-326.

Vroom, V. H. *Work and motivation*. New York: Wiley, 1964.

THE CONTEXT OF
ACHIEVEMENT MOTIVATION

2 Old and New Conceptions of How Expected Consequences Influence Actions

John W. Atkinson
The University of Michigan

This book provides an occasion to remind the present generation of psychologists, many of whom are already strongly committed to a cognitive theoretical orientation, of some issues that were believed to be fundamentally important in the 1940s and 1950s when the grand conception of S–R behavior theory clearly dominated the scene. It also provides an opportunity to draw attention to some instructive things that we learned about the implications of an Expectancy ×️ Value theory of motivation while being guided by it in the analysis of achievement-related action in the 1950s and 1960s. Finally, and I think most importantly for the 1980s, this book provides exactly the right context in which to point out limitations of traditional explanatory schemes by drawing attention to new and different behavioral implications of subjective probabilities of consequences of actions and their subjective values when the motivational properties of these familiar variables are redefined within the more comprehensive theoretical framework of the new dynamics of action (Atkinson & Birch, 1970, 1974, 1978). These are the three themes of my discussion. I hope it will be apparent at the end that old wine poured into a new vessel has a decidedly new and different flavor.

SOME HISTORICAL ISSUES

For an aspiring motivational psychologist in training shortly after World War II, the psychological literature seemed to present convergent arguments that highlighted the potential theoretical importance of the expected consequences of an action. Tolman's (1938, 1951) rudimentary alternative to the more elegantly stated S-R theory had rats learning expectancies of what leads to what in a maze and then later expressing these expectancies in *selective performance* governed by the Law of Effect. This was not Thorndike's (1911) or Hull's (1943) hedonism of the past. It was, rather, a return to a more commonsensical hedonism of the anticipated future. Choice was presumed to be "guided by *expected pleasure,* which in turn is based on the remembrance of the pleasures actually experienced in the past" as pointed out by Jennings (1855), who much earlier had worked out the modern concept of utility for economics (Georgescu-Roegen, 1968, p. 236). Practically every chapter of Hebb's seminal book, *Organization of behavior: A neurophysiological theory* (1949), characterized central neural processes in terms of expectancies, not drives and habits. McClelland (1951) had concluded that Murray (1938) had bested Allport (1937) in the debate within descriptive personology when arguing that individuals are better understood when they are described in terms of the kinds of *effects* they typically strive to bring about (i.e., psychogenic needs) rather than in terms of their generalized patterns of action (i.e., traits). And most to the point of the really critical issue for motivational psychology, Meehl and MacCorquodale (1951; MacCorquodale & Meehl, 1953, 1954) were showing how Tolman's thoughtful rat could be freed from its chronic soliloquy at the choice point of a maze. One should realize, they argued, that a cognitive expectancy is inappropriately represented as merely an association involving S_1-S_2 in contrast to habit represented as S_1-R_1. A more adequate representation would include the behavior (R_1) that intervened between Tolman's Sign (S_1) and Significate (S_2) in specifying what the rat had learned. Expectancy then became ($S_1 R_1 S_2$.)[1] Once the long ignored response was included as a critical element in the formal representation of a cognitive expectancy, the concept—like the rat—could be off and running in the theoretical derby of the 1950s. It soon became apparent that Tolman's expectancy, or something very much like it, had won the long race to account for "the empirical law of effect." Sheffield's "drive induction" theory of reward (Sheffield, Roby, & Campbell, 1954) in particular, and Spence's (1956) "incentive motivation" embraced the motivational significance of the anticipated goal of a response for S-R psychology. A similar view, emphasizing the anticipation of affective consequences, was advanced by McClelland, Atkinson, Clark, and Lowell (1953, Ch. 2).

As far back as 1940, in discussing what then had to be considered the most systematic formulation of the expectancy principle, the Hilgard and Marquis classic, *Conditioning and Learning* (1940), exposed the conjectural, pretheory state of Tolman's (1938) cognitive alternative to the rapidly developing S-R behavior theory. Hull's (1943) formal statement of the latter, and the vigorous experimental programs of its various proponents, dominated motivational psychology for a quarter of a century. This may seem hard to appreciate now that

---

[1]We now can appreciate that these are the same three elements that constitute the important contingency in Skinner's (1953) analysis of operant behavior.

even more elaborate cognitive theories (Festinger, 1957; Kelley, 1967, 1973) have gained so many adherents. But reconsideration of the early problems of cognitive psychology, confronted first in the study of lower animals who cannot talk, should be instructive for contemporary cognitive psychologists who often seem as willing to leave their human subjects "buried in thought" as Tolman once did his rats, according to Edwin R. Guthrie's popular quip.

How is one to get from cognitions to actions? An expectation no more implies an action than does the streak of lightning imply the bang of thunder. There is no inherent logic in an observed or presumed correlation. The logical bridge between antecedent and consequent must be constructed. A neat phrasing of this lesson, one that many of us probably first learned reading Hume, is N. R. Hanson's (1958): "Causes certainly are connected with effects; but that is because our theories connect them not because the world is held together by cosmic glue [p. 64]."

In 1940, the pretheory state of conjectures about expectancies was made patently clear by Hilgard and Marquis: "The inference is made that the animal behaves in certain ways consonant with anticipated consequences [p. 88]." But, they went on, "explanation requires some manner in which the aroused expectation or signification leads to appropriate conduct." This, of course, was the point of Guthrie's criticism. During learning, according to Tolman's expectancy theory, what was strengthened was not a tendency to respond (as in S-R behavior theory) but a tendency to anticipate certain consequences. "The theory, stated in this form does not propose to predict the details of conduct, so that the most varied behavior, if it is consonant with anticipated consequences may be encompassed by it. . . . All that is learned, according to the expectancy principle, is a new anticipation. . . . An advance will be made in explanation according to the expectancy principle when more detailed analyses are given of the way in which signification leads to conduct [pp. 89-90]."

The response to this challenge began to appear when Meehl and MacCorquodale (1951) saw the need to represent expectancy in terms of three elements $(S_1R_1S_2)$. Soon after, MacCorquodale and Meehl (1953) advanced a principle of activation of R_1 borrowing the general ideas of reaction potential or excitatory tendency $(_sE_R)$, and oscillation, from Hull's familiar usage in the expression $_sE_R = D \times {_sH_R}$: "The activation of the $_sE_{R_1}$ in the presence of S_1," they argued, "is a multiplicative function of the strength of expectancy $(S_1R_1S_2)$ and the valence (retaining sign!) of the expectandum." Here is an early version of the now familiar logic of "Expectancy × Value" theory. It was soon more fully elaborated by these authors (1954) and by Tolman in very similar terms (Tolman, 1955, 1959; Tolman & Postman, 1954).[2]

---

[2]Tolman (1955) followed the lead of MacCorquodale and Meehl's attempts to formalize expectancy theory. Acknowledging the need to get his rats moving, he nevertheless wondered, in his own inimitable style, "Why should it be so shocking to leave a human being "buried in thought"? (p. 315).

Not included among the references in any of these papers, all of which focused on the development of a cognitive theory in the context of animal learning, were concurrent theoretical developments on the human side, which were saying essentially the same thing to a different audience and using different terms. Cartwright and Festinger (1943) had already introduced an oscillation principle comparable to Hull's to advance a quantitative theory of human decision making based on Lewin's cognitive conception of the determinants of psychological forces. And the Lewinian conceptual scheme, well off the mainstream of primary theoretical interest in animal behavior at that time, was gradually becoming more widely known in reference to level of aspiration (Escalona, 1940; Festinger, 1942; Lewin, Dembo, Festinger, & Sears, 1944) and from the systematic and influential organization of Lewin's papers by Dorwin Cartwright in *Field Theory in Social Science* (1951).

Missing from the references of both the Tolmanian and Lewinian literature was the seminal contribution of game theory (Von Neuman & Morgenstern, 1945) to the development of decision theory. This was another separate stream of thought to which psychology in general was soon introduced mainly by Edwards (1954).

In the middle of this period of construction of a viable formal statement of expectancy theory to challenge the already crowned champion (Hull, 1943) in the domain of animal behavior which was the locus of theoretical developments, the research on projective measurement of achievement motivation had gotten underway (McClelland, Clark, Roby, & Atkinson, 1949: McClelland et al., 1953). The very first attempt to represent the motivational impact of the situation on performance of persons who differed in strength of inferred achievement motive opted for the kind of cognitive conception that was being developed (Atkinson, 1950, 1953). Kurt Lewin's injunction to remember that the behavior of an individual was to be explained in terms of the *psychological environment* rather than the *geographic environment* was not taken lightly.

By the late 1950s it had become apparent that the basic conception of the contemporaneous determinants of behavior advanced by Kurt Lewin earlier (1938, 1946) and by Tolman (1938, 1955), by MacCorquodale & Meehl (1953, 1954; see also Meehl & MacCorquodale, 1951), by Rotter (1954) in reference to social learning, and in the context of achievement motivation (Atkinson, 1954, 1957, 1958b; Atkinson & Reitman, 1956) was formulated most clearly in the mathematical decision theory to which Edwards (1954) had called attention. It was apparent that the various conceptions were essentially similar though the terminology differed (Feather, 1959). This increasingly popular cognitive alternative to the long dominant S-R theory was christened "Expectancy × Value theory" (Atkinson, 1960) and then, soon after, for the first time treated as a scientifically respectable alternative to "Drive × Habit" theory in a motivation textbook (Atkinson, 1964) following Judson Brown's (1961) rather total preoccupation with drive in a popular and influential text.

Later in this chapter we take a good hard look at the behavioral implications of this traditional cognitive theory when the expected outcome has negative value.

Perhaps it will explain why investigators (MacCorquodale & Meehl, 1953), who did so much to make expectancy theory respectable before we all became familiar with the mathematical model of decision theory had felt the need to call attention emphatically to the sign (+ or −) of the valence (or subjective value) of the expected outcome.

An Expectancy Theory of Achievement Motivation

Adoption of "the expectancy principle" to represent the effect of the immediate situation in behavioral expression of individual differences in n Achievement was greatly influenced by Lewin's (1946) succinct statement of how the study of individual differences in personality and of basic behavioral processes are related:

> A law is expressed in an equation which relates certain variables. Individual differences have to be conceived of as various specific values which these variables have in a particular case. In other words, general laws and individual differences are merely two aspects of one problem; they are mutually dependent on each other and the study of the one cannot proceed without the study of the other [p. 794].

By the time Cronbach (1957) raised consciousness of the need to integrate "the two disciplines of scientific psychology," we had already made substantial progress in that direction in experimental and conceptual analysis of the interaction of personal and situational determinants of achievement motivation (Atkinson, 1957). The very earliest points made in reference to thematic apperceptive measurement of achievement motivation had to do with the two arguments for the validity of the n Achievement score obtained through disciplined content analysis of a sample of imaginative thought. First, it was sensitive to experimental induction or situational arousal of achievement motivation. Second, people who differed in n Achievement score obtained under neutral conditions had been found to differ in perceptual sensitivity (McClelland & Liberman, 1949) and in test performance (Lowell, 1952) in ways that were consistent with the inference that they must differ in strength of motivation to achieve. But how was this expression of individual differences in personality influenced, if at all, by the nature of the situation at the time of performance? That became my central interest in studying how experimental manipulation of instructions for performance of tasks (and other more subtle situational cues) might influence the recall of interrupted tasks of persons who were high or low in n Achievement (Atkinson, 1950). The Zeigarnik effect was then assumed to provide an adequate behavioral indicator of how strongly motivated a person had been to complete the tasks.

The language I used to describe my aim in confronting three groups of subjects with instructions that presumably would differ in their motivational significance reveals a preliminary tilt toward the cognitive position of Tolman and

Lewin. "The different instructions," I wrote (Atkinson, 1953); "were designed to vary the probability that S's would perceive completion of tasks as evidence of personal accomplishment (or success) and incompletion as evidence of personal failure [pp. 381–382]." The diametrically opposite trends across situations of S's classified high and low in n Achievement in that study, and their interpretation, foreshadowed the equivalent emphasis later to be given the tendency to achieve and the tendency to avoid failure in the theory of achievement motivation. But more to the immediate point, the discussion of the interpretation of personal and situational determinants of motivation

> lean[ed] heavily on an assumption that the achievement motive measured in imaginative behavior becomes a determinant of overt striving only to the extent that a particular performance is perceived as instrumental to the goal of personal accomplishment. The achievement motive [was] viewed as a latent characteristic of personality which is manifested in behavior only when engaged or supported by appropriate environment cues [p. 387].

A year later, I called attention to the relevance of the classic latent learning experiment as discussed by Tolman (1951) to analysis of achievement motivation and behavior (Atkinson, 1954):

> When [those high in n Achievement] find out, by means of verbal instructions, that the particular tasks they are asked to perform could lead to feelings of accomplishment if done well, their behavior shows more evidence of their knowing how to perform the tasks and more evidence of their wanting to perform the tasks than when they are told, in effect, that rewards for achievement are not possible in the situation. In the human experiment, verbal instructions to the subject have an effect on performance comparable to an actual learning experience in the rat when it associates food with the end of one of the routes through the maze for the first time [pp. 77–78].

This paper went on to discuss explicitly the relevance of the "recent formalizations of expectancy theory by Meehl and MacCorquodale and Tolman" (previously cited) to the problem of the interaction of personality and situation in achievement motivation, even to the point of trying to blend their S_1-R_1-S_2 notation and Hebb's (1949) analysis of interaction of central and sensory influences on behavior. That effort now appears to be a rather blurry anticipation of what was to be said more clearly in simple algebraic terms a few years later. There can be little doubt that I had to shift from thinking in traditional animal behavioral terms dominated by S–R language to an appreciation of the value of a simple mathematical statement to bring an evolving conception of *motive* (personality) and *expectancy of the goal* (situation) into contact with the basic concepts of decision theory (Atkinson, 1958b).

The programmatic guide previously provided by Lewin was reinforced by other considerations later made explicit (Atkinson, 1958a):

> The decision to employ the concept of expectancy to carry the burden of the meaning of the situation for the person is the result of another consideration. It is an appreciation of the extent to which an appeal to cognitive expectations is the core of what social scientists in other fields have in mind when they speak of the *norms* of a society and the definitions of *roles* within a society. Working in his own bailiwick, the psychologist has become sensitive to the need—argued forcefully by Sears (1951)—for a conception of personality which makes contact with a theory of action, so that the individual will be described in terms of potentialities for action for which there are known principles. The psychologist may also be susceptible to another kind of argument. It should influence his choice of concept when there are admittedly many different alternatives open to him. The ultimate point of contact between psychological and sociological conceptions lies in the analysis of the behavior of persons in particular concrete situations. The choice of concept and the development of methods for treating the effect of the situation on the individual can enhance or hinder the possibility of integrating the conception of personality and the conception of social structure in concrete research [p. 616].

Rotter (1955), working independently all the while in the context of social learning, had argued effectively for developing an adequate technique for assessing the cue characteristics of situations and for a taxonomy of situations in terms of expectancies aroused, something we also were pursuing with some initially promising results in reference to the pictures used to instigate imaginative behavior (Jacobs, 1958; Birney, 1958).

The connection between the theoretical argument anchored in animal research and the mathematical model of decision-making, on the human side, occurred, for me at least, in 1955–56 while at the Center for Advanced Study in the Behavioral Sciences. It was then that I really began to understand the role of mathematical models of motivation. In a paper entitled, "Towards experimental analysis of human motivation in terms of motives, expectancies, and incentives," first written that year but not published until later (Atkinson, 1958b), I took this view of the problem:

> Experiments which have dealt chiefly with the effects of individual differences in strength of n Achievement and n Affiliation on performance show fairly clearly that both a disposition to strive for a particular goal (a motive) and an expectancy that an act will be instrumental in attaining the goal must be present for the motive to be aroused and expressed in performance of the act. The crude qualitative nature of experimental attempts to manipulate the expectancies of Ss has unavoidably confounded two variables which are given independent status by Tolman (1955) and in other expectancy theories. These two variables are the strength of *expectancy*, an appropriate measure of which would normally be some index of the probability that performance of the act will have a certain consequence, and the

amount of *incentive,* i.e., the magnitude of the reward or potential satisfaction offered should the expected consequence occur.

The distinction between expectancy and incentive is exemplified in the animal experiment in which the probability of reaching food by turning left or right in a maze can be varied independently of the amount of food that is present in the goal box. Given any amount of hunger, the motive, a half-dozen food pellets constitutes a greater incentive than only one. . . .

Given our interest in motives for achievement, affiliation, and power, an ideal experiment would be one in which individual differences in the strength of one of these motives, the relevant expectancy, and incentive are measured or varied independently. Our measures of strength of motive and a suitable index of the relative amount of satisfaction of that motive offered as an inducement to perform (incentive) would together constitute an empirical basis for inferences about the "subjective value" or what in decision theory is called the "utility" of the consequence of the act for particular persons. And variations in strength of expectancy reduced to some index of probability would bring our experiments that much closer to a probability-utility model for decision and action (Edwards, 1954) that is implied in a motive-expectancy-incentive formulation of the problem.

But at this time, it is difficult to imagine exactly how to go about producing variations in incentives that would be appropriate for the particular human motives we are currently able to measure in thematic apperception. What would constitute a variation in achievement, affiliation, or power incentives? This is a question for future research [pp. 288–289].

The results of an experiment undertaken to isolate the effects of experimentally controlled differences in strength of expectancy and monetary incentive on human motivation (as measured by level of effortful performance) suggested that "satisfaction in winning" must be greater "the more difficult the feat," as had been assumed in earlier theory about the level of aspiration. What struck me then is that the very same variables that presumably influenced the strength of competing inclinations in human decision making also seemed to be the determinants of the strength of tendency expressed in the level or magnitude of human performance, as had already been assumed in the theories of animal behavior. Among some proposals then made concerning *"Motivation Theory and Decision Theory"* the following were most useful (Atkinson, 1958b):

As a guide for research in experiments like the present one, it may be helpful simply to list a series of proposals having to do with the use of various terms and possible linkages between a motive–expectancy–incentive conception of human motivation and the probability–utility model for decision and action:

1. The term, *incentive,* has been used to refer to some potential reward or goal that can be manipulated by the experimenter—the amount of food, the amount of money, the difficulty of the task as an index of achievement-incentive, etc. It has been suggested that the incentive to achieve is greater the more difficult the task and specifically that achievement-incentive value equals 1 minus probability of suc-

cess. It is a problem for future research to discover what constitutes a basis for varying the strength of affiliation, power, and other kinds of incentives.

2. The term, *motive*, has been used to refer to the disposition within the person to strive to approach a certain class of positive incentives (goals) or to avoid a certain class of negative incentives (threats). The definition of a particular class of incentives constitutes the general aim of a particular motive. At present, we infer the strength of various motives through content analysis of thematic apperception.

3. The term, *expectancy*, has been used to refer to a particular kind of cognitive association aroused in the person by situational cues. In the expectancy learning theory, an expectancy is designated S–R–S (MacCorquodale & Meehl, 1953). The initial S refers to the situational cue which arouses a chain of associations involving an act, the R, and the consequence of the act, the final S. We are interested in expectancies which signify consequences which are incentives, i.e., potential satisfiers of some motive. A crude inference can be made of the strength of certain expectancies, i.e., the probability of certain consequences, from qualitative experimental arrangements such as variations in instructions given to a group for performance of a task. But better methods for measuring expectancies are needed.

4. Given an objectively-defined incentive for a group of Ss, e.g., a glass of water, the subjective value or utility of that incentive for a particular individual depends upon the strength of his motive, e.g., thirst. The utility of a positive incentive is a positive function of the strength of the motive to approach. The disutility of a negative incentive is a positive function of the strength of the motive to avoid.

6. The arousal of motivation to approach, i.e., to perform the act, is equivalent to the expected positive utility of the consequences. Here, the term *motivation* is used to designate the activated state of the person which occurs when the cues of a situation arouse the expectancy that performance of an act will lead to an incentive for which he has a motive.

7. The arousal of motivation to avoid, i.e., not to perform the act, is equivalent to the expected negative utility of the consequences.

8. The resultant motivation, which is expressed directly in performance, is a summation of motivation to approach and motivation to avoid. In decision theory this summation is referred to as the overall expected utility of the consequences.

These suggestions are offered to bring a rather loosely stated theory of human motivation into contact with the more rigorously stated ideas of decision theory. They obviously contribute nothing to the problem of exact measurement of subjective probabilities and utilities which is currently engaging a good deal of experimental interest in the field of decision making. The objective is a very limited one: to try to make some theoretical sense of the observed relationships between thematic–apperceptive measures of the strength of motives and the expression of motivation directly in the vigor and persistence of goal-directed effort. The immediate objective is to increase the theoretical relevance of our future experiments.

The concept of "subjective probability" implies that future-oriented cognitions may differ from person to person *when the objective basis for these cognitions is the same for all persons....* The concept of "subjective value" or utility implies that individuals may differ in the degree of satisfaction or dissatisfaction accompanying certain kinds of events. It serves one of the same explanatory functions as the concept of motive. In assuming that the utility of an incentive will vary as a function of the strength of the motive for incentives of that class, we discover then a sound basis for predicting that the expected utility, and hence performance, will be greater for persons who have strong motives *when the objective circumstance (in this case the incentive offered) is the same for everyone.* Winterbottom (1953, 1958) has found that children who are strong in achievement motive are rated by their teachers as showing more pride and pleasure in success than children who are weak in achievement motive. This suggests that the strength of a motive determines the capacity for satisfaction in goal attainment. In the case of avoidance motive— fears, fatigue, guilt, etc.—the assumption will account for greater negative expected utility, and hence stronger avoidant behavior, the stronger the motive in the individual [pp. 303–305].

Although it had been recognized that the words "individual differences in strength of motive to achieve" could be restated "individual differences in subjective value or utility of achievement" within the framework of the SEU model for decision-making, this step was not explicitly taken in the initial statement (Atkinson, 1957) of what later would be called a theory of achievement motivation (Atkinson & Feather, 1966). Why not? It seems, in retrospect, that the equivalence of the conceptual analysis of activation of behavior by Tolman working with animals and decision theory had not yet been confidently accepted. It also seemed important *then* to preserve the order and distinction between personality and immediate environmental (or situational) determinants of motivation as expressed in Lewin's programmatic guide, $B = f(P,E)$. The conceptual analysis of achievement-oriented behavior still followed in Tolman's footsteps. Here, for example, is how the general conception was stated by Atkinson in 1957:

> *The principle of motivation.* The strength of motivation to perform some act is assumed to be a multiplicative function of the strength of the motive, the expectancy (subjective probability) that the act will have as a consequence the attainment of an incentive, and the value of the incentive: Motivation = f(Motive × Expectancy × Incentive). This formulation corresponds to Tolman's (1955) analysis of performance except, perhaps, in the conception of a motive as a relatively stable disposition. When both motivation to approach and motivation to avoid are simultaneously aroused, the resultant motivation is the algebraic summation of approach and avoidance. The act which is performed among a set of alternatives is the act for which the resultant motivation is most positive. The magnitude of response and the persistence of behavior are functions of the strength of motivation to perform the act relative to the strength of motivation to perform competing acts [pp. 360–361].

Then followed the initial discussion of the implications of this conception when applied to achievement-related behavior. It was assumed that motives to achieve success (M_S), and to avoid failure (M_F) were relatively stable dispositions of personality. The strength of expectancies was represented as subjective probabilities of success (P_s) and failure (P_f). And the incentive values of these particular outcomes were assumed to be inversely related to their respective subjective probabilities, e.g., $In_s = 1 - P_s$ and $In_f = -(1 - P_f) = -P_s$. The whole discussion had to do with the implications of individual differences in personality. What was to be expected when $M_S > M_F$ within the individual? When $M_F > M_S$?

By this time, the equivalence of concepts in decision theory and in the earlier Lewinian theory of psychological forces had been recognized as, for example, by Edwards (1954). The early algebraic discussion of the components of achievement motivation was considered an extension of ideas presented in the *resultant valence* theory of level of aspiration by Escalona and Festinger (cited in Lewin, et al, 1944).

IMPLICATION OF AN INHIBITORY TENDENCY WHEN THE VALUE OF EXPECTED CONSEQUENCE IS NEGATIVE

If one compares the initial statement of the theory of achievement motivation (Atkinson, 1957) with later ones (e.g., Atkinson, 1964; Atkinson & Feather, 1966), it is apparent that it took us quite a while to break the habit of using familiar but ambiguous terms (e.g., "strength of motivation") and of taking for granted some intuitively compelling conventional ideas (e.g., that strong fear of failure should motivate performance). We gradually substituted terms that could begin to be given more precise technical meanings (e.g., strength of *tendency*), and we gradually became more willing to listen to what new things the theory, once stated, was trying to say. We became more willing to comprehend what the algebraic statement of this kind of cognitive theory of motivation implied when the expected consequence of an act was negative (e.g., failure).

Our thinking about the additive motivational effect of separate tendencies to act, attributable to expectations of attaining several different goals (or incentives) through performance of a task (Atkinson & Reitman, 1956), corresponded to the explicitly stated assumption of additivity in the determination of subjectively expected utility (SEU) of some alternative in decision theory. That is, SEU $= p_1 u_1 + p_2 u_2 + \cdots p_n u_n$ where p and u refer, respectively, to the strength of expectancy or subjective probability of an outcome and its utility or subjective value for an individual. The additive algebraic combination of the strengths of the tendencies to approach the expected success (T_s) and to avoid the expected failure (T_{-f}) was fully appreciated in reference to risk-taking preferences, the choice problem, in the initial statement of theory (Atkinson, 1957). But somehow the implication of the theoretical statement was abandoned, then, in favor of intuition in a less than systematic initial discussion of how the strength of tendency to avoid failure should influence the vigor and effort of task performance.

In attempting to characterize (instead of deducing) the behavior of the person for whom resultant tendency to achieve was negative, because the motive to avoid failure dominated the motive to achieve success, these erroneous conjectures were initially advanced by Atkinson (1957):

> How does the more fearful person behave when offered only a specific task to perform? He can either perform the task or leave the field. If he chooses to leave the field, there is no problem. But if he is constrained, as he must be to remain in any competitive achievement situation, he will stay at the task and presumably work at it. But how hard will he work at it? He is motivated to avoid failure, and when constrained, there is only one path open to him to avoid failure—success at the task he is presented. So we expect him to manifest the strength of his motivation to avoid failure in performance of the task. He too, in other words, should *try hardest* when P_s is .50 and less hard when the chance of winning is either greater or less. The 50–50 alternative is the last he would choose if allowed to set his own goal, but once constrained he must try hard to avoid the failure which threatens him. Not working at all will guarantee failure of the task. Hence, the thought of not working at all should produce even stronger avoidant motivation than that aroused by the task itself [p. 364].

It was difficult, at the outset, to realize that one of the most important new things implied by a theory emphasizing the motivational significance of expected consequences ("retaining sign!") is the concept of an inhibitory tendency, a tendency *not* to perform the act, when the expected consequence is negative (Atkinson, 1964):

> These initial common-sense conjectures were misleading in that they missed what is clearly implied when failure is conceived as having a *negative* incentive value. If a particular act is expected to lead to a *negative* incentive, then the product of motive, expectancy, and incentive will be *negative* and the tendency (T_{-f}) must be conceived as a tendency *not* to perform the act—that is, as an inhibitory tendency. Thus, given this conception, the threat of failure does not directly *excite* avoidant actions *or* "task-relevant" actions. Instead, the threat of failure is conceived as producing a tendency to *inhibit* the performance of actions which are expected to produce failure. This inhibitory tendency, called the tendency to avoid failure, opposes and dampens the positive tendency to approach success which does *excite* actions that are expected to lead to the goal, success [p. 246].

It is presumed in the theory of achievement motivation that some persons are chronically more strongly motivated to avoid failure than to achieve success. This means that their resultant tendency to achieve, no matter what the circumstances, is always negative. They would, if they could, resist or avoid *all* activities in which the outcome of performance can be considered a success or a failure. Acknowledging this, researchers guided by the theory of achievement motivation (Atkinson & Litwin, 1960; Feather, 1961, 1962) found it convenient, reasonable, and necessary to assume the presence of other extrinsic sources of positive motivation to perform the same actions (social approval, deference to authority, etc.). The strength of such extrinsic tendencies, each considered the product of another motive, expectancy, and incentive, could compensate for the strength of the inhibitory tendency, thus overcoming the disinclination to act. The overall strength of tendency to act attributable to resultant tendency to achieve ($T_s + T_{-f}$) and extrinsic tendency (T_{ext}) would then be positive. Without this presumption of additional sources of positive tendency strength, there would be no action given the logic of the algebraic conception. Standing before the ringtoss game, the chronically "anxious" person would, otherwise, prefer not to engage in any of the alternative achievement-related activities. To argue that an individual should undertake the activity for which the resultant inhibitory tendency is weakest (i.e., minimization of disutility) leans rather heavily on the presumption that individuals are somehow compelled to act by factors not represented in the theory. It is a gratuitous presumption when one notices how many people in the world do, in fact, resist achievement-related activity completely. It rather surprised me that Lewin (1938), who had devoted great attention to defining the path-goal directional implications of psychological forces, had missed the implication of his conception of a force "away from" an anticipated threat. It specified only what act (path) would be avoided, not what would be done *instead* (Atkinson, 1964, pp. 76-77). Most students of Lewin have continued to view both forces to approach goals and to avoid threats as *driving* forces despite this lack of specification of the act to be performed when the anticipated consequence is negative.

One important general implication of our concept of a tendency *not* to do something that is expected to produce a negative consequence was an alternative to the S-R behavior theory account of the determinants of avoidance behavior summarized briefly by Atkinson and Feather (1966):

It is the idea that so-called avoidance or defensive behavior may not be caused by "anxiety" and reinforced by "anxiety reduction," as conceived within the framework of S-R behavior theory (Mowrer, 1939; Miller, 1948). In the case of achievement-oriented activity, anxiety about failure is associated with the tendency to inhibit a particular activity. What the individual in whom $M_{AF} > M_S$ does in an achievement-oriented context may be construed as avoidant behavior or defensive behavior. But a close look at the determinants of either an unrealistically high or low level of aspiration shows that the occurrence of one or the other of these alternatives is explained by the assumed presence of some extrinsic positive tendency to undertake the dreaded achievement-oriented action that is sufficient to overcome resistance. The individual is viewed as acting merely to comply with an authority or to gain approval for doing what is expected. In a very real sense, he is not achievement-oriented at all, but is merely going through the motions of what for others *is* achievement-oriented activity. He does what he does because other alternative activities (those representing intermediate or moderate risk) are inhibited.

Consequently, the final strength of the tendency to engage in a very safe or a very speculative venture, although weak, wins out in the competition among action tendencies.

The same sort of thing may happen to produce what is generally called avoidance behavior. Suppose that in a given situation, a number of different positive action tendencies are initially aroused in an individual, among them being one to engage in activity which would take him from the situation. Suppose that this positive tendency "to leave the field," whatever its determinants, stands relatively low in the initial hierarchy of activated tendencies. The individual will perform other activities which keep him in the stimulus situation instead of, or before, he expresses this tendency. If the individual is punished while, or immediately after, performing these other activities, he should later expect that they will lead to punishment. As a result, the activities should begin to suffer resistance. The so-called avoidance activity would then be more likely to occur, because even though nothing has happened to strengthen the tendency to engage in it, a lot has happened to weaken the *resultant* tendencies to engage in other activities. In time, the tendency to undertake the so-called avoidance activity would become *relatively* stronger than the others. In this conception, the so-called avoidance behavior is considered a weakly, but *positively* motivated activity which occurs at all only because each of the tendencies to engage in some other activity is now effectively blocked by an inhibitory tendency resulting from the expectancy of punishment.

This alternative to the anxiety-reduction theory of avoidance behavior is elaborated more fully elsewhere (Atkinson, 1964, Chapter 10). It suggests that "anxiety" be viewed as symptomatic that an individual is engaging in some activity with an expectancy of a negative outcome but not as the *cause* of the so-called avoidance response. Accordingly, there should be little or no anxiety when an individual is performing an activity with little or no expectancy of a negative outcome (i.e., when there is little or no resistance to the activity). As pointed out in the initial statement of the theory, the person in whom $M_S > M_{AF}$ should voluntarily place himself in a competitive activity which will *maximize* his anxiety about failure. But the person in whom $M_{AF} < M_S$, when given an opportunity, should voluntarily follow a strategy of *minimizing* his anxiety about failure [pp. 335–337].

In reference to extinction of the so-called avoidance response in studies of animal avoidance conditioning, other investigators who have employed Tolman's concept of expectancy (e.g., Ritchie, 1951) have emphasized that the animal must stay in the place where it has been shocked long enough and often enough to find out that the shock is no longer applied. I noted earlier (Atkinson, 1964), that this means, specifically: "*the animal must perform responses that are expected to be followed by shock, but without shock as the consequence so that the expectancy that the response is followed by shock can be weakened*. . . . But how is the animal to change its expectancy of the consequences of responses performed in the box unless it stays in the box and performs them [p. 290]?

To enhance the credibility of applying something learned from studying human achievement motivation to interpretation of avoidance behavior in animals, Stuart Karabenick and I once devised a simple experimental situation for use with human subjects that was, we thought, analogous to the way avoidance conditioning had been studied in animals by Solomon and Wynne (1956):

Subjects are seated at a table on which before them are five colored cards—white, yellow, red, blue, green. They are instructed that at each click of a timing device they may place their hand on one of the cards or none of them. They are also instructed that the amount of money (up to $5.00) which they will be paid at the end of the period will depend upon the number of points they accumulate relative to the total number of points it is possible to accumulate during the period. When the timing device clicks for the first time, the subject places his hand on one of the colors. The experimenter immediately reports "Win 25" or some "rewarding" or "punishing" consequence that has been predetermined. This procedure continues for more than an hour with the interval between responses set at approximately four seconds. If the subject passes, that is, does not touch one of the cards when the timing device clicks, the experimenter immediately reports the consequence of that particular act to the subject.

This situation is designed to provide an exhaustive account of what the subject is doing throughout the experimental period. At every click of the timing device, he has his hand on one of the colors or not. And each of the six alternatives (including "Pass") is considered a particular act having some immediate consequence to the subject, that is, a number of points won or lost.

In advance of the experiment, the investigators predetermined what the consequence of each response would be on each occasion when the timing device clicked. In one condition, it was decided to mold a hierarchy of responses by rewarding the subject for any response during the first 90 clicks of the timing device but varying the average amount of reward for the different colored cards and the pass response.

During the next 70 clicks, a signal light came on and remained on for a number of clicks of the timing device on several occasions but without producing any change in the amount of reward following each of the responses. This light did not produce much change in the hierarchy of response tendencies which had been established by differential reward.

After the hierarchy of responses in this situation had been established, "avoidance conditioning" was begun. During avoidance training, the signal light (CS) came on and stayed on until the subject placed his hand on "Blue," which was the second weakest response in the initial hierarchy. The rewards following any response were the same as usual for the first six clicks after the light (CS) came on, but on the seventh click and thereafter until the response "Blue" occurred, the consequence of any response other than "Blue" was "Lose 1000." When the subject placed his hand on "Blue," he both turned off the light and received the usual weak reward for the "Blue" response.

The investigators view this situation as analogous to the usual avoidance training situation with animals. There are a number of different responses an animal can make in the context in which he will later be shocked, including the response that the experimenter will later call the avoidance response. It is assumed that each of

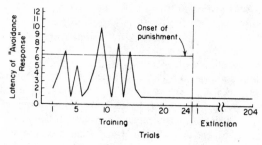

FIG. 2.1. Avoidance training and extinction series for one subject (6A) under conditions described in text. This subject took 24 trials to meet the arbitrary criterion of learning (10 consecutive trials on which the "avoidance response," Blue, occurred within six clicks following onset of the visual stimulus). He then continued to make this response immediately after the onset of the light for 204 trials with no sign of extinction. At this point the experiment was concluded. (Atkinson, 1964, p. 292.)

these responses is expected to have some rewarding consequence by the animal, or else it would not be performed. It is established that the stimulus which later will be the conditioned stimulus for the avoidance response (the light) has no effect on the behavior of the subject before avoidance training is begun. Then avoidance training is begun with a seven-click interval between the onset of the light (*CS*) and the onset of the report "Lose 1000," which is considered analogous to the extremely negative consequence, the shock, normally employed in animal studies.

The results for 10 subjects show that the so-called avoidance response, in this case putting the hand on "Blue," is learned within 11 to 55 trials by all subjects to a criterion of 10 successive "Blue" responses within six clicks following the onset of the light. After this criterion of learning has been met, the extinction trials begin, and the subject is never again punished for any response when the light comes on. Hand on "Blue," however, continues to turn off the light. Other responses are rewarded, as during the pre-training period, but do not turn off the light.

In this preliminary experiment, 4 out of 10 subjects continued to perform the so-called avoidance response within six clicks whenever the light came on until interruption of the experiment by the end of the planned experimental period (an hour and a half). Two subjects reached an extinction criterion of five successive trials with light on without putting their hand on "Blue" within 15 clicks of the timing device. These subjects took 18 and 21 trials to extinguish the "Blue" response. Four subjects were taking somewhat more than six clicks to put their hand on "Blue" by the end of the period, but had not yet reached the arbitrary extinction criterion.

Figure 2.1[3] shows the results obtained for the subject who had the most trials with the light on after training. It is obvious that his behavior begins to resemble the

---

[3]Numbers of tables and figures appearing in long extracts of earlier presentations have been renumbered for this chapter.

behavior of the dogs in the Solomon experiment which had been exposed to a traumatic shock during training. He had shown no signs of extinction after 204 trials.

According to Expectancy × Value theory, this subject continues to perform a weakly but positively motivated response because nothing has happened to change his expectancy that performance of one of the other responses, which normally produces more points when the light is off, will be followed by a great loss of points when the light is on. When the light was off, this subject showed the same preference for "White" and the other more highly rewarded responses that he had displayed before the avoidance training was instituted.

It seems very doubtful, in this instance, that the extreme resistance to extinction is to be explained in terms of an intense fear that is being aroused every time the light goes on and reduced every time the light goes off.

RECONSIDERATION OF "EXPECTANCY × VALUE" WITHIN THE FRAMEWORK OF THE NEW DYNAMICS OF ACTION

There have been two key developments concerning the theory of achievement motivation as presented in Atkinson and Feather (1966). First, it has been elaborated into a more general theory by Raynor (1969, 1974). He has taken into account the motivational impact on present behavior of the expectations concerning more distant future goals and threats that characterize lifelike achievement-oriented actions. These had been ignored completely in the earlier conceptual analysis based on performance of a simple laboratory task having only *immediate* rewarding or punishing consequences. Second, a clue provided in Feather's (1961, 1962) conceptual analysis of persistence within the framework of the early theory of achievement motivation, and explicit recognition of the limitations of the traditional conceptions of the motivation of behavior, provided the foundation for a reconstruction of the theory of motivation, *The Dynamics of Action* (Atkinson & Birch, 1970, 1974, 1978). The essentials of this new conceptual scheme have recently been summarized as follows (Atkinson, 1977):

Traditional theories of motivation, both cognitive (e.g., Cartwright & Festinger, 1943; Edwards, 1954; Lewin 1938; Tolman, 1955) and within S-R behavior theory (e.g., Hull, 1943; Miller, 1959; Spence, 1956), are stimulus bound. This means that the individual is implicitly viewed as at rest, not doing anything, and unmotivated *to do* anything, until exposed to the stimulus situation of critical interest. The theory of achievement motivation is also like that. It treats the person as if the individual were dead until confronted with the stimulus situation, e.g., a ring-toss game, at which time, as a result of some kind of sudden interaction of personality and environment there occurs—*instantaneously*—a set of competing motivational tendencies of certain magnitudes that control behavior. Life is not like that (Atkinson, 1964, Chapter 10; Atkinson & Cartwright, 1964).

The new dynamics of action exposes the simplistic character of this conventional *episodic* view of behavior, where every new action begins like an event at a track meet with a stimulus situation analogous to the starter's gun. This S–O–R *paradigm* of traditional psychological theory, to use Kuhn's (1962) term, is founded in the Cartesian concept of reflex that served the new science of physiology so well in the nineteenth century and was a great help to psychology during the first half of this century.

Now, however, we begin with a new premise: that an individual is already active in two senses of the word before being exposed to the traditional stimulus situation that in the past was supposed to get things started. The individual is already doing something when a scientific observer initially takes notice. Second, the individual is also already actively motivated to do many other different things before exposure to the stimulus situation of traditional interest. This was one of Freud's great insights: that wishes, inclinations, or tendencies, once aroused—whenever—persist until expressed in behavior, directly or substitutively, long past the point of direct exposure to their initial instigating stimulus.

This means, in effect, that we break out of the traditional mode of thought that has always considered behavioral episodes as isolated events and begin viewing the behavioral life of an individual as a continual stream characterized by change from one activity to another even in a constant environment. The focus of interest shifts from concern with the initiation, instrumental phase, and consummatory phase of particular isolated activities to the continuity of behavior and the juncture between different activities, a change from one to another.

To explain a simple change in activity coherently becomes the fundamental problem for a science of motivation. And to be able to do it gives one the conceptual tools needed to account for a series or sequence of changes, a much longer temporal unit of behavior, and the various measurable aspects of the stream of operant behavior, for example, relative frequency of various activities, operant level, proportion of time spent in an activity, and others (Birch, 1972).

In *The Dynamics of Action* (Atkinson & Birch, 1970, 1974), we conceived the impact of the immediate environment (or stimulus situation) on behavior to be the various instigating and inhibitory forces it produces. These influence the arousal of an individual's tendencies to engage or not to engage in certain activities. If a certain kind of activity has been intrinsically satisfying or rewarded in this kind of situation, there will be an *instigating force* (F) for that activity. This will cause a more or less rapid increase in the strength of an inclination to engage in that activity, an *action tendency* (T), depending on the magnitude of the force. If a certain kind of activity has been frustrated or punished in the past, there will be an *inhibitory force* (I) and a more or less rapid growth in the strength of a disinclination to act or *negaction tendency* (N). This is a tendency *not* to do it. The duration of exposure to these forces (t for time) will determine how strong the action or negaction tendency becomes. The latter, the tendency not to do something, will produce *resistance* to the activity. It opposes, blocks, dampens, the action tendency. That is, it subtracts from the action tendency to determine the *resultant action tendency* ($\bar{T} = T - N$). The resultant action tendency competes with resultant action tendencies for other incompatible activities. The strongest of them is expressed in behavior.

The expression of an action tendency in behavior is what reduces it. Engaging in an activity produces a *consummatory force* (C) which depends in part on the *consummatory value* (c) of the particular *kind* of activity and in part on the *intensity* of the activity as determined by the strength of tendency then being expressed in the activity ($C = c\overline{T}$). Similarly, resistance to an action tendency, produced by the opposition of a negaction tendency, constitutes an analogous *force of resistance* (R) which reduces, in a comparable way, the strength of the negaction tendency.

This, very briefly, introduces our conception of the causal factors involved in the continuous rise and decline in strength of tendencies illustrated in Fig. 2.2. These changes in motivation in turn account for the changes from one activity to another (x, y, z, etc.) that characterize the normal stream of an individual's behavior, even in a constant environment. The figure is the result of one of our earliest computer simulations of what should be expected to happen if an individual were exposed to instigating forces of different magnitudes for three incompatible activities in the same environment (Seltzer, 1973).

A single and fairly simple principle of change in activity can be derived. It yields hypotheses about how the magnitude of instigating and inhibitory forces will influence the initiation of an activity (latency of response), choice, the duration or persistence of a particular activity, the proportion of total time spent in a given activity, relative frequency of activities, and, derivately, the operant level or rate of an activity in a constant environment.

The basic concepts, presented in Table 2.1, should not seem totally unfamiliar. In the framework of the new dynamics of action, *the theory of achievement motiva-*

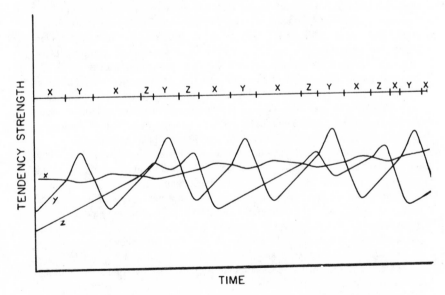

FIG. 2.2.   An example of a stream of activity (x, y, z) and its underlying tendency structure. (From Seltzer, 1973.)

TABLE 2.1
Analogous Concepts in the
Treatment of Instigation of
Action and Resistance to Action[a]

Instigation of action	Resistance to action
Instigating force, F	Inhibitory force, I
Action tendency, T	Negaction tendency, N
Action	Resistance
Consummatory force, C	Force of resistance, R

[a]From Atkinson and Birch (1970).

tion is now to be considered a theory about the determinants of instigating forces to achieve success (F_s) and inhibitory forces to avoid failure (I_f) in various activities and not, as heretofore assumed, of the final strength of tendencies to achieve success and to avoid failure in a particular situation. A distinction is made between the arousability (or rate of arousal) of a tendency, the magnitude of force (F), and the level of arousal or strength of that tendency (T) at a particular time. A similar distinction has been made by Whalen (1966) in analysis of sexual motivation.

To understand the new concepts, consider the various ways in which an observed change of activity, from A to B, might come about after a certain period of time (t) in a constant environment. In Fig. 2.3 we assume that initially (i) $T_{A_i} > T_{B_i}$, but when the change finally (f) occurs, $T_{B_f} > T_{A_f}$. The change in activity implies a change in the strength of one or both of the action tendencies. For example, think of an individual studying (achievement) who finally puts down a book and begins to talk to a nearby friend (affiliation). Or think of a student engaged in a friendly conversation (affiliation) who stops, at a certain point, and begins to study (achievement). In both simplified examples we are pitting the strength of tendency for affiliation against the strength of tendency to achieve.

What causes the change(s) in motivation implied by the observed change in activity? We begin very conservatively, eschewing the idea that action tendencies change in strength spontaneously by mere random oscillation from moment to moment (an assumption in traditional theory). Freud argued that the wish persists until it is expressed. We sharpen that language somewhat. A behavioral tendency, once aroused, will persist in its present state until acted upon by some psychological force that either increases or decreases its strength.

This first assumption explains why all of the tendencies in the graphs of Fig. 2.3 have some initial (or inertial) strength above zero at the beginning of the interval of observation. (The person is active—already doing something (activity A) and already actively motivated to do activity B, and certainly many other activities, should we care to complicate both the graphs and discussion.)

The cause of the change in the strength of a tendency must be something that occurs during the time interval. We suppose that the source of the *instigating force* (F), which functions to increase the strength of a particular inclination to act (T), is most often some discriminable feature of the immediate environment—a stimulus—to which the individual is exposed. And we suppose that the consummatory force (C), which reduces the strength of a particular tendency, is usually attributable to expression of that tendency in the activity itself, the other thing happening during the time interval. The change in strength of a particular tendency during the interval of time should then depend upon the relative strengths of instigating and consummatory forces. That is,

$$\frac{T_f - T_i}{t} = F - C.$$

Clearly if $F > C$, the tendency (T) will become stronger. If $C > F$, T will become weaker. And if $F = C$, the strength of T will remain constant.

Now consider what is different about the dominant tendency, T_A, which is initially being expressed in activity A, and T_B, a subordinate tendency which is not. Since activity B is not occurring, there is no consummatory force (C_B). But since there is an F_B, the strength of T_B is going to increase. The amount of increase, $T_f - T_i$, can be attributed to the exposure of the person to F_B throughout the time interval (t). That is, $T_{B_f} - T_{B_i} = F_B \cdot t$. Suppose F_B had been twice as strong? Then it would have produced an equivalent increase in strength of T_B in half the time. By strength or magnitude of F we refer to the arousability of a tendency as shown by the upward slope of the curves representing the strength of T_B in the graphs (see Figure 2.3) which describe the rate of change in the strength of that tendency.

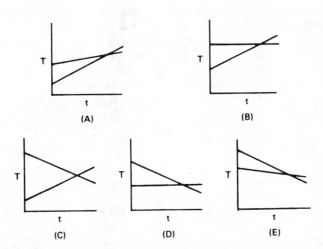

FIG. 2.3. Various ways in which a change in relative strength of T_A and T_B can come about during an interval of time (t). (From Atkinson & Birch, 1970, 1974.)

We can say it another way: $T_{B_t} = T_{B_1} + F_B \cdot t$. Look at any one of the graphs. At the outset, T_{B_1} has a certain strength above zero to which is added the increase in strength attributable to exposure to the magnitude of F_B times the duration of exposure to it, t.

The conditions are different for T_A. Since activity A is occurring, T_A is being expressed in behavior, and so there is the consummatory force (C_A) of activity A in addition to F_A attributable to some feature of the immediate environment. We have assumed (see above) that the magnitude of C_A depends upon the consummatory value (c_A) of the particular *kind of activity* that is occurring (eating a cherry pie versus eating a piece of celery serve as examples of different kinds of eating activities) and the *intensity of the activity*, which here depends on the magnitude of T_A being expressed in behavior. So $C_A = c_A \cdot T_A$.[4] We thus can determine when the strength of T_A will become relatively stable or constant, whether it is increasing because $F_A > C_A$ at the outset, or decreasing because $C_A > F_A$ at the outset. It will become stable when $F_A = C_A$, that is when $F_A = c_A \cdot T_A$, that is when $F_A/c_A = T_A$. The strength of T_A will become relatively constant when it begins to reach a level defined by the ratio of the instigating force for the activity (F_A) and the consummatory value of that activity (c_A). In general, then, T_A will tend to be strong when F_A (the numerator) is strong and weak when F_A is weak.

(This means that our now viewing the theory of achievement motivation as a theory about the determinants of instigating forces to achieve success (F_s), and inhibitory forces to avoid failure (I_f), as previously stated, does not change earlier conclusions dramatically. If $F_s = M_S \cdot P_s \cdot In_s$, as now assumed for the simplest case, the new deduction that the strength of T_s will become stable in a given situation at a level proportionate to the magnitude of F_s is not a great departure from the earlier idea that, in a given situation, $T_s = M_S \cdot P_s \cdot In_s$, a notion which we now discard.)

Now we can derive a basic principle of a change in activity, one which will tell us *when* the change from A to B will occur. When we observe activity A initially in progress, it implies that $T_{A_1} > T_{B_1}$. When we observe that activity A ceases and activity B is initiated, it implies that $T_{B_t} > T_{A_t}$ (or that $T_{B_t} = T_{A_t}$ plus a very small and negligible amount which we shall ignore). If we now substitute the determinants of T_{B_t} for T_{B_t}, we can say activity B is initiated *when* $T_{B_1} + F_B \cdot t = T_{A_t}$. And the principle of change in activity emerges when we solve that equation for *when*, the time, t:

$$t = \frac{T_{A_t} - T_{B_1}}{F_B}$$

If activity A has been going on for a while and T_A has become relatively stable, we may restate the principle to identify the motivational functions of both F_A and F_B, features of the immediate environment, by substituting F_A/c_A for T_{A_t}:

---

[4]The reader is reminded that it is the strength of the *resultant action tendency* ($\bar{T} = T\text{-}N$) that gets expressed in behavior. Thus, in general, $C_A = c_A \cdot \bar{T}_A$. But *here* we implicitly assume that $N_A = 0$. So $\bar{T}_A = T_A$ and $C_A = c_A \cdot T_A$ as stated in the text.

$$t = \frac{F_A/c_A - T_{B_1}}{F_B}$$

In reference to our first example of a change from achievement-related to affiliative activity, consider the effect of a very strong motive to achieve (M_S). If this strong M_S is sustaining the activity in progress by having an influence on F_A, it will be more difficult to interrupt studying than if M_S is weak. The time to change to affiliative activity will be long.

In reference to our second example, suppose the strong M_S is now influencing F_B. This should promote a greater willingness to initiate activity B (begin studying) promptly than would a weak motive. Thus, other things equal, the person strong in achievement motive should be more willing than others to initiate achievement activities when engaged in or confronted with other alternatives. And since the strength of the tendency expressed in an ongoing activity will approach a higher level when F_A is strong, the person strongly motivated to achieve should express a stronger tendency in behavior and be more persistent in achievement-related activity once he gets started.

Of course, the time to change from achievement to affiliative activity, and vice versa, will depend on the relative strength of the two motives within the person. This will influence the relative strength of F_A and F_B in these examples. Suppose M_S is weak and M_{aff} is strong in both examples we have just considered?

One, perhaps, can now begin to see how the principle of a change in activity provides a theoretical foundation for expecting to find correlations among different behavioral symptoms of individual differences in strength of motives. Probably most important, this principle constitutes a specification of how an individual with several motives that differ in strength will distribute time among different kinds of activity when it is applied to a continuous stream of behavior (see Fig. 2.2). Only when the achievement motive is very strong relative to the affiliative motive, within a person, will the person be very slow to leave an achievement activity for an affiliative activity and very prompt to go the other way. And only when the achievement motive is very weak relative to the affiliative motive within the person will he be quick to leave an achievement-oriented activity for affiliation and very slow to resume it. In between these imagined extreme types, we have the quantitative continuum of individual differences in strength of motives and of the relative strengths of different motives within the person. We only need to expand our conception to include a larger number of general motives in the basic personality structure (n Power, n Autonomy, n Sex, n Eat, etc.), to consider each as an important determinant of an instigating force for a different kind of activity, and to include further consideration of the more specific and situationally defined determinants of each force (competence in particular kinds of activities, (P_s), future orientation (or not), etc.) to see that the principle of a change in activity provides a very specific answer to the question of how various determinants of instigating force, differing in degree of generality—specificity, but all critical dimensions of personality, should be expressed in behavior [pp. 74–81].

Before moving on to the new conception of resistance, let us reconsider the behavioral implications of considering the earlier theory of achievement motivation as a specification of the determinants of instigating force to achieve success (F_s) in various activities in particular situations and not as previously assumed, of the static strength of tendencies to achieve success (T_s). Here we again summarize what is developed more fully elsewhere (Atkinson & Birch, 1970, 1974, 1978). And let us consider the implications of a more general proposal (Atkinson & Birch, 1970, pp. 175–183) that, in the language of the model for decision making, the product of the subjective probability (P) and the utility (U) of any consequence of an activity corresponds to the strength of an instigating force (or as we see later, an inhibitory force) for the activity that is expected to produce that consequence.

First, in reference to the initiation of an activity, the familiar assumption of adding the motivational implications of expecting some positive extrinsic goal to the strength of the tendency to achieve success is retained as shown in Fig. 2.4. So far, there is no departure from the traditional logic of $\mathrm{SEU} = P_1U_1 + P_2U_2 + \cdots P_nU_n$ except that the positive SEU is conceived as equivalent to the net instigating force that determines the rate of arousal of the inclination to act rather than its immediate static strength as before.

Second, it is obvious that coordinating expectation of positive outcome with instigating force, as conceived in the dynamics of action, provides a powerful

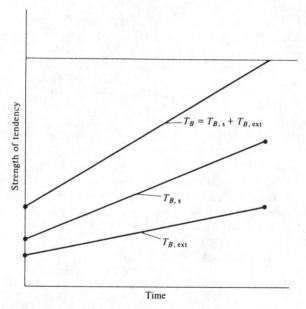

FIG. 2.4. *A compound action tendency.* When an individual is exposed to an instigating force to undertake activity B to achieve success ($F_{B,s}$), and to attain some extrinsic incentive ($F_{B,\mathrm{ext}}$), the strength of T_B equals $T_{B,s} + T_{B,\mathrm{ext}}$ at each moment as shown. (From Atkinson and Birch, 1978, p. 131.)

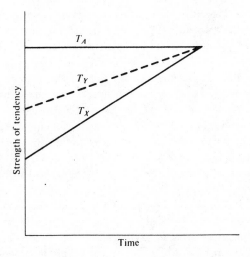

FIG. 2.5. *A special case of choice.* From inspection we deduce that preference follows the stronger instigating force *except* when the ratio of the initial gaps (i.e., $T_{A_f} - T_{X_i}/T_{A_f} - T_{Y_i}$) is greater than the ratio of the respective instigating forces (i.e., F_X/F_Y). In this graph, the ratio of both initial gaps and respective forces is 2 to 1. (From Atkinson and Birch, 1970.)

new basis for deducing effects of expectations on a number of different measurable aspects of action (viz., latency, persistence, choice, rate or operant level, time allocation among competing activities).

In reference to choice, the new dynamics of action has some new things to say. Given the principle of change in activity, the key question is which alternative, if presented by itself under the given conditions, would have the shortest latency of response? And since this time to initiate an activity may be influenced as much by the initial strength of a tendency, attributable to earlier instigation and carried over to the present situation unchanged in strength, one does not always expect that the alternative instigated by the stronger instigating force (i.e., the one having the greater magnitude of SEU) will be preferred. The choice of the "less attractive" of two alternatives need not be attributed to random oscillation in the strength of alternatives as traditionally assumed.

A special case of choice between alternatives X and Y is shown in Fig. 2.5. Under these circumstances the latencies of X and Y (if presented alone) would be equal. Because $F_X > F_Y$, as implied by the steeper slope describing *the more rapid arousal of T_X than T_Y*, alternative X, which is instigated by the stronger force, will become the dominant tendency (and chosen) in the next moment. But we can see that this would not be expected to happen if the initial strength of the other alternative (T_Y) had been stronger than shown in the graph or if the initial strength of the tendency for the chosen alternative (T_X) had been weaker than is shown in the graph. According to the dynamics of action, choice depends on the ratio of the magnitudes of the instigating forces (i.e., the ratio of the rates of arousal of competing inclinations) and not the difference between their magnitudes (Atkinson & Birch, 1970, pp. 107–118). Under certain conditions (viz., when the ratio of the initial gaps, $T_{A_f} - T_{X_i}/T_{A_f} - T_{Y_i}$, is greater than the ratio of the respective instigating forces), what might seem to an observer to be the less attractive of two alternatives will be chosen. This kind of apparently stupid or inconsistent behavior often occurs and is attributable to variations in the initial strengths of competing tendencies in choice situations.

An illustration of choice governed by the ratio of the magnitudes of instigating force (rather than the absolute difference in magnitude) is shown in Fig. 2.6. We once designed a simple experiment to show that if the monetary incentive value of a winning choice (In_w) among lotteries were arranged so that the prize for a lucky choice increased as the probability of winning (P_w) it decreased ($In_w = 1 - P_w$), people would prefer lotteries offering .50 probability of winning (Atkinson & Birch, 1970, pp. 178–185). This was a simple lottery model of achievement motivation in which the central assumption is $In_s = 1 - P_s$. Here quite obviously, the outcome was a matter of chance and not skill. Yet the monetary values of these outcomes were varied in a way that corresponded to the hypothesis concerning the relation of pride in accomplishment to task difficulty in achievement-oriented action. According to Atkinson and Birch (1978):

> College students were told they would be given an opportunity to make a series of choices among different containers. Each container, they knew, held 100 beads, among which a certain number, 10, 20, . . . 90, were distinctively colored "lucky" beads. If the person, in reaching "blind" into one or another container happened to draw a lucky bead from it, he knew he would be given a certain amount of money at the end of the experiment. Attached to each container was a small cardboard sign that stated accurately the number of lucky beads in the container (out of 100) and the monetary value of a lucky bead. Thus the sign on one container said, "10 lucky beads—win 9 cents"; another said "50 lucky beads—win 5 cents"; another said "70 lucky beads—win 3 cents"; and so on. One kind of information defined the objective probability of drawing a lucky bead (without looking); the other kind of information defined the monetary value of drawing a lucky bead. The former should have influenced the degree of certainty (expectancy) that reaching into the container would yield a lucky bead; the latter, the relative attractiveness (value) of drawing that particular lucky bead. The subject was prevented from seeing the bead he had drawn on each trial until the end of the experiment. And he knew that the experimenter would replace one just like the one he had drawn so that the information about the probability of winning remained constant throughout the series of choices in which each alternative was paired with every other one [p. 354].

Subjects clearly preferred the lottery offering .50 chance of winning when the prizes ranged from 1 to 9 cents, or from 5 to 45 cents, or from 25 cents to $2.25.

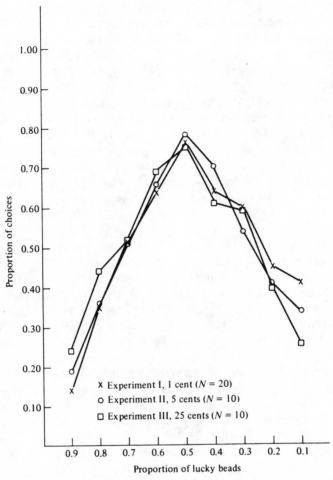

FIG. 2.6. Choices among containers having different proportions (*P*) of lucky beads when the dollar value of a lucky bead was equal to (1 − P) times 0.1, 0.5, and 2.5. (Based on Atkinson and Birch, 1970, p. 180.)

Multiplying the incentive value of the outcome by a constant of 5 or of 25 produced little change in the pattern of preference. Under the hypothesis that the instigating force, which determines the rate of arousal of the tendency for each alternative, is given by the product of the stated probability of winning and the stated value of winning, numerical values for each instigating force could be determined. Multiplication of all forces by a constant did increase the difference between magnitudes of force but did not change the ratio of forces in a particular paired comparison (e.g., *P* = .7 versus *P* = .5).

Why then, we immediately thought to ask, should preference for moderately difficult tasks be greater when M_S is strong than when M_S is weak if the theory of achievement motivation is to be taken as a theory concerning the determinants of instigating forces (i.e., $F_s = M_S \times P_s \times In_s$, where $In_s = 1 - P_s$)? With $M_S = 1$, F_s is .25 when P_s is .50, and F_s is .09 when P_s is .90. The ratio of the instigating forces is .25/.09 = 2.78. With $M_S = 3$, F_s is .75 when P_s is .50, and F_s is .27 when P_s is .90. The ratio is exactly the same, .75/.27 = 2.78!

In traditional theories of motivation, both cognitive and mechanistic, it has always been assumed that preference is a function of the magnitude of difference between strengths of competing tendencies (Hull, 1943; Cartwright & Festinger, 1943). Both involve the presumption of random oscillation in the strength of competing tendencies and decreased likelihood of the subordinate tendency being momentarily dominant by chance when the magnitude of the difference is large than small. This was the implicit logic of choice given the "traditional" theory of achievement motivation that presumed $T_s = M_S \times P_s \times In_s$ (1957 to 1970). In the context of traditional cognitive theory, the theory of achievement motivation had seemed to provide an adequate basis for deducing the observed greater preference for moderate risk among those more highly motivated to achieve because it accounted for this critical difference. (In our example, the difference favoring choice of moderately difficult over easy task is .16 when $M_S = 1$ and .48 when $M_S = 3$.) What can be said to resolve the problem that arises when the product of $M_S \times P_s \times In_s$ is assumed to define the rate of arousal of T_s rather than its static strength?

The proposal that has been offered does not go beyond the usual assumption in the earlier research that normally there are other extrinsic sources of motivation for achievement-oriented actions, as already shown in Fig. 2.4. And it has usually been assumed that the strength of extrinsic tendencies to undertake tasks varying in difficulty is constant. In the new theoretical framework that distinguishes the rate of arousal of a tendency (e.g., F_{ext}) from its strength at a particular time (e.g., T_{ext}), we ask a new question. What is the effect of adding a constant F_{ext} to each F_s on the ratio of the *net* forces to undertake a moderately difficult task ($P_s = .50$) versus an easy task ($P_s = .90$) when M_S is strong (3) and weak (1)? For simplicity, consider the ratio of instigating forces to achieve favoring choice of intermediate difficulty over easy task to be 3/1 when $M_S = 1$ and 9/3 when $M_S = 3$. Adding a constant of 1 (representing the magnitude of an F_{ext}) to each of the forces produces a ratio of 10/4 favoring choice of intermediate difficulty when $M_S = 3$ and 4/2 favoring choice of intermediate difficulty when $M_S = 1$. Clearly, 10/4 > 4/2. The effect of adding a constant is to change the ratio of forces in each case, but the change toward equalization of the net forces is greater the smaller the absolute magnitudes of instigating force to achieve. When M_S is strong, instigating forces to achieve have proportionally greater influence on the ratio of the total or net forces to undertake activities that differ in difficulty than when M_S is weak. (Atkinson & Birch, 1970, 1974, 1978).

Let us say the same thing another way to make explicit a very important implication of our proposal that the subjective probability (P) and the positive utility (U) of any consequence of an activity influence the strength of instigating force for the activity. In the case of achievement, or success, the hypothesis $F_s = M_S \cdot P_s \cdot I_s$ may be rendered $F_s = P_s \cdot U_s$ with no change in meaning. More generally, if $F_X = P_X \cdot U_X$ and $F_Y = P_Y \cdot U_Y$, then preferential behavior is governed by the ratio $(P_X \cdot U_X/(P_Y \cdot U_Y))$ according to the dynamics of action, not the magnitude of difference between $(P_X \cdot U_X)$ and $(P_Y \cdot U_Y)$. We have just pointed out that the addition of a constant to both numerator and denominator produces a greater change in the ratio (and preferential behavior) when the absolute magnitudes are small than large. A corollary of this is that an equivalent change in preferential behavior, favoring preference for X, requires a greater increase in the value of $(P_X \cdot U_X)$ when the initial magnitudes in the ratio $(P_X \cdot U_X/(P_Y \cdot U_Y))$ are large than small. For example, a change from indifference to a just noticeable preference for X resulting from an increment of 1 to the numerator when the initial ratio is 4/4 should require an increment of 2 when the initial ratio is 8/8. That is, $5/4 = 10/8$. This seems to refer to the kind of observation concerning increments of value needed to change preference that once prompted the assumption of diminishing marginal utility in economic theory. If a just noticeable difference in preferential behavior is taken to be the observable symptom of a just noticeable *difference* in the subjective motivational state (i.e., $(P_X \cdot U_X) > (P_Y \cdot U_Y)$), as traditionally supposed, then once must conclude that 2 more of some commodity added to 8 (the objective values) produces a change in *subjective* value or utility equivalent to that produced by 1 more of the commodity added to 4. Given the new conception of the motivational significance of the expected consequences of an act, the relationship between subjective and objective value may be assumed to be linear.

Turning now to the treatment of the tendency to avoid failure and resistance more generally in the new dynamics of action, we depart even more from the traditional logic of SEU $= P_1U_1 + P_2U_2 + \cdots + P_nU_n$. That formulation served as a useful model for the resultant tendency to achieve when the strength of tendency to achieve success (T_s) and of the tendency to avoid failure (T_{-f}) were conceived as static. They simply combined algebraically to determine the resultant tendency to achieve that, like the SEU of an option in decision theory, corresponded to the static strength of inclination or disinclination to act. Now, however, in the new conception that treats the product $(P_f \cdot U_f)$, or, as stated in the past $(M_F \times P_f \times In_f)$ as a specification of the determinants of an inhibitory force to avoid failure, the strength of the tendency to avoid failure has, so to speak, a life of its own. It is now explicitly referred to in terms of its motivational implication as a *negaction tendency* (N). It is conceived as the cause of *resistance* to action.

Here briefly, is the new conception of how expectancy of a negative outcome influences behavior from Atkinson (1977):

Resistance

How does the inhibitory force to avoid failure, or any other inhibitory force attributable to expectancy of a negative or punishing consequence, influence a change in activity? The essentials can be simply presented in reference to Fig. 2.7.

In Fig. 2.7 we picture what happens when there are both instigating and inhibitory forces for the same activity B to achieve (F_s) and to avoid failure (I_f).

A hatched line shows the arousal and linear growth of the action tendency, T_B, that is attributable to exposure to the F_B of the immediate environment. Simultaneously, below, another hatched line shows the trend of growth in the tendency *not* to engage in activity B, the negation action tendency (N_B) that is attributable to the I_B of the immediate environment.

As soon as N_B is aroused, it begins to oppose or resist T_B to determine the strength of the resultant action tendency ($\bar{T}_B = T_B - N_B$). This process of blocking the expression of T_B, resistance, produces a force of resistance (R), analogous to the consummatory force (C) that occurs when an action tendency is expressed in action. The negation tendency increases in strength as long as $I_B > R_B$. But as N_B becomes stronger, it is expressed in greater resistance, so R_B, the force of resistance, also becomes stronger. As it does, the initial difference in strength of I_B (which functions to increase N_B) and R_B (which functions to reduce N_B) di-

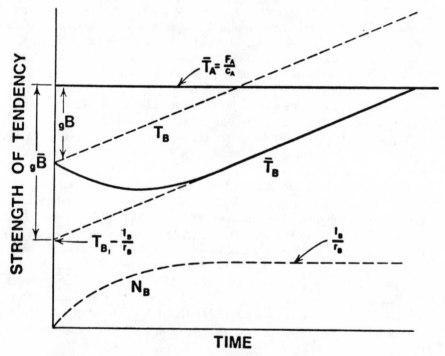

FIG. 2.7.   The effect of resistance to an activity on time to initiate that activity. See text for discussion. (From Atkinson & Birch, 1970, 1974.)

minishes. So N_B grows less rapidly. In time, $R_B = I_B$, so N_B approaches its maximum strength and becomes relatively stable as shown in Fig. 2.7.

(In the treatment of resistance, there is a parameter r (analogous to c in treatment of consummation) which represents the extent to which a negaction tendency (N) is reduced per unit of time in resistance to an action tendency (T). As a result, N becomes stable at a level defined by I/r as noted in Figure 2.7).

The effect of N_B, in opposition to T_B, is shown in the trend of $\overline{T}_B$, the resultant action tendency in Fig. 2.7. The effect of the resistance produced by N_B, and attributable to an inhibitory force is always a temporary suppression of the action tendency. It delays the initiation of activity B for a period of time. This amount of time is sufficient for T_B to continue to grow strong enough eventually to compensate for the maximum strength of N_B. That, too, is shown in the figure.

In brief, the trend of the curve describing the strength of the resultant action tendency, $\overline{T}_B$, is determined at every point by subtraction of the strength of N_B from T_B. In the case of achievement-oriented behavior, the resultant tendency to achieve success $\overline{T}_s = T_s - N_f$, would be temporarily suppressed and the initiation of achievement-oriented action delayed or less likely to occur at all if the inhibitory force is so strong that some other kind of activity X, also instigated in that situation, becomes dominant before $\overline{T}_s$, weakened by resistance, can do so. Often we call such an activity an avoidance activity when it removes the person from the situation posing the threat of a punishment that is the source of resistance to action.

The principle of a change in activity is easily rephrased to include the effect of the resistance. It can be seen in Fig. 2.7 that a negaction tendency has an effect equivalent to having a greater initial *gap* between T_{A_i}, the dominant tendency, and T_{B_i}, which motivates the new alternative activity. That is shown in the graph of Figure 2.7 and also in the algebraic statement when the principle of change of activity is modified to include the effect of the resistance that is attributable to, and proportionate to the strength of inhibitory force:

$$t = \frac{(F_A/c_A - T_{B_i}) + N_{B_t}}{F_B} = \frac{(F_A/c_A - T_{B_i}) + I_B/r_B}{F_B} \ .$$

In Fig. 2.8, we have superimposed the resultant action tendencies from Fig. 2.7 where there is and is not resistance, to show comparatively what should be expected concerning initiation and level of motivation for continuous performance of an achievement-related activity, perhaps an important test in a college course, when M_s is identical in two individuals but only one of them has any M_F. This means that F_s is equal for the two individuals but only one of them is exposed to I_f.

The positively motivated person will initiate the achievement-oriented activity sooner and become more completely involved in it sooner than his more anxious peer. After a period of time, however, the strength of motivation expressed in the task, $\overline{T}_s$, will become more nearly equal for the two individuals. How long this takes depends upon the magnitude of I_f. But by then, most of the detrimental effects on performance attributable to the tendency to avoid failure should have occurred—early rather than late in a test period. Here we assume (for simplicity) that the maximum level of $\overline{T}$ for both persons is in the low to moderate range and

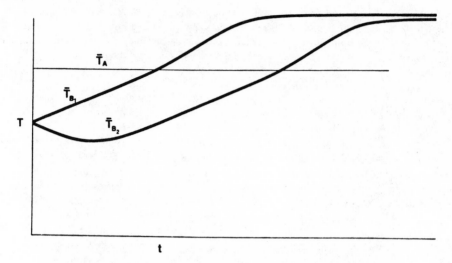

FIG. 2.8.   The effect of resistance on initiation of an activity ($\overline{T}_{B_1} = T_B$, and $\overline{T}_{B_2}$ $= T_B - N_B$) and the level of resultant tendency, $\overline{T}_B$, expressed in the activity. (Atkinson & Birch, 1974.)

not complicated further by the inefficiency attributable to overmotivation should $\overline{T}$ be beyond the optimal level for the task.

One important difference between the new dynamics of achievement-oriented action, here pictured, and the old static model of achievement motivation deserves comment. Previously it seemed essential always to assume the presence of some extrinsic motivational tendency to overcome an initially negative resultant achievement motivation (i.e., whenever $M_F > M_S$). Now it is evident that the effect of resistance is a temporal delay, a temporary suppression of achievement-oriented action, but that the initiation of an achievement-oriented activity should occur sooner or later without any necessary help of an extrinsic incentive *if* the individual stays in the situation long enough even when resistance is very strong.

The presence of additional extrinsic incentives for the achievement-oriented activity would produce additional instigating forces ($F_{approval}$, $F_{\$}$, etc.) which refer to the very same activity as F_s. The effect of the three positive tendencies simultaneously aroused is additive as previously assumed. That is $T_B = T_{B,s} + T_{B,app} + T_{B,\$}$, etc. The extrinsic tendencies, while not absolutely essential, still function to overcome the effects of resistance as previously supposed [pp. 81–84].

Quite obviously the old logic of mingling the expectations of rewarding and punishing consequences of an activity by algebraic addition to determine the strength of a single static inclination or disinclination to act has been eschewed. The systematic arousal and stabilization in the strengths of an action tendency (T_X), attributable to summed expectations of positive outcomes, and of a negaction tendency (N_X), attributable to summed expectations of negative outcomes, are treated separately. The resultant $(\overline{T}_X)$ of conflict between the strength of tendency to do X (T_X) and *not* to do X (N_X) can be specified at each moment as $\overline{T}_X = T_X - N_X$, but the strength of each component, T_X and N_X, is constantly changing because the individual is exposed to the instigating and inhibitory forces of the stimulus situation, the consummatory force of the activity in progress, and the force of resistance. The latter is the analog of consummatory force in its composition and in its effect on the strength of a negation tendency.

In reference to initiation of an activity, this new conception of the influence of the expectation of a negative consequence implies temporary suppression of the activity, the well-known effect of prior punishment. In reference to choice between alternatives, we again must refer to the ratio of the magnitudes of forces. Preference for the more strongly instigated of two alternatives is weakened when the ratio of the stronger to weaker inhibitory force exceeds the ratio of the corresponding instigating forces.

Taking the earlier theory of achievement motivation as a statement about determinants of instigating forces to achieve success (F_s) and inhibitory forces to avoid failure (I_f), the ratio of inhibitory forces attributable to expectations of failure at different tasks always equals the ratio of the corresponding instigating forces attributable to expectations of success. That is, whenever $F_{X,s}/F_{Y,s} = 3/1$, then $I_{X,f}/I_{Y,f} = 3/1$ given the symmetry of the theory of achievement motivation. However, given the presumption of some additional extrinsic incentive for all tasks and net instigating forces $(F_{X,s} + F_{X,ext})$ favoring preference for moderately difficult tasks in the ratio of 4/2 or 10/4, as discussed earlier, the ratio of the respective inhibitory forces to avoid failure will always be greater (i.e., $3/1 > 10/4 > 4/2$), and preference for moderate difficulty will be dampened. This is the ''new'' explanation of the generally observed weaker preference for moderately difficult tasks among ''highly anxious'' individuals (Atkinson & Birch, 1970, pp. 287–288; 1974, pp. 301–302; 1978, pp. 135–136).

The explanation of avoidance behavior, given the coordination of expectation of negative outcome with inhibitory force in the dynamics of action, is essentially unchanged.

Perhaps the most intriguing questions raised by the supposition that expectations of positive and negative outcomes should be conceived as determinants of instigating and inhibitory forces within the framework of the dynamics of action have to do with implications concerning the explanation of economic behavior. Certainly the behavioral effects of the anticipated costs of an action, shown graphically in Fig. 2.7, must differ from those of the traditional static quantity called ''subjectively expected disutility.'' Perhaps new light can be thrown on old stubborn questions that have arisen in the attempt to understand the motivation of economic behavior by substituting the new systematic account of the temporal process of motivation for the incomplete, quantified hedonism of traditional cognitive theory. It is a challenging sector in the frontier of our ignorance concerning expectations and actions.

REFERENCES

Allport, G. W. *Personality*. New York: Holt, 1937.

Atkinson, J. W. *Studies in projective measurement of achievement*. Unpublished doctoral dissertation, University of Michigan, 1950. Ann Arbor: University Microfilms Pub. #1945, 145.

Atkinson, J. W. The achievement motive and recall of interrupted and completed tasks. *Journal of Experimental Psychology*, 1953, *46*, 381–390. Also in D. C. McClelland (Ed.), *Studies in motivation*. New York: Appleton–Century Crofts, 1955.

Atkinson, J. W. Explorations using imaginative thought to assess the strength of human motives. In M. R. Jones (Ed.), *Nebraska Symposium on Motivation* (Vol. 2). Lincoln: University of Nebraska Press, 1954.

Atkinson, J. W. Motivational determinants of risk-taking behavior. *Psychological Review*, 1957, *64*, 359–372.

Atkinson, J. W. Thematic apperceptive measurement of motives within the context of a theory of motivation. In J. W. Atkinson (Ed.), *Motives in fantasy action, and society*. Princeton, N.J.: Van Nostrand, 1958. (a)

Atkinson, J. W. Toward experimental analysis of human motivation in terms of motives, expectancies, and incentives. In J. W. Atkinson (Ed.), *Motives in fantasy, action, and society*. Princeton, N.J.: Van Nostrand, 1958. (b)

Atkinson, J. W. Personality dynamics. *Annual Review of Psychology*, 1960, *11*, 225–290.

Atkinson, J. W. *An introduction to motivation*. Princeton, N.J.: Van Nostrand, 1964.

Atkinson, J. W. Motivation for achievement. In T. Blass (Ed.), *Personality variables in social behavior*. Hillsdale, N.J.: Lawrence Erlbaum Associates, 1977.

Atkinson, J. W., & Birch, D. *The dynamics of action*. New York: Wiley, 1970.

Atkinson, J. W., & Birch, D. The dynamics of achievement-oriented activity. In J. W. Atkinson & J. W. Raynor (Eds.), *Motivation and achievement*. Washington, D.C.: Winston, 1974 (Abridged edition, *Personality, Motivation, and Achievement*. Washington: Hemisphere, 1978.)

Atkinson, J. W., & Birch, D. *An introduction to motivation (Rev. Ed.)*. New York: Van Nostrand, 1978.

Atkinson, J. W., & Cartwright, D. Some neglected variables in contemporary conceptions of decision and performance. *Psychological Reports*, 1964, *14*, 575–590.

Atkinson, J. W., & Feather, N. T. (Eds.) *A theory of achievement motivation*. New York: Wiley, 1966.

Atkinson, J. W., & Litwin, G. H. Achievement motive and test anxiety conceived as motive to approach success and motive to avoid failure. *Journal of Abnormal and Social Psychology*, 1960, *60*, 52–63.

Atkinson, J. W., & Reitman, W. R. Performance as a function of motive strength and expectancy of goal attainment. *Journal of Abnormal and Social Psychology*, 1956, *53*, 361–366. Also in J. W. Atkinson (Ed.), *Motives in fantasy, action and society*. Princeton, N.J.: Van Nostrand, 1958.

Birch, D. Measuring the stream of activity. *Michigan Mathematical Psychology Publication*. MMPP 72-2. Ann Arbor: University of Michigan, 1972.

Birney, R. Thematic content and the cue characteristics of pictures. In J. W. Atkinson (Ed.), *Motives in fantasy, action and society*. Princeton, N.J.: Van Nostrand, 1958.

Brown, J. S. *The motivation of behavior*. New York: McGraw-Hill, 1961.

Cartwright, D., & Festinger, L. A quantitative theory of decision. *Psychological Review*, 1943, *50*, 595–621.

Cronbach, L. J. The two disciplines of scientific psychology. *American Psychologist*, 1957, *12*, 671–684.

Edwards, W. The theory of decision making. *Psychological Bulletin*, 1954, *51*, 380–417.

Escalona, S. K. The effect of success and failure upon the level of aspiration and behavior in manic-depressive psychoses. *University of Iowa Studies in Child Welfare*, 1940, *16*, 199–302.

Feather, N. T. Subjective probability and decision under uncertainty. *Psychological Review,* 1959, *66,* 150-164.

Feather, N. T. The relationship of persistence at a task to expectation of success and achievement related motives. *Journal of Abnormal and Social Psychology,* 1961, *63,* 552-561.

Feather, N. T. The study of persistence. *Psychological Bulletin,* 1962, *59,* 94-115. Also in J. W. Atkinson & N. T. Feather (Eds.), *A theory of achievement motivation.* New York: Wiley, 1966.

Festinger, L. A theoretical interpretation of shifts in level of aspiration. *Psychological Review,* 1942, *49,* 235-250.

Festinger, L. *A theory of cognitive dissonance.* New York: Harper and Row, 1957.

Georgescu-Roegen, N. Utility. In D. L. Sills, (Ed.), *International Encyclopedia of the Social Sciences* (Vol. 16). New York: The MacMillan Co. & The Free Press, 1968.

Hanson, N. R. *Patterns of discovery.* Cambridge, England: Cambridge University Press, 1958.

Hebb, D. O. *The organization of behavior.* New York: Wiley, 1949.

Hilgard, E. R., & Marquis, D. G. *Conditioning and learning.* New York: Appleton-Century-Crofts, 1940.

Hull, C. L. *Principles of behavior.* New York: Appleton-Century-Crofts, 1943.

Jacobs, B. J. A method for investigating the cue characteristics of pictures. In J. W. Atkinson, (Ed.), *Motives in fantasy, action, and society.* Princeton, N.J.: Van Nostrand, 1958.

Jennings, R. *Natural elements of political economy.* London: Longmans, 1855.

Kelley, H. H. Attribution theory in social psychology. In D. Levine (Ed.), *Nebraska Symposium on Motivation* (Vol. 15). Lincoln: University of Nebraska Press, 1967.

Kelley, H. H. The process of causal attribution. *American Psychologist,* 1973, *28,* 107-128.

Kuhn, T. S. *The structure of scientific revolutions.* Chicago: University of Chicago Press, 1962.

Lewin, K. *The conceptual representation and the measurement of psychological forces.* Durham, N.C.: Duke University Press, 1938.

Lewin, K. Behavior and development as a function of the total situation. In L. Carmichael (Ed.), *Manual of child psychology.* New York: Wiley, 1946.

Lewin, K., Dembo, T., Festinger, L., & Sears, P. S. Level of aspiration. In J. McV. Hunt (Ed.), *Personality and the behavior disorders.* New York: Ronald, 1944.

Lewin, K. *Field theory in social science.* (D. Cartwright, Ed.). New York: Harper & Row, 1951.

Lowell, E. L. The effect of need for achievement on learning and speed of performance. *Journal of Psychology,* 1952, *33,* 31-40.

MacCorquodale, K., & Meehl, P. E. Preliminary suggestions as to a formalization of expectancy theory. *Psychological Review,* 1953, *60,* 55-63.

MacCorquodale, K., & Meehl, P. E. Edward C. Tolman (Chap. 2). In Estes, W. K., Koch, S., MacCorquodale, K., Meehl, P., Mueller, C., Schoenfeld, W., & Verplanck, W. S. *Modern learning theory.* New York: Appleton-Century-Crofts, 1954.

McClelland, D. C. *Personality.* New York: William Sloane, 1951.

McClelland, D. C., Atkinson, J. W., Clark, R. W., & Lowell, E. L. *The achievement motive.* New York: Appleton-Century-Crofts, 1953.

McClelland, D. C., Clark, R. A., Roby, T. B., & Atkinson, J. W. The projective expression of needs. IV. The effect of the need for achievement on thematic apperception. *Journal of Experimental Psychology,* 1949, *39,* 242-255.

McClelland, D. C., & Liberman, A. M. The effect of need for achievement on recognition of need-related words. *Journal of Personality,* 1949, *18,* 236-251.

Meehl, P. E., & MacCorquodale, K. Some methodological comments concerning expectancy theory. *Psychological Review,* 1951, *58,* 230-233.

Miller, N. E. Studies of fear as an acquirable drive. I. Fear as motivation and fear-reduction as reinforcement in the learning of new responses. *Journal of Experimental Psychology,* 1948, *38,* 89-101.

Miller, N. E. Liberalization of basic S-R concepts: Extensions to conflict behavior, motivation, and social learning. In S. Koch (Ed.), *Psychology: A study of a science* (Vol. 2). New York: McGraw-Hill, 1959.

Mowrer, O. H. A stimulus-response analysis of anxiety and its role as a reinforcing agent. *Psychological Review*, 1939, *46*, 553–565.

Murray, H. A. *Explorations in personality.* New York: Oxford University Press, 1938.

Raynor, J. O. Future orientation and motivation of immediate activity: An elaboration of the theory of achievement motivation. *Psychological Review*, 1969, *76*, 606–610.

Raynor, J. O. Future orientation in the study of achievement motivation. In J. W. Atkinson & J. O. Raynor (Eds.), *Motivation and achievement.* Washington, D.C.: Hemisphere Publishing Co., 1974.

Ritchie, B. F. Can reinforcement theory account for avoidance? *Psychological Review*, 1951, *58*, 382–386.

Rotter, J. B. *Social learning and clinical psychology.* New York: Prentice-Hall, 1954.

Rotter, J. B. The role of the psychological situation in determining the direction of human behavior. In M. R. Jones (Ed.), *Nebraska Symposium on Motivation.* Lincoln: University of Nebraska Press, 1955.

Sears, R. R. A theoretical framework for personality and social behavior. *American Psychologist*, 1951, *6*, 476–483.

Seltzer, R. A. Simulation of the dynamics of action. *Psychological Reports*, 1973, *32*, 859–872.

Sheffield, F. D., Roby, T. B., & Campbell, B. A. Drive reduction versus consummatory behavior as determinants of reinforcement. *Journal of Comparative and Physiological Psychology*, 1954, *47*, 349–354.

Skinner, B. F. *Science and human behavior.* New York: The Free Press, 1953.

Solomon, R. L., & Wynne, L. C. Traumatic avoidance learning: The principles of anxiety conservation and partial irreversibility. *Psychological Review*, 1954, *61*, 353–385.

Spence, K. W. *Behavior theory and conditioning.* New Haven: Yale University Press, 1956.

Thorndike, E. L. *Animal intelligence.* New York: Macmillan, 1911.

Tolman, E. C. The determiners of behavior at a choice point. *Psychological Review*, 1938, *45*, 1–41.

Tolman, E. C. *Behavior and psychological man.* Berkeley: University of California Press, 1951.

Tolman, E. C. Principles of performance. *Psychological Review*, 1955, *62*, 315–326.

Tolman, E. C. Principles of purposive behavior. In S. Koch (Ed.), *Psychology: A study of a science* (Vol. 2). New York: McGraw-Hill, 1959.

Tolman, E. C. & Postman, L. Learning. *Annual Review of Psychology*, 1954, *5*, 27–56.

Von Neumann, J. & Morgenstern, O. *Theory of games and economic behavior.* Princeton: Princeton University Press, 1944.

Whalen, R. E. Sexual motivation. *Psychological Review*, 1966, *73*, 151–163.

Winterbottom, M. R. *The relationship of childhood training in independence to achievement motivation.* Unpublished doctoral dissertation. University of Michigan, 1953.

Winterbottom, M. R. The relation of need for achievement to learning experiences in independence and mastery. In J. W. Atkinson (Ed.), *Motives in fantasy, action, and society.* New York: D. Van Nostrand, 1958.

3

Actions in Relation to Expected Consequences: An Overview of a Research Program

Norman T. Feather
The Flinders University of South Australia

This chapter is a personal account of a research program that began over 20 years ago. It describes successive stages in this program and traces how ideas developed and how new interests emerged. A historical overview of this kind brings out continuities in theory and research over time. It may also reveal changes of direction that, for whatever reason, occur in the stream of research, and questions that have been put to one side and that perhaps deserve to be looked at again from new perspectives.

A dominant theme in this research program is the emphasis on relating aspects of behavior such as performance, persistence, and choice to a general class of theory that involves the concepts of expectation and valence (or subjectively perceived incentive value). This theme derives especially from Tolman and Lewin, whose ideas have had a profound influence on subsequent cognitive approaches to the psychology of motivation, including my own contributions to this area. The person is viewed as an active processor of information and as behaving in ways that reflect intervening cognitive processes and purposes. These intervening variables involve both personal characteristics that are assumed to be relatively stable (motives), and variables that are usually more closely related to the immediate situation (expectations and incentive values). Thus, the general analysis throughout the program explicitly allows for the interactive effects on behavior of variables that concern both the person and the situation. These are some of the constancies that run through the program as a whole.

OBJECT PREFERENCE

The earliest study in the program was concerned with the effects of varying a person's expectation of success in a choice situation that involved different goal objects (Feather, 1959a, 1959b). At the time there were a number of investigators who were interested in the study of object preference. For example, in an early study formulated within the context of Lewinian ideas, Wright (1937) tested the hypothesis that a barrier enhances a positive valence, that a goal object becomes more attractive if it is obstructed in some way. Child (1946) believed that the evidence for this hypothesis was somewhat inconclusive and discussed some of the conditions under which the hypothesis might be valid. Irwin and his colleagues (Irwin, Armitt & Simon, 1943; Irwin, Orchinik, & Weiss, 1946) were interested in temporal delay and its effect on object preference. Will a reward become more or less attractive the longer you have to wait for it? Filer (1952) investigated the effects of expectation and attainment and nonattainment on the attractiveness of goal objects. Does a goal object become more attractive when you expect to get it, when you actually have received it, etc? Similar sorts of questions were also asked about factors influencing the attractiveness of activities (Cartwright, 1942; Gebhard, 1948, 1949).

From the perspective of more recent theories one can advance a number of reasons why, under some conditions, a goal object that is obstructed or difficult to get may become more attractive. Perhaps people learn to like things for which they have had to suffer (dissonance theory). Perhaps threats to freedom of action increase the positive valence of obstructed goals (reactance theory). Perhaps the realities of choice in the wider environment are such that in general goal objects that are more attractive are indeed more difficult to attain. Perhaps frustration of action is associated with enhanced motivation that increases the perceived attractiveness of obstructed goals. No doubt the reader can think of other explanations as well.

My perception of the early literature was that it tended to ignore possible achievement-related rewards and punishments within a situation (Feather, 1959a). Thus, one can relate the attractiveness of a goal not only to the distinctive characteristics of the goal itself but also to the nature of the achievement. In the course of development and as they exercise emerging skills children come to learn that success at difficult tasks is more praiseworthy than success at easy tasks, and that failure at easy tasks is more blameworthy than failure at difficult tasks. They also learn to discriminate the conditions under which praise and blame are given. Hence, one would expect that obstructed goals, or goals that are difficult to attain, might be perceived by a person as more attractive because of the achievement value associated with their attainment, a value that would vary depending upon how test-like the situation was, how much the outcome depended on skill and could be attributed to the self, and so on.

The emphasis upon the attainment and nonattainment of goals in achievement situations was very apparent in the Lewin, Dembo, Festinger, and Sears (1944) model of level of aspiration behavior that represented choice of a level of aspiration as a problem in decision. When the level of aspiration was high, success would be more attractive (positively valent) and failure less repulsive (negatively valent) than when it was low. But attaining a high level of aspiration would be subjectively less likely (i.e., more difficult) than attaining a low level of aspiration. The level of aspiration that a person chose was assumed by Lewin et al. to be determined by a "weighting" of the valences by the corresponding subjective probabilities. The model proposed that a person would set a level of aspiration for which the multiplicative combination of valences and subjective probabilities was a maximum.

The level of aspiration model was an early example of "expectancy-value" theory because the decision to be made was assumed to depend on both a person's expectations about the possible outcomes (success or failure) and the subjective values (or valences) of these outcomes. The model, which strangely lay dormant for a number of years, was used by Lewin et al. (1944) to interpret the results of a large number of studies of factors influencing level of aspiration behavior.

My early study of object preference (Feather, 1959a, 1959b) involved a concern both with the effects of valences of success and failure that were a function of task difficulty, and with subjective probabilities of success that "weighted" these valences when a choice had to be made. The study, which was conducted with Australian schoolchildren, showed that the attractiveness of attaining a goal object (as defined by a "wishful" choice) increased as subjective probability of success decreased, that is, as the task, whose successful performance was a precondition of getting the reward, became more difficult. This relationship increased in strength as the choice situation became more test-like in character and where the person could attribute success to his own skill. Actual choice of a goal object, however, was constrained by the subjective probability of success in the direction of the easier alternative, but this "committed" choice was also influenced by the nature of the situation, being less apparent under testlike, skill conditions.

The interpretation of these results was in terms of past learning experiences. The possibility of loss of objective benefits would tend to bias preference in the direction of the easier alternative. In contrast, achievement values related to success under difficult conditions would bias preference toward the subjectively less likely alternative. The latter bias would be reflected in the "wishful" choice, whereas both biases would be reflected in the "committed" choice. The strength of the achievement values would depend not only on the difficulty of the task but also on the nature of the situation, being stronger in situations that were achievement oriented and where outcomes could be seen to depend on skill than in situations that were less testlike and where outcomes could be seen to depend on chance and therefore less attributable to a person's own ability and effort. The effect of possible loss of objective benefits in pushing choice toward the easier alternative would be more pronounced the greater the value of the objective benefits—see also Feather (1964b) for a discussion of level of aspiration behavior in relation to the payoffs and costs that follow success and failure. Thus, the potential loss of objective benefits would often override the effects of achievement values when choice involved actual commitment. These were some of the theoretical ideas that were used to interpret the results of this early study of object preference.

In the course of formulating these theoretical ideas it soon became apparent that a number of other expectancy-value models had emerged in the literature and that they were very similar in the types of concepts that they employed. One of these models has already been noted—the Lewin et al. (1944) level of aspiration model. In addition, Tolman (1955) had provided principles of performance to account for how his assumed cognitive and motivational variables issued into actual behavior. He discussed a hungry rat's performance of lever pressing in a Skinner box in terms of needs, expectations, and valences that, in combination, determined a resultant performance vector. Rotter (1954), in a book concerned with social learning and clinical psychology, had put forward an expectancy-reinforcement view of behavior that related the potential for a particular behavior to occur to concepts of expectancy and reinforcement value. Edwards (1954) had reviewed the literature concerned with the theory of decision making and had described a model that asserted that people choose so as to maximize subjectively expected utility (SEU), that is, they maximize the multiplicative product of utilities (the subjective values of possible outcomes) and their associated subjective probabilities. And Atkinson (1957), working within the area of achievement motivation, had developed a risk-taking model that involved concepts of motive, subjective probability, and incentive value relating to both success and failure that, in combination, determined the strength of resultant motivation. A fascinating aspect of these various models was that they emerged from quite different content areas yet converged in that each of them related a "resultant tendency" to a maximized combination of "valence" and "subjective probability" factors.

The main concepts used in these models were listed in an early theoretical report (Feather, 1959a, p. 154). The list can be extended so as to include some subsequent approaches that also involve concepts that fall within the expectancy-value rubric (Table 3.1). An interesting difference between the earlier models was that some of them assumed that, in general, utilities or valences were independent of subjective probabilities (Rotter, Edwards) or said nothing about their possible interaction (Tolman). Others (Lewin et al., Atkinson) explicitly assumed that utilities or valences were inversely related to subjective probabilities, increasing in strength as the corresponding subjective probabilities decreased. It is significant that both of these latter models were concerned with

TABLE 3.1
Examples of Expectancy-Value Models

Theorist	Determinants Involved in Resultant Tendency to Act
Tolman	Expectation, need–push, valence
Lewin et al.	Subjective probability × valence
Atkinson	Expectancy × (motive × incentive value)
Feather	Success probability, attainment attractiveness
Edwards	Subjective probability × utility
Rotter	Expectancy, reinforcement value
Peak	Instrumentality × attitude (affect)
Rosenberg	Instrumentality × importance
Vroom	Expectancy × valence; where valence is instrumentality × valence
Dulany	Hypothesis of the distribution of the reinforcement × value of the reinforcement
Fishbein	Probability × attitude

Note. Adapted from Feather (1959b) and Mitchell (1974). Table 3.1 presents the models in simplified form and focuses on the expectancy and valence concepts.

behavior in an achievement context. As indicated previously, my own study of choice between goal objects (Feather, 1959a, 1959b) was also based upon the assumption that achievement values would be inversely related to the subjective probability of success. So there was agreement that valences and expectations would not be independent in situations where success and failure could be evaluated against standards of excellence and where outcomes were relevant to a person's self-concept insofar as perceptions of ability, skill, and effort were concerned.

A THEORY OF ACHIEVEMENT MOTIVATION

My interest in Atkinson's (1957) risk-taking model was a major factor that took me to the University of Michigan in 1958 for a 2-year visit. The Atkinson model with its elaborations later became known as a theory of achievement motivation (Atkinson & Birch, 1978; Atkinson & Feather, 1966; Atkinson & Raynor, 1974) and the summary that follows refers to these more recent statements. In this model the strength of a person's tendency to achieve success through the performance of certain actions (T_s) was assumed to be determined by a relatively general and stable characteristic of the person—the motive to achieve success (M_S)—and by two other variables more closely tied to aspects of the immediate situation, namely the strength of the person's expectancy or subjective probability of success (P_s) and the positive incentive value of success (In_s). It was assumed that:

$$T_s = M_S \times P_s \times In_s$$

and that P_s and In_s were related as follows:

$$In_s = 1 - P_s$$

That is, the positive incentive value of success was inversely related to the subjective probability of success. In fact, according to the equation, it was completely determined by the subjective probability of success.

In a corresponding way the model assumed that a person's tendency to avoid failure (T_{-f}) was a multiplicative combination of a disposition to avoid failure called the motive to avoid failure (M_F), an expectancy or subjective probability of failure (P_f), and a negative incentive value of failure (In_f). That is:

$$T_{-f} = M_F \times P_f \times In_f$$

It was also assumed that the negative incentive value of failure would increase as the subjective probability of success increased, i.e.,

$$In_f = -P_s$$

Again, therefore, the incentive value depended only on the subjective probability of success. Both subjective probabilities $(P_s$ and $P_f)$ were assumed to add to unity. The tendency to avoid failure was viewed as a tendency not to undertake an activity. That is, it was conceived as an inhibitory tendency.

The equations involving the tendencies T_s and T_{-f} can be rewritten so that they take account of subjective probabilities and valences. It was assumed by Atkinson and Feather (1966) that the general motive to achieve success (M_S) and the positive incentive value of success (In_s) together determine what Lewinians call the *valence* or attractiveness of success (Va_s) and what decision theorists call the *utility* of success. That is:

$$Va_s = M_S \times In_s$$

and therefore, $T_s = P_s \times Va_s$

Similarly, the negative valence or repulsiveness of failure (Va_f) can be related to the general motive to avoid failure (M_F) and the negative incentive value of failure (In_f) as follows:

$$Va_f = M_F \times In_f$$

and therefore, $T_{-f} = P_f \times Va_f$

If one assumes that the amount of positive or negative affect that follows success or failure at a task is a reflection of these motive-related valences, then the two equations are consistent with the point of view put forward by Atkinson and Birch (1978), namely that: "Where the motive to achieve might be characterized as a capacity for reacting with pride in accomplishment, the motive to avoid failure can be conceived as a capacity for reacting with shame and embarrassment when the outcome of performance is failure [p. 96]."

One important implication of the two equations relating valences to general motives and incentive values is that the valences should change at a faster rate with increasing difficulty of the task when the motives are strong than when they are weak. This implication follows from the fact that the incentive values (In_s, In_f) in Atkinson's model are completely determined by the subjective probabilities (P_s, P_f)—see Atkinson and Feather (1966, p. 329). Table 3.2 illustrates the relationship between valences (Va_s, Va_f) and task difficulty (P_s, P_f) for motives (M_S, M_F) that differ in strength, and shows how the rate of change in valence across levels of subjective probability depends on the strength of the motives.

The model also allowed for the fact that task situations arouse other sources of motivation to act as well as the achievement-related tendencies. These other sources of motivation were called *extrinsic* tendencies (T_{ext}) and the final resultant tendency (T_x) to perform an act was assumed to be determined by the two tendencies that involved achievement-related motivation (T_s and T_{-f}) and by the other tendencies that together accounted for extrinsic motivation (T_{ext}). That is:

$$T_x = (T_s + T_{-f}) + T_{ext}$$

This early model, which has since been extended in important ways (Atkinson & Birch, 1978), generated a number of hypotheses of which perhaps the best known is the prediction that subjects with a stronger motive to achieve success ($M_S > M_F$), when given a choice, will prefer working at a task for which the subjective probability of success is intermediate ($P_s = .50$) than at a task that is either very easy or very difficult. In contrast, subjects with a stronger motive to avoid failure ($M_F > M_S$) will prefer to work at tasks that are either very easy or very difficult than at a task of intermediate difficulty. It is interesting to note that this prediction follows directly from the assumption in the model that incentive values and subjective probabilities are related in the manner stated. This assump-

TABLE 3.2
Relationship of Valences to Subjective Probabilities in
Atkinson's Model

	P_s	In_s	Va_s		P_f	In_f	Va_f	
			$M_S = 1$	$M_S = 4$			$M_F = 1$	$M_F = 4$
Easy	.9	.1	.1	.4	.1	−.9	−.9	−3.6
	.7	.3	.3	1.2	.3	−.7	−.7	−2.8
Moderate	.5	.5	.5	2.0	.5	−.5	−.5	−2.0
	.3	.7	.7	2.8	.7	−.3	−.3	−1.2
Difficult	.1	.9	.9	3.6	.9	−.1	−.1	− .4

Note. $In_s = 1 - P_s$; $In_f = -P_s$; $Va_s = M_S \times In_s$; $Va_f = M_F \times In_f$; $P_s + P_f = 1$. Adapted from Feather (1968b).

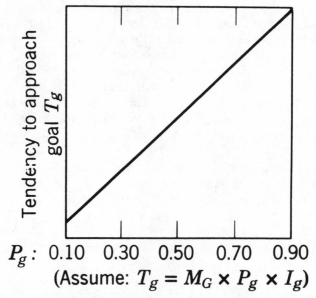

P_g : 0.10   0.30   0.50   0.70   0.90

(Assume: $T_g = M_G \times P_g \times I_g$)

FIG. 3.1.   Theoretical effect of increasing the strength of expectancy of attaining a goal (P_g) *when the incentive value of the goal (In_g) is constant and not affected by a change in P_g.* From this conception of the effect of "reward" on subsequent expectation concerning the consequence of an act are derived the behavioral phenomena summarized by the Law of Effect (Atkinson & Feather, 1966).

tion implies that the tendencies (T_s and T_{-f}) will be related in a curvilinear way to the subjective probability of success (P_s), with each tendency having its maximum value when $P_s = .50$.

If, however, one assumes that the incentive value of a goal is constant and is unaffected by the subjective probability of attaining it, then an expectancy-value model predicts that the tendency to approach the goal (holding strength of motive constant) will increase as the expectancy of attaining the goal increases. Thus, the idea that approach tendencies increase with increasing expectations of goal attainment may be valid for nonachievement contexts where incentive values and expectations are independent, but not when these variables are related.

Given that rewards confirm and strengthen expectations, then the positive relationship between an approach tendency and a person's expectation of goal attainment for a constant incentive can be used to derive the behavioral phenomena that are summarized by the Law of Effect (Fig. 3.1). Note, however, that in this interpretation the Law of Effect would be limited to situations not involving "ego" processes (Postman, 1947), and that it would break down where consequences affect one's self-evaluation and self-esteem—as they do under those testlike, achievement conditions where success and failure at different levels of task difficulty have implications about a person's ability, skill, and effort, and where the incentive values of success and failure are therefore a function of a person's expectation of goal attainment.

STUDIES OF PERSISTENCE

The early studies based on Atkinson's model had tested the model in situations where expectations were treated as if they were static or unchanging and where the focus was on the immediate task to be performed, isolated from the ongoing stream of activity. It was as if one were looking at a single snapshot photograph rather than at a movie version of the same event. A first step toward widening this limited vision was taken in a study of persistence that I conducted while at the University of Michigan (Feather, 1961, 1962b). I assumed that in order to study a person's persistence at a task it was necessary to specify not only the strength of the tendency to perform that task but also the strength of the tendencies to perform alternative tasks that were available. Persistence at a task could not be considered in isolation but had to be looked at in relation to the range of alternative activities to which a person could turn. In retrospect the point is obvious but it had far-reaching consequences for motivational theory, because it assumed that a person was already active and directed attention to change of activity as a basic aspect of the stream of behavior that all theories of motivation have to explain.

My analysis of persistence considered the relationship between the tendency to perform an initial task (Task A) and the tendency to perform an alternative task (Task B). It assumed that a person would keep working at Task A as long as the tendency to perform it (T_A) was greater than the tendency to perform the alternative (T_B), i.e., $T_A > T_B$. The person would turn to the alternative when $T_B > T_A$. As stated the principle was almost a tautology. It acquired meaning once the determinants of the tendencies were specified (motives, expectations, and incentive values) and once a basis for changes in the tendencies could be advanced. I assumed that a person's tendency to perform the initial task would increase or decrease as experience with the task produced changes in expectation of success. That is, increases or decreases in tendencies were assumed to be mediated by changes in expectation, a cognitive effect that followed from a person's actual task performance. Repeated failure at a task, for example, would tend to diminish a person's expectation of success, leading to consequent changes in task-related tendencies.

In the actual study, subjects worked at an insoluble puzzle and underwent repeated failure. Half of the subjects began the task with a high expectation of success induced by a fictitious group norm ($P_s = .70$). The remaining subjects began the task with a very low expectation of success induced by a fictitious group norm ($P_s = .05$). Subjects were selected so that half of them could be assumed to have a relatively strong motive to achieve success $(M_S > M_F)$. The remaining half could be assumed to have a relatively strong motive to avoid failure $(M_F > M_S)$. The initial task was presented as one of four items in a "Perceptual Reasoning Test" and subjects could work at it for as many trials as they wished before turning to the next item in the series.

The detailed hypotheses and assumptions for this study have been presented elsewhere (Feather, 1961, 1962b) and will not be repeated. Table 3.3 reports the main results, which were consistent with hypotheses. There it can be seen that persistence at the task in relation to initial expectation of success depended upon the person's motive structure. Subjects in whom, by assumption, $M_S > M_F$ persisted longer when the initial task was presented as easy than as very difficult. Subjects in whom, by assumption, $M_F > M_S$ persisted longer when the initial task was presented as very difficult than as easy. These results provide a compelling example of how the analysis of persistence can be advanced by considering the interaction of person variables (motives) and expectations and incentive values that are more closely tied to the situation. The study amply justifies this interactionist approach to the analysis of persistence.

In discussing the results of this early investigation it was noted that future studies should consider types of persistence situation that differ according to the nature of the alternative task, whether expectations and incentive values are related, and whether incentives are objectively present or absent (Feather, 1961, pp. 559–560). A later study provided further support for the analysis of persistence in terms of changes in tendencies (Feather, 1963d).

This early work had a seminal influence in directing attention to the importance of analyzing change in activity as a basic problem for motivational theory (Atkinson & Birch, 1970). It also stimulated other ideas about how tendencies might change. For example, Weiner, (1965, 1972) assumed that persisting,

TABLE 3.3
Number of Subjects Who Were High and Low in Persistence on
Item 1 in Relation to Stated Difficulty of the Task and Nature of
Motivation

	Motive Group			Persistence Trials	
Group	n Achievement	Test Anxiety	Stated Difficulty of Task	High (Above Median)	Low (Below Median)
A	High	Low	70% (easy)	6	2
B	High	Low	5% (difficult)	2	7
C	Low	High	70% (easy)	3	6
D	Low	High	5% (difficult)	6	2

Note. Adapted from Feather (1961).

unsatisfied inertial tendencies could also lead to an increase or decrease in resultant tendencies. Here was another dynamic, in addition to change in cognitive expectations, that provided a way of understanding how tendencies change. On a general level this early work emphasized that theories of motivation have to be able to deal with sets of changing tendencies that influence activity at any given time. It was argued (Feather, 1961) that this type of approach would require:

(a) specification of the nature of the motives, expectations, and incentives involved in the situation; (b) measures of the strength of these motives, expectations and incentives; (c) assumptions concerning how these basic variables combine to determine the various component motivations; (d) specification of the manner in which expectation changes with experience at the activity; and (e) assumptions concerning the resolution of the set of component motivations into a resultant motivation [p. 560].

DETERMINANTS OF EXPECTATIONS

An important implication of the persistence studies and the emphasis on expectation change as a dynamic principle was that one would have to specify the determinants of expectations and the conditions under which they would alter. There is not space to review the extensive literature that concerns the nature and determinants of expectations but four contributions (two early, two recent) will be briefly mentioned. Tolman (1932) distinguished between three different possible "moods" of expectations: perception, mnemonization, and inference. One's expectation that a certain means object (A) will lead to a demanded goal object (B) may occur because all the relevant stimuli can be perceived, or because one can remember from past experience in the same situation that A leads to B, or because one can infer in a novel situation that A leads to B from the information available. The latter "mood" allows for the apparently "insightful" construction of experience under changed conditions, whereas the former two "moods" are more closely tied to present perception and specific learning. In his writings Tolman (1932, 1958) provided many examples of how expectations develop and their effects on behavior.

Lewin, Dembo, Festinger, and Sears (1944), within the context of level of aspiration research, referred to a number of factors that determine the strength of a person's subjective probability of success. Past experience was seen as a major factor and Lewin et al. included here not only the average past performance of an individual in regard to his (or her) attempts to reach certain objectives but also the sequence of achievements (e.g., the effects of a gradually improving sequence of scores). They believed that the most recent success or failure will have particular influence on a person's expectation of future achievement but noted that one must also allow for "subjective hypotheses" that concern a given sequence of achievements. For example, they stated: "In the case of a nonachievement which is linked, for instance, to outside disturbances, the subject is not likely to lower his level of aspiration in the way that he would if he believed that the nonachievement reflected a genuine decrement in his performance ability [p. 367]." One is reminded of Weiner's (1972) assumption, 30 years later, that expectation change is mediated by attribution to stable causes such as ability or lack of ability, or the ease of difficulty of a task. Lewin et al. (1944) also referred to the goal structure of an activity as influencing expectations of future success and failure (e.g., whether a task is seen to have an upper or lower limit). Finally, they noted that expectations are not only determined by past experience and realistic considerations but also by wishes and fears. They asserted that:

> the various parts of the life space are an interdependent field: the realistic expectancy is based mainly on past experiences. The structure of the psychological past affects the structure of the psychological future. However, the expectancy or reality level of the psychological future is also affected by the wish and fear (irreality) level of the psychological future [p. 367].

Two recent discussions have distinguished between different types of expectations. Heckhausen (1977) relates expectations to a four-stage sequence of events that involves the initial situation as perceived, the person's own action, the outcome of the action or the situation, and the consequences of the outcome. The anticipated outcome is seen by Heckhausen as the pivotal point in the building of expectancies and he defines four different kinds of expectancies in terms of how the outcome relates to the other three stages in the sequence. Heckhausen (1977) calls these expectancies "situation–outcome expectancies (Eso), action–outcome expectancies (Eao), action-by-situation–outcome expectancies (Easo), and outcome–consequence expectancies (Eoc) [p. 287]." They are illustrated in Fig. 3.2. Heckhausen believes that the first two types of expectancy have typically been confounded in motivational theory (e.g., by Tolman), and that the fourth type of expectancy ("outcome–consequence expectancies") was relatively neglected until it became an important focus of instrumentality theories dealing with job satisfaction and work motivation (e.g., Mitchell, 1974; Vroom, 1964). The type of expectancy considered by Atkinson (1957, 1964) in his risk-taking model relates to the implications of a person's actions, to the subjective probability that an outcome (success or failure) will occur given a response.

Following his analysis of the concept of expectation, Heckhausen (1977) goes on to distinguish between different types of valence and to define his concept of action tendency, but this discussion is beyond the scope of the present chapter.

Finally, Bandura (1977) also has distinguished recently between different types of expectations, which he calls efficacy expectations and outcome expectations. The distinction is as follows: "An outcome expectancy is defined as a person's estimate that a given behavior will lead to certain outcomes. An efficacy

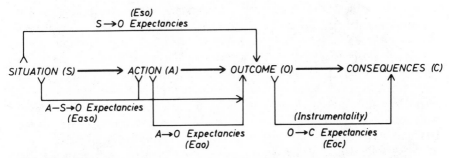

FIG. 3.2. Four kinds of expectancies relating different stages in a sequence of events (Heckhausen, 1977).

expectation is the conviction that one can successfully execute the behavior required to produce the outcomes [p. 193]." Bandura points out that a person can believe that a particular action will lead to some defined outcome but may also doubt that he (or she) can perform the action successfully. Thus, one can perceive the likely consequences of actions without being able to execute these actions. The distinction between outcome expectations and efficacy expectations is illustrated in Fig. 3.3. Bandura argues that "expectations of personal mastery affect both initiation and persistence of coping behavior [p. 193]." He discusses various dimensions and sources of efficacy expectations and notes that most theorizing about expectancies has been concerned with action–outcome expectations. Bandura does not mention Heider's (1958) "naive" analysis of action in which the personal components involved in a person's concept of "can" are quite similar to the concept of perceived self-efficacy.

These various discussions of the concept of expectation demonstrate increasing sophistication in the conceptual analysis of the term over a number of years, following the influential contributions of Tolman and Lewin. My own studies were concerned with the determinants of a person's subjective probability of success, that is, with outcome expectations rather than with efficacy expectations and they were initiated mainly because the theoretical analysis of persistence

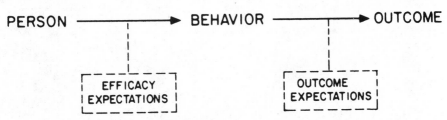

FIG. 3.3. Diagrammatic representation of the difference between efficacy expectations and outcome expectations (Bandura, 1977).

assumed that expectation change was an important dynamic principle involved in changes in tendencies. Hence there was a need to investigate how expectations are formed and how they change in response to various influences. The typical strategy in these early studies was to require subjects to rate their chances of success on a scale from 0 to 100, appropriately labeled at the extremes and middle of the scale. Subjects were also sometimes asked how confident they were about the probability estimates they provided. These dependent variables were related to a range of independent variables, such as information about the performance of other groups and subjects' actual experience at a task.

These studies demonstrated that knowledge of others' performance (e.g., group norms) affected probability estimates and so did the actual structure of the task (e.g., long lists of anagrams versus short lists of anagrams)—see Feather (1961, 1963b, 1963d, 1963e, 1965a, 1965b). These various cues affected initial expectations but once a person started to work at a task then task performance assumed the dominant role in influencing subjective probability of success. Evidence for the effect of actual task experience was obtained from the persistence studies (Feather, 1961, 1963d), from an early performance study (Feather, 1965a), and from a study in which amount of success was controlled by the experimenter (20%, 50%, or 80% success) and where subjects had to predict on each of 120 trials whether they would succeed or fail (Feather, 1963b). The results of this latter study, reported in Table 3.4, clearly indicate the effects of actual experience of success and failure on subjects' predictions. Subsequent research on the effects of prior success and failure at a task (Feather, 1966, 1968a; Feather & Saville, 1967) has also demonstrated the important role of actual performance on subjects' estimates of their chances of success at a task.

Success and failure are usually defined in terms of some criterion (e.g., a score of 50% or above is a pass, below 50% is a fail). Such information about

TABLE 3.4
Mean Number of Predicted Successes over Blocks of Trials for
High, Intermediate, and Low Success Conditions
(N = 20 for each condition)

| Blocks of Trials | Success Condition | | | | | |
| | High (80%) | | Intermediate (50%) | | Low (20%) | |
	Mean	SD	Mean	SD	Mean	SD
1–30	23.45	4.94	16.05	7.28	11.50	7.05
31–60	25.20	4.02	19.20	8.49	11.35	8.75
61–90	26.75	3.36	19.90	8.48	11.60	8.79
91–120	26.55	3.40	18.70	8.75	10.65	8.60

Note. Adapted from Feather (1963b).

meeting or not meeting the criterion affects expectations, but it is also necessary to take into account nearness to the criterion when analyzing expectation change. Failure can be a complete miss or a near miss, and success a near pass or a clear pass. Expectations of success are affected not only by success or failure defined by the criterion but also by the actual level of performance reflecting the degree of success or failure.

Some of the early studies (e.g., Feather, 1963e, 1966) also revealed a systematic tendency for subjects to overestimate their chances of success when the probability reported to them was low and to underestimate their chances of success when the reported probability was high. This tendency to overestimate chances when odds are long and to underestimate chances when odds are high had also appeared in other studies that used different procedures (e.g., Preston & Baratta, 1948).

There was also evidence from this early work that probability estimates and levels of aspiration were related to personality variables such as n Achievement, test anxiety, and external control (Feather, 1963e, 1965b, 1966, 1968a). Two main interpretations were offered for these findings, one a transfer effect from past experience, the other a direct motivational effect. Some motives, for example, may predict to expectations because these motives have been related to the quality of task performance in the past. For example, a person with high test anxiety may feel unconfident in a given situation because, in past situations like that one, he or she has not performed very well, partly because of the high anxiety. Any characteristic, whether it relates to aspects of the task or of the person, may therefore predict to a person's initial expectation of success, if that characteristic has been closely and reliably related to how well the person performed in the past at the same or similar tasks. In this interpretation of personality/expectation relationships, past performance was assumed to act as a mediating link.

The second interpretation assumed a more direct effect of motives on expectations. For example, a strong motive to achieve success (M_S) would, by assumption, determine relatively high levels of positive valence to achieve success (Va_s) at higher levels of task difficulty. The high positive valence or attractiveness of success may determine *autistic* distortions in judgments so that chances of success are overestimated. Similarly, a strong motive to avoid failure (M_F) would, by assumption, determine relatively high levels of negative valence to avoid failure (Va_f) at lower levels of task difficulty. This high negative valence or repulsiveness of failure may determine *defensive* distortions in judgment so that chances of success are underestimated. Some early studies by Marks (1951), Irwin (1953), and Crandall, Solomon, and Kellaway (1955), using a card guessing technique, had shown that stated expectations about an event are influenced by the desirability of that event. Some of the research from the achievement motivation literature had suggested that people with strong motivation to achieve success might bias their subjective probabilities of success upwards (i.e., are more optimistic in their expectations) whereas those with high anxiety about failure might bias them downwards (i.e., are more pessimistic in their expectations)—see Atkinson (1957); Atkinson, Bastian, Earl, and Litwin (1960). One would expect these motivational effects to be more evident under conditions where performance itself carries less weight as a cue that influences expectations (e.g., where there is considerable variability in task performance—see Feather, 1967c). Where present performance can be relied on as a cue, it should take over the dominant role in influencing expectations of success at a task.

It should be noted that most of the relationships involving expectations and personality variables that emerged from these early studies were fairly weak ones. Nevertheless these investigations did find relationships that were statistically significant and they also provided evidence about a wide range of variables that affect a person's expectations of success at a task.

STUDIES OF AFFECT

A number of the studies that have been mentioned also included questions about affective states (e.g., degree of anxiety about failure, disappointment about failure, concern about achievement) in postperformance questionnaires that were administered at the end of the studies. Some of these results were reported in a theoretical article that discussed Mowrer's concepts of fear, hope, relief, and disappointment in relation to expectancy-value theory (Feather, 1963c; Mowrer, 1960a, 1960b). In this expectancy analysis, motivational relief and motivational disappointment were defined in terms of reduction in fear motivation and hope motivation respectively, where this reduction was determined by nonconfirmation or partial confirmation of an expectation of punishment or an expectation of reward. Increments in fear motivation and hope motivation were assumed to follow confirmation or overconfirmation of expectations (Table 3.5). This analysis assumed that expectations and incentive values were independent. When expectations and incentive values were assumed to be related according to the Atkinson model (Atkinson, 1957, 1964), changes in hope and fear motivation following confirmation and nonconfirmation of expectations were rather more complex and depended on the strength of the expectation (Feather, 1963c, p. 510).

In another theoretical analysis (Feather, 1963b), degree of reported anxiety about failure was related to increases in the strength of the motivation or tendency to avoid failure (T_{-f}). These increases were discussed in terms of the Atkinson model in which the negative incentive value (In_f) varies with changes in the subjective probability of failure (P_f), and also in terms of a model in which In_f is set by the initial P_f and does not vary thereafter. These two models were called the ''varying incentive model'' and the ''fixed incentive model'' and their implications are presented in Table 3.6. The ''fixed incentive'' model predicts

TABLE 3.5
Fear Motivation, Hope Motivation,
Motivational Relief, and Motivational
Disappointment in Relation to Confirmation
and Nonconfirmation of Expectations
when Incentive Values and Expectations
are Independent

	Expectation of Punishment	Expectation of Reward
Confirmed or overconfirmed	Increase in fear motivation	Increase in hope motivation
Not confirmed or partially confirmed	Motivational relief	Motivational disappointment

Note. Strength of motivation is assumed to be positively related to strength of motive, level of expectation, and magnitude of incentive value. Adapted from Feather (1963c).

increasing T_{-f} with increasing P_f and therefore implies that reported anxiety about failure (as an index of T_{-f}) would increase with continuing failure at a task. The "varying incentive" model, on the other hand, implies curvilinear relationships. These two models still await detailed test, using experimental

TABLE 3.6
Changes in Tendency to Avoid Failure for Varying Incentive and Fixed
Incentive Models as Expectation of Failure Increases

	Varying Incentive Model				Fixed Incentive Model			
			Tendency to Avoid Failure When:				Tendency to Avoid Failure When:	
	Increasing P_f	Varying In_f	$M_F = 1$	$M_F = 2$	Increasing P_f	Fixed In_f	$M_F = 1$	$M_F = 2$
Low initial P_f	.1	−.9	−.09	−.18	.1	−.9	−.09	−.18
	.3	−.7	−.21	−.42	.3	−.9	−.27	−.54
	.5	−.5	−.25	−.50	.5	−.9	−.45	−.90
	.7	−.3	−.21	−.42	.7	−.9	−.63	−1.26
	.9	−.1	−.09	−.18	.9	−.9	−.81	−1.62
High initial P_f	.7	−.3	−.21	−.42	.7	−.3	−.21	−.42
	.8	−.2	−.16	−.32	.8	−.3	−.24	−.48
	.9	−.1	−.09	−.18	.9	−.3	−.27	−.54

Note. M_F = strength of motive to avoid failure; P_f = subjective probability of failure; In_f = negative incentive value of failure. Adapted from Feather (1965d).

situations in which the initial expectation of failure (P_f) is systematically varied and where the amount of failure at a task is controlled.

It would also be possible to relate affect to the positive and negative valences of the rewards and punishments that have either been experienced or not experienced. Attainment of a goal that has high positive valence for a person should be followed by more positive affect than attaining a goal with weak positive valence. So should avoidance of a punishment with high negative valence when compared with a punishment with weak negative valence. On the other hand, experiencing a punishment with high negative valence should be followed by more negative affect than experiencing a punishment with weak negative valence. And failure to attain a goal with high positive valence should also be accompanied by more negative affect than failure to attain a goal with weak negative valence. These predictions are summarized in Table 3.7.

Elaboration of this simple model depends on detailed specification of the determinants of valence. Some assumptions from achievement motivation theory about the determinants of the positive valence of success (Va_s) and the negative valence of failure (Va_f) have already been stated and tested (see earlier discussion and Feather, 1967e, 1969b). Furthermore, instrumentality theory (Mitchell, 1974; Vroom, 1964) has provided assumptions about how the valence of an outcome relates both to a person's expectation that the outcome will be instrumental in leading to positively or negatively valued consequences and to the value of those consequences (see also Heckhausen, 1977, pp. 289–291). Thus there is already a theoretical basis for relating the affect associated with the attainment or nonattainment of goals to the positive or negative valence of expected outcomes, as these valences existed prior to the actual behavior that led to attainment or nonattainment. Such variables as the general motives that a

TABLE 3.7

Degree of Positive Affect (+) and Negative Affect (−) in Relation to Attainment or NonAttainment of Positively Valent Goals and Avoidance or NonAvoidance of Negatively Valent Punishments

Event	Positive Affect	Event	Negative Affect
High positive valence attained	+ +	High positive valence not attained	− −
Low positive valence attained	+	Low positive valence not attained	−
High negative valence avoided	+ +	High negative valence not avoided	− −
Low negative valence avoided	+	Low negative valence not avoided	−

Note. The number of +s and −s indicates the degree of affect.

person holds, the particular characteristics of an incentive, the possible consequences of an outcome, the degree to which a person perceives that he or she has control over an outcome, the perceived difficulty of a task—all have an influence on valence and, by assumption, on subsequent affect.

These three approaches to the analysis of affect are relatively simple ones. The complete picture is likely to be a lot more complex. For example, Weiner, Russell, and Lerman (1978) differentiate between different kinds of affect; Solomon and Corbit (1974) have assumed that antagonistic processes may be involved in affective responses; and Klinger (1975) has described some consequences that follow commitment to and disengagement from incentives. There is plenty of scope for further investigation.

INFORMATION-SEEKING BEHAVIOR

So far in this review of a research program I have concentrated on theory and research concerned with the analysis of behavior in achievement-related situations. Another major interest has been with the way people deal with discrepancies and inconsistencies. My interest in this topic goes back to the early 1960s and has led to a series of studies dealing with such questions as how cigarette smokers react to dissonant information about their smoking behavior (Feather, 1962a, 1963a), how people evaluate arguments that are inconsistent with their attitudes (Feather, 1964a, 1967a), and how reactions to communications can be modeled by using balance theory (Feather, 1964c, 1967d). In later studies balance theory (Heider, 1958) has also been applied to the analysis of causal attribution (Feather, 1969b) and attitude-related recall (Feather, 1969a, 1970). A general theoretical statement concerning the question of organization and discrepancy in cognitive structures, which reviews earlier research, has also been published (Feather, 1971), and subsequently this analysis has been applied to the interpretation of the effects of discrepancies in value systems (Feather, 1975b).

My parallel interests in expectancy-value models and in the way people deal with discrepant information came together in a theoretical analysis of information-seeking behavior (Feather, 1967b). This paper deals with the conditions under which a person will voluntarily expose himself or herself to new information. If offers an alternative approach to dissonance theory (Festinger, 1957) which in its early version argued that: "If (a person) is led, for one reason or another to expect (an information source) will increase consonance, he will expose himself to the information source. If the expectation is that the cognition required through this source would increase dissonance, he will avoid it [p. 128]."

The evidence for this basic assumption from dissonance theory was mixed (Brehm & Cohen, 1962; Freedman & Sears, 1965). For example, I found in two separate studies that cigarette smokers did not avoid information that cigarette smoking leads to lung cancer—information that one would expect to be dissonant with their cognition that they were smokers. In fact they displayed more interest in this information when compared with nonsmokers (Feather, 1962a, 1963a).

Festinger (1964) later revised his earlier position and argued that a person may expose himself to dissonant information if he feels *confident* that he can deal with the information so as to reduce dissonance. For example, a cigarette smoker might feel confident that he or she can discover the flaws in any new information that is presented because he or she has successfully dealt with similar types of information in the past. Furthermore, Festinger (1964) argued that a person might expose himself or herself to dissonant information because it may be intrinsically *useful*. For example, a cigarette smoker may believe that dissonant information about smoking might involve suggestions about how to control cigarette smoking so that it becomes less dangerous. Thus, avoidance of dissonant information might not occur because there are other reasons for exposure.

This revised analysis suggested to me that it may be instructive to focus on the *instrumentality* of information-seeking behavior in relation to possible rewards and punishments within a situation and to develop an expectancy-value model that considered not only the effects of the immediate situation but also the influence of general personality dispositions (or motives). The analysis considered a person confronted by a number of different sets of information A, B, C, . . . any one of which he or she might decide to select. It was assumed that the problem of accounting for selective exposure to information could be conceptualized as the problem of accounting for the person's decision between the alternative sets of information, and that that set of information would be selected for which the resultant tendency (T_x) was a maximum. The theoretical problem then becomes that of specifying the component tendencies that together determine T_x.

It was assumed that the resultant tendency (T_x) is the resultant of positive tendencies to select X because it may lead to rewards or goals (g) and negative tendencies not to select X because it may lead to threats or punishments (p). That is:

$$T_x = T_{x,g} + T_{x,p}$$

Among the set of positive tendencies that may be elicted was one that I called $T_{x,c}$—a tendency to select X because X may lead to a consistent state of affairs. I assumed that $T_{x,c}$ was determined by a general motive to achieve consistency (M_C), an expectation that X may lead to consistency $(P_{x,c})$, and a positive incentive value of consistency (I_c). The general motive to achieve consistency allowed for the fact that individuals appear to differ in the degree to which they prefer consistent states of affairs, and it was conceived of as a general personality characteristic. The expectancy variable corresponded to the confidence variable introduced by Festinger (1964) that has just been described. The positive incentive value of consistency was introduced to allow for the possibility that consistency will be valued more in some situations than in others (e.g., a court of law in comparison with an informal ideas-generating discussion). It was assumed that:

$$T_{x,c} = M_C \times P_{x,c} \times I_c$$

and that $P_{x,c}$ and I_c are independent. Because the positive valence of consistency (Va_c) may be defined as:

$$Va_c = M_C \times I_c$$

it follows that: $T_{x,c} = P_{x,c} \times Va_c$

The theoretical analysis also assumed that, among the set of negative tendencies, there was a tendency *not* to select X because it may lead to an inconsistent state of affairs. This tendency ($T_{x,i}$) was assumed to be determined by a general motive to avoid inconsistency (M_{AI}), a subjective probability that X may lead to inconsistency ($P_{x,i}$), and a negative incentive value of inconsistency (I_i). That is:

$$T_{x,i} = M_{AI} \times P_{x,i} \times I_i$$

Again it was assumed that the subjective probability and the incentive value were independent. Because the negative valence of consistency (Va_i) may be defined as:

$$Va_i = M_{AI} \times I_i$$

it follows that: $T_{x,i} = P_{x,i} \times Va_i$

It was noted in the analysis that it may turn out to be more parsimonious in the long run to assume only one general motive instead of two different motives, but that the assumption of separate approach and avoidance motives was consistent with the logic involved in an expectancy-value model that postulated positive and negative tendencies (Feather, 1967b, p. 347).

Finally it was assumed that the consistency-related tendencies ($T_{x,c}$ and $T_{x,i}$) by no means exhaust the tendencies that may be elicited in any given situation. There may be positive tendencies, in addition to $T_{x,c}$, that influence selection of information. For example, a person may select a particular set of information because he or she wishes to gain the approval of the experimenter, because it helps the person to solve a problem in a test situation, because it is relevant to achieving some type of security, and so on. These are action tendencies other than the tendency to select X because it may lead to consistency.

Similarly, there may be negative tendencies elicited in a situation, in addition to $T_{x,i}$, that affect information-seeking behavior. A person may tend not to choose X in a problem situation because it might lead to failure. Or choice of X might be associated with the possibility of punishment or chastisement from another person, and so on. These inhibitory tendencies, like $T_{x,i}$, would block the positive tendencies to choose X.

The resultant of these other positive and negative tendencies elicited in a situation was called the extrinsic tendency (T_{ext}) and it was seen to correspond in a general way to what Festinger (1964) referred to as the usefulness of information in his revision of the earlier assumption about dissonance reduction and the seeking or avoidance of information. The complete expectancy-value model of information-seeking behavior could therefore be stated in the following equations:

$$T_x = T_{x,g} + T_{x,p}$$
$$= T_{ext} + (T_{x,c} + T_{x,i})$$
$$= T_{ext} + (M_C \times P_{x,c} \times I_c) + (M_{AI} \times P_{x,i} \times I_i)$$

Some specific implications of this model have been tested. These implications mainly concern the effects of differences in the motive variables. Two studies have supported the prediction that subjects high in intolerance of inconsistency will be more likely to seek out information consistent with their attitude toward an issue than subjects low in intolerance of inconsistency (Feather, 1967b, 1969c). The second study also indicated that personality variables (intolerance of ambiguity, dogmatism) not only influenced the degree to which subjects preferred supportive to nonsupportive information but also affected their preference for novel as opposed to familiar information (see Feather, 1969c, for details). These results are consistent with others in the literature (Miller & Rokeach, 1969).

Many of the assumptions and implications of the expectancy-value model of information-seeking behavior still remain to be explored. For example, what are some of the main extrinsic tendencies that would influence information-seeking behavior? What factors influence the motives, expectations, and incentive values involved in the tendency to approach consistency $(T_{x,c})$ and the tendency to avoid inconsistency $(T_{x,i})$? Under what conditions are these two tendencies elicited? What is the role of commitment and perceived volition? To what extent is information-seeking behavior an inevitable consequence of uncertainty following a decision or commitment to a course of action? How should one define consistency and inconsistency? These questions and many others that relate to the model still await detailed investigation. It is fair to say that the expectancy-value approach to selective exposure stands as a genuine alternative to dissonance-related models (Festinger, 1957, 1964) and to conflict theory (Janis & Mann, 1977).

EXPECTATIONS AND PERFORMANCE

During the 1960s I conducted four studies that tested predictions about level of performance at a task (solving anagrams), a dependent variable that has traditionally been an important one in the psychology of motivation. The first three of these studies (Feather, 1965a, 1966; Feather & Saville, 1967) involved motive measures (*n* Achievement, test anxiety) and the final study (Feather, 1968a) included internal-external locus of control as measured by the I-E scale (Rotter, 1966). All four studies obtained measures of expectation of success (ratings on a 0-100 scale) and most of them also included questions about affective reactions that accompanied or followed task performance (e.g., reported anxiety, reported disappointment). Predictions were based on the Atkinson (1957, 1964) model and took account of changes in positive and negative tendencies that were assumed to follow increases or decreases in subjective probability of success (P_s) as a person worked at the task over a series of trials and experienced success and failure. I also explored the applicability of alternative models when interpreting the results.

In general the studies did not provide clear-cut findings as far as the individual difference variables were concerned. The discussion section of each paper tended to be rather involved as I attempted to explain either the absence of individual difference effects or the complexity of these effects when they did occur. These studies discouraged me from pursuing further research into motive/performance relationships at that time. The prediction of performance differences from motive-expectancy-incentive models is not an easy task for a number of reasons. One has to allow for the fact that performance may be affected by residual, unsatisfied, inertial tendencies that carry over from the past, that performance differences between subjects in different motive conditions may be attenuated in noncontingent situations that have no future implications when compared with performance in contingent situations that do have long term implications, and that performance is probably related in a curvilinear fashion to the resultant tendency, with the optimum performance level corresponding to some intermediate level of resultant tendency (see Atkinson & Raynor, 1974, for discussion of these points). Moreover, one needs to track the pattern of expectation change as task performance proceeds and to make assumptions about the effects of this change on the various tendencies elicited within the situation (e.g., see earlier discussion of the assumptions involved in the variable incentive model compared with the fixed incentive model). One also has to take account of the effects on performance of other individual difference variables (e.g., abilities) and of specific situational variables (e.g., the social context of performance, the nature of the instructions). And, finally, one has to consider characteristics of the task itself (e.g., its level of difficulty and degree of complexity). No doubt there are other variables that one could add to this list that further complicate the use of task performance as a dependent variable.

Yet one should not be too pessimistic. The four performance studies did provide a number of firm findings, though these related more to the effects of situational variables than to the effects of person variables. There was some evidence that performance levels tended to be positively related to initial estimates of chances of success under conditions where the actual difficulty of the task was truthfully represented to subjects. One can assume that under such conditions subjects draw on their past experience at similar tasks of the same order of difficulty to guide them when they estimate their chances of success for the present task. The positive relationship between initial probability estimates and task performance would then reflect an underlying similarity between levels of performance in similar tasks undertaken in the past and levels of performance in the present task. For example, the person who has done well at similar tasks in the past may estimate his chances of success as high and may also tend to do well in the present task. The person makes an actuarial prediction that has some basis in reality. Where, however, the task is misrepresented to subjects (as by the use of false group norms), the actuarial prediction is based on misleading information and may be seriously in error. Other investigators have also noted a tendency for ratings of expectancy of success to predict to performance levels (Crandall, 1969; Crandall & McGhee, 1968).

The last three studies (Feather, 1966, 1968a; Feather & Saville, 1967) provided firm evidence that subsequent performance at a task is affected by initial performance. These studies used a procedure in which subjects who worked at an anagrams task either succeeded or failed on the first few items before they came to a final set of items that were of 50% difficulty. The results showed that subsequent performance on the final set of items was lower following initial failure than following initial success and that the extent of the effect of the initial experience depended on the amount of the prior success or failure. Table 3.8 shows, for example, that the enhancing effect of five initial successes and the depressing effects of five initial failures extended over the two successive five-item blocks from the final 10 anagrams of 50% difficulty. But, when there were three initial successes or three initial failures, the effects of this prior experience were more

TABLE 3.8
Mean Number of Anagrams
Correctly Answered in Block 1
(Trials 4–8) and Block 2
(Trials 9–13) Following Three
Successes or Three Failures and
in Block 1 (Trials 6–10) and
Block 2 (Trials 11–15) Following
Five Successes or Five Failures

Initial Experience	Block 1	Block 2
+ + +	2.59	1.83
– – –	1.17	2.09
+ + + + +	2.97	3.11
– – – – –	2.50	2.20

Note. Adapted from Feather and Saville (1967).

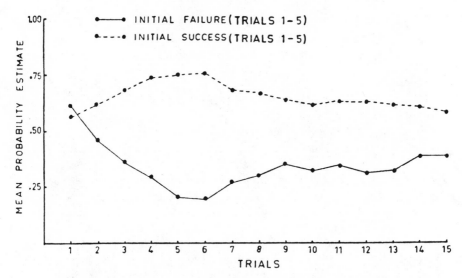

FIG. 3.4. Mean change in probability estimates for Trails 1–15 for combined initial failure groups and combined initial success groups (Feather, 1966).

localized within blocks. In recent years this type of experimental procedure has been used in studies of "learned helplessness" in which it is assumed that a person develops an expectation of uncontrollability of outcomes following the repeated failure experience (e.g., Abramson, Seligman, & Teasdale, 1978; Klein, Fencil-Morse, & Seligman, 1976; Maier & Seligman, 1976; Seligman, 1975). There is an obvious need to relate the theory and research from the learned helplessness and achievement motivation areas.

Each of my four performance studies revealed the powerful effects that task performance has on estimates of probability of success. Fig. 3.4 provides a graphic demonstration of these effects for subjects who either experienced five successes or five failures at a task before they worked on the final set of 10 anagrams of 50% difficulty level.

More detailed analyses of expectation change showed that typical changes in probability estimates (raising the estimate after a success, lowering it after a failure) were related to motive measures (n Achievement, test anxiety) and to internal–external control as measured by the I-E scale. Subjects, in whom it was assumed that $M_S > M_F$, were more likely to raise their probability estimates over a sequence of five initial successes than were subjects in whom, by assumption, $M_F > M_S$. The latter subjects were more likely to lower their probability estimates over a sequence of five initial failures than were the $M_S > M_F$ subjects—see Feather, 1966 for details. In a subsequent study (Feather, 1968a), "internals" tended to make a greater number of typical changes in their probability estimates over 15 trials involving success and failure than did "externals."

These results also relate to findings from the literature on learned helplessness (e.g., Klein, Fencil-Morse, & Seligman, 1976; Miller & Seligman, 1975), and suggest that some integration would be desirable.

VALENCE AND PERCEIVED CONTROL

Later in the 1960s I returned once more to the question of the determinants of the valences of success and failure (Va_s, Va_f). In one study (Feather, 1967e) subjects were presented with a hypothetical task situation in which the outcomes depended either on skill or on chance. Subjects were asked to make judgments about the chances of success, the attractiveness of success, and the repulsiveness of failure for each of 10 difficulty levels of a task, for a hypothetical person working at the first trial of the task and then again at the last trial of the task. Each subject also completed the projective measure of n Achievement, the Achievement Anxiety Test designed by Alpert and Haber (1960) to give separate measures of debilitating and facilitating anxiety, and the I–E scale (Rotter, 1966) which provided a measure of external control.

The main results of this study (Feather, 1967e) were summarized as follows:

(a) As a task becomes more difficult, success is seen as more attractive and failure as less repulsive, particularly when success or failure reflects upon the ability of the person. Attractiveness of success and repulsiveness of failure change more rapidly with task difficulty when success or failure involves personal skill and ability than when the outcome is determined by luck; (b) even under conditions where the outcome is determined by luck, an unlikely success is seen as more attractive than a likely success, particularly at the beginning of a task; (c) under conditions where the outcome is determined by luck, repulsiveness of failure is relatively low and there is little difference between the repulsiveness of a likely failure and the repulsiveness of an unlikely failure; (d) expectations of success are modified under conditions where a person can see that over trials success or failure depends upon his ability to influence the outcome, but not when success or failure is a matter of chance [pp. 383-384].

Measures of rate of change in probability estimates, attractiveness ratings, and repulsiveness ratings with change in levels of task difficulty (the regression coefficients or slope indexes) tended to be unrelated to the personality measures, but there were highly significant intercorrelations between the slope indexes when there was situational similarity with respect to whether or not performance could be seen as reflecting skill or chance (Feather, 1967e, pp. 380-382). Once more the situational manipulation appeared to dominate judgments.

In discussing the results of this study I speculated that it might be necessary to broaden the Atkinson (1957, 1964) model by considering the degree to which a person sees the outcome as internally controlled as an important variable that affects valence in any given situation. Thus, according to Feather (1968b): "rate of change in attractiveness of success and repulsiveness of failure with task difficulty will be a positive function of the degree to which an S sees himself as personally responsible for the outcome [p. 117]."

In particular, I suggested that a further variable called perceived internal control or responsibility (C), with positive values and a minimum of zero, might be incorporated in the Atkinson model. The basic assumptions would be modified so that:

$$Va_s = M_S \times C \times In_s$$

and, $Va_f = M_F \times C \times In_f$

It would be assumed that the motives to achieve success (M_S) and to avoid failure (M_F) would be engaged as long as perceived responsibility (C) were positive and as long as performance could be evaluated against standards of excellence. An obvious implication of these changes in assumptions is that the positive valence of success (Va_s) and the negative valence of failure (Va_f) would show little change with subjective probability of success (P_s) if C were low, but the rate of change in valence would increase as C increased in value.

These implications are apparent in Table 3.9, which shows the relationship of valences to subjective probabilities in relation to differences in motive strength ($M_S = 1$ or 4; $M_F = 1$ or 4) and differences in perceived internal control ($C = 1$ or 4). Table 3.9 indicates that any manipulation that increased the degree to which a person sees himself or herself as responsible for the outcome would be functionally equivalent to an increase in the strength of motive, when considering the effects on the relationship of valence to subjective probability. In both cases

TABLE 3.9
Relationship of Valences to Subjective Probabilities in Relation to
Differences in Motive Strength and Differences in Perceived Internal Control

		Va_s						Va_f			
		$M_S = 1$	$M_S = 4$	$M_S = 1$	$M_S = 4$			$M_F = 1$	$M_F = 4$	$M_F = 1$	$M_F = 4$
P_s	In_s	$C = 1$	$C = 1$	$C = 4$	$C = 4$	P_f	In_f	$C = 1$	$C = 1$	$C = 4$	$C = 4$
Easy .9	.1	.1	.4	.4	1.6	.1	−.9	−.9	−3.6	−3.6	−14.4
.7	.3	.3	1.2	1.2	4.8	.3	−.7	−.7	−2.8	−2.8	−11.2
Moderate .5	.5	.5	2.0	2.0	8.0	.5	−.5	−.5	−2.0	−2.0	−8.0
.3	.7	.7	2.8	2.8	11.2	.7	−.3	−.3	−1.2	−1.2	−4.8
Difficult .1	.9	.9	3.6	3.6	14.4	.9	−.1	−.1	− .4	− .4	−1.6

Note. $In_s = 1 - P_s$; $In_f = - P_s$; $Va_s = M_S \times C \times In_s$; $Va_f = M_F \times C \times In_f$; $P_s + P_f = 1$. Adapted from Feather (1968b).

the increase should be accompanied by a more pronounced rate of change in valence in relation to subjective probability.

This revision of the Atkinson model awaits further test. One line of research would be to explore the situational and personality determinants of perceived internal control (C). Immediate situational variables such as an emphasis on skill versus chance, and the degree to which a situation involves outside forces that facilitate or impede performance, are of obvious importance. Personality variables such as a person's generalized expectancy about locus of control (Rotter, 1966) may also be important, though possibly overshadowed in most cases by the situational effects. Clues might come from the literature on attitude change and consistency where the concept of perceived responsibility or volition has been invoked to account for behavior in a lot of different contexts (see the early work of Brehm & Cohen, 1962; Feather, 1964c, 1967d). The emphasis should be on what determines a person's perception of internal control in a given situation *before* an action occurs rather than on how causes are attributed *after* an action has taken place.

One would expect, however, that positive affect following success and negative affect following failure would be a function of perceived internal control (C) before the event. As noted earlier (Table 3.7), affect can be assumed to be a function of valence that, in the present analysis, would increase with increase in C. Weiner (1972, 1974, 1980) has also argued that esteem-related affective reactions to success and failure will depend on perceived locus of control, being greater when outcomes can be attributed internally than externally.

Finally, it should be apparent that the interest in the perceived internal control (C) variable may be seen as continuous with the earlier research on the effects of skill and chance situations in the study of object preference (Feather, 1959a, 1959b) and with my assumption that perceived responsibility (or volition) is an important variable to consider when analyzing reactions to attitude-discrepant communications (Feather, 1964c, 1967d). From a current perspective, this line of research was an early signal of the interest in topics such as causal attribution (Weiner, 1972, 1974, 1980), personal causation (De Charms, 1968), perceived freedom (Steiner, 1970), learned helplessness (Abramson, et al., 1978; Miller & Norman, 1979; Seligman, 1975), and perceived self-efficacy (Bandura, 1977), topics that were to claim the attention of a lot of psychologists during the 1970s.

EXPECTATIONS AND CAUSAL ATTRIBUTION

In 1969 I published an article on causal attribution (Feather, 1969b) that was the starting point of a research program that continued for a number of years and is still progressing. The paper also dealt with affect following success and failure in terms of a valence-difficulty model in a way that was consistent with ideas that I have already presented about the relationship of Va_s and Va_f to P_s (the subjective probability of success).

The analysis of causal attribution explored two models, both of which were derived from Heider's theoretical approach (Heider, 1958). The first model used balance theory and presented four structures that were completely balanced according to Heider's principle. Each structure involved three entities: *person, self,* and *outcome* (success or failure), and two types of relation: *attitudinal* (e.g., likes, dislikes) and *unit* (e.g., owns, disowns). Within each structure *self* and *outcome* were conceived as objects of attitudes, success was assumed to be positively valued and failure negatively valued, and relations within the structure were assumed to be seen from the point of view of the person. Fig. 3.5 presents four balanced structures represented as signed digraphs. In Fig. 3.5 the straight lines represent attitudinal relations and brackets represent unit relations. Solid lines represent positive relations and dashed lines represent negative relations. Arrows on the lines represent the direction of relations.

The four balanced structures in Fig. 3.5 were used to generate predictions about causal attribution. For example, signed digraph *a* implies that self and success will be linked together by a positive unit relation when the two attitudinal relations are positive, and signed digraph *b* implies that self and failure will

BALANCED ATTRIBUTION STRUCTURES

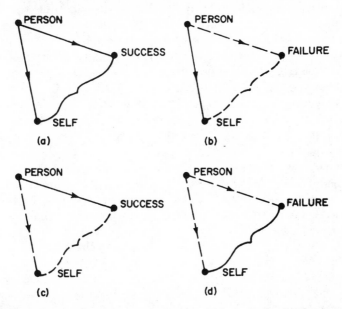

FIG. 3.5. Signed digraphs for the attribution model representing four balanced structures (Feather, 1971).

involve a negative unit relation when one of the attitudinal relations is positive and the other negative. It was assumed that a positive unit relation implies ownership and personal responsibility for outcome, whereas a negative unit relation implies that the outcome is seen as not belonging to the self, as disowned and not caused by the self. This assumption about positive and negative unit relations was consistent with a similar assumption made in a structural balance analysis of communication effects (Feather, 1964c, 1967d). Given these assumptions one can predict that when self-evaluation is positive, success will be attributed to the self and failure to outside influences. But when self-evaluation is negative, success will be attributed to external factors and failure to personal inadequacy.

The second model was influenced by Heider's "naive analysis of action," which relates the outcome of an action, x, to factors that reside in the person and factors that reside in the environment (Heider, 1958, Ch. 4). I assumed that causal attribution for success or failure at a task will be related to the specific expectation of success elicited within the task situation. This expectation may be due to a variety of determinants. For example, if the person has consistently succeeded or failed at this kind of task in the past (*consistency* information), then the expectation would reflect the person's estimate of his or her relatively stable ability or lack of ability at tasks of this kind. If the person knows that most others have succeeded at the task or most others have failed (*consensus* information), then the expectation would reflect the person's judgment that the task is easy or difficult. If the person intends to try very hard to succeed at the task or not to try at all, then the expectation would be influenced by this intention. If the task situation is seen to involve particular features involving good or bad luck or the presence or absence of some opportunity that may not recur again, or if the person is experiencing fatigue or a transient mood or emotional state, then the expectation would be affected by these special features. The point is that a person's expectation of success in a given task situation may be determined by a number of factors. One or more of these sets of determinants (e.g., ability, task difficulty) are, however, probably more important than others on any given occasion.

It can be assumed that outcomes that *confirm* a high or low expectation of success will be attributed to the factors that have most influence on the expectation. For example, if a person has a high expectation of success that is based on consistency information or other cues that determine ability estimates, then success (an outcome that confirms the high expectation) will tend to be attributed to ability. If a low expectation of success is based on consensus information that most others do poorly, then failure (an outcome that confirms the low expectation) will tend to be attributed to the difficulty of the task. On the other hand, outcomes that *disconfirm* high or low expectations of success will tend to be attributed to variable factors such as good or bad luck, or effort or lack of effort, when these expectations are based on *consistency* information. For example, a person with a high expectation of success that relates to consistently high performance in the past may tend to attribute the failure (an outcome that disconfirms the high expectation) to bad luck or lack of effort. But when expectations are based on *consensus* information, a disconfirming outcome may be attributed to stable factors such as the presence or absence of ability, or to unusual circumstances such as luck or opportunity. For example, a person whose expectation of success at a task is low because he or she knows that most others fail, may tend to attribute success (an outcome that disconfirms the low expectation) to unusual ability or to some "once only" cause that will not occur again.

My first study of causal attribution (Feather, 1969b) explored some of these ideas in a task situation in which subjects worked at a 10-item anagrams test. Before beginning they provided estimates of how confident they were, using a simple rating scale. Following their performance, they discovered whether they had passed or failed the test. They then rated the extent to which their success (or failure) was mainly due to good (or bad) luck or mainly due to ability (or lack of ability)—(see Feather, 1969b for details). The study also included measures of self-esteem and competence, based on semantic differential ratings, and a measure of feelings of inadequacy (Janis & Field, 1959).

Attribution scores were found to be related to level of initial confidence (Fig. 3.6). Subjects who succeeded at the task showed greater external attribution when they were initially unconfident (low expectation) than when they were initially confident (high expectation). Subjects who failed were more likely to show external attribution when they were initially confident (high expectation) than when they were initially unconfident (low expectation).

Note that in this early study the measure of causal attribution confounded two dimensions: internal/external locus of control and stability/instability. In most of my subsequent studies I have followed Weiner's (1972, 1974, 1980) example by distinguishing between these two dimensions in the rating scales that have been used. Weiner (1972, 1974, 1980) has argued that attributions along these two dimensions have different effects. Esteem-related affects that follow success or failure are assumed to be related to the internal/external locus of control dimension. Expectancy changes following success or failure are assumed to be related to the stability/instability dimension. Weiner has continued to explore the question of dimensions and their effects, elaborating and revising some of his earlier ideas (Weiner, 1980; Weiner, Russell, & Lerman, 1978; see also Chapter 6), and others have developed ways of classifying causes that use dimensions similar to Weiner's (Abramson, Seligman, & Teasdale, 1978; Deci, 1975).

It is interesting to note that the results of this initial attribution study (Feather, 1969b) showed that, although attribution ratings were related to the specific initial expectations held by subjects, they were unrelated to the general measures of self evaluation (self esteem, competence, inadequacy). Attribution ratings were, however, related to nearness to the pass/fail criterion—they were more external the closer the person's outcome (success or failure) was to the pass/fail

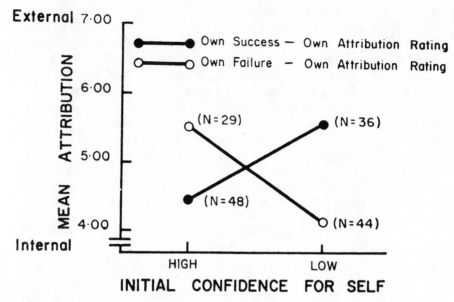

FIG. 3.6.   Mean attribution scores in relation to own outcome and initial confidence for self (Feather & Simon, 1971a).

criterion (Mann, 1974). Female subjects tended to be more external in their attributions than male subjects and their initial confidence ratings tended to be lower (Feather, 1968a, p. 42; Lenney, 1977). Other results can be found in the published report.

My program of research into causal attribution that followed this initial study has investigated a wide range of topics that include the following: person–other differences (Feather & Simon, 1971a), the effects of selective and manipulative control (Feather & Simon, 1971b), luck and the unexpected outcome (Feather & Simon, 1972), causal attributions for examination performance (Simon & Feather, 1973), causal attributions in relation to fear of success (Feather & Simon, 1973), how people explain poverty (Feather, 1974), how males and females attribute causality for success and failure in sex-linked occupations (Feather & Simon, 1975, 1976; Feather, 1977, 1978b), and the effects of different causal attributions on observers' reactions to an equal or equitable allocator (Feather & O'Driscoll, 1980). The balance model of causal attribution (Feather, 1969b) has been integrated into a general theoretical treatment of the question of organization and discrepancy in cognitive structures (Feather, 1971). Most of the later studies have been more concerned with the expectancy analysis of causal attribution (see especially, Feather, 1977).

AFFECT AND CONSISTENCY OF OUTCOME WITH SEX ROLES

A number of the studies just mentioned explored the question of sex differences in relation to various measures (e.g., causal attributions, initial confidence). A subset of them also involved an interest in male and female sex-roles in relation to different types of occupation—an interest that developed from research that included a projective measure of the fear of success (Feather & Raphelson, 1974; Feather & Simon, 1973). In the later sex-role studies questionnaire measures were used rather than the projective test, a wide range of occupations was sampled, and a variety of dependent variables relating to success or failure at sex-linked occupations were investigated—causal attributions being only one of these dependent variables.

Two studies have investigated perceived affect (happiness or unhappiness) in hypothetical situations where males or females either successfully entered or failed to enter defined occupations that varied both in their perceived status and sex-linked appropriateness (Feather, 1975a, 1978). The results of these studies showed that judgments of affect were higher for higher status occupations than for lower status occupations. Perceived affect was also higher when there was consistency between the sex of the person entering or failing to enter an occupation and the sex linkage of that occupation (see Table 3.10). For example, a male was seen as happier than a female if he succeeded in qualifying to become a company director (a male-dominated occupation); a female was seen as unhappier than a male if she failed to be selected to become a typist–stenographer (a female-dominated occupation). It was argued that the affect associated with success or failure at an occupation would be related to widely shared stereotypes about which jobs are seen as either appropriate or inappropriate for men and women in society, and to the perceived status of the occupation.

These findings have some general implications for the analysis of variables that influence the valence of success and failure, on the assumption that the affect associated with outcomes reflects the valences that existed before action occurred. The status of an occupation no doubt relates to the objective benefits that that occupation confers, to the value that society traditionally places on the type of work involved, to the difficulty of entering the job, to the preparation and qualifications required for the occupation, and so on. All of these variables may be seen to influence the perceived status of the occupation and the valence of succeeding or failing to enter it. The studies also suggest, however, that a success that confirms sex-role expectations (e.g., a male becoming a company director) will be more positively valent than a success that violates these assumptions (e.g., a female becoming a company director), whereas a failure that confirms sex-role expectations (e.g., a male failing to become a typist–stenographer) will be less negatively valent than a failure that violates these expectations (e.g., a

TABLE 3.10
Mean Rating of Happiness about Success and Unhappiness about
Failure by all Respondents for Male and Female Characters for
Different Occupations

Occupation	Happiness with success		Unhappiness with failure		Significant effects
	Male character	Female character	Male character	Female character	
Company director	12.97	11.88	13.49	10.59	C***, BC***
Solicitor	13.39	12.66	13.55	12.36	C***
Janitor	8.91	8.50	9.70	7.46	C***, AC**, BC***
Doctor	13.30	13.48	13.76	13.04	BC**
School principal	12.78	11.85	13.22	11.16	C***, BC**
Newspaper reporter	12.20	11.82	11.97	10.73	B**, C***
Secondary schoolteacher	11.84	12.11	12.82	12.65	B***
Laboratory assistant	10.63	12.20	10.14	11.32	B**, C***
Physiotherapist	12.08	13.16	12.23	13.02	A**, C***
Shop assistant	8.61	10.61	8.23	10.40	A*, C***
Domestic worker	6.06	9.34	5.82	9.95	A*, C***
Typist–stenographer	8.11	11.80	7.55	11.86	C***

Note. Higher numbers denote more happiness or unhappiness. On the rating scale the range was 1–15 with 8 as the theoretical neutral point. In the 2 × 2 × 2 analysis of variance, Factor A = sex of respondent, Factor B = outcome, Factor C = sex of character. Minor departures from sample Ns occurred in calculating item means due to missing data. Adapted from Feather (1975a).
$*p < .05$.
$**p < .01$.
$***p < .001$.

female failing to become a typist–stenographer). As noted previously, therefore, consistency pressures may have an effect on positive and negative valences.

VALUES AND VALENCE

My most recent research with expectancy-value models explores the conditions under which personal values predict to action (Feather, 1979). Because this topic is considered in another chapter in this book (Chapter 9), I limit the present description to a selective sketch of some of the main concepts involved in the analysis of the values/action relationship.

This recent research is the latest in a series of studies of values from a research program that is now several years old. I was convinced by Rokeach's argument that, although value had the status of a basic concept in many of the social sciences, it had not received the systematic treatment that it deserved from psychologists (Rokeach, 1968, 1973). Like Rokeach, I decided in the late 1960s to try to remedy this situation and began a program of research that is still continuing. Much of this research has been concerned with mapping values across different segments of the population and also across cultures. Some studies from the program have investigated the consequences of discrepancies between personal value systems and the perceived value systems of defined environments. Other studies have examined the accuracy with which the value systems of a group can be judged by others. And, most recently, I have attempted to move beyond the ecological task of mapping congruence and discrepancy in value systems to consider the relationship between values and behavior in terms of the expectancy-value approach. A lot of this research, with the exception of the recent motivational analysis, has been brought together in my book *Values in Education and Society* (Feather, 1975b).

Values may be conceived as a particular class of motives. They are those motives that involve normative considerations of "oughtness" and desirability, linked to an evaluative dimension of goodness and badness. Thus, a person may believe that freedom and equality are desirable states of affairs, general goals that all people should pursue. On the other hand, a person may see dishonesty and disobedience as undesirable modes of conduct, as ways of behaving that ought to be avoided. Values serve as standards or criteria to guide thought and action in various ways, and they are linked to affect, as is evident when one's important values are frustrated or challenged. I have suggested that values can be conceptualized as "abstract structures" (Feather, 1971, 1975b)—as abstractions from previous experience that have an oughtness quality about them and that comprise an associative network that can take different forms for different individuals. A person's values and value systems can be discrepant with those that particular environments are perceived to promote. The analysis of the consequences of these value disjunctions relates to my continuing interest in the concepts of consistency and structural discrepancy in relation to human thought and action.

This type of analysis owes a great deal to Rokeach (1973, 1979) who argues that values are enduring and transcendental beliefs that guide one's preferences about modes of conduct or end-states of existence and that serve as standards in many different ways. Rokeach distinguishes between *terminal* values, such as freedom, equality, and wisdom, that refer to general goals or end-states of existence, and *instrumental* values, such as being loving, helpful, and honest, that refer to modes of conduct. The relative importance of values within these two classes can be separately assessed by using Rokeach's Value Survey, which presents subjects with two lists of 18 terminal and 18 instrumental values with the instruction that subjects rank the values within each list in their order of importance. Rokeach assumes that the instrumental and terminal values become organized into hierarchies of importance that are called value systems and that the rank order obtained from the Value Survey reflects the terminal and instrumental hierarchies at that time. A value system may function as a "general plan" enabling a person to resolve conflicts between particular values (e.g., behaving politely or honestly in a given situation). Rokeach (1973, p. 25; 1979) argues that social institutions (e.g., the family, the church, one's political organization) maintain, enhance, and transmit selected subsets of values from generation to generation. Society does not, however, act on a passive organism. One must also allow for the biological makeup of the person, the basic needs involved, and the unique life experiences to which the person has been exposed. Ultimately, according to Rokeach (1979), human values: "provide us with a set of standards to guide us in all our efforts to satisfy our needs and at the same time maintain and, insofar as possible, enhance self-esteem, that is, to make it possible to regard ourselves and to be regarded by others as having satisfied societally and institutionally originating definitions of morality and competence [p. 48]."

How can one integrate the concept of value into the analysis of motivated behavior using the general expectancy-value approach? If one treats values as a particular class of motives, then like motives they can be assumed to have the power to induce valences on certain environmental objects, behaviors, or states of affairs (see also French & Kahn, 1962, pp. 11–12). McClelland (1971) has assumed that the "pulling power" of any positive incentive *for an individual* depends in part on the strength of the underlying motivational dispositions that the incentive satisfies. For example, money is an effective incentive generally, but it works better for some people than for others, depending on the underlying motives. In earlier discussion I argued that motives can be conceived as "weighting" factors that affect the valence of incentives. So too, it can be assumed that terminal and instrumental values can affect the valence of particular goals and ways of behaving. Money may be a very potent incentive for people who assign a high priority to *a comfortable life* in their value systems. Its incentive properties may also be bound up with the relative importance assigned by a person to *a sense of accomplishment* and to other values from Rokeach's list of terminal values. The alternative means of obtaining a particular incentive may also vary in their valence, depending on the importance of the relevant instrumental values. Thus, honest courses of action may be more attractive for persons who assign high importance to being *honest,* an instrumental value from Rokeach's list. In short (Feather, 1975b):

> One can speculate that terminal values may influence the valence of specific outcomes or "end-states"—some outcomes being seen as more attractive (or repulsive) than others, whereas instrumental values may influence the valence of specific instrumental behaviors or means to ends—some courses of action being seen as more attractive (or repulsive) than others [p. 302].

The distinctive contribution of this analysis is to treat value as a particular class of motive and to extend the valence-inducing properties so that values influence not only the valence of goals or ends but also the valence of means or types of activity that can lead to ends.

As an example of this type of analysis, let us show how it can be applied to the study of student activism. There is evidence that student activists assign a very high priority to *equality* in their terminal value systems (Ellerman & Feather, 1976). If we assume that values are sources of valence, then it follows, according to Feather (1975b) that:

> various outcomes involving the preservation of existing equalities and the removal of inequalities on the college campus would have higher subjective value (or positive valence) for these activists than for nonactivists, who ranked *equality* lower in importance. Similarly, some ways of achieving these outcomes would have higher valence than others, according to the relative importance assigned to particular instrumental values. Thus, courses of action corresponding to the instrumental values *courageous, helpful, imaginative,* and *loving* might be more attractive for activists than for nonactivists, and courses of action corresponding to the instrumental values *ambitious, capable, cheerful, clean, obedient, polite,* and *responsible* might be less attractive for activists than for nonactivists. . . . Some courses of action would be viewed as more likely to lead to success than others (that is, they would be associated with higher expectancies of success than others), depending upon each individual's past experience and the present circumstances. And, particularly on college campuses where sanctions are not always clear or easy to enforce, the strength of inhibitory forces that block action may be low. One could add other variables to this analysis, but already it should be clear that it captures many of the factors that have been mentioned in discussions of student activism [p. 304–305].

There is no reason why this kind of approach could not be applied to improve our understanding of many other topics, given the assumptions that values are central motives, that they tend to be more or less universally present (though varying in their relative importance within individuals), and that they are relatively few in number (Rokeach, 1979, p. 49). For example, knowledge of the importance within individual value systems of *freedom, logical,* and *helpful,* combined with an expectancy-value analysis, might significantly add to our understanding (respectively) of how individuals react to threats to their freedom, to cognitive inconsistencies, and to situations where altruistic actions are possible (Feather, 1975b, pp. 304–305). It should be noted that these analyses will need to recognize that typically, according to Feather (1975b): "behavior is overdetermined, embracing the effects of more than one motive or value and involving complex sets of instigating and inhibitory forces for which rules of combination have to be specified [p. 305].'' These analyses will need to consider, not only the combination of expectations and valences, but also the effects of other variables (like the availability of responses in a person's repertoire, the persisting inertial tendencies that carry over from the past, the long-term future goals that slot into contingent paths)—variables that have emerged as expectancy-value models have become more sophisticated (Atkinson & Birch, 1978; Atkinson & Raynor, 1974).

Thus, this type of approach clarifies the conditions under which values might be expected to lead to action and opens up new areas for research.

CONCLUSION

This overview of a research program indicates my continuing attempt to analyze the determinants of behavior in terms of a general class of theories that relate tendencies either to perform particular actions or not to perform them to the strength of *expectations* that these actions will lead to specific outcomes and to the *valences* (or subjectively perceived values) of these outcomes for the person. The research has extended beyond the achievement motivation domain to other areas as well, and it has explored some of the major variables that influence expectations and valence.

The theoretical analysis does not involve a static set of variables but explicitly allows for changes in expectations and valences and, therefore, for changes in positive and negative tendencies. It also acknowledges that persisting, unsatisfied sources of motivation may carry over from the past. The approach is not situation bound but acknowledges the importance of including both person and situation variables in the analysis. It recognizes that behavior is always ongoing and involves an active organism making its own distinctive contribution as it interacts with the environment and processes information from it. The expectations and valences involved in the analysis apply to segments or frames from the continuing stream of a person's behavior and they relate to that person's own structuring of reality. These variables together capture the cognition and purpose that most of behavior displays and, in their combination, provide a powerful lever for the understanding of human action.

REFERENCES

Abramson, L. Y., Seligman, M. E. P., & Teasdale, J. D. Learned helplessness in humans: Critique and reformulation. *Journal of Abnormal Psychology,* 1978, *87,* 49–74.

Alpert, R., & Haber, R. N. Anxiety in academic achievement situations. *Journal of Abnormal and Social Psychology,* 1960, *61,* 207–215.

Atkinson, J. W. Motivational determinants of risk-taking behavior. *Psychological Review,* 1957, *64,* 359–372.

Atkinson, J. W. *An introduction to motivation.* Princeton: Van Nostrand, 1964.

Atkinson, J. W., Bastian, J. R., Earl, R. W., & Litwin, G. H. The achievement motive, goal setting, and probability preferences. *Journal of Abnormal and Social Psychology,* 1960, *60,* 27–36.

Atkinson, J. W., & Birch, D. *The dynamics of action.* New York: Wiley, 1970.

Atkinson, J. W., & Birch, D. *An introduction to motivation.* Princeton, N.J.: Van Nostrand, 1978.

Atkinson, J.W., & Feather, N. T. (Eds.). *A theory of achievement motivation.* New York: Wiley, 1966.

Atkinson, J. W., & Raynor, J. O. *Motivation and achievement*. New York: V. H. Winston (Halsted Press, Wiley), 1974.

Bandura, A. Self-efficacy: Toward a unifying theory of behavioral change. *Psychological Review*, 1977, *84*, 191–215.

Brehm, J. W., & Cohen, A. R. *Explorations in cognitive dissonance*. New York: Wiley, 1962.

Cartwright, D. The effect of interruption, completion, and failure upon the attractiveness of activities. *Journal of Experimental Psychology*, 1942, *31*, 1–16.

Child, I. L. Children's preferences for goals easy or difficult to obtain. *Psychological Monographs*, 1946, *60*(No. 280).

Crandall, V. C. Sex differences in expectancy of intellectual and academic reinforcement. In C. P. Smith (Ed.), *Achievement-related motives in children*. New York: Russell Sage Foundation, 1969.

Crandall, V. C., & McGhee, P. E. Expectancy of reinforcement and academic competence. *Journal of Personality*, 1968, *36*, 635–648.

Crandall, V. J., Solomon, D., & Kellaway, R. Expectancy statements and decision times as functions of objective probabilities and reinforcement values. *Journal of Personality*, 1955, *24*, 192–203.

De Charms, R. *Personal causation: The internal affective determinants of behavior*. New York: Academic Press, 1968.

Deci, E. L. *Intrinsic motivation*. New York: Plenum Press, 1975.

Edwards, W. The theory of decision making. *Psychological Bulletin*, 1954, *51*, 380–417.

Ellerman, D. A., & Feather, N. T. The values of Australian student activists. *Australian Journal of Education*, 1976, *20*, 260–277.

Feather, N. T. Subjective probability and decision under uncertainty. *Psychological Review*, 1959, *66*, 150–164. (a)

Feather, N. T. Success probability and choice behavior. *Journal of Experimental Psychology*, 1959, *58*, 257–266. (b)

Feather, N. T. The relationship of persistence at a task to expectation of success and achievement related motives. *Journal of Abnormal and Social Psychology*, 1961, *63*, 552–561.

Feather, N. T. Cigarette smoking and lung cancer: A study of cognitive dissonance. *Australian Journal of Psychology*, 1962, *14*, 55–64. (a)

Feather, N. T. The study of persistence. *Psychological Bulletin*, 1962, *59*, 94–115. (b)

Feather, N. T. Cognitive dissonance, sensitivity and evaluation. *Journal of Abnormal and Social Psychology*, 1963, *66*, 157–163. (a)

Feather, N. T. The effect of differential failure on expectation of success, reported anxiety, and response uncertainty. *Journal of Personality*, 1963, *31*, 289–312. (b)

Feather, N. T. Mowrer's revised two-factor theory and the motive–expectancy–value model. *Psychological Review*, 1963, *70*, 500–515. (c)

Feather, N. T. Persistence at a difficult task with alternative task of intermediate difficulty. *Journal of Abnormal and Social Psychology*, 1963, *66*, 604–609. (d)

Feather, N. T. The relationship of expectation of success to reported probability, task structure, and achievement related motivation. *Journal of Abnormal and Social Psychology*, 1963, *66*, 231–238. (e)

Feather, N. T. Acceptance and rejection of arguments in relation to attitude strength, critical ability, and intolerance of inconsistency. *Journal of Abnormal and Social Psychology*, 1964, *69*, 127–136. (a)

Feather, N. T. Level of aspiration behavior in relation to payoffs and costs following success and failure. *Australian Journal of Psychology*, 1964, *16*, 175–184. (b)

Feather, N. T. A structural balance model of communication effects. *Psychological Review*, 1964, *71*, 291–313. (c)

Feather, N. T. Performance at a difficult task in relation to initial expectation of success, test anxiety, and need Achievement. *Journal of Personality*, 1965, *33*, 200–217. (a)

Feather, N. T. The relationship of expectation of success to need achievement and test anxiety. *Journal of Personality and Social Psychology*, 1965, *1*, 118–126. (b)

Feather, N. T. Effects of prior success and failure on expectations of success and subsequent performance. *Journal of Personality and Social Psychology*, 1966, *3*, 287–298.

Feather, N. T. Evaluation of religious and neutral arguments in religious and atheist student groups. *Australian Journal of Psychology*, 1967, *19*, 3–12. (a)

Feather, N. T. An expectancy-value model of information-seeking behavior. *Psychological Review*, 1967, *74*, 342–360. (b)

Feather, N. T. Level of aspiration and performance variability. *Journal of Personality and Social Psychology*, 1967, *6*, 37–46. (c)

Feather, N. T. A structural balance approach to the analysis of communication effects. In L. Berkowitz (Ed.), *Advances in experimental social psychology* (Vol. 3). New York: Academic Press, 1967. (d)

Feather, N. T. Valence of outcome and expectation of success in relation to task difficulty and perceived locus of control. *Journal of Personality and Social Psychology*, 1967, *7*, 372–386. (e)

Feather, N. T. Change in confidence following success or failure as a predictor of subsequent performance. *Journal of Personality and Social Psychology*, 1968, *9*, 38–46. (a)

Feather, N. T. Valence of success and failure in relation to task difficulty: Past research and recent progress. *Australian Journal of Psychology*, 1968, *20*, 111–122. (b)

Feather, N. T. Attitude and selective recall. *Journal of Personality and Social Psychology*, 1969, *12*, 310–319. (a)

Feather, N. T. Attribution of responsibility and valence of success and failure in relation to initial confidence and task performance. *Journal of Personality and Social Psychology*, 1969, *13*, 129–144. (b)

Feather, N. T. Preference for information in relation to consistency, novelty, intolerance of ambiguity, and dogmatism. *Australian Journal of Psychology*, 1969, *21*, 235–249. (c)

Feather, N. T. Balancing and positivity effects in social recall. *Journal of Personality*, 1970, *38*, 602–628.

Feather, N. T. Organization and discrepancy in cognitive structures. *Psychological Review*, 1971, *78*, 355–379.

Feather, N. T. Explanations of poverty in Australian and American samples: The person, society, or fate? *Australian Journal of Psychology*, 1974, *26*, 199–216.

Feather, N. T. Positive and negative reactions to male and female success and failure in relation to the perceived status and sex-typed appropriateness of occupations. *Journal of Personality and Social Psychology*, 1975, *31*, 536–548. (a)

Feather, N. T. *Values in education and Society*. New York: Free Press, 1975. (b)

Feather, N. T. Causal attributions for male and female success and failure at occupations differing in perceived status and sex-linked appropriateness. *Australian Journal of Psychology*, 1977, *29*, 151–165.

Feather, N. T. Perceived affect following male and female success and failure at occupations. *Australian Journal of Psychology*, 1978, *30*, 133–145. (a)

Feather, N. T. Reactions to male and female success and failure at sex-linked occupations: Effects of sex and socio-economic status of respondents. *Australian Journal of Psychology*, 1978, *30*, 21–40. (b)

Feather, N. T. Values, expectancy, and action. *Australian Psychologist*, 1979, *14*, 243–260.

Feather, N. T., & O'Driscoll, M. P. Observers' reactions to an equal or equitable allocator in relation to allocator input, causal attributions, and value importance. *European Journal of Social Psychology*, 1980, *10*, 107–129.

Feather, N. T., & Raphelson, A. C. Fear of success in Australian and American student groups: Motive or sex-role stereotype? *Journal of Personality*, 1974, *42*, 190–201.

Feather, N. T., & Saville, M. R. Effects of amount of prior success and failure on expectations of success and subsequent task performance. *Journal of Personality and Social Psychology*, 1967, *5*, 226–232.

Feather, N. T., & Simon, J. G. Attribution of responsibility and valence of outcome in relation to initial confidence and success and failure of self and other. *Journal of Personality and Social Psychology*, 1971, *18*, 173–188. (a)

Feather, N. T., & Simon, J. G. Causal attributions for success and failure in relation to expectations of success based upon selective or manipulative control. *Journal of Personality*, 1971, *39*, 527–541. (b)

Feather, N. T., & Simon, J. G. Luck and the unexpected outcome: A field replication of laboratory findings. *Australian Journal of Psychology*, 1972, *24*, 113–117.

Feather, N. T., & Simon, J. G. Fear of success and causal attribution for outcome. *Journal of Personality*, 1973, *41*, 525–542.

Feather, N. T., & Simon, J. G. Reactions to male and female success and failure in sex-linked occupations: Impressions of personality, causal attributions, and perceived likelihood of different consequences. *Journal of Personality and Social Psychology*, 1975, *31*, 20–31.

Feather, N. T., & Simon, J. G. Stereotypes about male and female success and failure at sex-linked occupations. *Journal of Personality*, 1976, *44*, 16–37.

Festinger, L. *A theory of cognitive dissonance.* Stanford: Stanford University Press, 1957.

Festinger, L. *Conflict, decision, and dissonance.* London: Tavistock, 1964.

Filer, R. J. Frustration, satisfaction and other factors affecting the attractiveness of goal objects. *Journal of Abnormal and Social Psychology*, 1952, *47*, 203–212.

Freedman, J. L., & Sears, D. O. Selective exposure. In L. Berkowitz (Ed.), *Advances in experimental social psychology* (Vol. 2). New York: Academic Press, 1965.

French, J. R. P. Jr., & Kahn, R. L. A programmatic approach to studying the industrial environment and mental health. *Journal of Social Issues*, 1962, *18*, 1–47.

Gebhard, M. E. The effect of success and failure upon the attractiveness of activities as a function of experience, expectation, and need. *Journal of Experimental Psychology*, 1948, *38*, 371–378.

Gebhard, M. E. Changes in the attractiveness of activities: The effect of expectation preceding performance. *Journal of Experimental Psychology*, 1949, *39*, 404–413.

Heckhausen, H. Achievement motivation and its constructs: A cognitive model. *Motivation and Emotion*, 1977, *1*, 283–329.

Heider, F. *The psychology of interpersonal relations.* New York: Wiley, 1958.

Irwin, F. W. Stated expectations as functions of probability and desirability of outcomes. *Journal of Personality*, 1953, *21*, 329–335.

Irwin, F. W., Armitt, F. M., & Simon, C. W. Studies in object preferences: I. The effect of temporal proximity. *Journal of Experimental Psychology*, 1943, *33*, 64–72.

Irwin, F. W., Orchinik, C. W., & Weiss, J. Studies in object-preferences: The effect of temporal proximity upon adults' preferences. *American Journal of Psychology*, 1946, *59*, 458–462.

Janis, I. L., & Field, P. B. Sex differences and personality factors related to persuasibility. In C. I. Hovland & I. L. Janis (Eds.), *Personality and persuasibility.* New Haven: Yale University Press, 1959.

Janis, I. L., & Mann, L. *Decision making: A psychological analysis of conflict, choice and commitment.* New York: Free Press, 1977.

Klein, D. C., Fencil-Morse, E., & Seligman, M. E. P. Learned helplessness, depression, and the attribution of failure. *Journal of Personality and Social Psychology*, 1976, *33*, 508–516.

Klinger, E. Consequences of commitment to and disengagement from incentives. *Psychological Review*, 1975, *82*, 1–25.

Lenney, E. Women's self-confidence in achievement settings. *Psychological Bulletin,* 1977, *84,* 1-13.

Lewin, K., Dembo, T., Festinger, L., & Sears, P. S. Level of aspiration. In J. McV. Hunt (Ed.), *Personality and the behavior disorders* (Vol. 1). New York: Ronald, 1944.

McClelland, D. C. *Assessing human motivation.* New York: General Learning Press, 1971.

Maier, S. F., & Seligman, M. E. P. Learned helplessness: Theory and evidence. *Journal of Experimental Psychology: General,* 1976, *105,* 3-46.

Mann, L. On being a sore loser: How fans react to their team's failure. *Australian Journal of Psychology,* 1974, *26,* 37-47.

Marks, R. W. The effect of probability, desirability, and "privilege" on the stated expectations of children. *Journal of Personality,* 1951, *19,* 332-351.

Miller, I. W. III, & Norman, W. H. Learned helplessness in humans: A review and attribution-theory model. *Psychological Bulletin,* 1979, *86,* 93-118.

Miller, G. R., & Rokeach, M. Individual differences and tolerance for inconsistency. In R. Abelson, E. Aronson, W. McGuire, T. Newcomb, M. Rosenberg, & P. Tannenbaum (Eds.), *Theories of cognitive consistency: A source book.* Chicago: Rand McNally, 1969.

Miller, W., & Seligman, M. E. P. Depression in humans. *Journal of Abnormal Psychology,* 1975, *84,* 228-238.

Mitchell, T. R. Expectancy models of job satisfaction, occupational preference and effort: A theoretical, methodological, and empirical appraisal. *Psychological Bulletin,* 1974, *81,* 1053-1077.

Mowrer, O. H. *Learning theory and behavior.* New York: Wiley, 1960. (a)

Mowrer, O. H. *Learning theory and the symbolic processes.* New York: Wiley, 1960. (b)

Postman, L. The history and present status of the law of effect. *Psychological Bulletin,* 1947, *44,* 489-563.

Preston, M. G., & Baratta, P. An experimental study of the auction-value of an uncertain outcome. *American Journal of Psychology,* 1948, *61,* 183-193.

Rokeach, M. A theory of organization and change within value-attitude systems. *Journal of Social Issues,* 1968, *24,* 13-33.

Rokeach, M. *The nature of human values.* New York: Free Press, 1973.

Rokeach, M. (Ed.). *Understanding human values: Individual and societal.* New York: Free Press, 1979.

Rotter, J. B. *Social learning and clinical psychology.* New York: Prentice-Hall, 1954.

Rotter, J. B. Generalized expectancies for internal versus external control of reinforcement. *Psychological Monographs,* 1966, *80*(1, Whole No. 287).

Seligman, M. E. P. *Helplessness: On depression, development, and death.* San Francisco: Freeman, 1975.

Simon, J. G., & Feather, N. T. Causal attributions for success and failure at university examinations. *Journal of Educational Psychology,* 1973, *64,* 46-56.

Solomon, R. L., & Corbit, J. D. An opponent-process theory of motivation: I. Temporal dynamics of affect. *Psychological Review,* 1974, *81,* 119-145.

Steiner, I. D. Perceived freedom. In L. Berkowitz (Ed.), *Advances in Experimental Social Psychology* (Vol. 5). New York: Academic Press, 1970.

Tolman, E. C. *Purposive behavior in animals and men.* New York: Century, 1932.

Tolman, E. C. Principles of performance. *Psychological Review,* 1955, *62,* 315-326.

Tolman, E. C. *Behavior and psychological man: Essays in motivation and learning.* Berkeley & Los Angeles: University of California Press, 1958.

Vroom, V. H. *Work and motivation.* New York: Wiley, 1964.

Weiner, B. The effects of unsatisfied achievement motivation on persistence and subsequent performance. *Journal of Personality,* 1965, *33,* 428-442.

Weiner, B. *Theories of motivation: From mechanism to cognition.* Chicago: Markham, 1972.

Weiner, B. *Achievement motivation and attribution theory*. Morristown, N.J.: General Learning Press, 1974.

Weiner, B. *Human motivation*. New York: Holt, Rinehart, & Winston, 1980.

Weiner, B., Russell, D., & Lerman, D. Affective consequences of causal ascriptions. In J. H. Harvey, W. Ickes, & R. F. Kidd (Eds.), *New directions in attribution research* (Vol. 2). Hillsdale, N.J.: Lawrence Erlbaum Associates, 1978.

Wright, H. F. The influence of barriers upon strength of motivation. *Contributions to Psychological Theory*, 1937, *1*, No. 3.

Future Orientation, Self-Evaluation, and Achievement Motivation: Use of an Expectancy × Value Theory of Personality Functioning and Change

4

Joel O. Raynor
State University of New York at Buffalo

In this chapter we present some implications for the study of achievement motivation of an expectancy × value theory of personality functioning and change (Raynor, 1981b) that has evolved from earlier theory and research on achievement-related behaviors (Raynor, 1968b, 1969, 1974a, 1974b). The earlier theory in turn represented an elaboration of an expectancy × value theory of achievement motivation (Atkinson, 1957, 1964; Atkinson & Feather, 1966) and was developed to account for the effects of anticipated future goals on the motivation of immediate activity. The ideas applied here can be seen as both an extension and refinement of the earlier expectancy × value theory of achievement motivation, and as part of a theory of personality functioning and change in its own right. Although the newer theory builds on the earlier ideas and is able to recapture earlier predictions and to account for research findings relevant to the earlier ideas, it is no longer restricted to the domain of achievement-oriented activity. In addition, it utilizes several variables not included in the earlier theory so that it can apply to a broader range of conceptual and empirical issues. The evolution and statement of this theory of personality functioning and change has been presented in detail elsewhere (Raynor & Entin, 1981c). Here we provide a review of the research upon which it is in part based so that the reader is able to see the context in which it developed.

INITIAL EXPECTANCY × VALUE THEORY OF ACHIEVEMENT MOTIVATION

The newer ideas applied here have evolved primarily in an attempt to extend the initial expectancy × value theory of achievement motivation (Atkinson, 1957, 1964; Atkinson & Feather, 1966) so that it can account for an increasing number of research findings not dealt with by the initial formulation. The initial theory can be seen as an extension and refinement of the resultant valence theory of level of aspiration (Lewin, Dembo, Festinger, & Sears, 1944) so as to include: (1) relatively stable personality dispositions (or motives) assumed to influence the valences of success and failure; and (2) precise specification of the inverse relationship between subjective incentive value (or valence) and potency (or subjective probability of success) that Lewin et al. (1944) assumed to exist. In the initial theory of achievement motivation it was assumed that $I_s = 1 - P_s$ and $I_f = -(1 - P_f)$, and $P_s + P_f = 1$, where I_s represents the incentive value of success, P_s the subjective probability of success, I_f the (negative) incentive value of failure, and P_f the subjective probability of failure.

The original equations of Lewin et al. (1944) stated that the resultant valence of success that determines choice of level of aspiration equals the difference between the valence of success (V_s) multiplied (i.e., weighted) by its potency or subjective probability of success (P_s), and the valence of failure (V_f) multiplied by the subjective probability of failure (P_f)—that is, $V_r = (V_s \times P_s) - (V_f \times P_f)$. The initial statement of the contemporary expectancy $\times$ value theory of achievement motivation (Atkinson, 1957, 1964; Atkinson & Feather, 1966) expanded the valence terms so that $V_s = M_S \times I_s$ and $V_f = M_F \times I_f$, where M_S is the motive to achieve success and M_F is the motive to avoid failure. The difference between the tendency to achieve success (T_s) and the tendency to avoid failure (T_{-f}) was assumed to determine *resultant* achievement motivation (T_r)—the term equivalent to resultant valence (V_r) in the earlier Lewin et al. (1944) formulation—so that $T_r = T_s + T_f$, where $T_s = M_S \times P_s \times I_s$ and $T_{-f} = M_F \times P_f \times I_f$.

Given the additional specific assumptions relating incentive value and the aforementioned subjective probabilities, it can be shown that, in summary form, $T_r = (M_S - M_F) \times [P_s \times (1 - P_s)]$. This last equation is the most useful statement of the determinants of resultant achievement motivation in that it shows that it is jointly determined by a personality component ($M_S - M_F$)—the difference in strengths of the motives to achieve success and to avoid failure— and a situational component $[P_s \times (1 - P_s)]$ that is completely defined by the subjective probability of success (where $I_s = 1 - P_s$) or the individual's perception of the difficulty of a task immediately confronting him or her. Thus the initial theory of achievement motivation could account for changes in the determinants of aroused achievement motivation (T_r) in either of two ways: (1) T_r was aroused or not; and (2) if aroused, changes in its value were completely determined by changes in an individual's expectancy of (immediate) success (P_s). In particular, the equations of the theory imply that, once aroused, an increase in T_r must be brought about by a movement of P_s toward a value of .5, where resultant achievement motivation (positive or negative) is maximum— assuming that the motives are relatively stable personality dispositions and do not change for an individual in a given situation. In later versions of this theory

(Atkinson, 1964, Ch. 9; Atkinson & Feather, 1966), positive extrinsic motivation (T_{ext}) was also considered as a determinant of the tendency to act (T_a) in a given situation, that is, $T_a = T_r + T_{ext}$, where $T_{ext} = M_{ext} \times P_{ext} \times I_{ext}$.

The behavioral implications of these assumptions and their empirical support are reviewed in a series of research monographs (Atkinson, 1958; Atkinson & Feather, 1966; Atkinson & Raynor, 1974).

A MORE GENERAL EXPECTANCY × VALUE THEORY OF ACHIEVEMENT MOTIVATION

An elaboration of this initial theory to produce a more general expectancy × value theory of achievement motivation (Raynor, 1968b, 1969, 1974a) assumed that component tendencies to achieve success (T_{sn}) and to avoid failure (T_{-fn}), each a multiplicative function of motive, subjective probability, and incentive value, were added to motivation of immediate activity when that immediate activity was contingently related to the opportunity to continue to strive, and hence to the possible achievement of some long-term future goal. The equations of the initial theory were elaborated so that summation over each future anticipated step of a contingent path now determined total resultant achievement motivation sustaining immediate activity. The summary statement of the more general theory closely resembles that of the initial one, which is now derived as a special case when immediate activity is not contingently related to future goal striving. That is, the more general theory in summary form states that

$$T_r = (M_S - M_F) \sum_{n=1}^{N} (P_1 s_n \times I s_n),$$

where $I s_n = 1 - P_1 s_n$, and $P_1 s_n = P_1 s_1 \times P_2 s_2 \times \cdots P_n s_n \times \cdots P_N s_N$. This more general theory applies in a contingent path situation, where the individual believes that immediate success earns the opportunity to try for some number of future successes but immediate failure means loss of the opportunity to continue and hence failure to achieve the future goal.

As noted earlier, the special assumptions concerning the inverse relationship between incentive values and subjective probabilities are retained but in an expanded form so that "perceived difficulty" (P_s) along a contingent path is still a critically important determinant of achievement motivation aroused for immediate activity in that contingent path. But now, in addition to P_s, two other variables are considered by the theory as determinants of aroused (resultant) achievement motivation: (1) the nature of the path or sequence of which immediate activity is but the first step (i.e., noncontingent, partial contingent, and contingent paths), and, if a contingent path; (2) the number of anticipated steps (N in the mathematical notation) or the length of the contingent path of which immediate activity is but the first step.

When precisely stated, the assumptions concerning incentive value and subjective probability indicate that in order to determine the degree of expectancy (subjective probability of success) that immediate activity will eventually result in some future success (as seen by the individual as he or she faces the first step of a contingent path), the anticipated values of subjective probability of success at steps intervening between the individual and a future success are to be multiplied to give the effective value of this expectancy. That is, for a contingent path of, let us say, four steps, $P_1s_4 = P_1s_1 \times P_2s_2 \times P_3s_3 \times P_4s_4$, where P_1s_1 is the subjective probability of success in the first step, P_2s_2 is the subjective probability of success in the second step as anticipated when faced with the first step, etc.[1] We refer to this as the "multiplicative assumption" (concerning subjective probabilities). The implications of the more general theory and the multiplicative assumption for contingent paths, and the supportive empirical evidence and problems, can be found in Atkinson and Raynor (1974) and Raynor and Entin (1981c). However, because the more general theory of achievement motivation outlined previously served as the basis for the theory of personality functioning and change (Raynor, 1981b) that we are concerned with here, it is worthwhile to deal with its implications and empirical support.

Although the more general theory of achievement motivation outlined earlier closely resembles the initial theory in its mathematical representation and derives the initial theory as the simplest case when immediate activity stands by itself ($N = 1$), the derivations of the more general theory are sometimes at variance with implications of the "single activity" theory if that earlier version of theory were applied to prediction of immediate behavior in a contingent path. When immediate activity is embedded in a long contingent path consisting of a series of easy, moderately difficult, or difficult tasks, it is predicted by the more general theory that so-called "success-oriented individuals" (those in whom $M_s > M_F$) will prefer the easy series, whereas if constrained to choose by positive extrinsic motivation that is equivalent for all choices, so-called "failure-threatened individuals" (those in whom $M_F > M_S$), will prefer the difficult series. Predictions from the single activity theory have been that individuals with $M_S > M_F$ will prefer an immediate single task with P_S of moderate difficulty ($P_S = .5$) and those with $M_F > M_S$, if constrained to choose by positive extrinsic motivation that is equal for all options, will prefer either an easy task or a difficult task and be indifferent as to whether easy or difficult is chosen. Also, predictions from the

---

[1]Note that use of conditional probabilities to represent these values of Ps along a contingent path was considered but rejected because use of conditional probabilities requires that the prior value (of Ps) would have to be specifiable, whereas in the psychological situation represented here, both P_1s_1 and P_2s_2, for example, are representative of *future* expectancies rather than the results of past activity. P_2s_2 represents the subjective probability of success at the second step of a contingent path, given the opportunity to try for it—an opportunity that is not yet guaranteed but that is represented by the subjective probability of success in the more immediate activity about to be undertaken.

two versions of theory are exactly opposite concerning persistence in the face of continued success in a series of tries not contingently related to the opportunity to continue (a *noncontingent* path) as implied using the earlier theory (Feather, 1961, 1963), and predictions for a series comprising a *contingent* path in the face of continued success using the more general theory (Raynor & Entin, 1981a, 1981d).

But it would be unfair to the earlier theory to apply it to contingent path behavior because the theory never considered situations where future orientation might influence immediate action. Thus for the reader who is familiar with predictions of the earlier theory, and who wonders why its elaboration must be taken seriously, we review the research findings concerning future orientation and achievement motivation.

EMPIRICAL EVIDENCE CONCERNING CONTINGENT FUTURE ORIENTATION

A review of research evidence concerning the role of contingent future orientation as a determinant of motivation of immediate activity (Raynor, 1974a; Raynor & Entin, 1981c, 1981d) shows a number of findings consistent with theoretical expectations, but with sufficient results at variance with them to have led to several important revisions in theory (Raynor, 1981b; Raynor & Entin, 1981d).

The original data concerning future orientation and achievement motivation showed an accentuation of predicted differences between success-oriented ($M_S > M_F$) and failure-threatened ($M_F > M_S$) college students in grades obtained in courses when students were classified as high in the perceived helpfulness/ importance of getting good grades for future career plans to work out (Isaacson & Raynor, 1966). Students low on test anxiety (success-oriented) received higher grades but students high on test anxiety (failure-threatened) received lower grades, as the perceived instrumentality (PI) of doing well now for future success increased from low, to intermediate, to high PI categories. The initial theory of achievement motivation (Atkinson, 1957, 1964; Atkinson & Feather, 1966) was elaborated to take this result into account and subsequently to derive this effect of perceived instrumentality on academic performance (Raynor, 1968b). In this and subsequent research individuals high on *n* Achievement (McClelland, Atkinson, Clark & Lowell, 1953) or the Mehrabian (1968, 1969) measure of resultant achievement motivation, low on test anxiety (Mandler & Sarason, 1952) or some other measure of test anxiety (Alpert & Haber, 1960), or high–low on *n* Achievement-test anxiety based on median breaks, are considered "success oriented" ($M_S > M_F$), whereas those high on test anxiety, low on *n* Achievement, or low–high on *n* Achievement-test anxiety are considered to be "failure threatened" ($M_F > M_S$). The basic pattern of interaction between measures of achievement-related motives and what was termed "perceived instrumentality" (PI) of grades for future success involved an increase in grades for the group with $M_S > M_F$ and a decrease in grades for the $M_F > M_S$ group with an increase in future orientation (PI). This result would have been accountable for by the earlier theory either by assuming that high but not low PI aroused T_r, and/or that T_r was greater in high than in low PI groups because the P_s of getting good grades was closer to .5 in high than in low PI conditions. Neither of these assumptions seemed plausible at the time, and subsequent research has confirmed that effects of future orientation are found when degree of achievement arousal and level of P_s are controlled (see the following).

This pattern of interaction has been replicated several times, using various questions to assess the perceived necessity of doing well *now* in order to eventually achieve *future* success (Raynor, 1970, Study I; Raynor, 1981a, male sample). The pattern of results—an increment for success-oriented subjects but a decrement for failure-threatened subjects from low to high PI—was also obtained when a resultant measure of concern about doing well relative to reported anxiety right before a final course examination (rather than actual grades) was used as a measure of aroused achievement motivation for academic performance (Raynor, Atkinson, & Brown, 1974). In these studies the predicted higher grades of success-oriented over failure-threatened students (and greater concern about doing well relative to anxiety) were apparent and were statistically reliable within groups high in PI, but the difference decreased as PI decreased, so that within the low PI condition it was not statistically reliable.

From the early research on academic performance a second pattern of results emerged—grades that were received and/or reported by students tended to be higher when these grades were seen as important for future success (e.g., under high PI conditions) (Raynor, 1968a; 1970, Study II; 1981a, female sample). For example, in a nationwide survey of high school boys, Bachman, Kahn, Mednick, Davidson, & Johnson (1967) reported that grades were higher for those classified as high–low than for those low–high on *n* Achievement-test anxiety, and they were also higher for those who rated high school grades as important for future success (high PI) than for those who rated grades as unimportant (low PI) (Raynor, 1968a). In a follow-up study, Atkinson, Lens, and O'Malley (1976) reported a similar pattern concerning pursuit of post-high school education— greater persistence in seeking education for the high–low *n* Achievement-test anxiety group and for the group high in PI—so that 59% of the high *n* Achievement-low test anxiety-high PI group were attending school 3 years later compared with only 27% of the low *n* Achievement-high test anxiety-low PI group. This second pattern failed to show the interaction between achievement-related motives and future orientation, but rather yielded a main effect due to motives, a main effect due to PI, and no accentuation of motive effects with an increase in PI.

We now interpret the difference between these two patterns of results as being a function of the amount of positive extrinsic motivation that is perceived to be dependent on future success. When large positive value is anticipated, all subjects are expected to be more motivated to do well in immediate activity so as to attain that future success than when small positive value is at stake, holding level of PI constant. However, as yet no a priori prediction of these two different patterns of results has been attempted. Perhaps the distinction between prerequisite and elective courses in the university will provide a convenient means of identifying circumstances where these patterns might differ. We would expect that prerequisite courses would offer substantially more positive extrinsic rewards contingent upon earning the opportunity to continue when compared with elective courses.

In the aforementioned research on academic motivation it has been assumed that those students who rate good grades as high in helpfulness/importance/ necessity for future success/career plans to work out (high PI) believe themselves faced with a *contingent path* linking immediate successful performance to the opportunity to try for later, and ultimately, distant future success, whereas those who rate good grades as low in this regard believe themselves faced with a *noncontingent path* linking immediate activity to future success—i.e., they believe that immediate success/failure has no bearing on earning the opportunity to continue. This interpretation has been tested directly in laboratory research when contingent and noncontingent paths have been created, and performance in the first step assessed for different motive groups, using various paper-and-pencil tasks-in-sequence. The predicted accentuation of motive group differences (the interaction effect between motives and contingent future orientation) has been routinely obtained in this laboratory work—an increment in performance level in the first task of a contingent series for success-oriented subjects but a decrement for failure-threatened subjects, when compared with performance in the first task of the noncontingent series (Entin, 1981; Entin & Feather, 1981; Entin & Raynor, 1973; Raynor & Entin, 1981a, 1981b; Raynor & Rubin, 1971). Usually the results show clearly superior performance of the success-oriented over the failure-threatened group in immediate activity in the contingent path condition. Sometimes this difference in the contingent path condition is not significant, but is accompanied by an unexpected reversal (i.e., failure-threatened subjects perform better than success-oriented ones) in the noncontingent path condition. Thus, in the laboratory situation, where large sources of positive motivation associated with future success are presumably lacking, the accentuation of positive motivation for success-oriented subjects coupled with the accentuation of negative (inhibitory) motivation for failure-threatened subjects is the usual pattern obtained under contingent path conditions. However, there are exceptions (Sorrentino, 1971, 1972, 1973) and, again, the difference between patterns of results in this laboratory research has not yet been successfully explained.

The most important point of theoretical significance in these studies of academic motivation and performance on laboratory tasks is that differences in future orientation systematically influence motivation of immediate activity. And, particularly in the laboratory studies, where subjective probability of immediate success is held constant across experimental conditions, it does not seem plausible to account for the results merely in terms of possible differences in the subjective probability of immediate success that involves a P_s closer to .5 for the consequences of immediate activity for the contingent path.

Additional research (Raynor & Entin, 1981b) has investigated whether arousal of resultant achievement motivation (T_r) rather than contingent future orientation could account for these differences, holding P_s constant across conditions. Both high arousal and low arousal achievement-oriented conditions were induced, with contingent and noncontingent paths created in each. The results showed that the predicted interaction between achievement-related motives and kind of path was found even under low achievement arousal. Success-oriented subjects tended to solve more problems but failure-threatened subjects tended to solve fewer problems in immediate performance in the contingent than in the noncontingent conditions. This finding suggests that the contingent path instructions was responsible for the predicted interaction effect.

Research by Teitelbaum, Raynor, and Entin (1981) suggests that, as would be expected, the predicted interaction between achievement-related motives and contingent future orientation tends to be stronger in the first task of a contingent path than in a one-step (single activity) task presented under either achievement-oriented or relaxed conditions, this time using recall of interrupted (e.g., failure) tasks to infer the strength of aroused achievement motivation (T_r). The data showed linear trends indicating greater recall of incompleted tasks for success-oriented subjects coupled will less recall of incompleted tasks for failure-threatened subjects from the relaxed (one-step) to the achievement (one-step) to the achievement-contingent (two-step) condition.

Use of the equations of the more general expectancy × value theory of achievement motivation summarized in the foregoing leads to the prediction that, other things equal, aroused positive or negative achievement motivation (T_r)—depending on whether M_S is stronger or weaker than M_F—should be greater for longer than for shorter contingent paths. Several studies have yielded mixed evidence in support of this hypothesis (Brecher, 1972, 1975; Raynor, Entin, & Raynor, unpublished data). However, the predicted interaction between motives and length of contingent path has been supported in two recent studies where effects due to anticipated elapsed time to complete the task sequence have been separated from those effects expected from the number of tasks in the sequence. In most life situations, a greater number of contingent steps in a path produces a greater anticipated amount of time to complete that path and/or achieve the final goal of the path. Gjesme (1974) has shown that increased anticipated time between practice and a real test *decreased* differences in aroused achievement motivation of success-oriented and failure-threatened individuals for that practice session. This "goal gradient effect" involved a reduction in positive motivation for success-oriented subjects (lower performance level) as well as a reduction in inhibitory motivation for failure-threatened subjects (higher performance level) as the anticipated time between the practice and the real test *increased*. Thus predicted effects of contingent tasks-in-sequence might be reduced, washed out, or even reversed by this opposite anticipated time effect, depending on its relative strength, unless time-to-complete contingent paths of varying lengths was somehow held constant and/or systematically varied independent of path length.

Pearlson's (1979, 1981) doctoral research accomplished this separation of the "task hierarchy" and the "time hierarchy" by creating 2- and 4-step contingent paths in which time to complete the path was held constant at two different amounts of time. In the short time conditions, the 2-step and the 4-step contingent paths were anticipated by subjects to take 20 minutes each to complete—(5) (15) versus (5) (5) (5) (5) represents the design, where each set of parentheses represents a step, and the number in each parenthesis represents the time in minutes announced as allowed for completing the task. In the long time conditions, the design is represented as (10) (30) versus (10) (10) (10) (10), so that 40 minutes was the anticipated elapsed time for each contingent path. Performance level was assessed during the first 5 minutes of the first step of each path, with instructions designed to minimize possible pacing effects by indicating to subjects in the 10-minute task conditions (10) that they would have a short rest after the first 5 minutes and therefore that they should not pace their effort. A measure of resultant achievement-related affect based on ratings of positive and negative affective reactions immediately prior to working the first task in each sequence was also obtained.

Both measures yielded a similar pattern of results. There were three findings of importance. First, the predicted motives × length of contingent path interaction was obtained: success-oriented subjects had significantly higher performance and reported more resultant positive affect but failure-threatened subjects performed (non)significantly lower (and reported more resultant negative affect) in the first step of the longer (4-step) contingent path than in the first step of the shorter (2-step) contingent path. Second, Pearlson's prediction of a motives × time interaction similar to that obtained by Gjesme (1974) was supported: success-oriented subjects performed higher and reported more resultant positive affect, but failure-threatened subjects performed lower and reported more resultant negative affect, in the first step of the *short* time-to-complete paths than in the first step of the long time-to-complete paths. Pearlson also obtained a significant triple-order interaction: The predicted effects of motives and length of contingent path were found only within the short time condition, where they were statistically reliable as an interaction between motive groups and length of path, whereas within the long time conditions the interaction between motive groups and length of path was in the opposite direction to that predicted by the more general theory of achievement motivation. Thus Pearlson's research not only provided important evidence concerning the interaction effects between motives and length of contingent path and between motives and anticipated elapsed time, but it also provided a plausible means of accounting for previous failures to obtain the predicted motives × length of contingent path interaction—effects of anticipated time-to-complete the paths were systematically confounded with number of steps in the path in the previous research studies, and the two opposite effects cancelled each other out.

Pearlson (1979, 1981) used male college students as subjects. Roeder's (1980) doctoral research attempted to replicate Pearlson's findings using 5th- and 7th-grade boys and girls as subjects. The digit-symbol substitution task used by Pearlson was presented to the younger subjects as a "Secret Coding Game," using identical time periods and functionally equivalent contingent path instructions to create the design described previously. However, resultant affect scores were not obtained. After performance scores were adjusted to eliminate significant differences between grades, schools, and individual classrooms in mean performance (by obtaining z-scores on digit-symbol output based on each classroom mean), the results showed a significant n Achievement × length of contingent path interaction: Subjects high in n Achievement showed higher performance but subjects low in n Achievement showed lower performance in the first step of the 4-step than the 2-step conditions, thus replicating Pearlson's motives × path length interaction. However, a significant test anxiety × time interaction was obtained that was opposite to what Gjseme (1974) and Pearlson (1979, 1981) found—the Roeder (1980) data showed an accentuation of differences between low and high test anxiety groups as time to complete the path *increased*. Thus, in the Roeder study, both number of steps in the path and time to complete the path worked in the same direction in interaction with motive measures—as both time and steps increased, predicted motive effects were accentuated. This overall pattern of results was similar to Pearlson's results for the short time periods only. The Roeder data also showed that the predicted motives × length of contingent path interaction was stronger within the short time paths than the long time paths, so that both studies were consistent in providing statistically reliable evidence supporting the accentuation of aroused achievement motivation with an increased length of contingent path from 2 to 4 steps, but only for relatively "short" time-to-complete-the-path sequences.

Although further research will be needed to understand the differences in how time interacted with motives in the Pearlson and Roeder studies, it seems apparent that anticipated time-to-completion will have to be conceptualized as an additional factor in theories about achievement behavior that use expectancy-value concepts. This time-to-completion variable functions along with number of anticipated steps in a contingent path to influence arousal of resultant achievement motivation. In life circumstances where both variables are operative but systematically confounded we can expect difficulty in replicating the predicted motives × length of contingent path interaction unless time-to-completion is taken into account.

Research has also systematically varied the constant subjective probability of success along contingent paths of equivalent length. Predictions for this situation that are derived from the more general theory of achievement motivation were discussed earlier in connection with the differences between the more general and initial theories. Two studies (Raynor & Entin, 1981d; Sorrentino & Raynor, 1972) initially suggested that, as predicted, differences between success-oriented and failure-threatened subjects in immediate performance level were greater when the contingent path consisted of a sequence of easy rather than intermediate or hard tasks, and that the performance of success-oriented subjects increased whereas that of failure-threatened subjects decreased as the constant value of P_s of tasks along the path increased from low to moderate to high. However, the modest levels of significance and inconsistency between results for n Achievement and test anxiety scores when viewed alone suggested that these two studies did not provide clearcut confirmation of hypotheses. More recently, Sorrentino, Short, and Raynor (unpublished manuscript) have replicated these predicted findings, but only for subjects assessed as high on a projective measure of n Uncertainty and low on a measure of authoritarianism. The predicted effects appear to be reversed for groups low on n Uncertainty and high on authoritarianism. These results may mean that uncertainty motivation plays an important role in the arousal of achievement motivation, particularly as the Sorrentino, Short, and Raynor data also show interactions between achievement-related motives, subjective probability of success, and uncertainty motivation for a one-step activity and for academic performance. At this point we are not clear as to the implications for theory of the possible role of uncertainty motivation, but the replication in several studies of these effects suggests that this may turn out to be an important new variable that has to be taken into account.

Finally, research concerning motivational arousal in descriptions of the future plans of college students has related the rated attractiveness/repulsiveness of a student's own future goal to variables from the more general theory of achievement motivation (cf. Raynor & Entin, 1981b). When subjects were separated into groups in terms of whether they faced primarily either a contingent or a noncontingent path to their future goal, success-oriented students saw the future goal as more attractive but failure-threatened students saw it as less attractive, when it was perceived to be part of a contingent path than when it was perceived to be part of a noncontingent path. When the subjective probability of achieving the future goal was taken into account, and when the majority of subjects included in the analysis appeared to see the future goal as part of a contingent path, it was found that attractiveness of the future goal increased for the success-oriented students but decreased for the failure-threatened students as the P_s of achieving the future goal increased. Both of these findings are consistent with predictions from the more general theory of achievement motivation if it can be assumed that attractiveness/repulsiveness ratings reflect aroused achievement motivation (T_r) for the path of which the future goal is the last step. However, there was no evidence to support the predicted motives × length of contingent path interaction—long as compared to short (in terms of number of steps) contingent paths did not accentuate motive group differences in rated attractiveness/ repulsiveness of the future goal. We would now interpret this failure to support hypotheses for length of contingent path in terms of the confounded effects of the time and task hierarchies of a contingent sequence as described earlier and disentangled in the Pearlson and Roeder experimental research. Our analysis of future plans was carried out prior to the distinction between anticipated time and number of steps, so that the assessment device provided no way of reducing the confounding between increased length of contingent path and increased time anticipated to complete it.

The accumulated weight of evidence reviewed in the foregoing provides some support for predictions derived from the more general theory of achievement motivation concerning the effects of contingent future orientation, but only when other factors not initially taken into consideration by the theory are controlled for—amount of positive extrinsic motivation, anticipated amount of time to complete a path, and (possibly) amount of uncertainty motivation aroused. We do not wish to claim confirmation of a theory that we know requires refinement based on the complications that have been discovered. Rather, we want to note that consideration of contingent future orientation as an important determinant of motivation of immediate activity seems a worthwhile endeavor, and that its role in influencing behavior in conjunction with other variables seems clearly to have been established.

FUTURE ORIENTATION AND SELF-EVALUATION

A potentially more serious threat to the validity of research on contingent future orientation arises from the fact that we have found a positive association between ratings of the helpfulness/importance/necessity of doing well now in order to achieve future success (*future-importance*) and ratings of the necessity of doing well now for feeling good about oneself, that is, for positive self-evaluation (*self-importance*). Raynor, Atkinson, and Brown (1974) first reported this association, which suggested the possibility that effects attributed to contingent future orientation in studies of academic motivation might in fact be due to differences in the importance of immediate behavior for positive self-evaluation. However, subsequent research in which both measures of future-importance and self-importance were obtained and related to behavior suggested that both variables influence achievement-oriented performance in an equivalent manner, and that effects of future-importance can be demonstrated when importance for self-evaluation is held constant.

In the first study concerning this issue Mitchell (1974) collected data that were analyzed and reported by Raynor (1974a, 1981a) so as to look at the joint influence of ratings of future- and self-importance. Students rated the necessity of getting a B or better grade for: (1) career plans to work out; and (2) self-esteem (feeling good about yourself). The data showed the same pattern of interaction between motive measures and each type of importance ratings on grades, and a strong positive association between future-importance and self-importance in the male sample. By classifying subjects as simultaneously high and low on both future-importance and self-importance it was possible essentially to "hold constant" one variable while looking at the pattern of interaction between motive measures and the levels of the other variable. It was found that for low self-importance students only, those classified as success oriented showed an increase in proportion of B or better grades from low future-importance (.20, $N = 10$) to high future importance (.60, $N = 5$) whereas those classified as failure threatened showed a decrease in proportion of B or better grades from low (.53, $N = 5$) to high (.20, $N = 4$) future-importance. Note that the Ns were small in these comparisons and that a comparable analysis using mean grades rather than proportion of B or better grades failed to show the increment for the success-oriented group, thus suggesting that we should not take this finding seriously by itself. In addition, however, a doctoral dissertation by Weinberg (1975) also obtained a positive association between ratings of future-importance and self-importance for laboratory performance on both a pursuit rotor and a verbal anagrams task. When subjects (males again) were classified simultaneously on both future- and self-importance, and the data for low self-importance subjects were inspected, the expected interaction between motive measures and levels of future-importance was again found for both tasks—within those low in self-importance. Success-oriented subjects performed better but failure-threatened subjects performed worse when they were high as opposed to low in future-importance. Although the Ns were again small, the consistency between these two data collections, one involving academic performance and the other laboratory performance, provides reasonable assurance that effects previously attributed to differences in contingent future orientation are not in fact the result of confounded differences in self-evaluation.

When future-importance was held constant, and the interaction between motive measures and differences in self-importance was inspected, the results of both of the studies cited suggested an interaction that involved accentuation of motive effects within the high self-importance group when compared with the low self-importance group—even within subjects low on future-importance. This, plus additional findings to be presented in the next section, suggested that of all the possible additional factors that might have to be taken into account in revising the theory of achievement motivation to account for the unexpected findings reviewed in the foregoing, the role of self-importance and self-evaluation in the arousal of achievement motivation was the most important one that needed to be dealt with, for the reasons to be discussed shortly.

FUTURE-IMPORTANCE, SELF-IMPORTANCE, AND
SELF-POSSESSION OF COMPETENCE

The discovery of a positive association between future-importance and self-importance, which has been replicated several times (Raynor, 1981a; Raynor, Atkinson, & Brown, 1974; Raynor & English, 1981), coupled with the suggestive evidence indicating that both variables function equivalently to accentuate arousal of individual differences in achievement-related motivation, poses a challenge to existing expectancy × value theory of achievement motivation because such theory does not consider the role of self-importance as distinct from future-importance. How can the effects of self-evaluation as well as the effects of future orientation be conceptualized within an expectancy × value framework? The additional finding that ratings of the degree of self-possession of an attribute of personality and/or some competence were also positively associated with future-importance (Gazzo, 1974), and with both self-importance and future-importance (Raynor & English, 1981), suggested that assessment of competence as a goal of immediate skill-demanding activity is a crucial variable in understanding these effects. We came to the conclusion that it is necessary to distinguish the goal of "doing well" (or "not failing") and/or "moving on" in achievement-oriented activity, on the one hand, from the goal of "finding out about oneself" in terms of the degree to which a person possesses competences believed to be assessed by the skill-demanding activity in question—particularly when "finding out" and "doing well" are both possible through the same immediate activity. We decided that the motivation of immediate activity involves two factors that have been systematically confounded in previous research that has used "tests of ability" to arouse resultant achievement motivation (T_r): (1) the subject's desire to find out *how much* ability he or she possesses by doing his or her best on the task; and (2) the subject's desire to do well on the task by *utilizing* his or her ability and/or effort. How else could we make sense out of the fact that subjects could rate doing well on a laboratory task as "very important" for future career success (Raynor & English, as discussed in Raynor, 1981a; Weinberg, 1975) when no contingent relationship existed between doing well on the laboratory task and being allowed to move on to any subsequent life activity? Ethical constraints on deception in laboratory research make it mandatory that subjects perceive that their performance in the laboratory will in no way be used to influence decisions about career advancement or any other life behaviors outside the laboratory. Thus future-importance in the sense of "earning the opportunity to continue along a contingent path" that relates performance at laboratory tasks to subsequent behavior outside the laboratory would appear to be irrelevant for an interpretation of laboratory research, because task performance is explicitly noncontingent in nature as far as future careers are concerned. However, presentation of such tasks as "tests of ability" that are perceived by the subject as having more or less validity for diagnostic assessment of competences *that the subject believes are necessary prerequisites for success in life striving* would make a high future-importance rating understandable—particularly if the competences assumed to be assessed were ones the subject regarded as involving highly valued attributes (such as intelligence), possession of which at a high level defined one as a "good person." What we have subsequently termed the positive *instrumental value* of a competence, and the positive individual *cultural value* of a competence, may be assumed to combine for a person and to produce a high degree of "importance" (e.g., value) in finding out how much of the desirable competence in question is possessed.

A theory of adult competence motivation (Raynor, 1981a) was proposed, which attempts to account for the willingness/resistance of a person to undertake a test of competence when the primary goal of the individual is to "find out about oneself." The theory concerns the motivation of the individual to seek information about the degree of possession of (positively or negatively) valued attributes, and in the achievement domain about positively valued competences, as a function of the value of possession of that competence to the individual and the expectancy that undertaking a test of competence will result in an *increment* in the perceived degree of possession of the competence. Willingness to undertake a test of competence is seen as a function of the magnitude of "positive value" (different sources of value are discussed in the next section), assumed to depend in part on the magnitude of the anticipated increment in degree of possession of that competence that is expected to result from the assessment, and of the subjective probability that the assessment will result in that amount of value—a subjective probability that is in part a function of the perceived validity of the assessment device. Resistance to undertaking diagnostic assessment of a positively valued competence is conceived as a function of the anticipated amount of *decrement* that is expected, and the subjective probability that such a decrement will result. Willingness/resistance to undertaking diagnostic assessment of a negatively valued attribute (such as stupidity or psychosis) is also a function of the (negative) value and subjective probability of attaining it.

This expectancy × value theory of information seeking builds upon an earlier analysis provided by Feather (1967), and provides a bridge between the more general theory of achievement motivation and the theory of personality functioning and change (Raynor, 1981b). It serves to emphasize the informational properties of many achievement-oriented tasks where "finding out" and "doing well" are both possible goals of immediate action. It makes explicit the distinction between motivation to "find out about oneself" and to "do well" when a task is seen as both an assessor of competence and one where ability and effort can be brought to bear to produce a performance. These two distinct kinds of motivation have been typically confounded in previous research on achievement motivation. In general, such research has neglected the self-diagnostic, information-seeking motivation aroused when a task is described as a "test of critical abilities."

We feel that recent research on information seeking and achievement motivation (Trope, 1975; Trope & Brickman, 1975) has emphasized to subjects the information-seeking goal of behavior while minimizing the goal of doing well on the tasks when presented as "tests of ability." This would make understandable the failure in this research to find evidence in support of hypotheses based on the theory of achievement motivation that emphasizes doing well as the goal that arouses achievement motivation. We believe that, usually, both kinds of motivation are aroused when skill-demanding activity is presented as a test of ability (or can be interpreted by the subject as a test of ability), but that one or the other goal of "finding out" or "doing well" can predominate depending on which aspects of the situation are emphasized by the researcher and/or perceived to be more valued by the individual confronted by such a task. Thus, in laboratory situations, where there is no contingent path that links success on the task to earning the opportunity to move on to other tasks outside the laboratory, a person's concern about "doing well" can still be substantial when the person believes that possessing the competence that he or she believes is assessed by the task is a necessary prerequisite for success in life and/or that it marks the person as "good" in his cultural context. And, when a contingent sequence is induced in the laboratory but is not linked to striving outside the laboratory, concern about "doing well" can be substantial because earning the opportunity to continue on in the laboratory situation is possible. When competence assessment is not explicitly related to later success in life, and when earning the opportunity to continue within the laboratory situation is not possible, then the informational/ diagnostic properties of a test of ability will tend to influence behavior maximally in that situation, if that ability has substantial positive value. Only when the opportunity to continue (either outside the laboratory or within the laboratory situation itself) is not at issue, when a task is not seen as a test of ability, and/or when the ability has low value to the subject, will subjective probability of (immediate) success be a potent determinant of behavior as predicted by the initial expectancy × value theory of achievement motivation (Atkinson, 1957, 1964; Atkinson & Feather, 1966).

THE SELF SYSTEM AND THEORY OF ACHIEVEMENT MOTIVATION

A general theory of personality functioning and change (Raynor, 1981a) has evolved in part as an attempt to generate theory that would account for the positive associations between self-importance, future-importance, and self-possession noted earlier, the functional equivalence of both future-importance and self-importance in interaction with achievement-related motives to influence immediate performance level, and the role of information seeking in arousing willingness/resistance to undertaking tests of critical abilities, as reviewed previously. The theory is presented in detail elsewhere as it evolved in these successive steps from the initial theory of achievement motivation to the more general theory to the theory of adult competence motivation (Raynor, 1981a, 1981b; Raynor & Entin, 1981c). Here we apply the newer theory to problems and issues in theory and research on achievement motivation as they concern the role of diagnostic assessment of ability, the correlation between self-importance, future-importance, and self-possession, and the functional equivalence of future- and self-importance. But first a review of the newer theory is in order.

The theory distinguishes between arousal in the *behavioral system* and arousal in the *self system* so as to account for the functional equivalence of striving to achieve a future goal per se and striving to become a particular kind of person dependent on that future goal attainment. The theory distinguishes between *affective value* and *information value* so as to account for the difference between striving to "do well" and striving to "find out" in skill-demanding (or other) activity. And the theory distinguishes between *time-linked* sources of *value* (past, present, and future) so as to distinguish between effects attributable to the anticipated future, the evaluated present, and the retrospected past as they influence motivation of immediate activity. Although these three dimensions are considered to be orthogonal, for our purposes we need consider some particular combinations along these dimensions so as to derive the effects we wish to account for. The major assumption of the theory is that individuals are motivated to maximize positive value and/or to minimize negative value, and that motivation with regard to any source of value is a joint function of the amount of value and its subjective probability of attainment. We have constructed a consistent and coherent expectancy × value theory of motivation, personality functioning, and change so as to more adequately account for research findings.

Arousal in the behavioral system refers to motivation to attain concrete achievement goals as outcomes of activity and is a function of the resultant expected value of the outcome(s) as referred to in earlier expectancy × value theories of achievement motivation (Atkinson & Feather, 1966; Lewin, et al., 1944; Raynor, 1969, 1974b). Arousal in the self system refers to motivation to become a particular kind of person and to attain a future self-image or sense-of-self, when limited to the future time-linked sources of value as future-expected outcomes of immediate activity. When so limited, this motivation is a function of the resultant expected value of the self-image to be attained. Thus the self system can be viewed in terms of an expectancy × value theory of self-identity and self-evaluation. When limited to the immediately evaluated present, arousal in the self system refers to motivation to find out (informational value) and feel good about (affective value) oneself.

The newer theory distinguishes between five sources of (positive and negative) value, each of which can be time linked (past, present, and/or future), can refer to information (value) or affect (value), and can refer to concrete outcomes of action (behavioral system) and/or self-images or senses-of-self (self system).

Intrinsic value is determined by the properties of the particular task as seen by a particular individual and is included not so much on the basis of evidence from the achievement domain of activity but because other domains of human activity (particularly sexual activity) seem to require such a concept. *Difficulty value* refers to value determined by the subjective probability of attainment per se and is equivalent to the incentive values of success and failure when limited to behavioral outcomes of skill-demanding activity as in the previous (initial) theory of achievement motivation. *Instrumental value* refers to value determined by the number of opportunities for action that are at stake and is equivalent to the perceived instrumentality of immediate success/failure when limited to contingent paths linking skill-demanding activity-in-sequence as in the previous (more general) theory of achievement motivation. *Extrinsic value* refers to value determined by factors other than intrinsic value, difficulty value, and instrumental value, and is used to refer to expected outcomes such as money, prizes, etc. that can be linked to the outcomes of skill-demanding activity, or to other qualitative kinds of motivation (affiliation, power, etc.) that in previous research have been systematically manipulated or assessed at different levels. *Cultural value* refers to value determined by a moral/evaluative judgment of good/bad within a given cultural context and, when conceived of in the achievement domain as individual cultural value, refers to the individual's belief that success is "good" and failure is "bad" (behavioral system), and that a successful person is a "good" person and a "failure" is a "bad" person (self system).

Within the self system the goal of becoming a particular kind of (positively valued) person contingent upon future success combines a future time-linked self-image, an individual cultural valuation on becoming a good (successful) person, and/or the consequences of becoming a (rich, powerful, etc.) person (extrinsic positive value). We now expect that when immediate activity has positive future instrumental value and is rated high on future importance (as we assume occurs when "moving on" in a contingent path is possible for a success-oriented individual), and when this instrumental value refers to the concrete future achievement only so that becoming a particular self-image is not at issue, arousal in the behavioral system accounts for the effects of contingent future orientation identified in studies of academic motivation and laboratory performance. However, when the immediate activity also has positive future instrumental value in the self system so that it is rated high on both future-importance and self-importance, arousal is attributable to both the behavioral and self systems and produces for the success-oriented individual more positive achievement motivation than would be the case if arousal is limited to the behavioral system. Thus we account for the accentuation of resultant achievement motivation when both future-importance and self-importance are rated as high, with effects for the failure-threatened individual producing greater inhibition of immediate activity because instrumental value is negative when the opportunity to continue to other skill-demanding activity is at stake.

Note that in previous research no distinction was made between the importance of the anticipated future for self-evaluation and of the evaluated present for self-evaluation, so that although the above explanation is plausible, it does not rule out the possibility that accentuation of motivational effects may have been due to an increase in resultant achievement motivation caused by a desire to demonstrate an upward evaluation of competence in the present rather than to become a culturally valued (future) kind of person. In fact, we suspect that both the evaluated present and the anticipated future in the self-system contribute to the motivation of immediate activity in these studies because both the competences involved and the future self-images at stake probably have substantial positive value for many of the college students who serve as subjects. Also note that the interaction effect between motives and both self-importance and future-importance is expected when the extrinsic (positive) sources of value in the self system are weaker than the other sources of value referred to here. When the opposite is the case we expect a main effect due to both future- and self-importance when both are tied to the attainment of future goals.

SOURCES OF VALUE AND POSSESSION OF COMPETENCE

In the newer theory, sources of value are summed to determine total value when these sources are compatible. When an individual is committed to undertaking a skill-demanding activity, the affective value of the present (both positive and negative) evaluation of competence from performance on the task can come from: (1) *difficulty value*—the higher the performance, the greater the perceived degree of possession of the (positively valued) competence based on the subject's assumption that the more difficult the task, the more ability will be required to accomplish it, and the greater value of possession of that competence based on that performance; (2) *instrumental value*—the higher the performance, the greater the perceived degree of possession of the competence believed assessed, and when that competence is perceived as a necessary prerequisite for some later success because its possession is believed to be required in order to achieve that success, instrumental value is implicated, and the greater the number of opportunities believed to be earned by that level of possession of the competence, the greater the instrumental value of its possession; (3) *extrinsic*; and (4) *cultural value,* as discussed in the previous section of this chapter.

However, information and affective value are not necessarily compatible sources of value, particularly when an individual is faced with *choice* of some version from among alternative versions of some test of competence. For example, we suspect that a sequence of ability test items that maximizes (positive) affective value will not necessarily maximize (positive) information value. In our previous treatment (Raynor, 1981c) we have suggested that instrumental value is maximized by a choice of a sequence of relatively easy items in a *contingent* path sequence, but that information value is maximized by choice of a *noncontingent* path sequence consisting of items that begin as easy but are seen as becoming increasingly more difficult (a decreasing noncontingent path). However, we have no adequate theory that allows us to determine a priori the perceived information value to an individual of a particular alternative on an ability test, although others have either suggested such a theory (Trope, 1975; Trope & Brickman, 1975) or have used intuition to speculate about this issue.

What is needed at this point are empirical data that will allow respondents on tests of ability to tell us the relative amount of expected information value from various items and items-in-sequence in order to be able to construct such an expectancy × value theory. Note that in this discussion we have omitted reference to intrinsic value, either affective or informational, concerning possession of a competence, because we have no data that unambiguously seems to require this concept to account for the results. Despite claims to the contrary (Deci, 1974; Kruglanski et al., 1975), previous research is not compelling in this regard, primarily because other sources of value referred to here have not been systematically held constant in this research. We feel that both information and affective (intrinsic) value may be useful concepts for a complete theory of human action, but research must systematically vary the nature of the activity while holding other sources of value constant in order to demonstrate the explanatory value of sources of value linked to the activity per se, rather than to its perceived difficulty, its instrumental value, its extrinsic value, and its cultural value for a particular individual. Put another way, we see no convincing evidence that differences in the substantive nature of different skill activities (running versus throwing, mathematical versus verbal, musical versus artistic) rather than other sources of value are better able to account for the manner in which individual differences in achievement-related motives affect behavior in these activities. This does not mean that such evidence might not be obtained. Rather, research designs are thus far inadequate to separate intrinsic value per se from other sources of value in the domain of skill-demanding activity—whether seen as presenting an opportunity to "do well," or to "find out," or both.

TIME-LINKED SOURCES OF VALUE AND EXPECTANCY × VALUE THEORY: THE PAST

The newer theory distinguishes between the anticipated future and the evaluated present (as previously discussed) by linking evaluation of competence to the present and striving for goals to the future. It also considers for the first time in the expectancy × value theory of action the possible effects of the *retrospected past* on the motivation of immediate activity. Previous theory of achievement motivation within the context of the dynamics of action (Atkinson & Birch,

1970, 1974, 1978) has considered the concept of inertial motivation—the automatic carry-over of a previously aroused but not reduced tendency to achieve. Previous theory has also considered the concept of a cognitive learning effect (Atkinson, 1964, 1974; Atkinson & Feather, 1966) produced when success and failure change the individual's subjective probability of success for similar achievement-oriented activities and has used this assumed cognitive change to account for changes in level of aspiration (e.g., choice) that follow success and failure at a task. Our earlier discussion concerning competence can also be viewed as dealing with how the effects of (past) success/failure bear on the evaluation of the present level of competence that is brought to a given skill-demanding activity seen to require that competence for effective performance.

However, we believe there is an additional effect of the past, that is linked to an individual's striving to maintain the value of past success and/or to minimize the value of past failure, that is independent of the other effects noted above. This effect is a function of the stage of striving along a sequence of tasks. In early striving, anticipated future goals (along with evaluation of competence) provide the greatest amount of anticipated value, but the retrospected past is irrelevant because past successes and failures have not yet occurred to provide for possible sources of value. In late striving, retrospection of past success/failure so as to maximize positive value and minimize negative value provides the greatest amount of anticipated value, but the anticipated future is irrelevant because future goals along that path (termed a closed path) are no longer seen as possibilities. In middle striving, effects of the anticipated future, evaluated present, and retrospected past can all influence the motivation of immediate activity because all time-linked sources of value are potentially available. Thus we expect that late-stage striving in a closed contingent path will be influenced more by trying to maintain the value of past success and to minimize the value of past failure than trying to attain the (positive) value of future success and to minimize the (negative) value of future failure. In early-stage striving, however, the effects of the anticipated future rather than the retrospected past will predominate, holding effects of the evaluated present constant. As a consequence, we predict that individuals starting out along the contingent career paths of society will be influenced primarily by anticipated future success/failure, and accentuation of motive effects as predicted by the more general theory of achievement motivation referred to earlier in this paper will be most pronounced for such individuals (e.g., as for those college students faced with introductory psychology who are now presumed to face early-stage striving).

In a study (Raynor & Teitelbaum, 1981) bearing directly on the concept of time-linked motivation in the self system, male and female college students enrolled in the day school (and a smaller number of older students enrolled in evening school for whom data were analyzed separately) were presented with past, present, and future time-linked sentence leads in place of the usual pictures or sentences used to elicit TAT stories. All other procedures were identical to those used to obtain the n Achievement score (Atkinson, 1958, Appendix III; McClelland, Atkinson, Clark, & Lowell, 1953). The sentence leads were constructed using the appropriate alternative versions of the following material: "A person is thinking about (who they are becoming) (who they are) (who they have been). The person is thinking about the most important (future) (immediate/ present) (past) event that defines (who they are becoming) (who they are) (who they have been)." Subjects received either future, present, or past sentence leads as the first sentence to write a story about. Protocols were scored for n Achievement in the usual manner (Atkinson, 1958, Chapter 12 and Appendix III; McClelland et al., 1953) and, in addition, if a story was scored for "achievement imagery" (AI), which of the three criteria for AI it fulfilled was noted— competition with a standard of excellence (CWS), unique accomplishment (UA), and/or long-term involvement (LTI). No a priori hypotheses were explicitly derived. However, given earlier arguments concerning the relationship between future orientation and the n Achievement score (Raynor, 1968b) and the fact that the subjects were all relatively young and/or starting out in the presumed early stages of an educational/occupational path of society, it was expected that the future-oriented lead would elicit stories having the highest n Achievement scores, and also the most future-oriented n Achievement scores. In fact, both these results were obtained for males and females taken separately, and the pattern of results did not differ for the night school and day school samples.

We would now interpret these findings as consistent with the notion that arousal of achievement motivation is dependent primarily on the possibility of future success at a stage of relatively early path striving, and that the use of "ego involvement" to arouse achievement motivation elicits striving toward a future sense of self as well as toward concrete future achievement goals. We would predict a quite different pattern of results either if much older subjects were used in the sample or if the sentence leads distinguished between "an older (mature) person" versus "a younger person" or "an old person" versus "a young person." At the extreme, for an older sample of subjects faced with a sentence lead describing an old person, we would expect a much greater percentage of past-oriented stories concerned with maintaining the values (either intrinsic, difficulty, instrumental, extrinsic, and/or cultural sources of value) of past success. Note, however, that the current means of scoring for n Achievement might not be sensitive to such past-oriented concerns abour doing well to maintain past success because the scoring system seems to have been developed and validated primarily using future-oriented (goal-directed) concepts and using relatively young individuals as subjects (McClelland, et al., 1953).

A behavioral test of the foregoing hypothesis concerning the future versus the past as sources of value would be possible if subjects were asked "How important is doing well in this academic course you are currently enrolled in for: (1) achieving future success; and (2) maintaining past success?", preceded by two fill-in questions asking subjects to write in their future goals and their past successes. We would predict a motives × importance × stage of striving interaction on grades such that the motives × future-importance effects of previous research would be obtained for individuals faced with early-path striving, whereas a motives × past-importance interaction would be predicted for individuals faced with late-path striving. Note here that chronological age might not be a good indicator of stage of striving if 60-year-old individuals were returning to school and thus faced early-stage striving, and if 20-year-old individuals were finishing school with no future-oriented thoughts concerning what they would do next with their lives and thus faced late-stage striving. The theory defines psychological age and aging in terms of the time-linked preponderance of future-oriented versus past-oriented sources of value rather than dealing with age per se.

The study could also test the idea that "ego involvement" involves achievement arousal that implicates the self system by assessing "How important is doing well . . . for: (1) becoming the person you want to become; and (2) remaining the person you have become?", in addition to the questions noted earlier concerning concrete future/past accomplishment. Perhaps in doing so the earlier reference should be to a specific life accomplishment like "graduating from college" so that this behavioral goal could be distinguished from a self-goal like "becoming a college graduate." According to our analysis, time-linked sources of value in the behavioral system alone versus in both the behavioral and self systems should arouse different amounts of resultant achievement motivation—if individuals perceive a difference between attaining a goal and becoming a particular kind of person contingent on attainment of that goal. The predicted motives × future-importance or motives × past-importance interaction should be stronger for those seeing the goal as involving both the concrete achievement and the self-image defined by that goal than for those who only see the goal as involving the concrete achievement. The particular interaction expected for these effects consists of an increase in grades for success-oriented individuals coupled with a decrease in grades for the failure-threatened individuals from low to high importance, given weak positive extrinsic sources of value.

CULTURAL VALUE AND THE THEORY OF ACHIEVEMENT MOTIVATION

Application of the concept of individual cultural value to the achievement domain involves the notion of an achievement value that is independent of subjective probability of success. This value functions to accentuate the amount of positive or negative resultant achievement motivation that is aroused for success-oriented and failure-threatened subjects. This is a return to the concept of achievement value (Rosen, 1959) from a different perspective, and as yet there is no direct evidence bearing on its validity. We speculate that individuals differ in the extent to which an achievement outcome is believed to be good/bad in their cultural context. We do not know whether this might be a relatively stable characteristic of individuals or whether it might vary from task to task, or whether such individual differences are independent of or correlated with individual differences in the motives to achieve success and/or to avoid failure.

Evidence suggesting the utility of this concept comes from data showing an accentuation of individual differences in achievement motivation when neither the subjective probability of success nor the instrumental value of immediate success seem plausible reasons for the accentuation. In particular, the data reported by Pearlson and Raynor (1981) indicated that the ratings of the importance of achieving a future goal interacted with n Achievement scores to accentuate differences between high and low n Achievement groups from low to high future goal importance.

We feel that when important future goals are conceived as defining a future self-image, the notion of becoming a positively valued ("good") person or becoming a negatively valued ("bad") person has promise for providing a more complete understanding of the arousal of achievement motivation in important life activities. From the point of view of the experimental analysis of behavior, the concept of individual cultural value suggests a means of manipulating achievement arousal independent of subjective probability of (immediate) success and independent of the contingent nature of a sequence of tasks, and its effects can be tested by using arousal in the self system, particularly as both possession of certain competences ("intelligence") but not others, and achievement of success on certain tasks but not others, are often seen as marking the person as "good"/"successful." Moral evaluation in the arousal of achievement motivation was most recently suggested by Weiner's (1974) analysis of the development of attributions for skill-demanding activity. His consideration of the similarities in the development of moral and achievement attributions provides a basis for understanding the development of individual cultural value in the achievement context. Of course, the original concern of McClelland and his coworkers regarding the link between the Protestant ethic, the spirit of capitalism, and the development and functioning of the achievement motive (McClelland, 1961) has always implicated a strong moral/evaluative element that up to now has not been formally recognized as a factor in the arousal of achievement motivation by systematic theory in this area.

SUMMARY

In this chapter we first reviewed predictions and evidence concerning the elaboration of the initial expectancy $\times$ value theory of achievement motivation that takes into account the effects of contingent future orientation on the motivation of immediate activity. Evidence concerning academic performance, comparison of contingent and noncontingent path performance, and effects of both length of contingent paths and subjective probability of success along contingent paths was reviewed. The data suggested that, despite complications concerning the effects of extrinsic motivation, time-to-completion of task sequences, arousal of uncertainty motivation, and simultaneous arousal of motivation concerning self-evaluation, predictions were supported to a sufficiently great extent so as to merit taking contingent future orientation seriously as a variable that influences the motivation of immediate activity.

A newer theory of personality functioning and change, which in part was developed in an attempt to deal with some of these complications, was then discussed in relation to evidence concerning arousal in what was termed the "self system," where motivation to find out about oneself in the context of assessment of competences, and/or motivation to attain future goals so as to become a desired future sense-of-self, were assumed to be reflected in the interaction between measures of achievement-related motives and ratings of importance for self-evaluation—in regard to both academic performance and performance on laboratory tasks.

The concept of time-linked sources of value was introduced to differentiate effects of the anticipated future, evaluated present, and retrospected past, and evidence concerning arousal of achievement motivation in fantasy-thought samples was reviewed to suggest that early stage striving of younger individuals has served as the primary basis for development and validation of the theory of achievement motivation and the assessment of the achievement motive itself. The possible effects of motivation to maintain the value of past success were discussed in relation to previous research studies. The distinctions between intrinsic, difficulty, instrumental, and extrinsic value on the one hand, and individual cultural value, on the other, were also discussed as they related to the arousal of achievement motivation and value in the self system. The concept of individual cultural value was discussed as a possible source of achievement arousal that interacts with achievement-related motives but is independent of either subjective probability of success or instrumental value in a contingent path. Research was suggested that might help to demonstrate the utility of including this moral/evaluative dimension of achievement arousal.

The distinction between affective and information value made in the newer theory has been used to distinguish between the goals of "doing well" and "finding out." Although previous research on achievement motivation has been more concerned with the goal of doing well and its affective value, the competitive instructions for tests of ability probably also aroused motivation to find out about one's competences and their instrumental value. Newer research concerning ability assessment seems to provide for the goal of finding out while minimizing the goal of doing well on such tests. Choice of tests of competence can arouse both information and affective value, but these sources of value need not be compatible so that the individual may be faced with trying to maximize one or other kinds of (information and affective) value. In some situations, undertaking a test of competence involves simultaneous maximization of "finding out" and "doing well" through trying to do one's best. Such arousal is expected to accentuate characteristic differences between success-oriented and failure-threatened individuals, so that, once constrained to perform, motivation to assess competence by doing well is expected to function in a manner equivalent to motivation to utilize one's competence in doing well.

REFERENCES

Alpert, R., & Haber, R. N. Anxiety in academic achievement situations. *Journal of Abnormal and Social Psychology*, 1960, *61*, 207–215.

Atkinson, J. W. Motivational determinants of risk-taking behavior. *Psychological Review*, 1957, *64*, 359–372.

Atkinson, J. W. (Ed.). *Motives in fantasy, action, and society*. Princeton: Van Nostrand, 1958.

Atkinson, J. W. *An introduction to motivation*. Princeton: Van Nostrand, 1964.

Atkinson, J. W. The mainsprings of achievement-oriented activity. In J. W. Atkinson & J. O. Raynor (Eds.), *Motivation and achievement*. Washington, D.C.: Hemisphere Publishing Corporation, 1974. Also in J. W. Atkinson & J. O. Raynor (Eds.) *Personality, motivation, and achievement*. Washington, D.C.: Hemisphere Publishing Corporation, 1978.

Atkinson, J. W., & Birch, D. *The dynamics of action*. New York: Wiley, 1970.

Atkinson, J. W., & Birch, D. The dynamics of achievement-oriented activity. In J. W. Atkinson and J. O. Raynor (Eds.), *Motivation and achievement*. Washington, D.C.: Hemisphere Publishing Corporation, 1974.

Atkinson, J. W., & Birch, D. *An introduction to motivation* (Second Ed.). New York: Van Nostrand, 1978.

Atkinson, J. W., & Feather, N. T. *A theory of achievement motivation*. New York: Wiley, 1966.

Atkinson, J. W., & Raynor, J. O. *Motivation and achievement*. Washington, D.C.: Hemisphere Publishing Corporation, 1974.

Bachman, J. B., Kahn, R. L., Mednick, M. T., Davidson, N. T., & Johnson, L. D. *Youth in transition* (Vol. 1). *Blueprint for a longitudinal study of adolescent boys*. Ann Arbor, Michigan: Survey Research Center, Institute for Social Research, 1967.

Brecher, P. J. *Examination of achievement-oriented performance decrement in contingent pathways*. Unpublished masters thesis, Ohio University, 1972.

Brecher, P. J. *The effect of extrinsic incentives on achievement-oriented performance in contingent paths*. Unpublished doctoral dissertation, Ohio University, 1975.

Entin, E. E. Achievement motivation, future orientation, and acquisition. In J. O. Raynor and E. E. Entin (Eds.) *Motivation, career striving, and aging*. Washington, D.C.: Hemisphere Publishing Corporation, 1981.

Entin, E. E., & Feather, N. T. Attribution to success and failure in contingent and noncontingent paths. In J. O. Raynor and E. E. Entin (Eds.), *Motivation, career striving, and aging*. Washington, D.C.: Hemisphere Publishing Corporation, 1981.

Entin, E. E., & Raynor, J. O. Effects of contingent future orientation and achievement motivation on performance in two kinds of task. *Journal of Experimental Research in Personality*, 1973, *6*, 314–320.

Feather, N. T. The relationship of persistence at a task to expectation of success and achievement related motives. *Journal of Abnormal and Social Psychology*, 1961, *63*, 552–561.

Feather, N. T. Persistence at a difficult task with alternative task of intermediate difficulty. *Journal of Abnormal and Social Psychology,* 1963, *66,* 604–609.

Gazzo, B. *The effects of achievement motivation, self-future orientation, and competent vs. nurturant role descriptions on interest and expectancy of success in a tutorial program.* Unpublished honours thesis, State University of New York at Buffalo, 1974.

Gjesme, T. Goal distance in time and its effect on the relations between achievement motives and performance. *Journal of Research in Personality,* 1974, *8,* 161–171.

Kruglanski, A. W., Riter, A., Amitai, A. Margolin, B., Shbtai, L., & Zaksly, D. Can money enhance intristic motivation?: A test of the context-consequence hypothesis. *Journal of Personality and Social Psychology,* 1975, *31,* 744–750.

Lewin, K., Dembo, T., Festinger, L., & Sears, P. S. Level of aspiration. In J. McV. Hunt (Ed.), *Personality and the behavior disorders* (Vol. 1). New York: Ronald Press, 1944.

Mandler, G., & Sarason, S. B. A study of anxiety and learning. *Journal of Abnormal and Social Psychology,* 1952, *47,* 166–173.

McClelland, D. C., Atkinson, J. W., Clark, R. A., & Lowell, E. L. *The achievement motive.* New York: Appleton–Century–Crofts, 1953. Reissued with a New Preface by J. W. Atkinson. New York: Irvington Publishing, Inc. (Halstead Press/Wiley), 1976.

Mehrabian, A. Male and female scales of tendency to achieve. *Educational and Psychological Measurement,* 1968, *28,* 493–502.

Mehrabian, A. Measures of achieving tendency. *Educational and Psychological Measurement,* 1969, *29,* 445–451.

Pearlson, H. B. *Effects of temporal distance from a goal and number of tasks required for goal attainment on achievement-related behavior.* Unpublished doctoral dissertation, State University of New York at Buffalo, 1979. Also in J. O. Raynor and E. E. Entin (Eds.) *Motivation, career striving, and aging.* Washington, D.C.: Hemisphere Publishing Corporation, 1981.

Pearlson, H. B., & Raynor, J. O. Motivational analysis of the future plans of college men: Imagery used to describe future plans and goals. In J. O. Raynor and E. E. Entin (Eds.), *Motivation, career striving, and aging.* Washington, D.C.: Hemisphere Publishing Corporation, 1981.

Raynor, J. O. *Achievement motivation, grades, and instrumentality.* Paper presented at the meetings of the American Psychological Association, San Francisco, September, 1968. (a)

Raynor, J. O. *The relationship between distant future goals and achievement motivation.* Unpublished doctoral dissertation, University of Michigan, 1968. (b)

Raynor, J. O. Future orientation and motivation of immediate activity: An elaboration of the theory of achievement motivation. *Psychological Review,* 1969, *76,* 606–610.

Raynor, J. O. *The engagement of achievement-related motives: Achievement arousal vs. contingent future orientation.* Paper presented at the meetings of the American Psychological Association, New Orleans, September, 1974. (a)

Raynor, J. O. Future orientation in the study of achievement motivation. In J. W. Atkinson and J. O. Raynor (Eds.), *Motivation and achievement.* Washington, D.C.: Hemisphere Publishing Corporation, 1974. (b) Also in J. W. Atkinson and J. O. Raynor (Eds.), *Personality, motivation, and achievement.* Washington, D.C.: Hemisphere Publishing Corporation, 1978.

Raynor, J. O. Motivation and career striving. In J. W. Atkinson and J. O. Raynor (Eds.), *Motivation and achievement.* Washington, D.C.: Hemisphere Publishing Corporation, 1974. (c) Also in J. W. Atkinson and J. O. Raynor (Eds.), *Personality, motivation, and achievement.* Washington, D.C.: Hemisphere Publishing Corporation, 1978.

Raynor, J. O. Self-possession of attributes, self-evaluation, and future orientation: A theory of adult competence motivation. In J. O. Raynor and E. E. Entin (Eds.), *Motivation, career striving, and aging.* Washington, D.C.: Hemisphere Publishing Corporation, 1981. (a)

Raynor, J. O. A theory of personality functioning and change. In J. O. Raynor and E. E. Entin (Eds.), *Motivation, career striving, and aging.* Washington, D.C.: Hemisphere Publishing Corporation, 1981. (b)

Raynor, J. O., Atkinson, J. W., & Brown, M. Subjective aspects of achievement motivation immediately before an examination. In J. W. Atkinson and J. O. Raynor (Eds.), *Motivation and achievement*. Washington, D.C.: Hemisphere Publishing Corporation, 1974.

Raynor, J. O., & English, L. D. Relationships between self-importance, future-importance, and self-possession. In J. O. Raynor and E. E. Entin (Eds.), *Motivation, career striving, and aging*. Washington, D.C.: Hemisphere Publishing Corporation, 1981.

Raynor, J. O., & Entin, E. E. Achievement motivation as a determinant of persistence in contingent and noncontingent paths. In J. O. Raynor and E. E. Entin (Eds.), *Motivation, career striving, and aging*. Washington, D.C.: Hemisphere Publishing Corporation, 1981. (a)

Raynor, J. O., & Entin, E. E. Effects of high vs. low achievement arousal on level of performance in contingent and noncontingent paths. In J. O. Raynor and E. E. Entin (Eds.), *Motivation, career striving, and aging*. Washington, D.C.: Hemisphere Publishing Corporation, 1981. (b)

Raynor, J. O., & Entin, E. E. *Motivation, career striving, and aging*. Washington, D.C.: Hemisphere Publishing Corporation, 1981. (c)

Raynor, J. O., & Entin, E. E. Theory and research on future orientation and achievement motivation. In J. O. Raynor and E. E. Entin (Eds.), *Motivation, career striving, and aging*. Washington, D.C.: Hemisphere Publishing Corporation, 1981. (d)

Raynor, J. O., & Rubin, I. S. Effects of achievement motivation and future orientation on level of performance. *Journal of Personality and Social Psychology*, 1971, *17*, 36–41. Also in J. W. Atkinson and J. O. Raynor (Eds.), *Motivation and achievement*. Washington, D.C.: Hemisphere Publishing Corporation, 1974.

Roeder, G. P. The effects of future orientation as time and task variables on children's present achievement. Unpublished doctorial dissertation. State University of New York at Buffalo, 1980.

Rosen, B. C. Race, ethnicity and the achievement syndrome. *American Sociological Review*, 1959, *24*, 47–60.

Teitelbaum, R. C., Raynor, J. O., & Entin, E. E. Recall of interrupted and completed tasks under relaxed, achievement, and contingent conditions. In J. O. Raynor and E. E. Entin (Eds.), *Motivation, career striving, and aging*. Washington, D.C.: Hemisphere Publishing Corporation, 1981.

Trope, Y. Seeking information about one's ability as a determinant of choice among tasks. *Journal of Personality and Social Psychology*, 1975, *32*, 1004–1013.

Trope, Y., & Brickman, P. Difficulty and diagnosticity as determinants of choice among tasks. *Journal of Personality and Social Psychology*, 1975, *31*, 918–925.

Weiner, B. *Achievement motivation and attribution theory*. Morristown, N.J.: General Learning Press, 1974.

5

The Expectancy-Value Approach within the Theory of Social Motivation: Elaborations, Extensions, Critique

Julius Kuhl
Ruhr University, Bochum, West Germany

Stating that modern theories of social motivation are expectancy-value theories amounts to a tautology. Expectancy-value conceptions are so pervasive in most theories of social motivation that they are rarely contrasted against any alternative conceptions. There seems to be implicit consensus among many theorists concerned with social motivation that expectancy-value theory is for motivation theory what evolution theory is for biology: a firm, universally accepted foundation for all theories of specific phenomena to build upon (Atkinson & Birch, 1978, Weiner, 1972). Consequently, expectancy-value theories are often the basis rather than the target of empirical investigations. There are, of course, exceptions: Some investigators take explicit interest in testing the validity of expectancy-value theory against alternative conceptions (Graen, 1969; Hackmann & Porter, 1968; Lawler & Porter, 1967; Pritchard & Sanders, 1973; Schmidt, 1973). This line of research has not been absorbed, however, by research on social motivation. The latter has been preoccupied with generalizing (Heckhausen, 1977; Kuhl, 1978b; Raynor, 1969), or reformulating (Atkinson & Birch, 1970; Weiner, Frieze, Kukla, Reed, Rest, & Rosenbaum, 1971) expectancy and value parameters. Later in this chapter, it is argued that the methods used within this *elaboration paradigm* cannot answer the questions regarding the interindividual and cross-situational generality of expectancy-value theory. It need not be emphasized that the elaboration paradigm is still a perfectly legitimate approach because it is based on an indispensable method of scientific research: Formulating basic postulates and deriving testable hypotheses. Without assuming something that is not questioned for a while we cannot test anything: We cannot test hypotheses about mediators of motivational determinants without any preliminary postulates concerning the nature of those determinants. Within the elaboration paradigm, expectancy-value theory seems to have received that status of a preliminary postulate to start from. The elaboration paradigm has rendered a great deal of valuable information about the mediators of expectancy and value parameters.

In the first part of this chapter, some elaborations of original expectancy-value conceptions are reviewed. Because the theory of achievement motivation has received a paradigmatic status for the development of the theory of social motivation, the theoretical examples are taken from that theory. The second part deals with the question of whether motivation theory should confine itself to the two basic dimensions suggested by the expectancy-value framework. As an example for one possible extension of the two-dimensional approach, a third dimension ("action orientation") is discussed that has proved to be useful as an additional assumed determinant of motivation in explaining results from experiments on "learned helplessness" (Seligman, 1975).

The third part of this chapter describes attempts to test the basic postulate underlying expectancy-value theory. Specifically, alternative methods are discussed that have been of some use in investigating the interindividual and cross-situational validity of expectancy-value theory.

THE ORIGINAL THEORY OF ACHIEVEMENT MOTIVATION

As the reader may recall, Atkinson's (1957) risk-taking model considered resultant motivational tendency (T_r) a function of the product of expectancy of success (P_s) and incentive of success (I_s) weighted by the difference of two dispositional motive factors (striving for success, M_S, and avoiding failure, M_F):

$$T_r = (M_S - M_F) \times P_s \times I_s$$

Given Atkinson's assumption that I_s is an inverse linear function of P_s (i.e., $I_s = 1 - P_s$), the model results in the well-known inverted U-shaped preference function with its peak at intermediately difficult tasks ($P_s = .5$), for subjects with $M_S > M_F$ (success oriented) and a U-shaped negative curve implying strongest avoidance at intermediately difficult tasks for subjects with $M_F > M_S$ (failure oriented). For success-oriented subjects subsequent empirical tests of the model resulted in relatively consistent findings that are basically compatible with the model except for the fact that the peak of the preference function seems to be located at moderately difficult tasks ($.3 > P_s > .4$). Attempts to reconcile this finding resulted in appropriate curve-fitting suggestions (Heckhausen, 1967b; Hamilton, 1974; Schneider, 1973), and various elaborations of the model, which are dealt with later in this chapter.

A recent summary of one of the most extensive research programs aimed at testing the validity of the risk-taking model (Schneider, 1978), boils down to the conclusion that—as far as summary data (averaging preferred P_s across subjects) is concerned—there is no need to adjust the original Atkinson model by making curve-fitting manipulations. Schneider (1973) took great pains in developing various direct and indirect methods of assessing subjective probability of success. Schneider's analyses suggest that the most widely used assessment procedure (i.e., subjective ratings of P_s for the next trial or the next 10 trials) yields a distorted index of the latent, behaviorally relevant P_s construct. When indirect, apparently less distorted, measures of P_s (e.g., decision time) are used, the peak of the curve describing *mean* preferences among success-oriented subjects does not differ noticeably from the intermediate P_s level.

Figure 5.1 illustrates Schneider's results, which were obtained from a risk-taking experiment using a psychomotor task. The objective of this task is to strike a steel ball through a gap of nine different widths at the end of the table. The upper figure (5.1a) represents his empirical preference function peaking at the third facility level. On the basis of Atkinson's risk-taking model and a typical rating measure of subjective probability of success, the peak of the preference function would be expected at the fifth facility level (fig. 5.1b), which is easier than the one where the empirical preference function peaks. Up to this point, the results suggest a modification of the risk-taking model to account for the "fact" that subjects choose moderately difficult tasks (i.e., $.3 > P_s > .4$). Figure 5.1c shows, however, that decision time taken to predict a hit or miss at every gap peaks at the same facility level where the preference function peaks. Maximum decision time seems to indicate maximum uncertainty (Johnson, 1955), which, in turn, should represent the point of intermediate probability of success (Schneider, 1978). Intermediate P_s also should be located at that point on the difficulty scale, where the proportions of predicted hits and misses are equal (i.e., 50%). Also this indirect measure of P_s suggests intermediate P_s at the preferred third facility level (fig. 5.1c). The discrepancy between reported P_s and inferred P_s seems to be a result of a greater pressure for realism when forced to state a P_s estimate (Schneider, 1978). In other words, subjects seem to be implicitly more optimistic about their chances of success than they are inclined to express explicitly.

Lest it be believed, however, that it may be concluded from Schneider's data that elaborations of the risk-taking model are not necessary, it should be noted that his results pertain to group data only. Individual preference functions may depart considerably from averaged group functions. To accommodate individual departures from the "ideal" preference function, additional individual parameters affecting risk taking have to be taken into account.

Before turning to examples of elaborations of the original risk-taking model that introduce additional parameters, we should devote some thoughts to the less

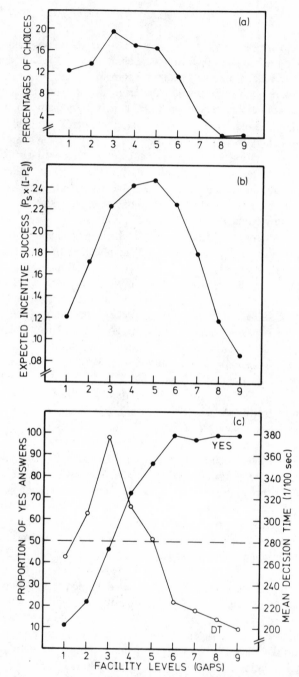

FIG. 5.1. Percentages of choices (a), expected incentive of success (b), decision time (DT) and proportion of yes answers (YES %) (c) as a function of 9 levels of facility (after Schneider, 1978).

confirmed part of the risk-taking model describing a U-shaped negative preference function for failure-oriented subjects. Empirical studies yielded inconsistent findings (i.e., maximum preferences for easy, intermediate, or difficult levels or combinations thereof resulting in bimodal or trimodal preference functions [Heckhausen, 1977]). Heckhausen offered an attempt to explain those inconsistent findings on the basis of his elaborated model of motivation to be discussed later. The model predicts preference of easy tasks by failure-oriented subjects provided the situation is threatening enough to arouse avoidance motivation (i.e., the goal not to evaluate one's own ability), which is conceptualized in Heckhausen's model by negative perceived instrumentality of internal causation of results. Experiments suggesting preference for difficult tasks by failure-oriented subjects seem to have been based on less threatening situations, though performance outcomes were made explicit to the subjects, to the experimenter, and—in group situations—to other subjects. According to Heckhausen, this situation should prevent subjects from pursuing avoidance goals because it leaves no opportunity to avoid information about one's own ability. Mixed preference patterns having preference peaks at the difficult and the easy end of the scale of difficulty are attributed to a differential perception of the situation (i.e., as threatening by one part of the failure-oriented group and as not threatening by another part of this group [Heckhausen, 1977]).

Measurement Problems

A recent investigation of the dimensional status of the measurement instrument used to assess motive strength (i.e., M_S and M_F) revealed—among other things—an additional potential reason for the lacking consistency of risk preference observed among failure-oriented subjects (Kuhl, 1978a). One thousand thirty four sets of six TAT stories each were scored according to Heckhausen's (1963) scoring system, which yields scores for "hope of success" (M_S) and "fear of failure" (M_F). These data were analyzed so as to discover how compatible they were with Rasch's stochastic measurement model (Rasch, 1960). Rasch's model is based on the assumption of *specific objectivity*, which may be considered the mathematical formulation of several attributes that seem indispensable from a measurement point of view. The most important attribute is based on the assumption of interindividual consistency as to the determinants of test behavior. In this respect, specific objectivity requires that, for all subjects to be compared with regard to motive strength: (1) the same response classes and the same situations should be associated with the motive; and (2) the rank order of incentive values associated with those motive-related response classes and situations should be the same. If one of those criteria is violated within a given sample of subjects, it must be concluded that the determinants of test behavior differ across subjects (i.e., the test does not measure the same construct for different subjects).

The assumption of specific objectivity is tested by dividing a sample of subjects into two or more groups according to an internal (test score) or an external (age, intelligence, anxiety, etc.) criterion and estimating person and item parameters independently in each group on the basis of the test model. This model describes the relationship between manifest test behavior (i.e., the probability of a positive or negative response r_{vi} by person v on item i) and the assumed latent personal (x_v) and situational (e_i) determinants by a logistic function:

$$p(r_{vi} \mid x_v, e_i) = \frac{(x_v e_i)^{r_{vi}}}{1 + (x_v e_i)^{r_{vi}}}$$

with $r_{vi} = 1$ for a positive response and $r_{vi} = 0$ for a negative response. If the data are compatible with the model (i.e., if specific objectivity holds), any estimation of an item parameter based on one group should not differ from the estimated parameter of the same item derived from another group of subjects. This was not the case for the subscale "fear of failure" (FF) when two subject groups were formed according the internal criterion (FF score).

A chi-square test of goodness of fit (Fischer & Scheiblechner, 1970) revealed a highly significant difference between item parameters from both groups [χ^2 (25) = 90.57, $p < .001$]. Comparisons based on additional criteria for forming subject groups (age, education, "hope for success" score) resulted in significant deviations from the model. It must be concluded from these results that the FF measure does not indicate the same construct for all subjects.

Further analyses of the data suggested one hint as to what might be confounded in the FF measure. The deviation from the model seemed to be caused by two distinct subgroups of scoring categories, one comprising the categories "need to avoid failure" and "instrumental activity to avoid failure," whereas the second group consisted of the categories "anticipation of blame" and "failure theme." Interestingly enough, the first group of categories was associated with "hope for success" (HS score), whereas the second one was related to "fear of failure" (FF score). It was concluded that the original FF construct comprises two distinct ways of dealing with failure threats, an *action-oriented* approach (trying to avoid or overcome failure) and a *state-oriented* approach (focusing on failure and its consequences). The two FF-related constructs seem related to the distinction between facilitating and debilitating anxiety (Alpert & Haber, 1960). In contrast to this distinction, the constructs of action and state orientation imply an assumption about the cognitive mediators of facilitating versus debilitating effects of anxiety. The effect of anxiety on performance depends on the particular coping mechanism employed. To the extent that state and action orientation are associated with different risk preferences, inconsistent findings would be in part due to the confounding of both concepts in the FF measure.

The Measurement of Hope for Success

In contrast to the analysis of *FF*, the comparison of *HS* parameters between groups yielded virtually constant estimations across subject groups formed according to the internal criterion. In spite of the high number of subjects (1034), the statistical test of the difference between parameter estimations was not significant. This remarkable finding implies that: (1) all scoring categories (need for success, instrumental activity to gain success, expectation of success, praise, and positive affect) belong to a motive-related class of equivalent responses; and (2) that all pictures of the Heckhausen TAT describing diverse situations belong to a motive-related class of equivalent situations. It has been argued that current personality tests measure "summary constructs" (i.e., combine heterogeneous information about a person [Gewirtz, 1969]). The compatibility with Rasch's unidimensional model suggests that this criticism does not apply to the TAT measure of *HS*. There are theoretical and empirical reasons, however, suggesting that questionnaire measures that are based on a similarly diverse repertoire of subconstructs as the TAT-scoring categories do, in fact, measure a heterogeneous summary concept. Self-report measures of the achievement motive have often failed to yield consistent results (Atkinson & Birch, 1978, p. 102; Heckhausen, 1967a).

What should be the reason for this incongruence between projective and self-report measures of motive strength? An answer may be found by analyzing the process underlying imaginative behavior. One major attribute that makes fantasy so distinct from other kinds of cognitive activity is that the entire thinking process seems to be dominated by principles that relate to the attractiveness of goals and the possible fulfilment of wishes. People fantasize about goals they want to reach, no matter whether or not they think they actually can reach them (Singer, 1966). Under fantasy conditions, expectational cognitions, for instance, may be more a function of a *pleasure principle* than of a *reality principle*. Thus, it may be assumed that the unidimensional nature of the TAT measure of *HS* is due to the effect of a unifying, value-focused principle that relates to the value of the general goal of success and that governs diverse cognitions that are categorized by the scoring system. A similar unifying principle cannot be assumed when a subject is responding to a questionnaire. A question regarding expectation of success may not be determined primarily by value cognitions ("I always get what I want"), but it may tap an independent process aiming at a realistic assessment of the chances of succeeding. Summarizing across such truly diverse concepts yields, in fact, a summary measure that will produce less consistent relationships to behavioral criteria than the relationships obtained on the basis of a projective measure (Heckhausen, 1977). A recommendation for future development of self-report instruments can be derived from the foregoing discussion: Items should exclusively be related to value parameters. One questionnaire (Gjesme &

Nygård, 1970), which is based on similar considerations, seems to yield very promising results (Nygård, 1977).

There are, of course, more shortcomings of self-report measures compared to projective techniques. A major problem is that subjects may be unable or unwilling to verbalize the motivational determinants of their behavior. Attempts to formulate simple, concrete, and phenomenologically representative items with answer categories that control for social desirability may help overcome those problems (Kuhl, 1980).

Heckhausen (1977) raised the question whether motive constructs should be abandoned in favor of more specific parameters such as expectancy and incentive. The foregoing discussion is not to say that global motive constructs are *sufficient* for explaining behavior. Research during the past 10 years has shown clearly that achievement-related behavior cannot be explained unless additional, situation-specific parameters are taken into account (Heckhausen, 1977). The results from the TAT analyses based on Rasch's model do suggest, however, that global motive constructs should be retained as *necessary* determinants of behavior. The problem left for future research is not whether or not motive concepts are useful parameters for explaining behavior. Instead, future efforts should concentrate on determining what type of behavior may be explained by motive constructs and what kind of behavior depends on the more specific motivational parameters. A plausible hypothesis may be that the more global aspects of behavior such as structuring a novel situation with regard to what goals should be strived for may be explained by (global) motive constructs, whereas the more specific aspects of behavior (e.g., level of aspiration, persistence, and performance at a particular task) may depend on more specific parameters (e.g., expectancy and incentive of success). Current research on motivation tends to focus on specific behavioral measures rather than on more global ones. Typical experiments do not leave much room for free choice between goals such as achievement, affiliation, or power-related goals. Instead, specific behavioral indices are obtained while observing the subject approaching a goal that has been chosen in advance by the experimenter. Heckhausen's recent suggestion to abandon summary constructs in favor of specific process variables is only justified to the extent that future research continues to selectively attend to specific behavioral phenomena (Heckhausen, 1977).

ELABORATIONS OF THE THEORY OF ACHIEVEMENT MOTIVATION

Early attempts to elaborate the risk-taking model focused on the relationship between incentive of success and probability of success. These attempts range from numerical curve-fitting suggestions, like letting I_s be equal to $(.7 - P_s)$ (Heckhausen, 1967b) to have the peak of the preference function shift to moderately difficult tasks, to introducing additional determinants of incentive to the model (e.g., Feather, 1967; Kuhl, 1978b; Raynor, 1969). Several authors assumed a curvilinear rather than a linear relationship between I_s and P_s mainly to account for the observed shift of maximum preference to moderately difficult tasks (Schneider, 1973; Heckhausen, 1977; Wendt, 1967). It is hard to evaluate the validity of this assumption, however, (1) because a direct test is not possible as long as we are not able to measure latent expectancy and incentive parameters on an interval scale, and (2) because an indirect test based on the implied asymmetric preference function is equivocal since asymmetric preference functions are implied by all existing elaborations of the original model. For the present, it seems wiser to maintain the simple linear model and focus on testable assumptions concerning additional determinants of incentive.

Generalizations of The Original Theory

Several determinants of this kind have been proposed.

Perceived Responsibility for Outcomes. Feather (1967) suggested perceived own responsibility (C) for outcomes as a weighting factor of incentive parameters [e.g., $I_s = C(1 - P_s)$]. Though Feather's empirical results lent some support to this hypothesis, his generalization of the original theory did not receive much attention in subsequent research, which may be partly due to the fact that the implications of Feather's generalized model for risk-taking behavior were neither formulated nor tested empirically in his article. Also, Feather's generalized model may have had less impact than it deserved because effects of personal control of outcomes had been studied in the following years by authors who chose to reformulate rather then generalize the original theory of achievement motivation (e.g., Weiner et al., 1971; Meyer, 1973b).

Instrumentality for Future Goals. Raynor elaborated the original model on the basis of the assumption that motivation for immediate activity is also a function of perceived instrumentality of immediate success for attaining future goals. Whenever success at an immediate task is necessary to continue to future tasks, motivation is assumed to be intensified by all component tendencies related to each step along that *contingent path* leading toward some future goal. The model implies that, with increasing length of a contingent path, success-oriented subjects show an increasing shift of maximum preference towards the easy end of the scale of difficulty, whereas failure-oriented subjects choose—if constrained to make a choice—increasingly more difficult tasks. Raynor's own results from laboratory experiments support the predictions derived for success-oriented subjects only, whereas results reported by Wish and Hasazi (1972, cited after Raynor, 1974) from an ecologically more representative field setting lent strong support to the elaborated model with regard to both motive groups. Because instrumentality of immediate success for future goals should be more typical of field settings than of laboratory settings, the better fit of the elaborated model in field settings is not surprising.

Perceived Goal Distance.   Future time orientation (FTO) is considered a dependent variable in Raynor's model: The distance of the phenomenologically represented future goal is defined by that step along a contingent path where component motivation reaches a maximum value. FTO is assumed to be large, for instance, in a contingent path consisting of easy tasks provided $M_S > M_F$, or tasks of intermediate to high difficulty provided $M_F > M_S$. High FTO should be associated with relatively low perceived distance of a goal.

In contrast to Raynor's conception, Gjesme speculated that perceived distance to a future goal may be a separate determinant rather than a result of motivational tendency. In that case, temporal distance should be (inversely) related to motivation also if immediate motivation is not intensified by any instrumentality of immediate success for future opportunities (i.e., in a noncontingent path). Gjesme (1974) found empirical support for this conclusion: Motivation on an immediate task increased with decreasing temporal distance of an announced future "test" consisting of tasks that were allegedly similar to the immediate task. This relationship was found in spite of the fact that immediate success was not necessary in order to get the opportunity to work on the future task. Recently, Gjesme (1979) proposed an extension of the theory of achievement motivation which formally incorporates perceived goal distance as an independent determinant of motivation. In this theory, psychological distance is considered not only a function of expectancy of success (as in Raynor's theory), but also a function of the distance in time between the present state and the future goal as well as future time orientation as a personality trait.

Personal Standards.   Another determinant of achievement motivation recently integrated within the formal model of achievement motivation is the *personal standard* for self-evaluation (Kuhl, 1978b). The personal standard is defined as that point on the scale of subjective difficulty where the midpoint of the incentive scale ($I_s = .5$) is anchored. According to this conception, the incentive associated with a certain task is not only a function of subjective difficulty (i.e., $1-P_s$) of the task, but it is also a function of the difference between subjective difficulty and that point on the scale where the personal standard is located. The more the difficulty of a task exceeds the difficulty criterion for self-evaluation (personal standard), the greater will be the incentive of succeeding at that task. Consequently incentive of success is defined as the difference between perceived difficulty ($1 - P_s$) and the departure of the personal standard (S) from the point of intermediate difficulty ($.5 - S$). Making a similar assumption for the negative incentive of failure, the elaborated model predicts—for success-oriented subjects—a shift of maximum preference towards difficult tasks when the standard is difficult (S < .5) and a shift towards easy tasks when the standard is easy (S > .5); for failure-oriented subjects, the model predicts an inverse relationship between difficulty of standard and preferred difficulty. Empirical results are in line with these predictions (Kuhl, 1978b). The supporting evidence for failure-oriented subjects is especially interesting. The nonobvious implication of the model predicting that failure-oriented subjects having difficult standards prefer easy tasks and vice versa suggests a maladaptive mechanism that explains the quick stabilizing of failure-motivation once it has been aroused for a while. By choosing easy tasks, failure-oriented subjects having difficult standards rarely give themselves a chance to meet their standards, whereas failure-oriented subjects having easy standards rarely experience success because of their preference for difficult tasks.

Reformulations of The Original Theory

Several theoretical developments reformulated the parameters of the original model rather than generalizing them by adding new determinants.

Attribution Theory. The most influential reformulation has been the application of attribution theory to the theory of achievement motivation (Weiner et al., 1971). According to this approach, the motive to achieve success is no longer defined as a disposition to experience pride when succeeding at a task; instead, that motive is related to a pattern of attribution that involves attributing success to internal causes (i.e., own ability and effort) and failure to internal and variable causes (i.e., effort). Further the reformulated theory proposed by Weiner and his associates relates fear of failure to a pattern of attribution that involves attributing success to external causes and failure to an internal and stable cause (i.e., lack of ability). Perceived locus of control is considered to be the critical determinant of affective parameters (incentive), whereas stability of perceived causes is assumed to affect the stability of expectancy parameters. Though it is possible to integrate attributional parameters within the formal model of achievement motivation (Feather, 1967), Weiner and coworkers decided to part with the original model by conceiving of the achievement motive as a personality variable that is associated with distinctive patterns of attribution rather than as a variable that affects the degree to which a person seeks pride in accomplishment. This reformulation of the original theory *reduces* achievement related incentives to attributional activity rather than regarding attribution as one among several moderators of incentive parameters.

Because attributional parameters are considered cognitive mediators of expectancy and value parameters, attribution theory is perfectly compatible with an expectancy-value framework. An integration of the extensive work done on attributional mediators of achievement motivation within an expectancy-value theory of motivation would require explicit statement of the relationship between measurable attributional antecedents and incentive or expectancy parameters. This goal cannot be achieved, however, until some fundamental problems of measurement are solved. So far, the dimensional status of attributional factors is unclear (e.g., Kruglanski, 1975; Abramson, Seligman & Teasdale, 1978). Ability, for instance, need not be perceived as a stable factor (Weiner et al., 1971), it may as well be considered a factor that may be changed as a result of learning. Similarly, effort may be perceived as either stable (industriousness vs. laziness) or variable. These and similar examples suggest that the measurement of attributional factors does not yet meet the requirement of specific objectivity. Empirical results based on an application of Rasch's measurement model are in line with this hypothesis (Kuhl, 1977). A possible solution to the problem of obtaining interindividually comparable measurements of attributional parameters may be reached by asking subjects to assess the dimensional properties of perceived causes directly rather than merely labeling the causes themselves.

Self-concepts of Ability.   Another reformulation of the original theory was a direct result of research on attributional mediators. The findings that success-oriented subjects tend to explain success by internal causes, whereas failure-oriented subjects tend to attribute failure to lack of ability suggest a difference between both motive types with regard to the personal concept of own ability. Accordingly, Meyer (1973b) and Kukla (1972) developed two similar, though independently formulated models of achievement motivation based on concepts of personal ability. In these models, the achievement motive was equated with the self-concepts of own ability, which should be high in success-oriented subjects but low in failure-oriented subjects. Kukla (1972), who developed a formal model of effort expenditure on the basis of an expectancy-value approach, assumes a need to expend the minimum amount of effort that is necessary and sufficient for attaining success. Accordingly, intended effort is considered a positive function of subjective difficulty up to a point of difficulty beyond which intended effort drops to zero because even maximum effort is not perceived as sufficient for having success.

Failure-oriented subjects should reach this point at easier tasks than success-oriented subjects because of the less favorable ability concept of the former group. Although the implication regarding "least necessary effort expenditure" received some empirical support from self-report data in predominantly fictitious situations (Meyer, 1973a; Meyer & Hallermann, 1974), recent results based on an objective measure of expended effort are not consistent with the model (Krug, Hage & Hieber, 1978).

Moreover, the identification of ability concepts and achievement motive has been criticized on logical and theoretical grounds (Heckhausen, 1977, p. 315). As elaborations rather than reformulations of the theory of achievement motivation, Kukla's and Meyer's models may be useful, however. Concepts of own ability can easily be integrated within the model as determinants of expectancy parameters. The assumption of "least necessary effort" may be a useful extension when the original expectancy-value theory is to be applied to explaining the intensity rather than the selectivity aspect of motivation. So far, the original model has been applied to both purposes (Atkinson, 1974). Choice between intensity levels at a given difficulty level may be—at least in some situations—governed by different laws than choice between difficulty levels. Future research would have to specify situational and personal parameters that tell us which model to apply in a given contact of a person with a situation. Further, it should be noted that Kukla's model is a pure expectancy model. Effort expenditure is not considered a function of an individual value parameter. It has been expected and found, however, that in situations where Kukla's model holds, intended effort is also a positive function of perceived incentive of success (Kuhl, 1977).

Optimal Stimulation.   A third reformulation of the original model has recently been proposed by Nygård (1977). According to this approach, the inverted U-shaped curve describing motivational tendency as a function of P_s is interpreted on the basis of an *optimal stimulation* hypothesis (Hebb, 1955; Berlyne, 1960) rather than by using the original logic of the theory. Maximum preference for intermediate difficult tasks in success-oriented subjects is attributed to optimal stimulation in this motive group rather than to a compromise between desirability (I_s) and (inversely related) attainability (P_s) of success. The curve does not drop to zero because of low attainability or low desirability of success at the extremes of the difficulty scale, but approaches negative values as a result of assumed understimulation at very easy or very difficult tasks (Fig. 5.2). Con-

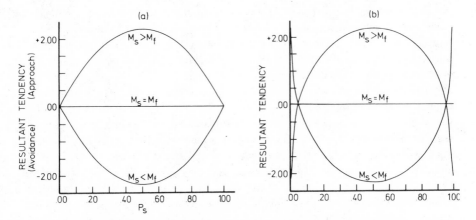

FIG. 5.2.   Theoretically expected resultant tendency as a function of subjective probability of success (P_s) for success-oriented ($M_s > M_f$) and failure-oriented ($M_s > M_f$) subjects according to Nygaard's optimal-stimulation hypothesis (after Nygaard, 1977).

versely, the maximum of avoidance at intermediate difficult tasks in failure-oriented subjects is interpreted in terms of overstimulation rather than maximum avoidance of realistic goals. Failure-oriented subjects are assumed to have high positive (rather than zero) motivation at the extreme ends of the difficulty scale as a result of optimal stimulation. This theory is better able than the original model to explain persistence data, suggesting greater persistence of failure-oriented than of success-oriented subjects at very easy or very difficult tasks (e.g., Weiner, 1965; Feather, 1961, 1963). Also, the revised model is consistent with the finding that failure-oriented subjects perform better at very easy tasks than success-oriented subjects (e.g., Heckhausen, 1963). Though the cited results may be explained differently (Feather, 1961, 1963; Kuhl & Blankenship, 1979b), Nygård's reformulation calls attention to a neglected component of achievement motivation.

The formal representation of the optimal-stimulation hypothesis may be improved, however. The function describing the reformulated model is based on a curve-fitting procedure rather than a theoretically derived equation containing theoretically meaningful parameters. An equation of this kind would have to specify the relationship between P_s, motive type, and degree of stimulation as well as the relationship between degree of stimulation and incentive. Nygård's theory implicitly assumes an inverted U-shaped relationship between degree of stimulation and P_s which starts and ends at a low (under-stimulating) level of arousal for success-oriented subjects and with a moderate (optimally stimulating) level of arousal for failure-oriented subjects. Though Nygård explicitly adheres to the original definition of the achievement motive as a capacity to take pride in accomplishment (Atkinson, 1964), he implicitly redefines the motive in terms of amount of (achievement-related) stimulation needed to reach the optimal level of stimulation. This definition is almost identical with Eysenck's construct of introversion vs. extraversion (Eysenck, 1967). It may be wiser to use the optimal-stimulation hypothesis for elaborating or extending the original model rather than replacing it by a theory that reduces achievement motivation to the striving for optimal arousal. Atkinson (1974) has proposed such an attempt to extend the original model with regard to degree of stimulation in order to explain its effect on efficiency of performance. This extension of the theory of achievement-motivation differs from Nygård's reformulation, however, in assuming that over-stimulation, in the sense of a very strong resultant tendency beyond some optimal level for efficient performance may also occur among success-oriented subjects, e.g., when their motivational tendency is intensified by several "extrinsic" sources of motivation. Failure-oriented subjects are not—as in Nygård's model—always optimally stimulated or overstimulated, but may also be under-stimulated in the sense that tendencies not to act may be very strong, e.g., when positive incentives are negligibly small and negative incentives are large.

Nygård's theory resembles Atkinson's theory as well as many other expectancy-value theories in assuming that incentive and expectancy are closely related rather than orthogonal determinants of motivation. Introducing additional determinants of incentive rather than reducing incentive to a "new" factor would help uncouple expectancy and value parameters. Such a liberalization of theory may be useful especially in future investigations of neglected extrinsic determinants of achievement motivation (Heckhausen, 1977) and, even more so, in studies concerned with thematic contents other than achievement (altruism, affiliation, power, etc.). Uncoupling expectancy and value parameters may be achieved by introducing stimulation-derived pleasure as an additional goal to the already existing number of achievement-related goals (e.g., demonstrating one's own ability; exceeding other people's performance; improving one's performance etc.). This approach may include an independent expectancy parameter describing the perceived probability of attaining the desired level of stimulation as well as a dispositional parameter describing the extent to which a person is interested in attaining optimal stimulation.

The Dynamic Theory of Action. The three reformulations of the original theory described earlier reinterpret achievement motivation in terms of assumed *antecedents* of the parameters of the original model. The last reformulation to be discussed in this chapter is based on a revised conception of the *effects* of the original parameters of motivation. In their dynamic theory of action, Atkinson & Birch (1970, 1974, 1978) redefine the original parameters as determinants of arousability rather than as determinants of absolute strength of motivational tendency. The product of motive, incentive and expectancy determines the rate of increase of a tendency described by the slope rather than the height of the curve that relates strength of motivation to time. This reformulation seemed necessary when the traditional theory of motivation was extended to explain temporal aspects of motivation which had been neglected earlier. Traditional expectancy-value theory has been called *episodic* because it describes motivational tendencies within a limited temporal episode. In *The Dynamics of Action* (Atkinson & Birch, 1970), a mathematical theory is formulated which overcomes this limitation. The new task for motivation theory is the explanation of the *stream of behavior,* i.e., the duration and frequency of diverse activities undertaken during an extended period of time.

The increase of motivational tendencies per time unit is described in terms of an *instigating force,* whereas a decrease is attributed to a *consummatory force.* Consummatory forces are operative when the respective tendency is dominant and—as a result—being expressed in behavior. The theory contains additional parameters controlling the onset and offset of consumption, selective attention to instigating stimuli as well as displacement, substitution and compatibility relations among tendencies. Tendencies directed toward *not* performing an activity (negaction tendencies) are aroused by *inhibitory forces* and "consummated" by *forces of resistance.* The theory has been programmed in order to permit computer simulations of theoretical predictions for complex situations (Bongort, 1975).

A series of computer simulations of a typical risk-taking experiment yielded predictions that run counter to predictions derived from the episodic risk-taking model (Kuhl & Blankenship, 1979b). The latter attributes shifts in risk preference to respective changes of expectancy parameters. When subjects perceive improvement at a task, P_s increases at all difficulty levels, and as a result the preferred level of intermediate difficulty moves toward the more difficult end of the scale. When expectancy of success has stabilized following an extended practice period, no shifts in risk-preference are expected. The dynamic reformulation predicts a shift to more and more difficult tasks also when P_s has stabilized because consummation is expected to be larger with easy than with difficult tasks. This is implied because of the higher frequency of success at easier tasks. This prediction rests on the assumptions (1) that the consummatory value of success is greater than that of failure, and (2) that consummatory value is a constant or a positive function of perceived facility of the task. Empirical results are consistent with the predictions: Subjects moved to more and more difficult tasks even when P_s had stabilized (Kuhl & Blankenship, 1979a). Though this effect should be limited to situations where the assumptions described earlier are valid, the cited study demonstrates one instance where the dynamic theory has shown to be superior to episodic formulations.

The shift to more difficult tasks in spite of stabilized P_s may, of course, be explained differently. One alternative explanation attributes that shift to an a priori strategy to move from easier to harder tasks rather than attributing it to motivational effects of success and failure experiences encountered when working on the tasks (Heckhausen, Schneider & Schmalt, in press). It should be noted, however, that those two explanations are not incompatible. On the contrary, a priori strategies and experience-based effects stressed by Kuhl and Blankenship's application of the dynamic reformulation may interact in that a strategy can only be effective when it is accompanied by the expected frequencies of success and failure experiences. A subject who initially plans to start with a certain level of difficulty and intends to proceed to successively more difficult tasks should maintain that strategy only after he or she has experienced success more often on the easier tasks than on the harder tasks. An interpretation of Kuhl and Blankenship's results which is based exclusively on the strategy-hypothesis is difficult to maintain because it would have to explain additional findings predicted by the dynamic theory, viz., a quicker shift to harder tasks in success-oriented compared with failure-oriented subjects and absence of that shift in a forced choice situation. The strategy-hypothesis may be coordinated with the dynamic model, however, by describing the strategy in terms of a pattern of dynamic parameters. An a priori strategy to move to more and more difficult tasks can be described, for instance, by a matrix of *conditional instigating forces* (CIF) which defines shifts in instigating force for the various difficulty levels (columns of the CIF-matrix) as a function of the number of successes required at each difficulty level (rows of the CIF-matrix) before switching to more difficult tasks. The most recent computer program simulating Atkinson and Birch's dynamic theory has an option to accomodate conditional forces defined on an a priori basis. Not only can the "cognitive" stragegy-hypothesis be coordinated to dynamic parameters, but the dynamic parameters describing the effects of success and failure experiences may also be coordinated with cognitive mediators. Increasing average consummatory value with increasing frequency of success may be coordinated, for instance, with increasing confidence in having mastered a certain difficulty level. This confidence may be the cognitive mediator of consummatory value. It seems more fruitful to search for coordinating definitions relating dynamic parameters to possible cognitive antecedents, than to construct a pseudo-incompatibility between cognitive and dynamic parameters (cf. Kuhl & Blankenship, 1979a).

An Integrative Theory of Motivation

Heckhausen (1977) formulated a cognitive model of motivation, which integrates most of the concepts proposed in the revised models discussed earlier. Though this integrative theory is not limited to achievement motivation, it contains specific assumptions for this thematic area. First, several motivational concepts are distinguished which are considered necessary to analyze the interaction of a person and a situation, i.e., the situation itself (S), the action (A), the outcome (O), and the consequences (C) of that outcome.

The first determinant of the motivational tendency supporting a certain action is the *valence* of an outcome (V_o). V_o is defined as "a monotonically increasing function of the algebraic sum of all products of incentive values and their corresponding instrumentalities" (p. 289). The latter are described in terms of *outcome-consequence* expectancies (E_{oc}) ranging from -1 (when an outcome is perceived as preventing the occurrence of a consequence 100% of the time) and $+1$ (an outcome is perceived as being associated with a consequence all the time):

$$V_o = f \sum_{j=1}^{n} (I_j \times E_{ocj}),$$

where n denotes the number of perceived consequences of an outcome. This part of the theory is closely related to Vroom's (1964) theory of job motivation. It incorporates Raynor's elaborations concerning instrumentality of immediate success for future goals, though Heckhausen's model is less restrictive than Raynor's: It is not limited to achievement-related outcomes nor does it project all consequences on a future time scale by emphasizing contingencies between the various consequences. In Heckhausen's model, the n consequences of an outcome may or may not be interdependent.

The second determinant of motivational tendency is the *Resultant Action-Outcome-Expectancy* ($E_{\overline{ao}}$) which is a generalization of the concept of subjective probability used in Atkinson's model. $E_{\overline{ao}}$ is defined as the sum of the expectancy that an action leads to a certain outcome (E_{ao}) and the *Action-by-Situation-Outcome Expectancy* (E_{aso}) which describes positive or negative shifts in an *action-outcome-expectancy* that are expected as a result of the interaction between a person's action and the situation (e.g., when the action is expected to elicit social support or fatigue). The valence of an action (V_a) is defined as the product of outcome valence and $E_{\overline{ao}}$:

$$V_a = V_o \times E_{\overline{ao}}.$$

Similarly, the *Situation Valence* (V_s) is expressed in terms of the product between outcome valence and a third expectancy parameter, namely *Situation-Outcome-Expectancy* (E_{so}), which describes the expectancy that the situation promises an outcome without personal intervention:

$$V_s = V_o' \times E_{so}$$

V_o is written as V_o' here to take account of the fact that it represents a restricted class of consequences because consequences related to self- and other-evaluation are related to an action only, which is not part of a situation valence. The action tendency (T) to strive for the outcome (o) is defined now by the difference between action valence and situation valence:

$$T = (V_o \times E_{\overline{ao}}) - (V_o' \times E_{so})$$

The inverse relationship between an action tendency and situation valence (i.e., $V_o' \times E_{so}$) assumed in this model introduces a principle of parsimony to motivation theory, which reminds one of the assumption of ''least necessary effort'' in Kukla's model of effort calculation (1972). To the extent that a person believes that desired outcomes may be obtained without his or her action, the action tendency is dampened or even inhibited.

With regard to achievement-related tendencies, Heckhausen formulates a number of coordinating definitions. Internal causal attribution is assumed to be expressed in the action-outcome expectancy (E_{ao}), whereas external attribution is thought to be represented by action-by-situation-outcome expectancies (E_{aso}). Internal attribution of success is considered the determinant of two consequences that are especially relevant in achievement-related settings, viz., self-evaluation and other-evaluation of one's outcomes. An inverted U-shaped function peaking at E_{ao} ($= P_s$) $= .5$ is assumed to describe the relationship between subjective difficulty and perceived instrumentality (E_{oc}) of success for positive self-evaluation and other-evaluation. Further, the relationship between incentive of success and P_s ($=E_{ao}$) is considered a power function rather than a linear function ($I_s = (1 - E_{ao})^2$). As can be seen from fig. 5.3, this bundle of assumptions results in a preference function which peaks at moderately difficult tasks ($E_{ao} = .30$). In addition, individual motive parameters are discussed in terms of weighting factors for V_o of success (V_{o+}) and V_o of failure (V_{o-}). The more heavily V_{o-} is weighted compared to V_{o+}, the more the peak of the function shifts towards

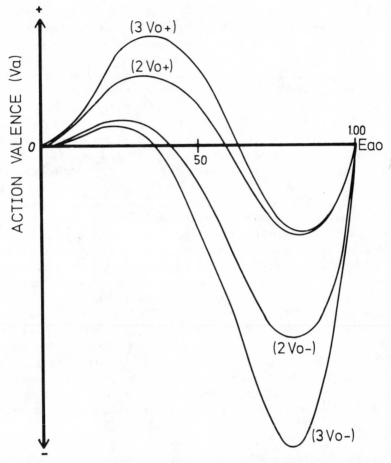

FIG. 5.3.   Action valences as a function of probability of success (Eao) when incentive values for success are wheighted twice or three times as heavily as those for failure (2Vo+; 3Vo+) or, vice versa, when incentive values for failure are weighted twice or three times as heavily as those for success (2Vo−; 3Vo−) (after Heckhausen, 1977).

extremely difficult tasks. A further coordinating definition states that *avoidance* of self-diagnostic information should be reflected in negative instrumentality of internal attribution which reverses those preference functions (Fig. 5.3) into their mirror images.

Though Heckhausen's model loses some of the beauty of simplicity when extended by a considerable number of coordinating definitions that can hardly be tested directly (for reasons to be discussed later), it does make testable predictions as to expected risk preference in various situations. Success-oriented subjects weighting V_{o+} more heavily than V_{o-} should prefer moderately difficult tasks, whereas failure-oriented subjects weighting V_{o-} more heavily than V_{o+} should prefer very difficult tasks unless they are motivated to *avoid* self-diagnostic information. In the latter case the preference function is expected to be the mirror image of the lowest one in fig. 5.3 resulting in predicted preference for very easy tasks. As mentioned earlier, Heckhausen was able to accommodate a great number of risk-taking studies by making some additional assumptions concerning the motivational effects of the situations created in those studies (Heckhausen, 1977). Because of the great number of assumptions made, the predictive power of the model is limited, however, because negative findings are equivocal as to what assumptions would be violated in a given context. This argument does not question the explicative and heuristic value of the model, however. The model is unique in integrating expectancy-value theory with such diverse theoretical developments as instrumentality theory, attribution theory, and the principle of parsimony as exemplified in Kukla's and Meyer's theories of effort calculation. Other theoretical developments could easily be incorporated within the model. The theory of personal standards (Kuhl, 1978b) could be used to define an additional determinant of incentive of success. Optimal stimulation theory (Nygård, 1977) may be discussed in terms of one particular class of consequences intended in achievement-related settings. Also, the episodic nature of Heckhausen's cognitive model may be remedied by coordinating the model to dynamic parameters which would yield a powerful and comprehensive theory of motivation. A coordination of a cognitive model and dynamic theory extends the scope of traditional expectancy-value theories to the ecologically more valid "stream of behavior" and improves the predictive power of dynamic theory by coordinating dynamic parameters with measurable cognitive antecedents (Kuhl, in prep.).

Empirical Evidence. Predictions derived from Heckhausen's model for a specific experimental setting were recently tested empirically (Kleinbeck & Schmidt, 1979). Apprentices from a German automobile plant were given a choice among 11 difficulty levels of a task requiring the modeling of a piece of metal. Ratings regarding probability of success at each difficulty level and instrumentality of immediate success for future success at the final exam were obtained. Subjects were subdivided into a success-oriented and a failure-oriented group, according to a self-report measure (Mehrabian, 1968). Within each motive group, subjects were further subdivided into a "low-instrumentality" and a "high-instrumentality" group, according to their respective ratings. Coordinating definitions were made in order to derive predictions from Heckhausen's model:

(1) The incentive of consequence 1 (getting closer to the ultimate goal of successfully finishing one's apprenticeship) was set at twice the amount of consequence 2 (testing one's own ability); (2) for the low-instrumentality group E_{oc}

was set equal to .20 compared to $E_{oc} = .80$ for the high instrumentality group; (3) for success-oriented subjects, the incentive of success for self-evaluation (consequence 2) was set at twice the amount of the respective incentive of failure, while failure-orientation was described by the reverse weighting procedure, plus a *negative* instrumentality of failure for their achievement-goal (i.e., avoiding negative self-evaluation).

On the basis of these assumptions, the model predicts (1) preference for intermediate difficult tasks by success-oriented, low-instrumentality subjects; (2) preference for easy tasks by failure-oriented, low instrumentality subjects, and (3) preference for easy tasks by both success-oriented and failure-oriented subjects from the high-instrumentality group. The second prediction is in contrast to Raynor's model, which predicts preference of the most difficult tasks by failure-oriented subjects in a contingent path. The results are perfectly consistent with the predictions derived from Heckhausen's model (Fig. 5.4).

Extension of Expectancy-Value Theory

All elaborations and reformulations of expectancy-value theory discussed so far, share the underlying assumptions regarding a two-dimensional theory of motivation: All determinants of motivational tendencies are assumed to be reflected in either a parameter of expectancy or a parameter of value. The necessary amount

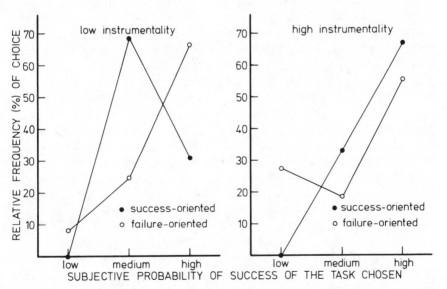

FIG. 5.4. Relative frequency of choice as a function of subjective probability of success, perceived instrumentality of success, and motive type (after Kleinbeck & Schmidt, 1979).

of expectancy of success along with the necessary amount of value is considered sufficient for resulting in a respective action. Motivational deficits are attributed to respective deficits regarding expectancy or value of the goal. This reasoning is also applied within the theory of learned helplessness, which explains debilitated performance at a test task following exposure to (objectively) uncontrollable outcomes at a training task on the basis of respective expectational deficits: People perform worse following exposure to uncontrollable events because they have developed a belief in uncontrollability resulting in low expectancy of success, which is generalized from the training task to the test task (Seligman, 1975; Maier & Seligman, 1976; Abramson, Seligman & Teasdale, 1978).

Recent experiments on learned helplessness (Kuhl, 1981) cast doubt on this interpretation of the results. Results from an earlier study (Kuhl, 1977) had shown that parameters of expectancy may be very task-specific. This finding suggests that subjects may not always generalize decreased expectancy of success at a seemingly too difficult training task to a test task, which in many experiments on learned helplessness differs considerably from the training task (Hiroto, 1974; Hiroto & Seligman, 1975; Klein & Seligman, 1976).

In two experiments (Kuhl, 1981) subjects rated expectancy of success and subjective controllability of success regarding training and test tasks both prior to and following helplessness training. The results are in contrast to the generalization hypothesis: Though expectancy and controllability ratings regarding the training task dropped significantly following exposure to uncontrollable outcomes, there was no respective drop regarding the test task. In spite of unaffected expectancy and controllability concerning the test task, however, subjects from some groups performed worse than control subjects at that task if the former had been exposed to repeated failure at the training task. Though these results are in contrast to helplessness theory, they may still be compatible with expectancy-value theory, if debilitated performance were associated with decreased value of performing well. Rated personal value of good performance was significantly greater or equal, however, in debilitated-performance groups compared to control groups. This finding, which was anticipated by a three-dimensional theory of "functional and motivational helplessness" (Kuhl, 1981), suggests a third dimension as an additional determinant of behavior.

Clues are available as to what type of determinant can account for debilitated performance following repeated failure in spite of a sufficiently high expectancy and value of success. In the study analyzing the dimensional status of a TAT-measure of fear-failure on the basis of Rasch's measurement model (Kuhl, 1978a), two distinct ways of dealing with failure became apparent: *action-oriented* behavior, i.e., focusing on action-alternatives that may help overcome failure and/or its cognitive consequences versus *state-oriented* behavior, i.e., focusing on the state of failure and its cognitive consequences. Heckhausen (1980) found an excessive amount of self-related state-cognitions in failure-oriented subjects that seemed to have interfered with proper cognitive functioning during an oral examination. Diener and Dweck (1978) found excessive state-related thinking in "helpless" children, whose performance was impaired following failure feed-back. These results suggest that action- vs. state-orientation represents an additional determinant of action.

This assumption was corroborated by the results in the helplessness-study referred to earlier (Kuhl, 1981). Performance decrements on the test task following failure on the training task were found only when subjects could be assumed to have been state-oriented either on the basis of a respective disposition assessed by a questionnaire or on the basis of experimental induction (asking subjects to respond to state-related questions following helplessness training). It is important to note that those performance deficits cannot be attributed to respective expectancy-related or value-related deficits. The results are consistent with an extension of expectancy-value theory which is based on the following assumption: Whether or not, a dominant motivational tendency (or an intention) that is supported by respective expectancy- and value-related cognitions will actually be executed and result in the performance of the *relevant* actions depends on an additional factor. This factor is assumed to have an attentional basis. The probability that an intended action is performed is assumed to increase with an increasing proportion of attention focused on action-related rather than state-related cues.

The occurrence of task-irrelevant cognitions in some subjects may be attributed to an inability to control the execution of activities intended to solve the task. In the study cited earlier (Kuhl, 1981), expectancy and incentive of success were apparently normal in those subjects that showed poor performance. Consequently, this performance deficit seems attributable to some disorder in a process that intervenes between motivation and performance rather than to a motivational deficit.

The dimension of action- vs. state-orientation may be relevant for performance behavior and free choice behavior rather than for forced preferential behavior. It is typical of preferential behavior that the person is assumed to actually make a choice. In a risk-taking experiment, subjects are not free to decide whether they want to choose any task at all. Thus observed risk-preference may be a choice of the least of several evils. When subjects are asked to work on a task, the experimenter does not have much control regarding the extent to which a subject actually performs the activities that are necessary for optimal performance. In this case, the degree to which a subject is "active" in the sense that his or her attention is focused on action-alternatives rather than his or her own state may gain central importance.

In this respect, action- vs. state-orientation may be considered a dynamic parameter explaining the energizing rather than the selective aspect of motivation. In typical experiments on human motivation, the situation is set up in a way to guarantee that virtually all subjects are "energized" to engage in some action. Subjects are not allowed to be "passive". Consequently, motivation theory tends to disregard the problem of passivity or even maintains that an organism is always "active" (Atkinson & Birch, 1970). Though this assumption seems reasonable in some sense—e.g., in a physiological sense—it deprives the pair of concepts of "activeness vs. passivity" of any meaning within motivation theory. It is proposed here that motivation theory should maintain the distinction between activeness and passivity by defining those concepts appropriately. One suggestion would be to define passivity within a theory of action by state-related activities. A person is *passive* when he or she is engaging in state-related thoughts, i.e., when he or she is preoccupied with activities that are not intended to transform a present state into a desired future state (e.g., thinking about possible reasons of outcomes or focusing on one's own emotional state without explicitly intending this kind of activity for accomplishing some future goal). In this sense, a person is not performing any action when he or she is engaging in state-related activities. This suggestion is consistent with current definitions of the concept of *action* (Schmalt, in press).

The dynamic nature of parameters describing action- vs. state-orientation becomes apparent by noting the similarity between possible antecedents of a change from state-orientation to action-orientation and the parameters that had to be introduced to the dynamic theory of action to account for a change from one activity to another. When constructing their dynamic theory of action, Atkinson and Birch (1970) faced the dilemma of *behavioral chatter:* On the basis of the assumption that an action tendency is consummated (reduced) while being expressed in behavior, but not so while being *dormant,* behavioral chatter is expected, i.e., quick oscillation between an activity and a new one that is about equal in strength: As soon as an action tendency supersedes a tendency that had been dominant for a while, the former drops immediately below the strength of the latter as a result of the onset of consummation. To overcome this theoretical problem, parameters had to be added, namely selective attention to action-related stimuli supporting the new activity, and *consummatory lags* (e.g., postponing the onset of consummation when a tendency has just become dominant). If it is assumed that consummation (i.e., reduction of an action tendency) is mediated by state-cognitions (e.g., comparing results with a standard), the similarity between action-orientation and delay of consummation becomes evident (Kuhl, in prep.).

The helplessness experiments referred to earlier demonstrated the effect of state- vs. action-orientation following exposure to uncontrollable outcomes. The effect of that parameter following success or during the phase of planning and executing an action (i.e., before an outcome has occurred) remains to be demonstrated. Recent empirical findings showed that correlations between reported strength of the intention to perform an activity and proportion of time actually spent in that activity were considerably greater in action-oriented than in state-oriented subjects. Further research suggested that action-oriented subjects accomplish that closer correspondence between their intentions and their actions by (1) focusing attention on facilitating action-related information rather than on debilitating task-irrelevant information, (2) minimizing the intensity of inhibiting emotional states following aversive events, and (3) minimizing the amount of information processed before making a decision. Although the last point is illustrated later in this chapter, a more detailed discussion of the experiments regarding some cognitive mediators of action control may be found elsewhere (Kuhl, in press). It may be concluded from those results that expectancy-value theory needs to be extended by parameters of action control to account for the relationship between motivation and performance. Until now expectancy-value theory has been used to predict both motivation and performance making the unrealistic assumption that people always do what they intend to do.

CRITIQUE OF EXPECTANCY-VALUE THEORY

The theoretical approaches discussed so far use expectancy-value theory as a basis rather than as a target of theory development and empirical research. The remainder of this chapter is devoted to the problem concerning the validity of the basic postulates underlying expectancy-value theory. Atkinson's risk taking model is typical of current expectancy-value models in regard to its deterministic nature and in regard to its universalistic validity claim. Do all people combine expectancy and value information in a multiplicative way when deciding about performing or not performing an action? Attempts to test this assumption have yielded equivocal results. Comparing correlations between theoretically expected motivation and observed indices of motivation (e.g., Hackman & Porter, 1968; Lawler & Porter, 1967) does not solve the problem because it is not possible to distinguish, for instance, between an additive and a multiplicative model unless parameters of expectancy, value, and motivation can be measured on an interval scale (Schmidt, 1973). Though methods for constructing interval scales at the manifest data level have been proposed (Thurstone & Jones, 1957), there is no consensus about any method that would guarantee interval scale measurement at the level of latent parameters. Initial enthusiasm concerning latent trait models (like Rasch's measurement model: Fischer, 1974) has been replaced by a more critical attitude (Wottawa, 1979): Interval scale measurement can only be expected by latent trait models when several assumptions are made that cannot be tested directly. It is safer, then, if not more realistic to look for methods of testing basic postulates of expectancy-value theory that do not require interval scale measurement.

A recent attempt to test Expectancy × Value theory (Lynch & Cohen, 1978) without justifying the assumed interval status of measurement is inconclusive. The fact that Lynch and Cohen's data almost perfectly fit into an expectancy × value model may be an artefact of the experimental situation. As subjects responded hypothetically to hypothetical situations, it seems plausible that stereotypes about "rational" behavior rather than determinants of actual behavior in ecologically representative situations guided action.

This study is an example of another drawback in prevailing methods for testing expectancy-value models. On the basis of the logic underlying traditional regression statistics, the validity of a model is tested across individuals only. Data from different individuals have to be pooled in order to estimate "error" variance. This aspect of traditional data analysis is not in conflict with psychological theory as long as the theory claims universal validity. Because data averaged across individuals may even be compatible with a model that does not hold for a single person, it would be safer to test models on an individual basis.

There is a very simple alternative to traditional methods for testing expectancy-value models. This alternative method requires; (1) formulation of logical statements describing the models to be tested and (2) counting how often those logical statements are true for a given person across various situations or for a given situation across individuals. An example of such a model would be: "If a person assumes that he is able to reach a goal (sufficient expectancy) by engaging in an available action alternative *and* he wants to reach it (sufficient value), he will perform that action". A different—disjunctive rather than conjunctive—model may combine expectancy and value by a logical "or—relation". Simpler models may be formulated, e.g., a pure expectancy model that considers expectancy as sufficient for an intention to act, or a pure value model that considers sufficient value as the only requirement for an intention to act.

This method, which may be called *logical statement analysis* (LSA) was employed in a recent study (Kuhl, 1977). In order to assess expectancy of success, subjects were asked to check all tasks from a series of twenty "perceptual reasoning" tasks, that they expected to be able to solve under a maximum effort condition. Subsequently, subjects checked those tasks at which they felt satisfied following success. Finally, subjects checked all tasks at which they intended to exert "as much effort as necessary for solving the task". On the basis of these responses the validity of the four models described earlier may be evaluated by counting the number of hits and misses of each model, for a given individual across the 20 tasks. In this particular study, this index was not used, however. Instead, the models were formulated in a stochastic way by assuming that the probability of an expectancy or value response is a function of (1) a respective latent person parameter (i.e., ability concept or personal value) and (2) a respective latent task parameter (i.e., difficulty or incentive). It could be shown that Rasch's stochastic measurement model mentioned earlier was compatible with the data. Therefore, Rasch's logistic function relating probability of response to assumed latent determinants was used to estimate the theoretical probability of an expectancy or value response for a given person at a given task on the basis of the respective person and task parameters. These parameters had been estimated in advance on the basis of appropriate self-report tests. By simulating the contact of each person and each task 1000 times, a theoretical distribution of predicted effort scores (number of tasks at which necessary effort was intended) could be generated. A person's behavior was considered compatible with a given model if his actual effort score lay between the 95%-confidence limits of the theoretical distribution of effort scores generated on the basis of that person's expectancy and value parameters and the particular model to be tested. Table 5.1 shows the results of these tests.

The fact that the sum of the numbers reported in Table 5.1 is greater than the number of subjects (N = 105) indicates that some subjects' responses were compatible with more than one model. This may be due to the broad confidence limits employed in this study. In spite of this overlap, 21 subjects could be identified, for instance, whose responses were compatible with a pure value model only, whereas the scores of 31 subjects were compatible only with a pure expectancy model. It must be concluded from these results that the implicit universalistic claim of expectancy × value theory is unwarranted. Different people may behave according to different models. Traditional statistical methods averaging across people have been blind regarding this fact. The results from a correlational analysis of the data (Table 5.1) illustrate this point: correlations between predicted and observed effort scores are significant, but rather low and do not distinguish between the models. This is what should be expected if different people behave according to different models (Bem & Allen, 1974).

If we have to assume different models for different people, the question arises how it can be anticipated according to which model a person behaves. The cited study also yielded some results regarding this problem. Failure-oriented subjects, for instance, behaved significantly more often according to a pure expectancy model than subjects low in fear of failure. This is consistent with results which suggest that performance of anxious people primarily depends on perceived difficulty of the task (which of course affects expectancy of success): Increased performance was observed in anxious subjects working at easy tasks, whereas deteriorated performance is the common finding when anxious subjects are confronted with difficult tasks (e.g., Weiner, 1965; Feather, 1965; Atkinson, 1958,

TABLE 5.1

Number of Subjects (N) Consistent with Various Models
of Intended Effort and Correlations (r) between Predicted
and Observed Effort Scores (N = 105)

Model:	Expectancy	Value	Exp. × Value	Exp. + Value
n	52	44	28	57
r	.20[+]	.26[+]	.19[+]	.29[+]

[+]Significant at the 5% level

pp. 288–305). It should be noted that the results from this study may be limited to achievement-related behavior and intended rather than actual effort. The failure to find interindividual validity of an expectancy × value model suggests, however, conducting future tests of that model on an individual level rather than on a group level.

The conjunctive logical model mentioned earlier does not test, of course, all implications of a multiplicative (algebraic) model. It was maintained earlier that a test of a multiplicative model may be impossible since no interval scale measurement of expectancy or value parameters may be assumed. Even if that quality of measurement could be accomplished, a test of a multiplicative model may be *less desirable* at the present stage of our knowledge. A conjunctive model represents only one basic postulate underlying a multiplicative model, namely, the assumption that an action is not intended unless both expectancy of success *and* perceived value are greater than zero. This conjunctive relation between P_s and I_s seems to be the main reason for assuming a multiplicative model (Atkinson, 1964). A multiplicative model makes, however, at least one additional assumption that may, in some cases, not even be intended: The effect of a standard increment in one predictor (say increasing P_s from .3 to .4) increases with increasing strength of the other predictor (here: value). For the present, it may be useful to test the conjunctive assumption *separately* from that additional assumption of a multiplicative model. The results reported in Table 5.1 demonstrate that even the less restrictive conjunctive model cannot claim universal validity.

The application of LSA in the study just reported was based on an additional reason. A model consisting of logical statements may be more appropriate to depict the cognitive processes affecting human behavior than traditional algebraic models of motivation. This statement is based on the assumption that people "think" rather than "calculate" before deciding about their course of action. Though an algebraic integration of information concerning expectancy and value may describe behavioral data, it may not describe the mediating cognitive process. A person who wants to decide whether or not to engage in a certain activity may not estimate the probability of succeeding nor its incentive value on a continous scale and compute the algebraic product of the two variables. Instead, he or she may decide in a dichotomous way, whether or not to *expect* success (i.e., reaching the goal) and whether or not he or she *wants* to attain the goal. If both conditions are met the person may decide to perform the activity in question. To the extent that it is the inferential structure of cognitions rather than some sort of algebraic manipulation of continous variables which affects human motivation, the use of algebraic models may have created unnecessary problems. Experimental manipulation and psychometric assessment of subjective probability for instance, has proved to be extremely difficult (Schneider, 1973). Those problems may be simply a result of the fact that subjective probability is not a phenomenologically representative construct. If people are not used to calculating probabilities it *should* be difficult to induce certain probabilities (cf. Feather

& Saville, 1967) or have subjects rate "their" probabilities on a continuous scale. Similarly, if people are not used to calculating the product between probability and value, a multiplicative model of motivation may be less than optimal.

In a recent study (Kuhl & Beckmann, in prep.), logical statement analysis was employed to test various models in a nonachievement related context. During a first phase of the experiment, subjects were asked to choose any number of games from a list of 100 games of dice. These games were the result of crossing ten levels of chance (from 0.01 to .91) with ten levels of prizes (from 10 to 100,000 points). The costs for participating in a game were 100 points for each game. It was expected that at the end of this phase subjects were sufficiently acquainted with chances and prizes of the games such that a consistent strategy for choosing among the games should have been established. In the second phase, subjects made their choices from 25 additional games that resulted from crossing 5 chance-levels with 5 prize-levels.

At the end of the experiment, subjects responded to a questionnaire that was designed to assess prospective state- vs. action-orientation. Typical items from this questionnaire were, for instance:

1. "When I know that something has to be done:
(a) I do it right away" (action-oriented)
(b) I wait until it's really necessary to do it" (state-oriented)
2. "If I stood in front of a movie theatre that played an interesting movie:
(a) I would first think about any alternatives that might be even more interesting" (state-oriented)
(b) I would buy a ticket" (action-oriented)

Choices from the second phase were analyzed as to their compatibility with any of the four logical models described earlier. It was expected that (1) subjects would differ in regard to the model that described individual choice behavior best, (2) action-oriented subjects should use less complex strategies than state-oriented subjects. The latter prediction was based on the assumption that prospective action-orientation may be described by the attempt to initiate an action on the basis of a minimum amount of cognitive evaluation of relevant information. In this particular experiment, value-information may be ignored because the amount to lose was constant in all games and only the lowest prize of winning was lower than the cost of participating. Thus, a parsimonious strategy would be to choose any game unless chances of winning are below a critical point.

Figure 5.5 illustrates the method of analysis. On the left side, the choice matrix of a subject is shown who obviously behaved according to a pure expectancy model, whereas the right side of Fig. 5.6 shows a choice matrix of a person that seemed to have employed a conjunctive expectancy- and-value-rule. In order to compare the goodness of fit of the four models tested for each individual, the

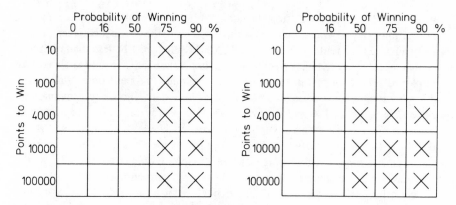

FIG. 5.5. Choice matrix based on the responses of a subject behaving according to an expectancy model (left side) compared to a choice matrix from a subject behaving according to an expectancy-and-value model (right side)(after Kuhl & Beckmann, in prep.)

number of errors encountered was counted for each model and each subject. Table 5.2 shows the results of this analysis.

From the 16 subjects included in this study, 6 had a choice matrix that yielded the best fit to a pure expectancy model ("a game is chosen if probability of winning exceeds the expectancy threshold"). The choice of 10 subjects yielded the best fit to the expectancy-and-value-model. Obviously, these results are not compatible with an expectancy-and-value approach claiming universal validity.

Table 5.2 further illustrates that the hypothesis concerning action- vs. state-orientation seems compatible with the data. All 8 state-oriented subjects based their choices on the more complex conjunctive rule, whereas most action-oriented subjects based their choices on the simpler expectancy rule. Analysis of the number of false predictions derived from either the expectancy or the conjunctive model revealed a considerably greater number of false predictions (38) for the expectancy model than for the conjunctive model (15) when the subject was state-oriented (t (14) = 5.06, p < .0001), and the reverse difference for

TABLE 5.2
Number of Subjects (N) Consistent with Various Models of Choice
Behavior for Action-Oriented and State-Oriented Subjects

Orientation	Pure Expectancy Model	Pure Value Model	Expectancy and Value (Conjunctive Model)	Expectancy or Value (Disjunctive Model)
State	0	0	8	0
Action	6	0	2	0

action-oriented subjects (i.e., 14 false predictions based on the expectancy model and 22 false predictions based on the conjunctive model). The latter difference approaches significance (t (14) $= -1.28$, p $< .10$).

The results provide additional support to the assumption that information about expectancy and value is not sufficient for predicting action. The construct of state- vs. action-orientation seems to convey additional explanatory value not only following helplessness experiences (cf. p. 146), but also prospectively, i.e., during the phase of planning an action when the outcome is still unknown.

LSA differs from traditional methods of data analysis in another way. LSA places more emphasis on the *inductive* part of scientific inquiry, which is always based on some combination of inductive and deductive steps. Traditional methods test hypotheses deduced from a theory by averaging across subjects rather than on an individual basis. Within group variance is attributed to experimental error. This logic may be more appropriate when a science has progressed far enough and error variance is rather small and is due to unsystematic chance factors. When error variance is still considerable and may reflect the effect of yet uncontrolled *systematic* determinants, traditional statistical methods should be accompanied by methods that take account of all information available for each single individual to explain his behavior. Though logical statement analysis starts like traditional methods with some hypotheses that are theoretically deduced, it takes some further steps in testing the validity of those hypotheses for each individual and it may proceed, then, to inductively formulate more general models on the basis of the data from individuals not described by any a priori model. Though these inductive steps had not been taken in the simple game-of-dice study reported earlier, they may be of central interest in more complex situations.

This aspect of LSA was illustrated in a recent study (Kuhl, 1979) in which after-school activities of six graders were to be explained on the basis of the various expectancy and value variables described in Heckhausen's integrative model of motivation. By examining all available information of subjects whose activities could not be explained by any of the a priori models, more complex models could be formulated that increased the number of subjects explained considerably. Successful cross-validation of those *inductively* constructed models supported the generality of the more complex models. The most interesting results from this study suggest that expectancy and value information explains leisure time activities, but not routine or obligatory activities. Examples of the latter type of activities are: Doing homework, brushing one's teeth, helping mother to do the shopping. Those activities are also performed when no personal value is attached to them. They are often *not* performed even though high expectancy of success and high values are associated with them, e.g., children did not learn for school when no explicit assignment was given by the teacher, no matter how they estimated expectancy of success and value (importance, instrumentality) of learning. The performance of an obligatory or routine activity seems to be more a function of the presence or absence of specific controlling stimuli than a function of expectancy and/or value considerations.

Computer programs performing LSA have been developed (Kuhl, 1977; Härtner, Mattes & Wottawa, 1980). A detailed discussion of LSA along with a description of the most elaborated LSA-computer program may be found elsewhere (Härtner et al., in press). In summarizing, the several purposes of LSA may be described as follows: (1) LSA may be an alternative to regression methods when assumptions concerning interval scale measurement, parameters of distribution, or multiplicative integration of parameters can not be made; (2) LSA permits the testing of hypotheses on a more elementary level than conventional algebraic models. (A conjunctive model focuses on one of the several assumptions implied by the corresponding multiplicative model); (3) LSA may yield a better fit between a model and the psychological process to be described (assuming that people ''think'' rather than ''calculate''), and (4) even if those assumptions may be made, LSA may be a useful supplement to traditional methods because it places more emphasis on inductive steps of scientific research. LSA is intended to supplement rather than replace traditional methods because the two methods serve different purposes. Although regression methods of data analysis are useful for an over-all test of theoretically deduced hypotheses, they usually do not take advantage of all information available from the data at hand. LSA may be employed for this latter purpose.

In concluding it may be said that expectancy-value theory has undergone a respectable number of revisions aimed at elaborating or reformulating original statements. The development of the theory of achievement motivation illustrates the problems encountered when original expectancy-value formulations seem to be insufficient. Recent research has focused on variables such as causal attribution of outcomes, instrumentality of an immediate goal for the attainment of future goals, personal standards for self-evaluation, temporal distance of the goal, self-concepts of own ability, tendency toward optimal stimulation, and ''situation-outcome'' expectancy. Some authors have attempted to integrate a neglected variable by generalizing an original model, others have chosen to reduce the constructs contained in an earlier formulation to hitherto neglected variables (i.e., causal attribution, self-concepts, optimal stimulation). In this chapter, it has been suggested that a neglected variable should be introduced by a generalization of old formulations rather than by a reformulation. This strategy may be more useful in a science that is struggling to understand such a complex subject matter as human behavior. The latter consideration was also the basis for a methodological reorientation suggested in this paper. We should not exclusively rely on methods that analyze data by testing the general validity of theoretical deductions only; we may also take advantage of methods that permit a more inductive analysis of our data. Logical-statement analysis has been discussed as an example of a method that permits the generation of hypotheses from individual data rather than from a presumably general theory.

REFERENCES

Abramson, L. Y., Seligman, M. E. P., & Teasdale, J. D. Learned helplessness in humans: Critique and reformulation. *Journal of Abnormal Psychology*, 1978, *87*, 49–74.

Alpert, R., & Haber, R. N. Anxiety in academic achievement situations. *Journal of Abnormal and Social Psychology*, 1960, *61*, 207–215.

Atkinson, J. W. Motivational determinants of risk-taking behavior. *Psychological Review*, 1957, *64*, 359–372.

Atkinson, J. W. *Motives in fantasy, action and society*. Princeton, N.J.: Van Nostrand, 1958.

Atkinson, J. W. *An introduction to motivation*. Princeton, N.J.: Van Nostrand, 1964.

Atkinson, J. W. Strength of motivation and efficiency of performance. In J. W. Atkinson & J. O. Raynor (Eds.), *Motivation and achievement*. Washington, D.C.: Winston, 1974.

Atkinson, J. W., & Birch, D. *The dynamics of action*. New York: Wiley, 1970.

Atkinson, J. W., & Birch, D. The dynamics of achievement-oriented activity. In J. W. Atkinson & J. O. Raynor (Eds.), *Motivation and achievement*. New York: Wiley, 1974.

Atkinson, J. W., & Birch, D. *An introduction to motivation*. Revised Edition. New York: D. Van Nostrand, 1978.

Bem, D. J., & Allen, A. On predicting some of the people some of the time: The search for cross-situational consistencies in behavior. *Psychological Review*, 1974, *81*, 506–520.

Berlyne, D. E. *Conflict, arousal and curiosity*. New York: McGraw-Hill, 1960.

Bongort, K. *Most recent revision of computer program for dynamics of action*. Unpublished program, University of Michigan, 1975.

Diener, C. I., & Dweck, C. S. Analysis of learned helplessness: Continous changes in performance, strategy and achievement cognitions following failure. *Journal of Personality and Social Psychology*, 1978, *36*, 451–462.

Eysenck, H. J. *The biological basis of personality*. Springfield, Ill.: Thomas, 1967.

Feather, N. T. The relationship of persistence at a task to expectation of success and achievement-related motives. *Journal of Abnormal and Social Psychology*, 1961, *63*, 552–561.

Feather, N. T. Persistence at a difficult task with alternative task of intermediate difficulty. *Journal of Abnormal and Social Psychology*, 1963, *66*, 604–609.

Feather, N. T. The relationship of expectations of success to need achievement and test anxiety. *Journal of Personality and Social Psychology*, 1965, *1*, 118–126.

Feather, N. T. Valence of outcome and expectation of success in relation to task difficulty and perceived locus of control. *Journal of Personality and Social Psychology*, 1967, *7*, 372–386.

Feather, N. T., & Saville, M. R. Effects of amount of prior success and failure on expectations of success and subsequent task performance. *Journal of Personality and Social Psychology*, 1967, *5*, 226–232.

Fischer, G. H. *Einführung in die Theorie psychologischer Tests*. Bern: Huber, 1974.

Fischer, G. H., & Scheiblechner, H. Algorithmen und Programme für das probabilistische Testmodell von Rasch. *Psychologische Beiträge*, 1970, *12*, 23–51.

Gewirtz, J. L. Levels of conceptual analysis in environment-infant interaction research. *Merill-Palmer Quarterly*, 1969, *15*, 7–47.

Gjesme, T. Goal distance in time and its effects on the relations between achievement motives and performance. *Journal of Research in Personality*, 1974, *8*, 161–171.

Gjesme, T. *Is there any future in achievement motivation?* Unpublished manuscript. Ruhr University, Bochum, W. Germany, 1979.

Gjesme, T., & Nygård, R. *Achievement-related motives: Theoretical considerations and construction of a measuring instrument*. Unpublished manuscript, University of Oslo, 1970.

Graen, G. Instrumentality theory of work motivation: Some experimental results and suggested modifications. *Journal of Applied Psychology*, 1969, *53* (Whole No. 2, Pt. 2).

Hackman, J. R., & Porter, L. W. Expectancy theory predictions of work effectiveness. *Organizational Behavior and Human Performance*, 1968, *3*, 417–426.

Hamilton, J. O. Motivation and risk-taking behavior. *Journal of Personality and Social Psychology*, 1974, *29*, 856–864.

Härtner, R., Mattes, K., & Wottawa, H. Computerunterstützte Hypothesenagglutination zur Erfassung komplexer Zusammenhänge. *EDV in Medizin und Biologie*, 1980, *11*, 53–59.

Hebb, D. O. Drives and the conceptual nervous system. *Psychological Review*, 1955, *62*, 243–254.

Heckhausen, H. *Hoffnung und Furcht in der Leistungsmotivation*. Meisenheim: Hain, 1963.

Heckhausen, H. *The anatomy of achievement motivation*. New York: Academic Press, 1967. (a)

Heckhausen, H. *The Atkinson model reshaped*. Paper presented at the American Psychological Association meeting, Washington, 1967. (b)

Heckhausen, H. Achievement motivation and its constructs: A cognitive model. *Motivation and Emotion*, 1977, *1*, 283–329.

Heckhausen, H. Task-irrelevant cognitions during an oral examination. In H. W. Krohne & L. Laux (Eds.) *Achievement, stress, and anxiety*. Washington, D.C.: Hemisphere, 1980.

Heckhausen, H., Schneider, K., & Schmalt, H. -D. *Advances in achievement motivation research* New York, N.Y.: Academic Press, in press.

Hiroto, D. S. Locus of control and learned helplessness. *Journal of Experimental Psychology*, 1974, *102*, 187–193.

Hiroto, D. S., & Seligman, M. E. P. Generality of learned helplessness in man. *Journal of Personality and Social Psychology*, 1975, *31*, 311–327.

Johnson, D. M. *The psychology of thought and judgement*. New York: Harper, 1955.

Klein, D. C., & Seligman, M. E. P. Reversal of performance deficits and perceptual deficits in learned helplessness and depression. *Journal of Abnormal Psychology*, 1976, *85*, 11–26.

Kleinbeck, U., & Schmidt, K. -H. Aufgabenwahl im Ernstfall einer betrieblichen Ausbildung: Instrumentalitätstheoretische Ergänzung zum Risikowahlmodell. *Zeitschrift für Entwicklungspsychologie und Pädagogische Psychologie*, 1979, *11*, 1–11.

Krug, S., Hage, A., & Hieber, S. Anstrengungsmotivation in Abhängigkeit von der Aufgabenschwierigkeit, dem Konzept eigener Tüchtigkeit und dem Leistungsmotiv. *Archiv für Psychologie*, 1978, *320*, 265–278.

Kruglanski, A. W. The endogenous-exogenous partition in attribution theory. *Psychological Review*, 1975, *82*, 387–406.

Kuhl, J. *Meβ- und prozeβtheoretische Analysen einiger Person- und Situationsparameter der Leistungsmotivation*. Bonn: Bouvier, 1977.

Kuhl, J. Situations-, reaktions- und personbezogene Konsistenz des Leistungsmotivs bei der Messung mittels des Heckhausen-TAT. *Archiv für Psychologie*, 1978, *130*, 37–52. (a)

Kuhl, J. Standard-setting and risk preference: An elaboration of the theory of achievement motivation and an empirical test. *Psychological Review*, 1978, *85*, 239–248. (b)

Kuhl, J. *Person- und situationsspezifische Validität der Erwartungs-×-Wert-Theorie: Freizeitaktivitäten von Hauptschülern*. Ruhr University Bochum, 1979.

Kuhl, J. Leistungsmotivation. In: H. Werbik, & H. J. Kaiser (Eds.), *Kritische Stichwörter zur Sozialpsychologie*. München: Fink, 1980.

Kuhl, J. Motivational and functional helplessness: The moderating effect of state- vs. action-orientation. *Journal of Personality and Social Psychology*, 1981, *40*, 155–170.

Kuhl, J. Action- and state-orientation as mediators between motivation and action. In W. Hacker, W. Volpert, & M. von Cranach (Ed.), *Cognitive and motivational aspects of action*. Amsterdam: North-Holland Publishing Co. in press.

Kuhl, J. Integrating cognitive and dynamic approaches: A prospectus for a unified motivational psychology. In: J. W. Atkinson & J. Kuhl (Ed.), *Motivation, thought, and action: Personal and situational determinants*. in prep.

Kuhl, J., & Beckmann, J. *Individuelle Prüfung von Erwartungs-×-Wertmodellen in einer Spielsituation*. Ruhr University, Bochum, 1979.

Kuhl, J., & Blankenship, V. Behavioral change in a constant environment: Shift to more difficult tasks with constant probability of success. *Journal of Personality and Social Psychology*, 1979, *37*, 551-563. (a)

Kuhl, J., & Blankenship, V. The dynamic theory of achievement motivation: From episodic to dynamic thinking. *Psychological Review*, 1979, *86*, 141-151. (b)

Kukla, A. Attributional determinants of achievement-related behavior. *Journal of Personality and Social Psychology*, 1972, *21*, 166-174.

Lawler, E. E., & Porter, L. W. Antecedent attitudes of effective managerial job performance. *Organizational Behavior and Human Performance*, 1967, *2*, 122-142.

Lynch, J. G., & Cohen, J. L. The use of subjective expected utility theory as an aid to understanding variables that influence helping behavior. *Journal of Personality and Social Psychology*, 1978, *36*, 1138-1151.

Maier, S. F., & Seligman, M. E. P. Learned helplessness: Theory and evidence. *Journal of Experimental Psychology: General*, 1976, *105*, 3-46.

Mehrabian, A. Male and female scales of the tendency to achieve. *Educational and Psychological Measurement*, 1968, *28*, 493-502.

Meyer, W.-U. Anstrengungsintention in Abhängigkeit von Begabungseinschätzung und Aufgabenschwierigkeit. *Archiv für Psychologie*, 1973, *125*, 245-262. (a)

Meyer, W.-U. *Leistungsmotiv und Ursachenerklärung von Erfolg und Mißerfolg*. Stuttgart: Klett, 1973. (b)

Meyer, W. -U., & Hallermann, B. Anstrengungsintention bei einer leichten und schweren Aufgabe in Abhängigkeit von der wahrgenommenen eigenen Begabung. *Archiv für Psychologie*, 1974, *126*, 85-89.

Nygård, R. *Personality, situation and persistence*. Oslo: Universitetsforlaget, 1977.

Pritchard, R. D., & Sanders, M. S. The influence of valence, instrumentality and expectancy of effort and performance. *Journal of Applied Psychology*, 1973, *57*, 55-60.

Rasch, G. *Probabilistic models for some intelligence and attainment tests*. Kopenhagen: Nielson and Lydicke, 1960.

Raynor, J. O. Future orientation and motivation of immediate activity: An elaboration of the theory of achievement motivation. *Psychological Review*, 1969, *76*, 606-610.

Raynor, J. O. Future orientation in the study of achievement motivation. In J. W. Atkinson & J. O. Raynor (Eds.), *Motivation and achievement*. Washington: Winston, 1974.

Schmalt, H.-D. Über des Handeln in Unterrichtssituationen. In K.-E. Schorr & N. Luhmann (Ed.), *Technologie und Selbstreferenz*. Stuttgart, West Germany: Klett-Cotta in press.

Schmidt, F. L. Implications of a measurement problem for expectancy theory research. *Organizational Behavior and Human Performance*, 1973, *10*, 243-251.

Schneider, K. *Motivation unter Erfolgsrisiko*. Göttingen: Hogrefe, 1973.

Schneider, K. Atkinson's "risk preference" model. Should it be revised? *Motivation and Emotion*, 1978, *2*, 333-343.

Seligman, M. E. P. *Helplessness*. San Francisco: Freeman, 1975.

Singer, J. L. *Daydreaming: An introduction to the experimental study of inner experience*. New York: Random House, 1966.

Thurstone, L. L., & Jones, L. V. The rational origin for measuring subjective values. *Journal of American Statistical Association*, 1957, *52*, 458-471.

Vroom, V. H. *Work and motivation*. New York: Wiley, 1964.

Weiner, B. The effects of unsatisfied achievement motivation on persistence and subsequent performance. *Journal of Personality*, 1965, *33*, 428-442. (a)

Weiner, B. Need achievement and the resumption of incompleted tasks. *Journal of Personality and Social Psychology*, 1965, *1*, 165-168. (b)

Weiner, B. *Theories of motivation: From mechanism to cognition.* Chicago: Markham, 1972.

Weiner, B., Frieze, I., Kukla, A., Reed, L., Rest, S., & Rosenbaum, R. M. *Perceiving the causes of success and failure.* New York: General Learning Press, 1971.

Wendt, H. W. Verhaltensmodelle des Nichtwissenschaftlers: Einige biographische und Antriebskorrelate der wahrgenommenen Beziehung zwischen Erfolgswahrscheinlichkeit und Zielanreiz. *Psychologische Forschung,* 1967, *30,* 226–249.

Wish, P. A., & Hasazi, J. Motivational determinants of curricular choice behavior in college males. Paper presented at the Eastern Psychological Association, Boston, April 1972.

Wottawa, H. Grundlagen und Probleme von Dimensionen in der Psychologie. *Psychologia Universalis,* 1979, *40,* 1–122.

THE CONTEXT OF
ATTRIBUTION THEORY

6

An Attributionally Based Theory of Motivation and Emotion: Focus, Range, and Issues

Bernard Weiner
University of California, Los Angeles

ABSTRACT

A theory of motivation based upon attributions of causality for success and failure is offered. The heart of the theory consists of an identification of the dimensions of causality and the relation of these underlying properties of causes to psychological consequences. Three central causal dimensions have been discerned: Stability, locus, and control; these dimensions respectively are linked with expectancy change, esteem-related emotions, and interpersonal judgments. Within achievement-related contexts, this theory is pertinent to a diverse array of phenomena and topics, including self-esteem maintenance, achievement-change programs, risk-preference, reinforcement schedules, hopelessness, sources of emotion, helping, evaluation, and liking. The range of the theory is further demonstrated by applications to hyperactivity, mastery, parole decisions, affiliation and loneliness, and depression. It appears that a general theory of motivation is under development.

The writing of this chapter was undertaken while the author was supported by a grant from the Spencer Foundation. Some of the material found in this chapter was presented in the *Journal of Educational Psychology*, 1979.

In prior publications (Weiner, 1972, 1974, 1976) I proposed a model of achievement strivings that applied some of the principles of social perception to human motivation. This model was influenced by three dominant trends in contemporary psychology: (1) the belief that behavior is guided by cognitive processes and that humans are best described as information processors and information seekers (see Estes, 1975); (2) the concern with perceived responsibility, as evidenced by concepts such as locus of control (Rotter, 1966), reactance (Brehm, 1966), personal causation (de Charms, 1968), perceived freedom (Steiner, 1970), intrinsic and extrinsic motivation (Deci, 1975), and learned helplessness (Seligman, 1975); and (3) the rise of attribution theory in social psychology (Harvey, Ickes, & Kidd, 1976, 1978; Heider, 1958; Jones, Kanouse, Kelley, Nisbett, Valins, & Weiner, 1972; Kelley, 1967).

It now appears that a general theory of motivation has evolved from this work and that success-failure manipulations merely provided a research site for the initial investigations. In the present chapter this general conception of behavior is elucidated. I first examine the theory as it applies to achievement strivings, for the achievement arena remains the focus of the conception. The discussion of achievement embraces diverse topics, such as skill versus chance settings, self-concept maintenance, reinforcement schedules, risk-preference, and behavioral change programs. Then additional areas of psychological research that document the range of the conception—hyperactivity, mastery, parole decisions, affiliation and loneliness, and depression—are presented.

THE SEARCH FOR CAUSES

A basic assumption of attribution theory, that sets it apart from pleasure-pain theories of motivation, is that the search for understanding is the (or *a*) basic "spring of action." This does not imply that humans are not pleasure seekers, or that they never bias information in the pursuit of hedonic goals. Rather, information seeking and veridical processing are believed to be normative, may be manifested in spite of a conflicting pleasure principle, and, at the least, comprehension stands with hedonism among the primary sources of motivation (see Meyer, Folkes, & Weiner, 1976).

In an achievement setting such as the classroom, the search for understanding often leads to the attributional question of "Why did I succeed or fail?" or, more specifically, "Why did I flunk math?" or "Why did Mary get a better mark on this exam than me?" But classrooms are environments for the satisfaction of motivations other than achievement. Thus, attributional questions also might pertain to, for example, interpersonal acceptance or rejection, such as "Why doesn't Johnny like me?''

Among the unknowns of this attributional analysis is a clear statement of when people ask "why" questions. It has been demonstrated that this search is more likely given failure (rejection) than success (acceptance) (Folkes, 1978). Furthermore, it is plausible to speculate that unexpected events are more likely to lead to "why" questions than expected events (Lau & Russell, 1978), and that subjective importance also will influence the pursuit of knowledge. Thus, frustration, dissonance, and centrality are likely precursors of the attribution process (see Wong & Weiner, 1981). Finally, it has been demonstrated that during task performance "failure-oriented" or "helpless" students especially tend to supply attributions (Diener & Dweck, 1978). Diener and Dweck also intimate that a subset of students, called "mastery-oriented," do not engage in attribution making. However, I suspect that attributional inferences often are quite retrospective, summarize a number of experiences, take place below a level of immediate awareness, and are intimately tied with self-esteem and self-concept. Thus, I believe that attributions are supplied by the "mastery-oriented" children as well, although not necessarily during or immediately following all task performances.

Our initial statement regarding the perceived causes of success and failure (Weiner, Frieze, Kukla, Reed, Rest, & Rosenbaum, 1971) was guided by Heider (1958) as well as by our own intuitions. It was postulated that, in achievement-related contexts, the causes perceived as most responsible for success and failure are ability, effort, task difficulty, and luck. That is, in attempting to explain the prior success or failure at an achievement-related event, the individual assesses his or her level of ability, the amount of effort that was expended, the difficulty of the task, and the magnitude and direction of experienced luck. It was assumed that rather general values are assigned to these factors and that the task outcome is differentially ascribed to the causal sources. In a similar manner, future expectations of success and failure would then be based upon one's perceived level of ability in relation to the perceived difficulty of the task (labeled by Heider as "can"), as well as an estimation of the intended effort and anticipated luck.

In listing these four causes we did not intend to convey that they were the *only* perceived determinants of success or failure, or even that they were the most salient ones in all achievement situations. Subsequently (e.g., Weiner, 1974; Weiner, Russell, & Lerman, 1978), it explicitly was indicated that factors such as mood, fatigue, illness, and bias could serve as necessary and/or sufficient reasons for achievement performance. Research restricting causality to the four causes given above at times might give rise to false conclusions. For example, assume that one is testing the hedonic bias notion that success primarily is self-ascribed. By not including help from others, for example, among the alternative causes, the hedonic bias hypothesis might be supported because the given external causes (task difficulty and luck) do not adequately capture the phenomenology of the subject.

In the last few years intuition has given way to empirical studies attempting to identify the perceived causes of success and failure. At least five investigations of *academic* attributions (Bar-Tal & Darom, 1977; Cooper & Burger, 1978; Elig & Frieze, 1975; Frieze, 1976; Simon & Feather, 1973) have been conducted (there undoubtedly are many more unknown to me), and there have been a number of studies that examine attributions outside of the classroom context (e.g., work experiences and athletics). The methodologies of the classroom inquiries have minor variations, with students or teachers stating the causes of success or failure at real or imagined events, and judging themselves or others. The responses are then categorized and tabulated.

Cooper and Burger (1978) provide a concise summary of the data from three of the studies (see Table 6.1). It is evident that ability, effort (both typical and immediate) and task difficulty are among the main perceived causes of classroom performance. Thus, the prior intuitions of Heider and my colleagues and I were not incorrect. In addition, Table 6.1 shows that others (teachers, students, and family), motivation (attention and interest), what Cooper and Burger label as acquired characteristics (habits and attitudes), and physiological processes

TABLE 6.1
A Summary of Previous Coding Systems

Frieze (1976)	Bar-Tal & Darom (1977)	Cooper & Burger (1978)
Ability	Ability	Academic ability
Stable effort	Effort during test	Physical and emotional
Immediate effort	Preparation at home	ability
Task	Interest in the	Previous experience
Other person	subject matter	Habits
Mood	Difficulty of the test	Attitudes
Luck	Difficulty of material	Self-perceptions
Other	Conditions in the home	Maturity
		Typical effort
		Effort in preparation
		Attention
		Directions
		Instruction
		Task
		Mood
		Family
		Other students
		Miscellaneous

(Adapted from Cooper & Burger, 1978)

(mood, maturity, and health) comprise the central determinants of success and failure. Luck is not reliably included with the dominant causes, but could be prominent on specific occasions, particularly in career or athletic accomplishments (see Mann, 1974).

In sum, there are a myriad of perceived causes of achievement events. In a cross-cultural study it was even reported that patience (Greece and Japan) and tact and unity (India) are perceived as causes of success and failure (Triandis, 1972). But, there is a rather small list from which the main causes repeatedly are selected. Furthermore, within this list ability and effort appear to be the most salient and general of the causes. That is, outcomes frequently depend on what we can do and how hard we try to do it. A clear conceptual analysis of only ability and effort would greatly add to our knowledge, given an attributional perspective.

Before moving on to this conceptual formulation, it should be recognized that Table 6.1 presents only a description of the perceived reasons for success and failure in achievement settings. Although attribution theory often is referred to as a "naive" conception, using the language of the "person on the street," it also has been appreciated that science has to go beyond mere phenomenology. That is, order must be imposed using scientific terminology that may not be part of the logic of the layperson. This is implicit in, for example, the work of Kelley (1967, 1971). Heider (1958) also clearly acknowledged the distinction between a naive psychology and a scientific psychology, stating: "There is no a priori reason why the causal description [scientific language] should be the same as the phenomenal description [naive language], though, of course, the former should adequately account for the latter [p. 22]."

I now turn from the layperson's perception of causality to the scientific language that is imposed on these causes. In this chapter I completely neglect how causal beliefs are reached, although this is the most common problem in the attributional field and is what is meant by the "attribution process" (see Kelley, 1967, 1971; Weiner, 1974). This void is left so that full space can be devoted to the psychological consequences of perceived causality, the topic most focal to my concerns, and the relation of these consequences to expectancy-value conceptions of motivation, which is the theme of this book.

DIMENSIONS OF CAUSALITY

Inasmuch as the list of conceivable causes of success and failure is infinite, it is essential to create a classification scheme or a taxonomy of causes. In so doing, similarities and differences are delineated and the underlying properties of the causes are identified. This is an indispensable requirement for the construction of an attributional theory of motivation.

The prior theoretical analyses of Rotter (1966) and Heider (1958) were available to serve as our initial guides in this endeavor. Rotter and his colleagues proposed a one-dimensional classification of causality. Causes either were within (internal) or outside (external to) the person. In a similar manner, Heider (1958), as well as de Charms (1968), Deci (1975), and many others have articulated an internal–external classification of causality. Rotter labeled this dimension "locus of control," whereas in the present context locus is conceived as a backward-looking belief and therefore is referred to as "locus of causality." Indeed, it will be contended that the concepts of "locus" and "control" must be separated.

The causes listed in Table 6.1 can be readily catalogued as internal or external to the individual. From the perspective of the student, the personal causes include ability, effort, mood, maturity, and health, whereas teacher, task, and family are among the external sources of causality. But the relative placement of a cause on this dimension is not invariant over time or between people. For example, health might be perceived as an internal ("I am a sickly person") or as an external ("The 'flu bug' got me") cause of failure. Inasmuch as attribution theory deals with phenomenal causality, such personal interpretations must be taken into account. That is, the taxonomic placement of a cause depends upon its subjective meaning. Nonetheless, in spite of possible individual variation, there is general agreement when distinguishing causes as internal or external.

A second dimension of causality that we have come to perceive as increasingly important is labeled "stability" (Weiner et al., 1971). The stability dimension defines causes on a stable (invariant) versus unstable (variant) continuum. Again Heider (1958) served as our guide, for he contrasted dispositional and relatively fixed characteristics such as ability with fluctuating factors such as effort and luck. Examining Table 6.1, ability, typical effort, and family would be considered relatively fixed, whereas immediate effort, attention, and mood are more unstable. Effort and attention may be augmented or decreased from one episode to the next, whereas mood is conceived as a temporary state. However, as indicated previously, the perceived properties of a cause can vary. For example, mood might be thought of as a temporary state or as a permanent trait. In addition, experimenters can alter the perceived properties of a cause. For example, although difficulty level of a task generally is considered a stable characteristic (Weiner et al., 1971), Valle and Frieze (1976) portrayed task difficulty as unstable by anchoring this concept to an assigned sales territory that could be shifted for any salesperson. Some researchers have classified task difficulty as stable, although their experimental manipulation strongly suggests it would be perceived by subjects as unstable (see Riemer, 1975 for this error).

Still a third dimension of causality that was identified by Heider and later incorporated into the achievement domain by Rosenbaum (1972) was labeled "intentionality." Causes such as effort or the bias of a teacher or supervisor were categorized as intentional, whereas ability, the difficulty of the task, mood, and so on were specified by Rosenbaum (1972) to be unintentional.

In prior writings this distinction was accepted (e.g., Weiner, 1974, 1976). But following a suggestion of Litman-Adizes (1978), it is now apparent that Rosenbaum mislabeled this dimension. Rosenbaum argued that the dimension of intentionality is needed to differentiate, for example, mood from effort. Both of these are internal and unstable causes, yet intuitively they are quite distinct. Rosenbaum invoked the intent dimension to describe this difference, with mood classified as unintentional and effort classified as intentional. However, it seems that the dimension Rosenbaum had identified was that of "control." Failure attributed to a lack of effort does not signify that there was an intent to fail. Intent connotes a desire, or want. Rather, effort differs from mood in that only effort is perceived to be subject to volitional control. Hence, it is proposed that a third dimension of causality categorizes causes as "controllable" versus "uncontrollable."

Causes theoretically can be classified within one of eight cells (2 levels of locus × 2 levels of stability × 2 levels of control). Among the internal causes, ability is stable and uncontrollable; typical effort is stable and controllable; mood, fatigue, and illness are unstable and uncontrollable; and temporary exertion is unstable and controllable. Among the external causes, task difficulty is stable and uncontrollable; teacher bias may be perceived as stable and controllable; luck is unstable and uncontrollable; and unusual help from others is unstable and controllable (see Table 6.2).

Some problems with this classification scheme remain unsolved, particularly among the external causes. For example, can an external cause be perceived as controllable? The answer to this question depends on how far back one goes in a causal inference chain, as well as whether controllability assumes only the perspective of the actor, which is not the case in Table 6.2 (e.g., teacher bias may be controllable from the vantage point of the teacher, but not given the perspective of the pupil). These questions, as well as the proposed independence of the dimensions, are difficult issues for future thought and research.

Although the main dimensions of causality in achievement-related contexts may have been identified, other dimensions doubtlessly will emerge with further

TABLE 6.2
Causes of Success and Failure, Classified According to Locus,
Stability, and Controllability

	Internal		External	
	Stable	Unstable	Stable	Unstable
Uncontrollable	Ability (aptitude)	Mood	Task difficulty	Luck
Controllable	Typical effort	Immediate effort	Teacher bias	Unusual help from others

analysis and will raise additional problems about the independence of the dimensions. Intention may be one of these dimensions and logically could be separable from control (although causes are certain to correlate highly on these two dimensions). A causal statement regarding a neglected homework assignment illustrating the separation of intent from control is, "I wanted to study, but could not control myself from going out." A conceptually similar example disassociating intent from control concerns a criminal who does not want to commit a crime but cannot control the compulsion. Criminal justice also accepts the possibility of control without intent, as in negligence.

Still another possible dimension of causality, identified by Abramson, Seligman, and Teasdale (1978), has been labeled "globality." The global versus specific ends of this dimension capture the concept of stimulus generalization (whereas stability expresses temporal generalization). For example, one's ability may be perceived as task-specific ("I failed because I am poor at math") or as a general trait influencing performance in a wide variety of settings ("I failed because I am dumb").

The dimensions of causality introduced above were derived from a logical examination of perceived causes. More recently, a number of investigators have employed techniques such as factor analysis or multi-dimensional scaling to discover the dimensions of causality (e.g., Meyer, 1980, Michela, Peplau, & Weeks, 1978; Passer, 1977). In the inceptive study by Passer, male and female subjects rated the similarity of either the causes of success or failure. Eighteen causes were presented in all possible pairs to the subjects. The similarity judgments provided the input for a multi-dimensional scaling procedure. This method is akin to a cluster analysis and depicts the underlying judgment dimensions.

Passer found two clear dimensions of causality: (1) a locus dimension, anchored at the internal end with causes such as bad mood and no self-confidence and at the external extreme with causes such as bad teacher and hard exam; and 2) an intentional-unintentional dimension (that I will call controllable-uncontrollable), anchored at the controllable end with causes such as never studies hard and lazy, and at the uncontrollable extreme with nervous and bad mood. The findings reported by Passer (1977) were relatively similar for males and females in both the success and failure scaling solutions.

The proposed third dimension of causality, stability, was not displayed. Nevertheless, Passer's results are encouraging in that two of the three dimensions that had been presumed did emerge, and other unanticipated dimensions that had not been part of the logical analysis did not appear.

The data reported by Michela et al. (1978) are equally promising. Although they were concerned with the causes of loneliness, two familiar dimensions emerged in their study—stability and locus. There was some indication that control also appeared in the data, although it did not come through as an independent dimension, and was more evident among the internal causes. This suggests that perhaps control cannot be paired with externality.

The investigation by Meyer (1980) provides the best evidence for the dimensions portrayed in Table 6.2. Meyer gave subjects information relevant to the judgment of the causes of success and failure, such as past history and social norms (Kelley, 1967). The subjects then rated nine possible causes of the outcomes, including ability, effort, task difficulty, luck, mood, and teacher. A factor analysis of these ratings yielded the three dimensions given in Table 6.2.

It therefore appears that what dimensions emerge in part depends on the empirical procedure that is used. Given a multi-dimensional scaling method where subjects rate the similarity of the causes, the dimensions generated by the logical analysis may not be identical to those emerging with the empirical procedure. For example, as shown in the Passer (1977) data, a naive person might not spontaneously recognize that mood, luck, and effort are similar because they are unstable, and thus a stability dimension of causality will not be evident. On the other hand, factor analytic procedures are not subject to this limitation, and as Meyer (1980) has demonstrated, this procedure has yielded results fully supporting the logical analysis. For the scientist these dimensions are "second-order" concepts (Schütz, 1967, p. 59); they are concepts used by attribution theorists to organize the causal concepts of the layperson.

CONSEQUENCES OF CAUSAL PROPERTIES

I turn now from the dimensions of causality to the consequences or the implications of these dimensions for thought and action. It is contended that each of the three dimensions of causality has a primary psychological function or linkage, as well as a number of secondary effects. The primary relation of the *stability* dimension is to the magnitude of expectancy change following success or failure. The *locus* dimension of causality has implications for self-esteem, one of the emotional consequences of achievement performance; affect also is a secondary association for causal stability. The dimensional linkages with expectancy and affect (value) integrate attribution theory with expectancy-value formulations of motivation as outlined by Atkinson (1964), Lewin (1935), and others (see Weiner, 1972, 1974). Finally, perceived *control* by others relates to helping, evaluation, and liking. The theory thus addresses both self- and other-perception, and intra- as well as inter-personal behavior. The locus and control dimensions have a number of secondary effects that also will be very briefly discussed.

STABILITY—EXPECTANCY OF SUCCESS

The primary conceptual linkage of the stability dimension with expectancy of success was first explored by Weiner et al. (1971) and has not greatly changed since that time (see Weiner, 1972, 1974, 1976). I now more fully perceive the implications of this association, other secondary linkages with causal stability have been uncovered, and the empirical data have grown in clarity. But the following discussion is consistent with prior statements and is partially redundant with these earlier writings.

Research in the attributional domain has proven definitively that causal ascriptions for past performance are an important determinant of goal expectancies. For example, failure that is ascribed to low ability or to the difficulty of a task decreases the expectation of future success at that task more than failure that is ascribed to bad luck, mood, or a lack of immediate effort. In a similar manner, success ascribed to good luck or extra exertion results in lesser increments in the subjective expectancy of future success at that task than does success ascribed to high ability or to the ease of the task. More generally, expectancy shifts after success and failure are dependent upon the perceived stability of the cause of the prior outcome; ascription of an outcome to stable factors produces greater typical shifts in expectancy (increments in expectancy after success and decrements after failure) than do ascriptions to unstable causes. Stated somewhat differently, if one attains success (or failure), and if the conditions or causes of that outcome are perceived as remaining unchanged, then success (or failure) will be anticipated with a greater degree of certainty. But if the conditions or causes are subject to change, then there is some doubt that the prior outcome will be repeated.

Empirical Evidence

A large number of research investigations support the above theoretical contentions (e.g., Fontaine, 1974; McMahan, 1973; Meyer, 1980; Meyer, 1970; Ostrove, 1978; Pancer & Eiser, 1975; Rosenbaum, 1972; Valle, 1974; Valle & Frieze, 1976; Weiner, Nierenberg, & Goldstein, 1976). In the Weiner et al. (1976) investigation, it was demonstrated that expectancy changes are related to the dimension of stability, and are not associated with the locus of causality. This is an important finding, not only because two attributional dimensions are discriminated, but also because a vast competing literature relates expectancy changes to the dimension of locus (see Weiner et al., 1976 for a review).

Weiner et al. (1976) gave subjects either 0, 1, 2, 3, 4, or 5 consecutive success experiences at a block-design task, with different subjects in the six experimental conditions. Following the success trial(s), expectancy of success and causal ascriptions were assessed. Expectancy of future success was determined by having subjects indicate "how many of the next 10 similar designs you believe that you will successfully complete" (Weiner et al., 1976, p. 61). To assess perceptions of causality, subjects were required to mark four rating scales that were identical with respect to either the stability or locus dimensional anchors, but differing along the alternate dimension. Specifically, one attribution question was: "Did you succeed on this task because you are always good at these kinds of tasks, or because you tried especially hard on this particular task?'' ''Always good'' and ''tried hard,'' the anchors on this scale, are identical on the locus of causality dimension (internal), but they differ in perceived stability, with ability a stable attribute and effort an unstable cause. In a similar manner, judgments were made between ''lucky'' and ''tried hard'' (unstable causes differing in locus), ''these tasks are always easy'' and ''lucky'' (external causes differing in stability), and ''always good'' and ''always easy'' (stable causes differing in locus). Thus, the judgments permitted a direct test of the locus versus stability interpretation of expectancy change.

Expectancy estimates were examined separately for each of the causal judgments. The data revealed that both within the internal and the external causes, expectancy increments were positively associated with the stability of the ascription; that is, there were higher expectancies given ability and task ease ascriptions than given effort or luck attributions. Contrasting locus of causality differences within either the stable or the unstable ascriptions disclosed that the disparate causal locus groups did not differ in their expectancies of success.

Skill Versus Chance Settings, The "Gambler's Fallacy," and Locus of Control.   The previous discussion suggests that there should be differential expectancy shifts given ability (stable attribution) versus chance (unstable attribution) contexts. This supposition has been confirmed in many studies. For example, in games of chance atypical shifts (decrements in the expectancy of success following a success and increments after a failure) frequently are reported (e.g., Jarvik, 1951; Phares, 1957; Skinner, 1942). Such shifts have been labeled the ''gambler's fallacy,'' connoting the misconception that in games of chance events are not perceived as independent and the same outcome is believed unlikely to recur on successive occasions (the ''negative recency'' effect). Furthermore, in chance tasks the conviction that the future outcome will differ from the prior results increases as a function of the number of consecutive occurrences of the past event (Jarvik, 1951; Lepley, 1963). This finding is in marked opposition to data in skill situations, for with increasing success (or failure) at a skill-related task, there is increasing certainty that success (or failure) again will be experienced. That is, a ''positive recency'' effect is displayed (e.g., Diggory, Riley, & Blumenfeld, 1960; Zajonc & Brickman, 1969).

In other publications (e.g., Weiner et al., 1976) the attributional analysis of expectancy shifts has been compared with the beliefs espoused by social learning theorists (Phares, 1957; Rotter, 1966). According to the social learning conception, expectancy shifts are influenced by the locus of control (internal versus external), rather than the stability, of the perceived cause of an event. To test this hypothesis, experimental studies also have compared expectancy shifts in skill (internal control) versus chance (external control) settings (James, 1957; Phares, 1957; Rotter, Liverant, & Crowne, 1961). These investigations again confirmed that expectancies are differentially affected in these situational contexts. However, ability is an internal, stable cause, whereas luck is an external, unstable cause. Hence, the disparate expectancy shifts that have been observed can be logically imputed to either the locus of control or the stability dimension of causality. Subsequent research separating these two explanations conclusively has demonstrated that it is the stability, and not the locus, dimension of causality that accounts for the expectancy shift data (see review in Weiner et al., 1976).

One of my disappointments has been that investigators associated with social learning theory and locus of control have failed to recognize or admit the stability-expectancy linkage and the existence of other dimensions of perceived causality. Some researchers (e.g., Lefcourt, von Baeyer, Ware, & Cox, 1979) are incorporating the stability dimension into perceived causality scales. But this is in contrast to the position of other investigators. For example, Phares (1978) states:

> At the present time there does not appear to be a convincing body of data supporting the utility of adding the stability dimension. . . . Even should the addition of stability find support in laboratory studies of expectancy changes, it is not at all clear that . . . broader demonstrations of utility will be forthcoming [p. 270].

In opposition to this statement, the literature associating stability with expectancy change is unequivocal and the findings generalize outside of the laboratory as well as beyond the achievement domain (as will be documented later). It may indeed be that the concept of locus of control has great utility; my modest hope is that individuals in this area will acknowledge some of the prior shortcomings in their conceptual analysis of expectancy shifts at skill and chance tasks and in their limited approach to causality (for a fuller discussion of these issues, see Weiner et al., 1976).

Formal Analysis and Self-concept Maintenance

McMahan (1973) and Valle and Frieze (1976) have developed formal models of expectancy shifts based upon the concept of causal stability. Valle and Frieze postulate that predictions of expectancies (P) are a function of the initial expectancy (E) plus the degree to which outcomes (O) are attributed to stable causes (S):

$$P = f(E + O [f(S)])$$

In addition, Valle and Frieze (1976) also note that the perceived causes of success and failure are related to the initial expectancy of success. It has been clearly documented that unexpected outcomes lead to unstable attributions, particularly luck (Feather, 1969, 1977; Feather & Simon, 1971, 1972; Frieze & Weiner, 1971). Hence, Valle and Frieze (1976) conclude:

There is some value for the difference between the initial expectations and the actual outcome that will maximally change a person's predictions for the future. If the difference is greater than this point, the outcome will be attributed to unstable factors to such an extent that it will have less influence on the person's future predictions [p. 581].

These ideas have important implications for the maintenance of one's self-concept and for attributional change programs (see Weiner, 1974, 1976). For example, assume that an individual with a high self-concept of ability believes that he or she has a high probability of success at a task. It is likely that failure then would be ascribed to unstable causes such as luck or mood, which may not reduce the subsequent expectancy of success and sustains a high ability self-concept. On the other hand, success would be ascribed to ability, which increases the subsequent expectancy (certainty) of success and confirms one's high self-regard. The converse analysis holds given a low self-concept of ability and a low expectancy of success: success would be ascribed to unstable factors and failure to low ability. These attributions result in the preservation of the initial self-concept (see Ames, 1978; Fitch, 1970; Gilmore & Minton, 1974; Ickes & Layden, 1978). In addition, the above analysis suggests that in change programs involving expectancies or self-concept the perceived causes of performance must be altered, and a modification in self-perception would have to involve a gradual process (Valle & Frieze, 1976).

Reinforcement Schedules, Task Difficulty, and Extinction

Cognitive accounts of the effects of reinforcement percentages and schedules on behavior (resistance to extinction, rate of response) typically invoke the concept of expectancy (see Lewis, 1960; Rest, 1976). An attributional analysis of these relations starts with the assumption that given reward or nonreinforcement, the organism searches for a "why" answer. The perceived cause is then analyzed, in part, according to its stability. Given a perceived unstable cause for nonreinforcement, expectancy should be maintained. That is, the belief that reinforcement may be forthcoming is sustained. Hence, the organism should continue to respond (there is resistance to extinction). On the other hand, a causal explanation for nonreinforcement implicating stable factors intimates that reinforcement will not follow. The organism should therefore cease responding.

One hypothesis emerging from this line of reasoning is that any information giving rise to luck attributions for nonreinforcement should increase resistance to extinction. It has been demonstrated that variability in a series of outcomes elicits luck attributions (Weiner et al., 1971), and it is well known that partial reinforcement schedules do increase resistance to extinction. In a similar manner, chance rather than skill instructions also increase resistance to extinction (Phares,

1957). A second and related hypothesis is that information generating effort ascriptions for failure also should result in response maintenance in the face of nonreinforcement. Lawrence and Festinger (1962) have demonstrated that effortful responses (climbing up a steep incline) increase resistance to extinction. They explain this finding with cognitive dissonance theory, contending that the increased dissonance following nonreward results in more positive perceptions of the value of the goal object. However, if this were correct, then the animals should prefer a goal region associated with high effort. This apparently is not the case; a preference for the most easily attained goal has been relatively well documented given hunger motivation (see Tolman, 1925).

Although somewhat removed from the analysis of resistance to extinction, it is relevant to point out that fixed versus variable schedules, and ratio versus interval schedules, also give rise to differential perceptions of causality. For example, Pennebaker, Burnam, Schaeffer, and Harper(1977) found that there is greater perception of internal control (effort attributions) given fixed rather than variable schedules, presumably because of the clearer contingency or covariation between the response and the outcome in the former case. In a similar manner, it also may be contended that ratio schedules promote effort ascriptions, inasmuch as there is response-outcome covariation, whereas interval schedules lead primarily to an external ascription. In support of these hypotheses, Ferster and Skinner (1957) report that the variable-ratio schedule produces almost five times the rate of responding as the variable-interval schedule. Furthermore, given the attributional viewpoint, there should be (and are) differential response patterns as the ratio or intervals are lengthened: The ratio schedule alteration leads to response increments (''I must try harder''), whereas the interval schedule change produces response decrements (''It is pretty much beyond my control''). Rest (1976) has provided data in support of these interpretations.

I do not wish to contend that infrahumans such as rats make causal attributions. However, they might have the cognitive capacities to differentiate stable from variable environments, and the learned helplessness literature (Seligman, 1975) suggests that they apparently perceive effort-outcome covariation.

Achievement Change

These ideas have more than just a passing relevance to educational practices. Many of the burgeoning achievement-change programs make direct or indirect use of attributional principles. These programs often attempt to induce students to attribute their failures to a lack of effort, which is both unstable and under volitional control (see Andrews & Debus, 1978; Chapin & Dyck, 1976; Dweck, 1975; Sparta, 1978). This goal is expressly established for ''failure-oriented'' children who apparently ascribe their failures to a lack of ability, which is a stable and uncontrollable cause (see Diener & Dweck, 1978). Presumably, inasmuch as effort can be increased volitionally, ascriptions of nonattainment of a goal to lack of effort will result in the sustaining of "hope" and increase persistence toward the goal. On the other hand, because ability is stable and not subject to volitional control, ascription of nonattainment of a goal to low ability results in "giving up" and the cessation of goal-oriented behavior. This topic is further examined later in the chapter. In sum, it is suggested that the relations between diverse independent variables (reward schedules, effortfulness of the response, certain attributional biases, and task instructions), and the dependent variables of resistance to extinction or persistence in goal-related behavior are mediated by perceptions of causality:

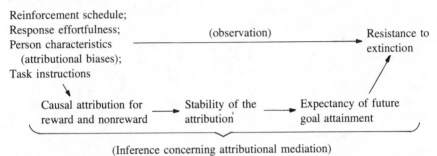

(Inference concerning attributional mediation)

LOCUS—AFFECT

In contrast to the rather stable beliefs about causal stability, our thoughts concerning locus of causality have fluctuated greatly. A temporary resolution is proposed here that is a synthesis of our previous antithetical positions and better accounts for the complexity of human affective responses.

Initially, Weiner et al. (1971) postulated that locus of causality is related to the affective consequences of success and failure. Emotional reactions were believed to be maximized given internal attributions for success and failure and minimized given external attributions. Thus, for example, pride and shame, the alleged dominant affects in achievement situations (Atkinson, 1964; McClelland, Atkinson, Clark, & Lowell, 1953), would be most experienced given personal responsibility for success and failure, as opposed to instances in which external factors such as luck or others were perceived as the causal agents. This postulated relation seemed intuitively reasonable, was consistent with Atkinson's '(1964) formulations concerning the incentive value of success and failure, and found support in a variety of research investigations. A detailed account of this position is not presented here (see Weiner, 1977).

Subsequently, it became evident that it is incorrect to presume an invariant positive relation between internality and the magnitude of emotional reactions in achievement settings. For example, failure ascribed to others, such as the bias of a teacher or hindrance from students or family, will presumably generate great anger and hostility. In this event, externality is positively related to emotional intensity. Thus, the position expressed in Weiner et al. (1971) cannot be correct (see Weiner, 1977; Weiner et al., 1978).

A series of studies therefore was initiated to determine the relation between attribution and affect (Weiner et al., 1978, 1979). In our first investigation, subjects were given a scenario that depicted a success or failure experience at an exam, along with a causal attribution for that outcome (e.g., Joan failed because she did not have the ability). The subjects then reported the affects that they surmised would be experienced in this situation. About 100 affects for success and 150 for failure were provided, with responses made on rating scales indicating the intensity with which the affects would be experienced.

There were two general findings of interest. First, there was a set of "outcome-dependent, attribution-independent" affects that represented broad positive or negative reactions to success and failure, regardless of the "why" of the outcome. Given success, pleased, happy, satisfied, good, and so on were reported as equally experienced in the disparate attribution conditions. In a similar manner, given failure, there were a number of outcome-linked emotions, such as uncheerful, displeasure, and upset. The outcome-dependent affects for both success and failure were reported as the ones that would be most intensely experienced.

But for both success and failure there were many emotions discriminably related to specific attributions. Given success, the unique attribution-affect linkages were: ability-competent and confident; typical effort-relaxation; immediate effort-activation; others-gratitude; personality-conceit; and luck-surprise. Therefore, if one perceived that success was caused by ability, then competent and confident were reported as intensely experienced; if one succeeded because of help from others, then the dominant reported affect was gratitude; and so on. In a similar manner, for failure the attribution-affect linkages were: ability-incompetence; effort-guilt and shame; personality-resignation; others-aggression; and luck-surprise (see Weiner et al., 1978).

It is of interest to point out that at times causal attributions yield opposite reactions for success and failure, as would be expected given diametric outcomes (respectively, competence versus incompetence given ability attributions; gratitude versus aggression for attributions to others). But at times the same emotion accompanies both positive and negative outcomes (surprise given a luck attribution); and given still other ascriptions, such as typical or immediate effort, the emotions that accompany success (respectively, relaxation and activation) are unrelated to the failure-tied affects (guilt and shame).

The data suggested we should reject the supposition that locus of causality mediates affective reactions in achievement contexts. Rather, emotions appeared to be either outcome or attributionally generated, without any intervening dimensional placement.

Additional evidence, however, has resulted in a synthesis of our prior antithetical stances. In a recent study (Weiner, Russell, & Lerman, 1979) subjects recreated a "critical incident" in their lives in which they succeeded (failed) at an academic exam because of ability, typical effort, immediate effort, help (hindrance) from others, personality, or luck. They then listed three affects they experienced in this situation. Table 6.3 includes only the emotions that were reported for *success* by more than 10% of the respondents for any particular attribution. The table shows the percent of subjects in all the attribution conditions reporting these relatively shared experiences.

The data in Table 6.3 are consistent with our previous findings. The most dominant affect, happy, is expressed regardless of the reason for the success. In addition to this outcome-linked emotion, there are significant attribution-affect linkages. These associations are: ability-competent and proud; other people-grateful and thankful; stable effort-content; personality-proud; and luck-surprise, relief, and guilty.

The failure data also revealed systematic patterns. There were significant outcome-linked emotions including disappointed, as well as attribution-affect associations consistent with prior research: ability-incompetence and resignation; effort-guilt; other people-anger; and luck-surprise.

Additional analyses of these data also demonstrated that causal dimensions play an essential role in affective life. Given internal attributions for success (ability, effort, personality), the affects pride, competence, confident, and satisfied were reported more frequently than given external attributions (others, luck). Internal ascriptions for failure generated the emotions of guilt and resignation. In

TABLE 6.3
Percentage of Respondents Stating a Particular Emotion for Success,
as a Function of the Attribution for Success

| Emotion | Causal Attribution | | | | | |
	Ability	Unst. Eff.	Stab. Eff.	Personality	Others	Luck
Competent	30	12	20	19	5	2
Confident	20	19	18	19	14	4
Content	4	4	12	0	7	2
Excited	3	9	8	11	16	6
Grateful	9	1	4	8	43	14
Guilt	1	3	0	3	2	18
Happy	44	43	43	38	46	48
Proud	39	28	39	43	21	8
Relief	4	28	16	11	13	26
Satisfied	19	24	16	14	9	0
Surprise	7	16	4	14	4	52
Thankful	0	1	0	0	18	4

(From Weiner, Russell, & Leiman, 1979)

sum, particular affects clustered with the internal causes. Reanalysis of Weiner et al. (1978) revealed virtually identical results.

It therefore appears that in achievement situations there are (at least) three sources of affect. First, there are emotions tied directly to the outcome. One feels "good" given success and "bad" given failure, regardless of the reason for the outcome. These probably are the initial and strongest reactions. Second, accompanying these general feelings are more distinct emotions, such as gratitude or hostility if success or failure respectively is due to others, surprise when the outcome is due to luck, and so on. Thirdly, the affects that are associated with self-esteem, such as competence, pride, and shame are mediated by self-ascriptions. Many emotional reactions are shared given success due to ability or effort, the two dominant internal attributions. It therefore may be that the central self-esteem emotions that facilitate or impede subsequent achievement performance are dimensionally-linked, referred by the actor to him- or herself. Some affects thus seem to be mediated by the locus dimension, but in a manner much more complex than was originally posited. It is likely that these dimension-linked affects have the greatest longevity and most significance for the individual.

Stability and Affect

In addition to the locus-affect linkage, there also is a relation between causal stability and emotions. Weiner et al. (1978) found that the affects of depression, apathy, and resignation were reported primarily given internal and stable attributions for failure (lack of ability, lack of typical effort, personality deficit). This suggests that only attributions conveying that events will not change in the future beget feelings of helplessness, giving up, and depression. Perhaps the control dimension also plays a role in generating these particular emotions. Hence, the dimensions of causality appear to relate to different sets of emotions.

In another research investigation supporting a stability-emotion union, Arkin and Maruyama (1979) assessed students' attributions for their success or failure at a college class. In addition, anxiety associated with school performance was measured. It was found that among successful students, the stability of their attributions was negatively correlated with anxiety. That is, when success is ascribed to stable causes, students report relatively little anxiety. On the other hand, among the unsuccessful students, attributional stability and anxiety correlated positively; most fear was reported when failure was perceived as likely to recur in the future.

The Cognition–Emotion Sequence in Achievement Contexts

On the basis of the earlier discussion, it is suggested that in achievement-related contexts (and, in particular, school settings), the actor progresses through something like the following cognition-emotion scenarios:

1. "I just received a 'D' on the exam. That is a very low grade." (This generates feelings of being frustrated and upset). "I received this grade because I never try hard enough" (followed by feelings of shame and guilt). "There really is something lacking in me, and it is permanent" (followed by low self-esteem or lack of worth and hopelessness).

2. "I just received an 'A' on the exam. That is a very high grade (generating happiness and satisfaction). "I received this grade because I always work very hard during the entire school year" (producing contentment and relaxation). "I really do have some positive qualities, and will continue to have them in the future" (followed by high self-esteem and feelings of self-worth, as well as optimism for the future).

Secondary Linkages

Because of the vast literature in the locus of control area, it might be anticipated that causal locus is directly linked with many psychological reactions in addition to esteem-related affects. This indeed is likely to be the case. For example, it has been reported that locus of control relates positively to behaviors such as information seeking and experiences such as feeling like an "origin" (de Charms, 1968). In most of this research, however, the concepts of "locus" and "control" are united. It is not reasonable to expect individuals who attribute failure to a lack of ability, which is internal but uncontrollable, to seek out information or feel like origins. Rather, it seems that the experiential state of an origin and correlated behaviors are exhibited because of the perceived personal control of the situation, or the belief that causality is both internal *and* controllable. Thus, the discussion of the secondary linkages with locus is postponed until the presentation of the control dimension of causality.

EXPECTANCY AND VALUE AS DETERMINANTS OF PERFORMANCE

Numerous investigations in the motivational literature have demonstrated that both expectancy and affect influence a variety of behaviors (see Atkinson, 1964; Weiner, 1972). Because of their influence on expectancy and affect, causal attributions are anticipated to influence motivational indexes such as the speed of performance, choice, and persistence of behavior (see Weiner, 1974).

Performance Intensity

One experiment perhaps best illustrates how the various linkages in the model influence intensity of performance. In an investigation by Weiner and Sierad (1975), subjects classified according to their level of achievement needs received four failure trials at an achievement task. Prior to the failure, the subjects in an experimental condition received a placebo pill that supposedly would interfere with their performance. Compared with subjects in a control condition, ascription of failure to the pill augmented the performance of subjects low in achievement needs while relatively decreasing the performance of subjects high in achievement needs.

The interaction between achievement needs and the causal manipulation was hypothesized on the basis of the attributional interpretation of expectancy-value theory. First, consider persons low in achievement needs. Prior research has suggested that these individuals have a bias to ascribe failure to low ability (see Weiner, 1974; Weiner et al., 1971). This attribution produces low expectancies of future success as well as arousing feelings of incompetence. Inducing ascription of failure to the placebo pill also generates a low expectancy of success, inasmuch as the effects of the pill were described as constant throughout the course of the experiment. But less esteem-related negative affect is generated given failure because of an experimenter-induced cause than to fail because of perceived low ability. Because the self-directed affective consequences of failure are lessened by the external pill attribution, it was anticipated that persons low in achievement needs would perform with greater intensity in the pill than in the control condition. That is, an external "rationalization" may serve as an adaptive defense for these individuals in that an inhibiting negative affect is lowered. Note in this example how closely attributions are related to defense mechanisms.

Now consider persons high in achievement needs. Prior research suggests that these individuals have a bias to ascribe failure to a lack of effort. This attribution results in the maintenance of a relatively high expectation of future success. Conversely, ascription of failure to a pill results in a low expectancy of success. For these individuals, future expectancy of success is believed to be the main determinant of achievement strivings and is given greater weight than the affective consequences of failure (see Weiner, 1970). It was therefore anticipated that persons highly motivated to achieve would perform with greater intensity in the control than in the pill attribution condition. As already indicated, the differential predictions concerning the effects of the pill attribution on persons low and high in achievement needs were confirmed.

Thought and Action.   Some investigators have reported behavioral change without finding attributional change, whereas others find attributional change without any modification of behavior (see Bem, 1974; Nisbett & Wilson, 1977). The relations between causal ascriptions and action are part of the broader controversial linkage between attitudes and behavior, and the even more embracing mind-body problem. I will not discuss this issue in the present context; suffice it to indicate that the theory presented here assumes a mind-body interaction with causal beliefs preceding and determining behavior. (This does not exclude the possibility that actions might also influence causal beliefs or that the causal beliefs at times are unconscious.) Furthermore, because of the affective and adaptive significance of attributions, it is likely that there are both primary and secondary causal appraisals, akin to the analysis of coping processes proposed by Lazarus (1966).

Risk Preference

Achievement theory as formulated by Atkinson (1964) and the attributional analysis that I have advocated differ in a number of respects. Of theoretical importance are the contrasting empirical predictions and conceptual analyses of risk-preference behavior. Atkinson's so-called "risk-preference" model leads to the prediction that individuals highly motivated to succeed will select tasks of intermediate difficulty, whereas persons low in achievement motivation prefer to undertake tasks that are very easy or very difficult. These disparate motive-group preferences theoretically maximize positive affect for the highly achievement-motivated person and minimize negative affect for the individual low in achievement needs. On the other hand, attribution theorists assume that humans are rational, information-gathering beings, seeking to understand the causal structure of the world (Heider, 1958). It has been contended that because of these information-striving tendencies there is a general desirability for intermediate difficulty choice. This is because performance at easy or difficult tasks yields relatively little information about one's ability and/or effort expenditure. The lack of personal feedback results from the fact that behavior consistent with social norms leads to situational or environmental causal inferences (Frieze & Weiner, 1971; Kelley, 1967; Weiner & Kukla, 1970). That is, if one succeeds and so do all others, or fails when others also fail, then the causal inferences are that the tasks were respectively easy or hard. Conversely, over a series of occasions a great deal of information about the self is gained given the selection of intermediate difficulty tasks. Inasmuch as some of the individuals undertaking these tasks succeed while others fail, the causal attribution for success or failure is to the person. That is, there is person-outcome, rather than task-outcome, covariation (see Kelley, 1967).

Meyer, Folkes, and Weiner (1976) conducted four experiments that examined the phenomenology of choice behavior by assessing the perceived affective and informational determinants of risk-preference. In two experiments, subjects classified according to their level of achievement needs expressed a preference among tasks varying in difficulty. In two of the experimental conditions, instructions conveyed that performance at the task chosen should either maximize satisfaction or the information gained about one's ability and effort expenditure. It was found that the majority of all subjects preferred to undertake tasks of intermediate difficulty and that both positive affect and information gain were perceived to be optimal at or near this difficulty level. The finding that intermediate risk taking is displayed by all subjects regardless of magnitude of achievement needs is consistent with a great amount of prior research (see review in Meyer et al., 1976), and contradicts the hedonic position advocated by Atkinson (1964).

Two additional experiments investigated at what level of task difficulty individuals most desire information about their performance. Police trainees and high school students with disparate self-concepts of respective target shooting and high-jumping ability were able to receive limited but self-selected performance feedback at a series of shooting and jumping tasks that varied in difficulty. The data revealed that the tasks selected for feedback became objectively less difficult as the self-perception of ability decreased. In addition, the tasks chosen for feedback were near the intermediate *subjective* certainty of success level for all subjects. These data provided support for attribution theory, while contradicting some of the predictions from Atkinson's conception. However, the information-seeking explanation of risk-preference remains to be clearly reconciled with, or integrated within, the expectancy-value framework.

An alternate informational explanation of choice behavior also has been proposed. Trope and Brickman (1975), replicated by Trope (1975), gave subjects a choice between tasks that varied in difficulty as well as in "diagnosticity." Diagnosticity was operationally defined as the difference in the percentage of success at a given task between individuals high versus low in ability. Their data indicated that individuals prefer to undertake tasks of high diagnosticity, relatively independent of the objective task difficulty level. That is, self-knowledge (ability feedback) was demonstrated to be a crucial determinant of risk-preference. These investigators contrasted the "diagnosticity" position with the "task difficulty" approach that I have advocated, although the two informational approaches have a great deal in common.

Trope and Brickman (1975) and Trope (1975) presented subjects with tabular diagnostic information about each task. Such summaries have few counterparts in our actual lives. I anticipate that if diagnostic information is presented in serial form, where individuals must synthesize the data, then such information is not used and subjective task difficulty again is the primary choice dimension. In addition, it is rare that we know the ability levels of individuals succeeding and failing at a task.

Persistence

The studies best demonstrating the relation of causal ascriptions to persistence in achievement contexts have been part of therapeutic treatment attempts to increase achievement strivings and were alluded to earlier in this chapter. Clearly, if causal attributions in part determine behavior, as has been contended, then it logically follows that a change in attributions should produce a change in action (Weiner & Sierad, 1975). The simple belief that alterations in thought are necessary and/or sufficient to give rise to behavioral change has been advocated by many clinical psychologists (e.g., Ellis, 1974; Kelly, 1955). Even within the behavioristic camp there is now a strong movement contending that internal speech can be used to control overt behavior (see Meichenbaum & Cameron, 1974).

Three distinct programs of research are pertinent to the efficacy of attributional training procedures. One research approach far removed from the achievement domain has demonstrated that misattribution of internal arousal or overt behavior influences emotional expression and the tolerance for pain (Davison & Valins, 1969; Nisbett & Schachter, 1966; Ross, Rodin, & Zimbardo, 1969; Schachter & Singer, 1962). A second program of research bearing upon attributional training emanates from broad-gauged achievement change programs (see McClelland & Winter, 1969). These training programs make use of a variety of techniques thought to be effective in changing behavior, including persuasion, reinforcement, and group and individual therapy (see McClelland, 1965). They also teach the importance of self-responsibility or internal control. Because the notion of internal control or personal causation (de Charms, 1968) is introduced, the programs are quite relevant to attributional approaches. However, the contribution of attributional training cannot be assessed, for the entire program is multifaceted and is not systematically linked with any single conceptual framework.

A third research strategy, which is directly relevant to the theory advocated here, is to train subjects to attribute failure to a lack of effort. Because effort is unstable and under volitional control, ascription of failure to insufficient effort should maintain "hope" and thus be an adaptive construal in certain situations. In these studies persistence of behavior generally is the indicator to assess the effectiveness of the attributional change procedure.

In the initial investigation in this area, Dweck and Reppucci (1973) demonstrated that there are attributional differences between children "giving up" in the face of failure, as opposed to those who persist when failing. More specifically, the persistent subjects were more likely to perceive that both success and failure are caused by effort expenditure than were the low persistent subjects.

Following this correlational finding, Dweck (1975) attempted to change the behavior of children characterized by "expectation of failure and deterioration of performance in the face of failure [p. 676]." To accomplish this change, an experimental treatment was imposed in which subjects received 80% success and 20% failure experiences at a series of training tasks. The failure trials were accompanied by an attribution to a lack of effort. This treatment was compared to one in which subjects received 100% success training without attributional information.

During the test phase of this experiment the effects of failure on performance were assessed. Dweck (1975) reports that only subjects in the attributional training condition handled failure better and exhibited improved performance, relative to pretraining behavior. In addition, only these subjects displayed increments in their general tendency to ascribe failure to a lack of effort.

Unfortunately, Dweck's procedure was somewhat faulty in that attributional training was confounded with reinforcement schedule. That is, the two treatment groups differed not only in the presence or absence of attributional information, but also in the percentage of success experiences. Subsequently, Chapin and Dyck (1976) replicated Dweck's finding, unconfounding these variables. Furthermore, they again used persistence of behavior as the dependent variable.

In the study by Chapin and Dyck (1976), subjects with learning difficulties received partial reinforcement training, either accompanied by effort attributions on both success and failure trials or else not paired with attributional information. The effectiveness of the training was determined by assessing persistence of behavior at a difficult reading test. Again it was found that attributional training facilitated achievement strivings (increased persistence), with its impact interacting with the type of reinforcement procedure used during training.

Finally, Andrews and Debus (1978) also induced effort ascriptions in their training procedure. Andrews and Debus first found that among sixth grade children there was a high positive correlation between persistence and ascription of failure to a lack of effort and a high negative correlation between persistence and ascription of failure to the stable factors of low ability and task difficulty. They then trained male subjects who least used effort attributions to ascribe failure to a lack of effort. This was accomplished by social and token reinforcement techniques applied in both success and failure situations. The attributional training was effective, for it not only increased the use of effort attributions, but also produced an increase in behavioral persistence in the face of failure.

In sum, successful attributional training procedures have been reported. Perceptions of the causes of failure can be altered, and these modifications influence the intensity and persistence of behavior.

CONTROL—HELPING, EVALUATION, AND LIKING

Attribution theory as formulated by Heider (1958), Jones and Davis (1965), and Kelley (1967) primarily concerns person perception, or inferences about the intentions and dispositions of others. But thus far in this chapter I have only been concerned with self-perception. I believe that one of the main contributions of our work has been the adaptation of some principles of social perception for the construction of a theory of motivation that has the individual as the unit of analysis.

In the discussion of the implications of causal dimensions, self- and other-perception were not distinguished. Considering changes in the expectancy of success, the same cause-effect logic pertaining to causal stability should hold when considering oneself or others. The discussion of affect also is equally applicable to both the self and others although, of course, the emotional experiences are limited to the self and inferred about others. But if success or failure is perceived as due to certain causes, then particular affective experiences should follow.

The following examination of the dimension of control centers upon inferences about others, and how beliefs about another's responsibility for success and failure influence an actor's reactions toward that person. The reactions examined are helping, evaluation, and sentiments.

Helping

Ickes and Kidd (1976), guided by Weiner et al. (1971) and Rosenbaum (1972), proposed an attributional analysis of helping behavior. A number of investigators prior to Ickes and Kidd (1976) had established that the tendency to help is influenced by the perceived cause of the need for aid (e.g., Berkowitz, 1969; Ickes, Kidd, & Berkowitz, 1976; Piliavin, Rodin, & Piliavin, 1969; Schopler & Matthews, 1965). The majority of these experimenters concluded that help is more likely when the perceived cause of the need is an environmental barrier, as opposed to being internal to the person desirous of aid. For example, Berkowitz (1969) reported that individuals are more inclined to help an experimental subject when the experimenter caused a delay in the subject's response, in contrast to a condition in which the subject was perceived as personally responsible for falling behind in the experiment.

In their review, Ickes and Kidd (1976) argued that this locus of control explanation of helping confounds the causal dimensions of locus and intentionality (that I again will call controllability). They suggest that in the study conducted by Berkowitz (1969), the causal ascription to the experimenter is both external and uncontrollable (from the perspective of the actor), whereas an attribution to the subject's own mismanagement is internal to the actor and is perceived by the potential helper as under volitional control. Hence, two dimensions of causality are confounded and it is impossible to determine which of the two causal dimensions is responsible for the differential help giving. Ickes and Kidd, in contrast to Berkowitz, suggest that it is the controllable aspect of the perceived cause, and not the locus, that mediated the disparate help giving. The reader should note how similar this analysis is to the one pertaining to expectancy shifts in skill and chance tasks. Both controversies point out that the locus of control literature has been plagued by an inadequate analysis of perceived causality. Furthermore, what is required is research that separates the various causal dimensions.

Other data support the Ickes and Kidd (1976) interpretation of helping behavior. For example, Piliavin, Rodin and Piliavin (1969) found that there is a bias to aid a blind person in distress as opposed to helping a drunk. According to the above argument, this is because drunkenness is perceived as subject to volitional control, whereas blindness is not. When "failure" is perceived as controllable, then help is withheld; the persons presumably should help themselves. For this reason, it is much easier to raise charity funds for battered children or blindness than for alcoholism centers.

Guided by the prior research of Barnes, Ickes, and Kidd (1977), Weiner (1980) applied these ideas to one instance of altruism in the classroom—lending class notes to an unknown classmate. In this investigation, two themes were created for a student's failure to take class notes. One theme involved a professor, whereas the second concerned an employer. In the professor theme, the student always (stable) or sometimes (unstable) did not take notes because of something about himself (internal) or something about the professor (external). Either he was unable to take good notes (uncontrollable) or he did not try (controllable), whereas the professor either was unable to give a clear lecture or did not try. Thus, for example, an internal, stable, and uncontrollable cause was that the student never was able to take good notes (low ability), whereas an external, unstable, and uncontrollable cause was that the professor at times could not give a clear lecture. Each story within the eight possible causal combinations (2 levels of stability × 2 levels of locus × 2 levels of control) elaborated the basic scenario. The second theme involved a work situation in which the student did not have the notes because he (or the boss) always (sometimes) was responsible for his coming late to school, that could (could not) have been avoided.

Following each causal statement the subjects rated the likelihood of lending their notes to the student. Judgments were made on a ten point scale anchored at the extremes with "Definitely would lend my notes" and "Definitely would not lend my notes".

The mean helping judgments for four conditions (2 levels of locus × 2 levels of control) are shown in Table 6.4. Stability did not effect the judgments and thus is ignored in the analysis. Table 6.4 reveals that helping is reported to be relatively equal and reasonably high in all conditions except when the cause is internal and controllable; in that case aid is unlikely to be given. That is, if the student did not try to take notes (professor theme), or could have avoided being

TABLE 6.4
Mean Likelihood of Helping as a
Function of Perceived Locus of
Causality and Controllability

	Controllable	Uncontrollable
Internal	3.13[a]	6.74
External	7.35	6.98

[a]High numbers indicate greater likelihood of note lending.

(From Weiner, 1980)

absent (employer theme), then help is withheld. The findings concerning the influence of intent information on moral judgments and criminal justice support this line of reasoning (see Carroll & Payne, 1976, 1977, discussed later in this chapter).

Evaluation

Some of the early experimental work conducted by my colleagues and I was undertaken to promote the distinction between various causes of success and failure. In particular, we attempted to provide evidence that ability and effort should be distinguished, although both are internal in locus of causality.

In one reference experiment that was employed, subjects were asked to pretend that they were teachers and were to provide evaluative "feedback" to their pupils (e.g., Eswara, 1972; Kaplan & Swant, 1973; Rest, Nierenberg, Weiner, & Heckhausen, 1973; Weiner & Kukla, 1970; Weiner & Peter, 1973). The pupils were characterized in terms of effort, ability, and performance on an exam. The data from these investigations conclusively demonstrated that effort is of greater importance than ability in determining reward and punishment. High effort was rewarded more than high ability given success, and lack of effort was punished more than lack of ability given failure.

To explain these findings, it was stated by Weiner (1977) that:

> There appear to be two reasons for the discrepancy between ability and effort as determinants of reward and punishment. First, effort attributions elicit strong moral feelings—trying to attain a socially valued goal is something that one "ought" to do. Second, rewarding and punishing effort is instrumental to changing behavior, inasmuch as effort is believed to be subject to volitional control. On the other hand, ability is perceived as nonvolitional and relatively stable and thus should be insensitive to external control attempts [p. 508].

Thus, both the moral and control aspects of evaluation were considered. But it was not realized that evaluation is conceptually similar to behaviors and feelings such as help giving, altruism, liking, and blame. That is, there is a pervasive influence of perceived controllability or personal responsibility on interpersonal judgments in achievement-related contexts, including how students are graded.

Sentiments

Investigations linking liking to perceptions of controllability primarily have been conducted in the area of loneliness (see Peplau, Russell, & Heim, 1979). Michela, Peplau, and Weeks (1978) found that persons lonely for reasons thought to be controllable (e.g., does not try to make friends) are liked less than individuals lonely for uncontrollable reasons (e.g., no opportunity to meet people). In addition, when a lonely person puts forth effort to make friends, that person is liked and elicits sympathy (Wimer & Peplau, 1978). In contrast, if it is believed that the lonely individual is responsible for his or her plight, then sympathy is not forthcoming and respondents indicate they would avoid such persons. I assume that this pattern of results will also be evident in achievement-related contexts. Surely a teacher will not particularly like a student who does not try, and failure perceived as due to lack of effort does not elicit sympathy.

Self-perception of Control

Although perceived control in others relates to interpersonal judgments, self-perceptions of control have quite a different array of consequences. These intrapersonal effects appear to be vast, ranging from experiential states such as feeling as an origin (de Charms, 1968) and perceiving freedom of choice (Steiner, 1970), to specific behaviors such as information search (see Rotter, 1966) and normal functioning rather than learning, cognitive, and motivational deficits that are postulated to accompany the loss of control (Seligman, 1975). This is a complex subject matter in need of systematic examination and synthesis that goes well beyond the scope of our present knowledge.

SUMMARY

A variety of sources of information (not discussed here) are used to reach causal inferences in achievement-related contexts. The perceived causes of success and failure primarily are ability and effort, but also include a small number of other salient factors such as home environment and teacher, and a countless host of idiosyncratic factors. These causes can be comprised within three primary dimensions of causality: stability, locus, and control. There also are an undetermined number of subordinate causal dimensions, including perhaps intentionality and globality. The three main dimensions respectively are linked to expectancy changes, esteem-related affects, and interpersonal judgments (decisions about helping, evaluation, and sentiments). In addition, there are secondary linkages between the causal dimensions and psychological effects: stability relates to depression-type affects and control is associated with particular feeling states and behavior. The dimension-consequence linkages influence motivated behaviors such as persistence and choice. This theory is depicted in Table 6.5.

THEORETICAL RANGE

The theory rather sketchily conveyed in Table 6.5 has been shown to be relevant in many achievement-related contexts. The topics already examined in this chapter include the perceived reasons for success and failure, expectancy changes,

TABLE 6.5
Partial Representation of an Attributional Theory of Motivation

Antecedent Conditions	Perceived Causes	Causal Dimensions	Primary Effects	Other Consequences
	Ability	Stability ⟶	Expectancy change	Performance intensity
	Effort (typical	Locus ⟶	Esteem-related	Persistence
	and immediate)		affects	Choice
	Others (students,	Control ⟶	Interpersonal	Others
	family, teacher)		judgments;	
	Motivation (atten-		Intrapersonal	
	tion, interest)	Intentionality	feeling states	
	Etc.	Globality		

self-concept maintenance, achievement change programs, risk-preference, reinforcement schedules, hopelessness, sources of emotion, self-esteem, helping,
evaluation, and liking. Still other achievement-related topics have been demonstrated to be encompassed within this attributional conception (see Weiner, 1974,
1976). The breadth of the phenomena incorporated within this attributional
framework intimates that a general theory of motivation is being constructed. In
the remainder of this chapter I document other areas to which the theory is
applicable.

Hyperactivity and Psychostimulants

Whalen and Henker (1976) have outlined an attributional analysis of the effects
of drug treatment for hyperactive children. They contend that when hyperactivity
is combatted with a drug, the belief is conveyed to both the child and his or her
parents that the cause of the hyperactivity is a physiological dysfunction. Hence,
the involved individuals are not responsible for, or in control of, the maladaptive
behavior that is exhibited. Because this physiological deficit is perceived as an
uncontrollable cause, neither the child nor the parents need feel guilty or blame
themselves for the aberrant behavior. That is, the shift in perceived causality
from ''lack of effort'' minimizes self-blame, and negative evaluations from
others. This appears to be a beneficial and an unanticipated side-effect of the
treatment technique.

On the other hand, Whalen and Henker (1976) also state that ''the reputed
physiological dysfunctions used to explain the failure of the hyperactive child are
frequently viewed as stable and relatively unresponsive to behavioral change
effects [p. 1123].'' Thus, according to Whalen & Henker (1976), the preception
of fixed causation ''leads to demoralization about problem solutions . . . and
interferes with effective coping [p. 1124].''

In sum, again there is an analysis of a psychological phenomenon from the perspective shown in Table 6.5. Individuals utilize information (treatment technique) to infer causation about an event (hyperactivity). The perceived cause (a genetic deficit) is perceived as uncontrollable and stable. This minimizes certain negative affects and unfavorable evaluations (beneficial effects) but also weakens the perceived possibility of recovery (a harmful consequence). These two factors, in turn, influence the long-range influence of the treatment (negatively, according to Whalen and Henker, inasmuch as they perceive expectancy to be the more potent determinant of long-term behavioral change).

Mastery

The labels "mastery" and "competence" are prominent among the writings of many psychologists (e.g., Nissen, 1954; White, 1959). However, in my opinion systematic experimental work elucidating these alleged motivators of behavior has not been conducted. An investigation by Nuttin (1973), described as demonstrating "causality pleasure," could provide an important experimental paradigm for this area. Nuttin placed 5-year-olds in an experimental room containing two "machines." The machines each had colored lights and movable handles. For one machine (A), the onset of the lights was preprogrammed by the experimenter. On the other hand, the lights in the alternate machine (B) went on or off when the handle was moved beyond a certain point. Thus, although both machines stimulated the viewer perceptually, the children were the producers or the cause of the stimulation only with machine B.

The subjects in this experiment were free to spend their time with either machine. The experimenters recorded various indexes of choice or preference, such as the time spent with each machine and verbal reports of liking. Both observational and self-report data revealed that the children strongly preferred machine B over machine A. These findings have been replicated by Weiner, Kun, and Benesh-Weiner (1980).

From the theoretical perspective shown in Table 6.5, the experiment by Nuttin (1973) illustrates a temporal sequence involving the use of information, inferences concerning locus of causality, positive affect, and some behavioral consequences of emotional states. That is, on the basis of the observed covariation between their own actions and the onset of the lights in machine B, the children infer that they are personally responsible (ability and effort) for the stimulation from that machine. Self-attribution for the outcome increases positive esteem-related affects, and the augmented affect increases the probability of engaging in the action again as well as increasing "liking" about playing with the machine.

This interpretation is applicable to another developmental study that has not been conceptualized as involving mastery-type behavior. Watson (1966, 1967) demonstrated that eight-week old infants can learn an instrumental response (a head turn) to increase stimulation (the movement of a mobile). He also reported that infants in the instrumental response condition apparently displayed more instances of positive affect (smiling and cooing) than children in a condition in which the mobile movement was controlled by the experimenter. This again suggests a temporal sequence of: response-outcome covariation—perceived internal causation—positive affects of competence and pride—choice. That is, the enhanced positive affect and subsequent performance of the instrumental response are mediated by perceptions of self-responsibility (perhaps the control dimension also plays a role here).

The underlying premise of this interpretation of Watson's (1966, 1967) research is that affect and choice can be used to infer cognitive processes (perceptions of causality). It may seem far-fetched to draw the inference that 8-week olds have the cognitive capacities to make causal deductions. However, it also may be that a differentiation between the self and the environment has developed by that age, and that primitive inferences about locus and control have been made using proprioceptive feedback information. If this interpretation has any validity, then Watson perhaps has identified the existence of attempts at mastery among very young infants.

Parole Decisions

A parole decision is a complex judgment in which causal attributions play a major role. Figure 6.1 depicts the parole decision process as conceptualized by Carroll and Payne (1976, 1977). The figure indicates that the decision maker is provided with a variety of information about the criminal, the crime, and other pertinent facts. This information is combined and synthesized, yielding attributions about the cause of the crime. The causal attributions, in turn, influence judgments about deserved punishment and social risk that are believed to be the basis for the final parole decision.

Carroll and Payne (1976), after reviewing an extensive literature, contend that the parole decision process is:

> based on a simple two-part model. In the first part, the primary concern of the decision maker is to make the punishment fit the crime. . . . At the second part . . . the primary concern . . . is with parole risk, i.e., the probability that the person being considered for release will again violate the laws of society [p. 15]."

According to Fig. 6.1, crimes that are ascribed to internal and/or intentional (controllable) factors (e.g., personality characteristics, evil intents) should result in harsher evaluation (punishment) than crimes attributed to external and/or unintentional (uncontrollable) causes (e.g., economic conditions, bad friends, etc.). In addition, the risk associated with parole should depend on the stability of the perceived cause of the crime. If, for example, the crime is attributed to some

Attributional Analysis of Perceptions of Crime and Criminals

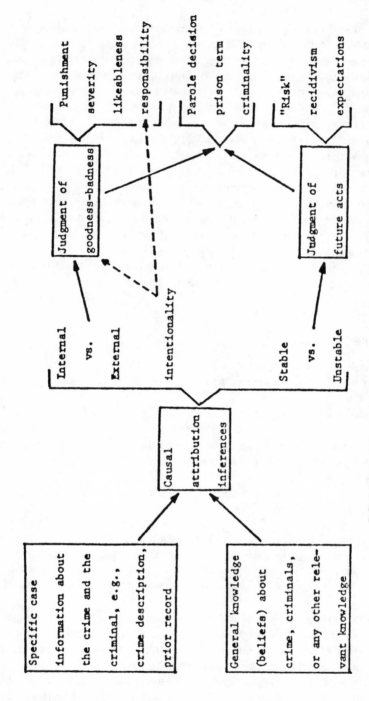

FIG. 6.1. An attributional framework for the parole decision process (From Carroll & Payne, 1977, p. 200).

fixed personality trait, then the decision maker will expect that a crime again will be committed if the prisoner is paroled. On the other hand, if the cause of the crime has been or can be altered (e.g., economic conditions have improved, a job can be found, etc.), then the criminal is perceived as a good parole risk.

Given the above analysis, a criminal is least likely to be paroled if the cause of the crime is perceived as internal and/or controllable but stable ("He is an evil person"). Conversely, parole will tend to be granted when the crime is perceived as caused by external and/or noncontrollable and unstable factors (e.g., prior economic conditions). The remaining causal combinations should fall between these extremes in terms of parole probability.

Carroll and Payne (1976, 1977) have furnished support for these hypotheses, examining professional parole decision makers and the judgments of college students when given simulated criminal cases. They find, for example, that perceptions of the locus, stability, and controllability of causes significantly relate to perceived responsibility for the crime, likelihood of recidivism, likability, prison term, and the purpose of the sentence.

In sum, according to Carroll and Payne (1976, 1977) the parole decision procedure is conceptually identical to the perceived sequence of events in the achievement domain: antecedent information is processed, a causal judgment is reached, and the cause is placed within the locus, stability, and intentionality (control) dimensions. This influences evaluation and expectancy, which are the main determinants of the parole decision.

Affiliation and Loneliness

It has been reasoned that in our culture two sources of motivation are most dominant: achievement and social recognition (or, in Freud's more general terms, *Arbeit und Liebe*). Hence, affiliative motivation is a natural area to turn toward in the development of a theory of motivation.

There have been two analyses of affiliative behaviors using the attributional principles specified in this chapter. Folkes (1978) examined causal communications during the initial stages of an affiliative relationship. In one of her investigations, Folkes asked female subjects to assume that they had been asked out for a date and they were to reject the male. The rejection was for one of 16 reasons subsumed within the eight causal dimension cells (2 levels of locus × 2 levels of stability × 2 levels of control) (see Table 6.6). The subjects were then asked to relate what they actually would tell the male concerning the reason for the rejection. Folkes thus was able to compare public and private causes. In addition, the subjects were asked "how hurt" the male would feel given each of these public and private attributions, what was the likelihood that the male would ask her for another date, and "how fair or deserved" the rejection was. These dependent variables tap affect, expectancy, and evaluation—the specified consequences of causal dimensions.

TABLE 6.6
Private Reasons for Rejection (from Folkes, 1978, pp. 99–102)

| | Internal | | External | |
	Stable	Unstable	Stable	Unstable
Controllable	1. Overweight (physically unattractive) 2. Negativistic personality	1. Scraggly beard (unattractive) 2. Temporary bad frame of mind	1. Don't want to date someone who went out with a friend 2. Want to devote all time to a hobby	1. Don't want to go to a sporting event 2. Want to see program on television
Uncontrollable	1. Physically unattractive 2. Not as smart as you	1. Ugly rash that will go away 2. Irritable because of medical treatment	1. Religion forbids dating him 2. Job transfer	1. Have the flu 2. Must wait for telephone call from parents

The data revealed that the females generally communicated external, unstable, and uncontrollable reasons for rejection (e.g., "I am ill"). External rather than internal causes were given for rejection in order not to hurt the male's feelings. In addition, there were clear linkages between the stability dimension of causality and the expectation of a future dating request, with stable causes for rejection leading to lower expectations. And finally, it was believed more "just" to reject a person for internal, controllable causes (being overweight or negative) than for internal, uncontrollable causes (being physically unattractive or irritable because of a drug treatment). Thus, the findings in the achievement area replicated perfectly in the affiliative domain.

Another attributional analysis of affiliative motivation guided by the theory shown in Table 6.5 concerns loneliness and conceives of loneliness as a social failure (Gordon, 1976; Stein & Bailey, 1973). Hanusa (1975) and Heim (1975) examined the perceived causes of social success and failure and found them to be similar to the causes of achievement success and failure. As already indicated, Michela et al. (1978) used scaling procedures to discover the dimensions of the causes of social failure and found them to be similar to the dimensions uncovered in achievement contexts.

The question that then remains is whether the attributional dimensions in the loneliness domain relate to psychological factors in the same manner as in the achievement domain. Research reveals that is indeed the case (see Peplau, Russell, & Heim, 1979). Stability relates to the perceived probability of remaining lonely in the future, locus is associated with esteem-related affects and, as previously stated, control is linked with liking and sympathy toward the lonely person.

Depression and Learned Helplessness

In accordance with the trend in loneliness research, recent explanations of depression have focused upon the cognitive, rather than the affective, aspects of this disorder (e.g., Beck, 1976). The work of Seligman (1975), captured under the label of "learned helplessness," has been especially influential. I will not dwell upon Seligman's use of this construct or the supporting empirical evidence in this context. Rather, my goal is to convey the pertinence of the learned helplessness literature to the attributional model depicted in Table 6.5 (see Abramson, Seligman, & Teasdale, 1978; Weiner & Litman-Adizes, 1980).

Learned helplessness communicates the belief that there is no perceived association between responding and environmental outcomes. That is, the actor believes that the likelihood of an event is independent of what he or she does. The belief in helplessness is alleged to produce deficits in motivation and learning, negative affect, and a syndrome that has been labeled "depression."

As this work progressed from infrahuman to human research, it became evident that it also is essential to consider why actions and outcomes are perceived to be independent. For example, Klein, Fencil-Morse, and Seligman (1976) found that only individuals making internal attributions for response-outcome independence exhibited aspects of the learned helplessness syndrome. Attributions of response-outcome independence to external factors did not produce any learning deficits. In a similar manner, Tennen and Eller (1977) found learned helplessness only under conditions that promote low ability attributions for prior lack of control.

Partially because of these data, Abramson et al. (1978) adopted an attributional framework for helplessness. They argue that depressed individuals attempt to make sense out of perceived evidence that their responses do not affect outcomes. A cause is determined that often is classified as stable, internal, and global. This leads to a low expectancy of success across a wide array of environments and a heightened negative affect (loss of self-esteem), which are sufficient precursors of depression. Abramson et al. (1978) also distinguish universal from personal helplessness. In the former case, for all individuals there is response-outcome independence (e.g., attempting to help a child with leukemia), whereas in the latter instance only the concerned individual cannot affect the environment. They contend that only in the latter instance will the person have lowered self-esteem and feelings of worthlessness. This is consistent with the postulated locus-affect relation that previously was discussed.

CONCLUSION

I have selectively reviewed the extensive literature outside of the achievement domain, including hyperactivity, mastery, parole decisions, affiliation, and depression. The data strongly suggest that a general conception of motivation, as well as a particular method of psychological analysis, is evolving.

REFERENCES

Abramson, L. Y., Seligman, M. E. P., & Teasdale, J. D. Learned helplessness in humans: Critique and reformulation. *Journal of Abnormal Psychology,* 1978, *87,* 49–74.

Ames, C. Children's achievement attributions and self-reinforcement: Effect of self-concept and competitive reward structure. *Journal of Educational Psychology,* 1978, *70,* 345–355.

Andrews, G. R., & Debus, R. L. Persistence and causal perceptions of failure: Modifying cognitive attributions. *Journal of Educational Psychology,* 1978, *70,* 154–166.

Arkin, R. M., & Maruyama, G. M. Attribution, affect, and college exam performance. *Journal of Educational Psychology,* 1979, *71,* 85–93.

Atkinson, J. W. *An introduction to motivation.* Princeton, N.J.: Van Nostrand, 1964.

Barnes, R. D., Ickes, W. J., & Kidd, R. F. *Effects of perceived intentionality and stability of another's dependency on helping behavior: A field experiment.* Unpublished manuscript, University of Wisconsin, Madison, 1977.

Bar-Tal, D., & Darom, E. *Causal perceptions of pupils' success or failure by teachers and pupils: A comparison.* Unpublished manuscript, University of Tel-Aviv, Israel, 1977.

Beck, A. T. *Cognitive therapy and the emotional disorders.* New York: International Universities Press, 1976.

Bem, D. J. Cognitive alteration of feeling states: A discussion. In H. London & R. E. Nisbett (Eds.), *Thought and feeling.* Chicago: Aldine, 1974.

Berkowitz, L. Resistance to improper dependency relationships. *Journal of Experimental Social Psychology,* 1969, *5,* 283–294.

Brehm, J. W. *Response to loss of freedom: A theory of psychological reactance.* New York: Academic Press, 1966.

Carroll, J. S., & Payne, J. W. The psychology of the parole decision process: A joint application of attribution theory and information processing psychology. In J. S. Carroll & J. W. Payne (Eds.), *Cognition and social behavior.* Hillsdale, N.J.: Lawrence Erlbaum Associates, 1976.

Carroll, J. S., & Payne, J. W. Judgments about crime and the criminal: A model and a method for investigating parole decision. In B. D. Sales (Ed.), *Prospectives in law and psychology: Vol. 1. The criminal justice system.* New York: Plenum, 1977.

Chapin, M., & Dyck, D. G. Persistence in children's reading behavior as a function of N length and attribution retraining. *Journal of Abnormal Psychology,* 1976, *85,* 511–515.

Cooper, H. M., & Burger, J. M. *Internality, stability, and personal efficacy: A categorization of free response academic attributions.* Unpublished manuscript, University of Missouri, Columbia, Missouri, 1978.

Davison, G. C., & Valins, S. Maintenance of self-attributed and drug-attributed behavior change. *Journal of Personality and Social Psychology,* 1969, *1,* 25–33.

de Charms, R. *Personal causation.* New York: Academic Press, 1968.

Deci, E. L. *Intrinsic motivation.* New York: Plenum, 1975.

Diener, C. I., & Dweck, C. S. An analysis of learned helplessness: Continuous changes in performance, strategy, and achievement cognitions following failure. *Journal of Personality and Social Psychology,* 1978, *36,* 451–462.

Diggory, J. C., Riley, E. J., & Blumenfeld, R. Estimated probability of success for a fixed goal. *American Journal of Psychology,* 1960, *73,* 41–55.

Dweck, C. S. The role of expectations and attributions in the alleviation of learned helplessness. *Journal of Personality and Social Psychology,* 1975, *31,* 674–685.

Dweck, C. S., & Repucci, N. D. Learned helplessness and reinforcement responsibility in children. *Journal of Personality and Social Psychology,* 1973, *25,* 109–116.

Ellis, A. Rational emotive therapy. In A. Burton (Ed.), *Operational theories of personality.* New York: Bruner/Mazel, 1974.

Estes, W. K. *Handbook of Learning and Cognitive Processes* (Vol. 1). Hillsdale, N.J.: Lawrence Erlbaum Associates, 1975.

Eswara, H. S. Administration of reward and punishment in relation to ability, effort, and performance. *Journal of Social Psychology,* 1972, *87,* 139–140.

Elig, T. W., & Frieze, I. H. A multidimensional scheme for coding and interpreting perceived causality for success and failure events: The Coding Scheme of Perceived Causality (CSPC). *JSAS Catalog of Selected Documents in Psychology,* 1975, *5,* 313(Ms. No. 1969).

Feather, N. T. Attribution of responsibility and valence of success and failure in relation to initial confidence and task performance. *Journal of Personality and Social Psychology,* 1969, *13,* 129–144.

Feather, N. T. Causal attributions for male and female success and failure at occupations differing in perceived status and sex-linked appropriateness. *Australian Journal of Psychology,* 1977, *29,* 151–165.

Feather, N. T., & Simon, J. G. Causal attributions for success and failure in relation to expectations of success based upon selective or manipulative control. *Journal of Personality and Social Psychology,* 1971, *39,* 527–541.

Feather, N. T., & Simon, J. G. Luck and the unexpected outcome: A field replication of laboratory findings. *Australian Journal of Psychology,* 1972, *24,* 113–117.

Ferster, C. B., and Skinner, B. F. *Schedules of reinforcement.* New York: Appleton-Century-Crofts, 1957.

Fitch, G. Effects of self-esteem, perceived performance, and choice on causal attributions. *Journal of Personality and Social Psychology,* 1970, *16,* 311–315.

Folkes, V. S. *Causal communication in the early stages of affiliative relationships.* Unpublished doctoral dissertation, University of California, Los Angeles, 1978.

Fontaine, G. Social comparison and some determinants of expected personal control and expected performance in a novel situation. *Journal of Personality and Social Psychology,* 1974, *29,* 487–496.

Frieze, I. H. Causal attributions and information seeking to explain success and failure. *Journal of Research in Personality,* 1976, *10,* 293–305.

Frieze, I. H., & Weiner, B. Cue utilization and attributional judgments for success and failure. *Journal of Personality,* 1971, *39,* 591–606.

Gilmore, T. M., & Minton, H. L. Internal versus external attributions of task performance as a function of locus of control, initial confidence and success–failure outcome. *Journal of Personality,* 1974, *42,* 159–174.

Gordon, S. *Lonely in America.* New York: Simon & Schuster, 1976.

Hanusa, B. H. *An extension of Weiner's attribution approach to social situations: Sex differences in social situations.* Paper presented at the Eastern Psychological Association Convention, New York, April 1975.

Harvey, J. H., Ickes, W. J., & Kidd, R. F. (Eds.). *New directions in attribution research* (Vol. 1). Hillsdale, N.J.: Lawrence Erlbaum Associates, 1976.

Harvey, J. H., Ickes, W. J., & Kidd, R. F. (Eds.). *New directions in attribution research* (Vol. 2). Hillsdale, N.J.: Lawrence Erlbaum Associates, 1978.

Heider, F. *The psychology of interpersonal relations.* New York: Wiley, 1958.

Heim, M. *Sex differences in causal attributions for achievement in social tasks.* Paper presented at the Eastern Psychological Association Convention, New York, April 1975.

Ickes, W. J., & Kidd, R. F. An attributional analysis of helping behavior. In J. H. Harvey, W. J. Ickes, & R. F. Kidd (Eds.), *New directions in attribution research* (Vol. 1). Hillsdale, N.J.: Lawrence Erlbaum Associates, 1976.

Ickes, W. J., Kidd, R. F., & Berkowitz, L. Attributional determinants of monetary help-giving. *Journal of Personality,* 1976, *44,* 163–178.

Ickes, W. J., & Layden, M. A. Attributional styles. In J. H. Harvey, W. J. Ickes, & R. F. Kidd (Eds.), *New directions in attribution research* (Vol. 2). Hillsdale, N.J.: Lawrence Erlbaum Associates, 1978.

James, W. H. *Internal vs. external control of reinforcement as a basic variable in learning theory.* Unpublished doctoral dissertation, Ohio State University, 1957.

Jarvik, M. E. Negative recency effect in probability learning. *Journal of Experimental Psychology,* 1951, *41,* 291–297.

Jones, E. E., & Davis, K. E. From acts to dispositions: The attribution process in person perception. In L. Berkowitz (Ed.), *Advances in experimental social psychology* (Vol. 2). New York: Academic Press, 1965.

Jones, E. E., Kanouse, D. E., Kelley, H. H., Nisbett, R. E., Valins, S., & Weiner, B. *Attribution: Perceiving the causes of behavior.* Morristown, N.J.: General Learning Press, 1972.

Kaplan, R. M., & Swant, S. G. Reward characteristics of appraisal of achievement behavior. *Representative Research in Social Psychology,* 1973, *4,* 11–17.

Kelley, H. H. Attribution theory in social psychology. In D. Levine (Ed.), *Nebraska Symposium on Motivation*. Lincoln: University of Nebraska Press, 1967.

Kelley, H. H. *Attribution in social interaction*. Morristown, N.J.: General Learning Press, 1971.

Kelly, G. A. *The psychology of personal constructs*. New York: W. W. Norton, 1955.

Klein, D. C., Fencil-Morse, E., & Seligman, M. E. P. Learned helplessness, depression, and the attribution of failure. *Journal of Personality and Social Psychology*, 1976, *33*, 508–516.

Lau, R. R., & Russell, D. Attributions in the sports pages: A field test of some current hypotheses in attribution research. *Journal of Personality and Social Psychology*, 1978, *39*, 29–38.

Lawrence, D. H., & Festinger, L. *Deterrents and reinforcement*. Stanford, Calif.: Stanford University Press, 1962.

Lazarus, R. S. *Psychological stress and the coping process*. New York: McGraw-Hill, 1966.

Lefcourt, H. M., von Baeyer, C. L., Ware, E. E., & Cox, D. J. The multidimensional-multiattributional causality scale: The development of a goal specific locus of control scale. *Canadian Journal of Behavioral Science*, 1979, *11*, 286–304.

Lepley, W. M. The maturity of the chances: A gambler's fallacy. *Journal of Psychology*, 1963, *56*, 69–72.

Lewin, K. *A dynamic theory of personality*. New York: McGraw-Hill, 1935.

Lewis, D. J. Partial reinforcement: A selective review of the literature since 1950. *Psychological Bulletin*, 1960, *57*, 1–28.

Litman-Adizes, T. *An attributional model of depression: Laboratory and clinical investigations*. Unpublished doctoral dissertation, University of California, Los Angeles, 1978.

Mann, L. On being a sore loser: How fans react to their team's failure. *Australian Journal of Psychology*, 1974, *26*, 37–47.

McClelland, D. C. Toward a theory of motive acquisition. *American Psychologist*, 1965, *20*, 321–333.

McClelland, D. C., Atkinson, J. W., Clark, R. A., & Lowell, E. L. *The achievement motive*. New York: Appleton, Century, & Crofts, 1953.

McClelland, D. C., & Winter, D. *Motivating economic achievement*. New York: The Free Press, 1969.

McMahan, I. D. Relationships between causal attributions and expectancy of success. *Journal of Personality and Social Psychology*, 1973, *28*, 108–115.

Meichenbaum, D., & Cameron, R. The clinical potential of modifying what clients say to themselves. In M. J. Mahoney & C. E. Thoresen (Eds.), *Self-control: Power to the person*. Monterey, Calif.: Brooks-Cole, 1974.

Meyer, J. P. Causal attributions for success and failure: A multivariate investigation of dimensionality, formation, and consequences. *Journal of Personality and Social Psychology*, 1980, *38*, 704–718.

Meyer, W. U. *Selbstwortlichkeit und Leistungsmotivation*. Unpublished doctoral dissertation, Ruhr Universität, Bochum, Germany, 1970.

Meyer, W. U., Folkes, V. S., & Weiner, B. The perceived informational value and affective consequences of choice behavior and intermediate difficulty task selection. *Journal of Research in Personality*, 1976, *10*, 410–423.

Michela, J., Peplau, L. A., & Weeks, D. *Perceived dimensions and consequences of attributions for loneliness*. Unpublished manuscript, University of California, Los Angeles, 1978.

Nisbett, R. E., & Schachter, S. Cognitive manipulation of pain. *Journal of Experimental Social Psychology*, 1966, *2*, 227–236.

Nisbett, R. E., & Wilson, T. D. Telling more than we can know: Verbal reports as mental processes. *Psychological Review*, 1977, *84*, 231–259.

Nissen, H. W. The nature of drive as innate determinant of behavioral organization. In M. R. Jones (Ed.), *Nebraska Symposium on Motivation*. Lincoln: University of Nebraska Press, 1954.

Nuttin, J. R. Pleasure and reward in motivation and learning. In D. Berlyne (Ed.), *Pleasure, reward, preference.* New York: Academic Press, 1973.

Ostrove, N. Expectations for success on effort-determined tasks as a function of incentive and performance feedback. *Journal of Personality and Social Psychology,* 1978, *36,* 909–916.

Pancer, S. M., & Eiser, J. R. *Expectations, aspirations, and evaluations as influenced by another's attributions for success and failure.* Paper presented at the American Psychological Association Convention, Chicago, September 1975.

Passer, M. W. *Perceiving the causes of success and failure revisited: A multidimensional scaling approach.* Unpublished doctoral dissertation, University of California, Los Angeles, 1977.

Pennebaker, J. W., Burnam, M. A., Schaeffer, M. A., & Harper, D. C. Lack of control as a determinant of perceived physical symptoms. *Journal of Personality and Social Psychology,* 1977, *35,* 167–174.

Peplau, L. A., Russell, D., & Heim, M. The experience of loneliness. In I. Frieze, D. Bar-Tal, & J. Carroll (Eds.), *New approaches to social problems: Applications of attribution theory.* San Francisco: Jossey-Bass, 1979.

Phares, E. J. Expectancy changes in skill and chance situations. *Journal of Abnormal and Social Psychology,* 1957, *54,* 339–342.

Phares, E. J. Locus of control. In H. London & J. E. Exner, Jr. (Eds.), *Dimensions of personality.* New York: Wiley, 1978.

Piliavin, I. M., Rodin, J., & Piliavin, J. A. Good samaritanism: An underground phenomenon? *Journal of Personality and Social Psychology,* 1969, *13,* 289–299.

Rest, S. Schedules of reinforcement: An attributional analysis. In J. H. Harvey, W. J. Ickes, & R. F. Kidd (Eds.), *New directions in attribution research* (Vol. 1). Hillsdale, N.J.: Lawrence Erlbaum Associates, 1976.

Rest, S., Nierenberg, R., Weiner, B., & Heckhausen, H. Further evidence concerning the effects of perceptions of effort and ability on achievement evaluation. *Journal of Personality and Social Psychology,* 1973, *28,* 187–191.

Riemer, B. S. Influence of causal beliefs on affect and expectancy. *Journal of Personality and Social Psychology,* 1975, *31,* 1163–1167.

Rosenbaum, R. M. *A dimensional analysis of the perceived causes of success and failure.* Unpublished doctoral dissertation, University of California, Los Angeles, 1972.

Ross, R., Rodin, J., & Zimbardo, P. G. Toward an attribution therapy: The reduction of fear through induced cognitive–emotional misattribution. *Journal of Personality and Social Psychology,* 1969, *12,* 279–288.

Rotter, J. B. Generalized expectancies for internal versus external control of reinforcement. *Psychological Monographs,* 1966, *80* (1, Whole No. 609).

Rotter, J. B., Liverant, S., & Crowne, D. P. The growth and extinction of expectancies in chance controlled and skilled tasks. *Journal of Psychology,* 1961, *52,* 161–177.

Schachter, S., & Singer, J. E. Cognitive, social, and physiological determinants of emotional state. *Psychological Review,* 1962, *69,* 379–399.

Schopler, J., & Matthews, M. The influence of perceived causal locus of partner's dependence on the use of interpersonal power. *Journal of Personality and Social Psychology,* 1965, *2,* 609–612.

Schütz, A. *Collected papers. I. The problem of social reality.* The Hague: Martinus Nijhoff, 1967.

Seligman, M. E. P. *Helplessness: On depression, development, and death.* San Francisco: Freeman, 1975.

Simon, J. G., & Feather, N. T. Causal attributions for success and failure at university examinations. *Journal of Educational Psychology,* 1973, *64,* 46–56.

Skinner, B. F. The process involved in the repeated guessing of alternatives. *Journal of Experimental Psychology,* 1942, *30,* 495–503.

Sparta, S. N. *Treatment of "helpless" children through cognitive interpretations of failure: An examination of some therapeutic influences.* Unpublished doctoral dissertation, University of California, Los Angeles, 1978.

Stein, A. H., & Bailey, M. M. The socialization of achievement motivation in females. *Psychological Bulletin,* 1973, *80,* 345-366.

Steiner, I. D. Perceived freedom. In L. Berkowitz (Ed.), *Advances in experimental social psychology* (Vol. 5). New York: Academic Press, 1970.

Tennen, H., & Eller, S. J. Attributional components of learned helplessness and facilitation. *Journal of Personality and Social Psychology,* 1977, *35,* 265-271.

Tolman, E. C. Purpose and cognition: The determinants of animal learning. *Psychological Review,* 1925, *32,* 285-297.

Triandis, H. *The analysis of subjective culture.* New York: Wiley-Interscience, 1972.

Trope, Y. Seeking information about one's own ability as a determinant of choice among tasks. *Journal of Personality and Social Psychology,* 1975, *32,* 1004-1013.

Trope, Y., & Brickman, P. Difficulty and diagnosticity as determinants of choice among tasks. *Journal of Personality and Social Psychology,* 1975, *31,* 918-925.

Valle, V. A. *Attributions of stability as a mediator in the changing of expectations.* Unpublished doctoral dissertation, University of Pittsburgh, Pennsylvania, 1974.

Valle, V. A., & Frieze, I. H. Stability of causal attributions as a mediator in changing expectations for success. *Journal of Personality and Social Psychology,* 1976, *33,* 579-587.

Watson, J. S. The development and generalization of "contingency awareness" in early infancy: Some hypotheses. *Merrill-Palmer Quarterly,* 1966, *12,* 123-135.

Watson, J. S. Memory and "contingency analysis" in infant learning. *Merrill-Palmer Quarterly,* 1967, *12,* 55-76.

Weiner, B. New conceptions in the study of achievement motivation. In B. A. Maher (Ed.), *Progress in experimental personality research* (Vol. 5). New York: Academic Press, 1970.

Weiner, B. *Theories of motivation: From mechanism to cognition.* Chicago: Rand McNally, 1972.

Weiner, B. (Ed.). *Achievement motivation and attribution theory.* Morristown, N.J.: General Learning Press, 1974.

Weiner, B. An attributional approach for educational psychology. In L. Shulman (Ed.), *Review of research in education* (Vol. 4). Itasca, Ill.: Peacock, 1976.

Weiner, B. Attribution and affect: Comments on Sohn's critique. *Journal of Educational Psychology,* 1977, *69,* 506-511.

Weiner, B. A theory of motivation for some classroom experiences. *Journal of Educational Psychology,* 1979, *71,* 3-25.

Weiner, B. A cognitive (attribution)–emotion–action model of motivated behavior: An analysis of judgments of help-giving. *Journal of Personality and Social Psychology,* 1980, 39, 186-200.

Weiner, B., Frieze, I. H., Kukla, A., Reed, L., Rest, S., & Rosenbaum, R. M. *Perceiving the causes of success and failure.* Morristown, N.J.: General Learning Press, 1971.

Weiner, B., & Kukla, A. An attributional analysis of achievement motivation. *Journal of Personality and Social Psychology,* 1970, *15,* 1-20.

Weiner, B., Kun, A., & Benesh-Weiner, M. The development of mastery, emotions, and morality from an attributional perspective. In W. A. Collins (Ed.), *Minnesota symposium on child development* (Vol. 13). Hillsdale, N.J.: Lawrence Erlbaum Associates, 1980.

Weiner, B., & Litman-Adizes, T. An attributional, expectancy-value analysis of learned helplessness and depression. In J. Garber and M. E. P. Seligman (Eds.), *Human control.* New York: Academic Press, 1980.

Weiner, B., Nierenberg, R., & Goldstein, M. Social learning (locus of control) versus attributional (causal stability) interpretations of expectancy of success. *Journal of Personality,* 1976, *44,* 52-68.

Weiner, B., & Peter, N. A cognitive-developmental analysis of achievement and moral judgments. *Developmental Psychology,* 1973, *9,* 290-309.

Weiner, B., Russell, D., & Lerman, D. Affective consequences of causal ascriptions. In J. H. Harvey, W. J. Ickes, & R. F. Kidd (Eds.), *New directions in attribution research* (Vol. 2). Hillsdale, N.J.: Lawrence Erlbaum Associates, 1978.

Weiner, B., Russell, D., & Lerman, D. The cognition–emotion process in achievement-related contexts. *Journal of Personality and Social Psychology*, 1979, *37*, 1211–1220.

Weiner, B., & Sierad, J. Misattribution for failure and enhancement of achievement strivings. *Journal of Personality and Social Psychology*, 1975, *31*, 415–421.

Whalen, C. K., & Henker, B. Psychostimulants and children: A review and analysis. *Psychological Bulletin*, 1976, *83*, 1113–1130.

White, R. W. Motivation reconsidered: The concept of competence. *Psychological Review*, 1959, *66*, 297–333.

Wimer, S. W., & Peplau, L. A. *Determinants of reactions to lonely others.* Paper presented at the Western Psychological Association Convention, San Francisco, April 1978.

Wong, P. T. P., & Weiner, B. When people ask why questions and the heuristics of attributional search. *Journal of Personality and Social Psychology*, 1981, *40*, 650–663.

Zajonc, R. B., & Brickman, P. Expectancy and feedback as independent factors in task performance. *Journal of Personality and Social Psychology*, 1969, *11*, 148–156.

THE CONTEXT OF
INFORMATION FEEDBACK

7

Expectations and What People Learn from Failure

Ronnie Janoff-Bulman
University of Massachusetts, Amherst

Philip Brickman
University of Michigan

The tendency to work harder, after failure, by people who expected to succeed has uniformly been regarded as adaptive, while the tendency to stop working by those who did not expect to succeed has been regarded as maladaptive. In our view this is false. The tendency to give up when persistence would have paid off is certainly undesirable. But so is the tendency to persist in trying to solve a task that is essentially insoluble. Indeed, we will argue that in some ways the second kind of error leads to a more serious and debilitating form of pathology than the first kind of error. Mathematicians burn out by staking their careers on finding solutions to extremely difficult, perhaps insoluble problems. Ordinary people ruin their lives by persisting in efforts to maintain relationships with spouses, parents, or children in ways that may once have worked, but cannot work any longer.

Ultimately, it is neither persistence (as characteristically attributed to people who expect to do well) nor lack of persistence (as characteristically attributed to people who expect to do poorly) that is crucial. It is rather the ability to discriminate situations in which persistence will pay off from situations in which it will not. We will eventually offer an explanation of why our culture, and our field, has attached positive value only to persistence and not to quitting, while in our view the ability to quit is every bit as vital as the ability to persist. First, however, we need to establish that a pathological form of behavior is manifested both in the blind persistence exhibited by people with high expectations and in the lack of persistence exhibited by people with low expectations.

GIVING UP AND THE PATHOLOGY OF LOW
EXPECTATIONS

People who expect to do poorly are not always able to physically abandon a task after failing. Very often, as in social psychological experiments, they are required to continue working on that task or similar tasks. The evidence that they are motivated to quit is thus indirect. It may take the form of reduced interest in or attention to the task and, more generally, impaired performance on the task. In the paragraphs that follow, we review evidence that people with low expectations are less likely to persist at a task both following failure and following success, and also in the absence of further feedback.

The tendency for people with high expectations for success to work harder and do better after failure and for people with low expectations for success to do less well after failure has been found both in studies that have manipulated subjects' expectancies for success and failure on a task and studies that have measured the effects of naturally occurring expectancies. Miller, Brickman, and Bolen (1975) found that efforts by teachers to persuade fifth-graders to do better in math (which implicitly criticized their current performance in the subject) were more effective in stimulating the performance of children who had been doing well in the past than children who had not been doing well in the past. Using college student subjects, Means and Means (1971) found that failure feedback on an aptitude test resulted in enhanced performance on a subsequent examination by college students with high grade point averages but depressed performance by those with low grade point averages. Shrauger and Sorman (1977) found that college females with low self-esteem, who generally expected to do poorly, spent less time working on an anagram test and solved fewer anagrams after an initial experience of failure than did subjects with high self-esteem or subjects who had not been made to fail (cf. also Perez, 1973; Schalon, 1968). In a laboratory experiment, Brickman and Hendricks (1975) manipulated subjects' expectations for success on a reaction time task by providing them with false feedback during a series of training sessions. Subjects who expected to succeed improved their performance when they appeared to be failing, while subjects who expected to fail did not.

People who have previously been led to fail, and to expect failure on future tasks, often show impaired performance on these tasks even before they have received any further explicit feedback. Feather (1966, 1968), for example, found that subjects who were first given five insoluble anagrams not only expected to do much worse on subsequent anagrams but actually performed much worse than subjects initially given five very easy anagrams. Roth and Kubal (1975) found that subjects who had been led to fail on three major tasks showed debilitated performance on a subsequent test while subjects who had been led to fail only once (and who had not, presumably, been led to believe that they could generally expect to fail in the experiment) showed enhanced performance. Hiroto and

Seligman (1975) showed that, in this connection, a cognitive task involving a mental response and an instrumental task involving a physical response were functionally equivalent. Failure to solve a series of multidimensional discrimination problems and failure to press a button in time to escape bursts of aversive noise were both capable of disrupting subsequent performance. Moreover, both cognitive and instrumental performances were vulnerable to disruption by failure. Subjects who had been led to fail subsequently showed a decreased ability to manipulate a shuttlebox apparatus to escape an aversive tone and a decreased ability to solve anagrams.

We are concentrating in our analysis on how people respond to failure, as has most past literature. But it may be noted in passing that there are a series of studies suggesting that people who do not expect to do well are also less likely to persist following success. Many of these were stimulated by Aronson and Carlsmith's (1962) demonstration that subjects who expected to do poorly on a test of social judgment were more likely to undo an unexpectedly successful performance when (under the elaborate guise of a procedural failure) they were asked by the experimenter to retake that test. Low expectancy subjects changed many of their answers when they retook the test, despite their knowledge that in this instance almost all their answers had been correct. Subsequent experiments have found this effect hard to replicate (see Archibald, 1974, for a review). For example, Brickman and Hendricks (1975) found that low expectancy subjects were encouraged and worked harder when initial feedback indicated that they were succeeding. According to Mettee (1971) and Maracek and Mettee (1972), the tendency to abandon a successful course of action is to be found primarily when subjects are worried about their ability to sustain that level of success in the future, versus conditions in which they know that their success is a result of luck or irrelevant to future evaluation (see also Brickman, Linsenmeier, & McCareins, 1976).

Although it is beyond the scope of this paper to review the literature on either feelings of internal and external control (see Lefcourt, 1976) or test anxiety (see Sarason & Spielberger, 1975), it is worth noting that findings analogous to those we have been discussing for people with low expectations have been reported for subjects who believe events are externally controlled and for subjects who are very anxious. For example, Weiss and Sherman (1973) found that subjects who were low in their belief that they could control events, as measured by the Rotter (1966) Internal-External Control Scale, were less likely to persist in trying to solve an insoluble maze after having failed on an earlier task than subjects who were high in their belief that they could control events. Lavelle, Metalsky, and Coyne (1979) found that the anagram solving performance of subjects high in test anxiety suffered from prior exposure to uncontrollable noise, while the performance of subjects low in test anxiety did not. One would expect that, under many circumstances, people who believed that events were controlled by forces outside their control would also be high in anxiety and low in their expectation for positive outcomes (cf. Atkinson & Feather, 1966; Brockner, 1979). Thus it should not be surprising that analogous results are found in the three areas, or that explanations of value in one area should also prove helpful in understanding the results of other areas.

There are a number of possible explanations for this pattern of effects. The theory of learned helplessness (Seligman, 1975) postulates that when individuals are subject to uncontrollable aversive events like failure, they learn that their responding and their reinforcement are independent of one another. This expectation of response-outcome independence in turn reduces the individual's motivation to respond and thus their performance in subsequent situations where events are in fact controllable. Attribution theory (Weiner, Frieze, Kukla, Reed, Rest, & Rosenbaum, 1971) contends that people who fail repeatedly and expect to fail in the future come to attribute failure to internal and stable causes (their own lack of ability, or, more generally, deficiencies in their own character; see Janoff-Bulman, 1979). Believing that the cause of failure is internal and unchangeable lowers one's motivation to keep trying. People who expect to cope effectively attribute the difficulties they encounter to unstable causes, either internal (lack of effort or inappropriate behavior, both of which can be changed) or external (temporary bad luck). The reformulated version of learned helplessness also places great emphasis on the attributions people make for the causes of their failure (Abramson, Seligman, & Teasdale, 1978). Dissonance theory (Aronson, 1968; Yaryan & Festinger, 1961) suggests that the expenditure of effort on a task would be dissonant with the expectation that one would not do well on the task, and hence would be curtailed; and also that the experience of success on a task would be dissonant with the expectation that one would not do well, and hence would be rejected. Research on test anxiety (Sarason & Spielberger, 1975) emphasizes the tendency of individuals to avoid tasks on which they expect to fail or are anxious about failing and to attend instead to distracting features of the environment or their own behavior (Wine, 1971). This makes the performance of people who expect to do poorly more vulnerable to disruption by the presence of an audience, a mirror, or other distracting stimuli (Carver, Blaney, & Scheier, 1979; Shrauger, 1972).

All of these analyses, however, make the same essential prediction, that people who expect to do poorly will persist less in their efforts to solve problems, especially in the face of failure. This lack of persistence may show up in turning to some other activity in preference to the task at hand (Atkinson & Birch, 1970), behaving in a passive and seemingly helpless manner rather than actively attempting to find a solution, discounting or undoing attempts at solutions that initially appear successful, or having a hard time keeping attention focused on the task even while pursuing it. But, in one form or another, it is lack of persistence that is cited as the explanation for the deficits in problem solving behavior by people who do not expect to do well.

If people with low expectations do poorly because they do not persist long enough, think that lack of ability rather than lack of effort is keeping them from succeeding, or misperceive outcomes as not contingent on their own responding, treatments that encourage them to persist, to attribute failure to not trying hard enough, or to focus their attention more strongly on task contingencies should improve their performance, and indeed they do. Dweck (1975) showed that simply giving children who expected to fail experience with success did not improve their subsequent ability to cope with failure. Only if the children were specifically taught to attribute their failure on problems to a lack of effort, and shown that they could succeed with further effort, were they more likely to persist in the face of future failure. Subsequently, Diener and Dweck (1978, 1980) have demonstrated that children who appear helpless in the face of failure (as opposed to mastery-oriented children) start thinking too quickly about the possible causes of their failure (usually their presumed lack of ability), while mastery-oriented children maintain their concentration on the task, spur themselves on with admonitions and self-instructions, and avoid labeling their performance failure or wondering about its causes. Simply instructing subjects who do not generally expect to do well that it is extremely important for them to give the task their complete and undivided attention at all times may be sufficient to remove the deficit such subjects typically display (Brockner, 1979; Brockner & Hulton, 1978; Wine, 1971). Alternatively, their attention can be focused on the task by making the task itself clear, vivid, and engaging. After first making subjects feel helpless, Gregory, Chartier, and Wright (1979) tested them with an apparatus that made the relationship between their responding (setting a lever) and task outcomes (presence or absence of aversive noise) highly salient by the use of flashing lights. Focusing subjects' attention on the task in this manner removed the performance deficit previously found in such situations among subjects high in their belief in external control.

There are so many ways in which low expectancies and a lack of persistence are disadvantageous that it is hard to believe that high expectancies and dogged persistence can also have pathological consequences. But they can.

PERSISTENCE AND THE PATHOLOGY OF HIGH EXPECTATIONS

The most obvious cost of high expectations for success is that they will lead people to waste a great deal of time and energy working on tasks for which no satisfactory solution can be found. People are trapped into doing so not by a history and fear of failure but by a history and drive for success that allow them to maintain a course of action long after someone who had learned to fail would quit. It is confident and talented scientists, not their less well-endowed brethren, who are willing to defy group pressure (cf. Hochbaum, 1954; Gollob & Dittes, 1965) and persist in lines of research their fields regard as hopeless or passe. It is self-assured and attractive people, not their less fortunate peers, who can go from relationship to relationship without admitting that any of those that ended were failures or call for some reexamination of personal style. The weak may drift irresolutely from goal to goal, but only the strong can destroy themselves in the manner of Captain Ahab. People who expect to do well, like people who are high in achievement motivation (Atkinson & Feather, 1966), may prefer to choose tasks that are appropriate to their ability level rather than ones that are either too difficult or too easy. But when they make a mistake, when they do fix on a task that is in fact impossible, the same drives and talents that make them successful in other circumstances make them prone to disasters of the first magnitude.

There are a number of studies that show that people who expect to perform well do indeed spend much longer working on insoluble problems before they give up. Feather (1961, 1962) found that subjects who thought a tracing task would be easy persisted longer in trying to do it (it was actually insoluble) than subjects who did not expect it to be easy, though it should be noted that this held only for subjects high in achievement motivation. As mentioned, Weiss and Sherman (1973) reported greater persistence for subjects whose scores on the Rotter (1966) Internal-External Control Scale indicated that they had a high expectation that outcomes were under internal control. What should be noted is that, in an objective sense, this behavior is maladaptive on the part of the subjects with high expectations. It is not like working on soluble anagrams or trying to avoid shocks that could be avoided by appropriate vigilance, in which case greater persistence is eventually likely to lead to greater success. Greater persistence in these experiments actually meant more time and energy spent with, in the end, no more to show for it than what people who quit immediately had to show for their time and energy.

The cost of persistence is especially serious if it involves watching alternatives get worse and worse over time until one is forced to accept an outcome much less desirable than ones that were available earlier. People who search for the perfect house may find, to their regret, that they have passed by a number of opportunities that turn out to be better than anything they later encounter. Even if they do, after much searching, find a house that is as good as any they saw earlier, their net return is less because they have done without the house in the intervening time and incurred the additional, and perhaps substantial, costs of continued searching. People who search for the perfect mate may persist to the point where even if such a partner is found, they themselves no longer have the resources (physical attractiveness, enthusiasm, flexibility) to attract this partner. Brickman (1972) demonstrated that subjects will continue rejecting alternatives until they suffer a catastrophic loss if these alternatives fall below what early items have led them to expect and gradually get worse and worse over time. Many real-life disasters appear to follow this pattern. For instance, such a process would seem to be a reasonable characterization of the American involvement in Vietnam (see also Staw, 1976; Brockner, Shaw, & Rubin, 1979). Stock brokers feel that amateur investors fail to minimize their losses because they are too reluctant to sell a stock when it begins to drop. In one view, rationality consists precisely of minimizing the chances for this kind of worst possible outcome. This is the principle of minimax rationality, meaning behavior that minimizes one's maximum possible loss. Clearly, this principle represents a pessimistic view of what can be expected. Pessimistic or not, a policy that minimizes the risk of serious loss has been shown to be the best strategy in many conflict situations (Rapoport, 1966). It has also been endorsed as the only moral principle reasonable persons could agree upon in the absence of any information about their specific circumstances (Rawls, 1971).

High expectations, if mistaken, make people vulnerable to this kind of loss. There is a growing literature that suggests that people often hold expectations for their performances that are quite unrealistic. Fischhoff and Slovic (1980) have demonstrated that subjects are consistently and unjustifiably overconfident of their ability to answer many sensible but actually quite difficult questions (e.g., is an ulcer a benign or malignant condition; is a racehorse with particular characteristics a winner or a loser; is a sample of handwriting written by an American or European?). When people are asked to indicate their confidence by how much money they would risk on the correctness of their answers, results indicate that most would risk—and lose—substantial amounts of money. On inferential tasks, individuals appear both to jump too quickly to conclusions that cannot be justified by the evidence and to persist too long in these conclusions in the face of evidence that clearly disconfirms them (Nisbett & Ross, 1980).

People are most prone to be overconfident when they are psychologically involved in pursuing a desirable outcome. Langer (1975) found that subjects were more likely to overestimate their chances of winning a lottery when they were allowed to choose their lottery number, versus just being given it, and when they were induced to think about it on three different days, versus just on one day. Subjects also overestimated their control of a chance event when the task was made to seem familiar rather than strange and when an opponent appeared nervous rather than confident. All of these factors were logically irrelevant to subjects' chances of winning. Langer called this overestimation the illusion of control. Jenkins and Ward (1965) and Wortman (1975) found that subjects tended to believe that they had control over outcomes to the extent that they desired these outcomes and were involved in trying to produce them, even though the occurrence of the outcomes was strictly a matter of chance. Alloy and Abramson (1979) have shown that normal subjects differ from depressed subjects primarily in a tendency to believe that they have control in circumstances where no control is in fact possible.

People who expect to do well on the task they are pursuing and to do poorly on what they see as available alternatives may be especially likely to overestimate their chances of success at that task. Quitting a line of work or a relationship is easier when people have a reserve or a cushion to fall back upon. One reason professional or institutional investors can cut their losses better than amateurs is that for the professionals, any given investment is only one of many, with other investments providing a cushion to absorb the loss in a particular instance. Since privileged members of society are more likely to have such cushions, privileged individuals will, ironically, find it easier to quit when things are not working out well. Some minority group members who have just made it into the middle class say that they live with the feeling that if they fail at their present job, it is back to hauling garbage. We may expect people in this position to persist no matter how difficult the task becomes. It is not so much that they prefer either very difficult or very easy tasks (cf. Atkinson & Feather, 1966) as that they feel society has offered them only the choice between very difficult or very easy tasks.

Much of the strongest evidence for the negative effects of high expectations comes not from laboratory experiments on success and failure but from field studies of the relationship over time between expectations, achievement, and health. It may be no accident that the negative effects of high expectations have first been noted in studies that take a relatively long view of people's lives, since these negative effects, unlike the virtues of persistence, may emerge only slowly over time.

In certain settings, like nursing homes and hospitals, people are expected to be passive and to relinquish control over their daily routines to the staff and the rules of the institution. "Good patients," in the eyes of doctors and nurses, are patients who behave in this fashion rather than patients who are unwilling to give up control, question staff behavior, and resist recommendations and medications they do not understand or feel are unwise (Taylor, 1979). People who react to hospitalization with such resistive behavior are likely to be precisely those who have been most accustomed to controlling and managing their environment in the past and have the strongest expectations of controlling and managing it in the future. In the hospital, however, patients pay a price for expecting and insisting on control. The staff may ignore them, treat their complaints as less serious than those of other patients, overmedicate them, refer them to psychiatrists for treatment, or even discharge them prematurely (Taylor, 1979). Similarly, in a nursing home setting, Janoff-Bulman and Marshall (1978) found that the elderly residents who were most depressed and coping least successfully with their stay in the home were those who were highly educated and who felt that they had had a great deal of control over their lives before they entered the home. Felton and Kahana (1974) found that institutionalized elderly who made more external attributions for a variety of daily problems reported more positive feelings of adjustment to their environment than those who persisted in making internal attributions for events over which they in fact had little control.

Evidence has recently accumulated that the pursuit of high expectations can have negative consequences for individuals even if they largely succeed in obtaining the objective outcomes they have sought. Perhaps the most compelling documentation of these negative effects comes from the work on the Type A pattern of coronary prone behavior (Friedman & Rosenman, 1974; Jenkins, 1971). The Type A behavior pattern is characterized by a great sense of time urgency, competitive achievement striving, hostility when thwarted, and in general a high expectation and a high need for success and control. For example, Type A individuals typically have higher goals than Type B individuals. About 60% of Type A college students indicated plans to attend graduate or professional school, while 70% of the students exhibiting the alternative, more relaxed Type B style indicated that they planned to get a job after graduation. Type A's have been found to earn more academic honors than Type B's (Glass, 1977), and to attempt more complex arithmetic problems than Type B's on a test with no time limit (Burnam, Pennebaker, & Glass, 1973). Type A's are people who work at or near maximum capacity relative to Type B's, and whose first reaction to uncontrollable outcomes is hyper-responsiveness, or an intensified and repeated effort at reestablishing control (Glass, 1977). The negative health consequence of Type A behavior takes a simple and easily measurable form, heart attacks. Even controlling for other risk factors such as hypertension, cholesterol, and cigarette smoking, Type A behavior is reliably associated with a markedly increased incidence of heart disease (Rosenman, Brand, Jenkins, Friedman, Straus, & Wurm, 1975). Moreover, the Type A pattern of behavior is extraordinarily resistant to change even when its negative consequences are pointed out to people, since Type A's typically attribute all the good things that have happened to them in their lives to their hard-driving style. A heart attack, however, makes people more open to suggestions by physicians about the desirability of changing their habits.

Attribution theory, the theory of learned helplessness, dissonance theory, and the study of test anxiety offer explanations for why people who expect to do well persist in the face of failure. These are, of course, the reverse of their explanations for why people who expect to do poorly do not persist, reviewed earlier. People who expect to do well see failure as their own fault (Abramson, Seligman, & Teasdale, 1978; Weiner et al., 1971), or at least as something they can correct by their own efforts, even if caused by external forces (Brickman, Rabinowitz, Karuza, Coates, Cohn, & Kidder, 1980; Janoff-Bulman, 1979). Not working hard is dissonant with the cognition that failure can be avoided by hard work (cf. Aronson, 1968). People who are not anxious about failing at a task are not motivated to relieve this anxiety by avoiding or terminating their pursuit of the task (Wine, 1971).

If people who expect to do well experience stress more intensely for longer periods of time when they fail to obtain a goal, and if (in the manner of Type A's) they continually see themselves as having failed to obtain the next two or three or ten goals they are seeking, it is not surprising that they should display more serious stress-related consequences. Weiss (1971a,b) offers the simple proposition that the amount of stress an animal experiences is a strict function of the number of unsuccessful coping attempts it makes. If all its attempts are success-ful (which means receiving what Weiss calls relevant feedback from the envi-ronment, or feedback that is not associated with the aversive stimulus that ini-tially elicited the responding), the animal will experience no stress no matter how frequently and vigorously it responds. If the animal never attempts to respond, or ceases entirely its struggle to control the environment, it will also cease to experience stress no matter how frequent or intense the aversive stimulus. Maximum stress is associated with a situation in which, in our language, an animal persists in trying to control an environment that is in fact uncontrollable. In a number of experiments, Weiss (1971a,b) demonstrated that ulceration was greater in laboratory rats who made many efforts to cope with the uncontrollable aversive stimulation they received than in animals who tended to sit and take it. This analysis predicts more stress for people with high expectations in two ways. First, since they expect to be able to control things, they will be less likely to remove themselves from situations that are actually uncontrollable and thus more likely to suffer the aversive stimulation, augmented by their coping attempts, that these situations provide. Second, in uncontrollable situations from which escape is not possible, they will be more likely to augment their suffering by repeated and fruitless efforts at control.

This analysis suggests that people with high expectations may also profit from a kind of attribution retraining or immunization. People with high expectations need the ability to release themselves from the pursuit of tasks that have turned out to be impossible, at least within any reasonable budget of time and energy. It should be possible to immunize them against such maladaptive persistence by having them understand that some tasks, some combinations of tasks, or some deadlines, are impossible. We conducted a simple experiment (Janoff-Bulman & Brickman, 1976) to test this hypothesis.

AN EXPERIMENT IN IMMUNIZATION

The experiment had a 2 × 2 factorial design in which subjects had either high or low expectancies for success and either were or were not immunized against failure by being specifically told that some test problems were insoluble. Sub-jects were 28 male and 28 female undergraduates who were run individually and received course credit for their participation. All first worked on a pretest consist-ing of ten soluble five-letter anagrams. Subjects in the high expectancy condition were told that their pretest score, whatever it was, was one of the best received on the test and that they could certainly expect to do well on the larger anagram task to follow. Subjects in the low expectancy condition were told that their score was one of the poorest yet received and that they should not expect to do well on the larger task to follow. Subjects in the immunized condition were then told that not all of the anagrams on the test would be soluble, while subjects in the not immunized condition were merely told that test anagrams would vary in difficulty. The anagram test contained 70 items, of which 60% (six out of every set of ten) were soluble and 40% were insoluble. Subjects were allowed to spend as much or as little time as they chose on each anagram and also to spend as much or as little time as they chose on the test as a whole.

As shown in Table 7.1, high expectancy subjects attempted more anagrams when they were immunized against failure, while low expectancy subjects did not. This interaction was significant with an $F(1,55) = 4.06$, $p < .05$. Furthermore, high expectancy subjects solved more anagrams when they were immunized against failure, while low expectancy subjects did not. The difference between the two groups in number solved was significant only in the immunized condition ($F(1,27) = 6.35$, $p < .02$).

The results of the experiment indicate that high expectancy subjects are indeed better able to abandon unprofitable tasks when they are led to believe that some tasks may be insoluble. They are disinclined to waste their time working on insoluble tasks, and, once immunized, are better able to avoid wasting their time in this manner than are low expectancy subjects. Low expectancy subjects may not benefit in the same way because even soluble tasks may seem impossible to them. Thus, when confronted with a task that they cannot seem to solve, low expectancy subjects have difficulty deciding whether they are failing because they lack ability or because the task is insoluble. Since high expectancy individuals do not doubt that they have ability, they are better able to dismiss a task as insoluble—once they have been led to consider this possibility. Thus, while people who do not expect to do well may profit from attribution retraining that encourages them to see more of their failures as due to inadequate effort, people who generally expect to do well may profit from attribution retraining that allows them to see less of their failures as due to inadequate effort. The former profit from a greater ability to persist. The latter profit from a greater ability to quit.

TABLE 7.1
Performance of High and Low Expectancy Subjects When Immunized
Versus Not Immunized Against Failure

	Immunized		Not Immunized	
	High Expectancy	Low Expectancy	High Expectancy	Low Expectancy
Problems attempted	34.6	21.5	22.1	23.2
Problems correct	11.6	6.3	8.6	8.5

The results of the present study complement those of Brickman, Linsenmeier and McCareins (1976), who found that high expectancy subjects tend to pay less attention than low expectancy subjects to failures that they believe are irrelevant to their future performance (do not predict that performance one way or the other). Failing to solve an impossible task is, of course, completely unpredictive of whether one will succeed or fail on soluble tasks (cf. Linsenmeier & Brickman, 1978). If high expectancy subjects are readier to conclude that tasks they cannot solve are insoluble, they will be better able to believe that their failure to solve these tasks has no implications for their ability to solve future tasks. The present results also fit nicely with a recent study by Schwartz (1980) indicating that subjects who had previously been told about learned helplessness research in their introductory psychology course did not show performance deficits (on an anagram test) after prior exposure to uncontrollable noise. Knowing that the noise was uncontrollable in effect immunized subjects (most of whom, as college students, can be considered relatively high in achievement motivation and expectation for success; cf. Atkinson & Feather, 1966) against the debilitating effects of trying and failing to control it (cf. also Lavelle, Metalsky, & Coyne, 1979). Some research has suggested that individuals may become helpless when exposed to uncontrollable aversive stimulation even if they are told at the start that there is nothing they can do about this stress (e.g., Glass & Singer, 1972; see also the discussion in Wortman & Brehm, 1975). There may be kinds of stress that are debilitating no matter what attributions people make about the causes of the stress. In general, however, the literature indicates that knowing a task is impossible (or even very difficult; see Douglas & Anisman, 1975; Koller & Kaplan, 1978; Tennen & Eller, 1977) enables people to fail on that task without showing impaired performance on future tasks.

LEARNING WHEN TO CONTINUE AND WHEN TO QUIT

We have an ample number of proverbs reminding us that it is important to know when to quit. "Don't throw good money after bad." "If at first you don't succeed, try, try again. If you still don't succeed, quit. No use being a damn fool about it" (W. C. Fields). "Discretion is the better part of valor." "He who fights and runs away lives to fight another day." "It is better to have a horrible ending than horrors without end." "What is not worth doing is not worth doing well." Perhaps the most famous is a quotation attributed to, among others, Lord Acton and Reinhold Niebuhr: "God grant me the strength to change what I can, the courage to bear what I cannot, and the wisdom to know the difference." The most recent is probably the chorus of the 1979 Country and Western Song of the Year, "The Gambler," sung by Kenny Rogers: "You got to know when to hold them, Know when to fold them, Know when to walk away, Know when to run."

The repeated occurrence of such reminders tells us that people think this is an important lesson. But it also tells us that the lesson is one people tend to forget, and thus need to be reminded of. Repeated reminders to do something are necessary only when there is an opposing impulse motivating people to behave in a contrary way (Campbell, 1975). In this case, the opposing impulse is twofold. First, there is the sheer momentum of behavior. When people have become involved in pursuing a line of action and have invested time, money, and energy in that line of action, they are reluctant to quit, even when quitting is what observers would recommend (Staw, 1976; Teger, 1979). Second, there is the fact that messages reminding people that it is important to know when to quit are far less frequent than messages preaching the virtues of persistence. Winners never quit and quitters never win. Heroes defy the odds. Admiral Peary grew up with a sign pinned to his wall, "I will find a way or make one." People who persist are valued because they contribute to others' well-being, if not their own. People who quit are derogated not only because quitting is failing but because quitting is often refusing to continue with a line of action that other people wish to see pursued.

Psychological research, as we have seen, has begun to accumulate evidence that blind persistence is not an unmitigated virtue. There are even a few studies in which the issue of discriminating controllable from uncontrollable situations, or soluble from insoluble tasks, has been an explicit focus of concern. Gurin, Gurin, Lao, and Beattie (1969) have shown that black youths who distinguish between areas of personal life that are under their control and elements in the general situation of black Americans that are not under their control are more likely to have an active, realistic, coping orientation both toward personal achievement and toward social change. Rodin, Rennert, and Solomon (1980) have shown that subjects distinguish between situations in which they have control and feel competent to exercise it and situations in which they have control but do not feel competent to exercise it. In a number of studies, these investigators found that asking people to make decisions they did not feel competent to make (such as which of nine questionnaires to take) diminished rather than enhanced their self-esteem, as compared to other groups who were not given this control. Miller (1979) has shown that when a noncontingent aversive event (shock) is relatively unlikely to occur, subjects will be less aroused when they are distracting themselves with music than when they are listening for a warning signal that will predict the occurrence of the shock, and that most subjects will prefer distraction rather than vigilance under these circumstances. In studies where shocks are likely to occur, on the other hand, subjects generally prefer to be warned in advance (see Seligman, 1975, for a review), especially when they have an opportunity to avoid the shocks (Averill, O'Brien, & DeWitt, 1977). Taken together, these results imply that people can discriminate between situations in which it is useful to be vigilant and situations in which it is not.

Somewhat surprisingly, there is actually no consensus in the psychological literature on how important it is for individuals to be able to distinguish between controllable and uncontrollable outcomes, and no general theory which makes this ability its central feature. Wortman and Brehm (1975) suggest that when outcomes are truly uncontrollable, the most adaptive response may be to give up or not to try to exert control in the first place. But these authors, as well as Wortman (1976), also cite reports that victims of natural disasters or disease blame themselves or others for these events as evidence of an understandable and healthy tendency for people to believe that these events are controllable rather than random and uncontrollable. Likewise, Janoff-Bulman (1979) interprets self-blame by rape victims as a healthy effort by victims to believe that they can, by their own careful and responsible behavior, prevent the recurrence of the trauma of rape, though rape episodes may in fact be essentially independent of victim behavior. Langer (1975) and Seligman (1975) are unequivocal in taking the position that it is valuable for individuals to believe that they have control even when in fact they do not and this belief is an illusion. Furby (1979) surveys the psychological literature on perceived control and finds a general bias toward assuming that the belief that one has control is good. It is really quite remarkable that the literature has been so sensitive to the consequences of people's mistakenly assuming that they do not have control and so insensitive to the consequences of people's mistakenly assuming that they do have control.

The importance of distinguishing between soluble and insoluble problems, rather than blindly persisting on all problems, has probably been overlooked in part because the interests of the individual and the interests of society do not coincide on this matter. For any given individual it is a disaster to persist on a scientific problem that cannot be solved, or on a job with no prospects of success, or in a marriage with no possibilities for satisfaction. For society, however, the fact that some or even many individuals encounter disasters of this sort may be offset by the fact that others eventually make valuable discoveries and that even the victims or the unsuccessful continue to enact rather than abandon their social roles. The belief that people are personally responsible for their own successes and failures, that they are in control of their own fates, reconciles people towards accepting their own lot and the lot of others as fair and just (Lerner, 1975). In this domain, as in others, the culture appears to have two messages, one of them widely publicized and available to all and the other largely hidden and available only to the elect or the elite. The public message is that one should persist and persevere no matter how discouraging things appear, that good things will eventually follow if one only stays on the job, that the only real failure is to stop trying. People who follow orders need not be socialized to decide for themselves when to start and when to stop, but only to persist at whatever tasks they are assigned. Theirs not to reason why, theirs just to do or die. For the managerial elite, however, discretion rather than blind perseverence is the requisite social virtue. People responsible for making decisions and committing social resources to the realization of these decisions must, in theory at least, learn how to quit, how to call off disastrous enterprises, how to avoid being trapped in unpromising situations. Children of workers must learn to persist because changing careers, exploring alternatives, and failing are luxuries they cannot afford. Children of the elite not only have the cushion of parental resources that enable them to fail, but have access through these resources to a kind of learning—the ability to discriminate among tasks—that is vital to future success and not available to their less fortunate peers.

The public belief in persistence has led to a curious error of perception. People who suffer because they are foolishly, mistakenly, or hopelessly persisting in a futile attempt to exercise control are incorrectly identified as people who have given up! Heroin addicts are often seen as helpless in the face of addiction, frustrated by both personal inadequacies and lack of social support in their efforts to break free of their habit. We now know, however, that there is a population of heroin users whose habits are moderate and controlled (Zinberg, 1977). Such addicts practice what is called chipping, using heroin only on certain occasions (e.g., on weekends, with friends.). This, it turns out, is the ideal of every addict—a habit that is under control, not too costly to maintain, and not totally disruptive of ordinary relationships. A student of the junior author did his masters on heroin addicts (Sanders, 1973). The first step in working with any group of addicts, he reported, was to confront each member's image of a friend or an Uncle Harry who had been using heroin successfully for twenty years. That may be possible for Uncle Harry, the counselor had to point out, but it was obviously not possible for the client, since Uncle Harry was not there (did not need the clinic) and the client was (and usually had been before, after having messed up his life on previous occasions). The addiction, in other words, was maintained not by the addict's helplessness or hopelessness but by the addict's continuing to believe, against all evidence, that he could continue to use heroin and maintain a semblance of control over his life. A similar analysis can be made of alcoholism. The first step in therapy is to dismantle this illusion of control, a task made all the more difficult by the fact that therapists are often unable to recognize this control motivation.

This is also the only reasonable analysis that can be made of certain otherwise puzzling aspects of Jewish behavior in Nazi-occupied Europe. The puzzle is that Jews in many instances appeared to cooperate with Nazi authorities, donning yellow stars, accepting loss of citizenship and isolation in ghettos, walking to the trains and death camps rather than having to be dragged. In at least some instances, particularly the Netherlands and Salonica, these events may have been facilitated by an accommodating Jewish leadership that failed to recognize the possibilities that existed for resistance via alliance with a sympathetic church and native underground (Fein, 1979). On the face of it, this passive and accommodating behavior looks like helplessness, giving up, and a failure to try to exert control. A closer analysis reveals, however, that it is once again maladaptive persistence in pursuit of an impossible goal. The death camps were unbelievable even to many who heard the stories. Jews were told that they were being transported to resettlement camps in the East, and they, like many others, clung to this belief rather than accepting the horrible alternative (Arendt, 1965; Hughes, 1964). Accommodation with the Nazis was impossible, but the belief that it was possible, as it had been with many previous oppressors, was critical in leading Jews to choose passivity rather than resistance. According to Bettelheim (1960), even our admiration for the family of Anne Frank, at least as regards their strategy and tactics of hiding, is misplaced. Their chances of escaping would have been considerably greater if they had scattered rather than remained together. Like so many others, they tried for too long to pursue life as usual. Only when people realize that life as usual, and the goals of life as usual, are impossible will they adopt the radically different behavior that may be necessary for survival under the new conditions.

It is in fact quite difficult for people to learn that events are uncorrelated (Nisbett & Ross, 1980), and in particular to learn that events are uncorrelated with their own behavior (Jenkins & Ward, 1965; Wortman, 1976). This is especially true if they have had occasion to search for or construct explanations for these events (Ross & Lepper, 1980). Peterson (1978) has shown that maladaptive persistence can actually serve as the basis for an alternative explanation of the findings in learned helplessness experiments (see also Levis, 1980; McReynolds, 1980). Subjects in such experiments, he suggests, do not actually learn that the pretreatment problems are insoluble unless they are explicitly told that this might be the case (which Peterson did in his Experiment 2). Rather, they learn that simple solutions are not sufficient and therefore come to entertain more and more complex hypotheses about what the solutions are. When they are later given simple problems in the testing stage, their tendency to seek complex solutions, rather than their tendency to give up, is what impairs their performance. From this perspective, participants in learned helplessness experiments, like heroin addicts and Jews in Nazi Europe, suffer not because they give up too soon but because they persist too long in devising more and more elaborate efforts to make work what is essentially an unworkable arrangement.

More generally, the idea that depression comes from giving up or feeling helpless has been confused with the idea that depression comes from persisting on a task that is becoming, or has become, impossible. Giving up is not depression but, if it is done successfully, a first step toward relieving depression (cf. Klinger, 1975). The sense of loss comes from an attachment that can no longer be fulfilled but cannot yet be relinquished (Bowlby, 1961). The paralyzing effects of persistence at a hopeless task were described by George Vaillant as the overall conclusion he would draw from his 40-year study of 95 Harvard men, some of them happy and successful and some not: "No whim of fate, no Freudian trauma, no loss of a loved one is as devastating to the human spirit as some chronic ambivalent relationship that keeps us forever from saying goodbye"

("95 Harvard men: A psychiatrist examines who among them prosper in life, and why," 1977). Researchers have recognized an apparent paradox in depression, that depressed people feel both guilty (implying that they are responsible for their sad condition) and helpless (implying that they are not responsible for their sad condition; cf. Abramson & Sackeim, 1977). What they have failed to recognize is that this precisely defines a condition in which people are continuing to pursue a goal (feeling guilty or blaming themselves for their failure) that seems increasingly remote or impossible to attain (making them also feel increasingly helpless and become increasingly passive). Another perspective on the problem is indicated by Brickman, Rabinowitz, Karuza, Coates, Cohn, and Kidder (1980), who see depression as a state in which people feel responsible for the origin of a problem and helpless to find a solution to it. It is in part their blaming themselves for having been the cause of the trouble that makes them persist in trying to do something about it long after others would have recommended disengaging from the situation and embarking on a totally new course of action.

If inappropriate failures to give up have been misidentified as giving up, it is no wonder that no theory has emerged that treats both these errors as equally important (depending, of course, on the costs attached to each in particular situations) and places primary emphasis on the ability to discriminate between situations in which persistence is appropriate and situations in which it is not. If we could define the availability of a solution in a given situation as a "signal," such a theory would take the form of signal detection analysis (Green & Swets, 1966). Giving up in a situation where a solution was possible would be a miss. Persisting in a situation where a solution was not possible would be a false alarm. A signal detection analysis makes it clear that people can differ both in the accuracy with which they are able to discriminate soluble from insoluble problems and in the bias they may have toward labeling all problems soluble or all problems insoluble.

High expectations will be more advantageous than low expectations only when, as in the immunization condition of our experiment, people are aware of and accept the fact that some tasks are impossible to accomplish and not worth persisting on. The advantage of high expectations in these circumstances is not that they foster blind persistence, but that they foster selective persistence. The advantage of people with high expectations, when immunized in this fashion, is as much in their ability to quit as in their greater ability to persist. They appear more accurate in discriminating promising from unpromising situations, perhaps because they have learned in the past what cues to pay attention to and what cues to ignore. They can also better accept failure under these circumstances because they are better able to make an external attribution for it, and thus less likely to see one failure as implying that they will fail on future tasks. A key problem for future research is to discover what leads people with high expectations in the real world to believe that all tasks are possible and the only failure is to stop trying (comparable to the non-immunized condition of our experiment) and what leads them to recognize that some tasks may not be possible (comparable to the immunized condition of our experiment). In the first case, we would expect people with high expectations to display all the symptoms of pathology, and to risk the various kinds of disasters, we have previously described. In the second case, we would expect people with high expectations to appear as more accurate discriminators of promising from unpromising situations and better able to quit when situations are unpromising. There is evidence that there are at least some circumstances outside the laboratory in which people with high expectations are better characterized by their ability to discriminate than by their tendency to persist.

First of all, it may be useful to classify tasks according to whether they typically give people the critical information they need in order to assess their chances of mastery either early or late, gradually or suddenly (cf. Brickman & Hendricks, 1975). In chess, for example, it is clear quite early whether a person is talented, whereas in writing fiction it may not be clear for many years. In general, however, it may not be easy to tell on the basis of early returns whether a task will be soluble or not. It seems quite possible that this is an important instance in which a feeling, an intuitive or affective response, precedes any formal judgment that can be cognitively elaborated or rationally defended (Zajonc, 1980). For example, in the study of memory, investigators have found that people often have a "feeling of knowing" even when they cannot actually recall the answer (Hart, 1965). That is, they are confident that they would be able to recognize the correct answer if they were shown it on a list of alternatives. Shaughnessy (1979) has shown that students who performed best on a multiple-choice examination were also most accurate in their feeling of knowing, or best able to distinguish (by their confidence ratings) between items they knew and items they did not know. As Socrates said, the first sign of wisdom is to know the difference between what one knows and what one does not know (cf. Brickman, 1980, on the importance of understanding this in assessing what social psychology has so far accomplished).

People will become better over time at distinguishing between tasks they can handle and tasks they cannot if they receive unambiguous and informative feedback about their success and failure in particular situations. Individuals who expect to do well are more likely to seek such feedback than people who expect to do poorly. Trope (1975) found that people high in achievement motivation were more likely to choose to work on tasks that would tell them clearly whether or not they had a particular ability, though in subsequent research people who do not expect to do well have also been found to seek unambiguous information if that information was tailored to tell them exactly how little skill they had (Trope, 1979). People who do not expect to do well are less interested in social comparison (Brickman & Bulman, 1977) and, perhaps ironically, better able to respond to positive feedback (accept it and continue to work hard) when they believe this feedback is a matter of chance or irrelevant to their future performance

(Brickman, Linsenmeier, & McCareins, 1976; Maracek & Mettee, 1972; Mettee, 1971).

One interesting piece of evidence suggesting that people who think well of themselves and expect others to think well of them are better at discriminating promising from unpromising situations comes from the study of popular and unpopular children. Roistacher (1974) asked participants to list all their friends, rather than only the few best friends allowed in previous studies. Under these conditions, he found that the real difference between popular and unpopular children was not that popular children were more often chosen, but that they were more often chosen by children that they chose in return. If we can assume that others are valuable to a person as friends in large part simply by virtue of the fact that they like the person in the first place, people's task in making friends can be described as one of discovering who likes them. Children who expect to be liked thus also seem to be better able to tell who likes them and who does not, as well as better able to assume that others will like them (cf. Goslin, 1962). Their ability to discriminate may contribute as much or more to their popularity as their general expectation of being liked.

Compared to individuals who are clinically depressed or individuals who have been subject to inescapable bursts of noise, normal non-depressed subjects are more likely to respond to task contingencies and adjust their expectations for success in appropriate ways (Miller & Seligman, 1973, 1976). They are more likely to differentiate between a skill and a chance task, and to change their expectations in response to feedback on the skill task but not on the chance task. They are also more likely than depressed subjects to discriminate between success and failure on the skill task and to sharply lower their expectations following failure. These results remain to be reconciled, however, with the finding of Alloy and Abramson (1979) that non-depressed subjects are more likely to persist in an incorrect belief that they have control in a situation where they do not. It is possible that normal subjects are better able to discriminate skill from chance situations but distort their perceptions of control in an optimistic direction when the situation is ambiguous. This would be analogous to the finding by Jacobs, Berscheid, and Walster (1974) that subjects with high self-esteem distinguish sharply between others who like them and others who do not, but respond more favorably to an ambiguous message from another person (or are more willing to assume that this person likes them) than subjects with low self-esteem do.

A SEQUENTIAL MODEL FOR TESTING ONE'S LIMITS

If the ability to discriminate promising from unpromising situations or soluble from insoluble tasks were merely a matter of avoiding an occasional error, it would be an interesting but marginal element in a general theory of achieving or coping. It is much more than that. In our view, all achievement and coping consists of an alternation between periods of working, pushing, and concentrating and periods of regrouping, drawing back, and relaxing. We work in spurts, not continuously. The ability to discriminate we are talking about is the ability to know when in time to push, when to draw back, when to resume, and when not to resume. If all but the most fleeting effort is of this form, understanding how people make decisions to start and stop is vital to understanding how they succeed and fail.

A person turns away from a task, in our analysis, less as a function of whether they have succeeded or failed than as a function of whether or not they anticipate that further effort at that task will produce further, commensurate benefits. They may have done well, exceeding their initial expectations, and yet continue because they now feel that they can do better still. They may have done poorly, falling short of their initial expectations, and yet quit because they now feel that they cannot do even that well. The ability to discriminate is the ability to know that the point has been reached after which further effort will not result in further progress, after which there is nothing further to be learned about oneself, one's environment, or the relationship between the two.

Consider a racing car driver who is testing a new car, an executive who is planning the next round of investments, an author who is working on a manuscript, a radical organizer who is attempting to mobilize neighborhood sentiment against absentee landlords, or a paraplegic trying to learn to walk again. The person is not, in general, trying to achieve some minimum goal they have set in advance, though they may at any given point in time think of themselves as so doing. They are not doing what March and Simon (1958) call satisficing, i.e., merely aiming for any solution with minimally satisfactory features. But nor are they doing what March and Simon call optimizing, or trying to find the ideal solution or the best solution that anyone could possibly find. What they are in fact doing is trying to discover what is the maximum that they personally can reasonably expect to achieve. A racing car driver must take each turn as fast as possible to have any chance to win, because if he does not, he will lose to someone who does. On the other hand, if he tries to take a turn faster than his equipment, his skill, or the condition of the track will allow, he will not only fail to win but may fail to survive. Drivers gradually increase the speed with which they take each turn until they reach a point at which they feel they can no longer safely increase their speed any further. Their skill rests not only in being able to go fast but in being able to know when they can go faster and when they are already going too fast, and in being able to make the appropriate adjustments. Although the consequences of failure may be less dramatic, executives face structurally identical decisions in determining how far to push a particular product line, just as do military commanders or radical organizers in deciding how long to continue with a particular set of tactics, or scientists and authors in deciding how far to push their ideas or how long to continue revising their work before letting it go and turning, temporarily or permanently, to something else.

Several objections can be raised to our analysis. The first is that people only wish individuals to abandon mistaken means rather than to admit that a goal may be impossible. We want a military commander to abandon particular tactics, but not the goal of victory; a scientist to abandon particular lines of inquiry, but not the goal of discovery; a radical to abandon particular forms of protest, but not the goal of social change. We may admire these people all the more when they pursue goals that seem to be impossible. The problem with this sentiment is that it ignores the way in which means and ends blur. A means to which people have committed themselves becomes an end, as painful to abandon as any other end. But if scientists are to have the ability to pursue the larger, vaguely defined goal of discovery in a way we would admire, they must also have the ability to admit that any particular pathway they were pursuing is a dead end, and to turn their attention elsewhere. If this is a pathway that has been pursued for some time, abandoning it is, psychologically, failure, even though the task may be resumed at some later point in time. On the other hand, to the extent that goals are not simply undefined states that are desirable by definition, we want people to rethink them in terms of how promising they are as means to still further ends, and to abandon them if they seem unprofitable by this analysis. Thus we do indeed want our commanders to rethink, from time to time, what they mean by victory and what is to be gained by victory; our scientists to rethink what they mean by discoveries; and our radicals to rethink what they mean by social change.

It is also easy to misunderstand our analysis as recommending the setting of modest goals in order to avoid failure and impossible tasks. On the contrary, our model is precisely the formulation necessary to understand how people can set extreme, immodest, even impossible goals without destroying themselves in the process. If people do not expect as much as possible from themselves, they will not obtain as much as possible. They will exhibit, in some form, what we have called the pathology of low expectations, becoming too easily discouraged by failure and turning away or quitting too soon. Locke (1968) has reviewed a wide variety of studies indicating that the more difficult the goal people commit themselves to trying for, the more they actually accomplish (see also Linsenmeier & Brickman, 1978). We are in favor of dreaming impossible dreams, being willing to make a fool of oneself, letting one's reach exceed one's grasp (''or what's a Heaven for''). As Goethe once said (according to Levinson, 1977), ''For a man to achieve all that is demanded of him, he must regard himself as greater then he is.'' And here is a colleague expressing his admiration for art historian Vincent Scully: ''In one of our faculty meetings, Scully said about a graduate student, 'He's not living beyond his intellectual means.' I loved that, and it sticks in my mind, because that's exactly what it's all about. You're supposed to throw yourself into projects that are bigger than you are, and that's what Scully does'' (Stevenson, 1980, p. 47).

But this works only if a person knows how to fail, how to recognize when control has been lost and to reassert control by stopping, quitting, or drawing back. A person may have to periodically bump into his or her limits in order to discover them, but the knowledge is useless unless they are able to accept it and to draw back and operate effectively within these limits. People tend to promote themselves, as well as others, to the level of their incompetence—the famous Peter Principle. This principle is an effort to explain, half facetiously, why so many people in organizations appear to be holding positions they are incompetent to fulfill. The answer is that when people do a given job well, they are promoted to another, more demanding job. This continues until they are finally promoted to a job they cannot do well, where they remain, since they are no longer candidates for promotion and it is usually not possible to demote them. (Alternatively, if chances for promotion are remote because there are no vacancies at higher levels, people may become discouraged with their prospects and begin performing less well on this account.) The important point is that if people are to aim high, they must also be able to recognize when they have exceeded their level of competence and adjust their demands on themselves accordingly. Picasso said that if one could paint well with five colors, one should limit oneself to four colors and paint perfectly. A predictable consequence of being forced to continue pursuing goals that cannot be achieved with available means is burnout—a loss of caring and a retreat to routine, ritualized performance, especially noticeable in the human services professions (Cherniss, Egnatios, Wacker, & O'Dowd, 1981; Maslach, 1976).

Dreams can become nightmares. Control is not merely the ability to make things happen, to make things start. Equally important, perhaps more important, is control of the last resort, the ability to make things stop happening. Miller (1980) has argued that people's preference for control over aversive stimulation is at bottom their desire to minimize their maximum possible loss. They will ride a roller coaster as long as they feel they have the ability to get off when they want to. As Glass and Singer (1972) have shown, people are less disturbed and disrupted by aversive noise if they feel that they have the ability to terminate this noise if it gets too bad, even if they never use this ability.

The theory of achievement motivation (Atkinson & Feather, 1966; Atkinson & Raynor, 1974) predicted that achievement-oriented people would prefer tasks of intermediate difficulty (probability of success = .50) because it required people to attend simultaneously to the incentive value of success, if attained, and the probability of attaining success. People must choose a task that is not too difficult (so that they have a reasonable prospect of success) and not too easy (so that success, if achieved, will be satisfying). We agree with the assumption that people are interested both in the incentive value of success and the probability of success, but we suggest that they are not interested in them equally and simultaneously. In starting to work, or in choosing tasks, they focus primarily on the incentive value of success. In stopping work, or in deciding when little more can be expected from further effort, they focus primarily on the probability of success. Research to date has treated primarily the first of these questions, and has reliably found that people choose tasks more difficult or more according to their incentive value than predicted by the theory of achievement motivation (e.g., Heckhausen, 1968). It should be noted, however, that when ultimate success requires completing a series of tasks, each of which is contingent on prior items in the series, achievement-oriented subjects will prefer easy initial tasks (in order to keep the probability of ultimate success from falling too low; see Raynor, 1974).

If people, when they begin, have no fixed expectancy for how far they will be able to go or how much they will be able to achieve, what determines whether a stopping point is labeled failure or not? This is not a trivial question, especially if the stopping point is one at which people have surpassed what was their initial goal but remain short of what has become their current goal, or vice versa. A full treatment of this question is beyond the scope of this chapter. At this point it can merely be observed that failure is ordinarily the label people attach to experiences that cause them to stop what they are doing, take stock of their situation, and adopt a perhaps radically different orientation to this situation. A sense of failure is a signal that leads people to do two things that they would not have done otherwise. First, it leads them to consider alternative means. One is unwilling to change a line of action, and to invest large amounts of energy in highly problematic alternatives, unless one is ready to label further pursuit of that line of action a failure. Second, labeling an experience a failure leads people to consider alternative ends or other, noninstrumental elements of value in that situation. The experience was perhaps a useful lesson, perhaps amusing, maybe an inevitable part of growing and living, maybe something not really worth pursuing. This is, of course, dissonance reduction (Festinger, 1964). It is probably an essential step in allowing people to disengage from a situation without undue regret, distress, or ambivalence that would in turn interfere with their ability to pursue other lines of action. Bulman and Wortman (1977) have provided some evidence that paraplegics cope better with their disability if they see it as having been the inevitable result of an activity they had chosen and enjoyed (e.g. diving, playing football) versus the careless or avoidable result of an activity that had no particular meaning for them (e.g., being shot, being a passenger in an automobile accident).

Our analysis, although incomplete, predicts that the attributions people make for stopping will not fit easily into the traditional categories of internal or external and stable or unstable (Abramson, Seligman, & Teasdale, 1978; Weiner et al., 1971). When persons stop working on a task it is often unclear whether they will or will not resume working on it in the future. They may or may not be able to do more on it at some later date. The attribution for stopping must be sufficiently stable to make people stop, but not—at least not right away—so firm as to preclude their noticing if circumstances change and trying again. We would like to define the attribution that people typically make for stopping as an attribution of *circumstantial impossibility*. Further progress is impossible under current circumstances, but may become possible in the future. An attribution of circumstantial impossibility is to be distinguished from the belief that something will always be impossible (general or *universal impossibility*) and also the belief that failure is the fault of the people involved (personal or *unique impossibility*). In mountaineering, for example, climbers will often abandon a particular ascent as impossible yet retain the belief that it might be accomplished with better equipment or more favorable weather conditions in the future.

An attribution that partitions time into the certain and uncertain future is a *quasi-stable attribution*. Such attributions may prove to have a half-life or to decay over time. A number of recent studies have demonstrated that people tend to see events, including their own performances, as more typical, more predictable, more inevitable, and more uncontrollable as these events recede further back in time (Fischhoff, 1975; Miller & Porter, 1980; Moore, Sherrod, Liu, & Underwood, 1979). Women, for example, were more willing to see their performance on a test as in part due to their having their menstrual period when rating this performance a week later than when rating it at the time (Miller & Porter, 1980). People are also more likely to forget negative elements of past experiences (Holmes, 1970). Thus we may predict when people contemplate working again on something they have worked on in the past, they are more likely to be optimistic about it, or to differentiate the likely causes and controllability of their past and future performance, after some time has elapsed. The fact that there is likely to be a change in attribution and resurgence of optimism (cf. Tiger, 1979) over time may be in part what enables people to quit a task firmly and decisively without destroying their ability to take advantage of further chances at that task that may open up in the future. It may be as difficult to persist at quitting a task as it is to keep working at a task. To make either decision stick, a person probably has to make that decision not once but over and over again.

CONCLUSIONS AND DIRECTIONS FOR FUTURE RESEARCH

Effective work and effective coping consists of wholehearted, unambivalent pursuit of an activity or equally wholehearted turning away from that activity. This places a premium, not generally recognized in previous formulations, on people's ability to discriminate between situations in which such effort is appropriate and situations in which it is not. This ability is all the more fundamental, we have argued, since even in working on a single task people must generally discriminate between times when they have done all that is at the moment possible and times when further effort would yield a breakthrough to a new level of insight or a new level of skill.

We have hypothesized that the ability to discriminate between promising and unpromising tasks, rather than a blind tendency to persist on all tasks, is the reason people who expect to do well outperform those who expect to do poorly.

Without the ability to discriminate, and the ability to recognize, admit, and accept failure, their persistence would be a liability rather than an asset, leading them eventually into more and more costly disasters. If people with high expectancies set less realistic deadlines for themselves, they can do so only because they are also more willing to abandon these deadlines and to incur the costs that are involved in failing to meet them. This may be in the service of achieving a higher level of success by some later deadline, or it may be a willingness to abandon entirely lines of effort that do not seem sufficiently likely to pay off. We suggest that people who think well of themselves will both ask more of the relationships they enter into with others and also be more willing, over time, to accommodate themselves to the limits they discover in their exploration of these relationships. Investigating these propositions is clearly a task for future research.

More generally, and more speculatively, we think it may be useful to distinguish three stages of task involvement in which attributions and expectations play a characteristically different role. The first stage is a *preattribution stage* or an attribution-free stage. As Diener and Dweck (1978, 1980) have shown, children working on problems do not usually concern themselves with wondering whether they are doing well or poorly or trying to explain why they are doing well or poorly until after they have been working on the task for awhile. Mastery-oriented children, or effective copers, are especially likely to continue without making attributions for their preformance even in the face of a great deal of difficulty and frustration. We also suspect that in this first stage, especially when the task is novel, people have only weak expectations for how much they can accomplish or how well they will do.

The emergence of expectations and attributions is triggered by people's eventual sense that they are no longer making progress on the task, and that some change in orientation is called for. This is our second stage, which is characterized by what we may call *disengagement attributions*. This does not mean that people entering this stage immediately quit. On the contrary, they are first likely to show a burst of energy, sometimes called reactance (Wortman & Brehm, 1975), in which they try extra hard to overcome the difficulties they have been previously struggling with unselfconsciously. But even the attribution that more effort is called for is a disengagement attribution in our sense, since it prepares the individual for a possibility not previously considered, that the task may have to be abandoned. The period of disengagement attributions comes to a close when people accept that they have done all they can, be this a lot or a little.

After they have turned away from the task begins a period that may be called, ironically, a period of *reengagement attributions*. Beliefs about the causes for past performance, and expectations for future performance, may change, perhaps without the person's even being aware of any change. At some point the new attributions are likely to lead the person back to the task, or, if the person has had to keep working despite a period of discouragement, to a new burst of energy on the task. Then may follow another period that is relatively attribution free, then another period of disengagement attributions, then another period of reengagement attributions. The cycle probably ends gradually as the attribution-free periods become shorter and the disengagement attributions are made more unequivocally and forcefully. Again, it is a task for future research to assess the value of these hypothetical stages and, more generally, the characteristic and optimal rhythms of engagement and disengagement in different individuals.

Although there is no reason we cannot study these processes in the laboratory, in a number of respects they may be easier to observe in real life settings. Our model is perhaps best suited to understand how people behave when they are working simultaneously on a variety of different tasks, each of which can be pursued with a variety of possible means. In leading their lives, people find out how much they can do by accepting more and more obligations until they find that they are performing less and less of them in a satisfactory way. Whether a career or a relationship is possible or impossible is rarely something that is readily apparent to people but rather something they must assess and come to terms with gradually over a period of time and by a process of trial, error, and insight. Laboratory experiments have not, so far, typically confronted people with such a portfolio of tasks and complexity of means, and not observed the consequences of their persistence, lack of persistence, or selectivity over long periods of time. On the contrary, laboratory experiments have often given people the great luxury of being able to devote their full attention to a single task, pursued in a straightforward manner, with solutions that are obvious once they appear. Under these circumstances, persistence will rarely be maladaptive. The next step toward designing a more adequate set of laboratory experiments is observing closely how people cope with the complexity of problems they encounter over time in their lives.

ACKNOWLEDGMENTS

We wish to thank Gregory Davis, Jeffrey Howard, and William Marianes for their able assistance in running the immunization against failure experiment. We also wish to thank Fred Bryant, Norman Feather, Lita Furby, Anthony Greenwald, William Ickes, Jeffrey Paige, Linda Perloff, Richard Sorrentino, and especially Camille Wortman for their helpful comments on this manuscript.

REFERENCES

Abramson, L. Y., & Sackheim, H. A. A paradox in depression: Uncontrollability and self-blame. *Psychological Bulletin*, 1977, *84*, 838–851.
Abramson, L. Y., Seligman, M. E. P., & Teasdale, J. Learned helplessness in humans: Critique and reformulation. *Journal of Abnormal Psychology*, 1978, *87*, 49–79.

Alloy, L. B., & Abramson, L. Y. Judgment of contingency in depressed and nondepressed students: Sadder but wiser? *Journal of Experimental Psychology: General,* 1979, *108,* 441–485.

Archibald, W. P. Alternative explanations for self-fulfilling prophecy. *Psychological Bulletin,* 1974, *81,* 74–84.

Arendt, H. *Eichmann in Jerusalem: A report on the banality of evil.* New York: Viking, 1965.

Aronson, E. Dissonance theory: Progress and problems. In R. P. Abelson, E. Aronson, W. J. McGuire, T. M. Newcomb, M. J. Rosenberg, & P. H. Tannenbaum (Eds.), *Theories of cognitive consistency.* Chicago: Rand McNally, 1968.

Aronson, E., & Carlsmith, J. M. Performance expectancy as a determinant of actual performance. *Journal of Abnormal and Social Psychology,* 1962, *65,* 178–182.

Atkinson, J. W., & Birch, D. *The dynamics of action.* New York: Wiley, 1970.

Atkinson, J. W., & Feather, N. T. (Eds.), *A theory of achievement motivation.* New York: Wiley, 1966.

Atkinson, J. W., & Raynor, J. O. *Motivation and achievement.* Washington, D.C.: Winston, 1974.

Averill, J. R., O'Brien, L., & DeWitt, G. W. The influence of response effectiveness on the preference for warning and on psychophysiological stress reactions. *Journal of Personality,* 1977, *45,* 395–418.

Bettelheim, B. *The informed heart.* New York: Free Press, 1960.

Bowlby, J. Processes of mourning. *International Journal of Psychoanalysis,* 1961, *42,* 317–340.

Brickman, P. Optional stopping on ascending and descending series. *Organizational Behavior and Human Performance,* 1972, *7,* 53–62.

Brickman, P. A social psychology of human concerns. In R. Gilmour & S. Duck (Eds.), *The development of social psychology.* London: Academic Press, 1980.

Brickman, P., & Bulman, R. J. Pleasure and pain in social comparison. In J. M. Suls & R. L. Miller (Eds.), *Social comparison processes.* Washington, D.C.: Hemisphere, 1977.

Brickman, P., & Hendricks, M. Expectancy for gradual or sudden improvement and reaction to success and failure. *Journal of Personality and Social Psychology,* 1975, *32,* 893–900.

Brickman, P., Linsenmeier, J. A. W., & McCareins, A. G. Performance enhancement by relevant success and irrelevant failure. *Journal of Personality and Social Psychology,* 1976, *33,* 149–160.

Brickman, P., Rabinowitz, V. C., Karuza, J., Coates, D., Cohn, E., & Kidder, L. *Models of Helping and Coping.* Unpublished manuscript, University of Michigan, 1980.

Brockner, J. Self-esteem, self-consciousness, and task performance: Replications, extensions, and possible explanation. *Journal of Personality and Social Psychology,* 1979, *37,* 447–461.

Brockner, J., & Hulton, A. J. B. How to reverse the vicious cycle of low self-esteem: The importance of attentional focus. *Journal of Experimental Social Psychology,* 1978, *14,* 564–578.

Brockner, J., Shaw, M. C., & Rubin, J. Z. Factors affecting withdrawal from an escalating conflict: Quitting before it's too late. *Journal of Experimental Social Psychology,* 1979, *15,* 492–503.

Bulman, R. J., & Wortman, C. B. Attributions of blame and coping in the "real world:" Severe accident victims react to their lot. *Journal of Personality and Social Psychology,* 1977, *35,* 351–363.

Burnam, M. A., Pennebaker, J. W., & Glass, D. C. Time consciousness, achievement striving and the Type A coronary-prone behavior pattern. *Journal of Abnormal Psychology,* 1973, *84,* 76–79.

Campbell, D. T. On the conflicts between biological and social evolution and between psychology and moral tradition. *American Psychologist,* 1975, *30,* 1103–1126.

Carver, C. S., Blaney, P. H., & Scheier, M. F. Focus of attention, chronic expectancy, and responses to a feared stimulus. *Journal of Personality and Social Psychology,* 1979, *37,* 1186–1195.

Cherniss, C., Egnatios, E. S., Wacker, S., & O'Dowd, B. The professional mystique and burnout in public sector professionals. *Social Policy,* 1981, in press.

Diener, C. I., & Dweck, C. S. An analysis of learned helplessness: Continuous changes in performance, strategy, and achievement conditions following failure. *Journal of Personality and Social Psychology,* 1978, *36,* 451–462.

Diener, C. I., & Dweck, C. S. An analysis of learned helplessness: (II). The processing of success. *Journal of Personality and Social Psychology,* 1980, *39,* 940-952.

Douglas, D., & Anisman, H. Helplessness or expectation incongruency: Effects of aversive stimulation on subsequent performance. *Journal of Experimental Psychology: Human Perception and Performance,* 1975, *1,* 411-417.

Dweck, C. S. The role of expectations and attributions in the alleviation of learned helplessness. *Journal of Personality and Social Psychology,* 1975, *31,* 674-685.

Feather, N. T. The relationship of persistence at a task to expectation of success and achievement related motives. *Journal of Abnormal and Social Psychology,* 1961, *63,* 552-561.

Feather, N. T. The study of persistence. *Psychological Bulletin,* 1962, *59,* 94-115.

Feather, N. T. Effects of prior success and failure on expectations of success and subsequent performance. *Journal of Personality and Social Psychology,* 1966, *3,* 287-298.

Feather, N. T. Change in confidence following success or failure as a predictor of subsequent performance. *Journal of Personality and Social Psychology,* 1968, *9,* 38-46.

Fein, H. *Accounting for genocide.* New York: Free Press, 1979.

Felton, B., & Kahana, E. Adjustment and situationally-bound locus of control among institutionalized aged. *Journal of Gerontology,* 1974, *29,* 295-301.

Festinger, L. *Conflict, decision, and dissonance.* Stanford, California: Stanford University Press, 1964.

Fischhoff, B. Hindsight ≠ foresight: The effect of outcome knowledge on judgment under uncertainty. *Journal of Experimental Psychology: Human Perception and Performance,* 1975, *1,* 288-299.

Fischhoff, B., & Slovic, P. A little learning . . . : Confidence in multicue judgment tasks. In R. Nickerson (Ed.), *Attention and performance,* VIII. Hillsdale, N.J.: Lawrence Erlbaum Associates, 1980.

Friedman, M. *Pathogenesis of coronary artery disease.* New York: McGraw-Hill, 1969.

Friedman, M., & Rosenman, R. H. *Type A behavior and your heart.* New York: Knopf, 1974.

Furby, L. Individualistic bias in studies of locus of control. In A. R. Buss (Ed.), *Psychology in social context.* New York: Halsted, 1979.

Glass, D. C. Stress, behavior patterns, and coronary disease. *American Scientist,* 1977, *65,* 177-187.

Glass, D. C. & Singer, J. E. *Urban stress.* New York: Academic Press, 1972.

Gollob, H. F., & Dittes, J. E. Effects of manipulated self-esteem on persuasibility depending on threat and complexity of communication. *Journal of Personality and Social Psychology,* 1965, *2,* 195-201.

Goslin, D. A. Accuracy of self perception and social acceptance. *Sociometry,* 1962, *25,* 283-296.

Green, M. G., & Swets, J. A. *Signal detection theory and psychophysics.* New York: Wiley, 1966.

Gregory, W. L., Chartier, G. M., & Wright, M. H. Learned helplessness and learned effectiveness: Effects of explicit cues on individuals differing in personal control expectancies. *Journal of Personality and Social Psychology,* 1979, *37,* 1982-1992.

Gurin, P., Gurin, G., Lao, R. C., & Beattie, M. Internal-external control in the motivational dynamics of Negro youth. *Journal of Social Issues,* 1969, *25,* 29-53.

Hart, J. T. Memory and the feeling-of-knowing experience. *Journal of Educational Psychology,* 1965, *56,* 208-216.

Heckhausen, H. Achievement motive research: Current problems and some contributions towards a general theory of motivation. In W. J. Arnold (Ed.), *Nebraska symposium on motivation.* Lincoln, Nebraska: University of Nebraska Press, 1968.

Hiroto, D. S., & Seligman, M. E. P. Generality of learned helplessness in man. *Journal of Personality and Social Psychology,* 1975, *31,* 311-327.

Hochbaum, G. M. The relation between group members' self-confidence and their reactions to group pressures to uniformity. *American Sociological Review,* 1954, *19,* 678-688.

Holmes, D. S. Differential change in affective intensity and forgetting of unpleasant personal experience. *Journal of Personality and Social Psychology*, 1970, *15*, 234–239.

Hughes, E. C. Good people and dirty work. *Social Problems*, 1964, *10*, 3–11.

Jacobs, L., Berscheid, E., & Walster, E. Self-esteem and attraction. *Journal of Personality and Social Psychology*, 1971, *17*, 84–91.

Janoff-Bulman, R. Characterological versus behavioral self-blame: Inquiries into depression and rape. *Journal of Personality and Social Psychology*, 1979, *37*, 1798–1809.

Janoff-Bulman R., & Brickman, P. *When not all problems are soluble, does it still help to expect success?* Unpublished manuscript, Northwestern University, 1976.

Janoff-Bulman, R., & Marshall, G. *Coping and control in a population of institutionalized elderly.* Unpublished manuscript, University of Massachusetts, Amherst, 1978.

Jenkins, C. D. Psychologic and social precursors of coronary disease. *New England Journal of Medicine*, 1971, *284*, 244–255, 307–317.

Jenkins, H. M., & Ward, W. C. Judgment of contingency between responses and outcomes. *Psychological Monographs*, 1965, 79 (Whole No. 594).

Klinger, E. Consequences of commitment to and disengagement from incentives. *Psychological Review*, 1975, *82*, 1–25.

Koller, P. S., & Kaplan, R. M. A two-process theory of learned helplessness. *Journal of Personality and Social Psychology*, 1978, *36*, 1177–1183.

Langer, E. J. The illusion of control. *Journal of Personality and Social Psychology*, 1975, *32*, 311–328.

Lavelle, T. L., Metalsky, G. I., & Coyne, J. C. Learned helplessness, test anxiety, and acknowledgement of contingencies. *Journal of Abnormal Psychology*, 1979, *88*, 381–387.

Lefcourt, H. M. *Locus of control.* Hillsdale, New Jersey: Lawrence Erlbaum Associates, 1976.

Lerner, M. J. The justice motive in social behavior. *Journal of Social Issues*, 1975, *31*, 1–20.

Levinson, D. J. The mid-life transition: A period in adult psychosocial development. *Psychiatry*, 1977, *40*, 99–112.

Levis, D. J. The learned helplessness effect: An expectancy, discrimination deficit, or motivational-induced persistence? *Journal of Research in Personality*, 1980, *14*, 158–169.

Linsenmeier, J. A. W., & Brickman, P. Advantages of difficult tasks. *Journal of Personality*, 1978, *46*, 96–112.

Locke, E. A. Toward a theory of task motivation and incentives. *Organizational Behavior and Human Performance*, 1968, *3*, 157–189.

Maracek, J., & Mettee, D. R. Avoidance of continued success as a function of self-esteem, level of esteem certainty, and responsibility for success. *Journal of Personality and Social Psychology*, 1972, *22*, 98–107.

March, J. G., & Simon, H. A. *Organizations.* New York: Wiley, 1958.

Maslach, C. Burned-out. *Human Behavior*, September, 1976, 16–22.

McReynolds, W. T. Learned helplessness as a schedule-shift effect. *Journal of Research in Personality*, 1980, *14*, 139–157.

Means, R. S., & Means, G. H. Achievement as a function of the presence of prior information concerning aptitude. *Journal of Educational Psychology*, 1971, *62*, 185–187.

Mettee, D. R. Rejection of unexpected success as a function of the negative consequences of accepting success. *Journal of Personality and Social Psychology*, 1971, *17*, 332–341.

Miller, D. T., & Porter, C. A. Effects of temporal perspective on the attribution process. *Journal of Personality and Social Psychology*, 1980, *39*, 532–541.

Miller, R. L., Brickman, P., & Bolen, D. Attribution versus persuasion as a means of modifying behavior. *Journal of Personality and Social Psychology*, 1975, *31*, 430–441.

Miller, S. M. Coping with impending stress: Psychophysiological and cognitive correlates of choice. *Psychophysiology*, 1979, *16*, 572–581.

Miller, S. M. Why having control reduces stress: If I can stop the roller coaster I don't want to get off. In M. E. P. Seligman & J. Garber (Eds.), *Human helplessness*. New York: Academic Press, 1980.

Miller, W. R., & Seligman, M. E. P. Depression and the perception of reinforcement. *Journal of Abnormal Psychology*, 1973, *82*, 62–73.

Miller, W. R., & Seligman, M. E. P. Learned helplessness, depression, and the perception of reinforcement. *Behavior Research and Therapy*, 1976, *14*, 7–17.

Moore, B. S., Sherrod, D. R., Liu, T. J., & Underwood, B. The dispositional shift in attribution over time. *Journal of Experimental Social Psychology*, 1979, *15*, 553–569.

"95 Harvard men: A psychiatrist examines who among them prosper in life, and why." *People*, December 5, 1977, 56–60.

Nisbett, R. E., & Ross, L. *Human inference: Strategies and shortcomings of social judgment*. Englewood Cliffs, New Jersey: Prentice-Hall, 1980.

Peterson, C. Learning impairment following insoluble problems: Learned helplessness or altered hypothesis pool? *Journal of Experimental Social Psychology*, 1978, *14*, 53–68.

Perez, R. C. The effect of experimentally-induced failure, self-esteem and sex on cognitive differentiation. *Journal of Abnormal Psychology*, 1973, *81*, 74–79.

Rapoport, A. *Two-person game theory*, Ann Arbor, Michigan: University of Michigan Press, 1966.

Rawls, J. *A theory of justice*. Cambridge, Mass: Harvard University Press, 1971.

Raynor, J. O. Future orientation in the study of achievement motivation. In J. W. Atkinson & J. O. Raynor (Eds.), *Motivation and achievement*. Washington, D.C.: Winston, 1974.

Rodin, J., Rennert, K., & Solomon, S. K. Intrinsic motivation for control: Fact or fiction? In A. Baum, J. Singer, & S. Valins (Eds.), *Advances in environmental psychology*. Vol. 2. Hillsdale, New Jersey: Lawrence Erlbaum Associates, 1980.

Roistacher, R. C. A microeconomic model of sociometric choice. *Sociometry*, 1974, *37*, 219–238.

Rosenman, R. H., Brand, R. J., Jenkins, C. D., Friedman, M., Straus, R., & Wurm, M. Coronary heart disease in the Western Collaborative Group Study: Final follow-up experience of 8½ years. *Journal of the American Medical Association*, 1975, *233*, 872–877.

Ross, L., & Lepper, M. R. The perseverance of beliefs: Empirical and normative considerations. In R. A. Shweder & D. Fiske (Eds.), *New directions for methodology of behavioral science*. San Francisco: Jossey-Bass, 1980.

Roth, S., & Kubal, L. The effects of noncontingent reinforcement on tasks of differing importance: Facilitation and learned helplessness. *Journal of Personality and Social Psychology*, 1975, *32*, 680–691.

Rotter, J. G. Generalized expectancies for internal versus external control of reinforcement. *Psychological Monographs*, 1966, *80* (1, Whole No. 609).

Sanders, L. D. *A psychosocial analysis of the characteristics of 160 heroin addicts*. Unpublished masters' thesis, Northwestern University, 1973.

Sarason, I. G., & Spielberger, C. D. (Eds.), *Stress and anxiety*. Vol. 2. New York: Wiley, 1975.

Schalon, C. L. Effect of self-esteem upon performance following failure stress. *Journal of Consulting and Clinical Psychology*, 1968, *32*, 497.

Schwartz, B. *Knowledge of helplessness effects prevents helplessness effects*. Unpublished manuscript, Swarthmore College, 1980.

Seligman, M. E. P. *Helplessness*. San Francisco: Freeman, 1975.

Shaughnessy, J. J. Confidence-judgment accuracy as a predictor of test performance. *Journal of Research in Personality*, 1979, *13*, 505–514.

Shrauger, J. S. Self-esteem and reactions to being observed by others. *Journal of Personality and Social Psychology*, 1972, *23*, 192–200.

Shrauger, J. S., & Sorman, P. B. Self-evaluations, initial success and failure, and improvement as determinants of persistence. *Journal of Consulting and Clinical Psychology*, 1977, *45*, 784–795.

Staw, B. M. Knee-deep in the Big Muddy: A study of escalating commitment to a chosen course of action. *Organizational Behavior and Human Performance*, 1976, *16*, 27–44.

Stevenson, J. What seas, what shores. *New Yorker,* February 18, 1980, 43–69.

Taylor, S. E. Hospital patient behavior: Reactance, helplessness, or control? *Journal of Social Issues,* 1979, *35,* 156–184.

Teger, A. I. *Too much invested to quit: The psychology of the escalation of conflict.* New York: Pergamon Press, 1979.

Tennen, H., & Eller, S. J. Attributional components of learned helplessness and facilitation. *Journal of Personality and Social Psychology,* 1977, *35,* 265–271.

Tiger, L. *Optimism: The biology of hope.* New York: Simon & Schuster, 1979.

Trope, Y. Seeking information about one's own ability as a determinant of choice among tasks. *Journal of Personality and Social Psychology,* 1975, *32,* 1004–1013.

Trope, Y. Uncertainty-reducing properties of achievement tasks. *Journal of Personality and Social Psychology,* 1979, *37,* 1505–1518.

Weiner, B., Frieze, I., Kukla, A., Reed, L., Rest, S., & Rosenbaum, R. M. *Perceiving the causes of success and failure.* Morristown, N.J.: General Learning Press, 1971.

Weiss, H., & Sherman, J. Internal-external control as a predictor of task effort and satisfaction subsequent to failure. *Journal of Applied Psychology,* 1973, *57,* 132–136.

Weiss, J. M. Effects of coping behavior in different warning signal conditions on stress pathology in rats. *Journal of Comparative and Physiological Psychology,* 1971, *77,* 1–13. (a).

Weiss, J. M. Effects of punishing the coping response (conflict) on stress pathology in rats. *Journal of Comparative and Physiological Psychology,* 1971, *77,* 14–21. (b).

Wine, J. Test anxiety and direction of attention. *Psychological Bulletin,* 1971, *76,* 92–104.

Wortman, C. B. Some determinants of perceived control. *Journal of Personality and Social Psychology,* 1975, *31,* 282–294.

Wortman, C. B., Causal attributions and personal control. In J. H. Harvey, W. J. Ickes, & R. F. Kidd (Eds.), *New directions in attribution research.* Vol. 1. Hillsdale, New Jersey: Lawrence Erlbaum Associates, 1976.

Wortman, C. B., & Brehm, J. W. Responses to uncontrollable outcomes: An integration of reactance theory and the learned helplessness model. In L. Berkowitz (Ed.), *Advances in experimental social psychology.* Vol. 8. New York: Academic Press, 1975.

Yaryan, R. B., & Festinger, L. Preparatory action and belief in the probable occurrence of future events. *Journal of Abnormal and Social Psychology),* 1961, *63,* 603–606.

Zajonc, R. B. Feeling and thinking: Preferences need no inferences. *American Psychologist,* 1980, *35,* 176–186.

Zinberg, N. E., Harding, W. M., & Winkeller, M. A study of social regulatory mechanisms in controlled illicit drug users. *Journal of Drug Issues,* 1977, *7,* 117–133.

IV THE CONTEXT OF SOCIAL LEARNING THEORY

8

Social Learning Theory

Julian B. Rotter
University of Connecticut

ABSTRACT

In 1954 the author published a social learning theory of personality (SLT) that represented an attempt to integrate reinforcement theories and cognitive or field theories of behavior. As a personality theory, it included both a theory of how individual differences in stable behavior are acquired, generalized and changed (i.e., a process theory) and a descriptive system of individual differences, focusing on some of the dimensions on which individuals may differ.

The range of convenience of such a theory clearly goes beyond problems traditionally considered personality problems and applies to some of the problems presented in fields such as human learning and performance, development, social psychology and the social sciences, psychopathology, and psychotherapy. A description of such applications has been presented by Rotter, Chance, and Phares (1972).

In this chapter I shall attempt to describe briefly some of the basic principles of this theory and then to elaborate by applying them to four problem areas of special significance to this book. The four areas to be discussed are: (1) motivation, incentive and emotion; (2) beliefs, expressed social attitudes and social action; (3) attribution theory and defensive behavior; and (4) the psychological situation and interactionism.

241

SOME BASIC PRINCIPLES OF SOCIAL LEARNING
THEORY

In SLT, four basic concepts are used in the prediction of behavior. These concepts are: behavior potential, expectancy, reinforcement value, and the psychological situation. In addition, somewhat broader concepts are utilized for problems involving more general behavioral predictions; i.e., those dealing with behavior over a period of time and those including a number of specific situations. These variables and their relationships may be conveniently stated in the formulas that follow. It should be remembered, however, that these formulas do not at this time imply any precise mathematical relationships. Although the relationship between expectancy and reinforcement value is probably a multiplicative one, there is insufficient systematic data at this point that would allow one to evolve any precise mathematical statement.

The basic formula is stated thus:

1. $BP_{x_1, s_1, r_a} = f(E_{x_1, r_a, s_1} \ \& \ RV_{a, s_1})$

This formula is read: the potential for behavior x to occur, in situation 1, in relation to reinforcement a, is a fuction of the expectancy of the occurrence of reinforcement a, following behavior x in situation 1, and the value of reinforcement a in situation 1.

The above formula is obviously limited, inasmuch as it deals only with the potential for a given behavior to occur in relation to a single reinforcement. As noted earlier, description at the level of personality constructs usually demands a broader, more generalized concept of behavior reflected in the following formula:

2. $BP_{(x-n), s_{(1-n)}, R_{(a-n)}} = f(E_{(x-n), s_{(1-n)}, R_{(a-n)}} \ \& \ RV_{(a-n), s_{(1-n)}})$

The formula is read: the potentiality of functionally related behaviors x to n to occur, in specified situations 1 to n in relation to potential reinforcements a to n, is a function of the expectancies of these behaviors leading to these reinforcements in these situations, and the values of these reinforcements in these situations. To simplify communication, this second formula can be restated by introducing three terms—*need potential, freedom of movement,* and *need value*—to represent the three terms in Formula 2.

3. NP = f (FM & NV)

Thus, need potential is a function of freedom of movement and need value. In broader predictive or clinical situations, the latter formula would more likely be used, although the first formula would be appropriate in testing more specific, experimental hypotheses. A special significance of this formula is that when freedom of movement is low and need value is high, then the probability of defensive behavior increases. Such defensive behavior would include avoidance behaviors and attempts to attain the desired goal by irreal (Lewin) or symbolic means.

The fourth variable, *the psychological situation* is implicit in Formula 3. In SLT the psychological situation is considered to be of considerable importance. It is emphasized that behavior varies as the situation does. But, obviously, there is also transituational generality in behavior. If there were not, there would be no point in discussing "personality" as a construct or as a field of study. However, along with generality there is also situational specificity. Whereas it may be true that person A is generally more aggressive than person B; nonetheless, there may be certain situations in which person B behaves more aggressively than does person A. Predictions based solely on internal characteristics of the individual are not sufficient to account for the complexities of human behavior.

Our definition of *behavior* is a broad-gauged one. Any response to a meaningful stimulus (one that has acquired meaning as a result of previous experience) that can be *measured* either directly or indirectly would qualify. Behavior usually labelled as "cognitive" or "implicit" is included in this definition. Such behavior is not observed directly—it must be inferred from the presence of other behaviors. For example, the behavior of looking for alternative solutions, studied by Schroder and Rotter (1952), is a case in point. Looking for alternative solutions to problems was inferred to be present when the test for its occurrence—longer time taken by a subject for solution of a previously solved task, and shorter time for the solution of a new task requiring an alternative solution as compared to other subjects—took place. Likewise, rehearsal of thoughts about failure and its consequences may be measured, inferentially, by assessing subjects' performance on a difficult task where concentrated attention is necessary for problem solution.

Three different kinds of expectancies are postulated in social learning theory. (1) simple cognitions or labeling of stimuli; such as, "that's a chair," "I am warm," etc.; (2) expectancies for behavior-reinforcement sequences; such as, "If I cough, she will notice me," and (3) expectancies for reinforcement-reinforcement sequences; such as, "when I get my Ph.D., I will become rich and respected," "if my mother praises me now, the other boys will tease me later."

It is hypothesized in social learning theory that when a person perceives two situations as similar, then his or her expectancies for a particular kind of reinforcement, or class of reinforcements, will generalize from one situation to another. This does not mean that the expectancies are the same in the two situations, but that the changes in expectancies in one situation will have some small effect in changing expectancies in the other. *Expectancies in each situation are determined not only by specific experiences in that situation, but also, to some varying extent, by experiences in other situations that the individual perceives as similar.* One of the determinants of the relative importance of generalized expectancies versus specific expectancies developed in the same situation is the amount of experience in the particular specific situation. These relationships are expressed in the formula below (Rotter, 1954, p. 166):

4. $E_{s_1} = f(E'_{s_1} \& GE/f(N_{s_1}))$

In this formula, s_1 represents the specific situation and N is a function of the amount of previous experience the individual has had in that situation. E represents expectancy, E' represents a specific expectancy, and GE represents generalized expectancy. Clearly, if the formula is correct (and there is considerable empirical evidence to support it), then the relative importance of generalized expectancy increases as the situation becomes more novel or ambiguous and decreases as the individual's experience in that situation increases. This point is important in understanding under what conditions one might expect clear prediction from an accurate measure of generalized expectancy.

In social learning theory we have described two kinds of generalized expectancies. One of these, the generalized expectancy referred to in the formula for need potential, involves expectancies for a particular kind of reinforcement; e.g., achievement, dependency, conformity, social approval, etc. In this case it is the similarity of the reinforcement that provides the dimension for the generalization of expectancies. The second kind of generalized expectancy deals with expectancies that generalized from other aspects of a series of situations involving some decision or problem solving. In this case the nature of the reinforcements themselves may vary, but the similarity of the problem provides the dimension for the generalization of expectancies. For example, in situations involving different kinds of reinforcements, we may be asking ourselves if we can trust this individual to tell the truth or we may ask ourselves how we are going to find the solution when our previous attempt was blocked. The first kind of generalized expectancy we designate with the subscript r for reinforcement (GE_r); the second kind is designated as a problem-solving generalized expectancy (GE_{ps}). In considering the expectancy for some reinforcement to follow some behavior in a given situation, both kinds of generalized expectancies might be involved. The above discussion can be represented in the following formula (Rotter, Chance, & Phares, 1972, p. 41):

5. $E_{s_1} = \dfrac{f(E' \& GE_r \& GE_{ps_1} \& GE_{ps_2} \ldots GE_{ps_n})}{f(N_{s_1})}$

If we could accurately calculate all of the relevant variables in determining an expectancy, we would still be a long way from the prediction of a specific behavior. Expectancy is only one of the three major determinants of a behavior potential in social learning theory. The second is the value of the reinforcement. (The third, the psychological situation, will be discussed in detail later in this chapter). If we want to predict a specific behavior, such as studying for an exam, voting in an election, taking part in a student protest, etc., we would have to be able to assess the values of the available reinforcements to a particular person in that situation before anything resembling an accurate prediction could be made.

At this point, it would be useful to introduce a discussion of the determinants of the value of reinforcements generally. The notion that the current value of psychological goals depends upon past primary drive reduction is rejected, although for some goals drive reduction may have been important in their initial acquisition of reinforcement value. Instead, it is argued that psychological goals, needs, or reinforcements acquired during the individual's life depend on other psychological reinforcements for their value. The value of any given reinforcement depends on its association or pairing with other reinforcements. The value of a reinforcement is determined by the value of reinforcements that it has been associated and by the expectancy that its occurrence leads to the subsequent occurrence of the associated or related reinforcements. A generalized formula from which the value of a reinforcement may be predicted is:

$$6.\ RV_{a,\ s_1} = f(E_{Ra \rightarrow R(b\text{-}n),\ s_1}\ \&\ RV\ (b\text{-}n)_{s_1})$$

The formula reads: the value of reinforcement a in situation 1 is a function of expectancies that this reinforcement will lead to the other reinforcements b to n in situation 1, and of the values of these other reinforcements b to n in situation 1. To some extent, reinforcements may be expected to change value in different situations and under differing conditions. This formula provides a basis for determining these values given a variety of conditions. However, it should be recognized that quite often reinforcement values have considerable stability across both situations and time.

Once the value of reinforcement a has been firmly established through its relationship with reinforcement b, it is not necessarily true that subsequent failure of reinforcement b to occur with reinforcement a will lower the value of the latter. There are specific conditions under which lowering the value of a is more likely. Extinction is more likely under conditions of massed trials, where the original learning was not partially reinforced, or when the relationship between the two goals has been verbalized by the person. To a great extent, however, a reinforcement will maintain its value until new associations or pairings with other reinforcements of different values (more positive or more negative) occur. Because most goals acquire their value under spaced rather than massed conditions of training, under partial rather than 100% reinforcement, and because the relationships are frequently not verbalized, most reinforcements maintain their value except as they change on the basis of new pairings with other reinforcements.

Reinforcements may also become functionally related to other reinforcements, and be changed in value on the basis of cognitive activities. Either by means of symbolic manipulations or by attending to the behavior of another person and its consequences for him or her, an individual's reinforcement values are altered. By cognitive means, human beings are not only able to learn extremely complex methods of solving contemporary problems, but also to recreate the past and to create through imagination events that have not actually occurred. Imaginative rehearsal of events can affect reinforcement value. For example, in a choice situation in which the individual has to select only one of two possible alternative reinforcements, the reinforcement that is not chosen does not occur. However, in the process of deciding and imaginatively rehearsing its occurrence, its reinforcement value may change through pairings with other events that also take place in thought or imagination. In most cases, such changes may be small and subtle, but they must certainly exist, and in some instances, they may be very great indeed.

Similarly, when we attempt to obtain a reinforcement and fail to do so, not only is our expectancy for obtaining it reduced in future circumstances, but the reinforcement itself may become associated with the unpleasantness of failure and thereby decrease in value. It is equally possible that as a result of imaginative rehearsal of additional reinforcements obtainable through later success, the value of the "lost" reinforcement could actually increase. The central point here is that both expectancies and reinforcement values may change as a result of thinking. Description and prediction of the many cognitive processes subsumed under the term *thinking* is a great challenge.

More extensive definitions of these concepts, their assumptions, justifications, and elaborations are presented in Rotter (1954), Rotter, Chance and Phares (1972), and Rotter (1975). Further discussion of the psychological situation is reserved for the last section of this chapter.

MOTIVATION, INCENTIVE, AND EMOTION

This social learning theory adopts an empirical law of effect rather than a drive reduction theory to explain motivation. This does not negate cyclical physiological drives nor ignore their possible effects on the value of reinforcements.

A theory of motivation usually attempts to explain two aspects of behavior. One aspect deals with the directionality of behavior—the selection of one kind of reinforcement over another. The other aspect deals with the "energizing" of behavior, the "strength," or "force" of the behavior.

Social learning theory takes the position that both of these aspects can be understood and predicted from the concept of reinforcement value and that notions of "strength," "force," or "energy" are hangovers from a dualistic view of psychology. Although it is easy to provide examples of literal energy being expended in studies of lower organisms, there seems to be no reasonable analogue of motive strength and energy expenditure in humans. Everyone would argue that it take high "motivation" to shoot someone, but squeezing a trigger requires very little energy. The concept of energizing applied to human motivation is merely a bad analogue.

Can physiological cyclical drives affect the value of a reinforcement? Of course they can, since they produce internal cues that, along with external cues, determine not only expectancies for behavior-reinforcement sequences but also for reinforcement-reinforcement sequences (see Formula 6); hence, they affect the value of the reinforcement in that situation. The value of a glass of water increases when one's throat is dry, whether or not the dry throat is the result of true water deprivation or a "nervous" reaction to public speaking. For most human behavior beyond infancy and early childhood, however, the role of such internal stimuli is of lesser and lesser importance in contrast to that of social motives. Social values are learned through association with unlearned values but it is not necessary for social drives to lead to physiological drive reduction in order to be maintained (Rotter, 1954). In any case, it is the perceived stimuli we have to deal with and not the presumed physiological processes.

To regard the external reward as separate from the internal state makes a distinction similar to the one between drive as an energizing property and drive as a directional property of motivation. The concept of reinforcement value includes both of these. It is the *subjective* value placed on the external reward or incentive that is important and this is determined by past experience and present cues, whether they arise outside or inside the organism.

For example, "strength" of one's motivation for achievement, for some class of reinforcements and across some class of situations can be stated as the need value (see Formula 3) of these reinforcements relative to the values of other reinforcements available in the same set of situations. Behavioral prediction (need potential) would require knowing the expectancies for obtaining these reinforcements (freedom of movement) as well as the relative values placed on them. The notion that low freedom of movement and high need value leads to defensive behavior increases the potential for prediction over that of approaches that postulate only direct relationships. A person with a high need value for academic achievement and low freedom of movement may not simply show a moderate response in an achievement situation but one that announces to others that he or she does not care about academic achievement at all.

It is clear that both strong reinforcements—positive or negative—or the anticipation that such a reinforcement will take place shortly are accompanied by changes in autonomic nervous system activity. Such changes, that can be thought of as resulting in changes in the state of the organism are what some psychologists refer to as emotions. In spite of its obvious relationship the close connection between reinforcement and emotional state or emotional behavior has been ignored by most writers. Theorists of emotional behavior and reinforcement theorists tend to regard problems only from the perspective of their own tradition and ignore other approaches. In social learning theory we recognize that such autonomic changes can serve as cues and that, along with situational cues, they can affect learned behavior (Schachter, 1966; Lazarus, 1968). Clearly, individuals differ in the kinds of bodily changes that follow from the same reinforcement (Lacey, 1959); and some individuals are more aware of these bodily changes than others (Lazarus, 1968). Emotions have been a troublesome area for psychologists. To some extent this is the result of failure to separate behaviors from expectancies, and failure to separate bodily changes from the learned psychological patterns of response. Both physiological changes and learned response patterns have either strong reinforcement or its anticipation as a common antecedent. However, although strong reinforcement may be a common antecedent to both autonomic changes and learned behavioral responses, these two need not be highly correlated.

Occurrence of a negative reinforcement, or its anticipation, as already indicated, may lead to defensive or avoidant behaviors; and such behaviors can be understood as having a potential for a particular class of reinforcements. However, it may be characteristic of some people to respond with aggression, repression, withdrawal, projection, depression, and so forth, somewhat independently of the kind (need category) of reinforcement. These responses may be a function of the sign or strength of the reinforcement rather than its particular form. In other words, we can talk not only about a behavior potential to repress competitive failures but a behavior potential to repress all strong negative reinforcements. How functional or general such potentials are across need areas is an empirical question. Mild failure in an achievement related task may increase the potential for some individuals to narrow their attention, increase concentration or increase effort. However, mild failure might not have the same effect, should it occur in the process of initiating a social relationship.

The understanding and providing of an orderly description of this area is a current challenge to social learning theorists. In the meantime, it may be hypothesized that these psychological responses generally referred to as emotional behavior may be regarded as similar to other learned behaviors in that functional categories are related to the sign, strength, and nature of the reinforcements.

Anxiety (or certain behavioral referents for anxiety), aggression, repression, cautiousness, and rigidity are some of the characteristics that have been thought of by many investigators as consequences of "emotional" states. However, it has always been difficult to demonstrate the generality of these behaviors across different situations, at least in "normal" populations. Such behavioral characteristics appear to be more general among certain pathological groups and less general in the "normal" population. Behaviors elicited by strong positive reinforcements like elation or associated with mild positive reinforcements like relaxation have been investigated much less than those associated with negative reinforcements, but they are equally important for a comprehensive account of human behavior.

The description of states of the organism, the nature of reinforcement, and motivational states are intertwined problems. It is not necessary to explain all of these abstractions as if they were true facts of nature. From a social learning theory point of view, it is only necessary to have an integrated and efficient set of constructs to explain and/or predict complex human behavior.

BELIEFS, EXPRESSED SOCIAL ATTITUDES, AND SOCIAL ACTION

Simple expectancies or cognitions were briefly mentioned earlier in this chapter. In social learning theory such expectancies about the properties of some object(s) or event(s) may also be called a belief. A belief about a class of social objects is referred to here as a social attitude. Simple cognitions, expectancies or beliefs may appear phenomenally to have an all-or-none quality, but in fact they may vary in magnitude between zero and one, and they are subject to change. The child looking at the adult may believe that he *is* smiling or that he *may* be smiling. The four-legged creature *is* a dog or *may* be a dog. Additional experience may teach the child that it is a cat. Cats are likely to scratch; dogs are not likely to scratch, etc. In other words, simple expectancies, beliefs, or cognitions may be regarded as having the properties of subjective probabilities varying in magnitude from zero to one and constantly subject to change with new experience.

No *necessary* awareness, that is, ability to verbalize, is implied by the term simple expectancy. In casting the concept of cognition into the language of an expectancy-reinforcement social learning theory, I am implicitly hypothesizing that the laws governing the growth and change of expectancies as well as those governing the relationship of expectancies to observable behaviors will also apply to simple cognition.

The simple cognitions regarding the properties of objects determine, in part, expectancies for behavior-reinforcement sequences by defining the gradients along which generalization takes place. As a consequence they determine, in part, which kinds of behaviors are likely to be tried out for novel objects and consequently, which behavior-reinforcement sequences are likely to be experienced. In the prediction of stable behavior it is the expectancies for behavior-reinforcement sequences, however, that play the major role. Behavior-reinforcement sequences in which expectancies for reinforcement are concerned solely with the characteristics of the object alone or with its potential as a source of reinforcement are only one determinant of a specific behavior choice in a given situation (e.g., "Don't sit on the radiator . . . you may get burned"). In social situations particularly, a specific behavioral choice may involve a number of reinforcements that are relatively independent of the properties of the object but that are, in fact, dependent on other social agents present in the situation (e.g., "Don't sit on the radiator . . . it's not polite").

The formula for behavior potential, however, is limited for predictive purposes. That is, it deals only with the relationship between the potential of a single behavior and the expectancy for a specific reinforcement whereas in fact there is always a variety of potential reinforcements that follow from any given behavior. So, in order to make an actual prediction, it is necessary to measure not only the expectancy for one reinforcement and the value of that reinforcement but to measure the expectancy for many reinforcements and the values of all of the reinforcements. For example, the decision to study for an examination not only involves a potential grade and its value, but also involves the loss of other satisfactions and the potential reactions of parents, teachers, and schoolmates. Were we, in fact, able to measure most of the important variance involved in such a behavioral choice, we still would not know whether or not the individual would choose such a behavior until we knew the relative value of other behavioral choices in that situation. These points can be illustrated by examining some of the individual difference variables involved in predicting some kinds of social action-taking behaviors.

Let us assume that an individual is approached with a request to take part in some form of civil disobedience, a disapproved march on the Capitol or a sit-in strike aimed at doing away with black-white segregation in some locality.

In Fig. 8.1 potential determinants have been arranged in an hypothesized order of importance. Social approval has been placed at the top of the list. Situationally determined expectancies here would involve the nature of the person requesting participation and the degree to what the individual feels the *specific* action contemplated would or would not meet with social approval from significant others. Differences between E' and generalized expectancies could also account for those people who are in sympathy with the action but somehow manage not to actually carry through with their commitment. The generalized expectancies would involve expectancies for the general class of actions for a variety of social agents, and would be relatively independent of specific circumstances. Reinforcement values might differ in sign for different social agents, and the overall strength of a need value for social approval would, of course, differ among individuals.

The overall strength for such a need value as social approval in our culture is reflected in the actions of millions of people during time of war. Although thousands of persons, possibly millions, have no desire to endanger themselves, have no strong interests in the causes involved, and do not wish to interrupt the normal course of their lives: They nevertheless allow themselves to be drafted, or may, in fact, enlist largely because of the fear of social disapproval for any other action. Similarly, people will go into battle in spite of strong motives to the contrary partly because of the strong social disapproval involved in taking one of various other alternatives, such as feigning illness: Where feelings are intense,

$$B.P._{\text{Yes, } S_1} = f(E'_{S_1} \text{ \& G.E.}) \text{ \& } R.V._{1, S_1}^{+} \text{ Social approval}$$

$$B.P._{\text{Yes, } S_1} = f(E'_{S_1} \text{ \& } \boxed{G.E.}^{*}) \text{ \& } R.V._{2, S_1}^{+} \text{ Social change}$$

$$B.P._{\text{Yes, } S_1} = f(E'_{S_1} \text{ \& G.E.}) \text{ \& } R.V._{3, S_1}^{-} \text{ Loss of other satisfactions}$$

$$B.P._{\text{Yes, } S_1} = f(E'_{S_1} \text{ \& G.E.}) \text{ \& } R.V._{4, S_1}^{+} \text{ Consistency with public statements}$$

$$B.P._{\text{Yes, } S_1} = f(E'_{S_1} \text{ \& G.E.}) \text{ \& } R.V._{5, S_1}^{+} \text{ Consistency with private beliefs}$$

$$B.P._{\text{No, } S_1} = f(E'_{S_1} \text{ \& G.E.}) \text{ \& } R.V._{1, S_1}^{+} \text{ Social approval}$$

Etc.

(* Insert)

$$G.E._{\text{Yes} \rightarrow \text{ Social change}} = f \quad \begin{bmatrix} G.E._{\text{Internal-External Control}} \\ G.E._{\text{Efficacy of civil disobedience}} \\ G.E._{\text{Trust of leaders}} \end{bmatrix}$$

FIG. 8.1 Some Major Sources of Variance in the Determination of the Decision to Take Part in Social Action (From Rotter, J. B. Beliefs, social attitudes, and behavior. In Richard Jessor & Seymour Feshbach (Eds.) *Cognition, personality, and clinical psychology.* San Francisco: Jossey-Bass Inc., 1967, by permission).

as in the taking of social action in regard to segregation in the South: Expectancies for strong social disapproval can be very high and extremely important in determining behavioral choice.

In addition to different beliefs regarding the nature of blacks or of the injustice of present social conditions, people will still differ considerably in the degree to what they place value on effecting a social change. The strength of their belief in the injustice of present conditions may bear some relationship to the value they would place on social change, but it is probably far from a perfect relationship. Situational factors may again play a role in the expectancy that the behavior involved will lead to social change. The individual involved might consider it the wrong place, the wrong time, or the wrong leader. Generalized expectancies that this type of social action (i.e., civil disobedience) will lead to social change may also play a significant cross-situational role.

These generalized expectancies are illustrated at the bottom of Fig. 8.1. The first, internal versus external control, is a variable with which we have done considerable research (Rotter, 1966; 1975; Phares, 1976; Lefcourt, 1976). In general, internal-external control refers to the degree to which people believe that what happens to them results from their own behavior; versus the degree to which people believe that what happens to them is the result of luck, chance, fate, or forces beyond their control.

The second generalized expectancy is related to civil disobedience of many kinds. The individual may have developed, on the basis of previous experience, his or her own or that of others, an expectancy that such efforts do a great deal of good or none at all; the person may, in fact, believe that such behaviors actually delay rather than speed up social change.

The third generalized expectancy listed is one of trust of leaders for the civil rights movements. It is a more specific generalized expectancy than trust of other people, in general (Rotter, 1971, 1975), that might have been substituted in the figure for trust of leaders. Some individuals, although genuinely desiring social change and accepting the principle of civil disobedience, may expect that the leaders in the movement are dominated by Communists, are self-seeking, have ulterior motives, or cannot be relied upon to carry through. All such generalized expectancies are partial determinants of agreeing to take part in the social action.

The third formula, dealing with loss of other satisfactions, might well be placed second, depending again on the specific issue and place. Perhaps far more important is the case in responses to attitude questionnaires, this behavior potential will play a significant role in the determination of social action. Even the relatively mild behavior of signing a petition may involve specific and generalized expectancies for loss of business, physical harm, persecution via the telephone, and other significant negative reinforcements. It may in fact involve only an interruption of one's other activities, but there are undoubtedly thousands of individuals who would join various protest activities were it not for the loss of other satisfactions.

The fourth formula deals with the values involved in consistency with other public statements. Obviously, the specific situation will play a role, particularly with regard to whether the individuals present have also been present when the other public statements have been made.

Our fourth formula deals with the need to maintain consistency among public statements and has been studied experimentally by focusing on the effects of commitment. Mischel (1958) and Watt (1965) have demonstrated strong effects of public commitment on resistance to changing publicly expressed expectancies for reinforcement in task situations; and Hobart and Hovland (1954) have demonstrated that public commitment leads to more resistance to attitude change.

Consistency between two public statements may not be of as great importance to some people as consistency between public statement and public action. Inconsistency in the latter case is not an intellectual matter, but rather a fear of being viewed as a "hypocrite," of not having "the courage of one's convictions". This could play an important role for many individuals who would have relatively little concern about consistency with private beliefs. The generalized expectancies in this formula would involve expectancies that lack of consistency would lead others to perceive the individual as a phony hypocrite or "fourflusher". What one has said on an attitude questionnaire might in fact play some role here, but far more important are public statements made under other circumstances.

Finally, we come to consistency with private beliefs. Does the action involved represent what we truly believe to be right or proper? Our simple beliefs or cognitions regarding blacks and the issues involved play a more direct role here in affecting E's and generalized expectancies. The reinforcement value of such consistency will vary greatly within our culture. For a few individuals, it may, in fact, be the strongest motive of any we have described in Fig. 8.1. With the great majority of people in our society it appears that it plays a lesser role in determining social action behavior, than do the motives or reinforcement values we have previously discussed. If we use Benedict's (1946) distinction between shame and guilt, we can say that consistency with public beliefs avoids shame and consistency with private beliefs avoids guilt. For most Americans I believe that, in this situation at least, the avoidance of shame is probably the stronger motive.

One implication of this analysis is that although social psychologists are generally aware of the many sources of variance, they appear in their research to have overemphasized the significance of simple beliefs about specific social groups in determining answers to questionnaires. To an even greater degree, they have exaggerated the significance both of beliefs about social objects and of responses to attitude questionnaires in determining the behavior of a person when faced with the alternative of some kind of social action.

This model does not explain how change in behavior is effected. Previous publications (Rotter, 1954; Rotter, Chance & Phares, 1972) have dealt with principles of changing expectancies and reinforcement values. By changing any of the variables in Fig. 8.1 sufficiently, we can achieve behavior changes. The model in fact broadens considerably and the conventional approach to behavior change in providing many more variables that can be manipulated in order to achieve such change.

There are many possible additional variables and reinforcements that have not been included in this illustration. The *behavior* of responding to a social attitude questionnaire could be analysed similarly. In the latter case the value of consistency with private beliefs might be of much greater significance depending on the circumstances of testing and the controls for social approval exercised in the selection of items. Still it might not be the largest factor in determining a response in most circumstances.

This model does illustrate a method of analysis of a general problem and it presents a crude attempt to indicate the relationship of a simple cognitions, expressed attitudes and behavior. Whereas all these are related, the relationships are more complex than, perhaps, was originally thought. They are nevertheless amenable to systematic study.

SOCIAL LEARNING THEORY AND ATTRIBUTION THEORY

The purpose of this brief section is not to subsume attribution theory or to critically evaluate it, but rather merely to offer some comments on attribution theory from a social learning perspective.

At the outset, it should be made clear that expectations regarding causality before an event differ from beliefs after the event. Similarly, *expressed* beliefs after an event are not necessarily the same as implicit beliefs, but such verbal behaviors are subject to all the same kinds of determinants as those described in the section on social attitudes.

In the case of competitive activities it is clear that defensive behaviors are of extreme importance in failure situations; and these defenses are essentially a problem in individual differences as well evidenced by studies of level of aspiration techniques (Rotter, 1954, pp. 313–326). Even in dealing with attributions of causality for success a desire to be polite or socially acceptable may be reflected. Statements of expectancies for future success are influenced by ideas about negative sanctions for boasting, desire for conformity, etc., again, a function of individual differences. Of course, within a fairly homogeneous subculture, differences between groups subject to different conditions of success and failure are statistically significant.

Attribution theorists also study the effect of attributions for one behavioral outcome on subsequent behaviors. Here, also, there is a tendency to accept the attributions literally (and naively). Do people really believe their own expressed attributions? Surely not always. The polite response, "it was luck," is not really believed by the tennis player who catches the edge of the line on a tennis ace and the same defensive attribution of a loser ("it was the other player's luck") does little to dispel his or her gloom.

One contribution of social learning theory to attribution theory is the concept of generalized expectancies for problem solving. Perhaps the generalized expectancy most studied in this regard is internal versus external control of reinforcement. However, it is clear from several studies that the prediction of certain behaviors may require an individual difference distinction between passive or congruent externals and defensive externals (Hochreich, 1974, 1975; Davis & Davis, 1972). Generalized expectancies such as trusting others, looking for alternatives, etc. must also affect the nature of post-hoc attributions, whether one is dealing with competitive tasks or other events. Such expectancies may also account in part for differences in the kind of attribution made for one's self versus the kind of attributions made for others, as well as other variables such as characteristic defenses.

When and why do people make attributions of causality at all? Although there is little or no research describing the conditions under which people do make attributions of causality, it seems intuitively clear that usually people do not make post-hoc attributions. In social learning theory increments and decrements in expectancies are hypothesized to be a function of differences between expected and actual outcomes and the relative novelty of the situation (Rotter, 1954, pp. 176–177). It seems that a reasonable hypothesis would be that two factors determining the spontaneous occurrence of attributions would be the unexpected nature of the event—when it does not fit previous experience, we are more likely to look for reasons. When previous experience is lacking, we are perhaps also more likely to look for causal relationships than when we are experiencing a familiar event.

The second factor would be the occurrence of strong reinforcements, particularly negative ones. "Why is God punishing me!" occurs as a spontaneous thought much more frequently than "Why is God rewarding me!" In any case, when there is both a strong reinforcement and an unexpected one most people are more likely to make spontaneous attributions of causality.

If individual differences are an important aspect of attributions of causality then cultural differences would also account for considerable variance. Cultural differences in accepted defensive behavior, in concepts of reasonable causes, etc. should help us to understand both implicit beliefs and expressed attributions. The study of such cultural differences could reveal much about how attributions are learned and what variables control the expression of attributions.

THE PSYCHOLOGICAL SITUATION AND INTERACTIONISM

The first basic postulate of social learning theory is: "The unit of investigation for the study of personality is the interaction of the individual and his/her meaningful environment" (Rotter, 1954). This is clearly an interactionist position. It was stated earlier by Lewin (1935), Kantor (1924), and Murray (1938). Coutu (1949) in the field of sociology and Brunswik (1943) in his analysis of the field of perception expressed a similar principle. It should be noted, however, that all these theorists have had great difficulty in using the concept of the psychological situation, meaningful environment, life space, etc., systematically in a *predictive* fashion, because they have stressed the subjective or learned nature of the environment. The term "meaningful environment" as used here refers to the acquired significance or meaning of the environment to the individual. It is the psychological, not the physical, description of the environment that is important.

In social learning theory we define the psychological situation as a complex set of interacting cues acting upon an individual for any specific time period. *These cues determine, for the individual, expectancies for behavior-reinforcement sequences and also for reinforcement-reinforcement sequences.* Such cues may be implicit as well as explicit; that is, they may be thoughts, ideas, or internal stimuli such as pain, pleasure, excitement, or fear. Implicit responses may be carried over from a prior experience and may not be related to what are considered present external cues. It is *not* necessary that the person be able to verbally express conscious awareness of these cues, but only that it can be demonstrated that he/she was reacting to them. In order to make the concept of the psychological situation operational implicit cues must be identified by inference from immediately prior events or by inference from behaviors in the situation other than the behavior we are predicting, including physiological observations that serve as indirect measures of the psychological state of the organism.

We define the psychological situation as the interacting cues perceived by the individual over any defined time unit; thus, we may be interested in cues over a period of a moment, an experimental hour, or over much longer periods of time, as when we talk about a person's job situation or marriage situation. The definition, then, is not precise. What we call personal variables and what we call situational variables can extend over long period of time. The overall definition has to be in part arbitrary and relativistic, but it can be made workable and useful. The alternatives of either trying to predict behavior without paying attention to the present cues to which the individual is responding or of trying to predict behavior without taking into account what the individual brings into a situation in terms of relatively stable characteristics, limits one to extremely low levels of prediction. In other words, a useful distinction between person and situation is one that defines personal variables as a set of relatively stable characteristics and defines the other as the set of meaningful cues to which he or she is reacting at the present. Both sets of variables are presumed to be determined by past learning.

Problems Inherent in the Treatment of the Psychological Situation as a Systematic Variable. How can the psychological situation be defined independently of the person? If one defines the psychological situation as meaningful, or as truly psychological, rather than physical, or as subjective rather than objective, then the situation is a function of the person. We have already indicated that this is not a necessary barrier to problems of analysis, since we can treat situational variables as one aspect of the person and stable accumulated effects of experience, or personality variables, as a different aspect of the person. However, this does not tell us how to use the situation predictively.

In social learning theory this problem is treated by identifying the situation in the common sense terms of the social group, subculture, or culture. In other words, we can make clear the objective referent for what we are talking about and still treat the environment as a psychologically meaningful, or subjective environment. The subject's reactions to the environment and the scientist's descriptions of the environment need not be identical. In fact, the social scientist is often busily engaged in using the latter in order to better understand the former. In this way, we can talk not only about differences among situations, but about individual differences in response to the same objective situation. For example, we can generally obtain high agreement when we identify a situation as a classroom situation, a party, an authority situation, a frustration situation, etc. These are in themselves abstractions from a variety of cues, but at the common sense level. Note that we are not referring to an average of interpretations but to a descriptive level that will allow for high agreement among observers. If necessary or desirable, much more elaborate and detailed descriptions of the situation can be made, but always in the common sense terms of the subculture. Once we have identified a given situation, we can then make predictions about differences in behavior of individuals within that situation; differences of behavior of a group of individuals in one situation versus another, and interactions of the two. This is, of course, what social, clinical and personality psychologists have been doing for a long time. We are stating here explicitly what others have done implicitly over many years. By describing how situations can be identified objectively we have opened the way, but have not solved the problem of identifying or discovering the important dimensions of situations that can be used in defining classes of situations.

How Much Variance in a Person–Situation Interaction is Due to Personality Variables and How Much Variance is Due to Situational Variables? From the point of view of social learning theory, the foregoing question has to be regarded as a pseudoproblem. Although in the recent past, many investigators have been interested in this issue, most now recognize that the question is essentially meaningless, because both the personality variables and the situational variables depend on the person's previous experience. If we seek the answer to some specific, practical problem, the question may have some significance. For example, we may wish to know how much effect may be expected in measuring intelligence or school achievement when the examiner is black or white and the subjects are all black.

If one does ask the general question, there are at least seven aspects of the experimental design that will affect the answer.

The first of these is the homogeneity of subjects. If we are studying adjustment under conditions of mild and no stress, then an unselected group of college freshmen represent a much more homogeneous sample than would a group of subjects who range from hospitalized psychotic patients through the professional personnel who work at the institution. In the latter case, it is obvious that more variance is attributable to people than to situations.

The second aspect is the question of what is being measured, or the criterion behavior being studied. That is, if we want to see how Moslem and Protestant Americans respond to success and failure situations, a measure of attributions to fate will probably show stronger between-group (person) differences than will a measure of perserverance.

The third experimental consideration that affects the relative importance of situational and individual differences is the degree of situational homogeneity. If we are examining the effects of success and failure on behavior, and we design our experiment to include passing or failing on a test of arithmetic reasoning given to high school subjects for "research purposes," with confidentiality of test scores assured, the situational variable will not account for as much variance as when we are studying the effects on behavior of passing or failing an examination in which failure would lead to the exclusion of any further educational goals.

The fourth variable affecting the relative variance attributed to behavior by situational and personality variables is the nature of the culture or subculture. This may be regarded as a special case of the first variable; namely, homogeneity of subjects. For example, consider a study of attitudes towards big-time athletics in college in which individual differences were predicted from a measure of need for achievement. The study is done in two colleges, one in which the football team has just won a national championship and the other in which they have just lost the national championship. With these situational and personality measures we might expect the degree of variance contributed by the individual difference variable to be much higher for females (who may vary more in their interest and involvement) than it is for males and for seniors (some of whom may become more cynical with longer time exposure) than it is for freshmen. In relationship to specific situations and when studying particular behaviors, one subculture may be much more homogeneous than another.

Many studies usually done by social psychologists with a secondary interest in individual differences often show little or no contribution of these individual differences to the prediction of criterion behavior. In many studies of person-situation interactions the individual differences measures employed by the investigator are invalid or irrelevant. In part, this is the result of the lack of good measures developed for specific purposes. The development of such measures requires years of careful work and modern test construction theory and technology. It is relatively easy to construct two situations which differ clearly and markedly in the degree of threat they present or in the kinds of reinforcements that it is possible to obtain. It is not nearly so easy to find a good measure of individual differences relevant to the criterion behavior being studied. And it is both difficult and time-consuming to construct such a measure and to validate it carefully. Literally hundreds of studies have thrown in a scale for measuring attitudes towards internal versus external control of reinforcement, as an afterthought in a study whose main focus is situational differences. However, it seems clear that in a significant proportion of such studies, it can be reliably established that the measure was in fact irrelevant to the behavior being studied.

The sixth variable, similar to the one just discussed, is the relevance of the situational variable that is being manipulated to the criterion behavior. If we are studying the interaction of academic aptitude and sex of the examiner during the giving of final examinations in a math course, then it is common sense that the situational variable—sex of the examiner—will have little or no effect on the criterion behavior— grade on the examination. It is not a relevant dimension for the criterion of examination grade in a math course, although it would be a relevant dimension if the test were a Rorschach test being given to college students for research purposes.

Finally, the seventh dimension is the degree of familiarity or novelty of the situation used in the experiment. For example, Schwarz (1969) has shown that several measures of a generalized expectancy for success on a relatively novel motor skill task correlated significantly with the first trial on the task. The correlation was lowered eventually to zero with increased massed trials. In social learning theory this follows from our formula that an expectancy is a function of a specific expectancy learned in that situation and related generalized expectancies. The generalized expectancies have less influence on the situation as the number of trials increase.

It is clear from the previous analysis that one can easily design an experiment to either maximize variance accounted for by personality measures or by situational differences in some specific person-situation interaction.

To make use of the psychological situation for predictive purposes it is necessary to identify functional dimensions of situational similarity. Methods for doing this have been described by Rotter (in press) in another source.

REFERENCES

Benedict, Ruth F. *The crysanthemum and the sword*. Boston: Houghton Mifflin, 1946.

Brunswik, E. Organismic achievement and environmental probability. *Psychological Review*, 1943, *40*, 255-272.

Coutu, W. *Emergent human nature*. New York: Knopf, 1949.

Davis, W. L., & Davis, D. E. Internal-external control and attribution of responsibility for success and failure. *Journal of Personality*, 1972, *40*, 123-136.

Hobart, Enid M., & Hovland, C. I. The effect of "commitment" on opinion change following communication. *American Psychologist*, 1954, *9*, 394. (Abstract)

Hochreich, D. J. Defensive externality and attribution of responsibility. *Journal of Personality*, 1974, *42*, 543-557.

Hochreich, D. J. Defensive externality and blame projection following failure. *Journal of Personality and Social Psychology*, 1975, *32*, 540-546.

Kantor, J. R. *Principles of psychology* (Vol. 1, 2). New York: Knopf, 1924.

Lacey, J. I. Psychophysiological approaches to the evaluation of psychotherapeutic process and outcome. In E. A. Rubinstein & M. B. Parloff (Eds.), *Research in psychotherapy*. Washington, D.C.: American Psychological Association, 1959.

Lazarus, R. S. Emotions and adaptation: Conceptual and empirical relations. In W. J. Arnold (Ed.), *Nebraska Symposium on Motivation*. Lincoln: University of Nebraska Press, 1968.

Lefcourt, H. M. *Locus of control*. Hillsdale, N.J.: Lawrence Erlbaum, 1976.

Lewin, K. *A dynamic theory of personality*. New York, London: McGraw–Hill, 1935.

Mischel, W. The effect of the commitment situation on the generalization of expectancies. *Journal of Personality*, 1958, *26*, 508–516.

Murray, H. A. *Explorations in personality: A clinical and experimental study of fifty men of college age, by the workers at the Harvard psychological clinic*. New York, London: Oxford University Press, 1938.

Phares, E. J. *Locus of control in personality*. Morristown, N.J.: General Learning Press, 1976.

Rotter, J. B. Generalized expectancies for internal versus external control of reinforcement. *Psychological Monographs*, 1966, *80* (Whole No. 1).

Rotter, J. B. *Social learning and clinical psychology*. Englewood Cliffs, N.J.: Prentice–Hall, 1954. New York: Johnson Reprint Co., 1980.

Rotter, J. B. Generalized expectancies for interpersonal trust. *American Psychologist*, 1971, *26*, 443–452.

Rotter, J. B. Some problems and misconceptions related to the construct of internal versus external control of reinforcement. *Journal of Consulting and Clinical Psychology*, 1975, *43*, 56–67.

Rotter, J. B. The psychological situation in social learning theory. In D. Magnusson (Ed.), *The situation: An interactional perspective*. Hillsdale, N.J.: Lawrence Erlbaum Associates, in press.

Rotter, J. B., Chance, J. E., & Phares, E. J. *Applications of a social learning theory of personality*. New York: Holt, Rinehart & Winston, 1972.

Schachter, S. The interaction of cognitive and physiological determinants of emotional state. In C. D. Spielberger (Ed.), *Anxiety and behavior*. New York: Academic Press, 1966.

Schroder, H. M., & Rotter, J. B. Rigidity as learned behavior. *Journal of Experimental Psychology*, 1952, *44*, 141–150.

Schwarz, J. C. Contributions of generalized expectancy to stated expectancy under conditions of success and failure. *Journal of Personality and Social Psychology*, 1969, *11*, 157–164.

Watt, N. F. The relation of public commitment, delay after commitment, and some individual differences to changes in verbalized expectancies. *Journal of Personality*, 1965, *33*, 284–299.

V THE CONTEXT OF VALUES AND ATTITUDES

9

Human Values and the Prediction of Action: An Expectancy-Valence Analysis

Norman T. Feather
The Flinders University of South Australia

Over the past 20 or 30 years we have witnessed an increasing use of cognitive concepts in psychology and this trend has been a general one, not restricted to any particular area. We find cognitive concepts employed in theories about how individuals acquire, organize, and use information from their environments; in theories about changes in the thought process that occur as children mature; in motivational theories that are concerned with identifying the immediate determinants of the vigor, direction, and persistence of purposive behavior; in theories about the labelling of emotional experience; in theories about the memory process—indeed, throughout all of psychology. There has been a movement away from a strictly mechanistic view of the person as something akin to a sophisticated, modifiable robot responding in predictable ways to incoming stimulation and to internal drive states, to an alternative view of the person as continually active as well as reactive, as engaged in processing information constructively so as to achieve meaningful views of physical and social reality, as behaving in ways that reflect intervening cognitive processes, and as having the power to control and change environments. I leave it to the historian of ideas to explain this shift in emphasis. Remembering the old debate between the associationists and the cognitivists, however, it appears that Hull has lost and that Tolman and Lewin have won. Some may quibble with that conclusion but I believe that it has the ring of truth, at least at this stage of our history.

Social psychology has been in the vanguard of this cognitive revolution. Lewin's emphasis on the importance of relating an individual's behavior to an interdependent set of immediate determinants that include both the person conceived structurally and the structured situation as experienced by the person, was a pioneer contribution that had wide influence and whose legacy still persists

(Cartwright, 1978; Lewin, 1935, 1936, 1951). Tolman (1955) in his discussion of the principles of performance and Lewin and his colleagues in their analysis of level of aspiration behavior (Lewin, Dembo, Festinger, & Sears, 1944) were early advocates of expectancy-value theories of motivation, a cognitive approach that first came to my attention over 20 years ago and that has continued to influence my work ever since (Atkinson & Feather, 1966; Feather, 1959, 1961, 1967, 1975). One could point to many other examples of the use of cognitive concepts by social psychologists and by others in cognate areas. Lack of space precludes a detailed survey of these concepts but a sample list will suffice to indicate their widespread use: cognitive dissonance, naive theory of action, perceived self-efficacy, abstract structure, prototype, subjective probability, belief system, perceived control, hypothesis, category, scripts, accounts, plans, rules, and so on. You can play the game of linking the concept to the theorist.

Some of the cognitive concepts that have been introduced recently give one the feeling of déja vu, as if one is being presented with old wine in new bottles. Perhaps one should not complain as long as the wine is good. The invention of new labels for old ideas may be productive in its own right, if it is accompanied by new research techniques that can be used to further knowledge, if it draws attention to an old concept from a different angle and relates it to new conceptual developments, and if the old concept in new guise is so central and important that it continues to force attention and evokes the interest and efforts of a new generation of psychologists.

It is always useful, however, to put ideas into their historical context and to determine to what extent they improve on what we had before and whether they overcome difficulties that may have plagued similar theoretical approaches in the past. One early criticism made of Tolman and Lewin was that their theories were deficient in explicating how intervening variables such as expectancies and life-space were related to overt behavior or performance. Guthrie (1935) accused Tolman of leaving the rat in the maze "buried in thought" and Brunswik (1943) argued that Lewin's concept of the life-space focussed upon determinants of behavior that were "post-perceptual and pre-behavioral [p. 266]." Both Tolman and Lewin responded to these criticisms in their subsequent work—Tolman by developing his "principles of performance" (Tolman, 1955) and Lewin by introducing new concepts that stemmed from action research (Cartwright, 1979; Lewin, 1951). But the problem of the relationship between "knowledge" and "thought", on the one hand, and overt action on the other is still with us today. The new wave of social psychologists, in their concern with cognitive structure and cognitive process, have little to say about the link between cognition and behavior and one wonders now whether the person is left buried in scripts, accounts, prototypes, causal attributions, or whatever, and whether these cognitive events precede behavior or are interpretations of behavior after it has occurred. Theories about social cognition and theories about the dynamics of action clearly need to make contact with one another.

I have been concerned with this issue in some of my recent research in the psychology of values. Specifically, I have become interested in the question of how a person's behavior relates to the values held by that person. To what extent will knowledge of a person's value priorities enable us to understand that person's actions within defined situations, and what other variables may have to be taken into account in making that prediction. This is a complex and difficult question that also has a long history—see, for example, the studies conducted over 50 years ago by Hartshorne and May (1930). My analysis of this question is still at an early stage but I do have some research findings that are relevant. There are two recent studies that I will describe. The first relates social interaction between groups to degree of similarity in their value systems (Feather, 1980c). The second and most recent study explores the relationship between values and willingness to lend support to social movements. The two studies demonstrate rather different theoretical approaches. The first was conceived within the general framework of discrepancy theory, of which a particular case involves the fit between a person's value systems and those the person attributes to social environments or groups (Feather, 1971, 1975, 1979a). The second study made use of expectancy-value theory, a class of motivational theory that has already been mentioned. This type of theory is cognitive in its emphasis and it has emerged from many different areas of psychology (Feather, 1959, see also Chapter 3). It is a theoretical approach that I have found congenial in my previous work—for example, in the analysis of both achievement behavior (Atkinson & Feather, 1966) and information-seeking behavior (Feather, 1967), and I have been drawn to it again as a source of hypotheses about the relationship between values and overt action.

Before describing these new developments, however, I want to clear some ground and provide a context by briefly describing the direction that my research on values has taken over the past few years.

THE FLINDERS VALUE PROGRAM

The research program on values was initiated for a number of different reasons. An important aim was to explore an area that has been relatively neglected by social psychologists. Textbooks in social psychology have little to say about values despite the fact that the term "value" is one that emerges in many different disciplines—for example, in psychology, sociology, anthropology, philosophy, politics, economics, and religion. It seemed to me to to be foolish to ignore a concept that is so central and so, over 10 years ago, I began investigations in this area.[1]

---

[1]Rokeach (1978-79) has also noted the relative lack of concern among social psychologists with the conceptual analysis and empirical study of values. His pioneering efforts in this field have been a major influence in stimulating my interest in this area of research.

The program to date has concentrated on two main questions: (1) What are the value systems of different groups?; (2) How do the value systems of groups and individuals relate to those of the social environments with which they commonly interact? The approach may be seen as an attempt to develop an *ecology of values*. Just as one can map the economic and geographical resources of an environment and relate these to characteristics of the people who inhabit that environment, so, I believe, one can also map the values of persons and groups and look at the effects of disjunctions between these values and those values that the environment is perceived to promote. The greater part of my recent book *Values in Education and Society* was concerned with reporting theory and research relevant to these ecological questions over a very wide area of application (Feather, 1975). The focus was on the value systems that people attributed to themselves, on the value systems that they attributed to their environments, and on the correlates of discrepancies in these two sets of value systems. Some studies were also reported that examined the accuracy of perceptions of value priorities, considered in the aggregate. Finally, in the last chapter of the book, there was some discussion of how the relationship between values and action could be approached by using expectancy-value theory. The research program has been guided by theory and it has been cumulative, each study building on but also to some extent replicating what has been found before. Where possible, I have tried to use convergent validation procedures, approaching problems by employing a variety of methods.

The major instrument used for measuring value systems has been the Rokeach Value Survey (Rokeach, 1973). Two classes of values are included in this Value Survey—terminal values and instrumental values. The terminal values are concerned with general goals or "end-states of existence" and they include such values as *freedom, equality, self-respect, wisdom, an exciting life, true friendship,* and *inner harmony*. The instrumental values are concerned with means to goals or "modes of conduct" and they include such values as being *ambitious, courageous, honest, loving, responsible, imaginative,* and *obedient*. Table 9.1 lists the two sets of values as they are presented to respondents in the Value Survey. In the standard use of this test the respondent has to rank each set of values in their order of importance for self, "as guiding principles in *your* life." This rank order for each set of values provides two value systems or hierarchies of importance for each person, a terminal value system and an instrumental value system, and respondents can be compared in regard to their value systems considered as a whole, and also in relation to the rank orders they assign to particular values.

In those studies that have been concerned with the correlates of person-environment fit, I have taken the further step of asking respondents to rank the values in regard to specified social environments (for example, the school situation) to try to discover how they perceive the value systems of these defined environments. One can then compare the value systems of the respondents them-

TABLE 9.1
Terminal and Instrumental Values from the Rokeach Value Survey

Terminal Values	Instrumental Values
A comfortable life (a prosperous life)	Ambitious (hardworking, aspiring)
An exciting life (a stimulating, active life)	Broad-minded (open-minded)
A sense of accomplishment (lasting contribution)	Capable (competent, effective)
A world at peace (free of war and conflict)	Cheerful (lighthearted, joyful)
A world of beauty (beauty of nature and the arts)	Clean (neat, tidy)
Equality (brotherhood, equal opportunity for all)	Courageous (standing up for your beliefs)
Family security (taking care of loved ones)	Forgiving (willing to pardon others)
Freedom (independence, free choice)	Helpful (working for the welfare of others)
Happiness (contentedness)	Honest (sincere, truthful)
Inner harmony (freedom from inner conflict)	Imaginative (daring, creative)
Mature love (sexual and spiritual intimacy)	Independent (self-reliant, self-sufficient)
National security (protection from attack)	Intellectual (intelligent, reflective)
Pleasure (an enjoyable, leisurely life)	Logical (consistent, rational)
Salvation (saved, eternal life)	Loving (affectionate, tender)
Self-respect (self-esteem)	Obedient (dutiful, respectful)
Social recognition (respect, admiration)	Polite (courteous, well-mannered)
True friendship (close companionship)	Responsible (dependable, reliable)
Wisdom (a mature understanding of life)	Self-controlled (restrained, self-disciplined)

selves with the value systems they attribute to the social environment under consideration and study the effects of disjunctions between these two sets of value systems, one a personal set, the other an environmental set (Feather, 1975, 1979a). The Rokeach Value Survey is a useful instrument for this purpose. Moreover, it does involve a wide range of different kinds of values, unlike some other instruments.

The first study concerning values and action that I want to describe involved this kind of methodology in which discrepancies between personal and environmental value systems were related to a dependent variable—in this case, social interaction between groups.

VALUE SYSTEMS AND SOCIAL INTERACTION

This study was conducted in the newly independent nation of Papua New Guinea in 1976. It was designed to test the hypothesis that groups who perceive their value systems to be similar are more likely to interact socially than groups who perceive their value systems to be dissimilar. There is a long line of research both from the laboratory and from the field that is compatible with this hypothesis—for example, the work by Byrne (1971), by Newcomb (1961), and, more recently, by Brewer and Campbell (1976). The hypotheses tested in this prior research have been developed from a variety of theoretical frameworks—involving consistency theory, reinforcement theory, exchange theory, or some other conceptualization that relates to the interaction process (Secord & Backman, 1974). In the case of my own investigation I assumed that a shared set of value priorities between groups would tend to facilitate social interaction because each group would be a compatible social environment for the other, providing both support and reinforcement for deeply held views, and thereby satisfying basic needs and validating self-conceptions (Feather, 1980c).

The setting for the research was Port Moresby High School—the only secondary school in Papua New Guinea that contains a sizeable number of both Australian expatriate students and indigenous Papua New Guinean students. The hypothesis relating social interaction to value similarity was tested in relation to these two groups. The students, who were all in the upper forms of the high school, first ranked either the terminal or the instrumental values from the Rokeach Value Survey (Rokeach, 1973) in relation to their own priorities, using the standard instructions. The Australian expatriate students then ranked the same set of values (terminal or instrumental) "in the order of importance you think most Papua New Guineans of about your age who were born in Papua New Guinea would assign them—as guiding principles in their lives." The indigenous Papua New Guineans ranked the set of values ". . . in the order of importance you think most Australian expatriates of about your own age in Papua New Guinea would assign to them—as guiding principles in their lives." Respondents in each group therefore provided two rank orders of importance for the one set of values (terminal or instrumental)—the first set of rankings applying to self and the second set to the other group. These two sets of rankings were compared for similarity for each respondent by using the Spearman rank-order correlation coefficient (*rho*), higher positive values of *rho* implying increasing similarity in the value systems being compared. Either a terminal *rho* or an instrumental *rho* was calculated for each respondent, depending on whether respondents ranked the terminal values or the instrumental values.

Subsequently the respondents answered a number of questionnaire items of which I will describe only those that provided relatively direct measures of extent of social interaction. Further details can be found in the published report (Feather, 1980c). Two direct measures were obtained. The first was a social interaction index based on each respondent's answers to five items. These items concerned being invited home, being asked to parties, playing sport, sharing recreation, and mixing informally at school with members of the other group. The second direct measure was obtained by asking each respondent how many good friends he or she had in the other group.

Subjects also responded to an item presented in Likert format that asked them how much they thought they had in common with the other group. This item was included to obtain a general measure of perceived similarity in addition to the Spearman *rhos* that were based on comparison of each respondent's value rankings for self and other group. This general measure is called perceived commonality. I expected that increasing perceived commonality, like increasing value similarity, would be associated with increasing social interaction.

The results are presented in Table 9.2. It can be seen that they provided selective support for the hypothesis. The predictions were not confirmed for the indigenous students. The predictions were supported, however, for the Australian expatriate group when perceived commonality was used as the measure of similarity and when similarity in value systems referred to the instrumental values.

One should not be discouraged by this limited support. When considered in context these results are very informative. Let us consider some possible reasons why the predictions were not supported for the Papua New Guineans. In the first place it could be argued that the Rokeach Value Survey was an inappropriate instrument for this group, given their different cultural background, and that the particular way that it was used to obtain both own and attributed rankings made it even more difficult for the Papua New Guineans. Note, however, that my previous research in Papua New Guinea with the Value Survey has shown that it yields meaningful and replicable results when used with indigenous students who possess a good command of English (Feather, 1975, 1980a). Note also that the relatively simple measure of perceived commonality, that should not have pre-

TABLE 9.2
Correlations of Direct Measures of Social Interaction with
Terminal and Instrumental Similarity Indexes (*Rhos*) and
with Perceived Commonality

		Correlations		
Variable	*With:*	*Terminal rho*	*Instrumental rho*	*Perceived Commonality*
Australian expatriate students				
Social interaction index		−.02 (35)	.31* (39)	.24* (74)
Number of good friends in other group		.19 (35)	.40** (35)	.30** (70)
Papua New Guinean students				
Social interaction index		−.13 (14)	−.04 (16)	.25 (30)
Number of good friends in other group		.11 (14)	.09 (14)	−.02 (28)

Note. Ns involved in correlations are listed in parentheses after the correlations. Note that subjects ranked either the terminal or the instrumental values, not both.

*p < .05 (one-tailed)
**p < .01 (one-tailed)
***p < .001 (one-tailed)

sented any special difficulties for the indigenous students, did not predict to social interaction either.

A second explanation of why the predictions were not supported for the Papua New Guineans could be that value similarity and perceived commonality might not be especially relevant factors for understanding social interaction in this new nation. The similarity/attraction hypothesis has been formulated by psychologists from a Western culture and it may not generalize from one culture to another, especially if the cultures are different in many respects. Cross-cultural psychologists and anthropologists are fond of pointing out the dangers of treating hypotheses as if they had universal cultural application (eg., Berry, 1969; Cole & Scribner, 1974; Feather, 1975). Note, however, that the similarity/attraction hypothesis was confirmed in the Brewer and Campbell (1976) study that involved 30 East African tribes.

In my opinion, the most likely explanation of the negative results for the Papua New Guineans is that support for the similarity/attraction hypothesis may be hard to find under conditions where one is attempting to predict the extent to which a relatively low status group interacts with a group of higher status. One hardly needs to be reminded that for many years Australians have occupied the positions of status and power within Papua New Guinea, a situation that is now beginning to change as, with nationhood, the roles involved in government and administration are transferred. But social psychological analysis must take account of historical forces. The past leaves a legacy. The Australian hegemony in Papua New Guinea has probably shaped deep-seated attitudes, social norms, roles and expectations, that render perceived similarity largely irrelevant as a determinant of social interaction between the indigenous students and the Australian expatriates—especially where the interaction occurs outside of the formal structure of the school. The Australian students, accustomed to the higher status conferred on them by the fact that their parents occupy or have occupied relatively high status positions within the social fabric, may have been freer to initiate social interaction with the indigenous group than vice-versa. Perceived similarity in values and in other characteristics may have been more relevant considerations for them in deciding who to interact with.

The fact that the predicted relationships were found for the Australian group when the instrumental values were involved but not for the terminal values may be due to differences between the two value sets in their behavioral visibility. One can speculate that the effects of instrumental values may be easier to observe at the behavioral level and that measures of perceived similarity involving the instrumental values may therefore be somewhat more reliable, especially when perceived value similarity involves comparisons across different cultures.

There are two final lessons that we can draw from this first study. One is that research in social psychology must go beyond the laboratory to the field situation. Research in the field provides vital information about the extent to which social psychological hypotheses based on laboratory investigations can be generalized, and often alerts one to new variables that need to be included in a more complete account of social behavior.

The second lesson is that prediction of overt behavior from measures concerned with person-environment fit (in this case similarity in value systems) is likely to be hazardous. There is a very long jump from "fit" to behavior and undoubtedly many other variables need to be considered when making predictions. I will speculate that "fit" measures are probably most successful in predicting to variables concerned with affect and satisfaction such as how happy one is with the school situation (Feather, 1972, 1975, 1979a) or how much one likes another person (Byrne, 1971). Going beyond affect to actual behavior introduces a whole new level of complexity, however, not allowed for in person-environment fit models.

It is to this higher level of complexity that I now want to turn by considering our most recent attempt to relate values and overt behavior. This approach involved the use of expectancy-value theory. Before describing the second study, however, I want to set it within its theoretical context, first by describing some of the attempts that have been made to conceptualize the relationship of behavior to attitudes and values and then by suggesting how values may be integrated into the expectancy-value framework so as to permit the prediction of action.

ATTITUDES, VALUES, AND BEHAVIOR

There has been considerable discussion in recent years about the conditions under which attitudes predict to behavior. Recent articles have summarized the relevant literature (e.g., Ajzen & Fishbein, 1977; Calder & Ross, 1973; Fishbein & Ajzen, 1975; Kelman, 1974; Rokeach, 1968, 1978–79, in press; Schuman & Johnson, 1976; Triandis, 1977; Wicker, 1969) and I will not attempt to review this literature again. Most of these discussions assume that a thorough conceptual analysis of the attitude-behavior relationship must take account of other variables in addition to attitudes. It is not so much a question of whether or not attitudes predict to behavior. Rather the questions are what other variables have to be included in the analysis and what form the extended relationship might take. I will illustrate these points by referring to two recent discussions, one by Fishbein and Ajzen (1975), the other by Rokeach (1968, 1978–79).

Fishbein and Ajzen (1975) relate overt behavior to the concept of behavioral intention that refers to "a person's subjective probability that he will perform some behavior [p. 288]. "Behavioral intentions are assumed to be a function of a weighted combination of two main variables: attitude toward performing the behavior and a subjective norm for that event.[2] Consistent with some other

---

[2]Fishbein and Ajzen (1975) note that their approach was influenced by Dulany's (1961, 1968) theory of propositional control.

related formulations (e.g., Carlson, 1956; Peak, 1955; Rosenberg, 1956; Vroom, 1964), *attitude toward behavior* is conceived as the sum of the beliefs or subjective probabilities that the behavior will lead to salient consequences multiplied by the evaluations of those consequences. Fishbein and Ajzen (1975) refer to this conceptualization of attitude as an "expectancy-value" model. The *subjective norm* aspect takes account of the influence of the social environment on behavior. The general subjective norm involves the person's perception about whether reference groups or individuals whose expectations are seen to be relevant in the situation would or would not perform the behavior in question, and it is assumed to be related to the person's expectations about these specific referent individuals or groups, and the motivation to comply with these expectations. In summary, therefore, the behavioral intention to perform a specific behavioral act under a particular set of circumstances is assumed to depend on a personal or "attitudinal" factor and a social or "normative" factor. These two components of the theory are assumed to combine additively in a weighted combination.

Algebraically the model can be expressed as follows:

$$B \sim BI = (A_B) \ w_1 + (SN) \ w_2$$
$$= \left[\ \sum_{i=1}^{n} B_i E_i \ \right] w_1 + \left[\ \sum_{i=1}^{m} NB_i MC_i \ \right] w_2$$

where B = the particular behavior; BI = the behavioral intention to perform the behavior B; A_B = the attitude toward performing behavior B; SN = the subjective norm; B_i = the belief (subjective probability) that performing the behavior will lead to consequence X_i; E_i = the evaluation of X_i; NB_i = the perceived expectation of Referent i; MC_i = the motivation to comply with Referent i; n = the number of salient consequences; m = the number of salient normative beliefs; and w_1 and w_2 are empirically derived regression weights.

There are a number of recent studies that have tested the Fishbein and Ajzen (1975) model and related alternatives (e.g., Bearden & Woodside, 1978; Bentler & Speckart, 1979; Davidson & Jaccard, 1979; Schlegel, Crawford, & Sanborn, 1977). These tests typically try to clarify the conditions under which the model can best be applied and include such variables as the degree to which a given behavior involves a sequence of prior events, the extent of volitional control over behavior, whether there are opportunities for attitudes to change before the behavior occurs, the time interval between the measurement of the behavioral intention and the behavior, and the degree to which there is correspondence between the attitudinal and behavioral variables in relation to specific aspects such as *action, target, context,* and *time.* Ajzen and Fishbein (1977), in a comprehensive review of the attitude-behavior literature, argue that this last requirement of measuring both attitude and behavior at a similar level of specificity is especially important if correlations between attitudes and behavior are to be enhanced, and the evidence supports this contention.[3]

Let me now briefly describe Rokeach's approach. In an important series of publications Rokeach (1968, 1973, 1979b, 1978-79, in press) develops the idea that a person's beliefs, attitudes, and values should be considered as a total system serving the function of maintaining and enhancing self-conceptions that are concerned with issues of competence and morality and that are derived in large part from societal demands. Rokeach develops the concepts of belief, attitude, and value in considerable detail and shows how they are ultimately in the service of the self. Beliefs are assumed to involve expectancies concerning existence, evaluation, prescription-proscription, or cause, whereas an attitude is defined as a relatively stable organization of beliefs around an object or situation that predisposes a person to respond preferentially to that object or situation. An attitude is also assumed to be associated with discriminatory responses to persons whose corresponding attitude is discrepant, and with differential responses to social controls or pressures that relate to expression of the attitude. Rokeach argues that in order to predict behavior from attitudes one needs to consider not only attitudes toward objects but also attitudes toward situations. Objects and situations are not conceived of in a specific sense but more in the nature of the conceptual categories that they evoke. A specific object or situation may involve many conceptual categories or attributes toward which a person holds attitudes. Behavior is assumed to be a function of all of these attitudes relating to objects and situations, weighted according to their relative importance. Among these attitudes would be those pertaining to social pressures and constraints.

It is clear, however, that Rokeach prefers to subsume the question of the attitude-behavior linkage under the broader question of the relationship between values, attitudes, and behavior. The preferential, discriminatory, and differential responses characteristic of an attitude are assumed to be instrumental to realizing societally-originating values and to be congruent with one another. Moreover, the total belief-attitude-value system is assumed to be hierarchically organized and to remain stable to the extent that self-conceptions about competence and morality can be maintained or enhanced. Within this system, therefore, a person's values occupy central positions. Rokeach agrees with Kluckhohn (1951) that individual values are socially shared conceptions of the desirable, and with Williams (1970, 1979) that they serve as standards or criteria. In particular, they are criteria, according to Rokeach (1979a):

---

[3]I do not find this conclusion surprising given the fact that one would expect increasing similarity or congruence between attitudinal and behavioral measures to be associated with higher correlations. But the specification of *action, target, context,* and *time* is a useful aid for classifying and comparing the range of attitude-behavior studies.

that we learn to employ transcendentally across objects and situations in various ways: to guide action; to guide us to the positions that we take on various social, ideological, political, and religious issues; to guide self-presentations . . . and impression management . . . ; to evaluate and judge ourselves and others by; to compare ourselves with others, not only with respect to competence . . . but also with respect to morality. We employ values as standards, moreover, to decide what is worth and not worth arguing about, worth and not worth persuading and influencing others to believe in and to do. And, finally, we employ values to guide processes of conscious and unconscious justification and rationalization of action, thought, and judgment. Thus, the ultimate function of human values is to provide us with a set of standards to guide us in all our efforts to satisfy our needs and at the same time maintain and, insofar as possible, enhance self-esteem, that is, to make it possible to regard ourselves and to be regarded by others as having satisfied socially and institutionally originating definitions of morality and competence [p. 48].

As noted previously, Rokeach distinguishes between values that concern end-states of existence (the terminal values) and values that concern modes of behavior (the instrumental values). He argues that the universe of values is relatively small when compared with the total number of beliefs and attitudes that a person holds. Moreover, according to Rokeach (1979a), the small set of values is assumed to be more or less universally present: "for there are just so many end-states of existence that people everywhere are capable of striving for, and just so many idealized modes of behavior that are instrumental for their realization [p. 49]." Rokeach asserts that these core values are capable of being ordered into hierarchies of importance or value systems and that a person's value systems reflect underlying needs as well as societal demands. Changes in basic values are assumed to have widespread effects upon thought and action, having important implications for attitudes and beliefs and for personal and social behavior.

An important part of Rokeach's research program has been concerned with investigating the relationship between values and attitudes and values and behavior (Rokeach, 1973, 1979b), and with tracing the effects on behavior of confronting a person with contradictions that involve the implications of a person's important values for cognitions about the self (Rokeach, 1973, 1979b, in press). Such contradictions can give rise to feelings of self-dissatisfaction, that the person attempts to eliminate or reduce by cognitive and behavioral change. Thus the total system of beliefs, attitudes, and values may be reorganised and overt behavior may be redirected in the interests of maintaining and enhancing a consistent sense of self-identity and self-esteem.

These two approaches to the question of the relationships between attitudes, values and behavior—the first from Fishbein and Ajzen (1975), the second from Rokeach (1973, 1979a)—obviously differ in many respects. They both reveal a concern, however, with a basic psychological question and they advance solutions that have stimulated useful research. The Rokeach analysis, in particular, provides a context for introducing my own approach that is developed within the general framework of expectancy-value theory.

VALUES AND MOTIVES

I want to argue that values may be conceptualized as a particular class of motives. Like Rokeach, I conceive of values as relatively stable and general beliefs about what is and what is not desirable. They transcend situations and function as standards or criteria to guide thought and action. Our attitudes, evaluations, judgments, justifications, decisions, commitments, and so on, are influenced by the value systems that we hold. Value systems emerge in the course of development and they undergo some rearrangement throughout life as we take on new roles and responsibilities and react to social change and historical events (Feather, 1975, 1979d). Values reflect both the impact of social institutions and the influence of underlying psychological needs, and they are regarded as basic to our sense of self.

As I have noted before (Feather, 1975, pp. 297–300) there are both conceptual and empirical grounds for assuming that values and motives may be related. On the conceptual side, sometimes the general concept of motive is defined in such a way that it is hard to distinguish it from the concept of value. There are some similarities, for example, between Rokeach's treatment of value and McClelland's analysis of motive. McClelland (1965) argues that:

> . . . all motives are learned. . . . Clusters of expectancies or associations grow up around affective experiences, not all of which are connected by any means with biological needs . . . Motives are ''affectively toned associative networks'' arranged in a hierarchy of strength or importance within a given individual [p. 322].

Values for Rokeach are also assumed to be arranged in hierarchies within individuals and to have affective consequences—for example, when they are challenged. My own concept of value structure (Feather, 1975, pp. 15–16, 1980b) treats value as a relatively stable network of associations linked to affect—the network being describable in various ways—for example, in regard to its degree of differentiation, integration, isolation, centrality, and so on. Values and value systems are therefore particular examples of what I have called abstract structures or schemata—organised summaries of experience that capture the focal, abstracted qualities of past encounters, that have a normative or oughtness quality about them, and that function as criteria or frameworks against which present experience can be tested (Feather, 1971, 1975). But they are not affectively neutral abstract structures. They are tied to our feelings and can function as general motives.

French and Kahn (1962) also treat values (together with needs) as motives. They describe both needs and values as having:

> ... the basic conceptual property of the ability to motivate goal directed behavior in the person by inducing valences (or incentive values) on certain environmental objects, behaviors, or states of affairs [pp. 11–12].

Sometimes values may function to control need-induced behavior. But in other cases a motivational system may have both need and value properties in that what a person *wants* to do corresponds to what the person thinks *ought* to be done. French and Kahn believe that values have the ability to induce evaluations of good and bad and that need does not have this conceptual property. But both values and needs function as motives in their ability to induce valences, and these valences may be positive or negative, corresponding to attractive or repulsive regions of the psychological environment.

Finally, Rokeach (1973) views values as involving the cognitive representation and transformation of needs and argues that the transformation takes account of societal and institutional demands. As we have seen, he believes that ultimately values are in the service of the self and that they are employed to maintain and enhance self-esteem, a superordinate function that encompasses other functions such as ego-defense, adjustment, and understanding reality.

There is an obvious need for further conceptual analysis of the motive and value concepts and for relevant empirical studies. To what extent are motives and values functionally distinguishable in their effects? Is there a basic similarity in the antecedent conditions underlying their development? Or are there some distinctive differences, despite overlap between them in their antecedents and consequents, that justifies continuing to differentiate between motives and values. For example, as I have pointed out before (Feather, 1975), values:

> are commonly held to be normative, to involve conceptions of what is desirable and undesirable. As such they serve as standards that are employed in many contexts where evaluation is a consideration.... No necessary connection seems to exist, however, between motives and normative evaluations of goodness and badness. The desired is not always the desirable; goodness and badness are not identical to pleasure and pain; sometimes "want" and "ought" coincide, but by no means always; and action often takes place in the absence of conscious evaluation.
>
> Perhaps motive should be regarded as the more general concept to be used as one important variable in theoretical accounts of the determinants of the direction, persistence, and amplitude (or vigor) of sequences of purposive behavior—sequences that can be abstracted from the ongoing stream of activity. Values may then be seen as a particular class of motives: those tied to a normative base relating to an evaluative dimension of goodness-badness. Thus, motive would be the more inclusive concept and value would be a member of this general class. There may, therefore, be some motives that are not values but no values that are not motives.

Clearly, we need further conceptual and empirical inquiry to resolve some of these issues. In the meantime, however, there is no reason why values should not be treated as basic personality characteristics similar and perhaps identical to motives, and integrated into expectancy-value models in the same way that motives have been included in the past [p. 300].

I continue to hold this view that values can be treated as general motives in terms of which people differ and which affect the major defining characteristics of purposive behavior. But how can the concept be integrated into an expectancy-value approach?

VALUES, VALENCE, AND EXPECTANCY

It can be assumed that, as motives, values will induce valences (positive or negative) on certain environmental objects, behaviors, and states of affairs (Feather, 1975, pp. 297-300; French & Kahn, 1962). To continue with the Lewinian terminology, certain regions of the psychological environment may be assumed to become attractive or repulsive—that is, they are viewed or evaluated positively or negatively, and the direction that behavior takes is influenced by these positive and negative regions. The theoretical basis for the linkage between general values and the valence of specific objects, events, and activities within a means-end structure is an issue that I do not want to take up at this time. It is sufficient to say that I conceive of a value as an associative structure involving affect, and that aspects of a present situation may be tested against this structure, the general value "informing" the individual about what is good and bad, what is worth approaching and what should be avoided (see Feather, 1975, pp. 13–17).

There is plenty of support from cognitive and motivational theory to support the assumption that motives may selectively sensitize the individual to certain objects and activities within an existing situation. A hungry man, for example, is sensitized to food and ways of getting food. A whole class of objects and activities relating to food and to getting food become salient, command attention, acquire demand characteristics, or are seen as having positive or negative valence—to sample from some of the concepts that have been used by different theorists. I am suggesting that values as motives have this function also, sensitizing the person to perceive some potential events and activities as desirable and worth approaching or continuing with, and other aspects as undesirable, to be avoided or terminated. These statements are not tautologies. They underline the fact that general values influence our definition of particular situations, and in this way have implications for action.

Note that I am not saying that motives and values are the only influences on valences. Obviously, valences will depend also on other factors, such as the qualitative and quantitative aspects of events and activities. Some foods, for example, may be more attractive to a hungry person than others, depending upon their amount and quality. The precise relationship between valences and their determining factors may turn out to be quite complex. Indeed, one of the important future tasks of motivational psychology is to give more theoretical and empirical consideration to the various factors that influence valences.

Are these distinct roles for terminal and instrumental values as sources of valence? I have previously argued (Feather, 1975) that:

> terminal values may influence the valence of specific outcomes or "end-states"—
> some outcomes being seen as more attractive (or repulsive) than others, whereas
> instrumental values may influence the valence of specific instrumental behaviors or
> means to ends—some courses of action being seen as more attractive (or repulsive)
> than others. In a specific situation, therefore, different means to the same end may
> vary in their valence, contingent in part upon a person's dominant instrumental
> values, and different ends or goals that might be pursued may differ in their
> valence, contingent in part upon a person's dominant terminal values. The behavior
> that emerges in any given situation, then, depends not only upon the relative
> valence of different possible outcomes, but also upon the valence of alternative
> courses of action relating to the same possible outcome. And, in each case relevant
> values may be assumed to be important sources of these valences [p. 302].

But overt action may be related on the theoretical level, not only to valences but to other variables as well, of which an important class are the expectancies that the individual holds about whether specific actions will lead to positively valent, desired or desirable outcomes, or away from negatively valent outcomes that are threatening or undesirable. As noted previously (Feather, 1975), the concept of expectancy:

> . . . is especially important in capturing the idea that actions have different implica-
> tions, each of which is associated with some *perceived likelihood* of occurrence.
> The concept is particularly congenial to theorists who conceive of behavior in
> means-end terms where actions are seen as embedded in a structured network of
> possible outcomes—some of which are sequentially linked to others, depending
> upon the nature of the actions [p. 300].

Achievement behavior, for example, may be related not only to the valences of success and failure induced by general motives but also to the expectations of success and failure that a person holds. Expectancies are influenced not only by situational characteristics such as task difficulty, the nature of response-outcome contingencies, and information about the performance of others. They are also affected by a person's perception of self-efficacy in relation to the required response—whether the person sees himself or herself as able to perform the response (Bandura, 1977; Feather, 1975, p. 301; Heider, 1958; Weiner,

1972)—and by the person's past record of response outcomes in the same or similar situations.

Expectations in combination with valences may be assumed to determine the strength of tendencies to perform particular responses that might be expected to lead to positive incentives and the strength of tendencies not to perform particular responses that might be expected to lead to negative incentives—or, to use the terminology introduced by Atkinson and Birch (1970, 1978), the strength of *instigating* and *inhibitory forces*. Knowing the set of forces and the residual, persisting tendencies that carry over from the past allows one to go a fair part of the way toward predicting which course of action will be selected by the individual, assuming that behavior will reflect some resultant of all of the competing tendencies that are present in any given situation.

A concrete example may help to illustrate some of the main features of this type of analysis. When freedom of action is blocked or threatened, the terminal value *freedom* may become especially salient, and certain possible outcomes that relate to the restoration of freedom may become more or less valent, depending in part on the relative importance of *freedom* within each person's terminal value system and also on other factors such as the amount and quality of the outcome[4] How the person copes with the loss of freedom would be related in part to the valence of these possible outcomes relative to other alternatives. But the ensuing behavior would depend not only upon these valences but also on the strength of the expectations associated with those available courses of action that are seen as relevant to the desired consequences. Some alternative courses of action may be viewed as more likely to lead to the restoration of freedom than others, depending in part upon present situational constraints and also on the past experience of the person. And some of these alternative instrumental actions may be more positively valent than others, depending on the relative importance of particular instrumental values. For example, individuals who assigned being *imaginative* a high position within their instrumental value systems may see novel and creative behaviors as especially attractive solutions to the problem of restoring freedom; courses of action that involve standing up for one's beliefs may have stronger positive valence for those individuals who assigned being *courageous* a key place, and so on.

Note, however, that the example is an over simplification because it has focused on single values only. Typically, behavior is overdetermined, in the sense that many motives or values may be involved and the final action will therefore depend upon complex sets of instigating and inhibitory forces whose rules of combination have to be specified. Moreover, other influences such as whether the necessary actions are available within the response repertoires of

---

[4]Consider, for example, a prisoner in a jail, or a person whose freedoms are obstructed by an oppressive political regime, or, at a less extreme level, a subject involved in an experimental study of psychological reactance (Brehm, 1966).

individuals, whether present actions can be related to future goals, and whether there are unresolved tendencies carrying over from past situations also have to be considered in any complete analysis. Note also that the example focuses on factors that would affect instigating forces to action. It should be clear that there may also be inhibitory forces and constraints of various kinds that block action within situations. In the present case, for example, some courses of action that could possibly restore freedom may also be seen to have high costs to the individual in the form of punishments and sanctions. These actions would, therefore, be resisted to some degree. The example does, however, underline the point that one should be able to consider the relationship of values to action within the context of expectancy-value theory, taking account of the valences of means and ends weighted by the individual's expectations about the likely consequences of the alternative behaviors that are available.

With this brief sketch of the theoretical context let us now describe the second study relevant to the question of how values relate to overt action.

VALUES AND SOCIAL MOVEMENTS

This study, designed and conducted with the collaboration of Dr. James Newton, involved the use of a specially constructed questionnaire that sought information about how many hours and in what specific ways respondents would be prepared to assist two hypothetical social movements, one of which was called *The Movement to Promote Community Standards* and the other *The Campaign to Safeguard Individual Rights*. The respondents, who were first year psychology students at Flinders University in 1978, were given a detailed description of the nature and aims of each organization as expressed in a fictional pamphlet from each organization. These descriptions were presented in counterbalanced order across all respondents. The descriptions provided contrasting value bases for the two organizations. For example, the description for the "Campaign" emphasized such concerns as "freedom to choose one's way of life," "equal opportunity to receive the benefits of society," "open-minded thought," "a peaceful world," and "harmony with one's environment," whereas the description for the "Movement" emphasized such concerns as "decency and responsible citizenship," "legitimate authority," "high standards of morality," "family life," and "hard work." The choice of the value base for each organization was not adventitious but drew on our own social experience and on the results of previous studies in the Flinders programme concerned with the value systems of student activists (Ellerman & Feather, 1976) and the value correlates of conservatism (Feather, 1979b).

After reading each description respondents answered a number of items designed to obtain information about their attitude toward the views of the organization, the ways in which they would be prepared to support the organization (assuming they had 10 hours of free time each week), how many of these 10 hours they would be prepared to contribute to the organization, how helpful they thought their efforts would be as a contribution to the organization's success (assuming they supported the organization and could devote all of their 10 hours to it), how likely they thought it was that the organization could make the public aware of its concerns, and how likely they thought it was that the organization could get the legislation it favors passed in the majority of Australian states. The questionnaire involved other items as well, and included the Wilson and Patterson Conservatism Scale (Wilson, 1973; Wilson & Patterson, 1968). Respondents had answered the Rokeach Value Survey (Rokeach, 1973) before they completed the questionnaire, under conditions designed to minimize situational demand characteristics (the two questionnaires were administered independently by different experimenters and were supposedly part of different investigations).

I will report some of the results that relate to willingness to support *The Movement to Promote Community Standards* in order to illustrate the application of the expectancy-value approach that I have just described. The corresponding results for the other organization (the Campaign) were also compatible with this approach.

Let us consider the operationalization of the valence variable first. We assumed that the valences (positive and negative) attached to components of the description of the Movement would be induced by the values that each person holds. Aspects of the description supporting "hard work and investment", "respect for legitimate authority", and "decent standards of morality", for example, would have positive valences for respondents who ranked such values as *ambitious, obedient,* and *salvation* high on their list of value priorities. Other aspects of the description denigrating "progressive intellectuals" and referring to a "misguided obsession with civil liberties", for example, would be negatively valent for respondents who ranked such values as *freedom* and being *intellectual* and *independent* high in their list of value priorities.

The actual pattern of valences elicited for each individual by the descriptions of organizations was not measured directly. Instead it was assumed that people were able to integrate the positive and negative valences that applied to aspects of the descriptions and that this cognitive integration would be reflected in their overall attitudes toward the organizations referred to in the descriptions. Thus each respondent's attitude toward the Movement can be viewed as a resultant or cognitive summation of all of the valences (positive and negative) attached to components of the description of the Movement. For any one person these valences relating to the goals and other features of the Movement were assumed to be combined into a resultant. The attitude measure was assumed to reflect the end product of this cognitive integration—a measure of *integrated* valences, further removed from the actual pattern of valences. Table 9.3 shows the terminal and instrumental values that were significantly related to the attitude measure concerned with the Movement ("To what extent do you personally agree or

TABLE 9.3
Product–Moment Correlations (Simple *rs*) between Attitude toward
Movement and Value Importance for Each Terminal and Instrumental
Value

Terminal Value	Agreement with Movement	Instrumental Value	Agreement with Movement
A comfortable life	.142	Ambitious	.189*
An exciting life	.007	Broadminded	−.346***
A sense of accomplishment	−.064	Capable	−.059
A world at peace	−.016	Cheerful	.100
A world of beauty	−.167*	Clean	.094
Equality	−.184*	Courageous	−.036
Family security	.143*	Forgiving	.175*
Freedom	−.150*	Helpful	−.089
Happiness	.103	Honest	−.024
Inner harmony	−.002	Imaginative	−.341***
Mature love	−.301***	Independent	−.177*
National security	.022	Intellectual	−.233**
Pleasure	−.104	Logical	−.080
Salvation	.393***	Loving	.025
Self-respect	−.134	Obedient	.348***
Social recognition	.137	Polite	.254**
True friendship	−.000	Responsible	.085
Wisdom	−.053	Self-controlled	.251**

Note. $N = 134$. As in previous studies, the measure of value importance was in terms of *z* scores obtained by transforming the rank orders for each set of 18 values, using the normal curve distribution (Feather, 1975, pp. 23–24).

　*$p < .05$ (one-tailed)
　**$p < .01$ (one-tailed)
　***$p < .001$ (one-tailed)

disagree with the views expressed in the pamphlet published by this organization?'')—and therefore, by assumption, to the pattern of valences. These values were those that we had expected to be related to the attitude measure. They overlap with those that emerged in my previous research into the value correlates of conservatism (Feather, 1979b). Indeed, there was a statistically significant positive correlation between attitude toward the Movement (scored in the positive direction) and scores on the Conservatism Scale ($r = .659$, $df = 132$, $p < .001$).

Finally, it was assumed that expectancy of success would be reflected in respondents' estimates of how helpful they thought their own personal efforts would be as a contribution to the organization's success, assuming they supported the goals of the Movement and could devote 10 hours of free time each

TABLE 9.4
Simple Correlations (*r*s), Multiple Correlations (*R*s), and
Proportion of Variance Explained (r^2 and R^2) from Regression
Analyses Predicting Action Measures from
Attitude, and Expectancy

| | Action Measures | | | | | | | |
| | Number of Volunteer Actions for Movement | | | | Number of Volunteer Hours for Movement | | | |
	r	r^2	R	R^2	r	r^2	R	R^2
Agreement with movement	.616	.380			.495	.245		
Expectancy	.341	.116			.309	.095		
Agreement × Expectancy	.673	.452			.579	.335		
Agreement + Expectancy			.672	.451			.554	.307

Note. *N*s ranged from 127 to 134 due to missing data. All correlations are highly significant ($p < .001$). Expectancy and Agreement with Movement were not significantly correlated ($r = .123$). The increment in the proportion of variance explained by the combination of Agreement and Expectancy over the variance explained by either Agreement or Expectancy taken singly was statistically significant beyond the .01 level in all cases.

week towards supporting it. Higher estimates about the efficacy of one's actions should reflect higher expectations that the person can assist the organization to achieve its goals.

Table 9.4 shows the relationship between two measures of behavioral support for the Movement, and attitude toward the Movement and expectancy considered a single variables. Table 9.4 also shows the effects of combining attitude with expectancy, both multiplicatively and additively, when predicting to each of the two dependent variables. The behavioral measures involved a count of the number of alternatives each respondent checked in an item listing various ways of supporting the Movement (e.g., signing a petition, telephoning people, handing out pamphlets, and so on) given 10 hours of free time each week, and how many of these available 10 hours they would be prepared to devote to the Movement.

Table 9.4 shows that the combination of attitude and expectancy provided a better prediction to each of the behavioral variables than either attitude or expectancy considered alone. This enhanced prediction occurred for both multiplicative and additive combinations of attitude and expectancy.[5] These results are consistent with an expectancy-value analysis and confirm our view that this

---

[5]The results from the multiplicative combination of attitude and expectancy are most relevant to the expectancy-value (valence) analysis given the fact that these models usually assume a multiplicative combination of expectancies and valences. Note, however, that the additive combination predicted to the action measures just as well.

theoretical approach may turn out to be very useful in the analysis of the conditions under which values relate to overt action.

These results have encouraged us to continue with this line of research Our most recent study has attempted to move away from hypothetical situations to a situation in which the decision to support an organization occurs under conditions of greater reality and commitment, and it has used a wider range of attitude and expectancy measures.[6]

SOME ISSUES

It should be clear that the expectancy-value approach does take us further than an analysis based only on a principle of person-environment fit. It views the individual as continually active, confronted by alternative goals and possibilities of action, and influenced both by unresolved tendencies carried over from the past and by motivational forces that relate to the present situation. This model is one that explicitly allows for the interaction of variables that concern both person and situation and, in this sense, is continuous with Lewin's (1935) programmatic equation, $B = f(P,E)$—Behavior is a function of an interdependent set of influences involving both the person and the psychological environment. Recent proponents of interactionism in psychology sometimes forget that the interactionist approach is not a new discovery but has a long history in psychology.

Are there any caveats? I will briefly consider two issues that are provocative and likely to be productive of a lot more research in the future. In the first place, it might be argued that the expectancy-value approach is too normative in its emphasis, that it ignores widespread defects and errors that are known to occur in information-processing, and that it is overly concerned with "cold" cognitive appraisal rather than with the "hot" cognition that occurs under stress or high emotional involvement. This would be a misreading of the expectancy-value approach, at least as it has been used in the analysis of basic questions from the psychology of motivation (Atkinson & Birch, 1978; Atkinson & Feather, 1966; Atkinson & Raynor, 1974; Feather, 1961, 1967, 1975). Defective information-processing and biases that may have a motivational or some other basis are certainly not excluded from consideration. The variables in the model are cognitive in nature and they may be in error at any given time when tested against

---

[6]This recent study (Newton, Feather, & Mann, 1980) has also provided support for the expectancy-valence analysis. In a situation involving heightened commitment, under conditions where the organization would be seen as actual rather than as hypothetical, prediction to willingness to assist the organization (called *The Campaign to Safeguard Individual Rights*) was enhanced when both attitude and expectancy measures were involved in the regression equation rather than either measure alone. This finding replicates the earlier results where the *Campaign* was presented as a hypothetical rather than as an actual organization.

objective reality. The model accepts the subjective reality as important for understanding a person's behavior—however defective that subjective reality might be—and it recognizes that motivational and emotional states can distort and, in extreme cases, disrupt the thought process, so that behavior may appear to be irrational. Moreover, the model is not normative in the sense that it prescribes how decisions *ought* to be made and pays little attention to how they *are* made. On the contrary, the model has been applied to behavior as it occurs, and often in situations of relatively high personal involvement (for example, achievement behavior, information-seeking behavior, and in the present context, values and action).

A second issue relates to how much thought or cognition precedes action. A lot of behavior seems to occur without conscious awareness. Whole sequences of organized action run off without much conscious thought about the details of the performance—as when a professional golfer plays a difficult stroke, a concert violinist performs a complicated cadenza, or a highly experienced motorist drives his car to work. Here also we find an issue that has a long history, especially among those theorists who have been concerned with the organization of skilled behavior and with the computer simulation of cognitive processes (e.g., Posner & Shulman, in press; Simon, 1979). Social psychologists have also noted the problem in recent discussions about cognition and behavior and the extent to which apparently thoughtful action is "mindless" (for example, Langer, 1978; Nisbett & Wilson, 1977; Weiner, 1980, pp. 296–303).

The point is well taken but can be handled in the expectancy-value approach by allowing for a progressive refinement and integration of expectancies with experience so that they become simplified and organized at higher levels, enabling a relatively automatic programming of response sequences without much intervening thought at all. Such behavior reminds us of William James' (1890) powerful metaphor—"the fly-wheel of habit". Thought would enter in at the earlier stages of learning when expectancies are being developed, and in the course of integration and refinement as higher order expectancies come to capture the implication structure of events across space and time. Thought would also enter in when expectancies are disconfirmed, that is where outcomes are unexpected and discrepant experience sets a problem to be solved (e.g., Miller, Galanter, & Pribram, 1960). Where expectancies are grounded in considerable experience, however, and where they continue to be confirmed by events and outcomes, one should find a relatively automatic sequencing of response without much consideration of the fine details.

Even under conditions where there is little thought about the precise mechanics of response, however, thoughts about the goal structure and the general planning of action in relation to this goal structure will almost certainly occur. And where the stream of behavior is punctuated by choice points and decisions or blocked by obstacles, one would also expect to find evidence of increasing cognitive activity.

It should be clear, therefore, that one can develop ideas within an expectancy-value framework about those conditions under which action is accompanied by thought and those in which action involves a minimum of conscious effort. Parenthetically, it is interesting to note that Lewin (1936) did not identify the life-space as consisting only of conscious determinants, even though he did insist on representing reality in terms of the individual's own perspective. The point is an obvious one to any clinical psychologist but it is only recently that social psychologists in the cognitive mold have come to recognize that a lot of behavior proceeds automatically and involves processes that are not consciously experienced. Although a person may be able to attribute reasons for the behavior retrospectively, these reasons may not have been present in consciousness at the time of action. They may be partial fictions—personal constructions that are informative but not necessarily accurate representations of reality. This whole area provides some fascinating opportunities for future research.

CONCLUDING REMARKS

Let me now conclude. I have described two studies concerned with the relationship between values and action, the first involving the principle of person-environment fit and the second developed in terms of an expectancy-value or, more accurately, an expectancy-valence framework. I have indicated that my preference is for the latter form of conceptualization. I have tried to put these ideas into historical perspective and to specify some issues that require further analysis and research. It should be obvious that the general question of the relationship between cognitive variables and behavior is a central one that confronts all of us who are involved in cognitive approaches to social psychology and motivation.

ACKNOWLEDGMENT

This chapter is an extension of my Presidential address delivered at the opening meeting of the fourteenth annual conference of the Australian Psychological Society on August 26, 1979 at the University of Tasmania. The chapter corresponds to this address in all details except for some additions. The address was published in the *Australian Psychologist,* (Feather, 1979c, *14*, pp. 243–260). This material is reprinted by courtesy of the Australian Psychological Society.

REFERENCES

Ajzen, I., & Fishbein, M. Attitude–behavior relations: A theoretical analysis and review of empirical research. *Psychological Bulletin,* 1977, 84, 888–918.
Atkinson, J. W., & Birch, D. *The dynamics of action.* New York: Wiley, 1970.

Atkinson, J. W., & Birch, D. *An introduction to motivation.* New York: D. Van Nostrand, 1978.

Atkinson, J. W., & Feather, N. T. (Eds.). *A theory of achievement motivation.* New York: Wiley, 1966.

Atkinson, J. W., & Raynor, J. O. (Eds.). *Motivation and achievement.* Washington: Winston, 1974.

Bandura, A. Self-efficacy: Toward a unifying theory of behavioral change. *Psychological Review,* 1977, *84,* 191–215.

Bearden, W., & Woodside, A. Situational and extended attitude models as predictors of marijuana intentions and reported behavior. *Journal of Social Psychology,* 1978, *106,* 57–67.

Bentler, P. M., & Speckart, G. Models of attitude–behavior relations. *Psychological Review,* 1979, *86,* 452–464.

Berry, J. W. On cross-cultural comparability. *International Journal of Psychology,* 1969, *4,* 119–128.

Brehm, J. W. *A theory of psychological reactance.* New York: Academic Press, 1966.

Brewer, M. B., & Campbell, D. T. *Ethnocentrism and intergroup attitudes: East African evidence.* New York: Wiley (Halsted Press), 1976.

Brunswik, E. Organismic achievement and environmental probability. *Psychological Review,* 1943, *50,* 255–272.

Byrne, D. *The attraction paradigm.* New York: Academic Press, 1971.

Calder, B. J., & Ross, M. *Attitudes and behavior.* Morristown, N.J.: General Learning Press, 1973.

Carlson, E. R. Attitude change through modification of attitude structure. *Journal of Abnormal and Social Psychology,* 1956, *52,* 256–261.

Cartwright, D. Theory and practice. *Journal of Social Issues,* 1978, *34,* 168–180.

Cole, M., & Scribner, S. *Culture and thought.* New York: Wiley, 1974.

Davidson, A. R., & Jaccard, J. J. Variables that moderate the attitude–behavior relation: Results of a longitudinal survey. *Journal of Personality and Social Psychology,* 1979, *37,* 1364–1376.

Dulany, D. E. Hypotheses and habits in verbal "operant conditioning." *Journal of Abnormal and Social Psychology,* 1961, *63,* 251–263.

Dulany, D. E. Awareness, rules, and propositional control: A confrontation with S–R behavior theory. In D. Horton & T. Dixon (Eds.), *Verbal behavior and S–R behavior theory.* Englewood Cliffs, N.J.: Prentice-Hall, 1968.

Ellerman, D. A., & Feather, N. T. The values of Australian student activists. *Australian Journal of Education,* 1976, *20,* 260–277.

Feather, N. T. Subjective probability and decision under uncertainty. *Psychological Review,* 1959, *66,* 150–164.

Feather, N. T. The relationship of persistence at a task to expectation of success and achievement related motives. *Journal of Abnormal and Social Psychology,* 1961, *63,* 552–561.

Feather, N. T. An expectancy-value model of information-seeking behavior. *Psychological Review,* 1967, *74,* 342–360.

Feather, N. T. Organization and discrepancy in cognitive structures. *Psychological Review,* 1971, *78,* 355–379.

Feather, N. T. Value similarity and school adjustment. *Australian Journal of Psychology,* 1972, *24,* 193–208.

Feather, N. T. *Values in education and society.* New York: Free Press, 1975.

Feather, N. T. Human values and the work situation: Two studies. *Australian Psychologist,* 1979, *14,* 131–141. (a)

Feather, N. T. Value correlates of conservatism. *Journal of Personality and Social Psychology,* 1979, *37,* 1617–1630. (b)

Feather, N. T. Values, expectancy, and action. *Australian Psychologist,* 1979, *14,* 243–260. (c)

Feather, N. T. Values in adolescence. In J. Adelson (Ed.), *Handbook of adolescent psychology.* New York: Wiley, 1979. (d)

Feather, N. T. Similarity of value systems within the same nation: Evidence from Australia and Papua New Guinea. *Australian Journal of Psychology*, 1980, *32*, 17–30. (a)

Feather, N. T. The study of values. *Journal of Asian-Pacific and World Perspectives*, 1980, *3*, 3–13. (b)

Feather, N. T. Value systems and social interaction: A field study in a newly independent nation. *Journal of Applied Social Psychology*, 1980, *10*, 1–19. (c)

Fishbein, M., & Ajzen, I. *Belief, attitude, intention, and behavior: An introduction to theory and research*. Reading, Mass.: Addison-Wesley, 1975.

French, J. R. P. Jr., & Kahn, R. L. A programmatic approach to studying the industrial environment and mental health. *Journal of Social Issues*, 1962, *18*, 1–47.

Guthrie, E. R. *The psychology of learning*. New York: Harper, 1935.

Hartshorne, H., & May, M. A. *Studies in the nature of character* (3 vols.). New York: Macmillan, 1930.

Heider, F. *The psychology of interpersonal relations*. New York: Wiley, 1958.

James, W. *The principles of psychology*. New York: Holt, 1890.

Kelman, H. Attitudes are alive and well and gainfully employed in the sphere of action. *American Psychologist*, 1974, *29*, 310–324.

Kluckhohn, C. Values and value-orientations in the theory of action. In T. Parsons & E. A. Shils (Eds.), *Toward a general theory of action*. Cambridge, Mass.: Harvard University Press, 1951.

Langer, E. Rethinking the role of thought in social interaction. In J. H. Harvey, W. Ickes, & R. F. Kidd (Eds.), *New directions in attribution research* (Vol. 2). Hillsdale, N.J.: Lawrence Erlbaum Associates, 1978.

Lewin, K. *A dynamic theory of personality*. New York: McGraw-Hill, 1935.

Lewin, K. *Principles of topological psychology*. New York: McGraw-Hill, 1936.

Lewin, K. *Field theory in social science*. New York: Harper, 1951.

Lewin, K. Dembo, T., Festinger, L., & Sears, P. S. Level of aspiration. In J. McV. Hunt (Ed.), *Personality and the behavior disorders* (Vol. 1). New York: Ronald, 1944.

McClelland, D. C. Toward a theory of motive acquisition. *American Psychologist*, 1965, *20*, 321–333.

Miller, G. A., Galanter, E., & Pribram, K. H. *Plans and the structure of behavior*. New York: Holt, 1960.

Newcomb, T. M. *The acquaintance process*. New York: Holt, Rinehart & Winston, 1961.

Newton, J. W., Feather, N. T., & Mann, J. W. Predicting action from values, attitudes, and expectancies. Paper presented at Annual Convention of The American Psychological Association, Montreal, 1980.

Nisbett, R. E., & Wilson, T. D. Telling more than we can know: Verbal reports on mental processes. *Psychological Review*, 1977, *84*, 231–259.

Peak, H. Attitude and motivation. In M. R. Jones (Ed.), *Nebraska Symposium on Motivation*. Lincoln: University of Nebraska Press, 1955.

Posner, M. E., & Shulman, G. L. Cognitive science. In E. Hearst (Ed.), *The first century of experimental psychology*. Hillsdale, N.J.: Lawrence Erlbaum Associates, in press.

Rokeach, M. *Beliefs, attitudes, and values: A theory of organization and change*. San Francisco: Jossey-Bass, 1968.

Rokeach, M. *The nature of human values*. New York: Free Press, 1973.

Rokeach, M. From individual to institutional values: With special reference to the values of science. In M. Rokeach (Ed.), *Understanding human values: Individual and societal*. New York: Free Press, 1979. (a)

Rokeach, M. (Ed.). *Understanding human values: Individual and societal*. New York: Free Press, 1979. (b)

Rokeach, M. Some unresolved issues in theories of beliefs, attitudes and values. To be published in the proceedings of the 1978–79 *Nebraska Symposium on Motivation*.

Rokeach, M. Value theory and communication research: Review and commentary. To be published in D. Nimmo (Ed.), *Communication Yearbook III*, Transaction Books.

Rosenberg, M. Cognitive structure and attitudinal affect. *Journal of Abnormal and Social Psychology*, 1956, *53*, 367–372.

Schlegel, R. P., Crawford, C. A., & Sanborn, M. Correspondence and mediational properties of the Fishbein model: An application to adolescent alchohol use. *Journal of Experimental Social Psychology*, 1977, *13*, 421–430.

Schuman, H., & Johnson, M. P. Attitudes and behavior. *Annual Review of Sociology*, 1976, *2*, 161–207.

Secord, P. F., & Backman, C. W. *Social Psychology* (2nd ed.). New York: McGraw-Hill, 1974.

Simon, H. A. Information processing models of cognition. *Annual Review of Psychology*, 1979, *30*, 311–396.

Tolman, E. C. Principles of performance. *Psychological Review*, 1955, *62*, 315–326.

Triandis, H. C. *Interpersonal behavior*. Monterey, Calif.: Brooks/Cole, 1977.

Vroom, V. H. *Work and motivation*. New York: Wiley, 1964.

Weiner, B. Theories of motivation: *From mechanism to cognition*. Chicago: Markham, 1972.

Weiner, B. *Human motivation*. New York: Holt, Rinehart, & Winston, 1980.

Wicker, A. W. Attitudes vs. actions: The relationship of verbal and overt behavioral responses to attitude objects. *Journal of Social Issues*, 1969, *25*, 41–78.

Williams, R. M. Jr. *American society: A sociological interpretation* (3rd ed.). New York: Knopf, 1970.

Williams, R. M. Jr. Change and stability in values and value systems: A sociological perspective. In M. Rokeach (Ed.), *Understanding human values: Individual and societal*. New York: Free Press, 1979.

Wilson, G. D. (Ed.). *The psychology of conservatism*. New York: Academic Press, 1973.

Wilson, G. D., & Patterson, J. R. A new measure of conservatism. *British Journal of Social and Clinical Psychology*, 1968, *7*, 264–269.

VI The Context of Organizational Psychology

10 Expectancy-Value Models in Organizational Psychology

Terence R. Mitchell

Expectancy theory's first major appearance in the organizational psychology literature was presented in 1964 in Vic Vroom's book, *Work and Motivation* (Vroom, 1964). Building on some earlier work by Georgopoulous, Mahoney and Jones (1957), Vroom described expectancy type models for the prediction of occupational choice, effort on the job, and job satisfaction. These writings have had a substantial impact on the field of organizational psychology and expectancy theory remains as one of the two or three most heavily researched theories of motivation.

Lots of work has been done since 1964 and numerous reviews of this research are available (Mitchell & Biglan, 1971; Heneman & Schwab, 1972; House & Wahba, 1972; Lawler, 1973; Mitchell, 1974; Wahba & House, 1974; Connolly, 1976; Schwab, Olian-Gottlieb & Heneman, 1979; Mitchell, 1979). Perhaps the most comprehensive review was one I wrote in 1974, which discussed the development of the theory, reviewed the results of over 50 published studies, and described a number of methodological and theoretical issues that were in need of resolution. Therefore, in this chapter I would like to use a format that first briefly summarizes the topic as of that 1974 paper and then discusses what has been accomplished since that time. Using this procedure, the theoretical, empirical, and methodological issues that have been resolved and unresolved will be highlighted. Finally, there is a section on a number of new topics that were unanticipated in the 1974 paper and that are currently important. An overall assessment concludes the chapter.

THEORETICAL DEVELOPMENT

Expectancy theory in the organizational area is similar in its underlying idea to the other theories described in this book. Lawler (1973) has stated it as follows: "The strength of a tendency to act in a certain way depends on the strength of an expectancy that the act will be followed by a given consequence (or outcome) and on the value or attractiveness of that consequence (or outcome) to the actor [p. 45]." Essentially, it is predicted that people choose behaviors that they think will result in the highest payoff for them.

Vroom's (1964) work presented two models, the first for the prediction of the valences of outcomes, and the second for the prediction of force toward behavior. An outcome is anything an individual might want to attain. The valence of an outcome for a person is defined conceptually as the strength of his positive or negative affective orientation toward it. Similar to Lewin's use of the term, valence refers to the anticipated satisfaction associated with an outcome, and is distinguished from the value of the outcome—the actual satisfaction resulting from attainment of the outcome.

The valence model states that the valence of an outcome to a person is a monotonically increasing function of the algebraic sum of the products of the valences of all other outcomes and his conceptions of the specific outcome's instrumentality for the attainment of these other outcomes. Symbolically,

$$V_j = f \sum_{k=1}^{n} (V_k I_{jk})$$

where

V_j = the valence of outcome j

I_{jk} = the cognized instrumentality of outcome j for the attainment of outcome K

V_k = valence of outcome K

n = the number of outcomes

Cognized or perceived instrumentality is defined conceptually by Vroom as the degree to which the person sees the outcome in question as leading to the attainment of other outcomes. Instrumentality varies from minus one (meaning that the outcome in question is perceived as always not leading to the attainment of the second outcome) to plus one (meaning that the outcome is perceived as always leading to the attainment of the second outcome).

Although this model can be used to predict the valence of any outcome, it has been applied most frequently to the prediction of job satisfaction, occupational preference (as an evaluation), and the valence of good performance. In essence the model says that the worker's satisfaction with his job or anticipated satisfaction with an occupation results from the instrumentality of the job for attaining other outcomes and the valence of those outcomes. In the remainder of the chapter it is referred to as the *valence model*.

Vroom's second model predicts the force toward behavior. The force on a person to perform an act is conceptualized by Vroom as a monotonically increasing function of the algebraic sum of the products of the valences of all outcomes, and the strength of his expectancies that the act is followed by the attainment of these outcomes (Vroom, 1964). Symbolically,

$$F_i = \sum_{j=1}^{n} (E_{ij} V_j)$$

where

F_i = the force on the individual to perform act i
E_{ij} = the strength of the expectancy that act i will be followed by outcome j.
V_j = the valence of outcome j
n = the number of outcomes

The individual's expectancy is defined by Vroom as his belief concerning the probability that the behavior in question is followed by the outcome of interest. An expectancy is a perceived probability and, therefore, ranges from zero to plus one. It is distinguished from instrumentality in that it is an action-outcome association, although instrumentality is an outcome-outcome association. Whereas expectancies are perceived probabilities, instrumentalities are perceived correlations.

Vroom suggests that this force model can be used to predict choice of occupation (a behavior), remaining on the job, and effort. We will refer to this model as the *force model* and its most frequently tested example as the *job effort model*. Specifically, Vroom states that the force on the individual to exert a given amount of effort is a function of the algebraic sum of the products of the person's expectation that the given level of effort will lead to various outcomes and the valence of those outcomes. The subject should choose that effort level with the greatest force. Note that the amount of effort, not performance, is predicted by Vroom; effort is considered to be a behavior, whereas performance would be an outcome. The early tests of this model (all of the pre–1974 research) measured the degree to which *both* working hard and good performance were likely to lead to a set of other organizational outcomes such as more pay or promotional opportunities. These scores were then combined into one expectancy measure (note that according to Vroom the performance-outcome link is an instrumentality, not an expectancy). This expectancy was weighted by the valence of each outcome and summed across outcomes to give a ΣEV for each subject. This ΣEV was then correlated across subjects with some criterion estimate of effort or performance on the job.

A number of modifications in the effort model have occurred whereas the valence model has remained essentially the same. Galbraith and Cummings (1967) extended Vroom's *job effort model*. They attempted to test empirically a distinction (first made by Vroom, 1964; Lawler & Porter, 1967) between first and second level outcomes. A first level outcome is one that has a valence that the investigator is interested in predicting—in their case, performance on the job. They defined second level outcomes as events to which the first level outcomes are expected to lead. Second level outcomes expected to result from performance might be money, fringe benefits, promotions, supportive supervision and an accepting work group. Figure 10.1 presents the Galbraith and Cummings model.

Although there are some differences in terms of the specific evolution of this model, in general the equation is as follows:

$$W = E(\sum_{j=1}^{n} I_{ij}V_j)$$

where

W = effort
E = the expectancy that effort leads to performance
I_{ij} = the instrumentality of performance for the attainment of second level outcomes
V_j = the valence of the second level outcome
n = the number of outcomes

Thus, the original effort and valence models presented by Vroom were combined. Job effort was being predicted from the expectancy that a given level of effort led to a given level of performance weighted by the valence of that performance level. The valence of this performance level was then determined by examining the degree to which it was instrumental for the attainment of second level outcomes weighted in turn by their valence. We have E(ΣIV) as opposed to ΣEV.

In practice this model was tested most frequently in the following manner. Each subject indicated the degree to which working hard (an effort level) was seen as leading to good performance (a performance level). He also indicated the degree to which good performance was likely to lead to each of a set of organizational outcomes (e.g. wages, promotions, security). Finally, he estimated the valence for each outcome. These variables were combined in the prescribed manner to generate a single E(ΣIV) score for each subject and these scores were then correlated across subjects with some criterion variable, usually self, peer, or supervisor ratings of effort or performance.

A number of points are raised here and discussed more fully later. First, note that this modified model has only *one* first level outcome: performance. Thus if one indicates that working hard has a zero probability of leading to good performance, the model predicts a zero level of effort. Vroom's original explanation in

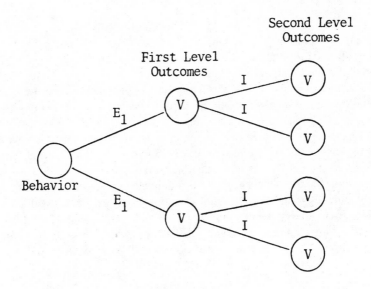

Behavior = effort

E_1 = expectancy

I = instrumentality

V = valence

Fig. 10.1.   A representation of the Galbraith and Cummings Model.

his 1964 book used a similar example but made no such restriction to one outcome. Second, the initial formulations by Vroom and also by theorists in other areas were within subjects, choice models. That is, the subject should have $E(\Sigma IV)$s for a whole series of effort levels and the analysis should predict that he will choose that level with the highest $E(\Sigma IV)$. Before 1974 there had been *no* investigations that tested the effort model in this fashion. Since 1974 there have been quite a few studies that have used the within-subjects approach and we will review these studies later.

Another modification was presented by Campbell, Dunnette, Lawler and Weick (1970). These authors stated more exactly the nature of task goals for which the individual is seen as striving to attain. They divided these goals into external task goals that are set by the employer or work group and internal task goals that the individual sets for himself. They also divided the original expectancy term into two terms: E_I where behavior leads to task goals and E_{II} where task goals lead to rewards. Thus, the model conceptually becomes $E_I E_{II}$ (ΣIV). Although the authors were reluctant to "propose explicit multiplicative combinations or other configural or higher order functions" (Campbell, et al., 1970, p. 348) for the interrelationship of these variables, the previous formula reflects how E_I and E_{II} have generally been combined in practice. We should note that these task goals are multiple in nature where the Galbraith and Cummings formulation was locked into only one first level outcome.

Since 1974 the minor and major modifications are simply too numerous to describe. Some authors have suggested simple additive models, others have dropped instrumentalities, others have suggested a ratio conceptualization and so on. Because many of these changes were prompted by the 1974 review we will discuss each suggested modification when we reach the topic that initiated the change. In summary, then, Vroom's original effort model was modified and elaborated quite extensively whereas the valence model remained relatively unchanged. We turn now to a review of the research evidence for both models.

RESEARCH RESULTS

The research results over the last 15 years are extremely impressive on the quantity dimension but they vary on the quality dimension. In general, there has been greater support for the valence model than for the effort model but more frequent tests of the latter. We will review each model by briefly summarizing the findings up to 1974 and then give a slightly more detailed description of more current studies.

Valence Model: Occupational Preference

This model assesses the degree to which an occupation is seen as leading to outcomes weighted by the valence of the outcome. This ΣEV or ΣIV (some researchers use expectancy, some use instrumentality) is then correlated with a separate global rating of the attractiveness of the occupation either across subjects for one occupation or within subjects across a set of occupations. In 1974 there were five studies reviewed and all of them provided substantial support. Three of the studies reported that the valence model controlled from 47% to 65% of the criterion. This support was the strongest of all the models tested.

In 1976 Mitchell and Beach (Mitchell & Beach, 1976) reviewed the use of expectancy as well as decision theory (traditional expected value) approaches to occupational preference and choice. Two additional expectancy studies by Sheridan, Richards and Slocum (1975) and Lawler, Kuleck and Rhode (1975) were included and both studies were supportive. The Sheridan, et al. study used expectancy theory to predict the occupational choices of nurses and the Lawler, et al. study focused on the preferences of accounting students for accounting jobs. We might add that some of these later tests (mentioned above and to follow) are not exact fits with the valence model. In some cases the criterion was occupational choice (behavior) rather than preference (an evaluation or attitude) and in some cases the model's components were not exactly as previously described. Also, some of the studies looked at job preference (a specific job evaluation) or some similar type of preference that was not an occupational preference. These differences are minor with respect to the intention of this review and interested readers can consult the original papers or other reviews for more details.

Since the Mitchell and Beach review a few more studies have appeared. Oldham (1976) found that the expectancy model did well in predicting sorority choice. Connolly and Vines (1977) reported that the valence model was able to accurately predict 68% of the actual choices of high school students selecting undergraduate colleges. Dillard (1979) reported that the expectancy model predicted about 45% of the variance in accounting employees' preferences for three positions within the subject's firm and four outside positions.

One somewhat more comprehensive approach has been presented recently by Forrest, Cummings and Johnson (1977) and Mobley and his colleagues (Mobley, 1977; Mobley, Hand, Baker & Meglino, 1979; Mobley, Griffeth, Hand & Meglino, 1979). These authors have used an expectancy type formulation to predict job turnover where the choice is defined in terms of the expected value of the present occupation or job versus other occupations or jobs. These authors have gathered data in a number of sites supporting the model and the underlying expectancy constructs.

A summary of this research suggests that the valence model continues to do well in this particular area. The research support has been consistent and strong over a variety of settings, criteria and subjects.

Valence Model: Job Satisfaction

This model is conceptually the same as the occupational choice model but job satisfaction is the criterion. The 1974 review cited nine studies all of which showed significant support but of a magnitude substantially lower than the occupational choice results (about half as much variance controlled).

Three more recent studies provided similar results. Reinharth and Wahba (1976) found a correlation of .40 (p < .01) across 260 subjects in three organizations between job satisfaction and the expectancy model. Kopelman (1977b) divided people into nine categories based on three levels of expectancy and three levels of valence for a set of rewards. The high expectancy, high valence people were significantly more satisfied than the low expectancy, low valence people. Finally, Pritchard, DeLeo and Von Bergen (1976) showed that in conditions where expectancies and valences were manipulated to be high (e.g. through the use of rewards and incentive systems) Air Force recruits were more satisfied with the Air Force in general and with their job than when those conditions did not exist. The differences though significant were not strong and this seems to fit the pattern of the other studies both before and after the 1974 review.

Force Model: Job Effort

The force model is used to predict behavior rather than an attitude and it has most frequently been used to predict effort exerted on the job. 21 studies using a variety of measures, models and criteria were reviewed in the 1974 paper and all but two of them displayed some support. This support, however, was the weakest for all the expectancy models tested. In general, support was greater for predictions of self reported effort than for objective or observer ratings of effort, and a more recent review including recent research by Schwab, Olian-Gottlieb and Heneman (1979) reaches the same conclusion. Also, the closer the model tested was to the original Vroom formulation the greater the support.

The more recent studies follow a similar pattern. Pritchard, DeLeo and Von Bergen (1976) manipulated behavior-reward contingencies in a series of training programs for first term Airmen at an Air Force base. They showed that these changes did indeed have an impact on instrumentalities and valences (not expectancies) but that there was little change in effort or performance. Reinharth and Wahba (1976) used expectancy models to predict the effort and performance of 321 people in 3 industrial organizations. They found only slight support in two of the organizations (i.e. the models controlled only about 5% of the criterion variance) and none in the third. Kopelman and Thompson (1976) however found more support. They reported correlations of .23 and .28 (p < .01) for predictions of self effort ratings for a sample of 399 design engineers at two different points in time (1969 and 1973). The correlations with supervisors' ratings were .24 and .33 (p < .01). A somewhat different analysis of these data (Kopelman, 1977b) based on a division of the sample into nine groups (three levels of expectancy by three levels of valence) showed similar support. Muchinsky (1977) reported an average correlation of .52 between the force model and self rated effort for 27 students describing their effort on academic tasks. Finally, Peters (1977) in a laboratory study with 89 female undergraduate students manipulated expectancy, instrumentality and valence. The correlation between the force model and effort on the task was .38 (p < .001). The pattern of all these more recent results is similar to that reported in 1974.

Force Model: Specific Behaviors

The force model can be used to predict any specific behavior—not just effort on the job. Five studies were reviewed in 1974 and all showed substantial support of a magnitude slightly better than the findings for job effort that suggests that effort may not be a very well defined criterion—a topic to which we will return.

The more recent results again show a similar pattern. Parker and Dyer (1976) were able to predict the retirement of Naval Aviation Officers with 63% accuracy using the force model. This percentage increased to 68% when only the 8 most important outcomes were used (rather than all 25 that were assessed). Turney and Cohen (1976) found modest support for the force model predicting 8 work related activities of 65 U. S. Army personnel. Matsui, Kagawa, Nagamatsu and Ohtsuka (1977) tested the force model with 62 female life insurance sales representatives. Using a within subjects analysis they generated force scores for six different types of insurance and then used actual insurance sales as the criterion. The average correlation across people was .50 (p < .001). Finally, Matsui and Ohtsuka (1978) used a within subjects force model to predict whether 76 first line supervisors would choose considerate or structuring leadership behaviors. The model predicted correctly 71% of the time.

Summary: Empirical Results

The strength of the empirical results has not changed much over the last five years. In general the valence model does better than the force model and self ratings of effort are easier to predict than objective measures. Predictions of specific behavior seem to be better than more general criteria such as effort.

However, the major changes in expectancy research appear to have occurred on other topics. The 1974 review pointed out a number of unresolved methodological, empirical and theoretical issues. Much of the current research has focused on these issues and we turn now to a review of these topics.

METHODOLOGICAL ISSUES

The major methodological topics discussed in earlier reviews had to do with how one determined the number and content of the outcomes and how one measured expectancies, instrumentalities and valences. Some recent work has helped to clarify some of the issues that were unresolved.

Outcome Content

First, with respect to outcomes, the most frequently researched problem has focused on the most appropriate number of outcomes to use. My earlier paper (Mitchell, 1974) suggested that a moderate number (5 to 8) might be best because more outcomes might be adding more error than predictive power. A study by Parker and Dyer (1976) reported the highest predictive power for a model with 8 outcomes (as compared to 5 or 25) and Connolly and Vines (1977) reported that a 9 outcome model did better than one with 23 outcomes. The recent Schwab, Olian-Gottlieb and Heneman (1979) review analyzed 32 studies and reported that studies using less than 9 or more than 16 outcomes controlled less variance than those using 10–15 outcomes suggesting a curvilinear pattern. Finally, Leon (1979) has questioned the data presented by Schwab, et al. (1979) and suggests that their results may only be valid for the self rated effort criterion. Analyzing other criteria suggested that the predictive validity generally decreased with an increase in the number of outcomes. Whether the curvilinear or linear pattern is correct is still undetermined but one point is relatively clear: large numbers of outcomes decrease predictability. This makes sense when you consider that less important outcomes probably add more error than substance to the force prediction.

The research on the content of the outcomes has not produced quite as clear an answer as the previous topic. For example, Rineharth and Wahba (1975) reported little difference in the predictability of positive and negative outcomes. Three studies have looked at the intrinsic-extrinsic distinction. Kopelman and Thompson (1976) reported that extrinsic outcomes do better, Parker and Dyer (1976) reported no difference and Turney and Cohen (1976) reported that intrinsic outcomes predicted better for some behaviors and worse for others than extrinsic outcomes. One must probably draw the conclusion that it is best to treat these categories separately in one phase of the analysis and only collapse across categories when it is warranted.

Measures

The measurement of the three models' components: expectancy, instrumentalities and valences, as well as the criteria: attitudes or behavior, has continued to generate controversy in the literature. We will discuss each of these concepts in turn.

The expectancy measure seems to have the least disagreement. It is seen as a probability and measured as such. Instrumentality, on the other hand, still causes some difficulty. The review by Connolly (1976) pointed out that perceived behavior-outcome linkages and outcome-outcome linkages can be assessed in many ways. One can look at existence, direction, form, strength and certainty with strength being the most common assessment. However, Connolly (1976) argues that instrumentality may be best conceived as a subjective probability. My earlier review concluded that instrumentality was more frequently measured as a probability but to date little evidence is available as to which strategy is most valid.

There does seem to be some agreement on the issue of the valence measurement. In the 1974 paper it was pointed out that importance was the meaning most frequently used but that Vroom conceptualized valence as the anticipated satisfaction or desirability of outcomes. Connolly (1976) has reiterated this argument and Schwab, et al. (1979) have shown empirically that, when valence is measured as desirability and numerically scaled with positive numbers only (instead of positive to negative), more variance is controlled in the 31 studies they reviewed than when other conceptualizations or procedures were used.

Finally, there seems to be some agreement about the "criterion problem." If one examines the support for the valence model or the force model it is clear that the more precise the criterion the better the prediction. Attitudes about specific jobs or occupations appear to be more predictable than more general attitudes and specific behaviors seem to be easier to predict than general concepts like effort. Connolly (1976) has argued for better clarity in our criterion and people like Ivancevich (1976) have shown that better prediction occurs when a behaviorally based criterion measure is used.

In summary, some of the methodological problems apparent in earlier expectancy work seem to have been resolved. We have a better idea of the number of outcomes to assess and it appears more valid to use separate analyses for different content outcomes. Measurement procedures for expectancy and valence seem fairly clear but ambiguity still surrounds the instrumentality measure. Also, the more clear and specific the criterion, the greater the predictability is likely to be.

EMPIRICAL ISSUES

The topics covered in this section have to do with some empirical or mathematical characteristics of the expectancy models. First we will review the reliability and validity of the model's components and then we will discuss the underlying mathematical assumptions of their combinatorial rules.

Reliability and Validity

Eight studies reviewed in the 1974 paper all showed adequate to substantial support for the reliability of the model's components. Support of a similar fashion has continued to be reported. Lied and Pritchard (1976) had test-retest (3 days) reliability of .59 for expectancy and .48 for valence. Turney and Cohen (1976) report test-retest (6 months) reliabilities for 3 expectancy measures as .70 to .75 and valence as .55. These data can be seen as adequate to good support.

The predictive validity of the models is best described by referring back to the review of the empirical studies. In general there is frequent support but at only a modest level depending on the model and criterion involved. The only construct validity findings were already discussed when we mentioned that Schwab, et al. (1979) found that valence as desirability was more valid than valence conceptualized as importance.

Mathematical Properties

The expectancy model requires certain sorts of mathematical operations such as multiplying Es times Vs and adding EVs over a set of outcomes. A number of controversies have surrounded the appropriateness of these operations.

One of these issues was raised by Schmidt (1973) and discussed in detail in the earlier Mitchell (1974) paper. Schmidt argues that ratio scales are required with a rational zero point if we wish the multiplication of Es and Vs to have any validity. Arnold and Evans (1978) have demonstrated the circumstances under which interval scales are also appropriate but even then it is unlikely that we can seriously argue that the measurement procedures for the expectancy model components meet the requirements of interval scales. Whereas this problem is probably not very serious in some general sense (Mitchell, 1974; Connolly, 1976) it does limit researchers in two ways. First, without such scaling procedures, we cannot in a strict sense see support for the model as support for some sort of underlying multiplicative psychological process. Second, because of this lack of validity we cannot competitively test this multiplicative model against alternatives in any really meaningful fashion.

This latter problem has been an issue in the literature for ten years. The Mitchell (1974) paper reviewed a number of studies where the multiplicative model (weighting Es or Is by Vs) was tested against an unweighted (Es or Is alone) or an additive model using Es, Is and Vs in a multiple regression. My conclusion was that the additive models often did as well or better than the multiplicative ones. Behling, Dillard and Gifford (1978) reached the same conclusions in a recent review. They then conducted a computer simulation of the problem and concluded that measurement error precludes any meaningful test of this sort of proposition. On the other hand, Connolly and Vines (1977) and Arnold and Evans (1978) showed support for the multiplicative model. It appears that when vigorous scaling procedures are used some evidence for the interactive approach is available. However, at the moment we are left with the somewhat vague conclusion that although Es, Is and Vs are related to a variety of job related attitudes and behaviors, their rules of combination require further clarification.

Another mathematical assumption is that EV products are summed over outcomes to produce an overall force score. An alternative combination rule might be averaging. Solomon, Messmer and Liddell (1977) recently compared the two processes using functional measurement procedures (Anderson, 1976). They found when comparing the judgments of 22 subjects making ratings of two work situations that averaging was widely used. The authors suggested that the original Vroom model may need to be altered.

Both of the previously discussed points call into question some mathematical procedures but at the same time they question some basic theoretical assumptions inherent in expected value formulations. We turn now to a discussion of these theoretical issues.

THEORETICAL ISSUES

In the 1974 paper a number of issues were discussed relevant to the theoretical foundations of an expectancy approach. Most prominent of these areas of controversy was the type of model used, the conditions under which expectancy approaches seemed most useful and some evaluation of competing alternatives. These topics have continued to be important and we will review the new research. Besides the progress on these problems there has also been a fairly new area of research that has focused on the causes of the model's components (expectancies, instrumentalities and valences). This topic will also be discussed before we attempt an overall summary.

Within-Subjects Analyses

One of the most important points made in the Mitchell (1974) paper was that most of the tests of the expectancy model up to that time had basically misconstrued the original formulation suggested by Vroom (1964). Vroom had clearly seen the expectancy model as a within-subjects, choice type model similar to subjective expected utility (SEU) approaches discussed elsewhere in this book. People were seen as having different ΣEVs (the Force Model) for different behaviors and were predicted to choose that alternative with the highest ΣEV (maximization). On the surface, this model is not very different from SEU or expected value in terms of its components and procedures for predicting behavior.

Instead of using the above approach the model was generally tested using an across subjects strategy. A ΣEV (or $E\Sigma IV$) would be generated for each subject for one behavior such as working hard and the score would be correlated across subjects with a criterion, usually self-rated effort. This process allows halo errors and response bias to degrade its predictions and is a misrepresentation of the theory.

Since 1974 a number of within-subjects tests have been conducted. Kopelman (1977a) and Muchinsky (1977) both found that within-subjects models did better in predicting effort on academic tasks than an across-subjects model. For example, Muchinsky reported the average within-subjects correlation as .57 whereas the across-subjects coefficient was .31. Matsui, et al. (1977) reported an average correlation of .50 for predicting the type of life insurance that will be sold by 62 female life insurance salespersons and Matsui and Ohtsuka (1978) reported 71% correct prediction for leader behavior.

Similar results are available in the broadly defined occupational choice area. Oldham (1976) found that a within-subjects model did better than an across-subjects model in predicting sorority choice, and Parker and Dyer (1976) reported a within-subjects model predicting the retirement of Naval Officers with 68% accuracy. Connolly and Vines (1977) reported a 68% prediction rate for choice of college and Dillard (1979) reported an average correlation of .70 for predicting the occupational choices of accounting students.

A couple of points are noteworthy about these results. First, the results are far stronger than the results reported for the across subjects tests summarized in the 1974 paper. Clearly, the closer the methodological procedures are to the theoretical formulation the better the prediction. The second point, however, is less optimistic. More specifically, these results show that *even at its best* (i.e. thorough, controlled, within subjects tests) the model seldom accounts for more than 50% of the variance in the criterion. Either our measurement and methodological procedures are inadequate or the theory is, or both.

The criticisms of the theory have progressed along two lines. One area of research has followed the criticisms originally raised by Behling and Starke (1973a). These authors pointed out that expectancy theory can be seen simply as an SEU model and should therefore be held to similar standards of support for some underlying mathematical properties. The type of issues debated here are whether people consistently order alternatives (transitivity), whether Es and Vs are independent, whether people are maximizers, and so on.

The empirical results in general suggest that people have few intransitivities (Dillard, 1979; Liddel & Solomon, 1977b) but that Es and Vs are not independent (Liddell & Solomon, 1977a; Connolly & Vines, 1977). Behling and Starke's (1973a) original review of research on these questions showed little support for a number of other propositions.

The second approach to criticizing the model has been either to test or suggest alternative models that are better. The Mitchell (1974) review discussed some of these approaches as did Behling and Starke (1973b), Feldman, Reitz and Hilterman (1976) and Connolly (1976). One empirical approach has been to look at different combinations of Es, Is, and Vs, alone or together, added or multiplied or split apart in various ways (e.g., types of outcomes) to see what generates the best predictions. As discussed earlier, this approach probably tells us very little about the underlying validity of the expectancy model due to the measurement error and the fact that the differences are usually very small. It is also true that these tests are essentially guided by empirical considerations rather than theoretical ones—the approaches tested often have little theoretical meaning and are not intuitively compelling.

A somewhat different approach to the alternative model question has guided other researchers. People like Sobel (1971), Feldman, et al. (1976) and Kopelman (1977a) have empirically tested alternative approaches that suggest somewhat different motivational mechanisms. For example, both Sobel (1971) and Kopelman (1977a) suggested that the individual's behavior is partly determined by the total outcomes available (some sort of ratio of EVs for specific acts compared to a total ΣEV). Behling and Starke (1973b), Locke (1975), Feldman, et al. (1976) and Connolly (1976) questioned the basic maximization strategy inherent in expectancy approaches and they have suggested alternatives (e.g., satisficing, minimum necessary reward).

This whole body of criticism is similar to the comments made about SEU approaches. The paper by Fischhoff, Goitein and Shapira elsewhere in this volume does an excellent job of summarizing those arguments. Their conclusion, and mine as well, is that expectancy models are not an exact description of what goes on in people's heads or of what motivates them. The variables in the model are undoubtedly important and clearly help in our prediction of behavior. They can be useful as normative type models as well. But to suggest that they are exact representations of the "true motivational process" is simply wrong.

The question has become rephrased. Instead of asking if expectancy theory is true or not, a number of authors have begun to inquire when it seems to operate best. The focus is on the conditions or environments in which an expectancy type analysis is likely to be helpful. We discuss this topic next.

Boundary Conditions

Perhaps the most important boundary condition for the expectancy model has to be with the employee's control over his or her behavior. The model is meant to predict the force on the individual to engage in some act. Obviously to the degree that this behavior is not in the repertoire, is an interdependent action, or is under the control of others, force will not be a good predictor. In two early studies (Mitchell & Nebeker, 1973; Mitchell & Pollard, 1973) it was shown that subjects who had high control over the predicted behaviors were more predictable using expectancy theory than subjects who indicated little control. Mitchell and Albright (1972) and Parker and Dyer (1976) indicated that prediction of military retention was increased by including a separate variable representing family wishes. Kopelman (1976) showed that people with task specific ability were more predictable than those who were low on the ability measure. So, the greater the control of the behavior, the better the prediction.

A second boundary condition was initially pointed out by Graen (1969) and Dachler and Mobley (1973). These authors indicated that expectancy theory seemed to work best in those environments where rewards were in fact contingent upon specific behaviors. This argument has recently been augmented by Mayes (1978a) and empirically supported by Kopelman (1976). Essentially, in noncontingent environments there is too much ambiguity. This ambiguity causes error and uncertainty and degrades the predictability of the expectancy model.

Finally, there is the question of time lags. There are two issues here. First is the question of the lag between behavior and the receipt of outcomes. An organization may utilize contingent rewards but the timing of the delivery of these rewards can vary. As Mayes (1978b) has pointed out, the longer the delay the lower the valence and the greater the uncertainty about how one feels about the reward. Again, lower validity is the result.

The second lag issue has to do with the time between the assessment of the predictors (Es, Is and Vs) and the criterion. Obviously expectancy theory is a forward looking theory but it should still be seen as generating scores that represent the immediate antecedents of action. The more time between the assessment of predictors and criterion, the greater the chance that the accuracy of prediction will decrease.

So, in summary, the theory seems to do best when (1) the behavior is in the repertoire of the subject; (2) the behavior is under the control of the subject; (3) the environment provides consistent contingent rewards; (4) the behavior-outcome links are unambiguous; (5) there is little delay between the assessment of predictors and observations of the criterion. Under these conditions expectancy approaches should do fairly well.

Predictors of the Theories Components

One relatively new area of research within the organizational context has been to investigate the causes of people's expectancies: that is, to what extent are expectancies caused by specific reward contingencies, personality variables, or group or organizational characteristics? The theory would suggest that reward contingencies would be a major determinant of expectancies and instrumentalities since these variables are defined as effort-performance or performance-outcome relationships. Two studies that actually manipulated reward contingencies and assessed resultant expectancies found support for this proposition (Peters, 1977; Pritchard, DeLeo & Von Bergen, 1976). The Peters study was particularly impressive in that expectancies (the behavior-performance link), instrumentalities (the performance-outcome link), and valences (the value of the outcomes) were all influenced strongly in the predicted direction when performance evaluations, the distribution of rewards, and the desirability of the rewards were manipulated. Also, some work by Kopelman (1976) suggested that people's expectancies were related to the "reward responsiveness" of the organization. These results provide strong support for the notion that expectancies do indeed reflect the subjects' perceptions of behavior-outcome relationships.

Some personality and organizational variables have also been shown to be related to expectancies. Oldham (1976) found that people with higher self-esteem had higher expectancies, and a number of studies (Lied & Pritchard, 1976; Mitchell, Smyser & Weed, 1975; Sims, Szilagyi & McKemey, 1976) have reported that people with an internal locus of control have higher expectancies than those with an external locus of control. These studies make sense; people who are confident about their ability to influence the world around them see stronger relationships between what they do and the results of their actions than do people who see these outcomes occurring as a function of fate or luck.

Finally, a few investigations (James, Hartman, Stebbins & Jones, 1977; Sims, et al., 1976; Turney & Cohen, 1976) have found positive relationships between leader behavior (e.g., support) and expectancies. The James, et al. study (1977) also found that expectancies were higher in a supportive organizational climate and lower where role ambiguity existed. These results make intuitive sense and are not contradictory in any fashion with the propositions of the theory.

In reviewing this whole section one is left with some optimistic conclusions. If we test a within subjects model within certain boundary conditions the theory does fairly well. By gaining a better understanding of what causes high expectancies, instrumentalities and valences we are better able to have some impact on them. In this way we may increase our understanding as well as perhaps increasing people's satisfaction and productivity.

SUMMARY AND CONCLUSIONS

The results from expectancy theory as used in the organizational context suggest the following set of conclusions:

First, most researchers agree that the model is not descriptive of the actual motivational process. People do not compute probabilities and values, multiply them together, add the products, and base their choice on these computations. It is far too taxing and complex a process. It is also true that the underlying assumptions of the model are frequently violated. The empirical results reflect these inadequacies.

Why, then, do researchers and theoreticians continue to utilize such models? What are its positive points? Well, clearly at an intuitive, and definitely nonscientific level, it feels right. Both the underlying assumptions of maximizing and the components of the model (expectancies and valences) are appealing. And there is more. Although the theory is not exact it has been helpful. It has helped to point out that behavior-outcome links are important as well as the evaluation of outcomes. It emphasizes that different people will want different things. It helps us to focus on some variables that might have been overlooked (e.g. listing alternatives, listing outcomes, thinking about contingencies).

Also, as we mentioned earlier, the question being asked is shifting from "*Is* expectancy theory right or wrong?" to "*When* is expectancy theory right or wrong?" Some environments, some people and some circumstances are more likely to result in an expectancy-like process than others. In other cases goals are the primary motivation whereas in others issues of fairness (equity) may guide behavior. It seems to me that the task of future research is even somewhat broader than pointing out when or where expectancy theory is useful or not. We must develop theories that attempt to integrate all of our motivational models. What is needed is an approach that describes those settings and times (developmentally) when equity, goal setting and expectancy theories are salient. Such an integration is reasonable and makes sense. But it will require more research designed to combine, compare, and competitively test different theories rather than the current approach that simply demonstrates the usefulness or lack of it of a given approach in a given setting. It should be a challenging but exciting task.

REFERENCES

Anderson, N. H. How functional measurement can yield validated internal scales of mental qualities. *Journal of Applied Psychology,* 1976, *61,* 677–692.

Arnold, H. J., & Evans, M. G. *A test for multiplicative models with internal scale data.* Faculty of Management Studies, University of Toronto, June 1978 (working paper).

Behling, O., Dillard, J. F., & Gifford, W. E. *Two demonstrations of the futility of expectancy theory research.* Columbus: The Ohio State University, 1977 (working paper).

Behling, O., & Starke, R. A. The postulates of expectancy theory. *Academy of Management Journal,* 1973, *16,* 373-388. (a)

Behling, O., & Starke, F. A. Some limits on expectancy theories of work effort. *Proceedings of the Midwest Meeting of the American Institute of Decision Sciences,* 1973. (b)

Campbell, J. P., Dunnette, M. D., Lawler, E. E., III, & Weick, K. E., Jr. *Managerial Behavior, Performance, and Effectiveness.* New York: McGraw-Hill, 1970.

Connolly, T. Some conceptual and methodological issues in expectancy models of work performance motivation. *Academy of Management Review,* 1976, *1,* 37-47.

Connolly, T., & Vines, C. V. Some expectancy type models of undergraduate college choice. *Decision Sciences,* 1977, *8,* 311-317.

Dachler, H. P., & Mobley, W. H. Construct validation of an instrumentality-expectancy-task-goal model of work motivation: Some theoretical boundary conditions. *Journal of Applied Psychology Monograph,* 1973, *58,* 397-418.

Dillard, J. F. Applicability of an occupational goal-expectancy model in professional accounting organizations. *Decision Sciences,* 1979, *10,* 161-176.

Feldman, J. M., Reitz, H. J., & Hilterman, R. J. Alternatives to optimization in expectancy theory. *Journal of Applied Psychology,* 1976, *61,* 712-720.

Forrest, C. R., Cummings, L. L., & Johnson, A. C. Organizational participation: A critique and a model. *Academy of Management Review,* 1977, *2,* 586-601.

Galbraith, J., & Cummings, L. L. An empirical investigation of the motivational determinants of task performance: Interactive effects between instrumentality-valence and motivation-ability. *Organizational Behavior and Human Performance,* 1967, *2,* 237-257.

Georgopoulous, B. S., Mahoney, G. M., & Jones, N. W. A path-goal approach to productivity. *Journal of Applied Psychology,* 1957, *41,* 345-353.

Graen, G. Instrumentality theory of work motivation: Some experimental results and suggested modifications. *Journal of Applied Psychology Monograph,* 1969, *53,* 1-25.

Heneman, H. G., III, & Schwab, D. P. An evaluation of research on expectancy theory predictions of employee performance. *Psychological Bulletin,* 1972, *78,* 1-9.

House, R. J., & Wahba, M. A. Expectancy theory in industrial and organizational psychology: An integrative model and a review of literature. *Proceedings of the 80th Annual Convention of the American Psychological Association,* 1972, *7,* 465-466.

Ivancevich, J. M. Expectancy theory predictions and behaviorally anchored scales of motivation: An empirical test of engineers. *Journal of Vocational Behavior,* 1976, *8,* 59-75.

James, L. R., Harman, A., Stebbins, M. W. and Jones, A. P. Relationships between psychological climate and a VIE model of work motivation. *Personnel Psychology,* 1977, *30,* 229-254.

Kopelman, R. E. Organizational control system responsiveness, expectancy theory constructs and work motivation: some interrelations and causal connections *Personnel Psychology* 1976, *29,* 205-220.

Kopelman, R. E. Across individual, within individual and return on effort versions of expectancy theory. *Decision Sciences* 1977, *8,* 651-662. (a)

Kopelman, R. E. Psychological stages of careers in engineering: An expectancy theory taxonomy. *Journal of Vocational Behavior,* 1977, *10,* 270-286. (b)

Kopelman, R. E., & Thompson, P. H. Boundary conditions for expectancy theory predictions of work motivation and job performance. *Academy of Management Journal,* 1976, *19,* 237-258.

Lawler, E. E., III. *Motivation in work organizations.* Monterey, Cal.: Brooks/Cole, 1973.

Lawler, E. E., III, Kuleck, W. J., Jr., & Rhode, J. G. Job choice and post decision dissonance. *Organizational Behavior and Human Performance,* 1975, *13,* 133-145.

Lawler, E. E., III & Porter, L. W. Antecedent attitudes of effective managerial performance. *Organizational Behavior and Human Performance,* 1967, *2,* 122-142.

Leon, F. R. Number of outcomes and accuracy of prediction in expectancy research. *Organizational Behavior and Human Performance*, 1979, *23*, 251-267.

Liddell, W. W. and Solomon, R. J. A critical analysis of a test of two postulates underlying expectancy theory. *Academy of Management Journal*, 1977, *20*, 460-464. (a)

Liddell, W. W., & Solomon, R. J. A total and stochastic test of the transitivity postulate underlying expectancy theory. *Organizational Behavior and Human Performance*, 1977, *19*, 311-324. (b)

Lied, T. R., & Pritchard, R. D. Relationships between personality variables and components of the expectancy-valence model. *Journal of Applied Psychology*, 1976, *61*, 463-467.

Locke, E. A. Personnel attitudes and motivation. *Annual Review of Psychology*, *1975*, *26*, 457-480.

Matsui, T., Kagawa, M., Nagamatsu, J., & Ohtsuka, Y. Validity of expectancy theory as a within person behavioral choice model for sales activities. *Journal of Applied Psychology*, 1977, *62*, 764-767.

Matsui, T., & Ohtsuka, Y. Within-person expectancy theory predictions of supervisory consideration and structure behavior. *Journal of Applied Psychology*, 1978, *63*, 128-131.

Mayes, B. T. Incorporating time-lag effects into the expectancy model of motivation: A reformulation of the model. *Academy of Management Review*, 1978, *3*, 374-379. (a)

Mayes, B. T. Some boundary considerations in the application of motivation models. *Academy of Management Review*, 1978, *3*, 51-58. (b)

Mitchell, T. R. Expectancy models of job satisfaction, occupational preference and effort: A theoretical, methodological, and empirical appraisal. *Psychological Bulletin*, 1974, *81*, 12, 1053-1077.

Mitchell, T. R. Organizational behavior. *Annual Review of Psychology*, 1979, *30*, 243-281.

Mitchell, T. R., & Albright, D. W. Expectancy theory predictions of the satisfaction, effort, performance, and retention of naval aviation officers. *Organizational Behavior and Human Performance*, 1972, *8*, 1-20.

Mitchell, T. R., & Beach, L. R. A review of occupational preference and choice research using expectancy theory and decision theory. *Journal of Occupational Psychology*, 1976, *99*, 231-248.

Mitchell, T. R., & Biglan, A. Instrumentality theories: Current uses in psychology. *Psychological Bulletin*, 1971, *76*, 432-454.

Mitchell, T. R., & Nebeker, D. M. Expectancy theory predictions of academic effort and performance. *Journal of Applied Psychology*, 1973, *57*, 61-67.

Mitchell, T. R., & Pollard, W. E. Instrumentality theory predictions of academic behavior. *Journal of Social Psychology*, 1973, *89*, 34-45.

Mitchell, T. R., Smyser, C. M., & Weed, S. E. Locus of control: Supervision and work satisfaction. *Academy of Management Journal*, 1975, *18*, 623-631.

Mobley, W. H. Intermediate linkages in the relationship between job satisfaction and employee turnover. *Journal of Applied Psychology*, 1977, *62*, 237-240.

Mobley, W. H., Griffeth, R. W., Hand, H. H., & Meglino, B. M. Review and conceptual analysis of the employee turnover process. *Psychological Bulletin*, 1979, *86*, 493-522.

Mobley, W. H., Hand, H. H., Baker, R. L., & Meglino, B. M. Conceptual and empirical analysis of military recruit training attrition. *Journal of Applied Psychology*, 1979, *64*, 10-18.

Muchinsky, P. M. A comparison of within and across subjects analyses of the expectancy valence model for predicting effort. *Academy of Management Journal*, 1977, *20*, 154-158.

Oldham, G. R. Organizational choice and some correlates of individual expectancies. *Decision Sciences*, October 1976, 873-884.

Parker, D., & Dyer, L. Expectancy theory as a within-person behavioral choice model: An empirical test of some conceptual and methodological refinements. *Organizational Behavior and Human Performance*, 1976, *17*, 97-117.

Peters, L. H. Cognitive models of motivation, expectancy theory and effort: An analysis and empirical test. *Organizational Behavior and Human Performance*, 1977, *20*, 129-148.

Pritchard, R. D., DeLeo, P. J., & Von Bergen, C. W., Jr. A field experimental test of expectancy-valence incentive motivation techniques. *Organizational Behavior and Human Performance,* 1976, *15,* 355–406.

Reinharth, L., & Wahba, M. A. A test of alternative models of expectancy theory. *Human Relations,* 1976, *29,* 257–272.

Schmidt, F. L. Implications of a measurement problem for expectancy theory research. *Organizational Behavior and Human Performance,* 1973, *10,* 243–251.

Schwab, D. P., Olian-Gottlieb, J. D., & Heneman, H. G., III. Between-subjects expectancy theory research: A statistical review of studies predicting effort and performance. *Psychological Bulletin,* 1979, *86,* 139–147.

Sheridan, J. E., Richards, M. D., & Slocum, J. W., Jr. Comparative analysis of expectancy and heuristic models of decision behavior. *Journal of Applied Psychology,* 1975, *60,* 361–368.

Sims, H. P., Jr., Szilagyi, A. D., McKemey, D. R. Antecedents of work related expectancies. *Academy of Management Journal* 1976, *19,* 547–559.

Sobel, R. S. Tests of preperformance and postperformance models of satisfaction with outcomes. *Journal of Personality and Social Psychology,* 1971, *19,* 213–221.

Solomon, R. J., Messmer, D. J., & Liddell, W. W. *A test of the addition hypothesis in Vroom's force model.* Williamsburg, Va.: College of William and Mary, School of Business Administration, April 1977 (working paper).

Turney, J. R., & Cohen, S. L. Influence of work content on extrinsic outcome expectancy and intrinsic pleasure predictions of work effort. *Organizational Behavior and Human Performance,* 1976, *17,* 311–327.

Vroom, V. H. *Work and motivation.* New York: Wiley, 1964.

Wahba, M. A., & House, R. J. Expectancy theory in work and motivation: Some logical and methodological issues. *Human Relations,* 1974, *27,* 121–147.

VII THE CONTEXT OF DECISION MAKING

11 The Experienced Utility of Expected Utility Approaches

Baruch Fischhoff
Decision Research

Bernard Goitein
University of Michigan

Zur Shapira
Hebrew University

A simple and comprehensive rule for making decisions is the following. List all feasible courses of action. For each action, enumerate all possible consequences. For each consequence, assess the attractiveness or aversiveness of its occurrence, as well as the probability that it will be incurred should the action be taken. Compute the expected worth of each consequence by multiplying its worth by its probability of occurrence. The expected worth of an action is the sum of the expected worths of all possible consequences. Once the calculations are completed, choose the action with the greatest expected worth.

Studying the prescriptive and descriptive validity of this model is the preoccupation of researchers in a diffuse field known as behavioral decision theory (BDT). Some look at the model as a whole, others concentrate on its components (e.g., assessments of worth or probability), and still others concern themselves with special cases. The most general form is known as the subjective expected utility (SEU) model. In it, probabilities are treated as being subjective whereas worth is expressed in *utility,* a generalized measure of desirability. The S is dropped if probabilities are considered to be ''objective'' (a distinction clarified below). The U, for utility, becomes a V, for value, if an absolute standard of worth, like dollars, is used. The E is dropped if probabilities are ignored, i.e., if there is no element of expectancy and receipt of all consequences is viewed as a certainty. Most of the expectancy-value (E-V) models described elsewhere in this book would in this jargon be called either EU or SEU models; they use subjective judgments of worth and consider uncertainty, but take no position on the meaning of probability.

The chapter that follows traces the history of SEU research, with particular emphasis on its varied intellectual roots and the insights and blind spots they have entailed. Like any other discipline, its progress has been speckled by fits, starts, and occasional extended pursuit of deadends. These are discussed in moderately blunt terms with an eye to highlighting the hard-earned lessons that seem to be most relevant to expectancy-valence (E-V) research. A final section considers less obliquely the question of what the two approaches, E-V and BDT, may have to learn from one another. To presage that discussion, the great advantage of E-V studies is the realism of their settings; their great disadvantage lies in the complexity of those settings. Many of the conclusions of behavioral decision theory regarding the intricacies of decision behavior and its study were slowly and painstakingly discovered and documented in highly constrained experimental situations. Such subtle signals might never have been detected in the flesh. Conversely, field research of the E-V type reminds us of the key variables that should be presented in laboratory work.

FORMAL MODELS OF DECISION MAKING

Attempts to describe how people make decisions took their initial marching orders from prescriptive models, telling how people should make decisions. Variants of the SEU model, as elaborated by statistical and Bayesian decision theory, were the most prominent. These models came from the vicinity of the intersection of economics and philosophy and, indeed, the first experimental studies of decision making were conducted by members of those professions. Two essays by Ward Edwards (1954, 1961) provide comprehensive and stimulating introductions to initial stages of this field.

The appeal of the models was obvious. They reduced the universe of decisions to a common set of primitives (options, probabilities, utilities) about which one could hope to derive universal truths (e.g., people exaggerate low probabilities) in due time. To some extent, this promise has been borne out by reality. Three hundred articles in behavioral decision theory written yearly probably produce more cumulative knowledge than the three thousand publications in personality research (Goldberg, 1974). A second enticement was the presence of an axiomatic basis for these models. Any individual who subscribes to a small set of reasonable rules (e.g., transitivity) should behave in accordance with the model. Prescriptive reasonableness is presumably a necessary condition for the descriptive validity of a law of conscious behavior. In mainstream American economics, the idea that people maximize V or U or EV or SEU or multiattribute SEU has the status of a meta-theory. It goes without saying that such maximization is what people try and manage to do. The goal of the theorist is not to test this assumption, but to divine just what it is that people are maximizing. Like other meta-theories, SEU is not falsifiable and thus not a theory at all from this perspective.

With sufficient ingenuity, one can always find something that a particular decision maker has maximized in a particular situation.

The story of behavioral decision theory has been the growing realization that SEU often does not describe the decision-making process either as it is designed or executed. The dramatic tension has been provided by SEU's remarkable ability to hang on despite mounting doubts about its descriptive competence. The climax of this yet-incomplete tale seems to have something to do with realizing that a clearly erroneous model still may serve some useful role. The denouement (or perhaps sequel) may involve elaborating and circumscribing that role.[1]

We believe that key clues to the future of the SEU model (and its E-V counterpart) can be found by going back and understanding how it has managed to hang on despite decades of withering attack. The retrospective look that follows suggests the secret to its longevity lies in the fact that the model (1) expresses some fundamental truth in some situations; (2) has a remarkable ability to be close to the mark in situations where its underlying logic is clearly inappropriate; and (3) has proponents of heroic tenacity.

Model Fitting

One way to use the SEU model is in explaining past decisions. A set of similar decisions is collected and the researcher sets about identifying a set of predictors (probabilities and utilities) that, when combined according to the SEU rule will account for those decisions. This search may involve not only trying different predictors, but also different ways of measuring and transforming those predictors.

Underlying this approach is a fairly reasonable research strategy. It is extraordinarily difficult to study simultaneously the form of the decision models that people use and the substantive considerations incorporated in them;[2] therefore, let us assume the truth of this general model and devote our efforts to seeing what inputs will make it work. Specifically, assume that people use the SEU model and find what their probabilities and utilities are. With such a strategy, it is hard

---

[1]One source of resistance only tangentially relevant to our story lies in the disciplinary prejudices of the economists and (to a lesser extent) the philosophers instrumental in launching SEU. The sophisticated mathematical derivations and elegant symbol manipulations which are the stock in trade of these two groups require a degree of formalism like that found in SEU. The theory did not fall over dead with the inconsistencies identified by Allais or Ellsberg, for example, because neither offered an alternative calculus on which these professionals could work their magic.

[2]Functional measurement is one of the few techniques designed to do this (Anderson, 1978). Whereas studies in this vein have produced useful insights, literal acceptance of their conclusions requires some heady assumptions, particularly regarding the verisimilitude of responses to involved factorial designs and highly schematic stimuli. For example, one must be convinced that subjects do not solve the problems presented by such tasks by concocting situation-specific decision rules that emerge, on analysis, as highly systematic behavior.

to lose in the short run. The clever researcher can usually find some set of values in a particular situation that will give good enough predictions or postdictions to maintain faith in the model.

Any descriptive failure by an SEU model can be explained away as a failure in measurement rather than the use of the wrong combination rule. The wrong consequences were included; their worth was assessed in an unreliable or confusing manner; uncertainties were ignored or elicited improperly and so on. Some of the more imaginative fudge factors fall into the categories of transaction costs. Decision making itself is seen as incurring such costs and the process is managed so as to keep those costs down. Thus a decision that seems to select a suboptimal alternative can be reinterpreted as the result of truncating or simplifying the model so as to minimize transaction costs.[3]

The complementary research strategy is to presume that one knows the probabilities and utilities to which people attend and then experiment with different combination rules until one is found that works. The price one pays for strict adherence to either strategy is that as the number of predictors (different variables, measurement techniques, data transformations, etc.) increases, the model becomes increasingly vague and imprecise. Given a sufficiently large set of probabilities and utilities, one can, of course, devise a rule "predicting" past decisions to any desired level of proficiency. In regression terms, by expanding the set of independent variables one can always find a set of predictors (or even one predictor) with any desired correlation with the dependent variable. The price one pays for overfitting is shrinkage, failure of the rule to "work" on a new sample of cases. With well-defined problems, the predictor/sample ratio allows one to "correct for shrinkage" and estimate the predictive validity of an SEU model for future decisions. Such corrections are impossible when it is unclear just how many variants of the model have been tried and discarded before the best-fitting one was identified. Thus, when an SEU model "works" on a set of data, it is difficult to know what that proves. Have we proven that the decision makers we are studying are using SEU, and here are their weights? Or has our fishing expedition finally stumbled upon an SEU-like model that mimics their actual behavior?

Simple Models or Simple Processes?

Growing unease with the elusiveness of the proper SEU model was compounded by results emerging from the study of clinical judgment, another intellectual tradition on which behavioral decision theory draws. Clinical judgment is exercised by a radiologist who sorts X rays of ulcers into "benign" and "malignant," by a personnel officer who chooses the best applicants from a set of

---

[3]See Beach and Mitchell (1978) for a predictive model using transaction costs, albeit not labeled as such, as a major determinant in the selection of decision-making strategy.

candidates, by a crisis center counselor who decides which callers threatening suicide are serious. In each of these examples, the diagnosis involves making a decision on the basis of a set of cues or attributes. When, as in these examples, the decision is repetitive and all cases can be characterized by the same cues, it is possible to model the judges' decision-making policy statistically. Following the logic of the SEU modeling described in the previous section, a set of decisions are gathered and multiple regression is used to determine the cue-weighting scheme that best accounts for the decisions actually made by the judge.

Two decades of such *policy-capturing* studies persistently produced a disturbing pair of conclusions: simple linear models, using a weighted sum of the cues, did an excellent job of postdicting judges' decisions, despite the judges' claim that they were using much more complicated strategies (Goldberg, 1968, 1970; Slovic & Lichtenstein, 1971). A commonly asserted form of complexity is called "configural" judgment, in which the diagnostic meaning of one cue depends on the meaning of other cues (e.g., "that tone of voice makes me think 'not suicidal' unless the call comes at mid-day").

Two reasons for this contrast have emerged, each with negative implications for the descriptive validity of SEU. One reason, fed by other developments in cognitive psychology (e.g., Miller, 1956; Simon, 1957), involved the growing realization that combining enormous amounts of information in one's head overwhelms the computational capacity of anyone but an *idiot savant*. A judge trying to implement a complex strategy simply would not be able to do so with great consistency. Indeed, it is difficult to learn and use even a nonconfigural, weighted-sum decision rule when there are many cues or unusual relationships between the cues and predicted variable (Slovic, 1974). Because the SEU model is such a weighted-sum rule, these results suggest that people could not use it even if they tried.

The second realization that emerged from clinical judgment research is that simple linear models are extraordinarily powerful predictors. If one can identify and reliably measure the attributes relevant to a decision maker, one can mimic his or her decisions to a large degree with simple models bearing no resemblance to the decision makers' cognitive processes. That is, one can misspecify weights and even combination rules and still do a pretty good job of predicting decisions under very general conditions (Dawes, 1979).

This discovery proves devastating from two perspectives. One is that whatever people are doing will look like the application of an additive linear model (like SEU or E-V). In Hoffman's (1960) term, such models are *paramorphic* in that they can replicate the input-output relations of the phenomena they are meant to describe without any guarantee of fidelity to the underlying processes. Thus, even if such a model predicts subjects' behavior, one cannot be certain that they are actually using such a decision rule.

Secondly, one cannot take the results of attempts to characterize decision makers' specific policies seriously. If one assumes that people are using an SEU or other additive linear model, their personal decision model could seemingly be captured by finding the weighting schemes that best predict their actual behavior. Unfortumately, the best predicting weights determined, say, by standard regression procedures, become increasingly unstable and uninterpretable when, as is usually the case, there is any dependence between the cues, or multicollinearity. Thus, even positing the (arguable) accuracy of the additive linear model, it is hard to tell what the judge is up to, even when behavior can be predicted quite well.

A possible solution to this problem is to create stimuli or tasks with no dependence between attributes. Slovic (1969), for example, used a factorial design to describe stocks that were evaluated by experienced investors. The variance explained by each dimension (or attribute) could be used to determine its importance in an additive linear decision model. A drawback to this solution is that it goes against another of the intellectual roots of behavioral decision theory, Brunswik's probabilistic functionalism (1952; Hammond, 1966). From this perspective, the study of behavior involves understanding how people adapt to an uncertain or probabilistic world. Central to their adaptation is learning the natural relationships between cues. A research design that destroys these relationships (e.g., the factorial one described above) lacks ecological validity. When confronted with such an unnatural stimulus environment, the individual can only effect some sort of (meaningless?) adaptation of natural behavior to this unique situation. That compromise may be distinctly unenlightening about real-world behavior, the world that E-V researchers wish to study.

The cumulative effect of these problems was to cast further doubt on the usefulness of research either testing the validity of the SEU model or attempting to explicate its usage through policy capturing. Despite the predictive validity of these attempts, they seemed to yield little trustworthy knowledge about how people actually make decisions. The response of the research community was a parting of ways between two camps that might be described as involving cognitive applied and applied cognitive psychologists (Baddeley, 1977; Wright, 1978). The latter were interested in how people think in the general applied context of decision making; their progress is described in subsequent sections.

The former were interested in specific applied problems whose locus was, at least in part, in cognitive decision making. For them, the predictive power of these models provided a highly useful tool. Often one doesn't care how decisions are made, as long as one can predict their outcome. If it works, a paramorphic model may be good enough for designing an effective marketing campaign or remuneration scheme. Such circumscribed successes are all that many applied E-V researchers need. Although even there, some understanding of how people process information might help present options in the most accessible manner possible.

At times, a valid predictive model might be used to replace clinical judges by formulae modeling their behavior. Called "bootstrapping," this approach calls for having decision makers identify the variables on which they base their decisions and then "capture" the policy they use with a set of trial cases. That policy, as embodied in a formula, is then used in place of the judges. Even if it does not embody their thought processes, it may mimic their decisions with greater reliability (and hence validity) than the judges themselves. Formulae never have off days nor suffer from fatigue or distraction by irrelevant cues (Slovic & Lichtenstein, 1971). Clearly people know more than what is included in such formulae. But there is little evidence to date indicating that they can convert this sensitivity to the richness of life situations into superior predictions.

Empirically discovering an analytical result by Wilks (1938), Dawes and Corrigan (1974) showed that considerable predictive success is possible without almost any modeling at all. All one has to do is to identify the variables (or attributes) to which a decision maker attends and decide whether they are positively or negatively related to the decision criterion. If these variables are expressed in standard units, they can be given unit weights (+1 or −1, as appropriate). Such a unit weighted model will, under very general conditions, predict decisions as well as a weighted-sum model using regression weights.

Thus, a simple substantive theory indicating what variables people care about when making decisions may be all one needs to make pretty good predictions of their behavior. If they like more of good things and less of bad things, just count up the number of good things an option leads to and subtract the number of bad things and you have a good idea of how favorably it is viewed. The predictive power of such a simple model provides a base line against which more sophisticated models could be compared.

Obviously, some goods (positive attributes) are more important than others. Therefore, a model using importance weights should, in principle, predict better than one using unit weights. Similarly, goods obtained with high probability should be valued more than those obtained with low probability. Therefore, a model using probability weights should in principle predict better than one using unit weights. However, any unreliability or misspecification of those weights, due to poor procedure or multicollinearity, reduces their contribution very rapidly. In the extreme, models using poorly conceived or executed weighting schemes may succeed in spite of rather than because of their differences from the unit-weight model.

All of these discoveries from the area of clinical judgment have rather chilling implications for the use of modeling techniques for determining whether people use E-V decision-making models and, if so, how. In short, the success of an E-V type model in predicting behavior proves very little besides membership of the model in the family of powerful linear models. Neither the degree of success, nor the specific importance weights used allow unambiguous interpretation.

Divide and Conquer

Feeling that the SEU model was inpregnable and inpenetrable when dealt with as a whole, the applied cognitive psychologists among behavioral decision theorists have largely turned to an examination of the model's parts and their validity. Do people accept the axioms on which the model is based? Are they capable of providing the inputs that it requires? Are their intuitions attuned to the kind of thinking embodied in SEU? In simplified situations, which relieve their computational load, do people exhibit SEU-like behavior? Are they sensitive to factors that have no representation in SEU?

PRESCRIPTIVE VALIDITY

One great attraction of SEU approaches is that they represent reasonable decision rules, ways in which people might want to make decisions; such an attractive prescriptive model would be a sensible point of departure for developing a valid descriptive model. The form of the SEU model ($\Sigma p_i u_i$) states that actions become more attractive as their good consequences become more appealing (u_i increases) and more likely (p_i increases) or as their less appealing consequences become less likely. Because the expected utilities of various possible consequences are added, low or negative utility associated with one consequence can, in principle, be compensated for by sufficiently high utility on others. If people wish to have their decision making guided by these rules, the study of decision making becomes an analysis of their ability to carry them out.

When might people reject these rules?

(1) When more of a good thing is not better. Such situations can, in principle, be handled by having a nonlinear or even nonmonotonic relationship between the magnitude of a consequence and its utility.

(2) When the appeal of a positive consequence does not increase linearly with the certainty of its being attained (p_i). Atkinson and Feather (1966) and others have shown that at times, people will forego an increment in probability of success in order to be challenged by a situation or to have some suspense associated with its outcome. For example, one might prefer a class in which the top 80% receive A's to one in which A's are given to everyone automatically. SEU models cannot directly accommodate assigning intrinsic values to probabilities of success. However, it is possible to redefine the consequences so as to save the model. In the example, the "cinch A" and the "earned A" are different consequences whose utilities may differ by more than the difference in probabilities (.8 and 1.0), whose values are treated as absolutes.

Because SEU researchers have been interested in developing a general descriptive theory of decision making, there have been relatively few attempts to describe the substantive situations in which such dependencies arise. One does not even know if they occur commonly or merely in a small, but important class of achievement-related circumstances.

One interpretation of such dependence of value on probability is as a reflection of risk aversiveness. Risk-averse individuals attach a value to certainty itself, whereas risk-seeking individuals do not. There have been some attempts to study individual differences in propensity to take risks, however, these have foundered on the apparent absence of such differences (e.g., Davidshofer, 1976; Wright & Phillips, in press). Poorly understood situational variables seem to overwhelm individual differences in determining risk aversion.[4]

(3) When options are evaluated by noncompensatory criteria. Two possible noncompensatory rules are the conjunctive and disjunctive. By the conjunctive rule, an option has to score fairly high on each consequence to be considered. For example, a vacation option must be reasonably priced, available when needed, suitably sunny and fairly quiet. If an option failed to pass muster on any one of these attributes, its rating on the others would be immaterial, e.g., no amount of sun will compensate for a lot of noise. These minimal levels are, in a sense, nonnegotiable demands. According to the disjunctive rule, an option that is adequate on any one attribute is acceptable. For example, an investment opportunity might be chosen if it were good enough as a speculation, tax shelter, or hedge against inflation, no matter how badly it rated on the other dimensions. Investment portfolios often include varied items chosen by the same disjunctive rule. Compound strategies are also possible, such as using a disjunctive or conjunctive rule to reduce a large set of options to a smaller one to which a compensatory rule is then applied (Svenson, 1979).

Either partial or total reliance on a noncompensatory rule could spell serious difficulties for the prescriptive (and hence descriptive) validity of SEU models. Einhorn (1971) provided one of the first such demonstrations, although the power of linear models is such that even where they were inferior to noncompensatory models, they still provided relatively good predictions. Lichtenstein, Slovic and Zink (1969) tried to convince people to abandon noncompensatory strategies in favor of using expected value as a decision rule, but to no avail. Choice theory offers a variety of other noncompensatory decision rules (e.g., minimax) whose use has been observed in one situation or another (e.g., Coombs, Dawes & Tversky, 1970). Here, too, our ability to characterize decision situations and the strategies they induce is limited. Attempts to predict the usage and nonusage of compensatory strategies have a distinctly ad hoc character.

(4) When consequences are not evaluated independently. Literal usage of an SEU model requires one to evaluate each consequence attribute of each option by itself and then combine the results. In some situations, however, the decision maker might want to evaluate a particular consequence differently depending on the value of other consequences. For example, one might like either a slightly uncomfortable chair or a moderate level of ambient noise when deciding where to sit in a lecture, knowing that either will help overcome a tendency to fall asleep.

---

[4]Influence in the opposite direction is also possible. Probabilities may be influenced by utilities, as when optimists exaggerate the probability of good things happening. There appears at the moment not to be any hard evidence of such distortions (Wallsten, 1971).

However, a seat that is both noisy and hard will be undesirable because it diverts too much attention to overcoming discomfort. In other words, worth is an interactive function of the attributes.

The concern of E-V researchers over the effects of extrinsic reinforcements on intrinsic motivation (Deci, 1975) relfects another such interaction, as it suggests that the value of intrinsic rewards may be affected by the specific extrinsic reward received. This can, in principle, be handled in SEU models, by evaluating the conjunction of attributes rather than each one separately. In the previous example, one would evaluate separately a noisy and soft seat, a noisy and hard seat, a quiet and soft seat, and a quiet and hard seat. With all but the simplest of attribute-attribute interactions, however, this would prove quite laborious in practice.

The prevalence of such interactive evaluations is the most extensively studied aspect of the search for configural judges mentioned earlier. To repeat the results of that search: whereas clinical judges often believe that they are using configural rules, evidence of consistent configurality is meager. However, it is still unclear whether this contradiction reflects the failure of these judges' introspection (i.e., they don't know what they're doing) or the power of additive linear models.

(5) When options are not evaluated simultaneously. Simon's (1957) notion of "satisficing" grew out of observing the predictive failures of the SEU-like models of classical economics. Satisficers look for decision alternatives that are good enough. In this process, they may use one of the noncompensatory rules described above or a compensatory rule, looking for adequate overall performance. In any case, their search terminates when a satisfactory option has been identified and evaluated. This option may, however, be inferior (in an SEU sense) to other options that are not considered.

An alternative approach to assessing the prescriptive reasonableness of the SEU model is to see whether people accept the axioms from which it is derived. In 1969, Tverksy found that though people like to be transitive in their choices (thus fulfilling one axiom), it is possible to design situations in which they are both intransitive and unable to resolve the inconsistency in their choices. He speculated that marketing approaches may be designed to exploit such difficulties. Another demonstration of inconsistency appeared in Zagorski (1975), who showed people pairs of gambles (A, B) and asked them to judge the amount of money $V(A-B)$ that would induce them to trade the better gamble (A) for the worse gamble (B). He demonstrated that one can construct quadruples of gambles $A, B, C,$ and D such that $V(A-B) + V(B-C) \neq V(A-D) + V(D-C)$. In other words, path independence was violated. The difference between gambles A and C depends on whether the intermediate gamble is B or D. The Allais and Ellsberg paradoxes (see Edwards, 1954, 1961) are two demonstrations of people rejecting Savage's independence axiom, according to which preferences between alternatives should be independent of any consequences they have in common.

Until recently, however, few theorists were convinced by these examples. By way of counterattack, MacCrimmon (1968) showed that business executives who violated various axioms could easily be led, via discussion, to see the error of their ways. However, Slovic and Tversky (1974) challenged MacCrimmon's discussion procedure on the grounds that it pressured subjects to accept the axioms. They presented subjects with arguments for and against the independence axiom and found persistent violations, even after the axiom was presented in a clear and presumably compelling fashion. Moskowitz (1974) used a variety of problem representations (matrix formats, trees, and verbal presentations) to clarify the principle and maximize its acceptability, yet still found that the independence axiom was rejected. Even MacCrimmon's faith in many of the key axioms has been shaken by recent data, leading him to suggest that reevaluation of the theory is in order (MacCrimmon & Larsson, 1976).

To be most useful, such a reevaluation would have to go beyond demonstrating that violation or rejection of the axioms is possible. It would have to give some guidelines as to the prevalence and distribution of violations. Are they just concocted curiosities? Or do they represent modal behavior in some important realms?

Kahneman and Tversky (1979) attempted this sort of reevaluation, presenting evidence for two pervasive violations of SEU theory. One, the "certainty effect," causes consequences, both positive and negative, that are obtained with certainty to be given more weight than uncertain consequences. The Allais paradox may be due to this effect. The second, labeled the "reference effect," leads people to evaluate alternatives relative to a reference point corresponding to their present status, expectation or adaptation level (Helson, 1947, 1959). By altering the reference point, formally equivalent versions of the same decision problem may elicit different preferences. These effects pose serious problems for the validity (prescriptive and descriptive) of SEU approaches. The power of Kahneman and Tversky's theory is its ability to predict responses to decision problems posed in particular ways and, in particular, to predict behavior that is contrary to predictions of the SEU model. It needs, however, to be complemented by a substantive theory regarding the way in which decision questions are posed by nature and interpreted by observers.

AVAILABILITY OF INPUTS

Let us restrict our attention to situations in which people might wish to engage in SEU-like behavior. Doing so means providing (and eventually integrating) lists of feasible options and possible consequences along with assessments of their probabilities and values. One needn't perform these tasks well in order to engage in SEU-like behavior. Poor performance will, however, lead to suboptimal decisions. As the lists become more and more incomplete and the quality of the assessments deteriorates, the resultant decision will tend to deviate from that obtained by the best possible usage of the SEU model.

Thus making decisions not in one's own best interests (as defined by the "best possible" SEU decision) need not mean that the SEU model is an invalid descriptor of what people are doing. Nonetheless, acute inability to provide the inputs required to use the SEU model well must cast some doubts on the extent of its usage. At some point, one must stop and ask, would people persist in doing something they do so poorly? To take an analogous problem, I may realize the essential wisdom of using the 1040 Form for income tax and itemizing my deductions in order to reduce my obligation. If, however, experience shows that I typically do it wrong and land in trouble, I may resort to less complicated decision rules. Whether or not it is reasonable to expect people to persist at suboptimal SEU behavior, rather than opting for some simpler rule, requires consideration of two questions: (1) Just how good or bad are they? and (2) How likely are they to learn about their mistakes? If people both could not perform these tasks and realized their limitations, the SEU model would be a less likely candidate for how people try to make decisions.

What else could people do, besides trying to list and assess the expected consequences of all courses of action open to them? For one, they could try not to think at all, but rely on nonanalytical decision rules like "this is (most like) what I've always done" or "this is what my (most expert) friends tell me to do" or "this is what everyone else is doing." Or they could refuse to make one final decision, preferring to muddle through by trial and error, making small incremental decisions that afford an opportunity to change courses if things aren't going well.

Relying on the collective wisdom of one's own experience (habit) or of one's predecessors' experience (tradition) or of one's peers' current feelings (norms) are all ways of externalizing the problem. Each recruits a number of people to think about issues too complex and poorly understood to analyze alone. Both common wisdom and such au courant techniques as Delphi advocate such thought sharing. One could, of course, consult these sources for opinions that would eventually be used in a personal SEU model. Or one could reject the methodological individualism of SEU decision making in favor of whatever conclusion emerges from these chaotic group processes. Such reliance on group rather than individual "rationality" is well documented in work situations (Salancik & Pfeffer, 1977, 1978; White & Mitchell 1979). Perhaps the best known example is the emergence of group production norms in defiance of piece-work pay schemes.[5]

One of the few exercises in complex and analytic decision making imposed on most people is completion of income tax forms. The success of H & R Block suggests the reluctance of the rest of us to face the challenge.

---

[5]A resolute SEU devotee could still claim that the group had been used to restructure the decision problem offered by management. Adherence to group production norms is actually the result of individual SEU maximizing in the context of the new decision problem that incorporates group action as a new option, group sanctions and collectively attained pay schemes as new consequences, and collective bargaining power as a new fact of life affecting the probabilities of all consequences.

Problem Structuring

Like other analytic approaches, SEU begins with a structuring of the problem, namely listing all relevant options and consequences. The obvious performance standard here is completeness. A modest amount of systematic and anecdotal evidence suggests that people have difficulty independently producing complete problem representations. When asked to judge completeness of problems presented by others, however, they do not seem to be very sensitive to these inadequacies. What is out of sight is effectively out of mind (Fischhoff, Slovic & Lichtenstein, 1977, 1978). Thus in the short run at least, people may not realize this limit on their analytical decision-making ability. In the long run, omitting options and consequences should lead to poor decisions. However, life seldom sends us large enough batches of unambiguous signals to make it clear just how good our decision making is and where the problems lie (Fischhoff, 1975; Einhorn & Hogarth, 1978). Although unrecognized incompleteness seems to be quite general, there presumably are decision problems whose most important features are readily uncovered by people's intuitive procedures. Identifying that set of problems would require the sort of substantive theory of people in situations that has interested E-V researchers.

Assessing Probabilities

A cornerstone of SEU thinking is that we all live in an uncertain world. According to the Bayesian or subjectivist position, that uncertainty reflects the limits of our understanding. From this position, all statements are implicitly or explicitly qualified by our degree of belief in them. Degrees of belief are numerically expressed in subjective probabilities, i.e., expressions with the form "My personal probability that Statement A is true is .XX." Such probabilities are entirely in the eye of the beholder and are not properties of the world. Two observers of a situation can in principle assign different probabilities of being true to the same statement about it, either because they interpret what they see differently or have different background information.

In fact, the whole notion of "objective probability" is confused. Assigning any probability requires some interpretation of the observed situation and that act of interpretation imputes a subjective element. What are commonly thought of as objective probabilities merely refer to situations in which there is consensus among reasonable observers about how to interpret existing evidence. The probability of a fair coin falling on "heads" on its next flip is commonly held to be .5, but that is only because observers agree on how to evaluate past performance and relate it to subsequent performance (e.g., what constitutes an adequate series of independent, equivalent trials). Bayesians do not talk about *estimating* probabilities, which implies that there is something "out there" in the world to be appraised, but of *assessing* probabilities, signifying the evaluation of an internal state.

If probabilities are subjective, does it make any sense to consider their validity? Individual probabilities can almost never be evaluated (except in the case where one says "There is *absolutely* no chance of this statement being wrong" regarding a statement that is, in fact, wrong).

Sets of subjective probabilities may, however, be evaluated according to two criteria. One is consistency with the laws of probability or (internal) coherence (Kyburg & Smokler, 1964). For example, the probabilities assigned to a statement and its complement should total 1.0. The second is "calibration," applicable when the truth of statements is known to the probability assessor. The well-calibrated probability assessor should have more true statements associated with high than with low probabilities. Specifically, XX% of the statements assigned probability .XX should be perceived to be true. That is, if I am well calibrated, 70% of the time when I say "there is a .7 chance of this statement being true," it should be true.

The earliest studies of probability assessment were restricted to situations in which consensus could be reached on "objective" probability values. These experiments used repetitive series of events (like drawing red or blue balls from an urn) and defined probability as relative frequency of occurrence. Research showed that people were quite good at appraising such frequentistic probabilities (Peterson & Beach, 1967).

More recently, the focus of research has turned to how people assign probabilities to statements, including unique events (e.g., Carter will be re-elected), where relative frequency has no meaning. This shift seems to reflect a growing acceptance of the subjectivist position, a feeling that one should study probabilities in their most general form, and a realization that relatively few important events in people's lives are thought of in terms of relative frequency.

Here, performance has been less than outstanding. Experiments using a variety of tasks, response modes and subjects have shown that probability assessments tend to be poorly calibrated (Lichtenstein, Fischhoff & Phillips, 1977). The most common type of error is overconfidence, i.e., people think that they know more than is actually the case. Where observed, this bias seems to be so robust that people are willing to engage in highly disadvantageous bets based on their confidence judgments (Fischhoff, Slovic & Lichtenstein, 1977).

Various forms of incoherence have also been observed, although without any clear indication of their prevalence. For example, Wyer (1974) found that people tend to exaggerate the probability of the conjunction of two events, relative to the probabilities assigned to the two individually. Kahneman and Tversky (1973) found that rather than combining background (base-rate) information with information regarding a particular case, people tend to ignore base-rate probabilities. Slovic, Fischhoff & Lichtenstein (1976) demonstrated situations in which the judged probability of compound events was larger than the probabilities of their constituent events.

It is disturbing that $P(A \cap B)$ should ever be greater than $P(A)$ or $P(B)$, but some notion of prevalence is needed to decide whether the problem is so bad as to indicate either (a) that people would realize their limits and avoid probabilistic thinking or (b) that the quality of people's probabilistic thinking is so poor as to suggest that they seldom engage in it. Such a study of prevalence and extent would have to be accompanied by an analysis of how bad performance would have to be for people to notice. In this context, the folklore of survey research may be instructive. Popular wisdom there holds that one cannot ask for numerical probability assessments from a random sample of the population without getting disturbingly high rates of nonresponse (i.e., over 20%). Regarding detailed verbal statements of probability, the experience of the 1977 Quality of Employment Survey (Quinn & Staines, 1978) is instructive. Pretest work resulted in probability assessments being gathered on a response scale with only two alternatives: "Yes, it is likely" and "No, it is not likely." The test-retest reliability of more detailed verbal probability assessment has been found at times to be surprisingly low ($r = .52 - .56$ for DeLeo & Pritchard, 1974; Lied & Pritchard, 1976). On the other hand, people do seem to have some appreciation of the meaning of probabilistic weather forecasts (Murphy, Lichtenstein, Fischhoff & Winkler, 1980). Perhaps they feel more comfortable with the probability of rain because the event is highly repetitive and their task is passive (listening).

Perhaps the most disturbing aspect of these results for a proponent of SEU descriptive models is not the presence of biases, but the thought processes that seem to underlie both erroneous and accurate probability assessments. Tversky and Kahneman (1974) have proposed that many probabilistic judgments are produced by using rules of thumb or heuristics whose internal logic bears little resemblance to the rules of probability. These are generally effective ways of coping with an uncertain environment that both deny its probabilistic character and preclude learning about some basic phenomena (like regression to the mean). Often they lead to substantially biased judgments and decisions not in the individual's best interest.[6] To the extent that these heuristics capture people's thought processes, they (1) argue strongly against the notion that we are efficient probabilistic functionalists, well-tuned to the uncertain structure of our environment, and (2) even when people do incorporate uncertainty in their decision making, they do so in terms quite different from the formally defined probabilities appearing in SEU models.

Assessing Values

The study of value judgments and their validity by behavioral decision theory researchers has languished relative to the study of probability judgments. The presumed reason for this apparent disinterest is the absence of an acceptable

---

[6]Although Kahneman and Tversky's research has come to be known for its identification of errors, they make no statement about how bad judgment is in general. They focus on errors because there are fewer ways to explain a pattern of errors than a pattern of success and because suboptimal behavior in conditions encouraging optimality suggests deep-seated cognitive tendencies.

criterion by which to evaluate value judgments. Such judgments would seem to be the last redoubt of unaided intuition. Who knows better than an individual what he or she prefers?

Recent research has, however, revived and elaborated a lesson long known to attitude researchers. Subtle changes in how value questions are phrased and responses are elicited can have marked effects on the preferences people express. This lability in value judgments seems to have important implications for both how values are conceptualized and how they are studied.

An article of faith among students of value, choice and attitude judgments is that people have reasonably well-defined opinions regarding the desirability of various events. Although these opinions may not be intuitively formulated in numerical (or even verbal) form, careful questioning can elicit judgments representing people's underlying values. From this stance, elicitation procedures are neutral tools, bias-free channels that translate subjective feelings into scientifically usable expressions. They impose no views on respondents, beyond focusing attention on those value issues of interest to the investigator.

It is by no means obvious, however, that people's values are well defined. Observed test-retest reliabilities in the values of desired outcomes (within situations) have been fairly modest (r = .48, .60 in DeLeo & Pritchard, 1974; Lied & Pritchard, 1976) and remarkably little consistency in the rated valence of outcomes across situations was observed by Muchinsky (1977). Lawler (1971) found wide variations in the importance attached to one central outcome of work, pay, at least partially due to variations in elicitation procedures.

What happens in cases where people do not know, or have difficulty appraising, what they want? Under such circumstances, these procedures may become major forces in shaping the values expressed, or apparently expressed, in the judgments they elicit. They can induce random error (by confusing the respondent), systematic error (by hinting at what the "correct" response is), or unduly extreme judgments (by suggesting clarity and coherence of opinion that are not warranted). In such cases, the method becomes the message, a reflection of the researcher's tools rather than the respondent's wishes.

People are most likely to have clear preferences regarding issues that are familiar, simple, and directly experienced.[7] Each of these properties is associated with opportunities for trial-and-error learning, particularly such learning as may be summarized in readily applicable rules or homilies. Those rules provide stereotypic, easily justifiable responses to future questions of values. When adopted by individuals, they may be seen as habits; when adopted by groups, they constitute traditions.

The power of these rules of thumb for assessing values comes from their development and application to simple and repetitive problems. Their viability

---

[7]For example, Ash, Levine & Edgell (1979) found that the reliability of the rated desirability of attributes increases with respondents' direct experience with the job.

becomes suspect when the issues are unfamiliar and complex, the old intuitions impotent, the old rules untested and perhaps untestable. Unfortunately, these are precisely those situations in which values are worth studying. In them, however, we may never have considered the implications of the values and beliefs acquired in simpler settings. As a result, we may have no articulated preferences. In some fundamental sense, our values may be incoherent, not thought through. In thinking about what are acceptable levels of risk, for example, we may be unfamiliar with the terms in which issues are formulated (e.g., social discount rates, minuscule probabilities, or megadeaths). We may have contradictory values (e.g., a strong aversion to catastrophic losses of life and a realization that we're not more moved by a plane crash with 500 fatalities than one with 300). We may occupy different roles in life (parents, workers, children) that produce clear-cut, but inconsistent values. We may vacillate between incompatible, but strongly held, positions (e.g., freedom of speech is inviolate, but should be denied to authoritarian movements). We may not even know how to begin thinking about some issues (e.g., the appropriate tradeoff between the opportunity to dye one's hair and a vague, minute increase in the probability of cancer 20 years from now). Our views may undergo changes over time (say, as we near the hour of decision or the consequence itself) and we may not know which view should form the basis of our decision.

Such inarticulated preferences are hardly compatible with the sort of rigorous systematic thinking required by SEU decision making. Furthermore, they give pause for thought about just what subjects are giving us when we elicit the values needed to test the conformity of their behavior with the SEU model.

Listing a few specific effects may indicate the power an elicitor may deliberately, or inadvertently, wield in shaping, distorting or even creating expressed preferences. The desirability of possible outcomes is often evaluated in relation to some reference point. That point could be one's current (asset) position, or an expected level of wealth (what someone with my talents should be worth at time t), or that possessed by another person. Shifts in reference point are fairly easily effected and can lead to appreciable shifts in judged desirability, even to reversals in the order of preference. Consider, for example, how one might think about the same safety program conceptualized in terms of lives saved or lives lost, with the respective reference points of the current situation or an ideal one. As one gets closer to an event with mixed consequences, the aversiveness of its negative aspects may increase more rapidly than the attractiveness of its positive aspects, making it appear, on the whole, less desirable than it did from a distance. People may have opposite orders of preference for gambles when asked which they prefer (that focuses their attention on how likely they are to win) and when asked how much they would pay to play each (that highlights the amount to win). People may prefer to take a chance at losing a large sum of money rather than absorb a smaller sure loss, but change their mind when the sure loss is called an insurance premium. A relatively unimportant attribute may become the decisive factor in choosing between a set of options if they are presented in such a way that the attribute affords the easiest comparison between them.

Three important features of these shifting judgments are: (1) people are typically unaware of the potency of such shifts in their perspective; (2) they often have no guidelines as to which perspective is the appropriate one; and (3) even when there are guidelines, people may not want to give up their own inconsistency (Fischhoff, Slovic & Lichtenstein, 1980; Tversky & Kahneman, 1981).

Elicitors must decide at some point whether or not they have adequately captured their respondent's values. The usual criteria are reliability and internal consistency (e.g., transitivity). However, where the task is poorly understood because of complexity or unfamiliarity, consistency of response within a given elicitation mode may tell us little beyond the power of that mode to impose a particular perspective. Consistency of response is a necessary but not sufficient condition for coherence of the underlying values. Greater insight into values may come from posing diverse questions in the hope of eliciting inconsistent responses. Therefore, one would want to start the study of values with methodological pluralism and treat inconsistency in expressed values as a success rather than a failure of measurement, for it indicates contexts defined sharply enough to produce a difference.

If one is interested in how people express their values in the real world, one question may be enough. That world often asks only one question (e.g., in a ballot measure). A careful analysis of how an issue is posed may allow one to identify that question and accurately predict responses.

If one is interested in what people really feel about a value issue, there may be no substitute for an interactive, dialectical elicitation procedure, one that acknowledges the elicitor's role in helping the respondent to create and enunciate values. That help would include a conceptual analysis of the problem and of the personal, social, ethical value issues to which the respondent might wish to relate.[8]

DECISION CONTEXTS

Although behavioral decision theorists have not developed a theory of decision situations to complement their evolving theory of the individual decision maker, they have on occasion attempted to replicate their laboratory studies in the real world. These experiments at roughing it have been prompted by (1) the feeling that decision theory like other areas in applied cognitive psychology should work

---

[8]As an example of the power of the interactive approach to assessing values, Matsui and Ikeda (1976) and Rosenberg (1956) were better able to predict people's decisions when using outcomes generated on the spot by subjects than with a more comprehensive list of outcomes that they, as experimenters, provided.

in the world; (2) the refusal of economists to accept (or even look at) laboratory data; (3) the hope of being able to elaborate their theories by embedding them in a broader context and (4) continued interaction with decision analysts, purveyors of SEU as a normative guide to decision making who are particularly attuned to the subjective quality of judgments of fact and value.

One obvious step in the direction of realism is to use real rather than hypothetical stakes in studies of decision making. A second is to use experts rather than naive subjects. Although available evidence is modest, neither manipulation has so far provided sufficiently dramatic results to cast serious doubt on most of the research conclusions cited above (Fischhoff, in press; Tversky & Kahneman, 1974). A third obvious step, using more realistic stimuli has, it seems, only strengthened conclusions regarding the lability of judgments of value and liabilities of judgments of fact (Lichtenstein et al., 1978; Fischhoff, Slovic & Lichtenstein, 1978).

None of these manipulations, however, leads to the study of actual judgments in situ. Probably the most elaborate excursion of behavioral decision theory into the real world has been a study of disaster insurance protection by Kunreuther et al. (1978). Despite massive investments in flood control projects, flood damage in the U.S. continues to climb. The main reason seems to be the overdevelopment of flood plains caused in part by the flood control projects themselves. By eliminating frequent minor floods, these projects have unduly reduced residents' feeling of flood danger. As a result, when a sufficiently large rain or thaw comes along and overwhelms the project, much more property is exposed. Thus floods are less frequent, but the loss from each is much greater than prior to the project. In order to reduce losses, the U.S. Congress enacted a flood insurance program that mandated land-use planning as the price for making insurance available at highly attractive rates. "Highly attractive" was determined by economists who assumed that residents shared the risk and cost data in the hands of the planners and combined them according to SEU principles. Unfortunately, almost no one bought the insurance.

A national survey of flood-prone areas designed to understand the failure of the program discovered that residents' judgments of risks and costs were very different than those of the experts. Often these misjudgments seemed to have the same roots as the judgmental biases observed in laboratory studies. Obviously, even if residents were SEU decision makers, they could not be expected to behave in the predicted way (i.e., purchase insurance) if they did not share the planners' information base. The design of Kunreuther's study allowed an appraisal of how favorable insurance should be to these individuals given what they thought to be the facts of the matter and assuming that they were SEU decision makers. A straightforward derivation translated attractiveness of insurance into an index R, with higher R values being associated with more attractive insurance situations. Comparison of individuals who had and had not purchased insurance revealed little difference in the distributions of R values. Thus whatever guided insurance purchase decisions, it was not an SEU analysis based on either the "real" (experts') or "imagined" (residents') view of the situation.

What did guide decisions? Kunreuther's best guess was that people relied on a series of informal decision rules like the answers to: Are my neighbors and relatives buying it? What does my insurance agent say? Do I have the capacity to worry about one more thing?

The application of E-V theory to predicting effort and performance in the work place may be considered a prolonged extension of SEU theory into the real world. In an extensive review of this effort, Schwab et al. (1979) found that on the average, only 9% of the variance in effort or performance is explained. Granting that their review considered only between-subject applications of this within-person behavioral choice theory (thereby increasing the amount of error variance), analogous within-person studies rarely explain more than 25% of the variance. Furthermore, with one exception, the few factors that Schwab and his colleagues identify as contributing to better prediction are either not those prescribed by E-V models, or antithetical to them. The authors conclude by noting that:

"Despite these qualifications, there is a nagging suspicion that expectancy theory overintellectualizes the cognitive processes people go through when choosing alternative actions (at least insofar as choosing a level of performance or effort is concerned). The results of the present review are consistent with this suspicion [p. 146]."

More pessimistically, Staw (1977) suggests that ordinary choice behavior is better modeled as "impulse buying" decisions of consumers than on the lines of SEU theory.

Perhaps more revealing than the contexts to which researchers have attempted to extend laboratory results are the contexts that they have avoided. Situations to which they have assumed that results will not generalize may provide an implicit partial theory of the environment. One characteristic of most behavioral decision theory experiments is that every attempt is made to eliminate any temptation for strategic responding. Rather, subjects are rewarded for responding as honestly as they can. However, there obviously are situations where it may pay to lie (e.g., when the boss asks me about my work environment) and they may engender rather different reporting behavior. A second characteristic is the absence of time and emotional pressure creating the sort of "hot cognition" studied by Janis and Mann (1977). A third characteristic is isolation of the individual from social interactions, which may deprive the individual of needed decision-making aids (i.e., talking to others) and foster individualism. A fourth characteristic of most studies is the preclusion of a no-choice or procrastination option (Corbin, 1980).

Each of these characteristics might in principle represent an environmental variable restricting the validity of behavioral decision theory results. Or each might provoke minor perturbations like the use of real stakes or the shift from naive to expert subjects.

CONCLUSION

The story of SEU research has in some senses been a tale of deadends and hard-earned lessons. An enormous amount of effort was devoted to "capturing" decision strategies before it was realized that the power of linear models virtually precluded learning what weights individuals were giving to different attributes or if they were using an SEU decision rule at all. Many studies of how people estimate relative frequencies were conducted before researchers realized that whatever their intrinsic interest such tasks were not particularly relevant to the sort of uncertainty in most decision situations. For years, researchers derived satisfaction from the elicitation of consistent, reliable value judgments, before beginning to worry that such orderliness was a product of their methods. Being rational individuals, decision scientists have repeatedly assumed that the inherent reasonableness of the SEU model would make it an acceptable normative guide to decision making. Those who doubted the model have naively felt that showing spot inconsistencies or rejection of axioms would cause the model to keel over.

Having disabused ourselves of these particular illusions, where do we go from here? Obviously, we should have better respect for the power of our methodology to produce orderly but misleading results. Substantively, we should begin to develop an understanding of decision environments that will enable us to understand how general laboratory results are and how far reaching their effects (Ebbesen & Konecni, 1980; Howell & Burnett, 1978). One key component of this understanding is an error theory explicating the implications of poorly structuring decisions, assessing probabilities and values, and combining the various components. The sensitivity of our decisions and their consequences to deviations from optimality will clarify which principles of decision making need to be and can be learned from experience (Einhorn & Hogarth, 1978; Fischhoff, 1980a, b).

Theoretically, we need to go beyond simply trying to falsify SEU theory; if only because of the power of linear models, it will typically provide at least mediocre predictions. Instead, we need to move on to sophisticated falsification (Lakatos, 1970), finding theories that do what SEU does and at least a little more. The shape of those theories might be new decision calculi with different primitives and combinations rules, like Kahneman and Tversky's Prospect Theory (1979); or process-tracing models that attempt to treat not only input-output relationships, but also the intervening thought processes (Payne, Braunstein & Carroll, 1978; Svenson, 1979); or contingency-based models that preserve some of the SEU logic but also incorporate a theory of the environment and the way that it is sequentially decomposed (Beach & Mitchell, 1978); or inventories of the rules of thumb that people use to supplement or replace analytical decision making (Kunreuther et al., 1978); or predictions of how the habits ingrained from making repetitive decisions with an opportunity for trial-and-error learning lead one astray when one must make analytic decisions and get them right the first time.

REFERENCES

Anderson, N. H. Progress is cognitive algebra. In L. Berkowitz (Ed.), *Cognitive theories in social psychology*. New York: Academic Press, 1978.

Ash, R. A., Levine, E. L., & Edgell, S. L. Exploratory study of a matching approach to personnel selection: The impact of ethnicity. *Journal of Applied Psychology*, 1979, *64*, 35–41.

Atkinson, J., & Feather, N. (Eds.). *A theory of achievement motivation*. New York: Wiley, 1966.

Baddeley, A. D. *Applied cognitive and cognitive applied psychology: The case of face recognition.* Paper presented at Uppsala Conference on Memory, June 1977.

Beach, L. R., & Mitchell, T. R. A contingency model for the selection of decision strategies. *Academy of Management Review*, 1978, *3*, 439–449.

Brunswik, E. *The conceptual framework of psychology*. Chicago: University of Chicago Press, 1952.

Coombs, C. H., Dawes, R. M., & Tversky, A. *Mathematical psychology: An elementary introduction*. Englewood Cliffs, N.J.: Prentice-Hall, 1970.

Corbin, R. M. A theory of choice should not be based on choice alone. In T. Wallsten (Ed.), *Cognitive processes in choice and decision behavior*. Hillsdale, N.J.: Lawrence Erlbaum Associates, 1980.

Davidshofer, L. O. Risk-taking and vocational choice: A reevaluation. *Journal of Counseling Psychology*, 1976, *23*, 151–154.

Dawes, R. M. The robust beauty of improper linear models. *American Psychologist*, 1979, *34*, 571–582.

Dawes, R. M., & Corrigan, B. Linear models in decision making. *Psychological Bulletin*, 1974, *81*, 2, 95–106.

Deci, E. L. *Intrinsic motivation*. New York: Plenum, 1975.

DeLeo, P. J., & Pritchard, R. D. An examination of some methodological problems in testing expectancy-valence models with survey techniques. *Organizational Behavior and Human Performance*, 1974, *12*, 143–148.

Ebbesen, E. B., & Konecni, V. J. On the external validity of decision making research. In T. Wallsten (Ed.), *Cognitive processes in choice and decision making*. Hillsdale, N.J.: Lawrence Erlbaum Associates, 1980.

Edwards, W. The theory of decision making. *Psychological Bulletin*, 1954, *51*, 380–417.

Edwards, W. Behavioral decision theory. *Annual Review of Psychology*, 1961, *12*, 473–498.

Einhorn, H. J. Use of nonlinear, noncompensatory models as a function of task and amount of information. *Organizational Behavior and Human Performance*, 1971, *6*, 1–27.

Einhorn, H. J., & Hogarth, R. Confidence in judgment: Persistence of the illusion of validity. *Psychological Review*, 1978, *85*, 395–416.

Fischhoff, B. Clinical decision analysis. *Operations Research* (issue devoted to decision analysis), 1980, *28*, 28–43. (a)

Fischhoff, B. For those condemned to study the past: Reflections on historical judgment. In R. A. Schweder & D. W. Fiske (Eds.), *New directions for methodology of behavior science: Fallible judgment in behavioral research*. San Francisco: Jossey-Bass, 1980. (b)

Fischhoff, B. Debiasing. In D. Kahneman, P. Slovic & A. Tversky (Eds.) *Judgment under uncertainty: Heuristics & Biases*, New York: Cambridge University Press, in press.

Fischhoff, B. Hindsight ≠ foresight: The effect of outcome knowledge on judgment under uncertainty. *Journal of Experimental Psychology: Human Perception and Performance*, 1975, *1*, 288–299.

Fischhoff, B., Slovic, P., & Lichtenstein, S. Knowing with certainty: The appropriateness of extreme confidence. *Journal of Experimental Psychology: Human Perception and Performance*, 1977, *3*, 552–564.

Fischhoff, B., Slovic, P., & Lichtenstein, S. Fault trees: Sensitivity of estimated failure probabilities to problem representation. *Journal of Experimental Psychology: Human Perception and Performance*, 1978, *4*, 342–355.

Fischhoff, B., Slovic, P., & Lichtenstein, S. Knowing what you want: Measuring labile values. In T. Wallsten (Ed.), *Cognitive processes in choice and decision behavior*. Hillsdale, N.J.: Lawrence Erlbaum Associates, 1980.

Goldberg, L. R. Simple models or simple processes? Some research on clinical judgments. *American Psychologist*, 1968, *23*, 483–496.

Goldberg, L. R. Man versus model of man: A rationale, plus some evidence, for a method of improving on clinical inferences. *Psychological Bulletin*, 1970, *73*, 422–432.

Goldberg, L. R. Objective diagnostic tests and measures. *Annual Review of Psychology*, 1974, *25*, 343–366.

Hammond, K. R. (Ed.). *The psychology of Egon Brunswik*. New York: Holt, Rinehart & Winston, 1966.

Helson, H. Adaptation level as frame of reference for prediction of psychophysical data. *American Journal of Psychology*, 1947, *60*, 1–29.

Helson, H. Adaptation level theory. In S. Koch (Ed.), *Psychology: A study of a science* (Vol. 1). New York: McGraw-Hill, 1959.

Hoffman, P. J. The paramorphic representation of clinical judgment. *Psychological Bulletin*, 1960, *47*, 116–131.

Howell, W. C., & Burnett, S. A. Uncertainty measurement: A cognitive taxonomy. *Organizational Behavior and Human Performance*, 1978, *22*, 45–68.

Janis, I. & Mann, L. *Decision making*. New York: The Free Press, 1977.

Kahneman, D., & Tversky, A. On the psychology of prediction. *Psychological Review*, 1973, *80*, 237–251.

Kahneman, D., & Tversky, A. Prospect theory. *Econometrica*, 1979, *47*, 263–291.

Kunreuther, H., Ginsberg, R., Miller, L., Sagi, P., Slovic, P., Borkan, B., & Katz, N. *Disaster insurance protection: Public policy lessons*. New York: Wiley Interscience, 1978.

Kyburg, H. E., Jr., & Smokler, H. E. *Studies in subjective probability*. New York: Wiley, 1964.

Lakatos, I. Falsification and the methodology of scientific research programmes. In I. Lakatos & A. Musgrave (Eds.), *Criticism and the growth of knowledge*. London: Cambridge University Press, 1970.

Lawler, F. E., III. *Pay and organizational effectiveness: A psychological view*. New York: McGraw-Hill, 1971.

Lichtenstein, S., Fischhoff, B., & Phillips, L. D. Calibration of probabilities: The state of the art. In H. Jungermann & G. de Zeeuw (Eds.), *Decision making and change in human affairs*. Amsterdam: D. Reidel, 1977.

Lichtenstein, S., Slovic, P., Fischhoff, B., Layman, M., & Combs, B. Judged frequency of lethal events. *Journal of Experimental Psychology: Human Learning and Memory, 1978, 4*, 551–578.

Lichtenstein, S., Slovic, P., & Zink, D. Effect of instruction in expected value on optimality of gambling decisions. *Journal of Experimental Psychology*, 1969, *79*, 236–240.

Lied, T. R., & Pritchard, R. D. Relationships between personality variables and components of the expectancy-valence model. *Journal of Applied Psychology*, 1976, *61*, 463–467.

MacCrimmon, K. R. Descriptive and normative implications of the decision theory postulates. In K. Borch & J. Mossin (Eds.), *Risk and uncertainty*. New York: St. Martin's, 1968.

MacCrimmon, K. R., & Larsson, S. Utility theory: Axioms vs. "paradoxes." In M. Allais & O. Hagen, (Eds.), *Rational decisions under uncertainty*, special volume of *Theory and decision*. Dordrecht, The Netherlands: D. Reidel, 1976.

March, J. G. Bounded rationality, ambiguity and the engineering of choice. *Bell Journal of Economics*, 1978, *9*, 587-608.

Matsui, T., & Ikeda, H. Effectiveness of self-generated outcomes for improving predictions in expectancy theory research. *Organizational Behavior and Human Performance*, 1976, *17*, 289-298.

Miller, G. A. The magical number seven, plus or minus two: Some limits on our capacity for processing information. *Psychological Review*, 1956, *63*, 81-97.

Moskowitz, H. Effects of problem representation and feedback on rational behavior in Allais and Morlat-type problems. *Decision Science*, 1974, *5*, 225-242.

Muchinsky, P. M. The consistency of intrasubject valence and instrumentality measures: A methodological consideration. *Academy of Management Journal*, 1977, *20*, 321-327.

Murphy, A., Lichtenstein, S., Fischhoff, B., & Winkler, R. L. Misinterpretations of precipitation probability forecasts. *Bulletin of The American Meteorological Society*, 1980, *61*, 695-701.

Payne, J. S., Braunstein, M. L., & Carroll, J. S. Exploring pre-decisional behavior: An alternative approach to decision research. *Organizational Behavior and Human Performance*, 1978, *22*, 17-44.

Peterson, C. R., & Beach, L. R. Man as an intuitive statistician. *Psychological Bulletin*, 1967, *68*, 29-46.

Quinn, R. P., & Staines, G. L. *The 1977 quality of employment survey*. Ann Arbor, Michigan: Institute for Social Research, University of Michigan, 1978.

Rosenberg, J. Cognitive structure and attitudinal affect. *Journal of Abnormal and Social Psychology*, 1956, *53*, 367-372.

Salancik, G., & Pfeffer, J. An examination of need-satisfaction models of job attitudes. *Administrative Science Quarterly*, 1977, *22*, 427-456.

Salancik, G., & Pfeffer, J. A social information-processing approach to job attitudes and task design. *Administrative Science Quarterly*, 1978, *23*, 224-253.

Schwab, D. P., Olian-Gottlieb, J. D., & Heneman, H. G., III. Between-subjects expectancy theory research: A statistical review of studies predicting effort and performance. *Psychological Bulletin*, 1979, *86*, 139-147.

Simon, H. A. *Models of Man*. New York: Wiley, 1957.

Slovic, P. Analyzing the expert judge: A descriptive study of a stockbroker's decision processes. *Journal of Applied Psychology*, 1969, *53*, 255-263.

Slovic, P. Hypothesis testing in the learning of positive and negative linear functions. *Organizational Behavior and Human Performance*, 1974, *11*, 368-376.

Slovic, P., Fischhoff, B., & Lichtenstein, S. Cognitive processes and societal risk taking. In J. S. Carroll & J. W. Payne (Eds.), *Cognition and social behavior*. Potomac, Md.: Lawrence Erlbaum Associates, 1976.

Slovic, P., Fischhoff, B., & Lichtenstein, S. Rating the risks. *Environment*, 1979, *21*(4), 14-20, 36-39.

Slovic, P., & Lichtenstein, S. Comparison of Bayesian and regression approaches to the study of information processing in judgment. *Organizational Behavior and Human Performance*, 1971, *6*, 458-479.

Slovic, P., & Tversky, A. Who accepts Savage's axiom? *Behavioral Science*, 1974, *10*, 368-373.

Staw, B. M. Motivation from the bottom up. In B. M. Staw (Ed.), *Psychological foundations of organizational behavior*. Santa Monica, Calif.: Goodyear, 1977.

Svenson, O. Process descriptions of decision making. *Organizational Behavior and Human Performance*, 1979, *23*, 86-112.

Tversky, A. Intransitivity of preferences. *Psychological Review*, 1969, *76*, 31-48.

Tversky, A., & Kahneman, D. Judgment under uncertainty: Heuristics and biases. *Science*, 1974, *185*, 1124–1131.

Tversky, A., & Kahneman, D. The framing of decisions and the rationality of choice. *Science*, 1981, *211*, 453–458.

Wallsten, T. S. Subjective expected utility theory and subjects' probability estimates: Use of measurement-free techniques. *Journal of Experimental Psychology*, 1971, *88*, 31–40.

White, S. E., & Mitchell, T. R. Job enrichment versus social cues: A comparison and competitive test. *Journal of Applied Psychology*, 1979, *64*, 1–9.

Wilks, S. S. Weighting systems for linear functions of correlated variables when there is no dependent variable. *Psychometrika*, 1938, *3*, 23–40.

Wright, G. N., & Phillips, L. D. Personality and probabilistic thinking. *British Journal of Psychology*, in press.

Wright, P. Feeding the information eaters: Suggestions for integrating pure and applied research on language comprehension. *Instructional Science*, 1978, *7*, 249–312.

Wyer, R. S. *Cognitive organization and change: An information processing approach*. Potomac, Md.: Lawrence Erlbaum Associates, 1974.

Zagorski, M. A. Risky decision: Attention effects or masking effects? *Acta Psychologica*, 1975, *39*, 487–494.

12 Conflict Theory of Decision Making and the Expectancy-Value Approach

Leon Mann
The Flinders University of South Australia

Irving Janis
Yale University

The conflict model of decision making (Janis & Mann, 1968, 1977) is primarily concerned with identifying factors that determine the major modes of resolving conflicts. It describes how the psychological stress of decisional conflict affects the ways in which people go about making their choices. Unlike expectancy-value models, it does not attempt to predict which choice alternative is selected.

Development of the conflict model owes a great deal to the ideas and concepts of a number of scholars who were prominent in formulating the expectancy-value approach to motivation and action. The conflict model draws on the work of Tolman (1938) who introduced the concept of cognitive expectations about consequences of action. The model has also been influenced by Kurt Lewin's (1951) pioneering studies, in particular his work on types of conflict, the concept of commitment, and the way in which positive and negative valences influence action. Both Tolman and Lewin emphasized the vital role of expectations about the consequences of an action.

We also recognize the compatibility of the conflict formulation with elaborations of expectancy theory in relation to achievement motivation (Atkinson & Raynor, 1974) and to problems of occupational choice, job satisfaction and organizational behavior (Vroom, 1964; Mitchell & Beach, 1977; Porter & Lawler, 1968). Our formulation is consistent with some of the basic assumptions of Ward Edwards' (1961) analysis of subjectively expected utility of alternative courses of action (the SEU model) as applied to economic decisions. However, despite a common intellectual ancestry and familial compatibility, the expectancy-value models and the conflict model have not had much impact on each other; indeed, the respective theorists barely refer to each other. Probably this is because the main problems to which expectancy theorists have applied their concepts are different from those with which our conflict theory is primarily concerned, namely, identifying factors that determine how people carry out the tasks of decision making and how they resolve decisional conflicts.

Our contribution to this volume is intended to examine the conflict model for the purpose of indicating in what respects it converges with and departs from the traditional expectancy-value theory in decision making. We shall try to show how the concept of expectancy is used quite broadly in conflict theory, and then explore how the two models might be combined in order to address problems of common interest.

CONFLICT THEORY: A MODEL OF DECISIONAL STRESS

Conflict theory offers a general theory of decision *making,* not a theory of choice behavior. It is concerned with *how* human beings arrive at the key consequential choices of living and working, but not with predicting the actual choices they make. Earlier versions of the model (Janis, 1958; Janis & Mann, 1968) dealt with components of decisional conflict using a balance sheet schema and described the stages in decision making. Our most recent formulations (Janis & Mann, 1977) draw heavily on the psychology of stress. The theory views behavior as goal-directed. People work toward pleasurable states and they avoid unpleasurable ones. These goals include obtaining desirable outcomes for oneself and for loved ones, social approval, and self-approval. Conflict arises when all of the available alternatives in a decisional choice are seen as uncertain means for attaining such goals or as leading to potential failures to attain one or another of the goals. We assume that decisional conflicts evoke stress in the decision maker. The distinct patterns of coping behavior associated with handling the stress of decision making is the core of the theory. When decision makers display one particular coping pattern, which we label as "vigilance", they respond in a manner broadly comparable to the "rational" decision maker postulated by decision theorists. But not when they resort to other coping patterns. If, for example, their coping pattern is "defensive avoidance", they are more intent on avoiding having to choose (through procrastinating, buck-passing, or rationalizing) than on searching for and weighing alternatives.[1]

---

[1]Our emphasis on psychological stress as a major cause of error in decision making does not imply denial of other causes of error—information overload and the limitations of information processing, blinding prejudice and ignorance, faulty heuristics, group pressures, organizational constraints, bureaucratic politics, etc. (Carroll & Payne, 1976; Janis, 1972; Nisbett & Ross, 1979; Simon, 1976; Tversky & Kahneman, 1974).

Role of Expectancy in Conflict Theory

Although expectancy is not a key concept in our conflict-theory formulations, it enters into our analysis in several crucial places. We assume that certain kinds of expectancies are:

1. Sources of stress arising from decisional conflict.
2. Determinants of decisional coping patterns.
3. Components of the decisional balance sheet.
4. Incentives for efforts to prevent the loss of choice alternatives.

Expectancy and the Sources of Stress

Central to the conflict model is the assumption that the prospect of consequential choice is stress producing. The act of decision is viewed as a form of conflict resolution. Psychological stress arising from decisional conflict stems from two principal sources. First, the decision-maker is concerned about the material and social losses he might suffer from whichever course of action he chooses—including the costs of failing to live up to prior commitments. Second, he recognizes that his reputation and self esteem as a competent decision-maker are at stake. The distinction between the two sources of stress is potentially important. The first source of stress relates to expected gains and losses *intrinsic* to the choice alternatives themselves. The second source of stress relates to the *generalized* expectation that the decision as a whole—how one goes about making it as well as its outcome—could prove to be satisfying or damaging. We see then, that the concept of expectancy is implicit in conflict theory.

Most of the conflict-theory propositions pertain to situational factors that affect the expectancies that give rise to decisional conflict and that determine the coping patterns. The theory also has some implications for individual differences among decision makers.

Individuals differ in their competence and confidence as decision makers. On the basis of their past experiences and opportunities, some develop generalized expectations that most, if not all, of their decisions will turn out well. Others, with a chronically low level of self esteem, expect failure in almost every decision they make. For people who have rigidly negative expectations, the usual warnings about the prospects of a decision going wrong will not necessarily produce the changes in patterns of conflict resolution specified by the conflict model. Persons with chronically low self esteem have a higher threshold of responsiveness to information that would induce confidence and vigilance in others. We hold that the conflict-theory propositions about the influence of situational factors are applicable to all persons who seek to avert stress and to exercise control over their decision making. There are wide individual differences in stress tolerance and motivation to exercise control; thus the situational factors that readily produce a specified pattern of conflict resolution in some decision makers may have to be quite extreme before others are induced to use the same pattern.

Expectancy as a Determinant of Decisional Coping Pattern

We postulate that there are five basic patterns of coping with challenges that are capable of generating stress by posing agonizingly difficult choices. Each pattern is associated with a specific set of antecedent conditions and a characteristic level of stress. These patterns are derived from an analysis of the research literature on psychological stress bearing on how people react to health and disaster-related warnings.

The five coping patterns are:

1. *Unconflicted adherence*. The decision maker complacently decides to continue whatever he or she has been doing, which may involve discounting information about risk of losses.

2. *Unconflicted change* to a new course of action. The decision maker uncritically adopts whichever new course of action is most salient or most strongly recommended.

3. *Defensive avoidance*. The decision maker escapes the conflict by procrastinating, shifting responsibility to someone else, or constructing wishful rationalizations to bolster the least objectionable alternative, remaining selectively inattentive to corrective information.[2]

4. *Hypervigilance*. The decision maker searches frantically for a way out of the dilemma and impulsively seizes upon a hastily contrived solution that seems to promise immediate relief. The full range of consequences of the choice are overlooked as a result of emotional excitement, perseveration, and cognitive constriction (manifested by reduction in immediate memory span and simplistic thinking). In its most extreme form, hypervigilance is known as "panic."

---

[2]A subsidiary analysis ties the cause of decisional stress to the preferred mode of defensive avoidance. If the decision maker is primarily concerned with his or her *reputation* as a decision maker, then either procrastination or shifting responsibility to someone else are the preferred modes of coping, because they enable the person to avoid having to make a decision or take responsibility for it. If, on the other hand, the decision maker is mainly concerned with the magnitude or probability of losses associated with the choice alternatives, then bolstering the least objectionable alternative by means of rationalizations is the preferred mode, because this enables the person to minimize the probability and magnitude of the expected losses. In general, however, we would expect the defensive avoidant decision maker to favor a low-effort coping pattern, such as procrastination or shifting responsibility, rather than a high-effort pattern such as rationalization, that requires time and effort.

5. *Vigilance*. The decision maker searches painstakingly for relevant information, assimilates information in an unbiased manner, and appraises alternatives carefully before making a choice.

Although the first two patterns are occasionally adaptive in saving time, effort, and emotional wear and tear, especially for routine or minor decisions, they often lead to defective decision making if the person must select a course of action that has serious consequences for himself, for his family, or for the organization whose policies he is determining. Similarly, defensive avoidance and hypervigilance may occasionally be adaptive but generally reduce the decision-maker's chances of averting serious losses. Consequently, all four are regarded as defective patterns of decision making. The fifth pattern, vigilance, although occasionally maladaptive if danger is imminent and a split-second response is required, leads to decisions that meet the main criteria for high-quality decision making.

The five coping patterns are represented in Fig. 12.1, which is a schematic summary of the conflict theory of decision making. This conflict model specifies the psychological conditions responsible for the five coping patterns.

The coping patterns are determined by the presence or absence of three conditions involving expectancies: (1) expectations of serious risks for whichever alternative is chosen (i.e., arousal of conflict); (2) hopeful or optimistic expectations about finding a better alternative; and (3) expectations of adequate time in which to search and deliberate before a decision is required. We assume that all five coping patterns are in the repertoire of every person when he or she functions as a decision maker and that the use of one pattern rather than another is determined by the mediating psychological conditions shown in Fig. 12.1.

What is unique about the model is the specification of conditions relating to expectancies that determine conflict, hope, and time pressure, that mediate the distinctive coping patterns. We do not claim that the five patterns occur only as a result of the specified conditions. A habitual procrastinator, for example, may almost invariably approach any decision, large or small, in a defensive manner. A flexible person may display vigilance in response to most threats but become hyper vigilant each time a situation is encountered in which he or she had once been traumatized. Our claim is that the patterns are linked dependably with the conditions specified in Fig. 12.1—a claim that has testable implications about environmental circumstances that generate vigilance and about deliberate interventions that would counteract the expectations responsible for defective coping patterns. It follows from this theoretical analysis that information inputs and special intervention procedures can modify the way people cope with the stresses of decisional conflict. A number of testable implications of the model have been investigated and at least partially confirmed concerning the conditions that determine whether information search is cursory or thorough, whether deliberations

ANTECEDENT CONDITIONS   MEDIATING PROCESSES   CONSEQUENCES

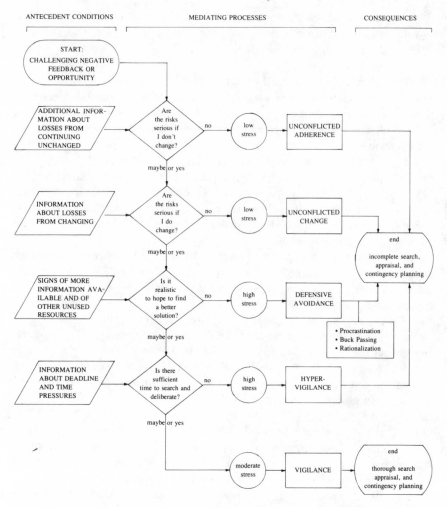

FIG. 12.1.   The conflict-theory model of decision making. (After Janis & Mann, 1977).

are biased or unbiased, and whether adherence to decisions is short-lived or persistent (see Janis & Mann, 1977, Chapters 4–14).

The conflict model consists of a set of interrelated hypotheses, derived from what is known about the antecedents and consequences of psychological stress. These hypotheses can be used to explain why people confronted with a choice dilemma frequently fail to make use of the resources available to them for engaging in effective search for and appraisal of alternatives—within the limits of their cognitive capabilities and within the limits imposed by powerful social constraints—with the result that they subsequently end up suffering severe losses that could have been averted. The model appears to be compatible with Herbert Simon's (1967) analysis of the role of motivation and emotion in controlling cognitive behavior. Drawing on concepts formulated by cognitive psychologists, Simon (1967), views man as "a basically serial information processor endowed with multiple needs (who usually) behaves adaptively and survives in an environment that presents unpredictable threats and opportunities [p. 39]." He conceptualizes the arousal of anxiety or any other unpleasant emotion as an interruption mechanism that allows the processor to respond adaptively to urgent needs. But he also emphasizes that when emotional arousal is extremely intense and persistent, it becomes disruptive and produces nonadaptive behavior. Our theory attempts to specify the contrasting conditions that determine whether the stress engendered by decisional conflict will facilitate or interfere with effective search for and appraisal of alternative courses of action.

Figure 12.1 shows the linkages between the conditions that produce conflict, the mediating expectancies, the level of stress generated, and the coping pattern adopted. The intensity of stress is related to the coping pattern: extremely low stress and extremely intense stress are likely to give rise to defective patterns, whereas intermediate levels are more likely to be associated with vigilant information-processing. We assume, then, a curvilinear nonmonotonic relationship between magnitude of stress and quality of decision making, like the relationship that has been described for emotional arousal and responsiveness to persuasive communications (Janis, 1967; McGuire, 1969).

In fine, not all stress is disruptive to decision making. A moderate degree of stress in response to a dilemma is optimal in that it motivates the person to think about the decision and to search for new information. When the decision maker experiences very little conflict, his level of stress is so low that he is unmotivated to give careful attention to the problem. When the decision maker experiences severe decisional conflict, the level of stress is so high that thought processes are disrupted: Immediate memory span is reduced, thinking becomes simplistic, fewer judgment categories are considered. We would expect a person in severe decisional conflict to fail miserably to assimilate and combine information relating to outcome expectancies and values.

Information-processing

The conflict model of decisional stress adopts an information-processing perspective, which emphasizes the responses made to challenging new information as well as the adequacy of information-processing characteristic of each coping pattern. But the kind of information-processing described by conflict theory is different from that examined by expectancy-value theorists. The expectancy-value model as a descriptive theory assumes that the only important information-processing involved in decision making is limited to the comparison of the expected values of alternative courses of action. These expected values are computed (perhaps not consciously) from the person's subjective estimate of the probability and utility of each possible outcome. A pertinent example is given in CRM *Psychology Today* (1975), p. 363.

> A door to door salesman stands at the gate of a house and reflects on the huge dog dozing inside the fence. The salesman considers the consequences of making a move onto the property. He estimates the probability of receiving a friendly reception from the householder is .90 and the utility value of that is 50, yielding an expected value of 45. But the probability of being attacked by the dog is .10 and the utility value of having his body savaged and clothes torn is −500 (an expected value of .10 × −500 = −50). Accordingly, a comparison of the expected values (45 versus −50) prompts him to decide he ought to forget that house and try next door.

Note how the information processing assumed by the expectancy-value model of decision making differs from that implied by conflict theory. Conflict theory specifies the distinctly different types of information-processing associated with each of the five coping patterns (see Table 12.1). From the standpoint of high-quality problem solving, the most adequate kind of information-processing is associated with the vigilance coping pattern. The vigilant decision-maker (1) thoroughly canvasses a wide range of alternative courses of action; (2) takes account of the full range of objectives to be fulfilled and the values implicated by the choice; (3) carefully weighs whatever he or she knows about the costs or drawbacks and the uncertain risks of negative consequences, as well as the positive consequences, that could flow from each alternative; (4) intensively searches for new information relevant for further evaluation of the alternatives; (5) conscientiously takes account of any new information or expert judgment to which he or she is exposed, even when the information or judgment does not support the course of action he or she initially prefers; (6) reexamines the positive and negative consequences of all known alternatives, including those originally regarded as unacceptable, before making a final choice; and (7) makes detailed provisions for implementing or executing the chosen course of action, with special attention to contingency plans that might be required if various known risks were to materialize. These activities are more comprehensive than the cognitive activities postulated by expectancy-value models, which essentially confine their attention to taking account of objectives and values and the weighing of consequences (activities 2 and 3 above).

Expectancy-value theory says little about such vital decisional behavior as the search for information and its assimilation, the formulation of new alternatives (including compromise solutions and refusal to make a choice) and the planning for implementation and contingencies. For this reason, we consider expectancy-value theory a model of choice (based upon a prescriptive or normative rule) rather than a comprehensive descriptive theory of decision making.

TABLE 12.1

Predecisional Behavior Characteristics of the Five Basic Patterns of Decision Making[a]

Pattern of Coping with Challenge	*Criteria for High-Quality Decision Making*							
	(1) Thorough Canvassing of Alternatives	(2) Thorough Canvassing of Objectives	(3) Careful Evaluation of Consequences of		(4) Thorough Search for Information	(5) Unbiased Assimilation of New Information	(6) Careful Reevaluation of Consequences	(7) Thorough Planning for Implementation and Contingencies
			a. Current Policy	b. Alternative New Policies				
Unconflicted adherence	NO	NO	NO	NO	NO	YES	NO	NO
Unconflicted change	NO	NO	YES	NO	NO	YES	NO	NO
Defensive avoidance	NO	NO	NO	NO	NO	NO	NO	NO
Hypervigilance	NO	NO	VARIES	VARIES	VARIES	NO	NO	NO
Vigilance	YES	YES	YES	YES	YES	YES	YES	YES

[a]From Janis and Mann 1977.

NO = The decision maker fails to meet the criterion.

YES = The decision maker meets the criterion to the best of his or her ability.

VARIES = The decision maker's performance fluctuates, sometimes meeting the criterion to the best of his or her ability and sometimes not.

All evaluation terms such as *thorough* and *unbiased* are to be understood as intrapersonal comparative assessments, relative to the person's highest possible level of cognitive performance.

Evidence for Conflict Theory

The conflict model is intended for decisions that have real consequences for the decision maker and thereby can generate some manifestations of stress. The model is not necessarily applicable to the simulated or hypothetical decisions so often investigated in the laboratory. Laboratory research seldom elicits the *hot* cognitions (emotionally arousing thoughts and judgments) that are generated by consequential decisions. We assume that a person who is acutely conflicted about a decision will exhibit very different information processing from that displayed when the same judgment is approached on a purely hypothetical basis.

A number of investigations have shown that when people face a consequential choice they often react in an entirely different way than when they confront the same problem as a purely hypothetical issue or intellectual exercise (e.g., Lanzetta, 1963; Sieber, 1974; Taylor, 1975). An example is provided by Taylor's (1975) study, in which young women were required to rate the attractiveness of young men. The purpose of the study was to determine how their ratings were affected when they were told that they had shown signs of strong physiological arousal while they were looking at the photograph of one particular man. Among the women who had to make a consequential decision about the young man, viz. whether to meet with him at a social gathering, the effect was a decrease in attraction toward him. But among women who were given the problem as a purely hypothetical exercise, with no consequences attached to their choice, the effect was an *increase* in attraction toward the man. Taylor's findings support our assumption that attitudinal and evaluational changes that accompany real-life decisions may be quite dissimilar from those that accompany hypothetical or trivial choices in the laboratory. Accordingly, we are extremely cautious about drawing any inferences about actual decision-making behavior from the large number of experiments, many of them conducted under the rubric of expectancy-value principles, that rely on purely hypothetical issues or revolve around inconsequential games and gambles in the laboratory.

Lynch and Cohen (1978) note that almost all research directly testing the implications of an SEU approach has involved gambling behavior, with few direct applications to other behavioral domains. One of the major reasons for the lack of discourse between conflict theory and the SEU model is the nature of the evidence preferred by the two theories. However, we note with interest the growing tendency for SEU theorists to apply their formulation to significant decisional problems capable of eliciting 'hot' cognitions, such as cigarette smoking (Mausner, 1973), occupational choice (Mitchell & Beach, 1977) and birth control (Beach, et al, 1976). This trend will undoubtedly lead to an increase in discourse about points of agreement and disagreement in interpretations of the findings.

Evidence in support of conflict theory is to be found in studies showing that under conditions predictive of defensive avoidance decision makers will tend to bolster or rationalize alternatives (Mann, Janis & Chaplin, 1969) and that under conditions predictive of vigilance decision makers will display high interest in supportive and nonsupportive information (Janis & Rausch, 1970). Indirect evidence in support of the theory has also been obtained from field experiments of decision counselling techniques designed to counteract defensive avoidance and promote vigilance (e.g., Mann, 1972; Hoyt & Janis, 1975; Langer, Janis & Wolfer, 1975).

Vigilance: The "Expected Information" Hypothesis

According to the conflict-theory model, distortion of expectancies and utilities relating to choice alternatives can occur before as well as after a decision is made. Individuals who are highly conflicted but have no means of selecting between alternatives will often resolve the conflict by seizing on one alternative and bolstering it. They invent rationalizations and use various defensive avoidance tactics, e.g., exaggerating favorable consequences and minimizing unfavorable consequences in order to "spread" the alternatives. In contrast, when the same individuals are led to believe that there is a possibility of obtaining new relevant information right up to the time of making a choice, they will show little or no tendency to distort or spread the alternatives. This "expected information" hypothesis was tested by Mann, Janis & Chaplin (1969), with female students who were told that the study had to do with the effect of unpleasant physiological stimulation on the ability to carry out intellectual tasks. They were given a choice between noxious taste and noise stimulation after being informed that each might possibly produce temporary side effects such as nausea, dizziness, headaches, and other disagreeable symptoms. In the "expected information" condition the experimenter told randomly assigned subjects that factual reports about the percentage of people suffering side effects from the different stimulations would be provided later on. In a contrasting "no additional information" condition, subjects were told that, regrettably, no such information would be available. Before and after these statements were made, the experimenter obtained ratings of the subjects' feelings about the two stimulations. After the second predecisional rating, the experimenter announced to subjects in both experimental conditions that the meager information in her files showed that the same small number of people had suffered side effects from the two stimulations. Each subject was then asked to state her actual choice.

The results supported the "expected information" hypothesis. When the subjects were led to expect no additional information bearing on the decision, they tended to bolster the least objectionable alternative, thus spreading the attractiveness ratings of the two choice alternatives. But when the subjects were led to expect more information relevant to the decision, there was virtually no tendency to bolster.

Mann et al's experiment illustrates one of the conditions that leads to systematic distortion in the evaluation of choice alternatives. When decision makers are highly conflicted and have little or no expectation of finding a satisfactory solution, they tend to bolster the least objectionable alternative. However, when highly conflicted decision makers expect new relevant information about the alternatives, they will remain hopeful (about finding a good solution), vigilant, and open-minded; as a result, they will delay their choice and abstain from distorting the attractiveness of alternatives.

Defensive Avoidance: The Construction of Rationalizations

There are three major forms of defensive avoidance: Procrastinating, shifting responsibility onto others, and bolstering the least objectionable alternative. Bolstering is an umbrella term that refers to a number of different cognitive tactics or defenses that enable the decision maker to rationalize that the decision will turn out well. Many of the main bolstering tactics we have specified (Janis & Mann, 1977, pp. 91–93) involve either distortion of the value or *utility* of an outcome or distortion of the *probability* of an outcome. These tactics enable the decision maker to arrive at subjective utility expectancies that put an end to painful indecision and, at least temporarily, resolve the conflict. Thus, our conflict-theory view of bolstering takes account of the two main components of the SEU model.

Examples of bolstering tactics that involve distortion of the utility or value of consequences are:

Exaggeration, or playing up the reward value of the favorable consequences of the chosen alternative, (e.g., "The prestige I'll get from becoming President of the P.T.A. will be incredible").

Minimization, or playing down the magnitude of loss from unfavorable consequences of the chosen alternative, (e.g., "Even if I get caught in this shady deal, the penalties won't be all that bad").

Denial of aversive feelings, for example by transforming the main negative feature into something positive, (e.g., "working with explosive chemicals on the job will give me a chance to prove myself").

Two bolstering tactics that involve the distortion of probability of outcomes are:

Exaggeration of the remoteness of action commitment: The person rationalizes that even after the choice is made, nothing will need to be done for such a long time that it can be safely forgotten. Here the probability that the choice will have to be implemented is distorted to make it appear quite remote.

Minimization of social surveillance: The person assumes it is very likely that others will take little or no notice of his choice, and even then will place no demands on him. This tactic refers to the expectancy of being permitted to get away with something that ordinarily entails social obligations.

The preferred bolstering tactic appears to depend partly on the nature of the unwelcome consequences of concern to the decision maker. In general, cognitive defenses such as these are fostered by ambiguities and uncertainties in the information available concerning the consequences of alternative courses of action. The more precise and exact the information, the less the opportunity for distortion in the service of defensive avoidance. According to Janis and Mann (1977):

> Whenever we have no hope of finding a better solution than the least objectionable one, we can always take advantage of the difficulties of predicting what might happen. We can bolster our decision by tampering with the probabilities in order to restore our emotional equanimity. If we use our imagination, we can always picture a beautiful outcome by toning down the losses and highlighting the gains [p. 94].

A study by Mann and Tan (1979) in which the antecedent conditions specified in the conflict model were directly manipulated provides further support for conflict theory. In this study, male students took the role of decision makers charged with the task of making choices on two decisional problems. In order to create conflict, subjects were informed that their reputations as decision makers were at stake. They were told that decision making is one of the most important of all human activities, that their solutions to the two problems would indicate their competence as decision makers, and that those students capable of making good decisions and those making poor ones would be publicly identified and interviewed. To create the conditions for the three specific coping patterns, both optimism/pessimism and time pressures were manipulated. For example, pessimism (an expectation of little hope for a good solution to the decision problem), was introduced by telling subjects that the problem they were about to tackle was tricky, with very few solutions possible. As predicted, subjects in the vigilance condition (who were made to feel optimistic about finding a good solution and were under no time pressure) produced better quality decisions than subjects in the hypervigilance and the defensive avoidance conditions (who were exposed to time pressure and pessimistic instructions respectively).

Expectancy as a Component of the Decisional Balance Sheet

Another important feature of the conflict model is the balance sheet schema for monitoring the ingredients of decision. The concept of a decisional balance sheet occupies a quite central but diverse role in the conflict model. The balance sheet is used as:

1. A schema for conceptualizing considerations that enter decisional conflict (here conflict theory addresses similar problems as behavioral decision theory, but in a different way).
2. A basis for predicting postdecisional stability and adherence to the chosen course of action (the defective balance sheet hypothesis).
3. A counseling procedure for fostering vigilance.

1. The Balance Sheet Schema.   In an earlier analysis of decision-making processes (Janis, 1959), a decisional "balance sheet" of incentives was proposed to take account of both the cognitive and the motivational aspects of planning for future action. It is intended to be broadly applicable to all important decisions made by a person—both personal and professional. We use the balance sheet as a *descriptive* schema to supplement the conflict model of coping patterns. The schema is valuable for analyzing the degree to which a decision maker explores the full range of alternatives open to him and considers the likely consequences of each alternative. There are several assumptions in the balance sheet schema that pertain to continuation or change in action.

A major assumption of the balance sheet schema is that a person will not decide to embark on a new course of action or to continue an old one unless he expects the gains to exceed the losses (cf. gain-loss models of social behavior). Our analysis of decisional conflicts as a kind of 'balance sheet' of expectations is consistent with expectancy-value theory. Implicit in conflict theory and explicit in the expectancy-value formulation, is the assumption that in order to choose among alternatives the person reduces each alternative to a single value on a scale of utility (desirability or preference) and that he chooses the alternative with the highest value. (But note that for conflict theory this is only one of several kinds of activity involved in the decision making process—see previous discussion on information processing).

Another assumption of the balance sheet schema is that there are four major kinds of expected consequences (incentives) that enter into a decisional conflict. The expected consequences of each alternative course of action can be exhaustively classified into the four main categories of the decisional balance sheet schema (see Janis, 1959; Janis & Mann, 1968, 1977):

1. Utilitarian gains and losses for self;
2. Utilitarian gains and losses for significant others;
3. Self-approval or disapproval;
4. Approval or disapproval from significant others.

In most important decisions all four types of expectancies are relevant to some extent, and the decision maker's choice is presumably determined by their relative strengths. Decisional conflicts are conceptualized in our schema in terms of a balance sheet containing positive and negative values corresponding to the potential gains (positive incentives) and potential losses (negative incentives) anticipated by the decision maker with respect to each alternative open to him. For most decisions in everyday life, the main considerations in the four categories are likely to be conscious, verbalized expectations. Occasionally, an important consideration may be temporarily preconscious, but readily accessible to consciousness if someone calls it to the decision maker's attention. By and large, all these considerations are subject to social influence through informational inputs and persuasive arguments presented either in the mass media or in interpersonal discussions. In exceptional instances, the individual remains unaware of an important consideration that is shaping his decision, because of the operation of repression and other psychological defense mechanisms.

In sum, whereas conflict theory assumes a substantial amount of rationality on the part of human beings, so that their decisions will occur largely on the basis of conscious expectations of positive and negative consequences, it recognises there are other possibilities—such as mood, that lead to biases and distortions. President Woodrow Wilson's sudden decision to stop trying to bring about "peace without victory" in Europe and to ask the U.S. Congress to declare war on Germany, following his shock and anger over the discovery that some members of the German government were trying to induce Mexico to attack the United States, is an example of an emotional reaction that may have influenced an important decision, with grave consequences for the lives of millions of people (see Janis, 1959; Tuchman, 1958).

2. Defective Balance Sheet Hypothesis.   One of the main hypotheses that has grown out of our analysis of the balance sheets of persons making stressful decisions is that *the more errors of omission and commission in the decision-maker's balance sheet at the time he commits himself to a new course of action, the greater is his vulnerability to negative feedback when he subsequently implements the decision* (Janis, 1959; Janis & Mann, 1977). We refer to this as the "defective balance sheet hypothesis". The defective balance sheet hypothesis asserts that the stability of a decision depends on the completeness and accuracy with which the decision maker has completed his decisional balance sheet *before he begins to implement the decision.* Errors of omission include overlooking the losses that will ensue from the chosen action; errors of commission include false, over-optimistic expectations about improbable gains.

Thus, the balance sheet schema provides a basis for making important predictions about postdecisional regret and the instability of the decision maker's subsequent actions. An incomplete or faulty 'balance sheet' at the time of decision will lead to postdecisional regret, inactivity, or reversal of action. The conflict-theory analysis of the dynamic relationship between pre- and post-decisional processes goes beyond the usual expectancy-value analyses of predecisional preferences. Unlike the expectancy-value analysis, it stipulates the entries in the decision maker's choice equation together with the gaps that are predictive of post-decisional behavior.

3. The Balance Sheet Procedure. It follows from the defective balance sheet hypothesis that if a person is induced to fill in gaps in his balance sheet by being encouraged to scan all of the information about the available alternatives before implementing a new decision, he will show less postdecisional distress and less instability when he subsequently encounters setbacks and losses.

The balance sheet procedure (Janis & Mann, 1977) was designed as a technique for preventing errors of omission in the predecision phase. The procedure, as used by Janis in pilot studies of Yale seniors facing career choices prior to graduation, attempts to elicit alternatives and probable outcomes (gains and losses), but does not obtain quantitative estimates of probabilities associated with each anticipated consequence. Typically, at the beginning of an interview, the person is asked to describe all of the alternatives he is considering and to specify the pros and cons for each. Then he is shown a balance sheet grid with empty cells (see Table 12.2). The meaning of each category is explained and he is helped to fill the entries for the most preferred alternatives. The person is then asked to reexamine each cell in the balance sheet, trying to think of considerations not yet mentioned. Most of the time is taken with categories with initially few entries—often those pertaining to self approval or disapproval.

The balance sheet procedure used in this way (as a technique for fostering vigilance) has been found in a series of controlled field experiments to be a successful counseling technique for promoting adherence to decisions and for preventing postdecisional regret (Mann, 1972; Colten & Janis, in press; Hoyt & Janis, 1975).

It is instructive to compare the balance sheet approach with the Optional Parenthood Questionnaire (OPQ) used by Beach, Townes, Campbell and Keating (1976) as a counseling device in decision making relating to family planning. Beach et al explicitly seek to apply SEU to family planning decisions with the aim of predicting the actual birth planning decision. This was done on the basis of couples indicating positive and negative considerations and probabilities of outcome for each consideration relating to choosing to have a child. Beach and Beach (this volume) point out a major nonobvious side benefit of the scheme. "It seems that the exercise of simply working through some sort of decision scheme can be valuable whether or not it is used to arrive at a final decision" (p. 389). Beach and Beach note that couples using the OPQ often remarked that it was helpful to go through the instrument—*it made them think of things they would not otherwise have thought of*—and thus learned where they differed from their spouse in terms of wanting and not wanting a (another) child.

Decision aids based on expectancy-value formulations may, as Mitchell and Beach (1977) surmise, assist the person to make a more effective and satisfactory decision. An interesting possibility for future research would be to compare the

TABLE 12.2
The Balance Sheet Grid

Alternative # _____		
	Positive Anticipations +	*Negative Anticipations −*
1. Tangible gains + and losses − for SELF		
2. Tangible gains + and losses − for OTHERS		
3. Self-approval + or self-disapproval −		
4. Social approval + or disapproval −		

effectiveness of different procedures for promoting vigilance, including the balance sheet procedure (listing outcomes for each alternative, rating each outcome for importance) and the Beach SEU procedure (rating the relative influence and value of various considerations, indicating the probability that each consideration would eventuate given a particular choice). Would the balance sheet procedure be (1) as predictive of choice; and (2) as effective in stabilising choice as the more complex SEU procedure? Could a simpler technique be devised to achieve substantially the same beneficial results?

It would be incorrect to overemphasize the "rational" aspects of these decision aids. Apart from the judgmental difficulties involved (e.g., how to estimate probabilities) many factors in major decisions are unverbalised and cannot be "scored", as for example, in many marital and "life and death" decisions. Consider two colleagues we know, both faced with the dilemma of leaving or retaining their University posts, who carefully filled out our balance sheets. One of them reported: "The damn balance sheet keeps on coming out wrong . . . I know what I want to do". (She wanted to leave—the balance sheet 'told' her to stay). The other found that her daily fluctuations in mood, as she wrestled with the decision, significantly affected the outcome pointed to by the balance sheet each day she worked on it. In brief, the balance sheet and similar procedures based on tallying values and/or expectancies should be regarded with extreme caution as a *guide* to decision. Its usefulness may be found primarily in stimulating essential cognitive activity, which could ensure that for whatever choice is made the decision is likely to be more stable.

The balance sheet score can, of course, serve as a rough predictor of the alternative subsequently chosen by the decision maker. A study by Mann and Tan (1980) reveals that in approximately two-thirds of cases the balance sheet score is an accurate predictor of actual choice. Mann and Tan had university students fill in balance sheets for two decisions—a decision to donate blood (N = 38 subjects) and a decision to undertake a jogging program (N = 39 subjects). On the first decision, the balance sheets of 68% of subjects predicted their actual decision, and on the second decision the figure was 67%. Inconsistencies between balance sheet and actual decision were almost always due to the failure of a *positive* net score in favor of taking action to predict the *chosen* policy. A *negative* score, i.e., in favor of not taking the action, invariably predicted that the alternative would be *rejected*. In brief, in a situation involving health-related decisions, where one course involves action and the other inertia, a positive "balance" of considerations in favor of action (donate blood, take up jogging) serves only as a very rough guide to the choice actually taken.

The failure of the balance sheet procedure to unerringly predict actual choice is hardly surprising, given the frequently observed discrepancy between judgment, attitude and action (cf. Wicker, 1969). A common example of this phenomenon is the smoker's positive balance sheet in favor of quitting, accompanied by the decision to continue smoking. Indeed, discrepancy between the balance sheet score and the subsequent choice is understandable when one recognises that the balance sheet is more than a mere tally of approach and avoidance motivation toward a course of action. The exercise of completing a balance sheet encourages vigilant behavior and thereby tends to make salient the importance of the decision, helps clarify the merits of the choice alternatives and stimulates a search for more information about the consequences. In brief, cognitive activity stimulated by the balance sheet exercise and following its completion sometimes produces marked shifts in preferences, leading to choices unheralded by the initial balance sheet itself.

To recapitulate, conflictful decision making is more than an activity of toting up the pluses and minuses according to their relative sizes to get a final equation on the "bottom line" pointing to the best course of action to choose. The decision maker becomes aware of gaps and uncertainties that require information search. To some extent, the decision maker may also scan relevant incentives that he or she had been ignoring or distorting because of preconscious emotional biases and irrational impulses.

Expectancies Regarding Loss of Choice Alternatives

Another area in which conflict theory introduces expectancies is the problem of how people react to expected or actual loss of choice alternatives. Reactance theory (Brehm, 1966; Wicklund, 1974) deals with the notion that people are motivated to reestablish their freedom whenever it is threatened or eliminated. One of the symptoms of reactive behavior is the common tendency to enhance the value (utility) of restricted acts and depreciate choice alternatives that are foisted on the person. Conflict theory, however, postulates that any attempt to usurp or narrow freedom of choice can lead to either an increase or a decrease in the value of the threatened alternative, depending on the decision maker's expectations concerning the consequences of struggling for and asserting his or her freedom of choice. The reaction of a vigilant decision maker to possible elimination of an alternative is a function of concomitant changes in the instrumental value of the threatened alternative. If the person expects to be able to restore the threatened alternative and to assert his power and independence in the process, then that alternative should *increase* in attractiveness. But when the person expects that the choice of a threatened alternative will lead to additional negative consequences (e.g., penalties, extra work, criticism), the alternative will *decrease* in attractiveness.

Mann and Dashiell (1975) conducted a field experiment which showed how changes in expectancy relating to vulnerability to the U.S. selective service draft led to systematic changes in the value of various draft-exempt and nonexempt career alternatives. This study is relevant to the present discussion because it bears out the conflict-theory assumptions about how *vigilant* decision makers will handle dilemmas arising from threats to constrain their freedom of choice. The theory assumes that such decision makers will examine and revalue the entire set of gains and losses to be expected from persisting in choosing an alternative they are no longer permitted to select without incurring severe new penalties.

The context of Mann and Dashiell's study was the first selective service draft lottery, drawn on December 1, 1969. This event affected many thousands of young American men, most of them anti-war and anti-draft. The government used the draft lottery to determine the draft status of all men 19–25 years. Those who drew low or "bad" numbers (1–120) were scheduled for early induction; those who drew high or "safe" numbers (241–365) knew that they would be safe from induction for at least a year and perhaps longer. The *exact* probability of being drafted was still uncertain, but the draft lottery threatened a large number of men with almost immediate induction into the army unless they chose career alternatives that carried draft exemption, viz. medical school, divinity school and teaching. Alternatives such as a full-time job, graduate school and travel, were not exempt from the draft. Mann and Dashiell asked: How would the attractiveness of these two types of career alternatives change among men who drew low, medium and high numbers in the draft lottery? On the basis of conflict theory the following predictions were made:

1. For the unlucky men who drew low numbers in the lottery, we should find:
    (a) a significant *decrease* in the attractiveness ratings of *vulnerable* choice alternatives (i.e., job, graduate school, and travel). These should be-

come unattractive because they now carried with them the strong possibility of a ticket to Vietnam.

(b) a significant *increase* in the ratings of *draft exempt* alternatives (i.e.,
medical school, divinity school, teaching). These should become more
attractive because they now promised safety from the imminent threat
of being drafted.

2. For the lucky men who drew high numbers, we should find:

(a) a significant *increase* in the attractiveness of the *vulnerable* alternatives, because the risk previously associated with them was markedly
diminished.

(b) a significant *decrease* in the value of *draft-exempt* alternatives, because
a major positive feature of those alternatives, viz., safety from the draft,
no longer figured as an important consideration during the coming year
or longer.

These predictions were tested in a study carried out with a group of Harvard
University students on the days preceding and following the drawing of the 1969
national draft lottery. Five days before the lottery, 84 Harvard seniors were asked
to rate various alternative activities "according to their attractiveness to you as
ways you would choose to spend the year following graduation". The alternatives were graduate school, medical school, divinity school, teaching, travel,
full-time job, and service in the armed forces. Following the lottery drawing,
either on the day after, or 10 days later, the same men were recontacted, asked to
indicate their lottery number, and then to rerate the choice alternatives.

The findings indicated that following an event that threatened to restrict freedom to choose among a set of career alternatives, the men altered the attractiveness of the various alternatives according to their utility for reducing or increasing the possibility of being drafted. As predicted, the men with low lottery
numbers, who regarded their highly vulnerable draft status as a threat not only to
their freedom of choice but also to their well-being, became more attracted to
low-risk career activities such as teaching, divinity school, and medicine. And
also as predicted, the men with high lottery numbers showed the reverse tendency.

Some Possibilities for Collaboration

We have argued that the decision maker's behavior is governed to a considerable
extent by the expectation that costs, including the loss of reputation, is the price
of a faulty decision. But what are the causes of people's expectancies? Specific
reward contingencies, personality variables, and organizational variables have
been shown to be related to expectancies (Mitchell, 1979). The person's self-
attributions relating to his or her repeated failures as a decision maker—such as
lack of competence, task difficulty, and a run of bad luck—will also affect
subsequent expectancies about his or her prowess as a decision maker (cf.
Weiner, 1974). Conflict theory has tended to overlook the question of how

attributions for success or failure on past decisions influence expectancy of success or failure on present decisions, a phenomenon with implications for the coping pattern adopted by the person.

The liberalization of traditional expectancy-value formulations to include cognitive concepts such as self evaluation, causal judgments and information processing (Heckhausen & Weiner, 1972) holds out the promise of stronger contacts with conflict theory. So far, the "new look" in expectancy-value theory has been confined to achievement-related behavior, with particular emphasis on factors affecting choice between tasks of varying difficulty. An obvious problem of common interest to the two theories is how best to modify people's self-attributions, including expectancies of failure as decision makers, in order to motivate increased self-control over their lives.

Another problem of mutual interest would be the investigation of stress-inducing conditions that produce departures from the SEU model. The SEU model presupposes a cool, vigilant decision maker who canvasses, weighs and computes all of the relevant subjective probabilities and utilities before making a choice. Several critiques (e.g., Slovic, Fischoff & Lichtenstein, 1977) reveal that the model is often wide of the mark. Our analysis would suggest that antecedent conditions governing the various decision coping patterns will create predictable defects in information-processing, some of which might be responsible for departures from the rational-utilitarian model. With reference to Table 12.1, we note that when the nonvigilant patterns are in operation, few of the activities associated with "rational-man" decision making are carried out adequately—e.g., canvassing a wide range of alternatives, taking account of all relevant objectives, weighing costs, risks, and positive consequences. It is possible that a close analysis of the conditions that apply when a decision maker confronts different decision tasks will help account for departures from the SEU model. For example, the hypervigilant (panicky) decision maker, under time pressure, might distort the magnitude of the *probabilities* of unfavorable consequences, whereas the defensive avoidant decision maker, feeling pessimistic about a good solution, might err when assessing and combining *utilities*. Unconflicted decision makers, on the other hand, might tend to show a generally sloppy approach to considering and combining all of the relevant parameters. Only the vigilant decision maker, buoyed by optimism and absence of extreme time pressure, might approximate the classical SEU pattern in his actual choice. Research testing predictions from the SEU model carried out under conditions antecedent to each coping pattern would seem to be an important next step.

CONCLUSION

This chapter has outlined a set of interrelated propositions about how people actually cope with the stresses of decision making, which we refer to as conflict theory. The core of the theory consists of an analysis of the five basic coping patterns that affect the quality of decision making. A key assumption is that only one of the patterns—vigilance—generally results in the kind of thorough information processing predicated by expectancy-value models of decision making. It was argued that the classic subjective-expected-utility model (the SEU model) constitutes a normative principle or rule for choice rather than a comprehensive descriptive theory of decision making. It was also argued that the principles that govern consequential decisions (in which *hot* cognitions are elicited by psychological stress) are probably quite different from those that come into play in inconsequential, hypothetical decisions. Accordingly, the relevance of studies testing SEU formulations in the laboratory by means of hypothetical or trivial choices was called into question.

The conflict model incorporates aspects of the concepts of expectancy and value (utility), although they are by no means used in a precise way. Expectancies enter the model in four ways:

1. They are sources of decisional conflict, in that expectancies of success or failure will influence how the person will respond to an opportunity or challenge.

2. They are determinants of the coping pattern adopted by the person to handle a high level of decisional conflict. The expectation of finding a better solution to the current alternative, and the expectation that time is available to find such an alternative will determine whether the person is vigilant, or resorts to defensive avoidance or hypervigilance, either of which leads to gross errors in decision making. Defensive avoidance, in particular, often takes the form of constructing rationalizations that distort both probability expectancies and utilities of consequences in order to bolster a shaky decision.

3. They are components of the decisional balance sheet. Analogous to the expectancy-value model, conflict theory postulates that the rational, vigilant decision maker will adopt as a decision rule the principle of choosing alternatives with the highest expected value. The balance sheet procedure is, however, not intended as a method for choosing but rather as an analytic device for encouraging vigilance.

4. They are determinants of efforts to prevent the loss of alternatives. Expectations regarding the consequences of attempting to protect or restore a threatened alternative can lead to major reevaluations of the choice alternatives.

The emphasis of conflict theory on the continuity between pre- and postdecisional processes has led to an examination of how people search for and evaluate information both before and after commitment. Even after commitment, there often are residues of conflict (or dissonance) left unresolved, which continue to exert an effect on how alternatives are valued. This points to the need for SEU formulations to take account of changes in expectancy and value that may occur postdecisionally, both before and after the decision is implemented. A good example of research within a value-instrumentality framework that takes this approach is the work of Vroom (1966).

Finally, several possible points of collaboration between the expectancy-value formulation and the conflict model were discussed. One problem relates to the factors that influence generalized expectations of success or failure as a decision maker and the other pertains to defective coping patterns in response to stress that might explain departures from the choices predicted by the SEU model.

REFERENCES

Atkinson, J. W., & Raynor, J. O. (Eds.). *Motivation and achievement.* New York: Wiley, 1974.

Beach, L. R., Townes, B. D., Campbell, F. L., & Keating, G. W. Developing and testing a decision aid for birth planning decisions. *Organizational Behavior and Human Performance,* 1976, *15,* 99–116.

Brehm, J. W. *A theory of psychological reactance.* New York: Academic Press, 1966.

Carroll, J. S., & Payne, J. W. (Eds.). *Cognition and social behavior.* Washington, D.C.: Lawrence Erlbaum Associates, 1976.

Colten, M. E., & Janis, I. L. Effects of self-disclosure and the decisional balance-sheet procedure in a weight reduction clinic. In I. L. Janis, (Ed.), *Counseling on personal decisions.* New Haven, Conn.: Yale University Press, in press.

CRM. *Psychology today: An introduction* (Third ed.). New York: CRM/ Random House, 1975.

Edwards, W. Behavioral decision theory. *Annual Review of Psychology,* 1961, *12,* 473–498.

Heckhausen, H., & Weiner, B. The emergence of a cognitive psychology of motivation. In P. Dodwell (Ed.), *New horizons in psychology.* London: Penguin Books, 1972.

Hoyt, M. F., & Janis, I. L. Increasing adherence to a stressful decision via a motivational balance-sheet procedure: A field experiment. *Journal of Personality and Social Psychology,* 1975, *31,* 833–839.

Janis, I. L. *Psychological stress: Psychoanalytic and behavioral studies of surgical patients.* New York: Wiley, 1958.

Janis, I. L. Motivational factors in the resolution of decisional conflicts. In M. R. Jones (Ed.), *Nebraska Symposium on Motivation* (Vol. 7). Lincoln: University of Nebraska Press, 1959.

Janis, I. L. Effects of fear arousal on attitude change: Recent developments in theory and experimental research. In L. Berkowitz (Ed.), *Advances in experimental social psychology* (Vol. 3). New York: Academic Press, 1967.

Janis, I. L. *Victims of groupthink.* Boston: Houghton Mifflin, 1972.

Janis, I. L., & Mann, L. A conflict-theory approach to attitude change and decision making. In A. Greenwald, T. Brock, & T. Ostrom, (Eds.), *Psychological foundations of attitudes.* New York: Academic Press, 1968.

Janis, I. L., & Mann, L. *Decision making: A psychological analysis of conflict, choice and commitment.* New York: Free Press, 1977.

Janis, I. L., & Rausch, C. N. Selective interest in communications that could arouse decisional conflict: A field study of participants in the draft-resistance movement. *Journal of Personality and Social Psychology,* 1970, *14,* 46–54.

Langer, E. J., Janis, I. L., & Wolfer, J. A. Reduction of psychological stress in surgical patients. *Journal of Experimental Social Psychology,* 1975, *11,* 155–165.

Lanzetta, J. T. Information acquisition in decision making. In O. J. Harvey (Ed.), *Motivation and social interaction.* New York: Ronald Press, 1963.

Lewin, K. *Field theory in social science.* New York: Harper, 1951.

Lynch, J. G., & Cohen, J. L. The use of subjective expected utility theory as an aid to understanding variables that influence helping behavior. *Journal of Personality and Social Psychology,* 1978, *36,* 1138–1151.

Mann, L. Use of a 'balance-sheet' procedure to improve the quality of personal decision making: A field experiment with college applicants. *Journal of Vocational Behavior*, 1972, *2*, 291-300.

Mann, L., & Dashiell, T. Reactions to the draft lottery: A test of conflict theory. *Human Relations*, 1975, *28*, 155-173.

Mann, L., Janis, I. L., & Chaplin, R. The effects of anticipation of forthcoming information on predecisional processes. *Journal of Personality and Social Psychology*, 1969, *11*, 10-16.

Mann, L., & Tan, C. *A test of the Janis and Mann conflict theory of decision making*. Presented at APA meetings, New York, 1979.

Mann, L., & Tan, C. *Studies with a mirror balance sheet*. Unpublished data, Flinders University, 1980.

Mausner, B. An ecological view of cigarette smoking. *Journal of Abnormal Psychology*, 1973, *81*, 115-126.

McGuire, W. J. The nature of attitudes and attitude change. In G. Lindzey & E. Aronson (Eds.), *Handbook of Social Psychology*. Addison-Wesley, 1969.

Mitchell, T. R. Organizational behavior. *Annual Review of Psychology*, 1979, 30, 243-281.

Mitchell, T. R., & Beach, L. R. Expectancy theory, decision theory, and occupational preference and choice. In M. F. Kaplan & S. Schwartz, (Eds.), *Human judgment and decision processes in applied settings*. New York: Academic Press, 1977.

Nisbett, R. E., & Ross, L. *Human inference: strategies and shortcomings in social judgment*. New Jersey: Prentice-Hall, 1979.

Porter, L. W., & Lawler, E. E. *Managerial attitudes and performance*. Homewood, Ill.: Irwin-Dorsey, 1968.

Sieber, J. Effects of decision importance on ability to generate warranted subjective uncertainty. *Journal of Personality and Social Psychology*, 1974, *30*, 688-694.

Simon, H. A. Motivation and emotional controls of cognition. *Psychological Review*, 1967, *74*, 29-39.

Simon, H. A. *Administrative behavior: A study of decision-making processes in administrative organization* (3rd ed.). New York: Free Press, 1976.

Slovic, P., Fischoff, B., & Lichtenstein, S. Behavioral decision theory: *Annual Review of Psychology*, 1977, *28*, 1-39.

Taylor, S. E. On inferring one's attitudes from one's behavior: Some delimiting conditions. *Journal of Personality and Social Psychology*, 1975, *31*, 1126-1133.

Tolman, E. C. The determiners of behavior at a choice point. *Psychological Review*, 1938, *45*, 1-41.

Tuchman, B. *The Zimmerman telegram*. New York: Viking Press, 1958.

Tversky, A., & Kahneman, D. Judgment under uncertainty. *Science*, 1974, *185*, 1124-1130.

Vroom, V. H. *Work and motivation*. New York: Wiley, 1964.

Vroom, V. H. Organizational choice: A study of pre- and post-decision processes. *Organizational Behavior and Human Performance*, 1966, *1*, 212-225.

Weiner, B. *Achievement motivation and attribution theory*. Morristown, N.J.: General Learning Press, 1974.

Wicker, A. Attitudes versus actions: The relationship of verbal and overt behavioral responses to attitude objects. *Journal of Social Issues*, 1969, *25*, 1-78.

Wicklund, R. A. *Freedom and reactance*. Potomac, Md.: Lawrence Erlbaum Associates, 1974.

13 Expectancy-Based Decision Schemes: Sidesteps Toward Applications

Barbara H. Beach
University of Washington

Lee Roy Beach
University of Washington

Much of the expectancy value/decision theory research has focused on the descriptive or predictive adequacy of the models. In this chapter, however, we will examine studies that have used the models as means to other ends. The ends are to aid personal or public decision making, to discover how people think or feel about the various components of these decisions, or to help them more carefully and systematically evaluate those components. The particular models we have chosen to discuss come exclusively from decision theory: probability theory, utility theory, and subjective expected utility theory. The personal and public decisions include such applied topics as medical diagnosis, weather forecasting, water quality, land use management, commuter transportation, family planning, and the like.

What follows is not a literature review. Instead, it is an assemblage of studies that we think represent a digestible cross-section of what is going on, so if your favorite study is not included, please do not be offended.[1] The framework is simple: We begin with a section on probability with primary emphasis on subjec-

---

[1]Wherever possible we have tried to limit citations to materials the reader might reasonably be able to obtain. Moreover, we have avoided studies that are so case-specific or situation-specific that no (or little) generalizable knowledge results. This means that we have not covered the vast amount of work done by decision analysis consultants such as Decisions and Designs, Inc., McLean, Virginia and the Stanford Research Institute, Menlo Park, California. These as well as other professional consulting groups such as Woodward–Clyde Consultants, San Francisco, California and the Social Science Research Institute, Los Angeles, California, have made major contributions—especially in measurement techniques and methods of problem structuring. Lists of available technical reports can be requested from these organizations.

tive probabilities because they are more likely to be used in personal and public decisions than objective probabilities—a short background to provide a bit of perspective and then some examples of current work. Next is a similar section on utility. Finally, there is a section on Subjective Expected Utility (SEU), that is left until last because, conceptually if not actually, it presupposes the previous two sections.[2]

An issue that cuts across all three sections involves the ultimate purpose of the various investigations. In some cases the purpose is to examine (evaluate) what a decision maker or some other person(s) thinks about the probabilities or utilities related to the consequences of some personal or public decision. In other cases the purpose is to help the decision maker actually reach a decision. In still other cases, of course, both the evaluation and the decision are important. We will not attempt to arrange the sections of the paper to reflect this evaluation-decision division because to do so becomes very formal, it detracts from the broader issues, and it usually is clear what the purpose is.

In the decision theoretic (analytic) framework, decisions require five basic steps—each of which can be more fully elaborated (e.g., Edwards' SMART, 1972; 1977).

1. Identify the available courses of action—the decision alternatives.
2. Identify the possible outcomes (i) of each decision alternative.
3. Assess the utility (U_i) or disutility of each outcome.
4. Assess the probability (P_i) of each outcome accruing to the decision maker should that decision alternative be selected.
5. Compute the expectation (usually the Expected Value or SEU) of each decision alternative

$$\sum_{i=1}^{n} P_i U_i$$

6. Apply some decision rule, usually maximization, to the expectations in order to select one of the decision alternatives.

Of course in some cases the interest may not lie in completing all six steps. For example, in some areas of medical diagnosis one can ignore utilities and merely look at the assessed probabilities of various diseases being the correct diagnosis in light of the presented symptoms. Or, one might be interested solely

---

[2]Two things should be made clear before continuing: First, some of the studies to be discussed involve a mixture of objective probabilities, subjective probabilities, objective values, and/or subjective utilities, but usually they use subjective probabilities and utilities. We prefer the term "assessed" probabilities and "assessed" utilities because they are merely what the subject says he or she has in mind, not necessarily what is really there. Second, some studies do not state specifically that they are using a subjective expected utility model, but because they involve the use of both probabilities and utilities and try to minimize cost and maximize benefit, we treat them as such.

in the assessed utilities of the outcomes (or of the attributes of those outcomes) as a way of examining a subject's value system in some particular realm. This is why it is necessary to look at both probability and utility as well as SEU if the current status of applied work is to be properly appreciated.

PROBABILITY

A Short Background

Until recently, the psychological study of subjective probability has been basically psychophysical. For example, in one of the earliest studies, Preston and Baratta (1948) derived a psychophysical function relating objective and subjective probabilities—the latter inferred from bids for bets. Subsequent research revealed that there apparently is no single function; it seems to vary greatly from individual to individual as well as with different experimental conditions.

The second phase of the psychophysical research was the Bayesian phase. Here Bayes' Theorem was used to generate objective posterior probabilities; subjects' own assessments of these probabilities provided the subjective probabilities. Series of data were presented and the Bayesian and assessed probabilities were compared to see if subjects revised their probabilities either more than or less than Bayes' Theorem did as a function of the presented data. Although later evidence casts doubt on their enduringness, two of the major conclusions reached in this research were that; (1) subjects are insufficiently sensitive to prior probabilities and (2) that subjects' revisions are "conservative" relative to Bayesian revisions (see review by Peterson & Beach, 1967).

Conservatism became something of a "phenomenon." The questions of interest were (1) what caused it; and (2) whether one could develop schemes to help people be less conservative. One of the answers proposed for the first question also pointed to a possible answer to the second. Lawrence Phillips, William Hays, and Ward Edwards (in whose laboratory the greater part of the Bayesian work had been done) suggested that conservatism resulted from subjects' inability to perform the necessary aggregation of the information as the series of data unfolded (Phillips, Hays, & Edwards, 1966). Whether this was inability to do the mental mathematics, or what, was not too clear. In any case, the point was that although subjects supposedly fully appreciated the information value of each individual datum in the series, they could not aggregate these information values optimally.

The "misaggregation" hypothesis suggests that the way to eliminate conservatism is to relieve the subjects of the task of having to aggregate. Instead, subjects should assess probabilities (actually, likelihoods) for single data only and a computer should aggregate these assessments across the series of data using

Bayes' Theorem. Thus was born Edwards' celebrated PIP system (Edwards, 1966; Edwards, Phillips, Hays, & Goodman, 1968).

In the PIP system, experts assess probabilities (likelihoods) for those aspects of the data about which they have expertise. The various experts' assessments are all aggregated by a computer using Bayes' Theorem and the final (posterior) probability is presented to the decision maker. Supposedly the decision maker then uses the probability in conjunction with his or her utilities, or the institution's utilities, to compute an expectation on which to base a decision.

The PIP system illustrates a very important idea that dominates much of the current work. This is the idea of decomposition and recomposition of decision problems. By decomposing the overall task into smaller tasks, PIP makes the overall task more manageable. Then by aggregating the assessments to get a single overall assessment, PIP recomposes the task again. (In this case decomposition also allows one to assign various parts of the assessment task to different individuals thus utilizing as much expertise as possible.) This is not to say that decomposition/recomposition originated with PIP or that subsequent uses of the idea grew out of PIP; certainly it has been around for a long time in operations research and is basic to the use of decision trees (Raiffa, 1968) and multi-attribute utility models (e.g., Shepard, 1964). However, it is an early and clever use of the idea.

Interest in the psychophysics of subjective probabilities faded. The death knell was struck by Tversky and Kahneman (1974) who presented evidence suggesting that assessed probabilities may be generated by processes that would only occasionally be expected to yield anything related to objective probabilities. This was followed by a series of studies that suggest that subjects are very poorly "calibrated"—that is, of all the questions a person answers with the accompanying statement that the probability of each answer being correct is, e.g., .75, then 75% of those answers should actually be correct. Similarly, for .65, .85, .30, etc., In fact, it appears that people grossly overestimate the probabilities of their answers being correct (reviewed in Slovic, Fischhoff & Lichtenstein, 1977). Although it is true that these studies have been criticized (Einhorn & Hogarth, 1978), the fact remains that the psychophysical line of research seems to have come to an end.

The decline of descriptive, psychophysical studies of subjective probability does not mean that interest in subjective probability has ceased; it merely has shifted. Kahneman and Tversky (1979) are working on what they call "Prospect Theory", L. Jonathan Cohen (1977) has published a book in which subjective probability is viewed as a system of implications, and Robert Goldsmith (1979) is exploring a similar system called the Evidentiary Value Model that derives from the use of evidence to arrive at a verdict in judicial settings. All three may help revitalize this important area; perhaps they will lead to a truly descriptive model of subjective probability (doubt, uncertainty, etc.) as opposed to the psychophysical functions that were sought by the psychophysical studies.

This change in direction in subjective probability research and theory reflects a general freeing-up in thinking about subjective probability. Formerly, when subjective probabilities failed to conform to objective probabilities it was almost as though in being incorrect they were illegitimate. Although it would have been more convenient if the natural calculus of doubt conformed to the calculus of probability theory, the fact remains that subjective probabilities still may be worth our interest. *If* it is the case that people's behavior is predicated on feelings of doubt or certainty and *if* these feelings can be measured to one degree or another, and *if* one wishes to regard these measured feelings as subjective assessments, then subjective probability, or some concept like it, is very much worth our interest. Clearly, the many successes of other models that use a concept like subjective probability (e.g., Fishbein, Atkinson, Vroom, etc.) indicate that the concept has value. Some of the work to be described here provides even further evidence.

Some Current Examples

It is a curious fact that throughout the decline in research on subjective probability, the researchers who were using it in applied or quasi-applied research seemed to have been almost unaware that anything was happening. Most seemed unconcerned about the theoretical subtleties of subjective probabilities; they simply plunged on, measuring subjective probabilities in all sorts of ways and multiplying and adding these measures just as though they had measured "real" probabilities. Indeed, such explorations of the use of subjective probabilities and/or Bayes' Theorem continues.[3]

Meteorology is one discipline in which the use of subjective probabilities is continuing and, perhaps, actually increasing. Murphy and Winkler (1974a), using information obtained from a nationwide survey of approximately 700 National Weather Service forecasters, continue to advocate use of probabilistic forecasts by meteorologists in all areas of weather forecasting. Particular progress is being made in the area of precipitation forecasts. As pointed out by Murphy and Winkler (1977a), "... [probability of precipitation] forecasts provide more information than precipitation forecasts not involving probability, and such additional information is valuable to potential users of the forecasts when decisions must be made in the face of uncertainty about the occurrence of precipitation [p. 62]."

Past research suggests that meteorologists appear to be quite able to give good, reliable probability forecasts for precipitation (e.g., Murphy & Winkler, 1974b; Murphy & Winkler, 1977c; Sanders, 1963; Winkler & Murphy, 1968). A recent study by Murphy and Winkler (1977a) demonstrates this ability. The

---

[3]For a review of the earlier use of subjective probabilities and Bayes' Theorem to deal with applied, real-world questions, see Beach, 1975.

researchers were interested in, among other things, the ability of practicing forecasters to make area precipitation forecasts as well as specific point recipitation forecasts within a general forecast area. A probability of precipitation forecast is simply the probability that .01 inch of precipitation will occur in a given forecast area; thus an area probability forecast refers to the probability of precipitation occurring anywhere in the forecast area whereas a specific point probability forecast refers to the probability of precipitation occurring at a specific point (e.g., a specific rain gauge). The experiment took place in Rapid City, South Dakota because this forecast area had a network of rain gauges that could be used to check for the accuracy of forecasts and because there were significant local effects that caused variation in the amount of precipitation falling at each rain gauge within the general forecast area. Because of the latter, Murphy and Winkler could evaluate how well forecasters could assess the probability of precipitation at specific points within the Rapid City area. Nine weather forecasters were asked to make probabilistic forecasts while on duty throughout June-September, 1974; 222 sets of forecasts were obtained. When the forecasters' probability of precipitation assessments were compared to the observed relative frequencies of precipitation it was found that not only did the forecasters' area probabilities correspond quite well with the observed relative frequencies for the forecast area, but the forecasters' probabilities for specific points also corresponded quite well with the observed relative frequencies of precipitation at these points (i.e., rain gauges). Thus, it appears that at least some weather forecasters can accurately assess probabilities of the occurrence of precipitation. They also appear to be able to give probability forecasts for other weather events such as tornadoes (Murphy & Winkler, 1977b) and temperature (see Murphy and Winkler, 1979, for a review of probabilistic temperature forecasts as well as an argument for public distribution of such forecasts).

The foregoing is an example of simply asking for probability assessments and using them as they are. In the medical arena more complex systems have been developed that ask for probability assessments from medical experts and then, using a computer and Bayes' theorem, aggregate these assessments to arrive at a final diagnosis. An example of such a system was developed by Gustafson, Greist, Stauss, Erdman, and Laughren (1977) for identifying potential suicide attemptors. It consists of a computer interview of patients who have reported having suicidal thoughts and Bayesian processing of the results of the interview to arrive at a probability that a given patient will attempt suicide within the following three months. The patient is questioned about symptoms that appear to be predictive of suicide, e.g., marital status, age, use of drugs, frequency of suicidal thoughts, existence of a suicide plan, etc. These symptoms were derived from the judgments of eight psychiatric residents who, through group consensus, arrived at a set of 32 symptoms with 246 levels. As the patient information comes in, the level (i.e., severity or the like) of each of the patient's symptoms is assessed by the computer. Then assessments of the likelihood ratios associated with each of the symptoms, which were obtained from a consensus of four experienced psychiatrists and two third-year residents in psychiatry and were stored in the computer, are retrieved and multiplied to yield the probability of the patient attempting suicide within the next three months.

To test the system, eight psychiatrists and 10 psychiatric residents were given case histories of 20 patients, half of whom had made a suicide attempt within three months after their initial interview by a psychiatrist and half of whom had not. After reading each case history they assigned a probability to each of two outcomes: That a suicide attempt would occur within the next three months and that no suicide attempt would occur within that time. The same case histories were processed by the computer system and probabilities were calculated for each outcome. The computer correctly identified attemptors more frequently (70% of the cases) than the average resident (33%) or average psychiatrist (38%). The computer was slightly less accurate in identifying nonattemptors (90% of the cases) than the average resident (97%) or average psychiatrist (93%). Moreover, the computer generally assigned a higher probability to the correct diagnosis than did the average resident or average psychiatrist.

The initial test of the system was based on the aforementioned past case histories; the system currently is being used to collect and process data from patients as they enter for care. They are interviewed by the computer and then seen by clinicians who are asked to estimate the probability of a suicide attempt. Follow-ups are conducted three and six months later. At last report, 30 patients have been interviewed by computer and clinician and have received a three-month follow-up interview. Four of these people had made a suicidal attempt. The computer identified three of the four attemptors (75%) whereas the clinicians identified an average of only one of the four (22%). Thus it appears that a computerized system that utilizes expert clinicians' assessed likelihoods and Bayesian processing of these likelihoods may improve on clinicians' ability to identify potential suicide attemptors.[4]

In a similar vein, Edwards (1978) has suggested using Bayesian methods to evaluate matters related to public policy. He describes an ongoing study by Lusted, Bell, Edwards, Roberts, and Wallace (in press) that utilizes Bayesian methods to evaluate the diagnostic usefulness of information from x-rays and other radiologic diagnostic procedures. The ultimate hope is to establish standards for use of such procedures because the procedures can be very costly compared to the benefits received from them. The basic procedure in this study was to collect judgments of the probabilities of possible diagnoses from the attending physician prior to the x-ray and then to obtain the judgments again after the physician saw the x-ray. Using the logic of Bayes' theorem it is possible to

---

[4]For summaries of numerous other examples of the use of subjective probabilities and Bayesian systems in medical diagnosis, see Beach, 1975; Krischer, 1980.

determine how much the information that is in the x-ray changed the physician's opinions about the diagnoses. If the physicians' opinions change a great deal then presumably x-rays yield valuable information that may be worth the cost; if the physicians' opinions do not change much one may question the use of the x-rays. By July, 1976, 9,000 cases of requests for x-rays by clinicians in an emergency setting (i.e., when x-ray information is needed within 12 hours or less) were collected. These cases were collected in 47 hospitals in 21 states and involved 400 physicians and 52 radiologists. So far the data from approximately 8000 cases have been analyzed to some extent. The investigators have drawn the following conclusions from their preliminary analyses:

1. It is feasible to measure the influence of X rays on the diagnostic thinking of physicians by elicitation of probabalistic assessments for tentative diagnoses before and after the X-ray information is available. That is, clinicians can be taught to make reliable probability estimates.

2. Overall, not more than 10% of the X-ray examinations had no apparent influence on diagnostic thinking.

3. At the time X-rays were requested, the requesting clinician was most often substantially uncertain about the correctness of his tentative diagnoses (4 times in 5 the probability of the most important tentative diagnosis was less than .50; over half the time it was less than about .15).

4. About 3/4 of the X-ray exams produced a lowering of the clinician's initial probabilities for the most important tentative diagnosis (which, as can be inferred from conclusion #3, tends to be an unlikely diagnosis, or as Edwards (1978) puts it, "a not-very-likely medical disaster"). Thus the information obtained from the X-rays tends to reassure rather than confirm some dreaded diagnosis.

5. The major effect of the X rays was to reduce uncertainty. Even after examination of the X rays, however, nearly 40% of the clinicians assessed probabilities for the most important tentative diagnosis at more than .02 but less than .98 suggesting that a great number of diagnostic decisions in emergency settings are based on weight of evidence rather than proof beyond a reasonable doubt.

From all of this it appears that in at least some circumstances clinicians can give meaningful probability assessments; moreover it appears that information obtained from X rays is valuable in that it usually changes the clinicians' diagnoses. Of course, further studies and analyses need to be done to determine whether the benefits of such diagnostic information outweigh the costs; the investigators are planning to do this.

It should be noted that although a great deal of research continues on the use of assessed probabilities and Bayes' theorem in personal and public decision making, judging from published reports, the great majority of such research remains quite laboratory-like in nature. To quote Feinstein (1977) who speaks about the use of Bayesian diagnosis in the medical field (but whose quote could apply to areas other than medical diagnosis):

> I know of no published work in which the initial claims of a Bayesian enthusiast have been confirmed by the results found in clinical reality. I know of no clinical setting or institution in which Bayesian diagnostic methods are being regularly used for practical diagnostic purposes in a routine or even specialized manner. I know of no specific, constructive, practical diagnostic decisions—involving real-world patients, data, and doctors—in which Bayesian methods have made a prominent contribution that could not have been achieved just as easily without Bayes' formula. (If readers know of any, I hope they will tell me.) . . . In the current absence of any evidence of sustained pragmatic value of Bayesian diagnosis, the process begins to resemble the alchemists' search for methods to transmute baser metals into gold. The chemical proposals are theoretically creative, imaginative, and sometimes even scholarly, but successful transmutations do not occur. [p. 489].

It is difficult to know why there appears to be so little use of subjective probabilities and/or Bayesian processing of assessed probabilities in applied situations. Perhaps they are being used but reports are not published about their use or results. Perhaps there is a reluctance to rely on such tools because of their impersonal and mechanistic nature. Perhaps people feel the systems are too costly and complicated. Perhaps people feel more research needs to be done before applying the tools in real-life situations. Certainly, lack of use of these tools is not due to lack of published reports explaining how to obtain and use assessed probabilities (e.g., Barclay, Brown, Kelly, Peterson, Phillips & Selvidge, 1977; Brown, Kahr & Peterson, 1974; Huber, 1974a; Spetzler & Staël von Holstein, 1975).

UTILITIES

A Short Background

Just as probability theory was developed outside of psychology and then adopted by psychologists to study subjective probability or doubt, utility theory developed outside of psychology and was adopted by psychologists to study subjective value or worth. The classic paper was by Daniel Bernoulli in 1738 (at which time he elaborated on maximization of expected utility as a strategy for gambling) and much has been done in economics since that time. In psychology the early studies of utility were, as they were for subjective probability, basically psychophysical. One direction was in terms of scaling using various psychometric techniques (e.g., Coombs, 1964; Thurstone, 1954). The other direction, and the one most identified with mainstream psychological decision research, involved inferences of utilities from bets (e.g., Davidson, Suppes & Siegel, 1957; Mosteller & Nogee, 1951). The point was to find the psychophysical function relating objective market value to subjective utility and to see if the function was concave as had generally been assumed since Bernoulli (1738/1954). For some subjects the functions look vaguely concave and for others they do not. However, in the Mosteller and Nogee (1951) study at least, the inferred utilities and the inferred subjective probabilities could be used to predict more complex betting behavior with fair accuracy, which implied that the inferred values had some legitimacy.

Probably the definitive psychophysical study was done by Amos Tversky for his PhD dissertation (1967). Using prison inmates as subjects and candy and cigarettes (the prison currency in those days) as payoffs, Tversky inferred utilities and subjective probabilities from prisoners' monetary bids for bets—the risky condition. In addition, he obtained the subjects' buying prices for various amounts of candy or cigarettes in a nonbet, riskless, condition. In the latter, utilities for the commodities were identical to the prison "fair-market" prices. However, in the risky condition there was some difficulty—it appeared as though the subjects had an additional utility for merely gambling that, when utility was inferred from the bids for the bets, inflated the utilities and made them larger than they were in the riskless condition. We doubt that it is cause and effect, but following this study there has been a steady decline in psychophysical studies of utility.

As with subjective probability, the decline in psychophysical studies of utility has not meant a decline in interest in utility in general. In fact, there has been a marked increase in interest with the advent of Multiattribute Utility Theory, MAUT, (Edwards, 1972; Keeney, 1972; Raiffa, 1969; Sayeki, 1972; Shepard, 1964).

The theoretical foundations of MAUT derive from decomposition models such as conjoint measurement (von Winterfeldt, 1976) and have been elaborated by Huber (1974b), von Winterfeldt and Fischer (1975), Keeney and Raiffa (1976), and Humphreys (1977). Deaton (1977) reviewed similar ideas from other disciplines. The general idea is that complex, multiattributed outcomes can be decomposed into their component attributes, the utilities of these attributes can be assessed, and then these assessments can be recomposed to derive the overall utility of the complex out-come. The theoretical elaborations define the conditions under which such procedures are appropriate and, as such, they are very important. Inappropriate application of MAUT, or violation of various of its requirements, can be dangerous if the problem to which it is applied is an important one. However, as Deaton (1977) and Bauer and Wegener (1977) have noted, actual applications of MAUT have been rather cavalier. Whether this has led to faulty decisions or not is hard to say because no checks have been done. On the face of it, however, most researchers seem to feel that everything works sufficiently well. There is a necessary trade-off between the simplification necessary for application and the rigor necessary for theoretical peace of mind; apparently simplification is judged to be more important because without it nothing gets done (see Edwards, 1977, for a defense of simplicity in the use of MAUT; also see Bauer & Wegener, 1977).

Some Current Examples

One of the earliest applications of MAUT was by Michael O'Connor in his PhD dissertation (1972). The goal was to devise two conceptually similar schemes that could be used for evaluating the quality of water supplies on the basis of samples from those supplies; one scheme was for public drinking water and the other was for water of lower, but sufficient, quality for fish and wildlife. Because many factors contribute to the degradation of water quality, the problem was viewed as one of evaluating the multiattribute utility of a water supply for either of these two uses.

The strategy was to use expert opinions to identify those attributes of a water supply that relate to its quality. Next, the relative importance of each attribute was ascertained. Then the functional relationships between water quality and various possible levels or states of each attribute were obtained. Next, equations were constructed for each of eight experts, using their own weights and functions. The equations were of the form:

$$\text{QUALITY } (X) = \sum_{i=1}^{n} w_i \, q_i \, (x_i)$$

where the quality of a water sample (X) is equal to the product sum of the quality (q_i) associated with a particular level (x_i) of an attribute (i) weighted by the importance (w_i) of that attribute relative to the other attributes. The quality (q_i) is obtained from the functions we just mentioned.

Finally, QUALITY (X) was calculated for each of 48 actual water samples for each of the eight experts using their personal equations. These values were then correlated with values generated for the same water quality samples using the averages of the experts' weights. The correlations were almost all about .90 indicating that the individual differences among the experts' equations were not too important. There were, of course, two equations for each judge—one for public water and one for fish and wildlife use. The results from using these two equations generally correlated about r = .70, which is about right. One would expect them to be similar up to a point, but public water was to be of a higher quality and so the equations should not be identical nor should the results generated by them.

O'Connor's report on the foregoing research is especially instructive because he unabashedly describes many of the blind alleys he encountered and much of the muddling through he had to do to complete the project. More recent publications (Edwards, 1977; Johnson & Huber, 1977) describe how to choose among and/or list step by step procedures to guide in the construction and use of MAUT schemes. Edwards (1972;1977) calls his series of steps the Simple Multiattribute Rating Technique (SMART). It consists of 10 steps:

1. Identify the person or organization whose utilities are to be maximized.
2. Identify the issue or issues (i.e., decisions) to which the utilities needed are relevant.
3. Identify the entities to be evaluated. Formally, they are outcomes of possible actions.
4. Identify the relevant dimensions of value for evaluation of the entities. The number of relevant dimensions of value should be modest.
5. Rank the dimensions in order of importance. This can be done by a single individual or by a group.
6. Rate dimensions in importance, preserving ratios. To do this, start by assigning the least important dimension an importance of 10. (Use 10 rather than 1 to permit subsequent judgments to be finely graded and nevertheless made in integers.) Consider the next least important dimension; how much more important (if at all) is it than the least important? Assign it a number that reflects that ratio. Continue up the list, rechecking each set of implied ratios as each new judgment is made. By the time you get to the most important dimensions there are many checks to perform; respondents may revise previous judgments to make them consistent with present ones.
7. Sum the importance weights, and divide each by the sum. This is a purely computational step that converts importance weights into numbers that, mathematically, are rather like probabilities.
8. Measure the location of each entity being evaluated on each dimension.
9. Calculate utilities for entities. The equation is

$$U_i = \sum_j w_j u_{ij}$$

remembering that $\Sigma_j w_j = 1.00$. U_i is the aggregate utility for the ith entity, w_j is the normalized importance weight of the jth dimension of value, and u_{ij} is the rescaled position of the ith entity on the jth dimension. Thus w_j is the output of Step 7 and u_{ij} is the output of Step 8. The equation, of course, is nothing more than the formula for a weighted average.
10. Decide. If a single act is to be chosen, the rule is simple: maximize U_i. If a subset of i is to be chosen, then the subset for which $\Sigma_i U_i$ is maximum is best.

The use of SMART is illustrated by its application to the problem of coastal land use regulation in Southern California. The goal was similar to O'Connor's goal—to devise a MAUT equation that could be used for evaluation and screening. In this case it was to be applied to land development proposals. Using

SMART, Gardiner and Edwards (1975) identified eight attributes of development proposals that were, to one degree or other, critical to acceptance or rejection of the proposal. Then 14 persons who were involved in one way or another in regulation of coastal land use were asked to evaluate 15 hypothetical proposals twice. First there was an intuitive, wholistic evaluation of the proposal and then an attribute-by-attribute (MAUT) evaluation was done. In addition, each person identified him/herself as being oriented toward conservation or development.

Comparison of the wholistic evaluations showed the conservation and development oriented groups' evaluations to be very different. However, the MAUT derived evaluations were amazingly similar. Edwards (1977) suggests that the reason for this is that:

> When making holistic (*sic*) evaluations, those with strong points of view tend to concentrate on those aspects of the entities being evaluated that most strongly engage their biases. The multiattribute procedure does not permit this; it separates judgment of the importance of a dimension from judgment of where a particular entity falls on that dimension [p. 333].

If this explanation of the results is accurate, and it certainly seems plausible, it is a strong argument for the use of MAUT (and SMART); anything that will reduce bias and help people take a broader range of attributes into account is likely to increase group satisfaction with decisions as well as the eventual effectiveness or correctness of the decision.

The final example of the use of MAUT is for identifying those people who, although they presently commute to work by automobile, might be most easily induced to switch to public transit (Beach, Mai-Dalton, & Marshall, 1979). The purpose here is quite different from the two previous examples—it is rather more similar to an attitude evaluation than to the more familiar decision paradigm.

In the autumn of 1978, METRO Transit, which serves all of the county in which Seattle, Washington is located, asked for a way of characterizing potential bus commuters. About 75% of the commuters in the county do so by automobile and nearly all the rest use the bus. An analysis (Davidson & Beach, 1979) of the mispredictions of people's decisions in other experiments suggested a way to do this using MAUT. In earlier studies it was found that when a decision involved change from the status quo versus staying with the status quo (as contrasted with "fork in the road" decisions in which staying with the status quo is not an option), there was an abundance of people for whom MAUT predicted change but who, in fact, did not do so. These "false positives" turned out to have utilities that were pro change, but only mildly so. Apparently for at least some people there is a disutility for change that was unmeasured in the studies but that was sufficient to tip the balance from mildly pro change to some degree of pro status quo (Jungermann, 1979).

TABLE 13.1
Predicted Versus Reported Transportation Mode

		Predicted Transportation		
		Bus	Auto	
Reported	Bus	47	6	53
Transportation	Auto	(62) 109	114 120	176

It occurred to us that changing from the status quo of driving one's automobile to work (and western American cities are designed for automobiles) to commuting by bus was much the same situation. And, false positive cases might be the potential bus riders METRO Transit was seeking. The idea was to see what was important to these people about commuting and then figure out how buses could meet those requirements in order to induce changes in commuting habits.

A MAUT-based questionnaire was designed using techniques similar to those described in Beach, Townes, Campbell, and Keating (1976).[5] This was sent to a sample of 575 commuters of whom 229 (40%) returned usable questionnaires. For each person, a prediction was made about whether or not he/she was a bus rider or an automobile driver. Each prediction was then compared to what each person had answered when asked how they go to and from work: the results are given in Table 13.1. The circled 62 respondents were the false positives that were sought. If the sample of 229 respondents was representative of the county population as a whole (demographic data suggested it was), these results suggested that about 27% of the county's commuters might be potential bus riders if conditions favored their switching.

This suspicion was strengthened by the data in Fig. 13.1. As a group, the 62 potential bus riders have overall MAUT values that are much nearer indifference than are those of the 47 regular bus riders; the latter's distribution of values looks like the mirror image of the distribution of the 114 "hard core" automobile drivers. This, of course, is exactly what Davidson and Beach (1979) had found.

The next question was to see what made the three groups in Fig. 13.1 so different. To do this we graphed the utilities for each of the attributes that comprised the MAUT-based questionnaire. These are graphed in Fig. 13.2. As

---

[5]The questionnaire had three major classes of topics related to commuting, each of which was divided into four subclasses. For each of the three classes respondents read descriptions of each of the four subclasses and indicated whether those topics inclined them to ride the bus or drive their automobile to work. Then they indicated the relative importance of the three major classes. As will be described in the family planning study later, this permits computation of an overall utility for the bus for each subject.

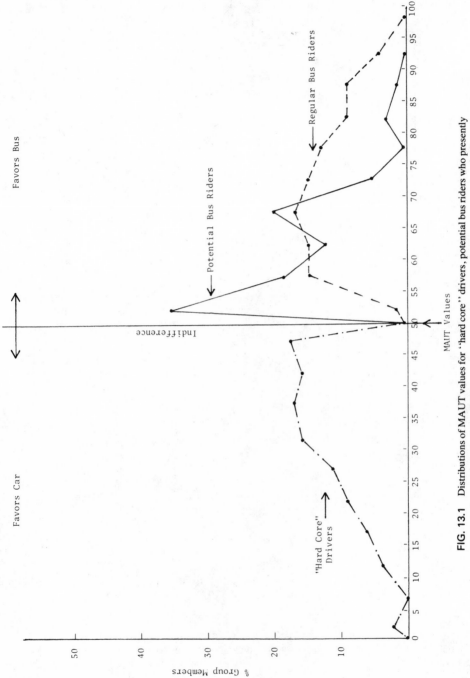

FIG. 13.1 Distributions of MAUT values for "hard core" drivers, potential bus riders who presently commute by car, and regular bus riders.

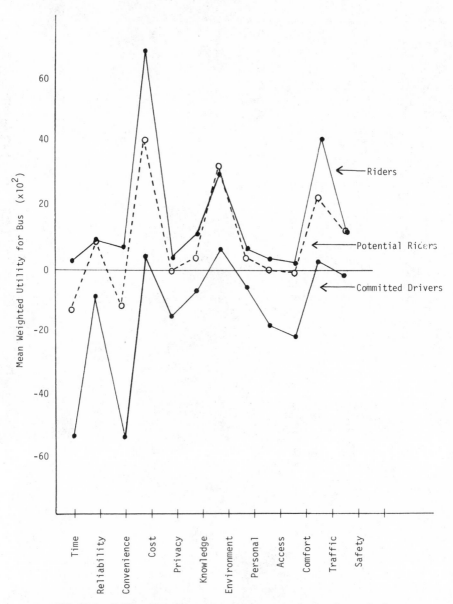

FIG. 13.2. Utilities for various aspects of commuting by bus for regular bus riders, potential bus riders who presently commute by car, and "hard core" drivers.

can be seen, the potential bus riders' utilities for the bus look very like the regular riders' utilities and not very much like the "hard core" automobile drivers' utilities. Moreover, the most important attributes are lower cost, improved environment, and avoidance of traffic. This suggests that the key to swinging the balance for potential bus riders is one or all of these three attributes.

On the basis of these results an experiment was conducted to see if potential bus riders could be induced to ride the bus. To do this 8 bus tickets that were good for one month were mailed to 40 potential bus riders and to 40 (one of whom never got the tickets, so it turned out to be 39) "hard core" automobile drivers. The hypothesis was that because cost is important to potential bus riders, they should be more likely to use the bus than "hard core" automobile drivers are when provided with free tickets—and, having used the bus, they might continue to do so. Of course, some automobile drivers cannot use the bus for perfectly legitimate reasons (e.g., need to use their automobile during the day for business). But, some percentage of both of these groups probably could use the bus if they chose to do so and the hypothesis was that a greater percentage of the people in the potential bus riders group would choose to do so with a little inducement.

As it happened, this rather weak cost manipulation was augmented by the simultaneous onset of a severe gasoline shortage in the Seattle area. Prices rose and long waiting lines for gas became the rule. In general bus ridership went up by roughly 25% in the first month of the shortage—which was the month that the tickets were valid. By recovering used tickets from bus drivers (who had been instructed to watch for them), and matching the serial numbers to a master list, it was possible to see which group of people had increased its bus usage most—the potential bus rider group or the "hard core" automobile drivers group.

At the end of the month, 58% of the 40 potential bus riders had used one or more tickets whereas only 31% of the 39 "hard core" automobile drivers had done so ($Z = 2.51$, $p < .01$). For both groups, those persons who used the tickets used an average of about 6 of the 8 tickets.

Ticket usage is not a very reliable dependent variable because the subjects may have merely given their tickets to other people. So, at this writing, a month after the tickets expired and people supposedly have either decided to stick with the bus or have reverted to driving again, a telephone interview is being conducted with all 79 subjects to see who is and who is not using the bus, and why they are or why they are not doing so.[6]

---

[6]For other interesting examples of the application or possible application of MAUT to personal and public decision making see Barclay and Peterson, 1976 (treaty negotiations); Edwards, 1979 (evaluation of desegregation plans); Ford, Keeney, and Kirkwood, 1979 (evaluation of nuclear power plant siting methodologies); Guttentag and Sayeki, 1975 (examination of cultural differences between American and Japanese social scientists); Huber, 1974b (a review); Humphreys and Humphreys, 1975 (evaluation of cinema films); Keeney, 1977 (evaluation of energy policies); Krischer, 1980 (a

SUBJECTIVE EXPECTED UTILITY

A Short Background

Recall that the subjective expected utility (SEU) for a decision alternative is the product sum of the assessed probability of the outcome (payoff) of that alternative and the assessed utility of the outcome. The research questions involve how well SEU represents subjects' preferences for decision alternatives and whether subjects actually select the maximally preferred alternative.

As was the case for probability and utility, much of the research on SEU has been psychophysical in nature. For example, Preston and Baratta (1948) compared subjects' competitive bids for bets with the bets' expected values. Under the bidding system that was used, the winning bids ideally should be equal to the bets' expected values. They were not. The lack of agreement was attributed to inaccurate subjective probabilities.

Similarly, Mosteller and Nogee (1951) inferred utilities from choices in paired comparisons of bets. Then they used these utilities to predict choices between other, often more complex, pairs of bets. They then constructed a psychophysical function relating increasing magnitude of SEU for the latter to increasing percentages of subjects electing to play the bets. There was, indeed, a fairly sigmoid arrangement to the plotted points; as the SEUs of the bets increased from negative to positive, a higher and higher percentage of subjects elected to play them.

Tversky (1967) used the logic of conjoint measurement to see if selling prices for bets were related to the bets' component probabilities and utilities in a manner congruent with the products of the latter; the data showed that they were. Shanteau (1974) using functional measurement in much the same way, showed that although behavior was congruent with the product hypothesis, the idea of summing over multiple aspects of outcomes is not quite accurate—subjects' behavior indicated that their sums were smaller than objective sums, a finding referred to as "subadditivity." Shanteau's results suggest that the definition of SEU as a product sum is not quite descriptively accurate. Whereas subadditivity probably increases as more products are summed, in Shanteau's experiment it was not very large.

Some Current Examples

Two studies using the same design but slightly different areas of emphasis have examined the correspondence between judged preferability of decision alternatives and the magnitudes of the alternatives' SEUs in a more applied situation.

---

review of MAUT applications to health care); Moskowitz, Evans, and Jimenez-Lerma, 1978 (evaluation of electrical generation expansion plans); Newman, 1977 (evaluation of automobiles); O'Connor, Reese, and Allen, 1976 (evaluation of alternative Naval aviation plans); Otway and Edwards, 1977 (evaluation of nuclear waste disposal sites—also described in Edwards, 1978).

Holmstrom and Beach (1973) studied the alternatives of entering any of eight different occupations in psychology (research and teaching, clinical practice, etc.). Utilities were obtained for 18 possible outcomes (salary, interesting work, etc.); these were assessed by having each subject rank order them and then assign a rating of 100 to the best outcome, 0 to the worst, and in-between numbers to in-between outcomes. Then, for each occupation, the subject assessed the probability of each of the 18 outcomes attaining a satisfactory level if the occupation in question were selected. Finally, using the 0–100 technique again, the occupations were rated for their relative preferability. For each subject, a SEU was computed for each of the eight occupations using their assessed utilities and probabilities. Then the eight computed SEUs were correlated with the subject's eight occupational preference ratings. For 30 subjects, 23 (77%) had positive correlations that were significant at or beyond the .05 level; the median correlation was $r = .83$.

Muchinsky and Fitch (1975) repeated the Holmstrom and Beach (1973) study using the taking of courses in any of six academic areas in an Industrial Relations program as the possible decision alternatives. They obtained assessed utilities and probabilities for 14 different kinds of outcomes. Of the 15 subjects in the study, 11 (73%) had significant positive correlations ($p < .05$) between computed SEUs and rated academic area preferences; the median correlation was $r = .81$.

Turning to the area of medical diagnosis and treatment, SEU and related cost-benefit analyses have been developed for helping physicians decide whether to select another diagnostic test or series of tests before arriving at a final diagnosis and/or what type of treatment to select to manage the disease once it has been diagnosed. For example, Gorry, Kassirer, Essig, and Schwartz (1973) devised a computerized system for both diagnosis and selection of treatment for acute renal failure. Their study was divided into two phases. The first phase involved using physicians' assessed probabilities (priors and likelihoods) and Bayes' theorem to arrive at a diagnosis of the cause of acute renal failure (the program considers a total of 14 possible causes). No utilities were considered. When given 33 hypothetical case histories the computer's diagnoses were identical to the physicians' diagnoses in 31 of the 33 cases when a probability of .90 was used as the threshold for establishing a final diagnosis; the computer's diagnoses were identical to the physicians' diagnoses in all 33 cases when a probability of .95 was used as the diagnostic threshold. What is interesting about the computer diagnostic system is that although up to 31 pieces of information were available for making a diagnosis, the computer used, on the average, only eight pieces of information before arriving at a final diagnosis (i.e., before reaching the diagnostic threshold).

The second phase of the system involved using the expected risks to the patient (disutilities) and expected benefits (utilities) of the various tests and treatments to determine whether it is best to treat the patient immediately or to carry out additional diagnostic tests before starting treatment. Thus the second phase utilizes both assessed probabilities and assessed utilities to arrive at subjective expected utilities for each test/treatment and chooses the test or treatment with the highest SEU; that is, the test or treatment that promises the largest benefit relative to its potential risk to the patient. When given 18 hypothetical cases of acute renal failure in which there were varying degrees of uncertainty about the true cause, the computer arrived at the same decision (i.e., choice of test or treatment) as that of a consensus of two physicians in 14 of the 18 cases. In the four cases in which the computer and the physicians disagreed, the physicians concurred that the computer's choice was a reasonable alternative.

Other systems have been developed that use both physicians' assessed probabilities (or, in some cases, objective probabilities, i.e., probabilities derived from the literature or actuarial data) and physicians' and/or patients' utilities (i.e., assessments of risks and benefits) and/or monetary values to select a test or a treatment. The goal is to minimize the costs and risks while maximizing benefits. For example, Pauker (1976) has developed a system for helping physicians determine whether to choose coronary by-pass surgery or medical therapy for patients suffering from coronary artery disease. Similarly, Safran, Tsichlis, Bluming, and Desforges (1977) have developed a series of computer programs to aid physicians in the management of patients with Hodgkin's disease. These programs help the physician decide whether further tests should be performed to determine the extent of a malignant tumor or whether treatment should begin immediately and, if so, which of two types of treatment it should be. Because choice of treatment depends to some extent on tumor extent, accurate diagnosis of tumor extent is advisable, and because some of the tests used to determine tumor extent are costly (in terms of money, morbidity, and mortality) one must balance the costs and benefits of further tests against the costs and benefits of immediate treatment. These computerized systems are flexible enough to allow the individual physician to adjust the probabilities and utilities to fit an individual case if he or she wishes to do so.

As is the case with Bayesian probabilistic systems for aiding the physician in making diagnoses, SEU or cost-benefit systems for helping physicians make both diagnostic and treatment decisions have not yet been used in a real, operational setting. They are primarily demonstrations of how decision analysis could aid the physician. Furthermore, only a few of the systems have been evaluated to any extent to see if they do as well as or better than the physician making a decision in his customary manner.

Weather forecasting is yet another domain in which SEU and similar models appear to have promise. Users of weather forecasts often face what is known as a "cost-loss ratio situation" (e.g., Murphy, 1976; 1977). That is, they must decide whether or not to take protective action, at a cost, in the face of uncertainty about whether adverse weather will occur; if no protective action is taken and adverse weather occurs, a loss is incurred. The basic notion is to take protective action only when the probability of adverse weather is equal to or greater than the cost divided by the loss. [This model was originally proposed by Thompson, 1952; see also Thompson & Brier, 1955.] Murphy (1977) has demonstrated that the best measure of uncertainty to use in such situations is assessed probability; if assessed probability forecasts are reliable they have more value when used in the cost/loss ratio than either categorical or climatological (i.e., relative frequencies) forecasts. Other investigators have provided demonstrations of how probabilities and utilities can be utilized by consumers of weather forecasts to make wise economic decisions; e.g., Baquet, Halter, and Conklin (1976), and Gregg (1977) discuss the use of probabilities and utilities by orchardists to decide whether to protect their crops against possible frost.

Our final example of the application of SEU is in the area of family planning. Six or seven years ago there was a major change of thinking on the part of at least some population researchers. Instead of viewing population growth as a strictly demographic question, these researchers (e.g., Fawcett & Arnold, 1973; Hoffman & Hoffman, 1973) called for increased attention to the factors that influenced individual couples' decisions to have or not to have a(another) child. This, of course, is an example of a complexly multiattributed, risky decision and, as such, is attractive for application of MAUT/SEU (Beach, Townes, Campbell, & Keating, 1976).

There were four goals for the Beach et al. (1976) project: The first goal was to demonstrate that it is possible to discover the factors that influence couples' birth planning decisions in some reasonably homogenous population. The second goal was to show that these factors' relative influence on decisions differ for different subgroups within that population. The third goal was to predict the birth planning decisions; ability to predict implies that the factors and their relative influence are accurate. Finally, the fourth goal was to use the results to develop a decision theory-based instrument for use in family planning counseling.

The "reasonably homogenous" population consisted of middle class, white, fairly well-educated married couples who were currently using contraception. The subgroups were couples having 0, 1, 2, 3+ children in their then existing families.

The "apparatus" was an experimenter-administered questionnaire that asked the subject to divide, what we shall call, "influence points" among factors to indicate their relative influence on his or her private considerations about having a(another) child. Then the subject indicated whether the influence of each factor was either positive or negative. Finally, the subject indicated how probable he or she thought it was that each factor would, in fact, eventuate were a positive decision (i.e., to have a child) to be made.

As described in Beach, Townes, Campbell, and Keating (1976), the factors were gleaned from the family planning literature and from probing interviews with seven couples who were in the throes of deciding whether to have a child or not. These same couples helped in the construction of a hierarchical arrangement of the factors; coherent subsets of factors were formed, these in turn were grouped to form higher level sets until everything was grouped together in one, all-inclusive, penultimate set.

The point of this scheme was to decompose the numerous and complex issues involved in such a decision into smaller, manageable "chunks." First, subjects divided 100 influence points among the *factors* in each of the subsets. Next they divided 100 influence points among the *subsets* in each of the sets. Finally they divided 100 influence points among the *sets* in the penultimate set.

Next the subject returned to the factors in the subsets and assigned each of them a plus or a minus to indicate whether its influence was positive (prochild) or negative (antichild). Finally the subject assessed a probability for each factor to indicate the chances that it would indeed eventuate should he or she decide to have a(another) child.

Later, the experimenter converted the influence points to decimal numbers and multiplied down the hierarchy (which looks rather like a conventional decision tree tilted 45° to the right and in which one multiplies from top to bottom instead of from, what in a decision tree would be, right to left). This yields a number between .00 and 1.00 for each factor, the sum of which, over all factors, equals 1.00. Regarding these as utilities, they, along with the pluses and minuses to indicate valence and the assessed probabilities, permit computation of an SEU for having a(another) child. This SEU can range between .00 and 1.00 with a number less than .50 being against having a child, a number greater than .50 being for having a child, and .50 indicating indifference.

The hierarchy was completed by 200 married couples, 50 of each family size (attrition reduced this to 165 couples). Each member of each couple completed the hierarchy separately and they were told to think of a 2-year time frame for deciding to have a child. It is important to stress that the subjects merely completed the hierarchy—they were not told what the results of the computations were and no decision was prescribed.

One year later the couples were contacted and asked to complete the hierarchy again. This was to assess test-retest reliability, that turned out to be .62. At the end of the second year they were again contacted and asked what their decision had been. If they had had a child, if the wife was pregnant, if they were trying to conceive (i.e., had stopped using contraception), or if they were attempting to adopt, they were regarded as having made a positive decision—everything else was regarded as a negative decision.

This is not the place for details, but significant and interesting differences in the relative influence of the various factors were found as a function of current family size (see Townes, Campbell, Beach, & Martin, 1977; Wood, Campbell, Townes, & Beach, 1977). Of greater interest here is the predictive ability of the scheme (Beach, Campbell, & Townes, 1979). Recall that couples were not told the predictions nor were decisions prescribed; they merely completed the hierarchy. The experimenter computed the husband's SEU and the wife's SEU and averaged them to make a prediction for the couple; if the average was greater than .50, a positive decision was predicted, if it was equal to or less than .50, a negative decision was predicted. After two years the results were as shown in Table 13.2.

Predictions were correct for 119 of the 165 couples (72%), which is not too bad. But, the large number (40) of "false positives" is troublesome. Closer examination of these couples' data revealed that although these couples' SEUs were indeed positive, they were, as a group, significantly closer to the .50 indifference point than were the SEUs of the 55 "hits." It appears that merely having a SEU above the indifference point is not sufficient; the impact of a child on a couple's life constitutes a major change and they apparently have to actively want the child, not just not be indifferent, before they will decide to have a(another) child. (It is this finding that suggested the idea for identifying potential bus riders in the METRO Transit study described earlier.)

After this study was completed (and another done on childless women in various professional training programs that showed marked differences in utilities for the various factors between women who wanted children "someday" and those who did not; Coleman, 1978), the scheme was modified in light of the results. For example, more factors were added that related to birth defects, a consideration of concern to older couples. It subsequently has been formulated as a self-administering questionnaire and, with the title Optional Parenthood Questionnaire (OPQ), has been published by the National Alliance for Optional Parenthood, which is an educational organization dedicated to rational decision making in family planning. The OPQ is sold in lots to family planning counselors and clinics and in one year has sold about 850 copies. A scoring and interpretation manual also is available from the Alliance and a computer scoring service is available through the Department of Psychiatry and Behavioral Sciences at the University of Washington. Use of the OPQ in family planning counseling, especially when the husband and wife have different utilities and/or probabilities is described in Wood, Campbell, Townes and Beach (1977).

TABLE 13.2
Predicted and Observed
Decisions About Having
A(Another) Child

		Predicted Decision	
		Positive	Negative
Observed	Positive	55	6
Decision	Negative	40	64

CONCLUSIONS

The primary theme that emerges from all of this is that many researchers in many laboratories are using decision theoretic/analytic ideas to devise schemes for dealing with many different kinds of personal and public decision problems. The secondary theme is that few, if any, of these schemes ever venture, let alone survive, outside of the laboratory. With so much creativity and so many good intentions behind them, one would expect the schemes to attract more interest from potential users or from people or institutions with similar problems. Of course, things may be different in the classified world of military decision making, although we tend to doubt it, but out here where the rest of us are, the market definitely is on the slow side. The question is, why?

Several researchers have discussed various possible reasons for these schemes' lack of use (e.g., Brown, 1970; Phillips, 1978; Ransohoff & Feinstein, 1976; Schwartz, 1979). Among these reasons are (1) distrust of the reliability and validity of assessed probabilities and utilities; (2) the time demands of the schemes; (3) the complexity of the schemes; (4) unwillingness on the part of the decision maker to expose how he/she arrived at a final decision; and (5) the threat posed by such schemes (or their superfluousness) in that decision makers often see themselves as experts who have the intuitive, educated, inborn, natural, or what-have-you, skill to make decisions.

The next question involves what can be done to make the schemes more acceptable. Schwartz (1979) suggests education to increase the understanding and use of decision schemes as well as the development of more accessible schemes. Lusted (1979) reports medicine is making progress in both education and accessibility. He mentiones, for example, an increase in availability of textbooks on decision analysis in medicine as well as the fact that medical schools are finally realizing medical education (both current and continuing) should involve acquisition of problem solving skills as well as acquisition of facts. As another sign of progress he mentions the formation and first meeting of the Society for Medical Decision Making in 1979. This society also plans to publish a journal entitled Medical Decision Making. Brown (1970) suggests greater promotion and better packaging; he suggests the development of more easily used schemes that can present results in a clear and appealing manner. One example of an attempt to develop a more easily accessible tool for physicians for a rather complex decision analysis technique (i.e., Bayesian diagnosis) is a program for computing Bayesian probabilities for up to nine diseases with up to 16 symptoms that will work on a pocket calculator (McNeil & Sherman, 1978; Sherman, 1978).

If our experience is any guide, and judging from conversations with others in the field, one of the biggest obstacles to acceptance is that virtually all of these schemes are almost more complicated than the original decision problem. Certainly, attempts to simplify abound (as discussed earlier, Edwards, 1977, is a major apologist for simplification as are Bauer & Wegener, 1977), but even at that, one often has the feeling that we are urging the use of a cannon to deal with a mouse. As Bauer and Wegener (1977) conclude, "... more emphasis should be placed on ... the implications of applying simple models to complex situations, rather than of applying complex models to simple problems [p. 214]."

The nonacceptance problem aside, there appears to be a major, nonobvious, side benefit of using these schemes. It seems that the exercise of simply working through some sort of decision scheme can be valuable whether or not it is sued to arrive at a final decision. For example when intelligence analysts were taught to assess probabilities instead of using common verbal phrases for communicating their opinions to each other, there was a considerable decrease in miscommunication and one analyst even remarked, "This is something; for the first time I know when I disagree" (Kelly & Peterson, 1970).

In his amazingly ambitious effort to create an MAUT scheme for evaluating several busing plans for the desegregation of Los Angeles' schools, Edwards (1979) found that perhaps the most important product of his project was having the school board members' utilities made explicit. These explicit utilities could very well be valuable as a guide to either evaluating busing plans or creating a new busing plan no matter what kind of procedure (decision theoretic or otherwise) is adopted to do the job. In short, when one knows what the clients want and do not want (and the relative degrees of wanting) one has cleared a major hurdle and the remainder may be relatively straight-forward.

In the same vein, couples using the OPQ often remarked that it was helpful to simply go through the questionnaire—it made them think of things they would not otherwise have thought of. Moreover, they learned where they differed from their spouse in terms of wanting or not wanting a(another) child (Wood, Campbell, Townes & Beach, 1977).

Even the most elementary instruction in the concepts underlying decision analysis may be useful. For example, Fryback and Thornbury (1978) performed an interesting study in which they asked six radiologists to decide independently for each of 50 cases which of two diagnostic tests, arteriography or needle aspiration, should be chosen to evaluate (i.e., diagnose) the space-occupying renal lesion discovered through excretory urography. Three possible diagnoses were considered. For ten cases the radiologists were asked to simply make their decision in their usual manner. Next they were told how such decisions would be approached using basic decision theory (i.e., to take uncertainty and costs into account). On the basis of this fairly informal instruction they were then asked to make a decision for each of 10 more cases; at no time were they asked to make any quantitative judgments. For each of the remaining 30 cases the radiologists were asked to quantitatively assess the probability that their diagnosis of the possible nature of the lesion was correct. Taking both monetary and nonmonetary (i.e., medical risk, patient discomfort, patient inconvenience) costs into account and assuming that the best method of decision making is the one that provides the greatest diagnostic benefit at the least cost, Fryback and Thornbury found that even "informal decision theory instruction" resulted in a decrease in costs relative to costs incurred when the radiologists used their usual decision making processes. Additionally, when they were asked to quantitatively assess their diagnostic probabilities, costs were reduced even more. Furthermore, if the experimenter combined the radiologists' assessed probabilities with the assessed costs for a formal, quantitative application of decision theory an even further reduction in cost could be made. Thus it appears that although formal application of decision analysis can greatly improve upon the radiologists' usual decision methods, even informal training in decision analysis can lead to improvement.

REFERENCES

Baquet, A. E., Halter, A. N., & Conklin, F. S. The value of frost forecasting: A Bayesian appraisal. *American Journal of Agricultural Economics,* 1976, *58,* 511–520.

Barclay, S., & Peterson, C. R. *Multi-attribute utility models for negotiations* (Technical Report 76-1). McLean, Va.: Decisions and Designs, Inc., March 1976.

Barclay, S., Brown, R. V., Kelly, C. W., III, Peterson, C. R., Phillips, L. D., & Selvidge, J. *Handbook for decision analysis* (Technical Report TR-77-6-30). McLean, Va: Decisions and Designs, Inc., September 1977.

Bauer, V., & Wegener, M. Applications of multi-attribute utility theory: Comments. In H. Jungermann & G. DeZeeuw (Eds.), *Decision making and change in human affairs.* Dordrecht, Holland: Reidel Publishing Company, 1977.

Beach, B. H. Expert Judgment about uncertainty: Bayesian decision making in realistic settings. *Organizational Behavior and Human Performance,* 1975, *14,* 10–59.

Beach, L. R., Campbell, F. L., & Townes, B. D. Subjective expected utility and the prediction of birth-planning decisions. *Organizational Behavior and Human Performance,* 1979, *24,* 18–28.

Beach, L. R., Mai-Dalton, R., & Marshall, M. *Characteristics of potential bus riders.* Unpublished manuscript, University of Washington, 1979.

Beach. L. R., Townes, B. D., Campbell, F. L., & Keating, G. W. Developing and testing a decision aid for birth planning decisions. *Organizational Behavior and Human Performance,* 1976, *15,* 99–116.

Bernoulli, D. Specimen theoriae novae de mensura sortis. *Comentarii Academiae Scientiarum Imperiales Petropolitanae,* 1738, *5,* 175–192. (Translated by L. Sommer in *Econometrica,* 1954, *22,* 23–36).

Brown, R. V. Do managers find decision theory useful? *Harvard Business Review,* 1970, *48,* 78–89.

Brown, R. V., Kahr, A. S., & Peterson, C. *Decision analysis for the manager.* New York: Holt, Rinehart & Winston, 1974.

Cohen, L. J. *The Probable and the Provable.* Oxford: Clarendon Press, 1977.

Coleman, M. B. *Values influencing professional women students' decision to parent.* Unpublished master's thesis, University of Washington, 1978.

Coombs, C. H. *A theory of data.* New York: Wiley, 1964.

Davidson, A. R., & Beach, L. R. *Error patterns in the prediction of fertility behavior.* Unpublished manuscript, University of Washington, 1979.

Davidson, D., Suppes, P., & Siegel, S. *Decision-making: An experimental approach.* Stanford, Calif.: Stanford University Press, 1957.

Deaton, M. D. Utility: Recent theory and some applications. *Catalog of Selected Documents in Psychology,* 1977, *7,* Ms. 1509.

Edwards, W. *Nonconservative probabilistic information processing systems.* Institute of Science and Technology, University of Michigan, Report Number ESD-TR-66-404, December 1966.

Edwards, W. Social utilities. In *Decision and risk analysis: Powerful new tools for management,* Proceedings of the Sixth Triennial Symposium, June 1971, Hoboken, N.J.: *The Engineering Economist,* 1972, 119-129.

Edwards, W. How to use multiattribute utility measurement for social decision making. *IEEE Transactions on Systems, Man and Cybernetics,* 1977, *SMC-7,* 326-340.

Edwards, W. Technology for director dubious: Evaluation and decision in public contexts. In K. R. Hammond (Ed.), *Judgment and decision in public policy formation.* Boulder, Colo.: Westview Press, 1978.

Edwards, W. *Multiattribute utility measurement in a highly political context: Evaluating desegregation plans in Los Angeles.* Paper presented at the 145th Annual Meeting of the American Association for the Advancement of Science, Houston, Tex., 1979.

Edwards, W., Phillips, L. D., Hays, W. L., & Goodman, B. C. Probabilistic information processing systems: Design and evaluation. *IEEE Transactions on Systems Science and Cybernetics,* 1968, *SSC-4,* 248-265.

Einhorn, H. J., & Hogarth, R. M. Confidence in judgment: Persistence of the illusion of validity. *Psychological Review,* 1978, *85,* 395-416.

Fawcett, J. T., & Arnold, F. S. The value of children: Theory and method. *Representative Research in Social Psychology,* 1973, *4,* 23-36.

Feinstein, A. R. Clinical biostatistics XXXIX. The haze of Bayes, the aerial palaces of decision analysis, and the computerized Ouija board. *Clinical Pharmacology and Therapeutics,* 1977, *21,* 482-496.

Ford, C. K., Keeney, R. L., & Kirkwood, C. W. Evaluating methodologies: A procedure and application to nuclear power plant siting methodologies. *Management Science,* 1979, *25,* 1-10.

Fryback, D. G., & Thornbury, J. R. Informal use of decision theory to improve radiological patient management. *Radiology,* 1978, *129,* 385-388.

Gardiner, P. C., & Edwards, W. Public values: Multiattribute utility measurement for social decision making. In M. F. Kaplan & S. Schwartz (Eds.), *Human judgment and decision processes.* New York: Academic Press, 1975.

Goldsmith, R. W. *Studies of a model for evaluating judicial evidence.* Paper presented at the Seventh Research Conference on Subjective Probability, Utility and Decision Making, Göteborg, Sweden, August 1979.

Gorry, G. A., Kassirer, J. P., Essig, A., & Schwartz, W. B. Decision analysis as the basis for computer-aided management of acute renal failure. *The American Journal of Medicine,* 1973, *55,* 473-484.

Gregg, G. T. Probability forecasts of a temperature event. *National Weather Digest,* 1977, *2,* 33-34.

Gustafson, D. H., Greist, J. H., Stauss, F. F., Erdman, H., & Laughren, T. A probabilistic system for identifying suicide attemptors. *Computers and Biomedical Research,* 1977, *10,* 83-89.

Guttentag, M., & Sayeki, Y. A decision-theoretic technique for the illumination of cultural differences. *Journal of Cross-Cultural Psychology,* 1975, *6,* 203-217.

Hoffman, L. W., & Hoffman, M. L. The value of children to parents. In J. T. Fawcett (Ed.), *Psychological perspectives on population.* New York: Basic Books, 1973.

Holmstrom, V. L., & Beach, L. R. Subjective expected utility and career preferences. *Organizational Behavior and Human Performance,* 1973, *10,* 201-207.

Huber, G. P. Methods for quantifying subjective probabilities and multiattribute utilities. *Decision Sciences,* 1974, *5,* 430-458. (a)

Huber, G. P. Multi-attribute utility models: A review of field and field-like studies. *Management Science,* 1974, *20,* 1393-1402. (b)

Humphreys, A. R., & Humphreys, P. C. An investigation of subjective preference orderings for multiattributed alternatives. In D. Wendt & C. Vlek (Eds.), *Utility, probability, and human decision making*. Dordrecht, Holland: Reidel Publishing Company, 1975.

Humphreys, P. Application of multi-attribute utility theory. In H. Jungermann & G. DeZeeuw (Eds.), *Decision making and change in human affairs*. Dordrecht, Holland: Reidel Publishing Company, 1977.

Johnson, E. M., & Huber, G. P. The technology of utility assessment. *IEEE Transactions on Systems, Man, and Cybernetics*, 1977, *SMC-7*, 311-325.

Jungermann, H. *'Decisionetics': The art of helping people to make personal decisions* (Technical Report 79-18). Seattle: University of Washington, Department of Psychology, March 1979.

Kahneman, D., & Tversky, A. Prospect theory: An analysis of decision under risk. *Econometrica*, 1979, *47*, 263-291.

Keeney, R. L. Utility functions for multiattributed consequences. *Management Science*, 1972, *18*, 276-287.

Keeney, R. L. The art of assessing multiattribute utility functions. *Organizational Behavior and Human Performance*, 1977, *19*, 267-310.

Keeney, R. L., & Raiffa, H. *Decisions with multiple objectives: Preferences and value tradeoffs*. New York: Wiley, 1976.

Kelly, C. W., & Peterson, C. R. *Probability estimates and probabilistic procedures in current intelligence analysis*. Gaithersburg, Md.: Federal Systems Division, International Business Machines Corporation, Report on Phase I, 1970.

Krischer, J. P. An annotated bibliography of decision analytic applications to health care. *Operations Research*, 1980, *28*, 97-113.

Lusted, L. B. Twenty years of medical decision making studies. *Proceedings of the Third Annual Symposium on Computer Applications in Medical Care*. (held in Silver Spring, Maryland, October 14-17, 1979) Washington, D.C.: *IEEE*, 1979 (#79CH1480-3C).

Lusted, L. B., Bell, R. S., Edwards, W., Roberts, H. V., & Wallace, D. L. Evaluating the efficacy of radiologic procedures by Bayesian methods: A progress report. In K. Snapper (Ed.), *Models and metrics for decision makers*. Washington, D.C.: Information Resources Press, in press.

McNeil, B. J., & Sherman, H. Example: Bayesian calculations for the determination of the etiology of pleuritic chest pain in young adults in a teaching hospital: Part B. *Computers and Biomedical Research*, 1978, *11*, 187-194.

Moskowitz, H., Evans, G. W., & Jimenez-Lerma, I. Development of a multiattribute value function for long-range electrical generation expansion. *IEEE Transactions on Engineering Management*, 1978, *EM-25*, 78-87.

Mosteller, F., & Nogee, P. An experimental measurement of utility. *Journal of Political Economy*, 1951, *59*, 371-404.

Muchinsky, P. M., & Fitch, M. K. Subjective expected utility and academic preferences. *Organizational Behavior and Human Performance*, 1975, *14*, 217-226.

Murphy, A. H. Decision-making models in the cost-loss ratio situation and measures of the value of probability forecasts. *Monthly Weather Review*, 1976, *104*, 1058-1065.

Murphy, A. H. The value of climatological, categorical, and probabilistic forecasts in the cost-loss ratio situation. *Monthly Weather Review*, 1977, *105*, 803-816.

Murphy, A. H., & Winkler, R. L. Probability forecasts: A survey of National Weather Service forecasters. *Bulletin of the American Meteorological Society*, 1974, *55*, 1449-1453. (a)

Murphy, A. H., & Winkler, R. L. Subjective probability forecasting experiments in meteorology: Some preliminary results. *Bulletin of the American Meteorological Society*, 1974, *55*, 1206-1216. (b)

Murphy, A. H., & Winkler, R. L. Experimental point and area precipitation probability forecasts for a forecast area with significant local effects. *Atmosphere*, 1977, *15*, 61-78. (a)

Murphy, A. H., & Winkler, R. L. *Probabilistic tornado forecasts: Some experimental results*. Preprint volume of the Tenth Conference on Severe Local Storms, Omaha, Nebraska, October 18-21, 1977. Boston: The American Meteorological Society. (b)

Murphy, A. H., & Winkler, R. L. Reliability of subjective probability forecasts of precipitation and temperature. *Journal of the Royal Statistical Society: Series C (Applied Statistics)*, 1977, *26*, 41-47. (c)

Murphy, A. H., & Winkler, R. L. Probabilistic temperature forecasts: The case for an operational program. *Bulletin of the American Meteorological Society*, 1979, *60*, 12-19.

Newman, J. R. Differential weighting in multiattribute utility measurement: When it should not and when it does make a difference. *Organizational Behavior and Human Performance*, 1977, *20*, 312-325.

O'Connor, M. F. *The application of multi-attribute scaling procedures to the development of indices of water quality.* Unpublished doctoral dissertation, University of Michigan, 1972.

O'Connor, M. F., Reese, T. R., & Allen, J. J. *A multi-attribute utility approach for evaluating alternative Naval aviation plans* (Technical Report 76-16). McLean, Va.: Decisions and Designs, Inc., September 1976.

Otway, H. J., & Edwards, W. *Application of a simple multi-attribute rating technique to evaluation of nuclear waste disposal sites: A demonstration* (Research Memorandum RM-77-31). Laxenburg, Austria: International Institute for Applied Systems Analysis, June 1977.

Pauker, S. G. Coronary artery surgery: The use of decision analysis. *Annals of Internal Medicine*, 1976, *85*, 8-18.

Peterson, C. R., & Beach, L. R. Man as an intuitive statistician. *Psychological Bulletin*, 1967, *68*, 29-46.

Phillips, L. D. *Decision analysis in the insurance industry* (Technical Report 78-7). Uxbridge, Middlesex, England: Decision Analysis Unit, Brunel Institute of Organization and Social Studies, Brunel University, November 1978.

Phillips, L. D., Hays, W. L., & Edwards, W. Conservatism in complex probabilistic inference. *IEEE Transactions on Human Factors in Electronics*, 1966, *HFE-7*, 7-18.

Preston, M. G., & Baratta, P. An experimental study of the auction-value of an uncertain outcome. *American Journal of Psychology*, 1948, *61*, 183-193.

Raiffa, H. *Decision analysis: Introductory lectures on choices under uncertainty.* Reading, Mass.: Addison-Wesley, 1968.

Raiffa, H. *Preferences for multiattributed alternatives* (Memorandum RM-5868-DOT/RC). Santa Monica, Calif.: The Rand Corporation, 1969.

Ransohoff, D. F., & Feinstein, A. R. Is decision analysis useful in clinical medicine? (Editorial). *The Yale Journal of Biology and Medicine*, 1976, *49*, 165-168.

Safran, C., Tsichlis, P. N., Bluming, A. Z., & Desforges, J. F. Diagnostic planning using computer assisted decision-making for patients with Hodgkin's disease. *Cancer*, 1977, *39*, 2426-2434.

Sanders, F. On subjective probability forecasting. *Journal of Applied Meteorology*, 1963, *2*, 191-201.

Sayeki, Y. Allocation of importance: An axiom system. *Journal of Mathematical Psychology*, 1972, *9*, 55-65.

Schwartz, W. B. Decision analysis: A look at the chief complaints. *The New England Journal of Medicine*, 1979, *300*, 556-559.

Shanteau, J. Component processes in risky decision making. *Journal of Experimental Psychology*, 1974, *103*, 680-691.

Shepard, R. N. On subjectively optimum selections among multi-attribute alternatives. In M. W. Shelley & G. L. Bryan (Eds.), *Human judgments and optimality.* New York: John Wiley & Sons, 1964.

Sherman, H. A pocket diagnostic calculator program for computing Bayesian probabilities for nine diseases with sixteen symptoms: Part A. *Computers and Biomedical Research*, 1978, *11*, 177-186.

Slovic, P., Fischhoff, B., & Lichtenstein, S. Behavioral decision theory. *Annual Review of Psychology*, 1977, *28*, 1-39.

Spetzler, C. S., & Staël von Holstein, C-A. S. Probability encoding in decision analysis. *Management Science*, 1975, *22*, 340-358.

Thompson, J. C. On the operational deficiencies in categorical weather forecasts. *Bulletin of the American Meteorological Society*, 1952, *33*, 223-226.

Thompson, J. C., & Brier, G. W. The economic utility of weather forecasts. *Monthly Weather Review*, 1955, *83*, 249-254.

Thurstone, L. L. The measurement of values. *Psychological Review*, 1954, *61*, 47-58.

Townes, B. D., Campbell, F. L., Beach, L. R., & Martin, D. C. Birth planning values and decisions: Preliminary findings. In S. H. Newman & V. D. Thompson (Eds.), *Population psychology: Research and educational issues*. Bethesda, Md.: U.S. Department of Health, Education, and Welfare, 1977.

Tversky, A. Additivity, utility, and subjective probability. *Journal of Mathematical Psychology*, 1967, *4*, 175-202.

Tversky, A., & Kahneman, D. Judgment under uncertainty: Heuristics and biases. *Science*, 1974, *185*, 1124-1131.

Winkler, R. L., & Murphy, A. H. Evaluation of subjective precipitation probability forecasts. *Proceedings of the First National Conference on Statistical Meteorology*. Boston: American Meteorological Society, 1968, 148-157.

von Winterfeldt, D. *Experimental tests of independence assumptions for risky multiattribute preferences* (SSRI Research Report 76-8). Los Angeles: Social Science Research Institute, University of Southern California, 1976.

von Winterfeldt, D., & Fischer, G. W. Multiattribute utility theory: Models and assessment procedures. In D. Wendt & C. A. J. Vleck (Eds.), *Utility, probability, and human decision making*. Dordrecht, Holland: Reidel Publishing Company, 1975.

Wood, R. J., Campbell, F. L., Townes, B. D., & Beach, L. R. Birth planning decisions. *American Journal of Public Health*, 1977, *67*, 563-565.

14
Expectancy-Value Approaches: Present Status and Future Directions

Norman T. Feather
The Flinders University of South Australia

In this chapter I intend to focus on some themes and issues that have emerged throughout this book and that relate to the expectancy-value approach. My intention is not to present a review or recapitulation of all that has gone before. To some extent this overview of the significant points in the various chapters has already been provided in the first chapter. Instead my concern is to draw out a number of points that seem to me to be important ones, not with the aim of presenting the reader with a neatly tied package because that is clearly impossible, but rather with the intention of providing some comparative appraisal of the different contributions and suggesting, sometimes directly and sometimes by implication, where we might go from here.

NEW PERSPECTIVES ON EXPECTANCY-VALUE THEORY

This book has been designed to inform the reader about how expectancy-value models have been used and/or discussed in a wide range of different contexts: achievement motivation, causal attribution, information feedback, social learning, values and attitudes, organizational psychology, and decision making. The different areas that have been sampled attest to the fact that the analysis of behavior in relation to expected consequences has had wide application. There is little question that the attempt to relate actions to expectations (or subjective probabilities) in combination with subjective values (or valences) has been a significant one by any standards. It has not only occupied the attention and efforts of psychologists across different contexts; it has done so in an enduring way. It is clear that the expectancy-value approach is not an ephemeral, fly-by-night model but one that has continued to interest theorists over the years.

Why the relatively long life? Perhaps because the approach is valid in many different contexts, with more than a grain of truth in its implications. Furthermore the approach is in tune with the current widespread interest in cognitive concepts and therefore benefits from a supporting *zeitgeist*. Alternatively, some critics might argue that the model endures because it is difficult to falsify—that subjective probabilities and valences can always be redefined after the event to fit the results. Whatever the explanation it is apparent that we are dealing with an approach that commands attention and respect, a significant form of theoretical analysis that has been applied quite generally, and that stands as a major alternative to competing, mechanistic theories of motivation such as traditional and neo-behavioristic analyses that invoke stimulus-response associations and internal drive states, and that pay less attention to the active, constructive properties of individuals.

Yet it is also clear that within the expectancy-value approaches there are some analyses that involve considerable extension and liberalization of the basic concepts and other analyses that remain quite close to earlier and more traditional models. It is interesting to note, for example, that neither expectancy-value models in organizational psychology nor subjectively expected utility (SEU) models in behavioral decision theory appear to have paid much attention to the new ideas that have emerged from some of the other areas described in the earlier chapters of this book. In these earlier chapters we find many new developments. Thus, several authors (Atkinson, Feather, Raynor) note the importance of viewing behavior as an extended and continuing stream rather than as a succession of discrete episodic events that involve a reactive rather than a continually active organism. This kind of focus has important implications, not the least of which is the need to recognize the effects on present actions of both persistent unresolved sources of motivation that carry over from the past and anticipations about long-term future goals that are linked contingently to sequences of possible actions and outcomes. We can add to the list of new perspectives the distinction between instigating and inhibitory forces and the new assumptions about resultant tendencies (Atkinson), the discussion of the various determinants of expectations and valences (e.g., Feather, Raynor, Kuhl, Weiner, Rotter, Mitchell), the interest in attributional concepts and their role in motivation (Weiner, Feather), the distinction between different kinds of expectations (Feather, Kuhl, Rotter), the analysis of the influence on behavior of self-related motivation, attitudes, and values (Raynor, Feather), the discussion of the concepts of generalized expectancy and psychological situation within the social learning framework (Rotter), the interest in both affect and perceived control (Feather, Weiner), the attention given to the information function of success and failure (Janoff-Bulman & Brickman), the distinction between action-orientation and state-orientation (Kuhl), the assumption that general human values function like motives to induce valences (Feather), and so on. One could keep adding to this list but the point is clear: Some areas seem to lag behind others in the extent to which expectancy-value models have been extended and liberalized. In particular, organizational psychology and SEU models of decision could profit from closer attention to some of these new ideas.

But the influence could also flow the other way. The considerable amount of knowledge gained from behavioral decision theory about subjective probabilities, utilities, and how well SEU models predict to choice when compared with alternative theories (Fischoff, Goitein & Shapira, Beach & Beach) have obvious implications for more general expectancy-value models—especially the recent emphasis on human errors in information-processing, the use of relatively simple heuristics, and exceptions to the prescriptive rules implied by the SEU model. The new ideas that emerge from how people go about making decisions in real-life (Mann & Janis, Beach & Beach) also have obvious relevance for theoretical approaches that have relied more on laboratory studies where behavior typically does not have important consequences and where high stress and conflict are usually the exception.

One hopes that some cross-fertilization will occur as the new ideas presented in this volume filter across the different areas of inquiry.

SCOPE OF THE EXPECTANCY-VALUE APPROACH

How generally can the expectancy-value approach be applied to the analysis of human action? What is its scope? Are there boundary conditions and limits to its application? These questions have been posed in various ways by Feather (Chapter 9), by Mitchell (Chapter 10), by Fischoff, Goitein, and Shapira (Chapter 11), and by Mann and Janis (Chapter 12).

There are no easy answers to these questions. Some critical comment has tended to simplify the issues by assuming that all expectancy-value models are essentially equivalent to SEU decision theory whereas, as we noted earlier, there are important differences across areas in the perspectives that are adopted and in the degree to which the traditional expectancy-value analysis has been extended. The claim that the expectancy-value approach fails to allow for human error and treats the person as overly rational is a misreading of those forms of analysis that are continuous with the early Tolman/Lewin models. The theoretical approaches of Atkinson (Chapter 2) and Feather (Chapter 3), for example, have never assumed that subjective probabilities and subjective values exactly mirror objective reality—however that is defined. They have always recognized that, because of insufficient information, or incorrect information, or defective information processing, or biases that have a motivational or some other basis, or for whatever reason, a person's expectations about the implications of particular actions could be serious distortions of reality. For example, a person desperate to succeed may be overly confident of success; a person threatened by failure may view the likelihood of success in an unduly pessimistic way; a person with limited information may develop an expectation that is based on misleading cues; a person overwhelmed by information may simplify to such an extent that expectations about the implications of actions are seriously in error; and so on. So too, the perceived values of incentives or reinforcements may be affected in various ways by motivational states and factors that are involved in the processing of information. The food that looks good to a starving man may be dry and unexciting to a well-fed person; success may be valued in different ways depending on the context. The concepts of expectation and perceived value that we use are framed at the level of subjective reality and that is what is held to be important for understanding a person's behavior.

We should note, however, that an emphasis on the subjective reality of events does not deny the importance of finding out how this subjective reality came about. We must not leave the person in an encapsulated life-space—a criticism leveled at Lewin (Brunswik, 1943), though one that field theory attempted to resolve in its later development (Cartwright, 1959, 1978). This means that the expectancy-value approach must pay close attention both to the determinants of a person's expectations and to what determines the perceived attractiveness and aversiveness of possible events for a person, as these expectations and valences are cognitively represented at any given time within a perceived situation. Thus, theorists who relate action to the combination of expectations (or related concepts) and valences (or related concepts) also have the task of providing a worthwhile theoretical analysis of the determinants of expectations and valences. Otherwise the general theory is incomplete and loose, with so much slippage that it may not be possible to falsify it, given the fact that the basic concepts are not clearly tied down but float in such a way that they can be reinterpreted in any retrospective analysis. We will return to this question later in this chapter.

Granted the emphasis on the subjective reality of expectations and valences, however, and the acceptance that this subjective reality is affected by motivational conditions and by those variables that influence the encoding of information, it is still possible that expectancy-value models may be more appropriately applied to some behaviors than to others. Impulsive behaviors, panic behaviors, habitual or automatic actions, irrational behaviors that involve bizarre symptoms, and so on, all seem to be less appropriate arenas for the application of these models. So do those behaviors that involve actual commerce with a goal object, where a person is not psychologically distant from a goal but is actually experiencing a goal and reacting affectively to it, as in consummatory behaviors associated with eating, drinking, and sex. All of these behaviors involve a relative absence of thoughtful planning at a distance and so, by implication, suggest that expectancy-value models may be more appropriate to actions where foresight and planning are possible.

It would be premature, however, to conclude that all seemingly unplanned behaviors are outside the limits of the expectancy-value approach, even though some probably are. Consummatory behavior, for example, could be treated as a limiting case where the subjective probability of goal attainment is certain and where action varies with the valence of the goal. Panic behavior might involve deficient processing of cues that provide information about the subjective probabilities of various means of escape, for example, so that the goal of escaping dominates action and the subjective probabilities carry less weight or are not clearly differentiated or are grossly distorted. So too, some other types of impulsive behavior that involve approach rather than escape may be dominated by valence considerations, as when a person gambles unrealistically on a large gain from a stock market investment without much heed for the probabilities. In each of these cases both valences and subjective probabilities continue to play a part, even though the rational-utilitarian model seems less appropriate than under other conditions.

A detailed analysis of the limits of the approach would require specifying those conditions that foster purposeful planning in contrast to those conditions that do not. The important psychoanalytic distinction between the primary process and the secondary process is relevant and may provide some clues that point to appropriate circumstances. Expectancy-value models might validly be applied to behaviors where the ego is in control and where secondary process thinking and conscious intentions dominate purposeful action. But where unconscious wishes strive for fulfilment and where primary process thinking is strongly in evidence, these models may be less appropriate—at least from the Freudian and neo-Freudian viewpoints. One is hard-pressed to explain slips of the tongue or the bizarre symptoms of psychotic behavior in terms of expectancy-value models. It should be noted, however, that recent more general approaches from the area of achievement motivation have included the concept of persisting unresolved action tendencies that may be augmented by forces acting over time or used up in behavior (Atkinson, Chapter 2). It remains to be seen whether this new analysis of the dynamics of action, that reflects upon the expectancy-value approach but that exists as an important contribution in its own right, can accommodate the phenomena described by Freud that led to his distinction between the secondary process and the primary process and to his analysis of the effects on thought and action of unconscious, unfulfilled wishes.

What conditions might be more likely to lead to foresight and planning and to behaviors relevant to an expectancy-value analysis? The following list combines suggestions from various chapters within this volume together with some additional ideas. In the first place, the models may be more appropriate where the situation *sets* the individual to structure possible actions within a means-end or instrumental framework. Under some conditions, for example, the response-outcome contingencies may be clearly laid out so that the person can easily structure a map of implications, drawing upon present information and relevant past experience. Similarly some situations may increase the salience of instrumental actions by encouraging the person to seek information about alternative courses of action and to assess the probabilities, to evaluate the possible consequences of actions, to reflect upon competencies in relation to possible behaviors, to note features of a situation that would facilitate or obstruct outcomes, and so on. These various conditions would have the effect of producing an instrumental and evaluative set and, by assumption, may be more likely to determine behaviors that are amenable to interpretation in terms of the combination of expectations and valences.

Second, the emphasis upon foresight and planning suggests that behaviors that are under intentional or volitional control should be more amenable to an expectancy-value analysis. Where external factors so dominate action that the individual has very little perceived choice about what happens, expectancy-value models may not be appropriate. The individual has to have some freedom of movement, believing that choices do matter and that intentions can have some effect.

Third, it may be true as Mann and Janis suggest (Chapter 12), that expectancy-value models are more appropriate under conditions that promote vigilance—that is, where there is moderate stress, where it is realistic to hope for a better solution, and where there is sufficient time to search and deliberate. Mann and Janis suggest that under these conditions the person is more likely to canvas alternatives and objectives thoroughly, to evaluate consequences carefully, to engage in a thorough search for information, to assimilate information in an unbiassed fashion, to reevaluate consequences carefully, and to engage in thorough planning for the implementation of a decision and for the possible contingencies. Where conditions depart from the vigilance condition—as when stress is either very low or very high, when there is little point in hoping for a better solution, and when the decision has to be made quickly under considerable time pressure—the rational-utilitarian model may be less appropriate.

Fourth, it is possible that the model may be more applicable to some individuals than to others. There may be individual differences in the extent to which people plan their actions in contrast to acting impulsively. These differences may be relatively stable, generalizing across a variety of situations so that some people may tend to be "planners" whereas others may tend to be "impulsives". Expectancy-value models would presumably be more appropriate forms of analysis for the former group.

Fifth, successful application of expectancy-value models, given the appropriate conditions, should be more likely when the time gap is minimal between the assessed probabilities and valences for an individual and the action to be predicted. It is obvious that, as the time gap increases, expectations and valences can change. In making predictions to behavior one would hope to assess the immediate determinants as they exist for the individual at the time action occurs.

THE ROLE OF THOUGHT

I have suggested that expectancy-value models may be more appropriately applied to the analysis of behaviors where planning and evaluation are possible in advance and where some freedom of choice is available. Does this imply that a high degree of conscious thought would precede the predicted actions? If so, the kinds of evidence presented by Fischoff, Goitein, and Shapira (Chapter 11) suggest that the thought may be of a relatively simple nature, given the difficulties of processing complex information. People may rely on simple heuristics for making probability judgments; they may not think much about the subjective values or utilities involved in a decision and, if they do, they may define these utilities rather inadequately. Moreover, they may make only a cursory analysis of the problem and the various possible courses of action; they may fall back on very simple decision rules; and so on. The rational, intelligent, analytic mode of thought that seems to be implied by the expectancy-value approach may therefore be a fiction as far as actual behavior is concerned.

But do cognitive models have to mirror exactly the thought processes that might take place? Tolman's cognitive theory was based on the analysis of the behavior of rats running through mazes and performing in other types of laboratory apparatus (Tolman, 1958). There was no implication that the rat somehow indulged in a complex thought process and then acted. The concept of expectation was defined as an intervening variable, as a construct that abstracted the relationship between antecedent (stimulus) and consequent (response) conditions, with no importation of meaning beyond this relationship. It was a concept that seemed to be demanded by observations of such behaviors as the rat's turning response at a choice point in a maze, its reactions when a different reward was substituted for one that had been usually presented, for its ability to display some degree of insightful behavior and to run a maze following latent learning, and so on. No doubt Tolman assumed that the rat could perceive, could structure information, and could learn within its biological limits, but his development of an expectancy-value approach in his later theorizing (Tolman, 1955, 1959) should not be taken to imply acceptance of complex thought processes. That would be to import additional meaning beyond the behavioral evidence, to move from an analysis in terms of intervening variables to one that employed hypothetical constructs—using the language of the 1940s (Marx & Hillix, 1973).

One should not, however, deny the importance of drawing upon a wide range of evidence so as to learn more about the assumed processes and mechanisms that relate to constructs involved in a model. At the human level, for example, one source of evidence not available from other species is a person's verbal report about possible intervening thought processes. But it would be a mistake to elevate this source of evidence so that it dominates all else, leading the investigator to discount evidence based upon other sources. Retrospective reports of conscious thought processes may be in error for a number of reasons. Thus, much thought may occur so rapidly that its details cannot be recaptured; people may present elaborated and manufactured accounts when asked to report their conscious thoughts so that the reports conform to internal theories about what the situation seems to demand rather than to the actual intervening processes; in the case of skilled behavior a lot of action may run off without conscious thought at all about the details of the performance (see Chapter 9, pp. 284–286). Given these difficulties it would be foolish to evaluate a theory or model only on the basis of how well it is supported by verbal reports of thought processes obtained after the event. A concert pianist who strikes a wrong note may not be able to say much about prior thought processes, if indeed there was much conscious thought. But the pianist's immediate annoyance and discomfort followed by more intensive practice of the passage so as to correct the error demonstrates that a particular standard of performance was expected—that expectations and subjective values were intertwined with the performance. Verbal reports should not be taken as critical sources of evidence for testing the expectancy-value approach. It is obvious that one has to appeal to a much wider range of behaviors.

More generally, the issue of thought and action has a long history in psychology and one to which I can only allude, given the summary scope of this chapter. Since Freud, all clinical psychologists and psychiatrists have recognized the importance of unconscious processes as determinants of behavior. Those of a Freudian persuasion refer to the effects of persisting, unconscious wishes, distinguish between the primary and secondary processes, and emphasize that conscious thought is only part of the overall picture for understanding human action. Indeed most people working with disturbed patients would agree that verbal reports can often give a distorted impression of the underlying personality dynamics. Note, for example, the over-intellectualization of some patients, the delusions of the paranoid patient, the rationalizations that are part of everyday life, and the secondary elaboration that occurs in dream reports.

In the development of systematic positions in psychology, the status of conscious experience and the use of the introspective method have been major issues for debate—as for example in the emergence of behaviorism. Even before then there were doubts that the analysis of conscious experience into fixed elements such as sensations, images, and feelings could give a true picture of conscious experience. The imageless thought controversy raised serious questions about the elementaristic approach (Posner & Shulman,   1979), as did the subsequent emphasis by Gestalt psychologists on organization and form (Koffka, 1935). William James (1890/1950) also pointed to deficiencies in attempts to isolate the basic elements of experience when he eloquently described the stream of thought, noting that: "A permanently existing "idea" or "Vorstellung" which makes its appearance before the footlights of consciousness at periodical intervals, is as mythological as entity as the Jack of Spades [p. 236]." One could provide many other examples from the history of psychology that relate to the nature and functions of conscious experience.

Over the last few decades there has been increasing recognition that cognitive models do not have to postulate that conscious thought necessarily precedes action. I have already noted that Tolman's main source of evidence for his cognitive approach was the behavior of the rat (Tolman, 1958), a species whose cognitive capacities are relatively limited. Lewin (1936) did not identify the life-space as consisting only of conscious determinants but used the criterion that what is real is what has effects. Psychologists concerned with human information processing, the organization of skilled behavior, and the computer simulation of cognitive processes have allowed for the progressive refinement and integration of expectancies (or related concepts) with practice so that they become simplified and organized at higher levels. In this way response sequences can be represented in terms of higher-order structures or programs without having to assume that a lot of intervening thought takes place (e.g., Hebb, 1949; Miller, Galanter, & Pribram, 1960; Simon, 1979).

Recently Shiffrin and Schneider (1977) and Schneider and Shiffrin (1977) have distinguished between controlled search and automatic detection in perception and memory, a point that has been taken up by Taylor and Fiske (1978) in their discussion of similarities between "top of the head" generation of salient responses and the automatic processing described by Shiffrin and Schneider. Taylor and Fiske assume that the generation of these "top of the head" salient responses is more likely to occur in situations that are commonplace and uninvolving and where overlearning has occurred. Other social psychologists have also recognized that a lot of routine actions appear to be "mindless" (Langer, 1978) and appear to involve "scripts" rather than "plans" (Schank & Abelson, 1977). Nisbett and Wilson (1977), Smith and Miller (1978), White (1980), and Weiner (1980, pp. 296–303) have looked at some of the limitations of verbal report and the question of whether or not people have access to cognitive processes that cause behavior. In summary, there seems to be general agreement that a lot of behavior goes on without much conscious planning and that cognitive models are not necessarily conscious thought models.

Perhaps the more important question to ask is when one would expect conscious thought to precede action. I have noted some of the conditions that might be involved (Feather, 1979; Chapter 9, p. 285). One might expect thought to enter in when expectancies are in the early stages of development and as they go through the process of becoming progressively integrated and refined so that they represent, in a more shorthand way, the implication structure of events over space and time. In learning to drive a car, for example, one might think about the details of the performance in the early stages of learning, but thoughts about the action sequence would apply to larger "chunks" as learning proceeds.

Thought would also intervene when expectations are disconfirmed, when what is expected does not eventuate, that is, when there is a discrepancy between expectation and input. Discrepant experience sets a problem to be solved, as when the motorist hits the accelerator rather than the brake, or when the road usually followed is blocked for repairs. Novel, unusual, discrepant information that does not conform to expectations may therefore elicit accessible processes of conscious thought, problem solving, or controlled search—to use Shiffrin and Schneider's (1977) term. Such thought may also be more likely to occur as the unexpected situation becomes more interesting and engaging (Smith & Miller, 1978). But where expectations are overlearned and firmly grounded in experience and where actions flow on in a routine way so as to confirm them, one would not expect to find much thought about the fine details of the performance. Under these conditions mental processes tend to run off quickly and automatically and to become inaccessible to conscious report (Shiffrin & Schneider, 1977; Schneider & Shiffrin, 1977). Conscious control is no longer necessary. The experienced driver who typically makes all the correct responses when driving to work along a familiar road can devote a lot of this thought and attention to other matters. He does not have to think about how to drive the car.

Even where automatic processing is dominant, however, thoughts may intrude about the goal structure and the general planning of the action, or about other intentions that await fulfilment. Thoughts may also intrude where a person is suddenly confronted by obstacles from the environment, or where new and difficult decisions have to be made, especially if these decisions have important consequences for the person (Mann & Janis, Chapter 12).

We are therefore led to the conclusion that the expectancy-value approach does not necessarily assume that a lot of conscious thought takes place in advance of action. Where a skill is in the early stages of development and where situations involve novel, unexpected, and involving events, conscious thought about the details of performance or about ways of making sense out of discrepant input may precede further action. But where an overlearned sequence of responses occurs under familiar conditions and runs off as expected, there may be a minimum of conscious thought. In the former case actions may be under conscious control and the cognitive processes that are involved may be accessible to verbal report. In the latter case actions may no longer involve conscious control and the cognitive processes may therefore be inaccessible to verbal report. Even where verbal reports are available, however, they should be regarded as one source of evidence relevant to the expectancy-value approach but not the only source. Like any other source of evidence, verbal reports should not be taken at face value but they should be weighed along with other information about the context of behavior and the behavior itself.

Expectancy-value models can be applied to actions where some conscious control appears to be involved and also to those response sequences that are not under conscious control. In the former case the role of expectations and subjective values may become evident from a person's verbal report as well as from the overt behavior itself. In the latter case, the role of expectations and subjective values become evident when the performance sequence is disrupted by novel or unfamiliar events and/or when the person is asked retrospectively to report on general overall plans and intentions. In both cases, the directed, purposive nature of behavior within a means-end or instrumental framework provides appropriate conditions for applying a conceptual analysis that relates actions to their expected consequences.

THE ROLE OF AFFECT

If we look at the general range of motivational theories in psychology it soon becomes evident that feelings occupy a central role in a number of them. In the early volume describing research on the achievement motive (McClelland, Atkinson, Clark, & Lowell, 1953), a theory of motivation was developed in which a motive was defined as "... a redintegration by a cue of a change in affective situation [p. 28]," and affect was related to the size of the discrepancy between a sensory or perceptual event and the adaptation level of the organism. Kagan (1972) similarly conceived of motives as cognitive representations of desired goals—anticipated future events that will make the person feel better. Young (1961, 1966) saw affect as basic to his theory of motivated behavior—a theory that is continuous with the long history of the application of hedonistic principles to the analysis of actions (see Cofer & Appley, 1964, for a review). There has been a lot of recent interest in the labeling of emotions (see Weiner, 1972, 1980, for some examples; Chapter 6), but in much of this work affect is treated as a passive state rather than as a possible determinant of action. Theories in the psychoanalytic tradition acknowledge the importance of cognitive-affective bonds (Dahl, in press; Holt, 1976; Klein. 1976). And affect is also central to the motivational system in theories developed by Tomkins (1962, 1963), Singer (1973, 1974), and Izard (1977). It is also a basic aspect of the opponent-process theory of motivation developed by Solomon and Corbit (1974) and a major variable in recent approaches to the analysis of depression (eg., Abrahamson, Seligman, & Teasdale, 1978; Blaney, 1977; Feather & Davenport, in press). It is evident, therefore, that there have been a number of recent attempts to relate affect and motivation, and to examine their role in regard to both cognition and behavior.

Among the contributors to this volume, Weiner (Chapter 6) presents a systematic account of how affect might be integrated into a more general view of motivated behavior—at least within an attributional context. My own contributions (Chapter 3) also demonstrate a continuing concern with the role of affect, evident in my attempts to assess degrees of achievement concern, anxiety, happiness, and disappointment after a success or failure outcome, in the development of some theoretical approaches to the analysis of affect (Chapter 3, pp. 68–71), and by the inclusion of affect as one of the defining characteristics of general human values and as a correlate of value system discrepancies (Chapter 9). More generally, Rotter (Chapter 8) comments upon emotional behaviors in relation to social learning theory, and Mann and Janis (Chapter 12) discuss the effects of different degrees of stress on decision making. There are also occasional references to feeling or affect in some of the other chapters.

These various contributions show that affect has not been neglected in this volume. But it is probably true to say that expectancy-value approaches need to give more attention to the role of affect. Decision theorists who use SEU (subjectively expected utility) models seem to neglect it altogether. When affect does appear in expectancy-value models it often seems to appear almost as an appendage or epiphenomenon, rather than as an integral part of the theory. Of course, that comment is relative. As I have noted, some authors in this volume do pay attention to affect. But, in general, its systematic status has not been developed in depth in relation to the expectancy-value approach. That is not to say that a systematic treatment is not possible. In fact, there are suggestions throughout this volume about how that development might proceed.

The question of how affect can be integrated into motivational theories of the expectancy-value type remains a challenge for future inquiry. I see affect as related in various ways to motives, to expectations, and to valences. Motives (including general values) have been assumed by some theorists to be linked to the affective system (Feather, 1975, and Chapter 9 in this volume; Atkinson & Birch, 1978, p. 96; McClelland, 1965). Discrepancies between present events and expectations or adaptation levels (Helson, 1964) have been regarded by some theorists as antecedent conditions for the development of affect (see Cofer & Appley, 1964, for a review). Valences have been taken to imply affective reactions when positively valent events and negatively valent events either occur or do not occur (Feather, Chapter 3, Table 3.7, p. 70). But what is the role of affect? Is the anticipation of positive or negative affect crucial to the direction that behavior takes? Does anticipated affect influence other characteristics of motivated behavior such as energy expenditure, latency of response, persistence in a given direction, and so on? How can the linkages between affect and cognition be represented? Can we spell out in more detail the relationships between motives and affect, expectations and affect, and valences and affect? These questions acknowledge that affective reactions are an integral part of the stream of behavior and that a complete analysis of the dynamics of action must allow for affective processes as well as cognitive processes.

DETERMINANTS OF EXPECTATIONS

Earlier in this chapter I noted that, in order to avoid encapsulating the individual within a subjective world, the expectancy-value approach should continue to investigate the determinants of expectations and valences. Having developed a detailed theoretical and empirical analysis relating to expectations on the one hand and valences on the other, one would then be in a better position to predict behavior in advance.

It first seems necessary to define the concept of expectation so as to capture its essential characteristics and so as to distinguish it from other related concepts. Several chapters in this volume contribute to this end. For example, Atkinson (Chapter 2) describes the early history of the concept and Feather (Chapter 3) adds to the picture by outlining some of the distinctions, made by Tolman (1932), Heckhausen (1977), and Bandura (1977a), between different kinds of expectations. Rotter (Chapter 8) distinguishes between specific expectancies and generalized expectancies. Other theorists, not included in this volume, make distinctions that correspond to some of those mentioned. For example, Bolles (1972) distinguishes between (S–S*) expectancies that relate to environmental stimulus-outcome contingencies and (R–S*) expectancies that relate to response outcome contingencies. And Mischel (1973) similarly distinguishes between expectancies that concern stimulus-outcome relations and expectancies that concern behavior-outcome relations. Mischel (1973), like Rotter (Chapter 8) and Bandura (1977b), emphasizes the importance of relating action to anticipated consequences and also develops his ideas from the perspective of a social learning theorist. Mischel's (1973) cognitive learning theory is therefore very congenial with the general theme of many of the contributions presented in this volume, given its emphasis on the individual's constructive competences and power to encode and categorize events, the expectancies that the individual holds about outcomes, the subjective values of these outcomes, and the role of self-regulatory systems and plans.

It is clear that the concept of expectation differs from some other concepts such as schema and prototype in that it is much more specific, relating to particular situations and particular responses. The behavior-outcome expectations that have been of special concern to expectancy-value theorists are elicited by cues within situations and they apply to defined responses and their possible consequences. They are not general abstracted structures without content. In terms of some current concepts from social cognition, they are more similar to scripts (Schank & Abelson, 1977) than to prototypes or schemata, because the *specific content* of both expectations and scripts is a fundamental aspect of their definition and both concepts are concerned with the structure of events within defined situations and the implications of particular actions within those situations. Scripts, however, are more extensive concepts, involving a whole sequence of interconnected events. Expectations are typically more limited in their scope, although they can be more extensive—as when an expectation applies to a well-practiced, integrated sequence of responses leading to a distant outcome. A set of specific expectations concerning the implications of particular actions might make up a script. If the expectations related to overlearned behavior, then the script would be a well-rehearsed one.

These comments suggest that it would be useful to analyze in some depth the similarities and differences among members of the family of cognitive concepts that include scripts, prototypes, schemata, plans, images, stereotypes, personal constructs, abstract structures, naive theories, expectations, and so on. These concepts cannot be used interchangeably and their comparison may bring out some important theoretical issues that relate to different shades of meaning. Taylor and Crocker (in press) have already made an important start in this direction and Goodnow (1979) has provided an excellent review of some of the concepts currently used in the general area of social cognition.

There are several references throughout this book to the determinants of expectations (especially Feather, Chapter 3) and what follows is by way of summary. It is clear that a person's own direct experience of response-outcome contingencies is a very important source of expectations. Past performance at tasks (the record of successes and failures) has a potent influence on initial expectations concerning similar tasks now to be performed. Present performance at a task may modify these initial expectations, especially if outcomes can be attributed to relatively stable causes (Weiner, Chapter 6). A person's expectations may also be influenced by cues in a situation that provides information about task difficulty. These cues might relate to the specific nature of the task itself (such as its length and complexity), to the conditions under which the task is performed (such as whether there is time pressure, whether there are distractions, whether help is available, and so on), or to the performance of others (whether similar others do well, whether one can learn vicariously from others, whether one is taught the response-reinforcement contingencies, and so on). In regard to the latter factors, Bandura (1977b) reminds us that "... learning is fostered by modeling and instruction as well as by informative feedback from one's own transactions with the environment [p. 91]." Expectations may also be influenced by motives and valences, either in an autistic or defensive way. A person who is dominated by a concern to do well or to win approval from others, for example, may have optimistic expectations that bear little relation to past performance and present reality; a person threatened by the possibility of failure may distort expectations of success downward and thus may be able to rationalize failure should it occur. These various determinants have received a lot of attention in the literature that deals with expectancies and subjective probabilities. The present volume provides some of the basic sources but by no means exhausts the list—see, for example, recent discussions by Bandura (1977b), Bolles (1972), Jones (1977), and Mischel (1973).

THE MEASUREMENT OF EXPECTATIONS

The measurement of expectations remains an important question for future research. Fischoff, Goitein, and Shapira (Chapter 11) indicate that procedures that rely upon direct self-report are fallible—for example, people often find it difficult to give numerical probability assessments concerning the possible occurrence of events. Moreover, as indicated earlier, verbal report has its problems as a source of evidence about conscious processes. Procedures that estimate subjective probabilities on the assumption that the SEU model is valid and that subjective probabilities and utilities are independent, thereby sidestep the issue as to whether the model is indeed a valid representation of choice behavior. One might estimate expectations from information about antecedent conditions (past performance, social comparison, the nature of the task to be performed, constraints within the present situation, and so on), but the weights to be assigned to each set of conditions would have to be estimated for each individual and the expectation itself would have to be operationalized.

One would hope that expectations could be assessed in advance of the behavior to be explained. When assessing expectations it is necessary to specify what kind of expectation is being assessed (for example, outcome expectations, efficacy expectations, generalized expectancies, and so on), and it also is probably necessary to consider expectations as having a number of dimensions. Bandura (1977a), for example, describes efficacy expectations as varying in their magnitude, their generality, and their strength. Presumably action-outcome expectations can also vary along similar dimensions. Some individuals, for example, may feel that their actions are very likely to lead to a desired goal; others may feel that the desired outcome is unlikely (magnitude). Some individuals may hold strongly to their expectancies; others may change them rapidly (strength). Some action-outcome expectancies may be elicited by a wide range of cues; others by a narrow range (cue generality). We can add to the list by suggesting that some expectancies may relate to a wide range of possible responses that could be enacted on the next step of a response sequence; others to a narrow band of responses or perhaps to only one response that could be enacted on the next step (response generality). Some expectancies may refer to sharply delimited parts of a sequence of response-reinforcement contingencies; others may refer to an integrated chain of events extending over a number of steps (response integration). Some expectancies may relate to a wide range of possible outcomes; others to a narrow range or perhaps to only one outcome (outcome generality). Some expectancies may be uniquely held by one person; others may be shared by a number of people (consensus). This list may not exhaust the possibilities, although it is fairly complete.

The measurement of expectations would involve some decision about which of the various dimensions is of major interest. Expectancy-value models have been most concerned with the magnitude dimension, as reflected in some estimate of the subjective probability that a response will lead to a defined outcome. But people could hold expectations that are of the same magnitude (for example, with a subjective probability or P_s equal to .50) but that differ in their strength. Thus, an expectation with the same magnitude might be relatively weak for one person and easily extinguished, whereas, for another person, its strength might be much greater and the expectation highly resistant to extinction. To complicate matters, the expectations could vary along the other dimensions as well. Clearly we need some theoretical treatment both of the conditions that lead to differences along these various dimensions and of the implications of these differences for behavior. This issue of the dimensions of expectations may turn out to be an important one for future development of the expectancy-value approach.

DETERMINANTS OF VALENCES

Just as continuing theoretical analysis of the concept of expectation is necessary, so too there is a need to develop detailed theories about valences, subjective values, or utilities. There are several references throughout this volume to factors that appear to affect valences—the subjective attractiveness or aversiveness of possible activities, events, or regions (to use the Lewinian language). Thus, Kuhl (Chapter 5), Rotter (Chapter 8), and Mitchell (Chapter 10) in various ways call attention to the importance of outcome instrumentality as a variable that affects valence; the valence of an outcome (for example, getting a job) is assumed to be related to the perceived likelihood that the outcome will lead to various desired or undesired consequences (for example, higher pay, longer vacations).

Other authors (Feather, Chapter 3) relate the valence of a goal to the strength of the relevant motive and to features of the goal itself—analogous to Lewin's (1938, pp. 106–107) treatment of valence as determined by an individual's tension systems and by the perceived nature of the object or activity to which the valence applies. More generally, in the Lewinian (1938) analysis: "The statement that a certain region of the life space has a positive or negative valence merely indicates that, for whatever reason, at the present time and for this specific individual a tendency exists to act in the direction toward this region or away from it [p. 88]." For a hungry person, food would be positively valent, the strength of the valence would be a function of the level of hunger and the nature of the food, and there would be a force to act in the direction of the food relating to the strength of the valence but also moderated by the psychological distance of the person from the positively valent region. In a corresponding way, in the Atkinson (1957) risk-taking model, the positive valence of success and the negative valence of failure are assumed to be related to the incentive values of success and failure (In_s, In_f) and to the strength of underlying motives, although in this case the motives are conceived as relatively stable personality dispositions—the motive to achieve success (M_S) and the motive to avoid failure (M_F).

In achievement situations the positive valence of success and the negative valence of failure are both assumed to be related to a person's expectations (or subjective probabilities) so that success becomes more attractive as expectations of success decrease and failure becomes more aversive as expectations of success increase—see Atkinson (Chapter 2), Feather (Chapter 3). The valences of success and failure in achievement situations are also assumed by Feather (Chapter 3) to depend on the extent to which a person believes that he or she has internal control over the outcome and can attribute the outcome to self. As success or failure is perceived as more under the control of self, so the positive valence of success and the negative valence of failure are assumed to increase. The effects of the attributional dimensions of locus and control are also discussed by Weiner (1980, Chapter 6).

Some other determinants of valences are also referred to in this volume. Feather (Chapter 9) assumes that general human values that are concerned with modes of conduct and with end-states of existence can function as motives to induce valences on means and ends. The level of aspiration model (Lewin, Dembo, Festinger, and Sears, 1944) mentioned in earlier chapters assumes that the norms established by a group can be used to define a scale of valences. Just as social comparison and observation of others can affect a person's expectations, so too the social context can function as a potent source for defining what is attractive and what is aversive. One can discover, therefore, several ideas in this volume about the determinants of valences.

Recent research has also suggested that the attractiveness of an activity may be diminished when an extrinsic reward is introduced for the first time (Lepper & Greene, 1978)—that is, that the valence of a previously unrewarded activity may be affected by an external reward. This area is a controversial one and the necessary conditions are still a matter for debate (see Bandura, 1977b; Lepper & Greene, 1978). For example, in a thoughtful discussion of extrinsic and intrinsic incentives, Bandura (1977b) emphasizes that ". . . one would be hard put to find any situations that lack external inducements for behavior [p. 108]," and that "Most human behavior is maintained by anticipated rather than by immediate consequences [p. 109]." It is clear, also, that the value of a reward or punishment will depend on the relational context. For example, according to Bandura (1977b), ". . . the same outcomes can have either rewarding or punishing effects on behavior depending on the type, frequency, and generosity with which behavior was previously reinforced" [pp. 117–118]." A reward or punishment may be seen as more or less attractive or aversive depending on what other rewards or punishments are available in the situation. Various kinds of contrast effects can operate depending on the comparison levels that have been established. The economists' concept of marginal utility and the extensive psychological and sociological research on reactions to relative deprivation both provide evidence that the valences or utilities of positive and negative reinforcements depend a lot on the relational context established by past experience and present situation.

Being able to specify determinants does not mean, however, that we have a theory about why some objects and activities are perceived as attractive or aversive at any given moment for an individual. There are many gaps in our understanding of the psychology of subjective values, utilities, and valences that still remain to be filled. The development of ideas in this area would be relevant to our understanding of how interests and preferences emerge, some of which are relatively stable and enduring and some of which may apply only to momentary situations. A reexamination of the Lewinian literature on such topics as substitution and satiation might provide some clues, as might attention to both the psychoanalytic treatment of the concept of cathexis and learning theory analyses of the formation of associations involving cognition and affect. It is likely that as we learn more about the dynamics of affect and the ways in which affects and cognitions become associated, so will our understanding of valences and their determinants be extended.

THE MEASUREMENT OF VALENCES

Just as there is an extensive literature on the measurement of expectations defined in terms of subjective probabilities, so too there is a large and related literature on the measurement of subjective values, utilities, or valences (see, for example, Jungermann & de Zeeuw, 1977; Wendt & Vlek, 1975). Much of this literature on the measurement of subjective probabilities and utilities comes from theorists concerned with mathematical models of the SEU type that can be applied to human decision making, and the measurement proceeds on the basis of stated assumptions demanded by the theoretical approach. This literature is too complex and specialized to summarize here, but typically the procedures make use of preference orderings to provide information about subjective probabilities and utilities (for recent discussions see Wallsten, 1980).

The Lewinian analysis of valences assumed that valences can be compared in choice situations in which psychological distance ($e_{P,G}$) between person (P) and goal region (G) is controlled. Given two goal objects that are equally psychologically distant from a person, the goal object chosen would have the higher positive valence (Lewin, 1938, p. 162). Rotter (1954) adopts a similar principle for the measurement of reinforcement values when expectancies are controlled. Given the same level of expectancy of achieving each goal object or reinforcement, the object chosen has the greater reinforcement value.

Again it would be an advantage to be able to specify the strength of valences in advance of behavior. Some studies have used direct verbal reports about how attractive or aversive possible future events would be if they were to occur, or how many points should be awarded for a success and how many subtracted for a failure, and so on (see Chapters 2 and 3). Note once more that one should be alert to the limitations of verbal reports and the extent to which they may reflect other influences (for example, situational demand characteristics) in addition to the variable of interest. They can, however, provide useful information.

Earlier in this volume (Chapter 3), I suggested that positive valences might be reflected in *wishful* choices where the constraints of reality are minimized. This procedure is analogous to the Lewinian one in that, by asking for choices that correspond to a person's wishes, one controls for the constraining effects of subjective probabilities on the choices to be made. Wishful choice occurs under conditions where the possibility of failure or loss is not an issue. Where failure or loss becomes an issue, however, realistic expectations constrain the choices that are made. A person may wish for success at a difficult task that carries with it the pride of achievement, but when required to make an actual choice may opt for an easier alternative where success is perceived to be more likely and where the benefits associated with success are therefore less at risk. Where both achievement rewards and extrinsic rewards are involved, choice of the easier alternative may become even more likely, especially if the extrinsic rewards are both salient and attractive.

It is possible that a person's affective reactions could be used to provide some evidence about the strength of valences as they existed prior to commerce with a positively or negatively valent object or activity. For example, a high degree of pleasure following successful attainment of a goal might indicate that the goal had a strong positive valence for the individual as he (or she) strove to attain it. Note, however, that there could be a discrepancy between the reality of goal attainment and the perceived attractiveness or aversiveness of the goal as perceived from a distance. The sweet that looks attractive to the child may turn out to have an unpleasant flavor. It would be a mistake to expect a perfect correlation between positive and negative valence on the one hand, and pleasure and pain on the other. The correlation may be higher, however, when pleasure or pain is anticipated than when positive or negative affect is subsequently experienced. The situation is analogous to the distinction between substitute valence and substitute value. Activities that are highly attractive from a distance may not always have high substitute value for interrupted tasks. Substitute valence and substitute value, like valence and affect, are not necessarily the same (Atkinson & Birch, 1978, p. 237; Lewin, 1938, pp. 163–164).

Finally, it should be clear that expectancy-value models deal with expectations and subjective values as they exist for the individual in the momentary situation. Measurement procedures that are applied considerably in advance of the behavior to be predicted run the risk that the assumed subjective probabilities and valences may have changed in the interval.

INTERACTION OF EXPECTATIONS AND VALENCES

As has been noted on a number of occasions, expectancy-value models that have emerged from the context of research into achievement motivation assume that valences and subjective probabilities are not independent but that the attractiveness of success increases as a task becomes subjectively more difficult, and the aversiveness of failure increases as a task becomes subjectively easier—see Part I of this volume and earlier discussion in this chapter. Various explanations of this relationship can be advanced but past learning experiences are of undoubted importance (see, for example, Feather, Chapter 3). Thus, a difficult accomplishment usually receives more positive reinforcement than an easy accomplishment, and failure at easy tasks is usually associated with more negative reinforcement than failure at difficult tasks. Decision theorists working in the area of behavioral decision theory tend to assume that subjective probabilities and utilities are independent, despite the evidence from the achievement context (Crozier, 1979; Feather, 1959).

The influence can also work in the opposite direction; expectations can be affected by the subjective values of possible events—see Jones (1977, pp. 134–140) and Crozier (1979) for reviews of relevant evidence. For example, a person may be unduly optimistic about his (or her) chances of success when a large reward is at stake than when the reward is small. I have argued that these effects of valence on subjective probability would be more likely to occur under conditions where cues about subjective probabilities are conflicting, ambiguous, or ill-defined and where a person's expectations are not solidly grounded in relation to a consistent past record of success or failure. That is, motivational factors tend to intrude when subjective probabilities are not or cannot be firmly based (Feather, 1967; Chapter 3).

The acknowledgement that expectations and subjective values are not always independent complicates expectancy-value models but is a proper reflection of the evidence. We need to be on the alert for cases where the independence assumption is violated and we need to be able to specify the implications that this lack of independence has for behavior. We also need to develop psychological theories that account for interdependence when it occurs.

THE COMBINATION OF EXPECTATIONS AND VALENCES

Expectancy-value models usually assume that expectations and subjective values combine multiplicatively to determine force, SEU, or whatever the combination is called. There is a need to test alternative rules of combination and, to an extent, this kind of research is proceeding, some of it using Anderson's (1974a, 1974b) functional measurement methodology—see, for example, recent articles by Shanteau (1975) and by Lynch and Cohen (1978).

Some of the authors in this volume also refer to the way variables are combined and/or to other points of a methodological nature that concern the testing of expectancy-value models. Thus, Fischoff, Goitein, and Shapira (Chapter 11) comment on the success of predictions that use simple linear models, and Kuhl (Chapter 5) supports the use of inductive methods, such as logical statement analysis, that enable one to generate hypotheses from individual data rather than proceeding deductively from a presumably general theory. On a different point, Mitchell (Chapter 10) argues that tests of expectancy-value models in organizational psychology should involve "within-subjects" analyses, consistent with the implications of Vroom's (1964) theory, rather than analyses across subjects.

These suggestions about methodology and about the need to compare different rules for the combination of expectations and subjective values are important ones to consider. They have already stimulated useful research and no doubt will continue to do so in the future.

THE STREAM OF BEHAVIOR

Several authors in the present volume have emphasized the need to consider the individual as continually active and constructive, behaving in terms of the present psychological reality that includes not only the immediate situation but legacies from the past and anticipations about the short-term and long-term future. Atkinson (Chapter 2) makes the point very clearly when he discusses the dynamics of action that relate to the stream of behavior, and Raynor (Chapter 4) also views behavior from a perspective that takes account of past, present, and future.

The emphasis by Mann and Janis (Chapter 12) on the need to assume continuity between pre- and post-decisional processes is also a recognition that thought and action should not be viewed simply in episodic terms without regard for continuing dynamic processes. Their "defective balance sheet" hypothesis, for example, asserts that the future stability of a decision depends on the extent to which a person has been able to fill in his or her decisional balance sheet accurately and completely before the decision is implemented. Thus, subsequent stability depends on how the decision was arrived at and on the persisting effects that follow from careful and complete consideration of possible gains and losses. The dynamic relationship between the pre- and post-decisional processes is seen by Mann and Janis to be continuous, even though the particular pattern of coping with a decisional conflict may vary according to such antecedent conditions as level of stress, hope for a better solution, and time pressure.

From a different perspective it is possible to conceptualize dissonance effects that have been shown to follow difficult and important decisions by assuming that persisting, unresolved tendencies carry over following a choice and influence subsequent thought and action. Instead of referring to a drive-like state of dissonance that is assumed to occur after a decision, however, one can use the concept of a persisting tendency that has not been satisfied (Atkinson & Birch, 1970). The alternative that is rejected in an important, conflictful decision would be associated with an unresolved tendency that would continue to persist after the decision was made. In contrast, the tendency associated with the chosen alternative would presumably be fully or partially satisfied after the decision. This form of analysis recognizes that the predecisional stage of decision making involves the elicitation of motivational tendencies, some of which are satisfied by the decision and some of which are not. Following the more general theory of the dynamics of action (Atkinson, Chapter 2; Atkinson & Birch, 1970), one would expect that the unfulfilled tendencies would persist following the decision and that they may have subsequent effects on thought and behavior. The detailed implementation of this type of analysis for the interpretation of decision making behavior and the effects of decisions is a task for the future. It is apparent, however, that this dynamics of action model, like the Mann and Janis approach, assumes an underlying continuity in the dynamic processes that are involved before and after decisions.

Atkinson (Chapter 2) has shown how concepts from the general theory of the dynamics of action (Atkinson & Birch, 1970, 1978) can be related to expectancy-value concepts, thereby giving some cognitive meaning to the assumed sets of tendencies and forces. Let me intrude one comment on this theory. The dynamics of action theory (Chapter 2) reminds one of models from physics that deal with continually changing patterns of force. The emphasis is on tendencies that change in a continuous manner, increasing as instigating forces operate, decreasing as action occurs, and so on. One wonders whether this approach can deal with discontinuous change as when insight or restructuring of relations occurs and a solution to a problem is suddenly found. It would be possible in an expectancy-value approach to account for abrupt changes in behavior that seem to imply some underlying discontinuities by considering conditions that determine sudden changes in expectations as when, following a sudden insight, a subjective probability changes from near zero to certainty. The rapid change in expectation would be expected to have a dramatic effect on behavior. Note that Tolman (1932) many years ago included inference as one of the three possible "moods" of expectations so as to allow for the apparently insightful construction of experience. The theory of the dynamics of action should keep in mind that change in cognitive expectations is a powerful dynamic mechanism that can underly change in behavior (Feather, Chapter 3).

Social learning theorists such as Rotter (Chapter 8), Mischel (1973), and Bandura (1977b, 1978) also deal with continuing behavior. In the more recent theoretical accounts there has been more emphasis on the self-regulation, monitoring, and planning that occurs as behavior proceeds. Thus Bandura (1977b) states that:

If actions were determined solely by external rewards and punishments, people would behave like weathervanes, constantly shifting in different directions to conform to the momentary influences impinging upon them . . . . Theories that explain human behavior as solely the product of external rewards and punishments present a truncated image of people . . . Behavior is . . . regulated by the interplay of self-generated and external sources of influence [pp. 128–129].

The component processes that are involved in the self-regulation of behavior by self-produced consequences have been discussed by social learning theorists—see, for example, Bandura (1977b, pp. 130–133, 1978) and Mischel (1973, pp. 274–275). The emphasis on self-regulatory systems and plans helps to free the individual from the immediate external environment and gives to the person an active and constructive role in determining the course of behavior.

The recent social learning approaches also recognize the intricate nature of the interplay between person, situation, and behavior. In this volume Rotter (Chapter 8) comments on interactionism and takes the position that both personality variables and situational variables depend on the person's previous experience, and that we should be concerned with the interaction of the person with his (or her) meaningful environment. Researchers in the achievement context have repeatedly asserted the need to consider both person and situation variables in the analysis of behavior—see, for example, Atkinson and Feather (1966). Bandura (1977b) argues from the viewpoint of a social learning theorist for the acceptance of the idea of reciprocal determinism that assumes that "... psychological functioning is a continuous reciprocal interaction between personal, behavioral, and environmental determinants [p. 194]." For example, a person is not only influenced by the environment but also has the power to change the environment that then becomes a new influence; the behavior that is enacted is influenced by both situation and personality variables, but person and situation are also affected by the behavior, and so on. The concept of reciprocal determinism implicitly recognizes the on-going nature of human action and the complex interplay between person, behavior, and situation (Bandura, 1978).

These various ideas draw us away from an episodic view of behavior to a more complex, dynamic treatment of the stream of human action. The future development of expectancy-value approaches must have regard for this relatively new perspective, along with the different forms of analysis that have been proposed. Each action that a person performs fits into the ongoing stream of that person's behavior and we need to discover how that action can be understood in the dynamic context that includes past, present, and future as represented in the immediate or momentary determinants. The present situation as perceived by the person, the residues of the past, and anticipations about the future all have their effect. Trying to analyze a single action separately without information about the dynamic context is like trying to make sense of a scene in a play without knowing the entire plot. It is an exercise that can yield only a partial understanding. One has to take a broader perspective on behavior, and at the same time acknowledge the role of the person as an active, constructive agent who structures and organizes information from many sources and who monitors and evaluates the consequences of actual and potential actions.

We assume that, within this broader context, expectations and subjective values are important components of the dynamic context of human action and that, as they undergo change, so too will the stream of behavior be affected.

In this final chapter I have attempted to review some general themes and issues that I see as important for the expectancy-value approach. It should be clear that we have moved toward models of greater sophistication and that the analysis of behavior in relation to expected consequences provides an important theoretical account that is relevant to a significant range of human action.

REFERENCES

Abramson, L. Y., Seligman, M. E. P., & Teasdale, J. D. Learned helplessness in humans: Critique and reformulation. *Journal of Abnormal Psychology*, 1978, *87*, 49–74.

Anderson, N. H. Cognitive algebra: Integration theory applied to social attribution. In L. Berkowitz (Ed.), *Advances in experimental social psychology* (Vol. 7). New York: Academic Press, 1974. (a)

Anderson, N. H. Information integration theory: A brief survey. In D. H. Krantz, R. C. Atkinson, R. D. Luce, & P. Suppes (Eds.), *Contemporary developments in mathematical psychology* (Vol. 2), San Francisco: Freeman, 1974. (b)

Atkinson, J. W. Motivational determinants of risk-taking behavior. *Psychological Review*, 1957, *64*, 359–372.

Atkinson, J. W., & Birch, D. *The dynamics of action*. New York: Wiley, 1970.

Atkinson, J. W., & Birch, D. *An introduction to motivation*. New York: D. Van Nostrand, 1978.

Atkinson, J. W., & Feather, N. T. (Eds.). *A theory of achievement motivation*. New York: Wiley, 1966.

Bandura, A. Self-efficacy: Toward a unifying theory of behavioral change. *Psychological Review*, 1977, *84*, 191–215. (a)

Bandura, A. *Social learning theory*. Englewood Cliffs, N.J.: Prentice-Hall, 1977. (b)

Bandura, A. The self system in reciprocal determinism. *American Psychologist*, 1978, *33*, 344–358.

Blaney, P. H. Contemporary theories of depression: Critique and comparison. *Journal of Abnormal Psychology*, 1977, *86*, 203–233.

Bolles, R. C. Reinforcement, expectancy, and learning. *Psychological Review*, 1972, 394–409.

Brunswik, E. Organismic achievement and environmental probability. *Psychological Review*, 1943, *50*, 255–272.

Cartwright, D. Lewinian theory as a contemporary systematic framework. In S. Koch (Ed.), *Psychology a study of a science* (Vol. 2), New York: McGraw-Hill, 1959.

Cartwright, D. Theory and practice. *Journal of Social Issues*, 1978, *34*, 168–180.

Cofer, C. N., & Appley, M. H. *Motivation: Theory and research*. New York: Wiley, 1964.

Crozier, W. R. The interaction of value and subjective probability in risky decision-making. *British Journal of Psychology*, 1979, *70*, 489–495.

Dahl, H. The appetite hypothesis of emotions. In C. E. Izzard (Ed.), *Emotions and psychopathology*. New York: Plenum Press, in press.

Feather, N. T. Subjective probability and decision under uncertainty. *Psychological Review*, 1959, *66*, 150–164.

Feather, N. T. *Values in education and society*. New York: Free Press, 1975.

Feather, N. T. Values, expectancy, and action. *Australian Psychologist*, 1979, *14*, 243–260.

Feather, N. T., & Davenport, P. R. Unemployment and depressive affect: A motivational and attributional analysis. *Journal of Personality and Social Psychology*, in press.

Goodnow, J. J. *Observations on some current topics in U.S. psychology*. Paper delivered at annual meeting at A.N.Z.A.A.S., Auckland, New Zealand, January, 1979.

Hebb, D. O. *The organization of behavior*. New York: Wiley, 1949.

Heckhausen, H. Achievement motivation and its constructs: A cognitive model. *Motivation and Emotion*, 1977, *1*, 283-329.

Helson, H. *Adaptation-level theory: An experimental and systematic approach to behavior*. New York: Harper, 1964.

Holt, R. R. Drive or wish? A reconsideration of the psychoanalytic theory of motivation. In M. M. Gill & P. S. Holzman (Eds.), Psychology versus metapsychology: Psychoanalytic essays in memory of George S. Klein. *Psychological Issues*, 1976, *9*, 158-197.

Izzard, C. E. *Human emotions*. New York: Plenum Press, 1977.

James, W. *The principles of psychology*. New York: Holt, 1890/1950.

Jones, R. A. *Self-fulfilling prophecies: Social, psychological, and physiological effects of expectations*. Hillsdale, N.J.: Lawrence Erlbaum Associates, 1977.

Jungermann, H., & de Zeeuw, G. *Decision making and change in human affairs*. Dordrecht, Holland: D. Reidel, 1977.

Kagan, J. Motives and development. *Journal of Personality and Social Psychology*, 1972, *22*, 51-66.

Klein, G. S. Freud's two theories of sexuality. In M. M. Gill & P. S. Holzman (Eds.), Psychology versus metapsychology: Psychoanalytic essays in memory of George S. Klein. *Psychological Issues*, 1976, *9*, 14-70.

Koffka, K. *Principles of gestalt psychology*. New York: Harcourt Brace, 1935.

Langer, E. Rethinking the role of thought in social interaction. In J. H. Harvey, W. Ickes, & R. F. Kidd (Eds.), *New directions in attributional research* (Vol. 2). Hillsdale, N.J.: Lawrence Erlbaum Associates, 1978.

Lepper, M. R., & Greene, D. *The hidden costs of reward: New perspectives on the psychology of human motivation*. Hillsdale, N.J.: Lawrence Erlbaum Associates, 1978.

Lewin, K. *Principles of topological psychology*. New York: McGraw-Hill, 1936.

Lewin, K. The conceptual representation and the measurement of psychological forces. *Contributions to Psychological Theory*, 1938, *1*. (Reprinted by Johnson Reprint Corporation, New York).

Lewin, K., Dembo, T., Festinger, L., & Sears, P. S. Level of aspiration. In J. McV. Hunt (Ed.), *Personality and the behavior disorders* (Vol. 1). New York: Ronald, 1944.

Lynch, J. G., Jr., & Cohen, J. L. The use of subjective utility theory as an aid to understanding variables that influence helping behavior. *Journal of Personality and Social Psychology*, 1978, *36*, 1138-1151.

Marx, M. H., & Hillix, W. A. *Systems and theories in psychology* (2nd ed.). New York: McGraw-Hill, 1973.

McClelland, D. C. Toward a theory of motive acquisition. *American Psychologist*, 1965, *20*, 321-333.

McClelland, D. C., Atkinson, J. W., Clark, R. A., & Lowell, E. L. *The achievement motive*. New York: Appleton-Century-Crofts, 1953.

Miller, G. A., Galanter, E., & Pribram. K. H. *Plans and the structure of behavior*. New York: Holt, Rinehart & Winston, 1960.

Mischel, W. Toward a cognitive social reconceptualization of personality. *Psychological Review*, 1973, *80*, 252-283.

Nisbett, R. E., & Wilson, T. D. Telling more than we can know: Verbal reports on mental processes. *Psychological Review*, 1977, *84*, 231-259.

Posner, M. I., & Schulman, G. L. Cognitive science. In E. Hearst (Ed.), *The first century of experimental psychology*. Hillsdale, N.J.: Lawrence Erlbaum Associates 1979.

Rotter, J. B. *Social learning and clinical psychology*. New York: Prentice-Hall, 1954.

Schank, R. C., & Abelson, R. P. *Scripts, plans, goals and understanding*. Hillsdale, N.J.: Lawrence Erlbaum Associates 1977.

Schneider, W., & Shiffrin, R. M. Controlled and automatic human information processing: I. Detection, search, and attention. *Psychological Review*, 1977, 84, 1–66.

Shanteau, J. An information-integration analysis of risky decision making. In M. F. Kaplan & S. Schwartz (Eds.), *Human judgment and decision processes*. New York: Academic Press, 1975.

Shiffrin, R. M., & Schneider, W. Controlled and automatic human information processing: II. Perceptual learning, automatic attending, and a general theory. *Psychological Review*, 1977, 84, 127–190.

Simon, H. A. Information processing models of cognition. *Annual Review of Psychology*, 1979, 30, 311–396.

Singer, J. L. *The child's world of make-believe: Experimental studies of imaginative play*. New York: Academic Press, 1973.

Singer, J. L. *Imagery and daydream methods in psychotherapy and behavior modification*. New York: Academic Press, 1974.

Smith, E. R., & Miller, F. D. Limits on perception of cognitive processes: A reply to Nisbett and Wilson. *Psychological Review*, 1978, 85, 355–362.

Solomon, R. L., & Corbit, J. D. An opponent-process theory of motivation: I. Temporal dynamics of affect. *Psychological Review*, 1974, 81, 119–145.

Taylor, S. E., & Crocker, J. *Schematic basis of information processing*. In E. T. Higgins, P. Hermann, & M. P. Zanna (Eds.), *The Ontario Symposium on Personality and Social Psychology*, Vol. 1. Hillsdale, N.J.: Lawrence Erlbaum Associates, in press.

Taylor, S. E., & Fiske, S. T. Salience, attention, and attribution: Top of the head phenomena. *Advances in experimental social psychology* (Vol. 11). New York: Academic Press, 1978.

Tolman, E. C. *Purposive behavior in animals and men*. New York: Century, 1932.

Tolman, E. C. Principles of performance. *Psychological Review*, 1955, 62, 315–326.

Tolman, E. C. *Behavior and psychological man: Essays in motivation and learning*. Berkeley & Los Angeles: University of California Press, 1958.

Tolman, E. C. Principles of purposive behavior. In S. Koch (Ed.), *Psychology: A study of a science* (Vol. 2). New York: McGraw-Hill, 1959.

Tomkins, S. S. *Affect, imagery, consciousness* (Vol. 1). *The positive affects*. New York: Springer, 1962.

Tomkins, S. S. *Affect, imagery, consciousness* (Vol. 2). *The negative affects*. New York: Springer, 1963.

Vroom, V. H. *Work and motivation*. New York: Wiley, 1964.

Wallsten, T. S. (Ed.) *Cognitive processes in choice and decision behavior*. Hillsdale, N.J., Lawrence Erlbaum Associates, 1980.

Weiner, B. *Theories of motivation: From mechanism to cognition*. Chicago: Markham, 1972.

Weiner, B. *Human motivation*. New York: Holt, Rinehart, & Winston, 1980.

White, P. Limitations on verbal reports of internal events: A refutation of Nisbett and Wilson and of Bem. *Psychological Review*, 1980, 87, 88–105.

Wendt, D., & Vlek, C. *Utility, probability, and human decision making*. Dordrecht, Holland: D. Reidel, 1975.

Young, P. T. *Motivation and emotion: A survey of the determinants of human and animal activity*. New York: Wiley, 1961.

Young, P. T. Hedonic organization and the regulation of behavior. *Psychological Review*, 1966, 73, 59–86.

Author Index

A

Abelson, R. P., 403, 407, *419*
Abramson, L. Y., 77, 83, *90,* 136, 146, *157,*
170, 197, 198, *198,* 210, 213, 215, 223, 225,
229, *232, 233,* 405, *418*
Ajzen, I., 10, *14,* 271, 272, 274, *286, 288*
Albright, D. W., 307, *311*
Allen, A., 151, *157*
Allen, J. J., 382, *393*
Alloy, L. B., 213, 225, *233*
Allport, G. W., 18, *50*
Alpert, R., 78, *90,* 101, *122,* 130, *157*
Ames, C., 175, *198*
Amitai, A., 116, *123*
Anderson, N. H., 304, *309,* 317, 336, 414, *418*
Andrews, G. R., 176, 186, *198*
Anisman, H., 218, *234*
Appley, M. H., 405, 406, *418*
Archibald, W. P., 209, *233*
Arendt, H., 222, *233*
Arkin, R. M., 180, *198*
Armitt, F. M., 54, *93*
Arnold, H. J., 304, *309*
Arnold, F. S., 385, *391*
Aronson, E., 209, 219, 215, *233*
Ash, R. A., 330, *336*

B

Bachman, J. B., 102, *122*
Backman, C. W., 268, *289*
Baddeley, A. D., 320, *336*
Bailey, M. M., 197, *203*
Baker, R. L., 299, *311*
Bandura, 9, *14,* 80, *91,* 278, *287,* 407, 408,
411, 416, 417, *418*
Baquet, A. E., 385, *390*
Baratta, P., 67, *94,* 367, 382, *393*
Barclay, S., 373, 381, *390*
Barnes, R. D., 188, *198*
Bar-Tal, D., 166, *199*

Atkinson, J. W., 4, 6, *14,* 17, 18, 20, 21, 22,
23, 24, 26, 27, 28, 29, 30, 33, 34, 37, 40, 41,
42, 43, 44, 45, 46, 48, 49, *50, 51,* 58, 59, 60,
62, 64, 68, 75, 78, 89, *90, 91,* 97, 98, 99,
100, 101, 102, 108, 110, 112, 113, 116, 117,
118, *122, 123, 124,* 125, 126, 131, 137, 138,
148, 151, 152, *157,* 171, 177, 181, 183, 184,
198, 201, 210, 212, 214, 218, 228, *233,* 264,
279, 284, *286, 287* 322, *336,* 341, *363,* 405,
406, 410, 413, 415, 416, 417, *418, 419*
Averill, J. R., 219, *233*

Bastian, J. R., 68, *90*
Bauer, V., 374, 375, 389, *390*
Beach, B. H., 369, 371, *390*
Beach, L. R., 298, *311,* 318, 328, 335, *336, 338,* 341, 350, 356, *363, 364,* 377, 378, 383, 385, 386, 387, 389, *390, 391, 393, 394*
Bearden, W., 272, *287*
Beattie, M., 219, *234*
Beck, A. T., 197, *199*
Beckmann, J., 153, 154, *159*
Behling, O., 304, 306, *310*
Bell, R. S., 371, *392*
Bem, D. J., 151, *157,* 182, *199*
Benedict, Ruth F., 253, *259*
Benesh-Weiner, M., 192, *203*
Bentler, P. M., 272, *287*
Berkowitz, L., 187, *199, 200*
Berlyne, D. E., 137, *157*
Bernoulli, D., 373, 374, *390*
Berry, J. W., 270, *287*
Berscheid, E., 225, *235*
Bettelheim, B., 222, *233*
Biglan, A., 293, *311*
Birch, D., 6, *14,* 17, 33, 34, 37, 40, 41, 42, 43, 44, 46, 48, 49, *50,* 58, 59, 62, 89, *90,* 116, *122,* 125, 131, 139, 148, *157,* 210, *233,* 279, 284, *286,* 406, 413, 415, 416, *418*
Birney, R., 23, *50*
Blaney, P. H., 210, *233,* 405, *418*
Blankenship, V., 138, 140, 141, *159*
Blumenfeld, R., 173, *199*
Bluming, A. Z., 384, *393*
Bongort, K., 139, *157*
Bolen, D., 208, *235*
Bolles, R. C., 407, 408, *418*
Borkan, B., 333, *337*
Bowlby, J., 222, *233*
Brand, R. J., 215, *236*
Braunstein, M. L., 335, *338*
Brecher, P. J., 104, *122*
Brehm, J. W., 71, 80, *91,* 164, *199,* 218, 220, 231, *237,* 279, *287,* 358, *363*
Brewer, M. B., 267, 270, *287*
Brickman, P., 112, 116, *124,* 173, 184, *203, 204,* 208, 209, 212, 215, 216, 218, 223, 224, 225, 227, *233, 235*
Brier, G. W., 385, *394*
Brockner, J., 210, 211, 213, *233*
Brown, J. S., 20, *50*
Brown, M., 102, 108, 110, *124*
Brown, R. V., 373, 388, *390*

Brunswik, E., 3, *14,* 255, *259,* 264, *287,* 398, *418*
Bulman, R. J., 224, 229, *233*
Burger, J. M., 166, *199*
Burnam, M. A., 176, *202,* 215, *233*
Burnett, S. A., 335, *337*
Byrne, D., 267, 271, *287*

C

Calder, B. J., 271, *287*
Cameron, R., 185, *201*
Campbell, B. A., 18, *52*
Campbell, D. T., 219, *233,* 267, 270, *287*
Campbell, J. P., 297, 298, *310*
Campbell, F. L., 356, *363,* 378, 385, 386, 387, 389, *390, 394*
Carlsmith, J. M., 209, *233*
Carlson, E. R., 272, *287*
Carroll, J. S., 189, 193, 194, 195, *199,* 335, *338,* 342, *363*
Cartwright, D., 4, *14,* 20, 33, 44, *50,* 54, *91,* 264, *287,* 398, *418*
Carver, C. S., 210, *233*
Chance, J. E., 241, 244, 246, 253, *260*
Chapin, M., 176, 186, *199*
Chaplin, R., 351, *364*
Chartier, G. M., 211, *234*
Cherniss, C., 228, *233*
Child, I. L., 54, *91*
Clark, R. A., 20, *51,* 101, 118, *123,* 177, *201,* 405, *419*
Clark, R. W., 18, 20, *51*
Coates, D., 215, 223, *233*
Cofer, C. N., 405, 406, *418*
Cohen, A. R., 71, 80, *91*
Cohen, J. L., 149, *159,* 350, *363,* 414, *419*
Cohen, L. J., 368, *390*
Cohen, S. L., 301, 302, 303, 308, *312*
Cohn, E., 215, 223, *233*
Cole, M., 270, *287*
Coleman, M. B., 387, *390*
Colten, M. E., 356, *363*
Combs, B., *337*
Conklin, F. S., 385, *390*
Connolly, T., 293, 299, 301, 302, 303, 304, 305, 306, *310*
Coombs, C. H., 323, 333, *336,* 373, *390*
Cooper, H. M., 166, *199*
Corbin, R. M., 334, *336*
Corbit, J. D., 71, *94,* 405, *420*

Corrigan, B., 321, *336*
Coutu, W., 255, *259*
Cox, D. J., 174, *201*
Coyne, J. C., 209, 218, *235*
Crandall, V. C., 76, *91*
Crandall, V. J., 67, *91*
Crawford, C. A., 272, *289*
Crocker, J., 408, *420*
Cronbach, L. J., 21, *50*
Crowne, D. P., 173, *202*
Crozier, W. R., 414, *418*
Cummings, L. L., 296, 299, *310*

D

Dachler, H. P., 307, *310*
Dahl, H., 405, *418*
Darom, E., 166, *199*
Dashiell, T., 359, *363*
Davenport, P. R., 405, *418*
Davidshofer, L. O., 323, *336*
Davidson, A. R., 272, *287*, 377, 378, *390*
Davidson, D., 374, *390*
Davidson, N. T., 102, *122*
Davis, K. E., 186, *200*
Davis, D. E., 254, *259*
Davis, W. L., 254, *259*
Davison, G. C., 185, *199*
Dawes, R. M., 319, 321, 323, *336*
Deaton, M. D., 374, *390*
Debus, R. L., 176, 186, *198*
deCharms, R., 80, *91*
deCharms, R., 164, 168, 181, 185, 190, *199*
Deci, E. L., 83, *91*, 164, 168, *199*, 324, *336*
DeLeo, P. J., 299, 300, 308, *312*, 329, 330, *336*
Dembo, T., 4, *14*, 20, *51*, 55, 63, *94*, 98, *123*, 264, *288*, 411, *419*
Desforges, J. F., 384, *393*
DeWitt, G. W., 219, *233*
Diener, C. I., 147, *157*, 165, 176, *199*, 211, 231, *233, 234*
de Zeeuw, G., 412, *419*
Diggory, J. C., 173, *199*
Dillard, J. F., 299, 304, 305, 306, *310*
Douglas, D., 218, *234*
Dittes, J. E., 212, *234*
Dulany, D. E., 271, *287*
Dunnette, M. D., 297, *310*
Dweck, C. S., 147, *157*, 165, 176, 185, *199*, 211, 231, *233, 234*

Dyck, D. G., 176, 186, *199*
Dyer, L., 300, 301, 302, 305, 307, *311*

E

Earl, R. W., 68, *90*
Ebbesen, E. B., 335, *336*
Edgell, S. L., 330, *336*
Edwards, 4, 11, *14*, 20, 24, 27, 33, *50*, 56, *91*, 316, 324, *336*, 341, *363*, 366, 367, 368, 371, 372, 374, 375, 377, 381, 382, 388, 389, *391, 392, 393*
Egnatios, E. S., 228, *233*
Einhorn, H. J., 323, 327, 335, *336*, 368, *391*
Eiser, J. R., 172, *202*
Elig, T. W., 166, *199*
Eller, S. J., 198, *203*, 218, *237*
Ellerman, D. A., 89, *91*, 280, *287*
Ellis, A., 184, *199*
English, L. D., 110, *124*
Entin, E. E., 97, 100, 101, 103, 104, 106, 107, 113, *122, 124*
Erdman, H., 370, *391*
Escalona, S. K., 20, *50*
Essig, A., 383, *391*
Estes, W. K., 164, *199*
Eswara, H. S., 189, *199*
Evans, G. W., 382, *392*
Evans, M. G., 304, *309*
Eysenck, H. J., 138, *157*

F

Fawcett, J. T., 385, *391*
Feather, N. T., 3, 4, 5, 9, 10, *14*, 20, 26, 27, 28, 29, 33, *50, 51*, 54, 55, 58, 59, 60, 61, 62, 63, 66, 67, 68, 69, 70, 71, 72, 73, 74, 75, 76, 77, 78, 79, 80, 81, 82, 83, 84, 85, 86, 87, 88, 89, *90, 91, 92, 93, 94*, 97, 98, 99, 101, 103, 111, 112, 113, 117, *122, 123*, 133, 135, 138 151, 152, *157*, 166, 174, *199, 200*, 208, 210, 212, 214, 218, 228, *233, 234*, 264, 265, 266, 267, 268, 269, 270, 271, 275, 276, 277, 278, 280, 282, 284, 285, *287, 288*, 322, *336*, 403, 405, 406, 414, 417, *418*
Fein, H., 221, *234*
Feinstein, A. R., 372, 388, *391, 393*
Feldman, J. M., 306, *310*
Felton, B., 214, *234*
Fencil-Morse, E., 77, 78, *93*, 198, *201*
Ferster, C. B., 176, *200*

Festinger, L., 4, *14*, 19, 20, 33, 44, *50, 51*, 55, 63, 71, 72, 74, *93, 94*, 98, *123*, 176, *201*, 210, 229 *234, 237*, 264, *288*, 411, *419*
Field, P. B., 83, *93*
Filer, R. J., 54, *93*
Fischer, G. H., 130, 149, *157*
Fischer, G. W., 374, *394*
Fischhoff, B., 213, *234*, 327, 328, 329, 332, 333, 335, *336, 337, 338*, 361, *364*, 368, *393*
Fishbein, M., 10, *14*, 271, 272, 274, *286, 288*
Fiske, S. T., 403, *420*
Fitch, G., 175, *200*
Fitch, M. K., 383, *392*
Folkes, V. S., 164, 165, 183, 195, 196, *200*, *201*
Fontaine, G., 172, *200*
Ford, K. C., 381, *391*
Forrest, C. R., 299, *310*
Freedman, J. L., 71, *93*
French, J. R. P. Jr., 88, *93*, 276, 277, *288*
Friedman, M., 215, *234, 236*
Frieze, I. H., 125, *160*, 165, 166, 168, 172, 174, 175, 183, *199, 200, 203*, 210, *237*
Fryback, D. G., 389, *391*
Furby, L., 220, *234*

G

Galanter, E., 3, 4, *14*, 285, *288*, 403, *419*
Galbraith, J., 296, *310*
Gardiner, P. C., 377, *391*
Gazzo, B., 110, *123*
Gebhard, M. E., 54, *93*
Georgescu-Roegen, N., 18, *51*
Georgopoulous, B. S., 293, *310*
Gewirtz, J. L., 131, *157*
Gifford, W. E., 304, *310*
Gilmore, T. M., 175, *200*
Ginsberg, R., 333, *337*
Gjesme, T., 104, 105, 106, *123*, 131, 134, *157*
Glass, D. C., 215, 218, 228, *233, 234*
Goldberg, L. R., 316, 319, *337*
Goldsmith, R. W., 368, *391*
Goldstein, M., 172, *203*
Gollob, H. F., 212, *234*
Goodman, B. C., 368, *391*
Goodnow, J. J., 408, *418*
Gordon, S., 197, *200*
Gorry, G. A., 383, *391*
Goslin, D. A., 225, *234*
Graen, G., 125, *157*, 307, *310*

Green, M. G., 223, *234*
Greene, D., 411, *419*
Gregg, G. T., 385, *391*
Gregory, W. L., 211, *234*
Greist, J. H., 370, *391*
Griffeth, R. W., 299, *311*
Gurin, G., 219, *234*
Gurin, P., 219, *234*
Gustafson, D. H., 370, *391*
Guthrie, E. R., 3, *14*, 264, *288*
Guttentag, M., 381, *391*

H

Haber, R. N., 78, *90*, 101, *122*, 130, *157*
Hackman, J. R., 125, 149, *158*
Hage, A., 136, *158*
Hallermann, B., 136, *159*
Halter, A. N., 385, *390*
Hamilton, J. O., 126, *158*
Hammond, K. R., 320, *337*
Hand, H. H., 299, *311*
Hanson, N. R., 19, *51*
Hanusa, B. H., 197, *200*
Harding, W. M., *237*
Harman, A., 308, *310*
Harper, D. C., 176, *202*
Hart, J. T., 224, *234*
Härtner, R., 156, *158*
Hartshorne, H., 265, *288*
Harvey, J. H., 164, *200*
Hasazi, J., 133, *160*
Hays, W. L., 367, 368, *391, 393*
Hebb, D. O., 18, 22, *51*, 137, *158*, 403, *419*
Heckhausen, H., 64, 65, 70, *93*, 125, 126, 129, 131, 133, 136, 138, 139, 140, 141, 143, 144, *158*, 189, *202*, 229, *234*, 361, *363*, 407, *419*
Heider, F., 65, 71, 81, 82, *93*, 164, 165, 167, 168, 183, 186, *200*, 278, *288*
Heim, M., 189, 197, *200, 202*
Helson, H., 325, *337*, 406, *419*
Hendricks, M., 208, 209, 224, *233*
Heneman, H. G. III, 293, 300, 301, *310, 312*, 334, *338*
Henker, B., 191, *204*
Hieber, S., 136, *158*
Hilgard, E. R., 18, *51*
Hillix, W. A., 401, *419*
Hilterman, R. J., 306, *310*
Hiroto, D. S., 146, *158*, 208, *234*

Hobart, Enid M., 252, *259*
Hochbaum, G. M., 212, *234*
Hochreich, D. J., 254, *259*
Hoffman, L. W., 385, *391*
Hoffman, M. L., 385, *391*
Hoffman, P. J., 319, *337*
Hogarth, R. M., 327, 335, *336*, 368, *391*
Holmes, D. S., 230, *235*
Holmstrom, V. L., 383, *391*
Holt, R. R., 405, *419*
House, R. J., 293, *310, 312*
Hovland, C. I., 252, *259*
Howell, W. C., 335, *337*
Hoyt, M. F., 351, 356, *363*
Huber, G. P., 373, 374, 375, 381, *391, 392*
Hughes, E. C., 222, *235*
Hull, C. L., 4, *14*, 18, 20, 33, 44, *51*
Hulton, A. J. B., 211, *233*
Humphreys, A. R., 381, *391*
Humphreys, P. C., 374, 381, *391, 392*

I

Ickes, W. J., 164, 175, 187, 188, *198, 200*
Ikeda, H., 332, *338*
Irwin, F. W., 54, 67, *93*
Ivancevich, J. M., 303, *310*
Izzard, C. E., 405, *419*

J

Jaccard, J. J., 272, *287*
Jacobs, B. J., 23, *51*
Jacobs, L., 225, *235*
James, L. R., 308, *310*
James, W., 285, *288*
James, W., 402, *419*
James, W. H., 173, *200*
Janis, I. L., 74, 83, *93, 334, 337*, 341, 342,
346, 347, 349, 351, 352, 353, 354, 355, 356,
363, 364
Janoff-Bulman, R., 210, 214, 215, 216, 220,
235
Jarvik, M. E., 173, *200*
Jenkins, C. D., 215, *235, 236*
Jenkins, H. M., 213, 222, *235*
Jennings, R., 18, *51*
Jimenez-Lerma, I., 382, *392*
Johnson, A. C., 299, *310*
Johnson, D. M., 127, *158*
Johnson, E. M., 375, *392*

Johnson, L. D., 102, *122*
Johnson, M. P., 271, *289*
Jones, A. P., 308, *310*
Jones, E. E., 164, 186, *200*
Jones, L. V., 149, *159*
Jones, N. W., 293, *310*
Jones, R. A., 408, 414, *419*
Jungermann, H., 377, *392*, 412, *419*

K

Kagan, J., 405, *419*
Kagawa, M., 301, *311*
Kahana, E., 214, *234*
Kahn, R. L., 88, *93*, 102, *122*, 276, 277, *288*
Kahneman, D., 325, 328, 329, 332, 333, 335,
337, 339, 342, *364*, 368, *392, 394*
Kahr, A. S., 373, *390*
Kanouse, D. E., 164, *200*
Kaplan, R. M., 189, *200*, 218, *235*
Kantor, J. R., 255, *259*
Karuza, J., 215, 223, *233*
Kassirer, J. P., 383, *391*
Katz, N., 333, *337*
Keating, G. W., 356, *363*, 378, 385, *390*
Keeney, R. L., 374, 381, *391, 392*
Kellaway, R., 67, *91*
Kelley, H. H., 19, *51*, 164, 167, 171, 183, 186,
200, 201
Kelly, C. W., III, 373, 389, *390, 392*
Kelly, G. A., 184, *201*
Kelman, H., 271, *288*
Kidd, R. F., 164, 187, 188, *198, 200*
Kidder, L., 215, 223, *233*
Kirkwood, C. W., 381, *391*
Klein, D. C., 77, 78, *93*, 146, *158*, 198, *201*
Klein, G. S., 405, *419*
Kleinbeck, U., 144, 145, *158*
Klinger, E., 71, *93*, 222, *235*
Kluckhohn, C., 273, *288*
Koffka, K., 3, *14*, 402, *419*
Kohler, W., 3, *14*
Koller, P. S., 218, *235*
Konecni, V. J., 335, *336*
Kopelman, R. E., 299, 300, 302, 305, 306, 307,
308, *310*
Krischer, J. P., 371, 381, *392*
Krug, S., 136, *158*
Kruglanski, A. W., 116, *123, 136, 158*
Kubal, L., 208, *236*

Kuhl, J., 125, 128, 132, 133, 134, 135, 136, 137, 138, 140, 141, 144, 146, 147, 148, 149, 150, 153, 154, 156, *158, 159*
Kuhn, T. S., 34, *51*
Kukla, A., 125, 136, 142, *159,* 165, 183, 189, *203,* 210, *237*
Kuleck, W. J. Jr., 298, *310*
Kun, A., 192, *203*
Kunreuther, H., 333, 336, *337*
Kyburg, H. E. Jr., 328, *337*

L

Lacey, J. I., 248, *260*
Lakatos, I., 335, *337*
Langer, E., 285, *288,* 403, *419*
Langer, E. J., 213, 220, *235,* 351, *363*
Lanzetta, J. T., 350, *363*
Lao, R. C., 219, *234*
Larsson, S., 325, *338*
Lau, R. R., 165, *201*
Laughren, T., 370, *391*
Lavelle, T. L., 209, 218, *235*
Lawler, E. E., 149, *159,* 341, *364*
Lawler, E. E. III, 294, 296, 297, 298, *310,* 330, *337*
Layden, M. A., 175, *200*
Layman, M., 333, *337*
Lawrence, D. H., 176, *201*
Lazarus, R. S., 183, *201,* 248, *260*
Lefcourt, H. M., 174, *201,* 209, *235,* 252, *260*
Lenney, E., 84, *94*
Leon, F. R., 301, *311*
Lepley, W. M., 173, *201*
Lepper, M. R., 222, *236,* 411, *419*
Lerman, D., 71, 83, *95,* 165, 178, 179, *20ʲ*
Lerner, M. J., 220, *235*
Levine, E. L., 330, *336*
Levinson, D. J., 227, *235*
Levis, D. J., 222, *235*
Lewin, K., 2, 4, *14,* 20, 21, 27, 29, 33, *51,* 55, 63, 64, *94,* 98, 113, *123,* 171, *201,* 255, *260,* 264, 284, 285, *288,* 341, *363,* 403, 410, 411, 412, 413, *419*
Lewis, D. J., 175, *201*
Liberman, A. M., 21, *51*
Lichtenstein, S., 319, 321, 323, 327, 328, 329, 332, 333, *337, 338,* 361, *364,* 368, *393*
Liddell, W. W., 304, 306, *311, 312*
Lied, T. R., 303, 308, *311,* 329, 330, *337*
Linsenmeier, J. A. W., 209, 218, 225, 227, *233, 235*

Litwin, G. H., 28, *50,* 68, *90*
Litman-Adizes, T., 169, 197, *201, 203*
Liu, T. J., 230, *236*
Liverant, S., 173, *202*
Locke, E.A., 227, *235,* 306, *311*
Lowell, E. L., 18, 20, 21, *51,* 101, 118, *123,* 177, *201,* 405, *419*
Lusted, L. B., 371, 388, *392*
Lynch, J. G., 149, *159,* 350, *363,* 414, *419*

M

MacCorquodale, K., 18, 19, 20, 21, 25, *51*
MacCrimmon, K. R., 324, 325, *337*
Mahoney, G. M., 293, *310*
Mai-Dalton, R., 377, *390*
Maier, S. F., 77, *94,* 146, *159*
Mandler, G., 101, *123*
Mann, L., 74, 84, *93, 94,* 167, *201,* 334, *337,* 341, 342, 346, 349, 351, 352, 353, 354, 355, 356, 358, 359, *363, 364*
Mann, J. W., 284, *288*
Maracek, J., 209, 225, *235*
March, J. G., 226, *235*
Margolin, B., 116, *123*
Marks, R. W., 67, *94*
Marquis, D. G., 18, *51*
Marshall, G., 214, *235*
Marshall, M., 377, *390*
Martin, D. C., 386, *394*
Marx, M. H., 401, *419*
Maruyama, G. M., 180, *198*
Maslach, C., 228, *235*
Matsui, T., 301, 305, *311, 332, 338*
Mattes, K., 156, *158*
Matthews, M., 187, *202*
Mausner, B., 350, *364*
May, M. A., 265, *288*
Mayes, B. T., 307, *311*
McCareins, A. G., 209, 218, 225, *233*
McClelland, D. C., 18, 20, 21, *51,* 88, *94,* 101, 118, 120, *123,* 177, 185, *201,* 275, *288,* 405, 406, *419*
McGhee, P. E., 76, *91*
McGuire, W. J., 347, *364*
McKemey, D. R., 308, *312*
McMahan, I. D., 172, 174, *201*
McNeil, B. J., 388, *392*
McReynolds, W. T., 222, *235*
Means, G. H., 208, *235*
Means, R. S., 208, *235*
Mednick, M. T., 102, *122*

Meehl, P. E., 18, 19, 20, 21, 25, *51*
Meglino, B. M., 299, *311*
Mehrabian, A., 101, *123*, 144, *159*
Meichenbaum, D., 185, *201*
Messmer, D. J., 304, *312*
Metalsky, G. I., 209, 218, *235*
Mettee, D. R., 209, 225, *235*
Meyer, J. P., 170, 171, 172, *201*
Meyer, W.-U., 133, 136, *159*, 164, 172. 183, 184, *201*
Michela, J., 170, 189, 197, *201*
Miller, D. T., 230, *235*
Miller, F. D., 403, 404, *420*
Miller, G. A., 3, 4, *14*, 285, *288*, 319, *338*, 403, *419*
Miller, G. R., 74, *94*
Miller, I. W., III, 80, *94*
Miller, L., 333, *337*
Miller, N. E., 29, 33, *51*
Miller, R. L., 208, *235*
Miller, S. M., 219, 228, *235*
Miller, W., 78, *94*
Miller, W. R., 225, *236*
Minton, H. L., 175, *200*
Mischel, W., 9, *14*, 252, *260*, 407, 408, 416, 417, *419*
Mitchell, T. R., 64, 70, *94*, 293, 298, 301, 303, 304, 305, 306, 307, 308, *311*, 318, 326, 335, *336, 339*
Mobley, W. H., 299, 307, *310, 311*
Moore, B. S., 230, *236*
Morgenstern, O., 20, *52*
Moskowitz, H., 325, *338, 382, 392*
Mosteller, F., 374, 382, *392*
Mowrer, O. H., 29, *52, 68, 94*
Muchinsky, P. M., 300, 305, *311*, 330, *338*, 383, *392*
Murphy, A., 329, *338*
Murphy, A. H., 369, 370, 384, 385, *392, 393, 394*
Murray, H. A., 18, *52, 255, 260*

N

Nagamatsu, J., 301, 305, *311*
Nebeker, D. M., 307, *311*
Newcomb. T. M., 267, *288*
Newman, J. R., 382, *393*
Newton, J. W., 284, *288*
Nierenberg, R., 172, 189, *202, 203*
Nisbett, R. E., 164, 182, 185, *200, 201,* 213, 222, *236,* 285, *288,* 342, *364,* 403, *419*

Nissen, H. W., 192, *201*
Nogee, P., 374, 382, *392*
Norman, W. H., 80, *94*
Nuttin, J. R., 192, *202*
Nygård, R., 132, 137, 144, *157, 159*

O

O'Brien, L., 219, *233*
O'Conner, M. F., 375, 382, *393*
O'Dowd, B., 228, *233*
O'Driscoll, M. P., 84, *92*
Ohtsuka, Y., 301, 305, *311*
Oldham, G. R., 299, 305, 308, *311*
Olian-Gottlieb, J. D., 293, 300, 301, *312,* 334, *338*
Orchinik, C. W., 54, *93*
Ostrove, N., 172, *202*
Otway, H. J., 382, *393*

P

Pancer, S. M., 172, *202*
Parker, D., 300, 301, 302, 305, 307, *311*
Passer, M. W., 170, 171, *202*
Patterson, J. R., 281, *289*
Pauker, S. G., 384, *393*
Payne, J. S., 335, *338*
Payne, J. W., 189, 193, 194, 195, *199,* 342, *363*
Peak, H., 272, *288*
Pearlson, H. B., 104, 106, *123*
Pennebaker, J. W., 176, *202,* 215, *233*
Peplau, L. A., 170, 189, 190, 197, *201, 202, 203*
Perez, R. C., 208, *236*
Peter, N., 189, *203*
Peters, L. H., 300, 308, *311*
Peterson, C., 222, *236,* 373, *390*
Peterson, C. R., 328, *338,* 367, 373, 381, 389, *390, 392, 393*
Pfeffer, J., 326, *338*
Phares, E. J., 173, 174, 175, *202,* 241, 244, 246, 252, 253, *260*
Phillips, L. D., 323, 328, *337, 339,* 367, 368, 373, 388, *390, 391, 393*
Piliavin, I. M., 187, *202*
Piliavin, J. A., 187, *202*
Pollard, W. E., 307, *311*
Porter, C. A., 230, *235*
Porter, L. W., 125, 149, *158, 159,* 296, *310,* 341, *364*

Posner, M. E., 285, *288*
Posner, M. I., 402, *419*
Postman, L., 19, *52,* 60, *94*
Preston, M. G., 67, *94,* 367, 382, *393*
Pribram, K. H., 3, 4, *14,* 285, *288,* 403, *419*
Pritchard, R. D., 125, *159,* 299, 300, 303, 308, *311, 312,* 329, 330, *336, 337*
Pritchard, R. D., 299, 300, 303, 308, *311, 312,* 329, 330, *336, 337*

Q

Quinn, R. P., 329, *338*

R

Rabinowitz, V. C., 215, 223, *233*
Raiffa, H., 368, 374, *392, 393*
Ransohoff, D. F., 388, *393*
Raphelson, A. C., 85, *93*
Rapoport, A., 213, *236*
Rasch, G., 129, *159*
Rausch, C. N., 351, *363*
Rawls, J., 213, *236*
Raynor, J. O., 33, *52,* 75, 89, *91,* 97, 99, 100, 101, 102, 103, 104, 106, 107, 108, 109, 110, 111, 112, 113, 115, 117, 118, *122, 123, 124,* 125, 133, *159,* 228, 229, *233, 236,* 284, *287,* 341, *363*
Reed, L., 125, *160,* 165, *203,* 210, *237*
Reese, T. R., 382, *393*
Reinharth, L., 299, 300, 302, *312*
Reitman, W. R., 20, 27, *50*
Reitz, H. J., 306, *310*
Rennert, K., 219, *236*
Repucci, N. D., 185, *199*
Rest, S., 125, *160,* 165, 175, 176, *202, 203,* 210, *237*
Rhode, J. G., 298, *310*
Richards, M. D., 298, *312*
Riemer, B. S., 168, *202*
Riley, E. J., 173, *199*
Ritchie, B. F., 30, *52*
Riter, A., 116, *123*
Roberts, H. V., 371, *392*
Roby, T. B., 18, 20, *52*
Rodin, J., 185, 187, *202,* 219, *236*
Roeder, G. P., 106, *124*
Roistacher, R. C., 225, *236*
Rokeach, M., 10, *14,* 87, 88, 89, *94,* 265, 266, 268, 271, 273, 274, 276, 281, *288, 289*

Rosen, B. C., 119, *124*
Rosenbaum, R. M., 125, *160,* 165, 168, 172, 187, *202, 203,* 210, *237*
Rosenberg, J., 332, *338*
Rosenberg, M., 272, *289*
Rosenman, R. H., 215, *234, 236*
Ross, L., 213, 222, *236,* 342, *364*
Ross, M., 271, *287*
Ross, R., 185, *202*
Roth, S., 208, *236*
Rotter, J. B., 4, 9, *14,* 20, 23, *52,* 75, 78, 80, *94,* 164, 168, 173, 190, *202,* 209, 212, *236,* 241, 243, 244, 246, 247, 252, 253, 254, 255, 259, *260,* 412, *419*
Rubin, I. S., 103, *124*
Rubin J. Z., 213, *233*
Russell, D., 71, 83, *95,* 165, 178, 179, 189, 197, *201, 202, 204*

S

Sackheim, H. A., 223, *232*
Safran, C., 384, *393*
Sagi, P., 333, *337*
Salancik, G., 326, *338*
Sanborn, M., 272, *289*
Sanders, F., 369, *393*
Sanders, L. D., 221, *236*
Sanders, M. S., 125, *159*
Sarason, S. B., 101, *123*
Sarason, I. G., 209, 210, *236*
Saville, M. R., 66, 75, 76, *93,* 153, *157*
Sayeki, Y., 374, 381, *391, 393*
Schachter, S., 185, *201, 202,* 248, *260*
Schaeffer, M. A., 176, *202*
Schalon, C. L., 208, *236*
Schank, R. C., 403, 407, *419*
Scheiblechner, H., 130, *157*
Scheier, M. F., 210, *233*
Schlegel, R. P., 272, *289*
Schmalt, H.-D., 140, *158, 159*
Schmidt, F. L., 125, 149, *159,* 303, *312*
Schmidt, K.-H., 144, 145, *158*
Schneider, K., 126, 127, 128, 133, 140, 152, *158, 159*
Schneider, W., 403, 404, *420*
Schopler, J., 187, *202*
Schribner, S., 270, *287*
Schroder, H. M., 243, *260*
Schuman, H., 271, *289*
Schütz, A., 171, *202*

Schwab, D. P., 293, 300, 301, 302, 303, *310, 312,* 334, *338*
Schwartz, J. C., 259, *260*
Schwartz, W. B., 383, 388, *391, 393*
Sears, D. O., 71, *93*
Sears, P. S., 4, *14,* 20, *51,* 55, 63, *94,* 98, *123,* 264, *288,* 411, *419*
Sears, R. R., 23, *52*
Secord, P. F., 268, *289*
Seligman, M. E. P., 77, 78, 80, 83, *90, 93, 94,* 125, 136, 146, *157, 158, 159,* 160, 170, 176, 190, 197, 198, *198, 201, 202,* 209, 210, 215, 219, 220, 225, 229, *232, 234, 235, 236,* 405, *418*
Seltzer, R. A., 35, *52*
Selvidge, J., 373, *390*
Shanteau, J., 382, *393,* 414, *420*
Shaughnessy, J. J., 224, *236*
Shaw, M. C., 213, *233*
Shbtai, L., 116, *123*
Sheffield, F. D., 18, *52*
Shepard, R. N., 368, 374, *393*
Sheridan, J. E., 298, *312*
Sherman, H., 388, *392, 393*
Sherman, J., 209, 212, *237*
Sherrod, D. R., 230, *236*
Shiffrin, R. M., 403, 404, *420*
Shrauger, J. S., 208, 210, *236*
Shulman, G. L., 285, *288,* 402, *419*
Sieber, J., 350, *364*
Siegel, S., 374, *390*
Sierad, J., 181, 184, *204*
Simon, C. W., 54, *93*
Simon, H. A., 226, *235,* 285, *289,* 319, 324, *338,* 342, 347, *364,* 403, *420*
Simon, J. G., 84, 85, *93, 94,* 166, 174, *199, 200, 202*
Sims, H. P., Jr., 308, *312*
Singer, J. E., 185, *202,* 218, 228, *234*
Singer, J. L., 131, *159,* 405, *420*
Skinner, B. F., 18, *52,* 173, 176, *200, 202*
Slocum, J. W., Jr., 298, *312*
Slovic, P., 213, *234,* 319, 320, 321, 323, 325, 327, 328, 332, 333, *337, 338,* 361, *364,* 368, *393*
Smith, E. R., 403, 404, *420*
Smokler, H. E., 328, *337*
Smyser, C. M., 308, *311*
Sobel, R. S., 306, *312*
Solomon, D., 67, *91*
Solomon, R. J., 304, 306, *311, 312*

Solomon, R. L., 31, *52,* 71, *94,* 405, *420*
Solomon, S. K., 219, *236*
Sorman, P. B., 208, *236*
Sparta, S. N., 176, *202*
Speckart, G., 272, *287*
Spence, K. W., 4, *14,* 18, 33, *52*
Starke, F. A., 306, *310*
Starke, R. A., 306, *310*
Spetzler, C. S., 373, *394*
Spielberger, C. D., 209, 210, *236*
Staël von Holstein, C-A.S., 373, *394*
Staines, G. L., 329, *338*
Stauss, F. F., 370, *391*
Staw, B. M., 213, 219, *236,* 334, *338*
Stebbins, M. W., 308, *310*
Stein, A. H., 197, *203*
Steiner, I. D., 80, *94,* 164, *203*
Stevenson, J., 227, *237*
Straus, R., 215, *236*
Suppes, P., 374, *390*
Svenson, O., 323, 335, *338*
Swant, S. G., 189, *200*
Swets, J. A., 223, *234*
Szilagyi, A. D., 308, *312*

T

Tan, C., 353, 358, *364*
Taylor, S. E., 214, *237,* 350, *364,* 403, 408, *420*
Teasdale, J. D., 77, 83, *90,* 136, 146, *157,* 170, 197, *198,* 210, 215, 229, *232,* 405, *418*
Teger, A. I., 219, *237*
Teitelbaum, R. C., 104, 117, *124*
Tennen, H., 198, *203,* 218, *237*
Thompson, P. H., 300, 302, *310*
Thompson, J. C., 385, *394*
Thornbury, J. R., 389, *391*
Thorndike, E. L., 18, *52*
Thurstone, L. L., 149, *159,* 373, *394*
Tiger, L., 230, *237*
Tolman, E. C., 2, 4, *14,* 17, 18, 19, 20, 22, 23, 26, 33, *52,* 63, *94,* 176, *203,* 264, *289,* 341, *364,* 401, 403, 407, 416, *420*
Tomkins, S. S., 405, *420*
Townes, B. D., 356, *363,* 378, 385, 386, 387, 389, *390, 394*
Triandis, H., 167, *203*
Triandis, H. C., 271, *289*
Trope, Y., 112, 116, *124,* 184, *203,* 224, *237*
Tsichlis, P. N., 384, *393*

Tuchman, B., 355, *364*
Turney, J. R., 300, 302, 303, 308, *312*
Tversky, A., 323, 325, 328, 329, 332, 333, 335, *336, 337, 338, 339,* 342, *364,* 368, 374, 382, *392, 394*

U

Underwood, B., 230, *236*

V

Valins, S., 164, 185, *199, 200*
Valle, V. A., 168, 172, 174, 175, *203*
Vines, C. V., 299, 301, 304, 305, 306, *310*
Vlek, C., 412, *420*
von Baeyer, C. L., 174, *201*
Von Bergen, C. W. Jr., 299, 300, 308, *312*
Von Neumann, J., 20, *52*
Von Winterfeldt, D., 374, *394*
Vroom, V. H., 10, *14,* 64, 70, *94,* 141, *159,* 272, *289,* 293, 294, 295, 305, *312,* 341, 362, *364,* 415, *420*

W

Wacker, S., 228, *233*
Wahba, M. A., 293, 299, 300, 302, *310, 312*
Wallace, D. L., 371, *392*
Wallsten, T. S., 323, *339,* 412, *420*
Walster, E., 225, *235*
Ward, W. C., 213, 222, *235*
Ware, E. E., 174, *201*
Watson, J. S., 192, 193, *203*
Watt, N. F., 252, *260*
Weed, S. E., 308, *311*
Weeks, D., 170, 189, *201*
Wegener, M., 374, 375, 389, *390*
Weick, K. E., Jr., 297, *310*
Weiner, B., 62, 64, 71, 80, 83, *94, 95,* 120, *124,* 125, 133, 135, 136, 138, 151, *159,* 164, 165, 167, 168, 169, 171. 172, 173, 174, 175, 176, 178, 179, 180, 181, 182, 183, 184, 187, 188, 189, 191, 192, 197, *200, 201, 202, 203, 204,* 210, 215, 229, *237,* 278, 285, *289,* 360, 361, *363, 364,* 403, 405, 411, *420*
Weiss, H., 209, 212, *237*
Weiss, J., 54, *93*

Weiss, J. M., 2i5, 216, *237*
Wendt, D., 412, *420*
Wendt, H. W., 133, *160*
Whalen, R. E., 36, *52*
Whalen, C. K., 191, *204*
White, P., 403, *420*
White, S. E., 326, *339*
White, R. W., 192, *204*
Wicker, A. W., 271, *289*
Wicker, A., 358, *364*
Wicklund, R. A., 358, *364*
Wilks, S. S., 321, *339*
Williams, R. M. Jr., 273, *289*
Wilson, G. D., 281, *289*
Wilson, T. D., 182, *201,* 285, *288,* 403, *419*
Wimer, S. W., 190, *204*
Wine, J., 210, 211, 215, *237*
Winkeller, M., *237*
Winkler, R. L., 329, *338,* 369, 370, *392, 393, 394*
Winter, D., 185, *201*
Winterbottom, M. R., 26, *52*
Wish, P. A., 133, *160*
Wolfer, J. A., 351, *363*
Wong, P. T. P., 165, *204*
Wood, R. J., 386, 387, 389, *394*
Woodside, A., 272, *287*
Wortman, C. B., 213, 218, 220, 222, 229, 231, *233, 237*
Wottawa, H., 149, 156, *158, 160*
Wright, G. N., 323, *339*
Wright, H. F., 54, *95*
Wright, M. H., 211, *234*
Wright, P., 320, *339*
Wurm, M., 215, *236*
Wyer, R. S., 328, *339*
Wynne, L. C., 31, *52*

XYZ

Yaryan, R. B., 210, *237*
Young, P. T., 405, *420*
Zagorski, M. A., 324, *339*
Zajonc, R. B., 173, *204,* 224, *237*
Zaksly, D., 116, *123*
Zimbardo, P. G., 185, *202*
Zinberg, N. E., 221, *237*
Zink, 323, *337*

SUBJECT INDEX

A

Abstract structures, 87, 275
Action orientation vs. state orientation, 7, 146–149, 153–154
Action tendency, 34, 36–42, 46–49, 142
Affect
  and causal attributions, 177–181
  and consistency theory, 85–86
  and espectancy confirmation/disconfirmation, 68–69
  and expectancy-value theory, 405–406
  and internal/external distinction, 135, 177–181
  and motives, 58, 275
  and reinforcement value, 248–249
  and specific attributions, 178–180
  and success or failure, 7, 58, 178–180
  and valence, 70–71, 406
  and value structures, 275
Affiliation and loneliness, attribution analysis of, 195–197
Altruism (*see* Helping behavior)
Attitude/behavior relationship, 10, 249–254, 271–273, 358
Attitude, as integration of valences, 281–282
Attributions
  and balance theory, 81
  conditions for making, 165
  and consensus information, 82–83

consequences of causal properties, 171–198
and consistency information, 82
dimensions of, 8, 83, 135, 166–171, 190
and expectancy-value theory, 135–136, 181–186
and expectations, 82–84, 171–177
and persistence, 177, 184–186, 215
and performance intensity, 181–182
and reinforcement schedules, 175–177, 186
and risk preference, 183–184
and self-concept maintenance, 174–175
and stage of task involvement, 231–232
types of, 165–198, 229, 230
Attribution therapy, 211, 216

B

Balance sheet hypothesis, 353–358, 415
Balance theory, 81
Bayes' Theorem, 367, 369–373, 384, 388
Behavior potential, 9, 242, 250–251
Behavioral chatter, 148
Behavioral decision theory (BDT), 315–317
Behavioral system, 7, 112–115
Belief-attitude-value system, 273–274
Belief, and subjective probability, 327
Beliefs, social attitudes, and social action, 249–254
Bolstering, as tactic in decision making, 352–353
Bootstrapping procedures, 320–321

C

Causal attribution (*see* Attributions)
Change in activity, and dynamics of action, 33–49
Cognitive map, 2
Cognitive revolution, 263–264
Cognition-emotion sequence, 180–181
Commitment, and choice, 55–56
Competence
    and information-seeking, 110–112
    learning about, 225–230
    and mastery, attributional analysis, 192–193
    self-possession of, 110–112, 136–137
    and sources of value, 115–116
Conflict theory, of decision making, 341–363
    coping patterns for consequential decisions, 344–347
    and information processing, 347–349
    and role of expectancy, 343–363
Conjunctive vs. disjunctive rules, 323
Conservatism Scale, 282
Conscious thought, 182–184, 231, 249, 285–286, 401–405
Consummatory force, 35, 37–38, 46, 139
Consummatory lags, 148
Consummatory value, 35, 38, 46–47, 140–141
Contingent vs. noncontingent paths, 7, 99–101, 103–107, 116–119, 133–134, 229, 396
Controllable vs. uncontrollable outcomes, discriminating between, 219–231
Control (*see also* Internal control)
    and adjustment, 214, 220–225
    as dimension of causal attribution, 169–181, 186–190
    illusion of, 213, 221
Controlled search vs. automatic detection, 403–404

D

Decision making (*see also* Conflict theory, Risk preference, SEU models)
    steps involved in, 366
Decision schemes
    applications of, 365–390
    problems in use of, 388
Defensive avoidance, and conflict theory, 344–346, 349–353, 361–362
Depression, attributional analysis, 197–198, 213, 222–223, 225

Discrepancy theory, 71, 87, 266
Dissonance theory, 54, 71–72, 209–210, 215, 229
Distance from goal, conceived as time, 104–105, 134
Drive theory, 20, 246–247
Dynamics of action model, 63, 33–49, 116–117 139–141, 416

E

Evaluation of worth, in SEU models, 323–324
Evaluative feedback, and causal attributions, 189
Expectancy (*see also* Expectation, Generalized expectancy)
    definition of in Atkinson's model, 25
    and related concepts, 1–3, 407–408
    Rotter's concept, 9, 56, 242–244, 246, 248–251, 254, 256
Expectancy theory
    Guthrie's criticism, 3–4, 18–19, 264
    Tolman's contribution, 17, 19, 56, 264
Expectancy-value models
    boundary conditions, 307–309, 322–325, 334, 397–401
    and conscious thought, 401–405
    general description, 1–12, 17–20, 278–280
    Heckhausen's integrative theory, 141–145
    measurement assumptions, 149–151, 302–304, 414
    multiplicative vs. additive models, 283, 304
    new perspectives, 395–397
    role of affect, 405–406
    scope of application, 397–400
Expectations (*see also* Subjective probability)
    and causal attributions, 80–84, 171–177, 360
    determinants of, 63–68, 75–77, 117, 278–279, 308–309, 360, 398, 406–408
    Heckhausen's analysis, 64–65, 278, 409
    maladaptive effects, 208–216
    measurement issues, 302–304, 408–410
    and motives, 67–68, 323, 397–398
    outcome vs. efficacy, 64–65, 278, 409
    and performance, 74–78, 208, 211
    and persistence, 61–63, 208–216
    problems in assessment, 327–329, 367, 408–410
    realism of, 213–214, 397–398
    refinement and integration of, 285, 403
    reliability and validity, 303, 329

as $S_1R_1S_2$ cognitive unit, 18, 25
Tolman's "moods", 63, 416
and valences, 59, 79-81, 213, 410-414
Expectation of failure (*see* Subjective probability of failure)
Expectation of success (*see* Subjective probability of success)
Expectation change
atypical vs. typical shifts, 77, 173, 225
and social learning theory, 225
and stable vs. internal attributions, 135, 173-174
Expected information hypothesis, in conflict theory, 351-352
Extrinsic tendency, 29, 44, 48-49, 59, 73, 99, 100, 103

F

Fixed incentive model, 68-69
Force, 36 (*see also* Instigating force, Inhibitory force)
Force of resistance, 35, 45-47, 139
Force model
in instrumentality theory, 295-298, 301
and job effort, 300
and specific behaviors, 300-301
Freedom of movement, 9, 242, 247
Future orientation
evidence concerning effects of, 101-108
in Raynor's model, 99-101, 118, 121, 134
and self-evaluation, 108-109

G, H

Gambler's fallacy, 173
Generalized expectancy, 9, 244, 251-255
Globality, as dimension of causal attribution, 170, 198
Helping behavior, and causal attribution, 187-189
Helplessness (*see* Learned helplessness)
Heuristics, use in information processing, 329
Hyperactivity and psychostimulants, attributional analysis, 191-192
Hypervigilance, and conflict theory, 344-347, 349, 361-362

I

Immunization against failure, 216-218, 223-224

Incentive, 24-25
Incentive value, 1-3, 24-25, 113-118, 142 (*see also* Reinforcement value, Utility, Valence)
of consistency, 73-74
of failure, 27-28, 45, 58, 68-69, 79, 98
of inconsistency, 73-74
of success, 27, 44, 57-58, 79, 98-99, 126, 132, 134, 137
and subjective probability, 7, 56-57, 60, 68, 306, 322
Information feedback, 8-9, 110-113, 115-116, 121-122, 183-184, 224-225
Information-seeking behavior
and competence, 110-113, 115-116, 121-122, 183-184
and conflict theory, 344-349, 351, 356, 358
and expectancy-value analysis, 7, 71-74, 111
Information value vs. affective value, 8, 111-113, 115-116, 121-122
Inhibitory force, 6, 34, 40, 47, 139, 279, 396
to avoid failure, 36, 38, 49
Inhibitory tendency, 6, 27-33
Instigating force, 6, 34, 36-38, 40-41, 48, 139-140, 279, 396
to achieve success, 36, 38, 40, 45, 48-49
Instrumentality theory, 11, 64, 70, 141, 245, 294-309
empirical findings, 298-301
force model, 295-298
measurement issues, 302
methodological issues, 301-303
valence model, 294-296
within-subjects tests, 297, 305-306, 415
Instrumental values
definition of, 87, 267
in Rokeach Value Survey, 266-267, 274
as sources of valence, 278
Intentionality, as dimension of causal attributions, 168-170
Interactionism, 255-256, 284, 417
Internal control (*see also* Control)
and related concepts, 80, 164, 190
as a weighting factor, 7, 78-80, 133, 410-411
Internal/external dimension of causal attributions, 168-170, 198, 229
Intrinsic motivation, 116, 324, 411

J, K

Job effort model
and force model, 300
in instrumentality theory, 295-298

Job satisfaction
  and instrumentality theory, 294-295
  and valence model, 299-300
Knowledge, and action (*see* Thought and action)

L

Law of effect, 18, 60, 246
Learned helplessness
  and depression, 197-198, 221-223
  and performance deficits, 77-78, 146-148,
    210, 215, 222
Level of aspiration model, 4, 20, 55-57, 63-64,
  411
Life space, Lewin's concept, 64, 255, 264, 284,
  286, 398, 403
Limits, sequential model of testing one's limits,
  225-230
Locus of causality, and affect, 177-181
Locus of control, 75, 77-78, 181, 187, 209,
  251-252, 254
Logical statement analysis, 7, 150-153, 155-
  156
Loneliness, and causal attributions, 189-190,
  195-197

M

Mastery and competence, attributional analysis,
  192-193
Motivation, incentive, and emotion in social
  learning theory, 246-249
Motive
  to achieve consistency, 73-74
  to achieve success, 26-30, 38, 44-45, 47-48,
    57-59, 62, 67, 77, 79, 98-104, 126, 129,
    134, 137
  Atkinson's definition, 25
  to avoid failure, 26-30, 38, 44, 47-48,
    58-59, 62, 67, 77, 79, 98-104, 126, 129,
    134, 137
  to avoid inconsistency, 73-74
  McClelland's definition, 275
Motives
  and attributional behavior, 136
  and latency of response, 39
  measurement problems, 129-132
  and performance, 75, 101-109, 138, 151-
    152, 181-182
  and persistence, 62, 138
  projective vs. self-report measures, 131-132

  and typical/atypical expectation change, 77
Mowrer's hope, fear, relief, disappointment, 68
Multiattribute utility theory (MAUT), 374-380
  and evaluating quality of water supplies, 375
  and public transit study, 377-380, 385, 387,
    389
  and SMART technique, 376-377

N, O

N Achievement, 21, 62, 77-78, 101-102, 106-
  107, 118, 129, 132
Need potential, 8, 242, 247
Need value, 8, 242, 247, 250
Negaction tendency, 34, 45-49
Object preference
  and achievement values, 54-57
  and expectation of success, 54-57
Objective probability, 327, 369
Occupational preference, in instrumentality
  theory, 298-299
Optimal stimulation hypothesis, 137-139
Optional Parenthood Questionnaire, 356, 387
Outcome content, in instrumentality theory,
  301-302
Outcome expectations, dimensions of, 409
Outcomes
  and consequences, 1-2, 141, 245
  first and second level, 296

P

PIP system, in assessing probabilities, 368
Parole decisions, and causal attributions, 193-
  195
Perceived instrumentality (*see* Contingent vs.
  noncontingent paths)
Perceived responsibility for outcomes (*see*
  Internal control)
Persistence
  attributional analysis, 177, 184-186
  expectancy-value analysis, 6, 33, 61-63, 212
  and learning when to quit, 218-230
  maladaptive aspects of, 207-216, 231-232
  and optimal stimulation hypothesis, 138
Person-environment fit, and value similarity,
  266-271
Predecisional/postdecisional processes, continuity assumption, 355, 362, 415-416
Procrastination, as tactic in decision making,
  352

Prospect theory, 325, 368
Psychological situation, 9, 243-244, 255-259

R

Reactance theory
    and loss of choice alternatives, 358-359
    and object preference, 34
Reciprocal determinism, 417
Reinforcement value, 9, 56, 242, 244-251, 256
Resultant tendency, 29-30, 34, 38, 46-47, 49,
    59, 74, 98, 126
Retrospected past, effects on motivation, 116-
    119
Risk-taking model (*see* Theory of achievement
    motivation)
Risk preference (*see also* Theory of achievement
    motivation)
    and action vs. state orientation, 153-155
    attributional analysis, 183-184
    and Heckhausen's theory, 142-145
Rokeach Value Survey (*see* Value Survey)
Rotter's I-E Scale (Locus of control), 75,
    77-78, 209, 212

S

Satisficing strategy, 324
SEU model (Subjectively expected utility
    model)
    and academic area preference, 383
    adequacy of real-life applications, 332-335
    assessing probabilities, 327-329, 408-410
    assessing utilities, 329-332, 373-374, 412-
    413
    conditions where inappropriate, 322-325,
    350, 361-362
    and expectancy-value model, 1, 11, 27, 40,
    45, 56-57, 315-336, 341, 366, 382
    and explaining past decisions, 317-320
    and family planning decisions, 356, 385-387
    and information processing deficiencies,
    322-332, 350, 361-362, 367-368, 397-
    398
    and medical diagnosis/treatment, 383-384
    and occupational preference, 383
    and problem structuring, 327
    research background, 382
    and simple linear models, 319-321, 414
    and weather forecasting, 384-385

Self-evaluation, and competence, 110-112,
    115-116, 225-232
Self-system, 7, 112-115, 119, 121
Self dissatisfaction, as motivating condition, 274
Sequential model for testing one's limits, 225-
    230
Sequential model of task involvement, 231-232
Shifting responsibility as decision making tactic,
    352
Similarity/attraction hypothesis, 267-268, 270
Simple multiattribute rating technique
    (SMART), 376-377
    applied to coastal land use, 376-377
Social interaction, and value similarity, 267-271
Social learning theory
    and attribution theory, 254-255
    and expectancy-value models, 9, 23, 241-259
    of personality, 241-259
Social movements, and values, 280-284
Soluble vs. insoluble tasks, importance of dis-
    criminating, 218-231
S-R behavior theory, 18-19, 20, 29, 33, 263
Stability, as dimension of causal attributions,
    168, 170-177, 188, 198, 229
Stream of behavior, 6, 39, 139, 144, 396, 415-
    418
Subjective probability (*see also* Expectations)
    and degree of belief, 327
    of failure, 27, 45, 55, 58-59, 68-69, 79, 98
    and medical diagnosis, 370-373, 389-390
    and meteorology, 369-370
    and objective probability, 369
    and public policy, 371-372
    research background, 367-373

T

Tendency to achieve success, 27-28, 40, 44,
    57-60, 98-99
Tendency to avoid failure, 27-28, 58-59,
    68-69, 98-99
Terminal values
    definition of, 87, 267, 274
    in Rokeach Value Survey, 266-267
    as sources of valence, 278-279
Text anxiety, 62, 77-78, 101-102, 210, 215
Theory of achievement motivation
    Atkinson's model, 6, 7, 21-40, 44-45,
    48-49, 56-61, 97-99, 126-132, 322
    and cultural value, 119-121
    and dynamics of action model, 33, 35-36, 40,

Theory of achievement motivation (*cont.*)
44-45, 48-49
elaborations and extensions, 33, 35-36,
39-40, 44-45, 48-49, 68-70, 78-80, 99-
101, 120-122, 132-156
and Heckhausen's theory, 141-145
and optimal stimulation hypothesis, 137-139,
144
and perceived internal control, 7, 78-80, 133
and personal standards, 134-135, 144
and Raynor's extended model, 99-101, 120-
122, 133-134
and risk preference, 59, 100, 126-127, 129,
133-138, 140, 183-184, 212, 228-229,
322
and self-system, 112-115
and time-related sources of value, 116-119,
121
Thought, and action, 18-21, 182-184, 231,
264, 285-286, 401-405, 415
TOTE units, 4
Type A behavior, 215

U, V, W

Unconflicted adherence, and conflict theory,
344-347, 349, 361
Unconflicted change, and conflict theory, 344-
347, 349, 361
Utility (*see also* Incentive value, Reinforcement
value, Valence)
in behavioral decision theory, 315
in economics, 18, 373, 411
research background, 373-382
Valence (*see also* Incentive value, Reinforcement value, Utility)
and affect, 70, 71, 294
of consistency/inconsistency, 73
and consistent outcomes, 85-86
determinants of, 55, 58, 70-71, 73, 79,

85-86, 107, 245, 277-278, 294, 396-398,
410-412
and expectation, 59, 79-81, 213, 410-414
of failure, 58, 67, 70, 78-79, 98
Heckhausen's analysis, 141-144
and motives, 58, 67, 398, 410
and perceived internal control, 78-80
problems of assessment, 302-303, 329-332,
373-375, 412-413
and relational context, 411
reliability and validity, 303, 332
of success, 58, 67, 70, 78-79, 98, 107
and general values, 10, 55, 86-89, 277-280,
411
Valence model
and force model, 10, 294-301
in instrumentality theory, 294-296, 301
and job satisfaction, 299-300
and occupational preference, 298-299
Value Survey, 87, 266-267
Value systems, and social interaction, 267-271
Values
and affect, 275
conceived as motives, 87, 275-277
and conservatism, 282
definitions, 87-88, 273-275
ecology of, 266
as inducing valences, 88-89, 277-280
and self-conceptions, 273-274
and social interaction, 267-271
and social movements, 280-284
Value/action relationship, 10, 265-286
expectancy-value approach, 277-284
person-environment fit approach, 267-271
Value structure, 275
Varying incentive model, 68-69
Verbal report, status of, 254, 401-404
Vigilance, in conflict theory, 345-351, 357-
359, 361-362
Wishful vs. committed choice, 55, 412-413
Zeigarnik effect, 21